KIERKEGAARD FOR THE CHURCH

KIERKEGAARD

"I will seek my refuge with... the Crucified One.... to save me from myself."

Christian Discourses (1848)

FIGURE 1: Bronze Kierkegaard stat
on display at First Lut

Kierkegaard for the Church

Essays and Sermons

Ronald F. Marshall

For Lee Snook,
Thanks for being my teacher + friend. Pages
121-22 are for you:

Ronald F. Marshall

Foreword by Carl E. Braaten

Epilogue by Robert L. Perkins

Wipf & Stock · Eugene, Oregon

KIERKEGAARD FOR THE CHURCH
Essays and Sermons

Wipf & Stock
An Imprint of Wipf and Stock Publishers
199 W. 8th Ave., Suite 3
Eugene, OR 97401

www.wipfandstock.com

ISBN 13: 978-1-62032-397-7

Cataloguing-in-Publication data:

Marshall, Ronald F., 1948–

    Kierkegaard for the church : essays and sermons / Ronald F. Marshall, with a foreword by Carl E. Braaten, and an epilogue by Robert L. Perkins.

    xxiv + 370 p. ; 23 cm. Includes bibliographical references and indexes.

    ISBN 13: 978-1-62032-397-7

    1. Kierkegaard, Søren, 1813–1855. 2. Christian life—Lutheran authors. 3. Lutheran Church—Sermons. I. Braaten, Carl E., 1929–. II. Perkins, Robert L., 1930–. III. Title.

BX8066 M35 P74 2013

Manufactured in the U.S.A.

For

Robert L. Perkins
quid nemis
(JP 2:1617)
&
angustiae
(JP 4:4700)

In memoriam

Martin J. Heinecken
(1902–98)

George E. Arbaugh
(1933–2002)

Edna H. Hong
(1913–2007)

Howard V. Hong
(1912–2010)

At Kierkegaard's Death

MY CONCEPTION OF JUDAS Iscariot would not be of a desperate man (which he probably was actually) who in a moment of rage sells his master. . . . No, Judas is constituted quite differently; he is a quiet man with an entirely different understanding of life—what profits. . . . According to my mind this is a whole shade more abominable—I really do believe that such an abomination could not occur in ancient times: it is reserved for our sensible age. It is easy to detect that I have conceived Judas somewhat *à la* the professor, who safely and quietly leads a tasteful, enjoyable life. . . . It is this quiet living on in perfect accommodation that makes assistant professors so odious. O, but in vain do you hope to influence assistant professors. When I am dead, all that is mine will also be exploited by assistant professors. (JP 2:2232)

Contents

Contents

Figures

Abbreviations

KIERKEGAARD'S WRITINGS

BA   *The Book on Adler*, trans. Howard V. Hong and Edna H. Hong. Princeton: Princeton University Press, 1998.

CA   *The Concept of Anxiety*, trans. Reidar Thomte in collaboration with Albert B. Anderson. Princeton: Princeton University Press, 1978.

CD   *Christian Discourses*, trans. Howard V. Hong and Edna H. Hong. Princeton: Princeton University Press, 1997.

CI   *The Concept of Irony*, trans. Howard V. Hong and Edna H. Hong. Princeton: Princeton University Press, 1989.

COR   *The Corsair Affair*, trans. Howard V. Hong and Edna H. Hong. Princeton: Princeton University Press, 1982.

CUP   *Concluding Unscientific Postscript*, trans. Howard V. Hong and Edna H. Hong. 2 vols. Princeton: Princeton University Press, 1992.

EO   *Either/Or*, trans. Howard V. Hong and Edna H. Hong. 2 vols. Princeton: Princeton University Press, 1987.

EUD   *Eighteen Upbuilding Discourses*, trans. Howard V. Hong and Edna H. Hong. Princeton: Princeton University Press, 1990.

FSE   *For Self-Examination* and *Judge For Yourself!*, trans. Howard V. Hong and Edna H. Hong. Princeton: Princeton University Press, 1990.

FT   *Fear and Trembling* and *Repetition*, trans. Howard V. Hong and Edna H. Hong. Princeton: Princeton University Press, 1983.

JFY   *Judge For Yourself!* and *For Self-Examination*, trans. Howard V. Hong and Edna H. Hong. Princeton: Princeton University Press, 1990.

JP   *Soren Kierkegaard's Journals and Papers*, ed. and trans. Howard V. Hong and Edna H. Hong. 7 vols. Bloomington and London: Indiana University Press, 1, 1967; 2, 1970; 3 and 4, 1975; 5–7, 1978.

LD   *Letters and Documents*, trans. Hendrick Rosenmeir. Princeton: Princeton University Press, 1978.

Pap   *Søren Kierkegaards Papirer*, I–XI, ed. P. A. Heiberg, V. Kuhr, and E. Torsting, 1st ed., Copenhagen: Gyldendal, 1909–48; 2nd ed., I–XIII, ed. Niels Thulstrup, Copenhagen: Gyldendal, 1968–70; with index, XIV–XVI, 1975–78, ed. N. J. Cappelørn.

P   *Prefaces*, trans. Todd W. Nichol. Princeton: Princeton University Press, 1998.

PC   *Practice in Christianity*, trans. Howard V. Hong and Edna H. Hong. Princeton: Princeton University Press, 1991.

PF   *Philosophical Fragments*, trans. Howard V. Hong and Edna H. Hong. Princeton: Princeton University Press, 1985.

PV   *The Point of View*, trans. Howard V. Hong and Edna H. Hong. Princeton: Princeton University Press, 1995.

R   *Repetition* and *Fear and Trembling*, trans. Howard V. Hong and Edna H. Hong. Princeton: Princeton University Press, 1983.

SLW   *Stages on Life's Way*, trans. Howard V. Hong and Edna H. Hong. Princeton: Princeton University Press, 1988.

SUD   *The Sickness unto Death*, trans. Howard V. Hong and Edna H. Hong. Princeton: Princeton University Press, 1980.

TA   *Two Ages*, trans. Howard V. Hong and Edna H. Hong. Princeton: Princeton University Press, 1978.

TDIO   *Two Discourses on Imagined Occasions*, trans. Howard V. Hong and Edna H. Hong. Princeton: Princeton University Press, 1993.

TM   *The Moment and Late Writings*, trans. Howard V. Hong and Edna H. Hong. Princeton: Princeton University Press, 1998.

UDVS   *Upbuilding Discourses in Various Spirits*, trans. Howard V. Hong and Edna H. Hong. Princeton: Princeton University Press, 1993.

WA   *Without Authority*, trans. Howard V. Hong and Edna H. Hong. Princeton: Princeton University Press, 1997.

WL   *Works of Love*, trans. Howard V. Hong and Edna H. Hong. Princeton: Princeton University Press, 1995.

OTHER WRITINGS

BC   *The Book of Concord* (1580), ed. T. Tappert. Philadelphia: Fortress, 1959.

IKC   *International Kierkegaard Commentary*, ed. Robert L. Perkins. 24 vols. Macon, Georgia: Mercer University Press, 1984–2010.

LHP   *Sermons of Martin Luther: The House Postils*, ed. E. F. A. Klug. 3 vols. Grand Rapids: Baker Books, 1996.

LW   *Luther's Works*, ed. Jaroslav Pelikan (1–30), Helmut T. Lehmann (31–54) and Joel W. Lundeen (55). 55 vols. Saint Louis and Philadelphia: Concordia and Fortress, 1955–86. Vols. 58–60, 69, 75, ed. Christopher Boyd Brown. Saint Louis: Concordia, 2009–2013.

RSV   *The New Oxford Annotated Bible with the Apocrypha: Revised Standard Version, Containing the Second Edition of the New Testament*, ed. Herbert G. May and Bruce M. Metzger. New York: Oxford University Press, 1973.

SML   *Sermons of Martin Luther*, ed. John N. Lenker. 8 vols. Grand Rapids: Baker, 1988.

Foreword

IT IS A DISTINCT honor for me to contribute a foreword to Ronald Marshall's remarkable book of scholarly essays and spirited sermons that, in addition to being solidly based on Holy Scripture, draw deeply from the well springs of his two favorite theological mentors, Martin Luther and Søren Kierkegaard. Marshall, essayist and preacher, has discovered in their writings much to teach us about what it means to be a believer in Christ and follower of Jesus today. His achievement is congruent with the aim of Kierkegaard's life-long authorship to present New Testament Christianity in sharp contrast to the established church, whether of nineteenth century Denmark or twenty-first century America.

It is impossible for me to think of Søren Kierkegaard without remembering Howard Hong (1912–2010), who became famous together with his wife Edna as editors and translators of twenty-six volumes of Kierkegaard's writings. Hong was my teacher of philosophy the years I attended Saint Olaf College from 1947 to 1951. Already at that time he was busy translating Kierkegaard into English, using the old A. B. Dick ink-bleeding copy machine to make his translations available to students. The little I knew about Kierkegaard before taking Hong's seminars came from reading portions of one of his devotional books that my father had in his library, *Purity of Heart is to Will One Thing* (UDVS 3–154). Among the many good teachers I had at Saint Olaf College, Howard Hong was for me the most influential, not primarily on account of the quantity of knowledge he disseminated in his classroom, but rather in the way he inculcated the love and joy of learning. His teaching method was maieutic, asking questions that engender reflection in accord with the Socratic method.

When it came time to write a senior's departmental honors paper, I chose the topic, *The Concept of Freedom in the Thought of Sören Kierkegaard and Jean-Paul Sartre: A Comparative Study*. That turned into good luck for me, for in applying for a Fulbright Scholarship, I submitted that identical topic as a research proposal for one year of study at the Sorbonne, University of Paris.

The Sorbonne turned out to be a hotbed of existentialist philosophy. Besides, Sartre's plays were all the rage at the time. I read a lot of Kierkegaard and Sartre that year in Paris, so much so that I came to feel deeply the existential condition both of them wrote so much about: negative feelings of angst, doubt, dread, despair, death, nausea, absurdity, ennui, giddiness, and so forth. Looking farther down that road I saw no salutary future for me. Still, one thing rang a bell from my reading of Kierkegaard. Being a Christian had been handed to me through no effort on my part, so how was I any different from the myriad of nominal Christians Kierkegaard described in the state church of Denmark? I felt his accusing finger pointing at me. But more important than Kierkegaard's accusation was his penetrating analysis of what is involved in *becoming* a Christian. That certainly involves a life of discipleship but with equal tenacity holding as true the apostolic faith. Kierkegaard was strong in stressing the subjective aspect of faith. Kierkegaard's description of the *fides qua creditur* as "infinite personal passionate interest" (CUP 1:29) is richer than Paul Tillich's definition of faith as "ultimate concern."[1] But what about the *fides quae creditur*—the objective content of faith, that to which faith clings as ontologically prior?

I left Paris and my flirtation with existentialism to pursue a career in learning and teaching the true doctrines of the biblical-Christian church. That is called dogmatics or systematic theology. In doing this I always felt the heat of Kierkegaard's scorn for the priests, prelates, and professors who admittedly had the traditional doctrines down pat, but still reeked of something rotten in the state church of Denmark. He looked around and saw millions of Christians, and yet could brazenly conclude that New Testament Christianity no longer existed (TM 39). The clergy were orthodox enough, certainly not heretics, but they were only "playing the game of Christianity." How was I any different? How could I be sure that the church of which I was a baptized and confirmed member was not itself a Judas-church, a betrayal of New Testament Christianity? How could I submit to the sacrament of ordination to become a Lutheran pastor and then later a professor of church dogmatics and hope to elude Kierkegaard's indictment?

I would have to accept the risk, knowing full well that I may be playing the same kind of game as Professor Martensen and Bishop Mynster, the two hapless targets of Kierkegaard's attack on the counterfeit Christianity of his time. For me—*pace* Kierkegaard—there was no alternative but to work hard to find out what Christianity essentially is, the doctrines it teaches in clear *undialectical* straightforward cognitive propositions. I went after that with gusto. Something Martin Luther wrote in his book, *Bondage of the Will*, to refute Erasmus' fuzzy teaching on free will, encouraged me: "For it is not the mark of a Christian mind to take no delight in assertions; on the contrary, a man must delight in assertions or he will be no Christian. . . . Nothing is better known or more common among Christians than assertions. Take away assertions and you take away Christianity" (LW 33:19–21). Luther aimed for dogmatic certainty and clarity, not for its own sake but for the sake of the pure preaching of the gospel.

Along with others I have struggled to determine what Kierkegaard could possibly have meant by asserting "Subjectivity is Truth" (CUP 1:207). I reject the views of religious pluralists who hold that it doesn't matter what you believe as long as you believe it passionately. They say there is no objective truth and, moreover, no way to prove that one's creed is more true than anyone else's. Everything in religion is relative, except the assertion that everything in religion is relative. I greatly appreciate the way in which Marshall's treatment of Kierkegaard's understanding of Christianity exculpates his teaching from such a subjectivist reductionism. Kierkegaard cared deeply about Christian truth, and that is why he lamented the nonchalant attitude of his

---

1. See Paul Tillich, *Dynamics of Faith* (New York: Harper & Row, 1957) and *Ultimate Concern: Tillich in Dialogue*, ed. D. Mackenzie Brown (New York: Harper & Row, 1965).

fellow Danes in matters of faith. Kierkegaard wrote: "Doctrine, as usually expounded, is on the whole correct. I am not disputing about that. My sole concern is how it can be effective" (JP 6:6702).[2] Marshall has mined out of Kierkegaard's voluminous authorship many assertions of orthodox Christianity, particularly those that bear on Christology, the way of salvation, and obedient discipleship.

My reading of Marshall's many citations from Kierkegaard's writings serves to remind me of how much I have been influenced by his way of thinking, without always being aware of it.

1. *Historical-critical research yields at best approximation knowledge.*

Kierkegaard built an argument to support this proposition in *Philosophical Fragments* and *Concluding Unscientific Postscript* while reflecting on Lessing's thesis that "Accidental truths of history can never become the proof of necessary truths of reason." Kierkegaard reformulated Lessing's thesis in the following terms: "Can there be an historical point of departure for a consciousness that is eternal in quality? Can eternal salvation be built on historical knowledge?" (PF 1; CUP 1:93).

In 1960 I submitted my doctoral dissertation to Harvard University on the modern problem of the historical Jesus. The question posed by Lessing and Kierkegaard became acute for me: How can the historical Jesus have decisive significance for our salvation, if our knowledge of the historicity of the whole phenomenon of Jesus as Savior must depend on the application of the historical critical method, the results of which never go beyond probability? Historically we can never establish with absolute certainty who Jesus was, what he said and what he did, let alone that he was the Christ, the Son of God, and the second person of the Trinity. The results of historical research are too fluctuating to provide a solid foundation for faith in Jesus Christ as our hope for eternal life. Kierkegaard showed that there is a better way, a position which greatly influenced the dialectical theologians, Karl Barth, Emil Brunner, as well as Paul Tillich. This is also the line of thinking I pursued in my recently published book, *Who Is Jesus? Disputed Questions and Answers*.[3] The question of the truth of Christianity cannot be answered objectively, though this is not to say the truth is not objective. The question of whether Christianity is objectively true coincides with the personal decision of faith. The historical event of Jesus Christ cannot be apprehended by reason alone, apart from faith.

---

2. See also FSE 24; JP 4:5049; 6:6727, 6753.

3. Carl E. Braaten, *Who is Jesus? Disputed Questions and Answers* (Grand Rapids: Eerdmans, 2011).

2. *Theology has a vocation of criticism vis-á-vis the Established Church.*

Kierkegaard's *Attack Upon Christendom* (TM 1–354)[4] opened my eyes to the prophetic task of theology. Just as the Old Testament prophets criticized Israel for its idolatrous ways, taking their stand from within the covenant that God made with his people, so Kierkegaard's blistering diatribe against the established church of his day was motivated by a deep love for the new covenant signed by Jesus by the blood of his cross.

In the words of Amos 7:14, I confess that "I am neither a prophet nor the son of a prophet," yet I believe it incumbent on a person called and ordained to preach the "whole counsel of God" to accept the onus of prophetic criticism of the established church, especially its leadership, when it drifts into various culture-conforming heresies and apostasies. Such criticism will inevitably trigger counter-attacks from the court theologians directing words of ignominy and obloquy at those who dare to criticize the establishment. The Catholic hierarchy effectively silences those who step out of line, the likes of Daniélou, de Lubac, Schillebeeckx, Boff, Gutiérrez, Küng, and others. Protestant bureaucracies have their own ways of silencing theologians who criticize their betrayals of scriptural truth and church doctrine. Ronald Marshall, faithful communicator in the spirit of Luther and Kierkegaard, knows something about the cost of speaking truth to power, and so do many others with similar courage.

Professor Joseph Sittler (1904–87) taught generations of seminary students in Chicago, both at the Lutheran School of Theology and at the University of Chicago Divinity School. He became famous for delivering now and then a juicy *bon mot*. One apropos in this regard goes like this: "The relation between a theologian and his bishop should be that of a dog to a fire hydrant." There could hardly be a better example of Sittler's point than the sort of things Kierkegaard wrote about his Bishop. About Bishop Mynster Kierkegaard said that his preaching "soft pedals, slurs over, suppresses, omits something decisively Christian, something which appears to us as inopportune, which would make our life strenuous, hinder us from enjoying life, that part of Christianity which has to do with dying from the world, by voluntary renunciation, by hating oneself, by suffering for the doctrine, etc.—to see this one does not have to be particularly sharp-sighted, if one puts the New Testament alongside of Mynster's sermons" (TM 3). Kierkegaard's description of a church in revolt against New Testament Christianity is probably closer to literal fulfillment here and now in North America than when he was walking the streets of Copenhagen.

---

4. See also Søren Kierkegaard, *Attack Upon "Christendom"* 1854–55, trans. Walter Lowrie, New Introduction by Howard A. Johnson (Princeton: Princeton University Press, 1968).

3. *The Lutheran doctrine of justification by faith apart from the works of the law does not mean that Christians are free to disobey the commandments of God and to neglect the works of love.*

I have been a huge supporter of the teaching of justification by grace *alone* through faith *alone* on account of Christ *alone*, as taught by the apostle Paul, the church father Augustine, and the church reformer Luther. The *sola*s are important, rightly understood. But wrongly interpreted, they lead smack into antinomianism, the Lutheran heresy *par excellence*, if ever there was one. And some Lutherans in the United States and Canada—bishops, pastors, professors, and laity—are reviving the old heresy of antinomianism. Gospel-reductionism is a relatively new term that refers to the same thing. The controversy in confessional Lutheranism has to do with making the proper distinction between law and gospel.

I will leave it to experts like Marshall to determine how Kierkegaard's writings measure up in relation to Article V of the *Formula of Concord*. There it states: "The distinction between law and gospel is an especially brilliant light which serves the purpose that the Word of God may be rightly divided and the writings of the holy prophets and apostles may be explained and understood correctly. We must therefore observe this distinction with particular diligence lest we confuse the two doctrines and change the gospel into law. . . . [Strictly] speaking, the gospel is the promise of forgiveness of sins and justification through Christ, whereas the law is a message that rebukes and condemns sin" (BC 558, 563).

Did Kierkegaard get it right? Did he observe the proper distinction between law and gospel so as to avoid the error of legalism, on the one hand, and the error of antinomianism, on the other? I believe he did. He did not believe that *sola fide* means that the works of love enjoined by the law of God are optional. He believed that a Christian believer, one with faith in Christ, will also be a disciple, following Jesus in one's daily life. Long before Bonhoeffer he warned against "cheap grace."[5]

This book by Ronald Marshall is a reliable guide as to what Kierkegaard teaches us about true Christianity. I need that because on my own I often have a hard time sorting out what Kierkegaard himself intends to teach us by means of the words of his pseudonymous authors. Marshall has renewed my interest in reading and learning from the writings of Kierkegaard, and I believe that there are many future readers who will benefit as much as I have from reading this book of essays and sermons.

Carl E. Braaten

---

5. See Dietrich Bonhoeffer, *Discipleship* (1937), trans. Barbara Green and Reinhard Krauss, Dietrich Bonhoeffer Works, Vol. 14 (Minneapolis: Fortress, 2001), 43–56.

Preface

Needing Kierkegaard—A Tribute

KIERKEGAARD WAS RAISED A Lutheran in Copenhagen, Denmark. He was highly educated at the university and developed a love for words and ratiocination—"the thorough kneading of reflection" (TA 111). In his book *Stages on Life's Way*, he praises the Danish language saying that it is "not without expressions for the great, the crucial, the eminent, yet has a lovely, a winsome, a genial partiality for intermediate thoughts and subordinate ideas and adjectives, and the small talk of moods and the humming of transitions and the cordiality of inflections and the secret exuberance of concealed well-being" (SLW 489–90).[1] These words also reveal his manner of thinking and writing.

But for all his learning and writing—nearly thirty books and thousands of pages of journal entries—his heart was with the ordinary fellow. Even though he was shy, he walked the streets of Copenhagen chatting with strangers—keeping the night hours for his secluded reading and writing. This was not because of any interest in politics, but for "the disjunctions . . . of good and evil, right and wrong, honesty and dishonesty, . . . of which the common man had an unshakable and instinctive grasp, quite apart from any reflection."[2]

Kierkegaard loved this instinct because he wanted to put a similar "intensity" back into Christianity (JP 2:1807)—when being a Christian in his day had "become a banality" (PV 78). So he took Matthew 7:13–14 to heart—reading it "primitively" for character building (JP 3:2916–17): that Christianity is difficult, and few practice it

---

1. In this regard, note also Kierkegaard's description of himself as a flutist: "Sometimes I have been able to sit for hours enamored with the sound of words, that is, when they have the ring of pregnant thought; I have been able to sit for hours like a flutist entertaining himself with his flute. Most of what I write is spoken aloud many times, frequently perhaps a dozen times; it is heard before it is written down. . . . In another sense most of what I have written has been written *currente calamo* [with flowing pen], as they say, but that comes from my getting everything ready as I walk" (JP 6:6883, 6885).

2. Jørgen Bukdahl, *Søren Kierkegaard and the Common Man*, trans. Bruce H. Kirmmse (1961; Grand Rapids: Eerdmans, 2001), 63. And so it is wrong of Altizer to say of Kierkegaard—especially in the concluding sentence of this passage—that he "was our first thinker to know an absolute *horror religiosus*, a horror whereby he could know himself as a second Job, and just as Job is the only ultimate No-sayer to God in the Bible, Kierkegaard is our only thinker until Nietzsche who could pronounce an ultimate No upon God. But Kierkegaard is a truly dialectical thinker, so that his No to God is at bottom an absolute Yes, and a Yes inseparable from that No, or a Yes inseparable from the most ultimate *Angst* . . . . And inseparable if only because we are now called upon to realize the greatest possible theological negation, a theology of every theology that is now manifest as theology, or every theology immediately nameable as theology today." Thomas J. J. Altizer, *The Call to Radical Theology*, ed. Lissa McCullough (Albany, New York: State University Press of New York, 2012), 8.

aright. Christian faith does not come from fine thinking but from acting "according to the . . . orders of Christ" (JP 3:3023). And Jesus said we should strive to follow his narrow way. This way opposes the easy life wherein "the gorgeous poisonous flower of excuses blooms," for all other ways are "wrong roads" (UDVS 153, 299). They do not "work against" ourselves (FSE 61) and our "mutually enchanting defraudation of love" (WL 107)—as Christ's true way does. So "woe, woe to the Christian church" when it craves being "victorious in this world," for then "the way to life is no longer narrow" and true (PC 223–24). For it is not a sign that you are on "the right way" when things are going so easily for you (TM 320).

Thank God for Kierkegaard, then, and learn from him. Thank God for Howard and Edna Hong who have translated his books into English—as well as for those who have translated them into German, French, Spanish, Portuguese, Dutch, Italian, Swedish, Norwegian, Chinese, Japanese, Korean, Hungarian, Polish, Romanian, Bulgarian, Croatian, Russian, Ukrainian, Czech, Hebrew, Greek, and Turkish.[3] Truly the world needs to hear from Kierkegaard—"that Christianity alone is able to give a solution to all the existential problems."[4]

---

3. For this information, go to oclc.org.

4. Gregor Malantschulk, *The Controversial Kierkegaard*, trans. Howard V. Hong and Edna H. Hong (Waterloo, Ontario: Wilfrid Laurier University Press, 1980), 74. This conviction contrasts bitterly with much of popular American culture. See, for instance, Richard Hell, *I Dreamed I Was a Very Clean Tramp: An Autobiography* (New York: HarperCollins, 2013), 127–29:

> The truth of our invention of our songs and our band preceded and transcended all the contentious opinions and stress and competitive junk that kept arising in the band, and that truth was the hilarious, incomparable intoxication of materializing into being these previously nonexistent patterns of sound and meaning and physical motion. It was as fraught and sublime as great Renaissance religious painting. . . . The power and beauty of it was unimaginable. . . . It can't be overstated, that initial rush of realizing, of experiencing, what's possible as you're standing there in the rehearsal room with your guitars and the mikes turned on and when you make a move this physical information comes pouring out and you can do or say anything with it. It was like having magic powers. The sounds that came from the amplifiers were absurdly moving and strange, the variety of them so wide in view of the fact that they came from flicks of our fingers and from our vocal noises, and the way that it was a single thing, an entity, that was produced by the simultaneous reactive interplay of the four band members combining various of their faculties. We were turned into sound, a flow of sound. . . . [To] be creating electronically amplified songs [felt like] being born. It was everything one wants from so-called God. The joy of it, the instant inherent awareness that you could go anywhere you wanted with it and everywhere was fascinatingly new and ridiculously effective. It was like making emotion and thought physical, to be undergone apart from oneself. . . . [Every] moment had that surging astonishment and pleasure—even if in the service of anger and disgust, as it often was—of anything being possible to make happen. It was like creating the world, and the feeling could never quite happen again, or be sustained, anyway, because familiarity and habit take the edge off.

Acknowledgments

THE FOLLOWING SECTIONS OF this book were previously published. Grateful acknowledgement is given to the original publishers for permission to republish these materials in this single volume. Slight changes have been made throughout to these articles—and major changes to chapters five and seven, and the postscript. Their original titles, noting where and when they were first published, are listed below:

Preface: "Tribute: Our Need for Kierkegaard" in *Lutheran Forum* 40 (Summer 2006): 17–18.

Chapter 1: "The Traversed Path: Kierkegaard's Complex Way to Religious Simplicity," IKC (Macon, Georgia: Mercer University Press, 2010), 22:117–56.

Chapter 2: "The Sickbed Preacher: Kierkegaard on Adversity and the Awakening of Faith," IKC (Macon, Georgia: Mercer University Press, 2007), 17:219–49.

Chapter 3: "News From the Graveyard: Kierkegaard's Analysis of Christian Self-Hatred," *Pro Ecclesia: A Journal of Catholic and Evangelical Theology* 11 (Winter 2000): 19–42.

Chapter 4: "Constraining the Berserk: Kierkegaard on Adler and the Ideal Pastor," IKC (Macon, Georgia: Mercer University Press, 2008), 24:35–66.

Chapter 5: "Kierkegaard's Worshipping Geese" in *The Bride of Christ: The Journal of Lutheran Liturgical Renewal* 17 (Saint Michael and All Angels, 1993): 8–15.

Chapter 6: "Driven by God: Kierkegaard's Parable of the Royal Coachman," in *Toward the Final Crossroads: A Festschrift for Edna & Howard Hong* (Macon, Georgia: Mercer University Press, 2009), 115–41.

Chapter 7: "Kierkegaard's Cure for Divorce," *Søren Kierkegaard Newsletter*, no. 44 (September 2002): 6–10.

Chapter 8: "No 'Quack Doctor': Kierkegaard's Dialectical Understanding of God's Changelessness," IKC (Macon, Georgia: Mercer University Press, 2009), 23:129–64.

Chapter 9: "Tears of Self-Forgetfulness: Kierkegaard on Self-Denial," in *Why Kierkegaard Matters: A Festschrift in Honor of Robert L. Perkins* (Macon, Georgia: Mercer University Press, 2010), 179–92.

Chapter 11: "Walking with Kierkegaard," *Lutheran Forum* 35 (Christmas 2001): 51–52.

Sermon 1: "Practice Your Faith," *Lutheran Forum* 40 (Summer 2006): 18–19.

Appendix 1, Part 2: "A Biographical Critique," first published as "Kierkegaard's Music Box," *Lutheran Forum* 39 (Fall 2005): 37–41.

Appendix 1, Part 3: "A Lutheran Heritage," first published as a book review of Christopher B. Barrett's *Kierkegaard, Pietism, and Holiness*, *Lutheran Quarterly* 26 (Summer 2012): 195–97; and "Martin Luther as Kierkegaard's Master," *Lutheran Quarterly* 27 (Autumn 2013): 344–48.

Postscript: "My Father in the Faith," first published as "Søren Kierkegaard," *The Messenger: Newsletter of First Lutheran Church of West Seattle*, November 1985.

I want to thank Patrick Sand and Sonja Clemente for the photo of the Rita Marie Kepner bronze statue of Kierkegaard that serves as the front piece to this book. In addition I want to thank United Media for permission to reprint the Guy & Rodd "Brevity" cartoon in chapter 2 (which first was published on August 30, 2005); the Society of St. James and the cartoonist Horatio for permission to reprint in chapter 4 the cartoon of "The Very Reverend Clarence Dimwitty" from the Summer 1990 issue of *Touchstone*; Paul D. Turnbaugh for permission to reprint his cartoon of Kierkegaard walking in chapter 11 (which first appeared in the January 17, 1986 issue of *Christianity Today*); Craig and Ellen Hinkson for the photo of Anders Stengaard[1] in appendix 1—part 1; and Broadman & Holman for permission to reprint the cover of *Loving Søren* in Appendix 2. And my special thanks to Heather Hudson for permission to print her drawing, "Kierkegaard's Fiancée," in Appendix 2.

I want to thank Princeton University Press for permission to quote from *Kierkegaard's Writings*, and Indiana University Press to quote from *Søren Kierkagaard's Journals & Papers*.

I also want to thank Carl E. Braaten for encouraging me to write this book and for writing his splendid foreword to it. While editor at *Dialog* journal, he published my first article on Kierkegaard, titled "Kierkegaard's Heavenly Whores" (1992). He did the same for me when he published in *Pro Ecclesia* my first major article on Kierkegaard, titled "News from the Graveyard: Kierkegaard's Analysis of Christian Self-Hatred" (2000). He also published my very first article, titled "God and Worship," back in 1975, also in *Dialog*. No one has supported my writing career more than he has. I will always be in his debt. I might also add that he preached at the seventy-fifth anniversary of our church in 1993, which was a wonderful day. A version of his sermon

---

1. Herr Stengaard, who is 95 years old at the writing of this book, is one of Kierkegaard's last known relatives. See the family resemblance? He is a direct descendent from Kierkegaard's maternal grandmother, Maren Andersdatter Stengaard (1726–1813). Both Herr Stengaard and his wife Maren, have also given permission to use Hinkson's 1990 photo of him.

is in *Preaching Christ in a Pluralistic Age: Sermons by Carl E. Braaten* (Minneapolis: Lutheran University Press, 2011), 120–24.

And I want to thank Robert L. Perkins, general editor of the *International Kierkegaard Commentary* (IKC), to whom this book is dedicated. He was my primary critic for the major previously published chapters of this book from the IKC. I clearly owe him a debt of gratitude for his many constructive criticisms and for his wonderful epilogue to this book.

I also want to thank my wife, Jane L. Harty, for her critiques of chapters 3 and 7, on the vexing matter of self-hatred.

I want to thank my congregation, First Lutheran Church of West Seattle, for supporting my study time. They believe it is important to have a learned pastor, and for that I am grateful. Our office manager, Sonja Clemente, helped me in cropping the illustrations and photos and in the formatting of the text. I owe her a great deal for her many hours of assistance.

I also owe a great debt of gratitude to two librarians—Bruce Eldevik at Luther Seminary Library, Saint Paul, Minnesota; and Wally Bubelis at The Seattle City Library, West Seattle Branch. Their bibliographic assistance was indispensible.

My thanks also go to Jeff Sagmoen and Jane L. Harty for reading the entire manuscript in its late stages and making many needed corrections. This is a better book because of their painstaking labor! My thanks also go to Dale Korsmo for keeping my computer equipment in good repair—always in a most timely and expert manner. And thanks to Patrick Harrison, at Wipf & Stock Publishers, for his diligence and expertise in helping get the text of this book ready for publication.

I also want to thank Lee E. Snook, my seminary professor, for his written comments on large portions of this book.

Finally I am grateful to that holy One Kierkegaard called Governance. Of him, Kierkegaard writes: "[Just] as juice is pressed from fruit, Governance time and again and in a wonderful way has pressed me into a necessary situation precisely in order to make me as productive as I should be" (JP 6:6360). This was his way of saying: "God be praised; I owe it all to him"—"God has led me to this task," even though Kierkegaard knew that even his "best work" was still "a bit squalid" (JP 6:6396, 6391, 6157). This admission of Kierkegaard's is not only glorious—but also humbling, as he states: "I deserve no credit whatsoever, because . . . Governance has helped me," and "he loves every man in the same way" (JP 6:6511, 6161). Even so he still thought his books were out of the ordinary—having "set forth the decisive qualifications of the whole existential arena with a dialectical acuteness and a primitivity not found in any other literature" (JP 5:5914).

Too many ideas and associations of thought came to mind unannounced while I was writing this book for me not to be thankful like Kierkegaard—especially in the sermons. These moments were many and uncanny. For Kierkegaard, God was "constantly" intervening while he was writing (JP 6:6207). But I am also chastened by

Kierkegaard's warning—do not say too much about this guidance. At one point he says: "Self-denial requires the consistency of silence on this subject" (JP 6:6352). That is because God sets the writers he inspires in a "frightful isolation [in which they] must persevere, continually alone" with him (JP 2:2093). Even so he still is able to say that "it seemed as if Governance itself inspired" him (JP 6:6820). He also had the conviction that after he was dead and gone, God would place

> the stamp of Governance upon my life so that it will be useful and lead men to be aware of God and of how frivolously they prevent themselves from leading the highest life, a life in fellowship with God. (JP 6:6152)

No wonder Kierkegaard was convinced that he had done nothing in his writings, but had put "everything into the hands of Governance"—even when arranging to have his books published (JP 6:6630, 6664)! And he says this makes his relationship to God "strangely childlike" (JP 6:6497). Even so he could still say, with some complexity: "Attention is not supposed to be called to me, and yet. . . . my existence as a person is also utilized, but always in order to point beyond me at the decisive moment: I am not that!" (JP 6:6525).

So in the end I agree with him and take his two-fold warning to heart:

> Although I work extremely hard as an author and see very well both what God gives and what he makes out of it, which I do not always understand in spite of my reflective powers, my true test is in being the poor, insignificant, sinful man that I am, to be that before God—my work as an author I actually do not dare talk about; in a way it is not my own. (JP 6:6216)

> To know that God is using one—this would be a dangerous thought for a man to have; this is why he does not get to know it until afterward. (JP 4:4460)

INTRODUCTION

Kierkegaard for the Church

The Viking was a northern barbarian who attacked settled countries in which civilization and Christianity were suffering from the ordinary and perpetually recurrent ills of complacency, ease, and wealth. The Viking was also like a fresh breeze from the sea. He was a storm of swift wind from the ocean who, though he destroyed houses and murdered the innocent, also reminded stay-at-home men of their manhood. For a long time he was a better raider than settler, though in due time his healthy stock contributed to the farming population that fed the nations; but the landing of the dread pirates from the north showed the hollow weakness of false fronts in government and society. His coming meant fighting, rapine, looting, and destruction; but afterward there were stronger individual units among the feudal groups.[1]

THE PASTOR WHO WROTE about these fierce Viking pirates, thought the picture he painted applied equally well to Søren Kierkegaard (1813–55)! As far as he was concerned, Kierkegaard was a latter day Viking.[2] This was because Kierkegaard also storms the settled minds of theological complacency in his writings to get the fires of faith burning again so that the character or stock of Christian believers might increase in quality. And because what holds us back is so persistent, Kierkegaard's barbarian-like invasion of our theological thinking, is on the scale of those old Viking assailants and turns out to be just what the doctor ordered. No wonder then that Kierkegaard is not well liked in the church. No one, after all, wants to be looted by a theological Viking! So ever since Christians figured out that Kierkegaard believed that subjectivity was truth (CUP 1:207) and that there was "more truth" in the sincere worship of an idolater than in the blasé prayers of half-hearted Christians (CUP 1:201), he has been *persona non grata* in the church, with no one adding his books to their book club lists.[3] I hope to change that with

---

1. William T. Riviere, *A Pastor Looks at Kierkegaard: The Man and His Philosophy* (Grand Rapids, Michigan: Zondervan, 1941), 215.

2. Albeit in Socratic form. On this qualification, see George Pattison, *Anxious Angels: A Retrospective View of Religious Existentialism* (New York: Saint Martin's, 1999), 36: "Like Socrates, Kierkegaard did not set himself up as the teacher of a finished doctrine but sought to be a midwife [PF 10, EUD 69], bringing others' thoughts to birth—or a gadfly [JP 4:4265, 6:6943], stinging them into a more urgent pursuit of truth." See also WL 276–77.

3. For a study of these contentious statements, see Herbert M. Garalick, *The Anti-Christianity of Kierkegaard: A Study of Concluding Unscientific Postscript* (The Hague: Martinus Nijhoff, 1965). Note as well Hal Lindsey, *Satan is Alive and Well on Planet Earth* (Grand Rapid, Michigan: Zondervan,

my book.[4] I want to make a case for Kierkegaard's place in the church today.[5] And his place, I will try to show, is to warn us of the pitfalls in following Jesus Christ and then encourage us to follow him in spite of those risks and hazards, dangers and difficulties.

I started reading Kierkegaard with intense interest in the summer of 1978 when my father bought me a set of the new seven volume translation of Kierkegaard's journals by Howard V. Hong and Edna H. Hong—making up nearly four thousand pages in translation. I remember the day that big box of books showed up on my front porch in Los Angeles from Indiana University Press. Once I opened up the box, I could not put down the books, dipping in again and again, here and there, to marvel at the theological treasures they contained. The arrangement of the entries was by topic rather than by chronology—except for the fifth and sixth volumes devoted to autobiographical materials. This topical arrangement put Kierkegaard's Christian themes at my finger tips.[6] So if I was writing or preaching on hope or despair, miracles or sin,

---

1972). Lindsey argues in this book that Kierkegaard's writings are "contrary to biblical principles," and constitute a direct "denial of the basic tenants of the Christian faith" (85, 87). I have tried—indirectly—to show in my book that Lindsey is wrong. Kierkegaard's influence on American has had an impact quite different from what Lindsey warned about. On this see "Kierkegaard Comes to America," in George Cotkin, *Existential America* (Baltimore: Johns Hopkins University Press, 2003), 45: "Kierkegaard placed himself squarely against that complacent form of Christianity wherein good works and outward acts of churchgoing and good manners equaled faith. While Kierkegaard respected outward forms of piety, he believed that they should not substitute for a strenuous faith that touched the inward soul of man."

4. This will not include domesticating him, however. On this see George Pattison, *Anxious Angels*, 41: "Kierkegaard did not himself proclaim the death of God, as Nietzsche [1844–1900] was to do, but it is clear that, for him, the life of the individual in society was a life denied the resources of religious tradition since even those institutions and systems of thought that claimed to represent tradition were profoundly anti-traditional. We can no longer believe on the basis of what the Church teaches or what our fathers have taught us. Kierkegaard's world is not atheistic, but it is atheous: there is no immediate presence of God in the world, no recognizable, unambiguous focus for religious belief. We are each thrown back on ourselves and challenged to find the truth by finding it first in ourselves." Otherwise we would turn Christianity into paganism. On this Kierkegaard's Climacus notes: "All paganism consists in this, that God is related directly to a human being, as the remarkably striking to the amazed. But the spiritual relationship with God in truth, that is, inwardness, is first conditioned by the actual breakthrough of inward deepening that corresponds to the divine cunning that God has nothing remarkable, nothing at all remarkable, about him—indeed, he is so far from being remarkable that he is invisible, and thus one does not suspect that he is there although his invisibility is in turn his omnipresence" (CUP 1:245). On how we—being created in the image of God—might resemble this invisible One, but only "inversely"—see UDVS 192–93.

5. On doing theology for the church, see the introduction, "Doing Theology *Pro Ecclesia*," in Carl E. Braaten, *That All May Believe: A Theology of the Gospel and the Mission of the Church* (Grand Rapids: Eerdmans, 2008). Doing theology *pro ecclesia* is harder than it seems, given Paul Tillich's (1886–1965) trenchant assessment of "the rather miserable reality of concrete churches." Paul Tillich, *Systematic Theology*, 3 vols. (Chicago: University of Chicago Press, 1951–63), 3:166. It is also resisted by those looking for a suitable religion for children. On this see Susan Tive and Cami Ostman, *Beyond Belief: The Secret Lives of Women in Extreme Religions* (Berkeley, California: Seal Press, 2013), 194: "I don't know a version of . . . any . . . religion that is kind, gentle, and compassionate enough to give to my child."

6. The new translation of his journals argues against this arrangement and follows a strict

I could turn right to that section in his journals and start reading. With the editors' notes appended to each section, connecting the journal entries to Kierkegaard's other writings and the secondary literature, this seven volume set became my tutor in things Kierkegaardian.[7] I had first read Kierkegaard in college with Donald A. Wells[8] and then at the seminary with Paul R. Sponheim.[9] But it was not until I delved into Kierkegaard's journals that I began to see what he could do for me as a Lutheran pastor. And since 1979, when I began my ministry, I have not stopped mining Kierkegaard's writings for my preaching and teaching. The essays and sermons in this book come, in large part, from those nearly thirty-five years of work on Kierkegaard's writing while serving as a Lutheran pastor.

In November 1980 my congregation began its annual commemoration of Kierkegaard—including sermons, music, and lectures on Kierkegaard—as well as folk dancing and Danish pastries after the church services. Twenty-five years later, at our Sesquicenntenial celebration of Kierkegaard's death in 2005, we commissioned a choir anthem by Carl Schalk on the William Cowper text, "Thankless for Favours From on High"—with Schalk naming the tune, KIERKEGAARD.[10] And at our 2013 celebration, for the bicentennial of Kierkegaard's birth, we will be dedicating a bronze commemorative statue of Kierkegaard[11] by the world renowned sculptor, Rita Marie Kepner,

---

chronological approach instead. See *Kierkegaard's Journals and Notebooks*, Volume 1, Journals AA–DD, ed. Bruce H. Kirmmse (Princeton: Princeton University Press, 2007). As of 2013, volumes 1–6 have been published.

7. And so I like very much the title given to the new edition of Alexander Dru's translation of the journals—*The Soul of Kierkegaard: Selections From His Journals* (Mineola, New York: Dover, 2003).

8. See Donald A. Wells, *God, Man, and the Thinker: Philosophies of Religion* (New York: Random House, 1962).

9. See Paul R. Sponheim, *Kierkegaard on Christ and Christian Coherence* (New York: Harper & Row, 1968). See also his Whiteheadian critique of Kierkegaard in *Love's Availing Power: Imaging God, Imagining the World* (Minneapolis: Fortress, 2011). His basic point is that Kierkegaard has an underdeveloped connection of "mind . . . with body, of the individual with other humans, of humans with nature" (31). Therefore Kierkegaard is not able to see clearly how we are "carried by the faith of our sisters and brothers," thinking that we instead are "alone to decide" our fate before God (72). Kierkegaard, Sponheim argues, is without much "creational relatedness" (86). Given this critique, Sponheim provides little room for Kierkegaard's insistence that the sinner stands alone before God, in fear and trembling (CD 167), struggling to believe in the sole Savior, Jesus Christ, and follow him (BA 33, 141). "How terrible, then," writes Kierkegaard, that God is the "eternally Changeless One! Yet you must at some time, sooner or later, come in conflict with this changeless will that wanted you to consider this because it wanted your good, this changeless will that must crush you if you in any other way come into conflict with it" (TM 272).

10. For background information on this anthem and a fine recording of it, go to our church web site, flcws.org.

11. Note that Kierkegaard warned against fashioning any depictions of him: "[My] literary work is dialectical in double-reflection; for that reason, it would be completely frustrating, yes, even high treason against the idea, if, for example, I allowed my portrait or picture to be published. On the other hand, it may be asked whether I am not even responsible for creating, for my work all the support that in complete consistency with the idea may result from the dissemination of my caricature, my trousers sketched with me in them. Only the idea, the thought, engages me; I follow it into whatever external

which is based on H. P. Hansen's famous profile drawing of Kierkegaard with his broad rimmed hat.[12] We will also be featuring the world premier of a fugue written for tenor voice and cello, by Josh Deutsch, using the text on "pernicious sureness" from Kierkegaard's *Christian Discourses* (CD 211–12),[13] as well as a new setting for Kierkegaard's favorite hymn, "Commit Thy Way, Confiding," by Paul Gerhardt (1606–1676) (JP 6:6673), and a commemorative poem by Dana Gioia.[14] These annual November commemorations over the years have helped me find ways to use Kierkegaard's writings in church. The Kierkegaard scholars, Howard V. Hong (1912–2010),[15] Martin Heinecken (1902–98), George E. Arbaugh (1933–2002) and Michael Plekon, have been among the better known guest speakers at our festivals. All of them, in their own ways, have helped me learn how to be a Lutheran pastor in a Kierkegaardian vein.

---

situation it leads me—to being admired or to being abused—I follow it confidently. Just as a child holding its mother's hand walks in danger without recognizing it, so I hold the hand of consistency and walk in danger, because I know that in the idea the danger has been surmounted" (COR 187). Therefore our Kierkegaard statue has a bronze plaque on the front of it with these words from his *Christian Discourses*: "I will seek my refuge with . . . the Crucified One . . . to save me from myself" (CD 280).

12. A photo of this statue is the frontpiece of this book. For information on the drawing by H. P. Hansen from 1854, which inspired the design of this statue, see Joakim Garff, *Søren Kierkegaard: A Biography*, trans. Bruce H. Kirmmse (Princeton: Princeton University Press, 2005), drawing number 31 after p. 715: "When Kierkegaard marched past, Hansen sat in his apartment with his pencil and pad at the ready and thus captured 'the police spy' [JP 6:6890] for posterity. The shadow cast by the hat and our view of the upper side of the brim make it clear that Hansen probably caught the figure from a window on the ground floor or one flight up. Kierkegaard aged early, and it is clear that he shed his aesthetic refinement as the years passed, but he still retained the little smile on his muzzle-like mouth, a smile that was sad and satirical in equal measure." A different photo of this same statue is on the cover of the Reformation 2013 issue of *Lutheran Forum*. See also my article "Commemorating St. Søren Kierkegaard," *Lutheran Forum* 47 (Reformation 2013): 64, 63.

13. For a discussion of this passage, see pp. 68–69 below.

14. On Gioia's poetry, see Matthew Brennan, *Dana Gioia: A Critical Introduction* (West Chester, Pennsylvania, 2012). See also Janet McCann, "Dana Gioia: A Contemporary Metaphysics," *Renascence* 61 (Spring 2009), 201: "Gioia's work has a compelling dark side. But what makes literature 'dark'—and what does darkness run counter too—light? Nihilism is dark, but this poetry isn't nihilistic, nor is it unforgiving. . . . [His poems] may be sardonic, or may reach through surface brightness to an unyielding darkness that seems to lie at the heart of things, as in Joseph Conrad's story. They are often uneasy and resistant to conclusion or solution. This admixture of religious elements or considerations does not lighten the experience of the poetry or of the world. It does, though, suggest other perspectives which make the experience of darkness meaningful.

15. For the story of Dr. Hong's visit, see my "Søren Kierkegaard Comes to Seattle," *Lutheran Forum* 19 (Pentecost, 1985), 15–16.

Figure 2: Kierkegaard drawing by H. P. Hansen (1854).

Most of what is written on Kierkegaard today is for the college classroom and scholarly conferences—featuring the philosophical aspects of his writings "concerning the limits of knowledge or the nature of ethics, forays into the history of ideas, reflection on aesthetics,[16] adumbrations of phenomenological description and so on."[17] In this book I go in a different direction.[18] In writing it I have kept in mind that

16. See Eric Ziolkowski, *The Literary Kierkegaard* (Evanston, Illinois: Northwestern University Press, 2011), 4: "Kierkegaard signals the essential literary as opposed to strictly theological or philosophical nature of his writings. We must therefore . . . decipher . . . the linkages between his writings and those of other literary masters by whom he was directly and manifestly influenced, such as Aristophanes, Cervantes, and Shakespeare." Note as well in this regard, that Kierkegaard said of himself, early on, in 1838: "If I am a literary weed—well, then at least I am what is called 'Proud Henry' [*Chenopodium bonus Henricus*]" (JP 5:5293). This plant is of the goosefoot family.

17. George Pattison, *The Philosophy of Kierkegaard* (Montreal: McGill-Queen's University Press, 2005), 1. See also Alastair Hannay, *Kierkegaard and Philosophy* (London: Routledge, 2003).

18. Others have done this too, but not in the way I have. See, for instance, *Provocations: Spiritual Writings of Kierkegaard*, ed. Charles E. Moore (Farmington, Pennsylvania: The Plough Publishing

book on Kierkegaard which I quoted at the beginning of this introduction by Pastor William T. Riviere, comparing Kierkegaard to the Viking marauders of old.[19] I would like to think of my book as a sequel to his—a second volume in the series, if you will. Pastor Riviere's book, *A Pastor Looks at Kierkegaard*,[20] inspired me to try to make use of Kierkegaard in the church. In what I have written, my guiding question, then, has been that if Kierkegaard's words about Christianity are true, how would they change the way we learn and practice the Christian faith today? My book is an answer to that question. So in these pages I do not enter into a critical discussion over the truth of

---

House, 1999); *Kierkegaard the Christian: An Anthology of Quotations*, ed. Robert B. Scheidt (Enumclaw, Washington: WinePress Publishing, 2003); *The Wisdom of Kierkegaard: A Collection of Quotations on Faith and Life*, ed. Clifford Williams (Eugene, Oregon: Wipf & Stock, 2009); C. Stephen Evans, *Søren Kierkegaard's Christian Psychology: Insights for Counseling & Pastoral Care* (Grand Rapids, Michigan: Zondervan, 1990); L. Joseph Rosas III, *Scripture in the Thought of Søren Kierkegaard* (Nashville: Broadman & Holman, 1994); and Timothy Houston Polk, *The Biblical Kierkegaard: Reading By the Rule of Faith* (Macon, Georgia: Mercer University Press, 1997).

19. In this regard, note also Paul L. Holmer, *On Kierkegaard and the Truth*, ed. David J. Gouwens and Lee C. Barrett III (Eugene, Oregon: Cascade, 2012), xxvi: "The evangelical hope of bringing the reader face to face with the God of Jesus Christ never forsakes him for a moment. But it is for others to say this at length about Kierkegaard." This is where, I would like to think, my book comes in. For a confirmation of Holmer's point, see Hugh Pyper, *The Joy of Kierkegaard: Essays on Kierkegaard as a Biblical Reader* (Sheffield, England & Oakville, Connecticut: Equinox, 2011), 1: "Kierkegaard . . . is an evangelist, in its root meaning as a bearer of good news. What he burns to communicate is good news, while knowing that the majority of his hearers cannot tell good news from bad and have a tendency to mistake the disease for the cure and the cure for the disease."

20. For another appreciative pastor, see Wallace Forgey, "A Pastor Looks at Kierkegaard," *Andover Bulletin* 44 (1955), 32: "Søren Kierkegaard is really a preacher's author. . . . S. K. had the faculty of seeing the sore spots of his day and generation, tried to do something about them in his thinking and writing, and had the courage to confront his generation with that which was truth for him, to pronounce judgment upon his church and his age, to face the tragedy of separation and loneliness, and to believe in the ultimate triumph of the things for which he lived and burned himself out, dying at the age of forty-two. Here is a man to know intimately. Here is meaty thought on which to chew. Here is a preacher who challenges one to use great themes. Here is a mind which is keen enough to cut through a pastor's complacency. Here is a life filled with divine discontent and passion. Here is a solution—a pastor's solution—to the problems faced by the 'amorphous despairing mass of displaced persons and paralyzed Hamlets' who make up our modern world." According to Forgey, Kierkegaard is like a biblical prophet. In this way he resembles Martin Luther, whom he deeply admired. See Martin Luther, "Appeal for Prayer Against the Turks" (1541), LW 43:223: "I am sure that I am a prophet, so much so that I suffer under the burden of it and wish that what I am saying were not true, as the prophet Micah did [Mi 7:1]. . . . [Even so] things are in about the same state as before the flood: 'And God saw the earth and behold, it was corrupt; for all flesh had corrupted their way upon the earth' (Gn 6:12). I myself am certain that if the world will not get better, . . . it will fall for the last time." Against Luther's view, see Steven Pinker, *The Better Angels of Our Nature: Why Violence Has Declined* (New York: Viking, 2011), 692–93: "Modernity [has brought] the transformation of human life by science, technology, and reason, with the attendant diminishment of custom, faith, community, traditional authority, and embeddedness in nature. . . . [It has greatly lessened] the trials of daily living [which plagued our ancestors who] were infested with lice and parasites and lived above cellars heaped with their own feces. Food was bland, monotonous, and intermittent. Health care consisted of the doctor's saw and the dentist's pliers. Both sexes labored from sunrise to sundown, whereupon they were plunged into darkness. Winter meant months of hunger, boredom, and gnawing loneliness in snowbound farmhouses."

Kierkegaard's philosophy and theology. Instead, I simply, by and large, believe what he wrote and run with it.[21] I do that by showing how his ideas shape our understanding of Christian identity, suffering and illness, worship and preaching, the Bible, baptism and the Christian minister. Interspersed are also many quotations from Martin Luther (1483–1546). That is because Kierkegaard's contributions are deeply shaped by the radical Christian view which he gleaned from Luther's theology. The book ends with a set of sermons inspired in various ways by Kierkegaard's writings—as well as with a biographical sketch coupled with a critique of Joakim Garff's new, major biography of Kierkegaard, and an assessment of Kierkegaard's failed engagement to Regine Olsen.

If my book adds anything to the scholarly understanding of Kierkegaard's thought, it would be in making a contribution to the place of the church in his thinking. Because of his criticisms of the Danish state church and his insistence on the necessity of the individual appropriation of Christian teachings, one might think that Kierkegaard had no regard for the church at all.[22] But that would be to throw the baby out with the bath. The fact is that he remained "a loyal son of the church" even while attacking it.[23] So a "Kierkegaard" whose alleged exaltation of subjectivity hatched a Christianity of "sheer privacy," suitable only for the "pious ghetto of the prayer house," is actually nothing but a "mythological Kierkegaard."[24] The real Kierkegaard attacked the church only in order to straighten out what he so dearly loved:

21. In so doing I add many long footnotes to enrich the argument in the main body of the book and to comment on the studies bearing upon my argument. On the zealous use of footnotes, see Anthony Grafton, *The Footnote: A Curious History* (Cambridge: Harvard University Press, 1997), 9: "To the inexpert, footnotes look like deep root systems, solid and fixed; to the connoisseur, however, they reveal themselves as anthills, swarming with constructive and combative activity." See also Kenneth L. Woodward, "In Praise of Footnotes," *Newsweek* (September 9, 1996), 75: "Footnotes . . . that yield the greatest pleasure are the kind that serve more than bibliographic purposes . . . . [They are the ones] like the cloakroom of Congress: they're the places where the author takes the reader into his confidence, revealing what he really thinks about his colleagues. I've read notes that resemble Russian dolls: footnotes within footnotes, aside piled on scholarly aside, sometimes running on for pages. There *are* books without footnotes, just as there are homes without porches, restaurants without bars. Millions have grown old without knowing the pleasures of these civilized appendages. Put books on tapes, if you must, but please include the footnotes." So I aim to please—Grafton and Woodward, at least. And maybe also David Foster Wallace (1962–2008). See his acclaimed novel, *Infinite Jest* (New York: Little, Brown and Company, 1996), with a hundred pages worth of endnotes! Note 110 is nineteen pages long, and note 304 has three footnotes in it. Note 216 may be the best: "No clue." On Wallace and his work, see James K. A. Smith, "David Foster Wallace to the Rescue," *First Things*, Number 231 (March 2013): 30: "If there is a moral to his own story, . . . it might be that transcendence continues to exert its pressure on contemporary fiction, piercing the confident boundaries of secularism."

22. See Bruce H. Kirmmse, "'Out With It!': The Modern Breakthrough, Kierkegaard, and Denmark," *The Cambridge Companion to Kierkegaard*, ed. Alastair Hannay and Gordon D. Marino (Cambridge: Cambridge University Press, 1998), 43: "The development of Kierkegaard's ecclesiology can be summarized as the progress from rather severe criticism of the Church, . . . to the decision that there must be rigorous separation of church and state, and finally to an apparent rejection of the Church . . . as such."

23. Howard A. Johnson, "Kierkegaard and the Church," *Kierkegaard's Attack Upon Christendom*, 1854–55, trans. Walter Lowrie (Princeton: Princeton University Press, 1968), xxi.

24. Per Lønning, "Kierkegaard: A Stumbling Block to 'Kierkegaardians,'" *Kierkegaard Studies*, ed.

His attack arose only when he felt the Church was *in a wrong way* a part of the culture, succumbing to a culture,[25] instead of so relating itself to eternity that it would be in possession of a transcendent principle of criticism by which to judge the culture to which God would have it responsibly related.[26]

It is just this transcendent principle of criticism that I have pursued in my essays and sermons. I offer them with the hope of strengthening the church that God established to call us "out from isolated subjectivity or out from engulfment in the masses and into a 'primitive God-relationship.'"[27] And I agree that we have "yet to take the full measure" of Kierkegaard's approach to renewing the church.[28] And it remains desperately needed because churches are still "selling their souls to the highest bidders, attracting consumers with a product whose appeal is success not faithfulness, self-esteem not discipleship, technique not truth."[29] But with this Kierkegaardian transcendent principle of criticism, there remains hope for the renewal of the faithfulness and discipline of the church. With that principle in hand, as we address in these essays and sermons, the various details of the Christian life, may the Christian, struggling to be faithful see, that

> When his only wish is to die,
> Not until then does Christianity truly begin.[30]

This is the sour note in Christianity that needs to be sounded if its truly saving power is to be known and believed. Therefore let us maintain that it is

> beneficial that the rigorous words are brought to recollection, are heard simultaneously, just as they inseparably belong together so that we at no time

---

Niels Jørgen Cappelørn and Hermann Deuser (Berlin and New York: Walter de Gruyter, 1997), 104.

25. On this same plague in our time, see Charles Taylor, *A Secular Age* (Cambridge: Harvard University Press, 2007), where he describes our society as one suffering from the "culturally hegemonic notion of a closed immanent order" (774).

26. Howard A, Johnson, "Kierkegaard and the Church," xxii. So "Kierkegaard desired essentially not the remodeling of the Church but its revival. . . . [And so] 'For Revival and Increase of Inwardness' . . . might well serve as the motto for Kierkegaard's whole endeavor in relation to the Established Church" (xxiv). Altizer, then, is also mistaken when he writes that "radical theology . . . understood as a solitary way, . . . cannot be an ecclesiastical theology, [it] cannot be bound to any established norms or traditions, and here Kierkegaard is . . . a primary model, and his final assault upon the church was a consistent fulfillment of the evolution of his thinking. Here, we can see all too clearly how the deepest religious or theological thinking . . . must be an anti-ecclesiastical thinking, or must be so in a genuinely modern world." Thomas J. J. Altizer, *The Call to Radical Theology*, ed. Lissa McCullough (Albany, New York: State University Press of New York, 2012), 3–4.

27. Howard A. Johnson, "Kierkegaard and the Church," xxviii.

28. Carl E. Braaten, "The Future of the Apostolic Imperative," *The Strange New World of the Gospel*, ed. Carl E. Braaten and Robert W. Jenson (Grand Rapids: Eerdmans, 2002), 161.

29. Carl E. Braaten, "The Gospel for a Neopagan Culture," *Either/Or: The Gospel of Neopaganism*, ed. Carl E. Braaten and Robert W. Jenson (Grand Rapids: Eerdmans, 1995), 18.

30. From "Kierkegaard's Jelly—for Pastor Ron Marshall," in Jim Bodeen, *The Jelly Poems* (Yakima, Washington: October Crush Publications, 2009), 73.

separate what God has joined together in Christ, neither add anything nor subtract anything, do not subtract the rigorousness from the leniency that is in them, do not subtract from the Gospel the Law that is in it, do not subtract from salvation the perdition that is in it. (CD 283)

EXCURSUS: ON THE ATONEMENT

Let me also note at the beginning of this book that I take it for granted[31]—especially in the sermons[32]—that Kierkegaard believed that Jesus was our "substitute," who was punished in our place to make satisfaction[33] for our sins before God (WA 123).[34] And thus by being our substitute, Christ "bought"[35] us back (CD 294) from condemnation

31. Not all students of Kierkegaard do, however. See, for instance, Lee C. Barrett, III, *Kierkegaard*, Abingdon Pillars of Theology (Nashville: Abingdon, 2010), 58: "Although Kierkegaard does use Anselm's language about Christ's satisfaction of God's justice, most frequently he describes the cross as manifesting God's forgiveness." Note as well, Murray Rae, *Kierkegaard and Theology* (London and New York: T. & T. Clark, 2010), 103: "Although this claim [WA 123] enjoins the concept of penal substitution, the emphasis here, and in Kierkegaard's further elucidations of the matter, is placed not at all upon the punitive aspect of the satisfaction but entirely upon the compassion of the Savior who bears for us the cost of sin." And so I agree with David J. Gouwens that "the substitutionary Anselmian aspects of Kierkegaard's thought on atonement" are substantial. *Kierkegaard as Religious Thinker* (Cambridge: Cambridge University Press, 1996), 147 n. 108.

32. So none of my sermons follow the judgment of Peter K. Stevenson and Stephen I. Wright, *Preaching the Atonement* (Louisville: Westminster John Knox, 2009), 112: "[Saint Paul avoids] driving a wedge between God and Christ. God did not 'punish' Christ . . . [and] Christ . . . did not set out to appease an alien and angry God. . . . In short, Calvary was the result of the unity of Father and incarnate Son, not of their somehow being pitted against each other." I reject this view, favoring instead the Lutheran Confessions, which state that only Christ can be "pitted against God's wrath" (BC 136). I also reject it because Jesus in fact does save us from the wrath of God (Jn 3:36; Rom 5:9), by intervening with the Father as our mediator (1 Tm 2:5), intercessor (Heb 7:25), and advocate (1 Jn 2:1). On this see Martin Luther, "There is grave discord between God . . . and us. . . . Therefore Christ has stepped into the breach as the Mediator between two utterly different parties separated by an infinite and eternal division, and has reconciled them" (LW 26:325).

33. See Is 53:11.

34. Let me also note at the beginning, that for all of Kierkegaard's emphasis on the imitation of Christ, his atonement is what actually has priority for him: "Atonement and grace . . . remain definitive. All striving toward imitation, when the moment of death brings it to an end and one stands before God, will be sheer paltriness—therefore atonement and grace are needed. Furthermore, as long as there is striving, the Atonement will constantly be needed to prevent this striving from being transformed into agonizing anxiety in which a man is burned up, so to speak, and less than ever begins to strive. Finally, while there is striving, every other second a mistake is made, something is neglected, there is sin—therefore the Atonement is unconditionally needed" (JP 2:1909). And he also notes that sometimes he shamefully forgets about this priority (JP 2:1852)! See also *Contemporary Worship 6: The Church Year, Calendar and Lectionary* (Minneapolis: Augsburg, 1973), 202: "In 1854 [Kierkegaard] began his assault upon the established church, accusing it of accommodating the Christian revelation to human desires. His thought, deeply original and ascetic in mood, reveals his Lutheran heritage in its basic concerns and emphases. Many of his writings are of great devotional value and reveal a profound understanding of the redemptive work of Christ and the significance of the cross."

35. See 2 Pt 2:1.

in hell, because of God's fierce anger against us, to keep us safe for all of eternity in heaven. Christ did all of this by carrying our sins in his body on the cross (UDVS 231), so that by his death, God would be reconciled to us (CD 289),[36] and out of mercy, love us when we repent[37] of our sins (JP 2:1329, 2300). Now I would like to make three notes on this view of atonement in Kierkegaard's writings, largely because it has caused "considerable dismay to the mind [and has been deemed] a notion which modern Christianity has no option but to discard."[38] And the first one of my notes is that his view is largely taken over from Luther. In his *Large Catechism* we have this classic formulation on the atonement:

> When we were created by God the Father, and had received from him all kinds of good things, the devil came and led us into disobedience, sin, death, and all evil. We lay under God's wrath and displeasure, doomed to eternal damnation, as we had deserved. There was no counsel, no help, no comfort for us until this only and eternal Son of God, in his unfathomable goodness, had mercy on our misery and wretchedness and came from heaven to help us. Those tyrants

36. David J. Gouwens misses this point. See his *Kierkegaard as Religious Thinker*, 168: "[The] change that God undergoes in atonement . . . cannot stand up under reflection [JP 2:1348]. . . . God's constancy (unchangeableness) in atonement calls, rather, for one to recognize sin and reconciliation." Kierkegaard, like Luther, does not however stumble over what Gouwens does, *viz.*, that if God is unchangeable he cannot be reconciled to sinners through Christ's crucifixion, for that would entail a change in God and he cannot change. Kierkegaard believed that God could be moved but without being changed (TM 268)—a distinction that is not apparent to many. So Kierkegaard carefully says that "Christ [is] the one who makes satisfaction and thus influences God's willingness to forgive" (JP 2:1223). Kierkegaard does say, as Gouwens notes, that "it is by no means necessary [that] for a reconciliation [to occur] . . . both parties [need to] be changed, for if one party is in the right, it would be madness for him to be changed" (JP 2:1348). But for Kierkegaard, that fact that God is right to send his only son Jesus Christ to die that sinners might be "brought . . . close to" him (CD 299), does not prevent that same death from also saving sinners from the wrath of God (Rom 5:9). In that sense, two parties can be reconciled without both being wrong.

37. See 1 Jn 1:9.

38. *The Glory of the Atonement: Biblical, Historical & Practical Perspectives: Essays in Honor of Roger Nicole*, ed. Charles E. Hill and Frank A. James III (Downers Grove, Illinois, 2004), 446. See also *The Redemption: An Interdisciplinary Symposium on Christ as Redeemer*, ed. Stephen T. Davis, Daniel Kendall, SJ, Gerald O'Collins, SJ (Oxford: Oxford University Press, 2004), 177: "We obtain [reconciliation] by the interceding death of the only Begotten and are justified by grace in the same blood. Why, you ask me, by blood when [God] could have done it by word. I, [Bernard of Clairvaux, 1090–1153], ask the same question." Against these two views, see Martin Luther, "Treatise on Good Works" (1520), LW 44:38: "[Faith] must spring up and flow from the blood and wounds and death of Christ. If you see in these that God is so kindly disposed toward you that he even gives his own Son for you, then your heart in turn must grow sweet and disposed toward God." This statement is also congenial to Kierkegaard's way of thinking. And for Luther's more general comment on the cross, see his "Commentary on Psalm 110" (1535), LW 13:319–20: "[The true sacrifice of Christ] deserves to be praised to the utmost and to have every honor given to it, especially over against those other false, lying sacrifices of our own works, which were invented to deny and blaspheme this sacrifice. He is also the Priest who ought to be called a priest above all others. What man can praise and exalt Him enough? . . . Willingly and without price He has mediated between God's wrath and our sin. By His blood and death He gave Himself as the sacrifice or ransom and thereby far outweighed both of them. No matter how great or burdensome sin, wrath, hell, and damnation may be, this holy sacrifice is far greater and higher!"

and jailers now have been routed, and their place has been taken by Jesus Christ, the Lord of life and righteousness and every good and blessing. He has snatched us, poor lost creatures, from the jaws of hell, won us, made us free, and restored us to the Father's favor and grace. . . . [How] much it cost Christ . . . to win us and bring us under his dominion. That is to say, . . . he suffered, died, and was buried that he might make satisfaction for me and pay what I owed, not with silver and gold but with his own precious blood.[39] (BC 414)

Kierkegaard is in basic agreement with this passage, even though he never comments on it directly, nor writes a treatise on the crucifixion in general to prove the "mystery of the atonement"[40]—which, as described by Luther, would be an Anselmian,[41] penal, substitution view of the atonement.[42] Nevertheless, he could still join in with generations of Lutherans and sing of Christ that

39. See also two passages from Luther's sermons. The first is from a "Sermon on 1 Corinthians 5:6–8" (1540), SML 7:190–91: "[Consider] . . . the greatness and terror of the wrath of God against sin in that it could be appeased and a ransom effected in no other way than through the one sacrifice of the Son of God. Only his death and the shedding of his blood could make satisfaction. And we must consider also that we by our sinfulness had incurred that wrath of God and therefore were responsible for the offering of the Son of God upon the cross. . . . Well may we be terrified because of our sins, for God's wrath cannot be trivial when we are told no sacrifice save alone the Son of God can brave such wrath. . . . Therefore, though your sins are great and deserve the awful wrath of God, yet the sacrifice represented by the death of the Son of God is infinitely greater." And the second passage is from a "Sermon on Luke 24:36–47" (1524), SML 2:344: "[If] God's wrath is to be taken away from me, . . . some one must merit this; for God cannot be a friend of sin nor gracious to it, nor can he remit the punishment and wrath, unless payment and satisfaction be made. Now, no one . . . could make restitution for the infinite and irreparable injury and appease the eternal wrath of God which we had merited by our sins; except that eternal person, the Son of God himself, and he could do it only by taking our place, assuming our sins, and answering for them as though he himself were guilty of them. This our dear Lord and only Savior and Mediator before God, Jesus Christ, did for us by his blood and death, in which he became a sacrifice for us; and with his purity, . . . which was divine and eternal, he outweighed all sin and wrath he was compelled to bear on our account; . . . and his merit is so great that God is now satisfied and says, 'If he wills thereby to save, then there shall be salvation.'"

40. Søren Kierkegaard, *Discourses at the Communion on Fridays*, trans. Sylvia Walsh (Bloomington: Indiana University Press, 2011), 26.

41. Saint Anselm (1033–1109), is one of the doctors of the church—*doctores ecclesiae*. See Bernard McGinn, *The Doctors of the Church: Thirty-Three Men and Women Who Shaped Christianity* (New York: Crossroad, 1999), 103–6.

42. These features make Luther's view quite controversial today. On this difficulty, see Stephen Finlan, *Problems With Atonement: The Origins of, and Controversy About, the Atonement Doctrine* (Collegeville, Minnesota: Liturgical Press, 2005), 75–76, 78–79: "Luther's teachings [on salvation are] more complex than one might realize if one reads only the interpretations of his works by others. . . . [He presents] a dramatic and frightening scenario of divine violence restrained by divine mercy, but a mercy that had to be mediated through violence [though he never explains why] a sacrificial death was required . . . [or] why God had to use a terrible killing as the means for salvation. . . . [His most influential doctrines] are absolute depravity, universal guilt, and a horrifying transfer of divine wrath to the undeserving son. When such doctrines sink in, they give rise to severe distress in most believers, ultimately contributing to the rejection of Christianity. . . . Luther thought he had to believe in a God who outraged his own deepest moral sensibilities. The ironic result of this is a God who is legalistic in condemning but arbitrarily extralegal in saving, who commands absolute obedience but

> He all the Law for us fulfilled,
> And thus his Father's anger stilled
> Which over us impended.[43]

And my second note is that, in his journals, Kierkegaard does discuss the atonement[44]—perhaps in lieu of a treatise on the topic. There he writes, for example, that we should join Anselm in declaring that "Christianity is God's invention and, in a good sense, God's interest," since it brings about his reconciliation to sinners. And "out of love God wants to be reconciled" to sinners—which shows how majestic and sublime he is:

> Alas, . . . Christianity is not presented at all any more; to that extent it has become meaninglessness, a thing of habit. The fact that Christianity is the divine combat of divine passion with itself,[45] so that in a sense we human beings

expects universal rebellion, who justifies a few who do not deserve it and condemns many who are not to blame. . . . Luther could declare independence from corrupt clerical practices but not from distorted dogma, and certainly not from his own internal conflicts and rage. The position of this important intellectual [i.e., Luther] ends up being anti-intellectual: dogma need not answer to reason; in fact, dogma must offend reason or 'it clearly would not be Divine' [LW 33:290]. . . . [Luther simplifies and hardens Paul's] sacrificial metaphors [into] the soteriology that most Christians now take for granted. All of Paul's subtleties . . . were forgotten by the latter and lesser minds of Christianity. I do not believe that Paul ever intended that one should interpret his metaphors with . . . the troubled self-loathing of Luther. Still, Paul's soteriological formulas about the death of Christ provided the seedbed for those frightening and rigid theologies of atonement that came later, [including Luther's. . . . Nevertheless] we cannot absolve Paul of responsibility for the fact that people have brought a transactional interpretation to bear on the idea that God 'did not withhold his own Son' (Rom 8:32), and that believers 'were bought with a price' (1 Cor 6:20)."

43. The text of this hymn, "Salvation Unto Us Has Come," is by Paul Speratus (1484–1551). See *Lutheran Book of Worship* (Minneapolis: Augsburg, 1978), Hymn 297. And note that this verse has been excised from the hymn, without telling us why, in the newer hymnal, *Evangelical Lutheran Worship* (Minneapolis: Augsburg Fortress, 2006), Hymn 590. One might imagine that it was because the editors disapproved of the view of the atonement expressed in these lines and so they took it out. This verse, however, has been maintained, under a slightly different translation, in another new Lutheran hymnal, *Lutheran Service Book* (Saint Louis, Missouri: Concordia, 2006), Hymn 555: "He has for us the Law obeyed and thus the Father's vengeance stayed which over us impended." These two worship books, published in the same year, show the Lutheran battle that is raging over the proper understanding of the atonement today. The same battle can be seen in the debate over the sacrifice of Christ in Romans 3:25 in the *Lutheran Study Bible* (Minneapolis: Augsburg Fortress, 2009), 1856, and in *The Lutheran Study Bible* (Saint Louis, Missouri: Concordia, 2009), 1914. The Concordia book says what the Augsburg Fortress book leaves unsaid: "Some thoughtless modern theologians have likened Paul's teaching on the atonement to child abuse because the Father sent the Son as a sacrifice. This assertion ignores Christ's willingness to make full satisfaction for sins. . . . The Father sent the Son the way a patriotic father sends his son to war for the good of his nation. A father does not send a son cheerfully, but sincerely, anticipating sacrifice, victory, and reunion."

44. Even so he still is no Danish Anselm. Alas, for a book length treatise from him on the atonement would have no doubt been splendid!

45. For a possible precursor to this view of divine combat, see Martin Luther, "Commentary on Psalm 51" (1538), LW 12:321: "[The] picture of a gracious and merciful God . . . shields the pronoun 'on me' [in Ps 51:1], throws wrath into the corner, and says, 'God is gracious.' This is not the theology of reason, which counsels despair in the midst of sin. David feels sin and the wrath of God, and yet he

disappear like ants (although it still is infinite love for us)—this is forgotten;
God is made into a lenient something or other which is neither God nor man.
(JP 1:532)

This internal divine combat pits his wrath against his love—and the sacrifice of Christ is precisely what appeases his wrath so that he can love sinners and forgive their sins.[46] The reason this sacrifice is needed is because "it is not simple for God to forgive sins"[47]—since he needs to be reconciled by way of a divine, blood sacrifice,[48] before

---

says, 'Have mercy on me, O God.' Reason does not know this teaching, but the Holy Scriptures teach it, as you see in the first verse of this psalm. The individual words are purely and chastely placed, but they are the words of the Spirit which have life. From them spiritual men learn to distinguish between sinner and sinner, between God and God, and learn to reconcile the wrath of God or the wrathful God with man the sinner."

46. This is stated in Romans 5:9 and prefigured in Hosea 11:8. On the Hosea verse see Hans Walter Wolff, *A Commentary on the Book of the Prophet Hosea*, trans. Gary Stansell, ed. Paul D. Hanson (Philadelphia: Fortress, 1974), 201: [There] will be . . . a change in Yahweh's heart. . . . Yahweh's will is directed against himself, i.e., against his wrath. . . . [So the] phrase 'my heart turns against me' . . . has a hostile sense. . . . His remorse (over his wrathful intention to judge), 'grows hot,' i.e., it provokes and dominates him." In this regard, note also Kierkegaard's point that "God's nature always joins opposites"—as in the case of linking the merciful with the scrupulous, for instance (CD 294). Against this reading of Hosea 11, see Ted Grimsrud, *Instead of Atonement: The Bible's Salvation Story and Our Hope for Wholeness* (Eugene, Oregon: Cascade, 2013). Grimsrud argues that God shows compassion to Israel because he is not human (Hos 11:9) rather than because his heart recoils within him (Hos 11:8) (35). But I would say that there is no wedge here. God has compassion in other than human ways *precisely beca*use he suffers the punishment himself. This is illustrative of the overall biblical theme of salvation through suffering—in this case, God's suffering. Grimsrud offers no argument for the necessity of this exegetical wedge, which I take to be his key point.

47. Paul Tillich, *A History of Christian Thought: From Its Judaic and Hellenistic Origins to Existentialism*, ed. Carl E. Braaten (New York: Touchstone, 1968), 166. See also Emil Brunner, *The Mediator: A Study of the Central Doctrine of the Christian Faith* (1932), trans. Olive Wyon (Philadelphia: Westminster, 1947), 519: "In . . . the Atonement. . . . God reconciles Himself in Christ to man. Here we stand in the presence of the central mystery of the Christian revelation: the dual nature of God. . . . Therefore the dualism of holiness and love, of revelation and concealment, of mercy and wrath, cannot be dissolved, changed into *one* synthetic conception, without at the same time destroying the seriousness of the biblical knowledge of God, the reality and the mystery of revelation and atonement." See also Jack Miles, *Christ: A Crisis in the Life of God* (New York: Knopf, 2001), 97, 99, 109: "When urging mercy, Jesus does not say 'Be merciful because mercy is better than vengeance.' What he says is 'Be merciful as your Father is merciful.' But how merciful has the Father shown himself to be in his previous career? How kind has the Most High typically been when confronted with the ungrateful and wicked? . . . The Lord can no longer be praised for smashing the heads of his enemies [Habakkuk 3:13], for he is no longer a head-smashing kind of god. But there is no denying that the Lord has been a head smasher—both by performance and in endlessly repeated aspiration. If he is such no longer, then he must have changed, but what accounts for the change? . . . The radical rejection of human difference, including the difference between friend and foe, does come on the cheap for God—unless and until God becomes a human being and suffers the consequences of his own confession."

48. See Heb 9:22: "[Without] the shedding of blood there is no forgiveness of sins" (RSV). Against this view, see Christopher D. Marshall, *Beyond Retribution: The New Testament Vision for Justice, Crime, and Punishment* (Grand Rapids: Eerdmans, 2001), 62: "[It] makes no sense at all to speak of God inflicting punitive retribution on himself, much less 'damning himself,' in order to satisfy divine justice!"

he can extend his eternal love to unworthy sinners. Because this sacrifice is needed before God can love us, rendering Christianity anything but "purely and simply sweet sugar candy," we may think he is anything but loving. This sacrifice, however, is actually his greatness, his majesty, his sublimity—that his love is not "plainly recognizable" to us, because "this love in a certain sense [looks] like cruelty" (JP 2:1447). For indeed,

> we human beings have no conception of divine sublimity! If we can just live on the fat of the land and God does not crack down on us—then we completely forget that his very calmness . . . [and] the very fact that he lets us get drunk on a life of ease and frothy gratitude can be an expression of his contempt and disfavor, whereas the lives of his beloved ones express that they must suffer . . . but which we harden ourselves against. (JP 3:2442)

This uncomfortable view of God is implied in a penal, substitution view of the atonement.[49] Such a stern deity—as is assumed in a penal, substitution view of the atonement—is hardly "a fuddy-duddy any preacher can twaddle about," as Kierkegaard sarcastically points out (JP 3:2573). No, this majestic, sublime view of God links him instead to ghastly natural calamities[50] in order to purge our conception of him of any "chummy idea" of a soft and cozy deity (JP 3:2569). To get a true biblical picture of God, we then need to think of him in terms of

> a storm, when a hurricane rages and uproots trees, and the birds in death-agony plunge to the ground. Or [when] the wind blows away the pollen of million of flowers, [and] the earth opens up and swallows entire cities. (JP 3:2853)

This is the divine rage that is appeased by the sacrifice of Jesus on the cross. If this wrath is missing from the picture of redemption, then Christ's atonement looks like much ado about nothing. Without this rage in God vented against sinners, Christ's sacrifice on the cross is meaningless. So while it is true that Jesus died on the cross to save us from our sins (1 Cor 15:3; Heb 9:26), the main point of the crucifixion for Kierkegaard is the reconciliation of God to sinners by way of Christ's sacrifice. On the cross God's wrath is being overcome so that sinners may be forgiven. And so Kierkegaard would agree with Luther that we should carefully "consider this price" that Christ offered up for sins.[51]

---

49. For Luther's classic statement on the theology of the cross, see his "Explanation of the Ninety-Five Theses" (1518), LW 31:227: "[The] theologian of glory . . . learns from Aristotle that the object of the will is the good and the good is worthy to be loved, while the evil, on the other hand, is worthy of hate. He learns that God is the highest good and exceedingly lovable. Disagreeing with the theologian of the cross, he defines the treasury of Christ as the removing and remitting of punishments, things which are most evil and worthy of hate. In opposition to this the theologian of the cross defines the treasury of Christ as impositions and obligations of punishments, things which are best and most worthy of love." If this inversion of values is honored, then opposition to Luther's view of the atonement ceases.

50. See Nm 11:1, 16:31–32; Job 38:1; Is 29:6, 30:30; Ez 13:13; Na 1:3.

51. Martin Luther, "Lectures on Galatians 1–4" (1535), LW 26:175–76: "[There] is so much evil in

A wonderful contemporary, visual depiction of this theological point of view, is Mel Gibson's controversial movie, *The Passion of the Christ*.[52] The "theological heart" of this movie is the Anselmian, substitutionary, objective[53] view of the atonement, wherein the "focus is on God himself and what he accomplished on our behalf in Christ Jesus. On the cross he took our place and bore our sins."[54] Because of this movie, Gibson has been dubbed "a latter day Kierkegaard," in as much as Christ cannot be "assimilated into our ordinary modes of thinking."[55] As so in the face of charges of excessive violence, Gibson's official interpreter notes that the movie in fact actually fails to show "the full reality" of the crucifixion—"toning it down just enough for the audience to actually watch it. . . . [But from] a Christian perspective, none of the violence is gratuitous. The purpose is not to make viewers squirm and say, 'How

---

my nature that the world and all creation would not suffice to placate God, but that the Son of God Himself had to be given up for it. [So] *consider this price carefully*, and look at this captive, the Son of God. You will see then that He is greater and more excellent than all creation. . . . If you looked at this price, you would take all your . . . works, . . . and you would . . . spit upon, and damn them. . . . [For God] cannot be placated except by *this immense, infinite price*, the death and the blood of the Son of God, *one drop of which is more precious than all creation*" (italics added).

52. *The Passion of the Christ* (2004), released on Ash Wednesday, February 25, 2004 (DVD–ASIN: B000–28-HBKM). Gross earnings worldwide have been over $611 million (boxofficemojo).

53. Even some critics of the penal, substitution view recognize the value in the objectivity that undergirds this view of the atonement—for as Kierkegaard noted: "The essentially Christian exists before any Christian exists; it must exist in order for one to become a Christian. It contains the qualification by which a test is made of whether someone has become a Christian; it maintains its objective continuance outside all believers, while it also is in the inwardness of the believer" (BA 117–18). So by establishing God's love for sinners through the crucifixion of Christ, despairing sinners have a sure and certain reference for their faith in the forgiveness of sins and a resolute hope for the possibility of a transformed life. On this need for objectivity, see J. Denny Weaver, *The Nonviolent Atonement*, Second Edition (Grand Rapids: Eerdmans, 2011), 315: "Critics of the moral theory [of the atonement] have pointed out that it has no objective character. As an act of God's love, the death of Jesus accomplishes nothing until a sinner responds to it. For [Abelard's version of the moral theory] nothing changes until the individual changes in response to the love of God, and then what changes is only the individual. In contrast, Anselm's satisfaction motif had a clear objective character. Jesus' death paid the debt which restored the order of the universe quite apart from whether individual sinners availed themselves of the opportunity of salvation thus provided. While [my] narrative Christus Victor [view] shares Abelard's rejection of the idea that Jesus' death is a debt payment, these two atonement motifs [Abelard's and mine] differ in a profound way. While the death and resurrection of Jesus clearly impacts the mind of the sinner, narrative Christus Victor envisions a change in the universe quite apart from any person's perception of it. With the death and resurrection of Jesus, the power structure of the universe is revealed to be different than it appears. The resurrection of Jesus is the definitive victory of the reign of God over the reign of evil, whether or not any individual sinner perceives the resurrection. When an individual does perceive the saving work of Christ and begins a transformed life under the rule of God, that individual is joining a reality already established by the resurrection of Jesus." The problem with Weaver's view, however, is that it is not really objective in that his altered universe has no positive impact on the sinner prior to going the way of the highly touted transformed life.

54. *Re-viewing the Passion: Mel Gibson's Film and Its Critics*, ed. S. Brent Plate (New York: Palgrave MacMillan, 2004), 62.

55. *Mel Gibson's* Passion *and Philosophy: The Cross, the Questions, the Controversy*, ed. Jorge J. E. Gracia (Chicago: Open Court, 2004), 3.

gross!' It's there because that's what Jesus suffered. Those are the wounds that heal. It really happened, and so, the film seems to say, if God let it happen, there must be a reason for it."[56] And that ghastly display of abuse and excruciating pain is good to see in a movie because it can change for the good "the perceived importance of how [one treats] other people"—replacing anger with forgiveness, and fear with love.[57]

And my third note has to do with the criticisms leveled against Kierkegaard's view. Over the last thirty years or so, this Anselmian view of Kierkegaard's has been widely attacked.[58] The charges against it have coalesced around the slogan of "divine child abuse"[59]—castigating God for sending his son with cruel intent to die for

---

56. John Bartunek, L. C., *Inside the Passion: An Insider's Look at the Passion of the Christ* (West Chester, Pennsylvania: Ascension, 2005), 88–89. See also Stephen Mansfield, *Killing Jesus* (Brentwood, Tennessee: Worthy, 2013), 137–38, 141, 167–68:

> [The] scourging [of Jesus] has been savage. Some of the bones in Jesus' back are exposed. He has lost vast amounts of blood. His flesh is shredded as though a wild animal had been gnawing on him. He is ghastly to look at, nauseating, even for those who have seen a scourging before. . . . He is almost dead though not quite. . . . [And so he] is now nearly unrecognizable. Until he moves in some small way, it is hard to tell whether he is alive or merely balanced upright by the guard. He does not look human. He looks freshly returned from the dead. . . . [Impaled on the cross, Jesus] realizes that the only way to keep from suffocating is to push down on the spike through his feet. This lifts him up to relieve the stress on his arms. It is an unspeakably tortuous move. It rotates his forearms around the spike in his wrists, scrapes his back over the jagged wood of the stipes, and grips his legs in agonizing cramps. It eases him slightly, though, by allowing him to breathe. He cannot hold the position long. Soon, he finds that pressing down on the spike through his feet is so exhausting that he has to lower himself and hang from his wrists again. . . . Then, the sadistic cycle repeats. In the barracks, grizzled legionnaires call this "the dance of death."

57. Jody Eldred, *Changed Lives—Miracles of the Passion* (Eugene, Oregon: Harvest House, 2004), 24, 41.

58. Some even say it has gone on longer than that. See Stephen Finlan, *Problems With Atonement*, 1: "What is most noticeable about the literature on atonement written in the last 150 years is the intense concern with *problems* that the authors (and presumably the readers) have with the traditional doctrine of atonement." And some say this debate is church-dividing. See *The Atonement Debate: Papers From the London Symposium on the Theology of Atonement*, ed. Derek Tidball, David Hilborn & Justin Thacker (Grand Rapids: Zondervan, 2008), 188: "[Since the debate over penal substitutionary atonement is] about who God is, about the creedal doctrine of the Trinity, about the consequences of sin, about how we are saved, and about views which are held to encourage the abuse of women and children, then [it is impossible for] those who disagree [to] remain allied without placing unity above truths which are undeniably central to the Christian faith." On this dilemma, see Peter Schmiechen, *Saving Power: Theories of Atonement and Forms of the Church* (Grand Rapids: Eerdmans, 2005), 118: "The theory of penal substitution presents us with a serious dilemma: on the one hand it is accepted by many traditions as the primary interpretation of the gospel of Jesus Christ; on the other hand it is perceived by others as so flawed that it converts the story of Jesus into divinely sanctioned violence."

59. See Joanne Carlson Brown, "Divine Child Abuse?" *Daughters of Sarah* 18 (June 1992), 28: "We must do away with the atonement, this idea of a blood sin upon the whole human race which can be washed away only by the blood of the lamb. This blood-thirsty God is the God of patriarchy who at the moment controls the whole Christian tradition. We do not need to be saved by Jesus' death from some original sin. We need to be liberated from this abusive patriarchy." See also *Perspectives on The Passion of the Christ: Religious Thinkers and Writers Explore the Issues Raised by the Controversial Movie*, ed. Jonathan Burnham (New York: Miramax, 2004), 142; *Cross Examinations: Readings on the*

sinners. For indeed, the "allied doctrines of original sin and vicarious atonement . . . are intellectually contemptible and morally outrageous,"—so much so that they make Christianity "the worst . . . of world religions."[60] What is more, logical inconsistencies within this view of the atonement have also been noted:

> [Although] it is possible to pay another's *debts*, it is not possible to bear per-
> sonal penalties which culminate in death. . . . We can see that the innocent are
> indeed often punished in the place of the guilty, but this is to be regarded as
> a tragic error and not a creative and redemptive fact.[61] Further, if an appeal
> is made to some unstated principle of equivalence, Christ's death might have
> paid the penalty for one death, but could not pay for all. He cannot be said to
> have died as the head of humanity, for that character did not yet belong to him
> during his earthly life. Moreover, the penalty for sin was eternal death, but
> Christ did not suffer this, but was raised from the dead. [And] Christ cannot
> both suffer in our place and fulfill the law as our substitute. If he did one, there
> [would be] no need for the other.[62] . . . [Furthermore, if] Christ has indeed
> made satisfaction then it follows that we are accepted; if Christ's merit must be
> "imputed" to us, then there can have been no satisfaction, for this implies that
> satisfaction has only limited validity. . . . [In addition, if] Christ was truly the
> God-Man, then he need not have suffered to such an extent, for the smallest
> of his sufferings would have weighed in the balance. The theory seems there-
> fore to imply a God who delights in torture. . . . The argument of this theory
> seems to show that we are more indebted to Christ than to God because Christ
> showed us kindness whereas God, by demanding the full penalty, showed us

---

Meaning of the Cross Today, ed. Margit Trelstad (Minneapolis: Augsburg Fortress, 2006), 41, 229, 238; and *Stricken by God? Nonviolent Identification and the Victory of Christ*, ed. Brad Jersak and Michael Hardin (Grand Rapids: Eerdmans, 2007), 411. On two other significant factors in this attack, see *The Nature of the Atonement: Four Views*, ed. James Beilby and Paul R. Eddy (Downers Grove, Illinois: IVP Academic, 2006), 10–12. Added to this slogan about divine child abuse are (i) the critique of scapegoat theory and its endorsement of sacred violence by René Girard (1923–), and (ii) the argument in favor of the *Christus Victor* motif over the sacrificial view in the writings of Gustaf Aulén (1879–1978).

60. *The Glory of the Atonement*, 15.

61. Other critics concede this neuralgic point. See for an example, Peter Schmiechen, *Saving Pow-er*, 118: "[One of the] positive assumptions . . . of penal substitution [is that] Jesus dies the death of a sinner and in this way does in fact *take our place*. Why he does this, however, needs to be explained without suggesting that it is compensation offered to God [*contra* Eph 5:2; Heb 9:14] to enable God to redeem us."

62. But both are covered under the clearing of God's name. On this view see Ben Cooper, *Just Love: Why God Must Punish Sin* (Surrey, United Kingdom: The Good Book Company, 2005), 90: "When we sin, when we rebel against God, we assault his authority, we disbelieve his justice, we defame his name, we wish he weren't God, we stupidly wish he were dead. We circulate a great lie, saying he is not God. And rather as you and I would want to set things straight and clear . . . your name if you were slandered, so God acts to clear his name. A repeated refrain in the Bible is that God punishes so that people may know he is the LORD. He will not be satisfied until he has dealt with every one of those lies our rebellion has leveled at him. He will not be satisfied until he has demonstrated his authority and justice. And the cross proves it."

no kindness at all.[63] Finally it is ethically dangerous, in that it invites indolence or even licentiousness.[64]

None of these point in this passage are convincing however—due to the unsubstantiated assumptions that undergird them. Take the last one, about the fractured Holy Trinity—with Christ being kinder than God the Father. It has been pointed out that within God there can be "mutual involvement of the persons without implying symmetrical involvement."[65] This distinction allows for differences within God that do not result in divisions in his very nature—as this criticism alleges. And on the last point regarding indolence, Kierkegaard writes that Christian practice disrupts or turns Christianity all around when we think that because Christ died and made "satisfaction for our sins," that we can then "enjoy life properly and at most thank him once in a while, although that is not really necessary" (JP 2:1836).[66] This lackadaisical

63. This criticism rests on the view that if God's wrath has to be placated in order for him to show mercy, then there is no mercy at all—because mercy is only shown when wrath is all that can be reasonably expected. Mercy is wild and woolly, on this view. So if divine mercy depends on God first being reconciled by the blood of Christ, then it is nothing but rank legalism—simply following legalistically the dictates of divine satisfaction, and not the freely flowing gifts of mercy. Against this view I have written in "Praying in Jesus' Name," *The Bride of Christ* 22 (Lent and Easter 1998): 5: "God's Law explains only the need for salvation and one accomplishment of salvation [*viz.*, God being placated], but neither the motive nor the means of salvation. God wants to save us because he loves us. This is the motive of salvation. And God saves us by accepting the death of his only Son as sufficient payment for the punishment all people had earned by violating God's Law. If God had not deemed Christ's death meritorious, it would have not saved us. This judgment of God is the means of salvation. So God's Law does not determine our salvation [which would be legalism], but God's love alone [which is mercy]. God's Law is the grist in the mill of salvation, but not the ox that moves the mill stone." This is the point of Ephesians 5:2 which says that God accepts Christ's sacrifice to him as a fragrant offering. Therefore the sacrifice of Christ to God the Father does not automatically save us—by the necessities of the Law. No, God first has to accept the offering as salvific—a fragrant offering, and we then have to believe in it, by the grace of God (Gal 2:8), before there can be any salvation. Therefore all the steam in the charge of legalism is drained out of it.

64. Timothy Gorringe, *God's Just Vengeance: Crime, Violence, and the Rhetoric of Salvation*, (New York: Cambridge University Press, 1996), 145–46. Against this overall view, see Ian J. Shaw and Brian H. Edwards, *The Divine Substitution: The Atonement in the Bible and History* (Leominster, United Kingdom: Day One, 2006), 124–25: "J. C. Ryle (1816–1900) . . . lamented the rise of [jelly-fish] Christianity—a Christianity without bone, or muscle, or sinew—without any distinct teaching about the atonement or work of the Spirit, or justification, or the way of peace with God—a vague, foggy, misty Christianity."

65. Steve Jeffery, Michael Ovey, Andrew Sach, *Pierced For Our Transgressions: Rediscovering the Glory of Penal Substitution* (Wheaton, Illinois: Crossway, 2007), 284.

66. This misuse of the atonement tries to "eliminate conscience . . . in the following manner: You have a God who has atoned—now you may really enjoy life. This is the greatest possible relapse" (JP 1:534)! So Kierkegaard would disagree with Stephen J. Patterson, *Beyond the Passion: Rethinking the Death and Life of Jesus* (Minneapolis: Fortress, 2004), 3: "[We] leap over Jesus' life to take in his death in all its significance, as if it could be significant without his life to make it so. But so it has become to us: his death is the sacrifice that ensures our forgiveness before a God torn between anger and compassion. What need do we have of his life if it is his death that ensures our salvation?" Kierkegaard believes that the relationship between Christ as our redeemer and example is complex: "[It] is not simply a matter of Christ's being the prototype and that I simply ought to will to resemble him. In the

attitude conflicts with redemption which requires all Christians to maintain an ethical bearing. Kierkegaard expresses this correlation well in one of his prayers:

> O Redeemer, by your holy suffering and death you have made satisfaction for everyone and everything; no eternal salvation either can or shall be earned—it has been earned. Yet you left your footprints, you, the holy prototype for the human race and for every individual, so that by your Atonement the saved might at every moment find the confidence and the boldness to want to strive to follow you. (JFY 147)[67]

Here we see how ethics requires the power—which is manifest in redemption—to live out the moral life by striving to be like Jesus.[68] Kierkegaard does not believe that

---

first place I need His help in order to be able to resemble Him, and, secondly, insofar as he is the Savior and Reconciler of the race, I cannot in fact resemble him. The medieval conception of Christ as the prototype, its beautiful zeal to resemble him—this is youthfulness which wants to get along right away. But the older one becomes, the deeper becomes the qualitative distinction between the ideal and the man who wants to resemble it. Therefore Luther actually fought against a too zealous and too enthusiastic desire to make Christ only the prototype—and now it appears all the more that the prototype is also something else, as the Atoner whom we cannot resemble, who can only help us. Finally, this was emphasized so much that His being the prototype almost evaporated as something altogether too transcendent. This, however, must not be done" (JP 1:693). So deep down it is all grace—"but this does not mean that one is to sneak out of self-denial, no, no" (JP 2:1490)!

67. For a similar distinction, see Martin Luther, "Lectures on Galatians 5–6" (1535), LW 27:34: "Scripture presents Christ in two ways. First, as a gift. If I take hold of Him this way, I shall lack nothing whatever. 'In Christ are hid all the treasures of wisdom and knowledge' (Col 2:3). As great as He is, He has been made by God my wisdom, righteousness, sanctification, and redemption (1 Cor 1:30). Therefore even if I have committed many great sins, nevertheless, if I believe in Him, they are all swallowed up by His righteousness. Secondly, Scripture presents Him as an example for us to imitate. But I will not let this Christ be presented to me as exemplar except at a time of rejoicing, when I am out of reach of temptations (when I can hardly attain a thousandth part of His example), so that I may have a mirror in which to contemplate how much I am still lacking, lest I become smug. But in time of tribulation I will not listen to or accept Christ except as a gift, as Him who died for my sins, who has bestowed His righteousness on me, and who accomplished and fulfilled what is lacking in my life. For He 'is the end of the Law, that everyone who has faith may be justified' (Rom 10:4)."

68. For a position squarely opposed to this correlation, see James H. Cone, *The Cross and the Lynching Tree* (Maryknoll, New York: Orbis, 2011), 163, 149–50, 166, xviii: "The church's most vexing problem today is how to define itself by the gospel of Jesus' cross. . . . Delores Williams. . . . [rejects] the view common in classic texts of the Western theological tradition as well as in the preaching in African American churches that Jesus accomplished human salvation by dying in our place [*contra* Rom 8:3–4; 2 Cor 8:9; Col 2:13–14; 1 Pt 2:24]. According to Williams, Jesus did not come to save us through his death on the cross [*contra* 1 Cor 15:3; Col 1:19; Heb 9:26]. . . . I accept Delores Williams's rejection. . . . I find nothing redemptive about suffering in itself [*contra* Rom 5:3–5; 1 Pt 2:18–24]. . . . The lynching tree is a metaphor for white America's crucifixion of black people. It is the window that best reveals the religious meaning of the cross in our land. In this sense, black people are Christ figures, not because they wanted to suffer but because they had no choice. Just as Jesus had no choice in his journey to Calvary [*contra* Mt 26:39, 27:39–43; Jn 10:18; Phil 2:6–7], so black people had no choice about being lynched. . . . Reading and writing about the lynching nightmare, looking at many images of tortured black bodies, has been my deepest challenge and the most *painful* experience I have had as a theologian. At times it was almost too heavy for me to bear." Consistent with Cone's view would be Ted Grimsrud, *Instead of Atonement*, 231: "[The crucifixion of Jesus Christ] reveals the logic of retribution to be the tool of evil, not the God-ordained rule of the universe." One of his

when redemption is properly understood that it throws out all ethical deliberations and moral efforts genuinely inherent in following Christ.[69] A famous example of this correlation is in the witness of Kim Phuc, who was severely burned by napalm as a little girl in the Vietnam War, and shown naked and screaming from her injuries in the iconic photo by Pulitzer Prize winner, Nick Ut. Kim explains her convictions:

> Jesus Christ came to the world to die on the cross to pay for our sins. Only if we believe that can we go to heaven. . . . Jesus said, "I am the way, the truth, and the life." I believe in and I pray through Jesus Christ. God opens the door for me and gives me faith to overcome my burdens. You see that I am not sorrowful. I am not complaining. I think only of the present and the future, not of the past. I live with my faith, because without my faith I am nothing. . . . You need to be saved. I know that people who die and are not saved will go to hell like the fire of the napalm bomb. So I pray that people will be saved and go to heaven. . . . I receive blessings because I was burned badly. You see me? I look normal. My face and my hands were not burned. My feet were not burned in order that I could [run from] the fire, and have my picture taken. That gave me a chance to receive rescuers . . . to help me.[70]

---

prime examples to prove this is the Parable of the Prodigal Son (Luke 15)—wherein we see that God forgives without any sacrifice being needed to appease his wrath—which he ironically calls "the gospel in miniature" (83–84).

69. For a consonant view on how "true Good Friday" theology engenders moral behavior, see *Against the Third Reich: Paul Tillich's Wartime Radio Broadcasts into Nazi Germany*, trans. Matthew Lon Weaver, ed. Ronald H. Stone and Matthew Lon Weaver (Louisville: Westminster John Knox, 1998), 240: "[If] you grumble, just like one of those crucified on Good Friday [Lk 23:39], if you amass bitterness, hatred, and a desire for retribution within yourselves, then your suffering will have just as little reconciling power as the suffering the German people had after the First World War. Then the true Good Friday has not come for the German people. Then you will again proceed among those who crucify others, and the end of this war will be a suffering without reconciliation and a death without resurrection." On Tillich's praise of Kierkegaard, see *A History of Christian Thought*, 458–59: "In the years 1905–7 we were grasped by Kierkegaard. It was a very great experience. . . . [We] had a feeling of moralistic distortion and amystical emptiness, an emptiness in which the warmth of the mystical presence of the divine was missing, as in the whole Ritschlian school [Albrecht Ritschl, 1822–89]. We were not grasped by this moralism. We did not find in it the depths of the consciousness of guilt as classical theology had always had. So we were extremely happy when we encountered Kierkegaard. It was this combination of intense piety which went into the depths of human existence and the philosophical greatness which he had received from Hegel that made him so important to us. The real critical point would be the denial that Hegel's idea of reconciliation is a genuine reconciliation. Man is not reconciled by the reconciliation in the philosopher's head."

70. Denise Chong, *The Girl in the Picture: The Story of Kim Phuc, the Photographer, and the Vietnam War* (London: Simon & Schuster, 2000), 319–20.

1

On Simplicity and Complexity

> What a pleasure it is to have written a book that does not
> owe its origin to an inexplicable inner need and therefore is ignorant
> of whether it fits into the world, indeed, is bashful and ashamed
> like an ambivalent witness to a sinful love affair. (P 13)[1]

READING KIERKEGAARD CAN BE a bewildering experience. "The dialectical verbal pyrotechnics, the paradoxical turns in the argument, the pseudonyms[2] that mask the author who refuses to make his point straightforwardly—all of these and other characteristic features of Kierkegaard's strategy of indirect communication disorient even the most sophisticated reader."[3] This is so even when most readers of his works who are

1. On fitting into the world, see Martin Luther, "Commentary on Psalm 101" (1534), LW 13:224: "I hope I have done a good job. I shall call it good if it is well-pleasing to a few people and quite disgusting to many people. . . . [If] it pleases everyone, then it certainly is a bad and disgraceful job that I have done. . . . But if it pleases everyone, as God may see fit, then in God's name may it be a labor lost and no one be served thereby. But whoever lets it be noticed that he is not pleased with it will certainly feel smitten and know that he is guilty." On Kierkegaard's deep regard for Luther, see Johannes Sløk, "Kierkegaard and Luther," trans. A Rousing, in *A Kierkegaard Critique*, ed. Howard A. Johnson and Niels Thulstrup (New York: Harper & Brothers, 1962), 86: "[Kierkegaard] was a constant reader of Luther's *Postil*, and, let it be noted, he read it for edification." See also David J. Gouwens, *Kierkegaard as Religious Thinker* (Cambridge: Cambridge University Press, 1996), 48: "Although Kierkegaard came to him quite late, Martin Luther (1483–1546) was the object of his appreciation for the fact that his life exemplified his theology." Throughout this book I will be correlating passages from Luther with those of Kierkegaard's, not because of any direct influence from Luther to Kierkegaard, but because "Luther's theology is the matrix" of Kierkegaard's authorship, and as a result, there are "many affinities between his point of view and Luther's theology" which can be drawn out. Jaroslav Pelikan, *From Luther to Kierkegaard* (Saint Louis: Concordia, 1950), 21, 118.

2. On Kierkegaard's pseudonymous writings, as in *Prefaces* by Nicolaus Notabene, see: "For many years my depression has prevented me from saying 'Du' to myself in the profoundest sense. . . . This is what I partially discharged in the pseudonyms" (JP 5:5980). See also: "Some people might be disturbed by my sketch of an observer in *The Concept of Anxiety*. It does, however, belong there and is like a watermark in the work. After all, I always have a poetic relationship to my works, and therefore I am pseudonymous" (JP 5:5732). Therefore "every major edition of any of the pseudonymous works is ascribed to 'Søren Kierkegaard'—not the pseudonymous author—and . . . every edition of the collected works, in any language, includes the pseudonymous books and articles among *Kierkegaard's Writings* or *Søren Kierkegaards Skrifter*." Joseph Westfall, *The Kierkegaardian Author* (Berlin and New York: Walter de Gruyter, 2007), 127 n. 13.

3. Paul B. Anderson, "Reading Kierkegaard—Disorientation and Reorientation" in *Kierkegaard's Truth: The Disclosure of the Self*, ed. Joseph H. Smith (New Haven: Yale University Press, 1981), 23.

"preoccupied above all with discovering his thought, fail to realize how much attention the author paid to construction and style."[4]

That disregard for style, or how Kierkegaard expressed himself, only adds to the confusion because then the reader would not see that the inherent difficulty in what Kierkegaard had to say is in part due to how he said it.[5] Kierkegaard's goal in his authorship was to show how one becomes a Christian according to New Testament teachings (PV 23, 90; TM 39)—in contrast to being "nominal Christians" according to cultural norms (PV 125, 141).[6] Because taking on the genuine Christian way of life includes the cross, suffering, and rigor (PV 16, 79, 130, 229), reading about this must also be difficult—even though reading about becoming a Christian is not the same as becoming one. But Christianity seldom is presented "in its true form" (PV 80, 138) because it has been allowed to drift away from its historical norms. To offset this diminishment, Kierkegaard uses his many writings to draw a map to explain how one properly becomes a Christian (JP 6:6283). He does this because, to an "unusual degree," he believes he knows "with uncommon clarity and definiteness what Christianity is, what can be required of the Christian, what it means to be a Christian" (PV 138).

In his writings, then, all "protective devices like closure and foreshortening are sabotaged."[7] His map therefore covers the full "traversed path" (PV 7)—bumpy, harrowing and "narrow" though it may be (PV 118). So just as it would be a mythological

---

See also Harvie Ferguson, "Before the Beginning: Kierkegaard's Literary Hysteria," IKC 9:51: "The Kierkegaardian authorship is the work of many hands. The dizzying multiplicity of pseudonyms, the parallel publication of aesthetic and edifying works, the merging of fictional biography and autobiographical confession, deliberate confusion of editorial and authorial roles, the inconclusive character of every argument, and the subjunctive character of every description exhausts each volume with baroque paratextuality."

4. F. J. Billeskov Jansen, "The Literary Art of Kierkegaard," trans. Margaret Grieve in *A Kierkegaard Critique*, 11.

5. See M. Jamie Ferreira, *Kierkegaard* (West Sussex, United Kingdom: Wiley-Blackwell, 2009), 10: "[If] we cease to care about the literary strategies in [Kierkegaard's] texts, we will fail to understand the ideas in the text." See also Bjarne Troelsen, *Søren Kierkegaard: Ideens Politispion* (Herning: Systime, 1984), 7, quoted in Michael Strawser, *Both/And: Reading Kierkegaard From Irony to Edification* (New York: Fordham University Press, 1997), xxviii: "Kierkegaard's writings stand out, consistently enough, as a very motley and uneven textual mass with passages at a nearly inaccessible level of abstraction, formulated in an esoteric, forced, Germanic philosophical jargon, side by side passages of great simplicity and pictorial clarity, again alternating with diffusely garrulous digressions and sections bred of high-flown lyrical pathos."

6. On nominal Christians, see Eddie Gibbs, *In Name Only: Tackling the Problem of Nominal Christianity* (Tunbridge Wells, United Kingdom: BridgePoint, 1994). See also Gibson Winter, *The Suburban Captivity of the Churches* (New York: MacMillan, 1962), 91: "The nominal members [of middle-class churches] are willing to contribute to buildings that will ennoble their local communities; they are much less willing to contribute to benevolences for others or to provide ministries in remote places . . . . Such buildings are monuments to middle-class consumption. The churches are identified with consuming communities in a society which segregates consuming from producing communities. The net effect is a cult of consumption rather than mission and ministry."

7. Naomi Lebowitz, *Kierkegaard: A Life of Allegory* (Baton Rouge, Louisiana: Louisiana State University Press, 1985), 72.

fantasy to imagine that we could reach the top of Mount Moriah by way of the "winged horse" Pegasus (FT 52) and get the same blessing Abraham did without having to traverse by foot, in "anxiety and distress" (FT 53, 64–66, 74, 113), that three day journey, so it would be wrongheaded to expect Kierkegaard's books to make Christianity easier than it is. Rather than trying to make life easier—following the genre of the modern self-help book—Kierkegaard's authorship does the opposite by protecting "the difficulties of the life of faith."[8] According to Kierkegaard, books on Christianity should be like Christianity itself, where the "help looks like a torment" and we stick with it whether it is "a help or a torment" (PC 114–15).

In this chapter I will show how this difficulty ends up in clarification and simplicity—rather than being mired down in puzzlement, confusion and ambiguity (EUD 306, 324). This movement from difficulty to simplicity is in large part the burden of Kierkegaard's argument in *The Point of View* on the meaning of what and why he wrote. In the first section of this chapter I will discuss the illusions that Kierkegaard's method of indirection sets out to combat in order to maintain clarity and simplicity. These are the theological illusions that faith is free of any duty to God and that quantity matters more than the quality of our life before God. Here I also show that self-denial is what these illusions are trying to avoid. In the second section I will show how his method of indirection—the new science of arms—tackles these illusions by way of humor, sarcasm and counter-sentences. I will illustrate this technique of counter-sentences by way of Kierkegaard's view that love does not seek its own. In the third section I will illustrate Kierkegaard's move from indirect to direct statements through his discourse on James 1:22–27 on being doers of the word. And in the fourth section I will show how this clarity and simplicity in Kierkegaard's authorship drives toward a Pythagorean version of Christian identity.

EMPTYING THE JAR OF ILLUSIONS

"In relation to pure receptivity, like the empty jar that is to be filled, direct communication is appropriate," writes Kierkegaard, "but when illusion is involved," which is a blight on Christianity that needs eradication, then "direct communication is inappropriate" (PV 8). Because Denmark in Kierkegaard's time was plagued by philosophical and theological illusions, he believed that a direct prescribing of a remedy would fail, and so indirection would first have to be used to empty out the jar before filling it with any directly stated solutions. In this section I want to describe those illusions that Kierkegaard seeks to eliminate by way of indirection. Chief among them is that belief in God does not imply that people have a duty to him (PV 41) and that quantity matters more than quality (PV 125–26; TM, 37). Both of these illusions are grounded

---

8. Naomi Lebowitz, *Kierkegaard: A Life of Allegory*, 210. For this reason Kierkegaard preferred big books because by their very size they cut off all "connection with the momentary," for indeed "all moral upbringing consists first and foremost in being weaned away from the momentary" (JP 2:2157).

in a disregard for religious appropriation which, when ignored, fosters hypocrisy and spiritual lethargy. These illusions have been around since the beginning of Christianity.[9] This is because the principal duty we have before God is so demanding—that we must die to ourselves, our understanding and to the world (FSE 76–82). Not surprisingly, Christians have shrunk back from this duty. They have recoiled from this self-denial as a veritable "living death."[10] Even so the Christian message continues to beckon us to become "intimate with the death-thought of self-denial" (EUD 288) and the power it brings to transform us:

> It is only all too easy to understand the requirement contained in God's Word ("Give all your goods to the poor." "If anyone strikes you on the right cheek, turn the left." "If anyone takes your coat, let him have your cloak also." "Rejoice always." "Count it sheer joy when you meet various temptations" etc.).[11] It is all just as easy to understand as the remark "The weather is fine today," a remark that could become difficult to understand in only one way—if a literature came into existence in order to interpret it. The most limited poor creature cannot truthfully deny being able to understand the requirement—but it is tough for flesh and blood to will to understand it and to have to act accordingly. In my view,[12] it is human for a person to shrink from letting the Word really gain

9. See, for instance, Gal 5:25: "If we live by the Spirit, let us also walk by the Spirit" (RSV). On this verse, see Martin Luther, "Lectures on Galatians 5–6" (1535), LW 27:98: "Paul is very serious [and it] is as though he were saying: 'If it is true that we live by the Spirit, then let us proceed in an orderly fashion and walk by the Spirit. For where the Spirit is present, He renews men and creates new attitudes in them. He changes men who are vainglorious, wrathful, and envious into men who are humble, gentle, and loving. Such men seek not their own glory but God's. They do not provoke and envy one another; they yield to one another and outdo one another in showing honor (Rom 12:10).'" Note also Martin Luther, "Sermon on Titus 2:11–15" (1521), SML 6:137: "[The] effort of our entire lives should be to purge from body and soul unrighteous, unregenerate, and worldly conduct. Until death our lives should be nothing but purification. While it is true that faith instantly redeems from all legal guilt and sets free, yet evil desires remain in body and soul, as odor and disease cling to a dungeon. Faith occupies itself with purifying from these. Typical of this principle, Lazarus in the Gospel was raised from the dead by a single word (Jn 11:44), but afterward the shroud and napkin had to be removed."

10. Sylvia Walsh, "Dying to the World and Self-Denial in Kierkegaard's Religious Thought," IKC 21:195.

11. See Mt 19:21; 5:39,40; 1 Thes 5:16; Jas 1:2.

12. This is also Luther's view. See his "Sermons on John 1–4" (1538), LW 22:389, 397: "Christ did not come that you might remain in your sin and in condemnation. You will not be saved unless you stop your sinning. To be sure, sin has been forgiven; but you must cease your covetousness, adultery, and fornication. The life of all of us is under condemnation and subject to the judgment of God, but Christ appeared in order to deliver us from this. Yet you have the effrontery not only to remain in your sin but also to spring to its defense. . . . Wherever faith is genuine, there is no love for sin. Nor does a true believer remain in sin, but shuns it. . . . Just as a person who has been healed and cured of a disease can find no delight in sickness or do anything to impair health, so anyone who persists in false teaching and in an offensive life is under judgment and condemnation. . . . It is bad enough if I refuse to admit a sin which I really feel and for which the Son of God was given to us as the Man who is to forgive sins. But the devil does not stop there; he bids us defend ourselves. . . . To commit a sin and then to deny it and try to justify it, is not human; no, that is devilish and reveals a real dragon's tail."

power over him. . . . But . . . it is not human to give the matter a totally different
turn . . . [and] cast it as far away as possible. (FSE 34–35)

In addition to this living death, there is also the duty to love others—and this love
is not just for those whom we like or for those who will love us in return (WL 373,
349). This sort of love goes against the grain and incurs disfavor (WL 109). And that
is not because it is unloving, but because of the nature of the love itself—and so we
"must always be on the watch" for attacks when we love in this way (WL 130). Because
of this danger, God's way of loving will always be unpopular. And again, this is not
because we have been unloving. The low success rate is instead due to the inherent
difficulty in the love which we share.[13] It would therefore be a disaster to water down
Christian love in order to make it more palatable. While that might seem like a good
idea so that more could embrace this love, it actually will not help at all but only keep
it further away from those who need it (PV 131, 134).

Kierkegaard called this intensification of Christian life and love a "jacking up"
of the cost of being Christian (PV 95, 138–39).[14] Martin Luther also did this.[15] In a

13. "The gate is narrow and the way is hard that leads to life, and those who find it are few" (Mt
7:14) (RSV). But it is "not the way as such that is narrow, although quite a few people walk along it
single-file; no, the narrowness is simply that each one separately must become the single individual
who must press forward through this narrow pass along the narrow way where no comparison cools,
but also where no comparison kills with its insidious chill. The broad way, on the other hand, is broad
because many are walking on it. . . . There the gorgeous poisonous flower of excuses blooms; . . . the
chilling breezes of comparison are there—that way does not lead to life" (UDVS 153–53). However,
not every single individual follows Christ. This is because the way "certainly can be narrow when
you are still allowed to use all your powers to push your way through when the opposition is outside
yourself, but when you must use your powers to work against yourself, then it seems infinitely too little
to say that the way is narrow—it is, instead, impassable, blocked, impossible, insane! And yet it is this
way of which it holds true that Christ is the way; this is precisely how it is narrow" (FSE 61).

14. See Lk 14:28: "Count the cost" (RSV). Note as well: "The method increasingly used in the
course of the centuries is this: we have lowered the standard for being a Christian and thus have caught
all the more. Instead of whales, we caught sardines—but countless millions of them" (JP 3:2979).

15. On Kierkegaard's admiration of Luther, see: "I could be tempted to take Luther's book of sermons and extract a great many sentences and ideas, all of which are marked in my copy, and publish
them in order to show how far the preaching nowadays is from Christianity, so that it shall not be said
that I am the one who hits upon exaggerations" (JP 3:2516). On the importance of Luther's sermons,
see Fred W. Meuser, *Luther the Preacher* (Minneapolis: Augsburg, 1983), 38: "[Almost] everything
Luther did was preaching. We divide his works into categories such as academic, theological, sermonic, devotional, pastoral, catechetical, and polemic—and there are significant differences between
them in approach, intent, content, and style. But these differences are not nearly as sharp as we might
assume. His lectures were never technical or objective, no matter how precise his treatment of a word
or how incisive his analysis of a theological issue. Always he aimed at the heart as well as the mind
of a student. He felt he had not dealt responsibly with any text . . . if the hearer's understanding and
personal appropriation had not been deepened and strengthened." See also *The 1529 Holy Week and
Easter Sermons of Dr. Martin Luther*, trans. Irving L. Sandberg, annotated by Timothy J. Wengert
(Saint Louis: Concordia, 1999), 11–12: "The Reformation itself was more than anything else a result
of Luther's preaching. The attack on indulgences began not with the 95 Theses on October 31, 1517, as
is often imagined, but in sermons delivered earlier that year to his congregation. . . . His most popular
publications were not the carefully argued polemics or the dense biblical exegesis—intended for the
most part for pastors and scholars—but his sermons and devotional literature."

time when Christian hypocrisy was running rampant and the church profited from indulging our sins, Luther called for greater dedication to one's Christian life. He admonished parents, for instance, to raise their children in a more strenuous Christian way, warning that if they refused to do so, they would "earn hell" for themselves:[16]

> Thus it is true . . . that parents could attain salvation by training their own children, even if they were to do nothing else. . . . [God] sets you over them as a hospital superintendent, to wait on them, to give them the food and drink of good words and works. He sets you over them that they may learn to trust God, to believe in him, to fear him, and to set their whole hope upon him; to honor his name and never curse or swear; to mortify themselves by praying, fasting, watching, working; to go to church, wait on the word of God, and observe the Sabbath. He sets you over them that they may learn to despise temporal things, to bear misfortune without complaint, and neither fear death nor love this life.[17]

These indeed are strong words for children. But only this sort of instruction on trusting, fearing, fasting, hoping, mortifying, waiting and despising brings about true Christian practice. All of this hinges on self-denial and dying to the self—which stretches throughout Kierkegaard's entire authorship, from early to late (EUD 288, 325; TM 189, 312).[18] This wonderful training Kierkegaard calls "the blessed soil of self-denial" for it continually holds out the promise of a "soft breeze of self-denying joy" that can even be "sensed in the thunder of . . . judgment" (EUD 285). It is no surprise then that self-denial is the criterion upon which we will be judged in the end:

16. On Luther's advocacy of Christian vocation, see Gustaf Wingren, *Luther on Vocation*, trans. Carl C. Rasmussen (Philadelphia: Muhlenberg, 1957), 212: "An unexpected power flows forth in work when a man knows that he is truly under divine command in discharging the vocation at hand, a power greater than any to be found in the words of orators." See also Paul Althaus, *The Ethics of Martin Luther*, trans. Robert C. Schultz (1972; Minneapolis: Fortress, 2007), 100: "A hidden majesty dwells in parents. It deserves to be feared—and Luther understands this fear to be more than what we call reverence. We honor our parents primarily by obeying them. This obedience is limited only when parents wish to train and educate their children contrary to God's commandment. In such a situation, children ought not to obey." On a strict upbringing, Kierkegaard writes: "If a child is so unfortunate as to have a father who does not know how to command, or the horses a second-rate driver, it seems as if the child and the horses would not have half the powers they actually do have. Alas, and when the adult who is a sufferer surrenders his soul to the power of vacillation, he is actually weaker than a child. But then it is indeed also a joy that hardship is the road, because then the task is immediately at hand and stands unshakably fixed and firm" (UDVS 300).

17. Martin Luther, "Treatise on Good Works" (1520), LW 44:85–86.

18. See Sylvia Walsh, "Dying to the World and Self-Denial in Kierkegaard's Religious Thought," 193: "Strictly speaking, Kierkegaard does not move from one view to another on this matter. He does not discard the inward definition of self-denial in the later writings but simply adds the external to the internal, the outward response that is commensurable with inwardness, and views it as decisive for the determination and recognition of the Christian's inward self-denial or dying to selfishness and worldliness."

In eternity you will not be asked about how large a fortune you are *leaving behind*—the *survivors* ask about that; or about how many battles you won, about how sagacious you were, how powerful your influence—that, after all, becomes your *reputation for posterity*. No, eternity will not ask about what *worldly things* remain *behind* you in the world. But it will ask about what riches you have gathered in heaven, about how often you have conquered your own mind, about what control you have exercised over yourself or whether you have been a slave, about how often you have mastered yourself in self-denial, . . . about how often you in self-denial have forgiven your enemy, . . . about how often you in self-denial endured insults patiently, about what you . . . in self-denial have suffered for God's sake. And the one who will ask you, the judge, . . . does not merely know what self-denial is, he does not merely know how to judge in such a way that no malpractice can hide itself—no, his presence is the judging that makes everything that looked so good, which was heard and seen with admiration in the world, become silent and turn pale; his presence is the judging, because he was self-denial. He who was equal with God took the form of a lowly servant, . . . he walked about defenseless; he who was lord of creation constrained nature itself to keep quiet, for it was not until he had given up his spirit that the curtain tore and the graves opened and the powers of nature betrayed who he was: if this is not self-denial, what then is self-denial? (UDVS 223–24)

This criterion of self-denial makes judgment day a *dies irae, dies illa* (a fearful and awesome day) (PV 136). Self-denial is a most stringent standard—to be carried out in the most exacting way by Christ himself—and made manifest to us now, before the fact, as "a helping hand," in order to lead us back to God's "righteous Governance" (UDVS 51, 55). Because the prevailing Christian view in Kierkegaard's day did little to prepare one for such judgment through the discipline of self-denial, Christendom was mired in illusions.

It was also deluded because it stressed quantity over quality. Rather than pursuing the qualitative enhancement of individual Christian lives through self-denial, the emphasis was placed on building up the numbers of people claiming to be Christian. This superficial approach to Christianity violates the individual relationship between the sinner and God. Even though God "without the tremor of dizziness" watches over us all, as "the great examiner" he addresses only "each and every individual" one by one (PV 107). Wanting to reach the goal of true Christian blessedness "jointly" because it would be "more certain and . . . easier for each one individually" is a travesty because that can happen only one at a time (PV 106).[19] We cannot believe in groups.

19. See 1 Cor 9:24: "Do you not know that in a race all the runners compete, but only one receives the prize?" (RSV). See also Martin Luther, "Temporal Authority" (1523), LW 45:108: "[Every] man runs his own risk in believing as he does, and he must see to it himself that he believes rightly. As nobody else can go to heaven or hell for me, so nobody else can believe or disbelieve for me; as nobody else can open or close heaven or hell to me, so nobody else can drive me to belief or unbelief. How he

This is because "the object of all faith's work is to get rid of egotism and selfishness in order that God can actually . . . rule in everything" (UDVS, 259).[20] We cannot get rid of egotism in groups. For this reason Kierkegaard used "Christian fervor and zeal" to pursue "the thankless . . . task of relieving Christianity of some of those battalions of Christians" (PV 125–26)—to help a person "become a Christian when in a way one is a Christian" already (PV 56). This is a thankless task because one has to do it by "jacking up the price or the requirement for being what they already think they are" (PV 138). Only then can Christianity "make a genuine idea-impression" on the individual (PV 51). By putting this sort of pressure on the individual, the "essentially religious author is always polemical" (PV 67). Because Christendom eschews these polemics it is engulfed in illusion.

A NEW SCIENCE OF ARMS

It will not be easy to disabuse ourselves of these illusions. Trying to crush them with the standard of self-denial will not solve the problem. Coming in with the "full marching equipment of orthodoxy" (BA 93) to attack those illusions directly, will misfire. Therefore

> the entire old science of arms, all the apologetics and everything belonging to it, serves instead, to put it bluntly, to betray the cause of Christianity. At every point and at every moment, the strategy must be constituted on the basis of having to contend with a delusion, an illusion. (PV 52–53)

This is because a choice is needed (PC 140) if one is to move away from these illusions.[21] And that choice cannot be forced because our ability to decide against these illusions is not "entirely in order" (PV 54).[22] Because of this handicap, an indirect approach is a better way to proceed. More straightforward information on denying oneself will not bring about self-denial.[23] But indirection with its sarcasm,

---

believes or disbelieves is a matter for the conscience of each individual. . . . For faith is a free act, to which no one can be forced. Indeed, it is a work of God in the spirit."

20. See also Martin Luther, "Sermon on Titus 2:11–15" (1521), SML 6:116–17, 126: "Ungodliness . . . is the sin of failing to honor God; that is, of not believing, trusting, fearing him, not surrendering to him, not submitting to his providence, *not allowing him to be God*. . . . Observe, they are pious and filled with grace, who do not walk by reason, do not trust in human nature, but rely only on the grace of God, ever fearful lest they fall from grace into dependence upon their reason, their self-conceit, good intentions and self-devised works" (italics added).

21. See Acts 14:15: "[Turn] from these vain things to a living God" (RSV).

22. See Is 30:9–10: "For they are a rebellious people, . . . who will not hear the instruction of the Lord; who say to . . . the prophets, 'Prophesy not to us what is right; speak to us smooth things, prophesy illusions'" (RSV).

23. See George Pattison, "If Kierkegaard is Right About Reading, Why Read Kierkegaard?" in *Søren Kierkegaard: Critical Assessments of Leading Philosophers*, 4 vols, ed. Daniel W. Conway with K. E. Gover (London: Routledge, 2002), 1:198: "The text works upon us . . . by a careful and slow deconstruction of all our pretensions . . . which, till now, we have believed or claimed ourselves to be."

irony, and humor can accomplish this (JP 1:818; PV 54).[24] These techniques stir us up so that we can open up to self-denial—having been caught off guard by their wily, unexpected ways.[25] By "luring and teasing," Kierkegaard frustrates the reader "out of habitual thought" and "into a need for faith."[26] An abstract linear argument cannot do this because the emotional and volitional elements are not taken into account. But even with the help of humor and sarcasm, self-absorption still is difficult to overcome.

24. See *The Humor of Kierkegaard: An Anthology*, ed. and introduced by Thomas C. Oden (Princeton: Princeton University Press, 2004), 1–2, 25, 36: "Kierkegaard's humor ranges from the droll to the rollicking, from farce to intricate, subtle analysis, from nimble stories to amusing aphorisms. Some [instances] are merely a brief fantastic flight of imagination or an amusing word picture. . . . All these levels of musings, from wild fancy to cerebral philosophical humor, are a part of the always dialectical and sometimes preposterous buffoonery we find in SK. . . . Humor, in Kierkegaard's view, . . . does not move merely within this-worldly premises and humanistic assumptions. Rather it points implicitly but constantly toward the incarnational premise. . . . Christianity is nowhere more intensely comic to Kierkegaard than in the Christmas story. There we meet the Absolute Paradox, the Incarnation itself, and there we find the decisive expression of the comic—God's coming to humanity in the least expected way, with the greatest depth of contradiction." See also Eric W. Gritsch, *The Wit of Martin Luther* (Minneapolis: Fortress, 2006), 83: "According to Luther, poetry, music, and humor are better means to express God's love of the sinner in Christ than logic." For a more measured analysis, see Adam Buben, "Kierkegaard and the Norm (MacDonald) of Death" in *Family Guy and Philosophy: A Cure for the Petarded*, ed. J. Jeremy Wisnewski (Oxford: Blackwell, 2007). In the Family Guy episode, "Death is a Bitch," the personification of death, sprains his ankle, and cannot kill anyone until it gets better. Commenting on this, Buben writes: "Since [the personification of death] in this situation can be seen as a comic symbol of the foolishness of failing to remember the certainty and uncertainty of death, it's doubtful that Kierkegaard would condemn this particular [episode, even though he stressed the fear of death] (TDIO 81, 98–99). . . . In fact, how could Kierkegaard reject this example when he derives a similar lesson from a comic story about another failure to take the certainty and the uncertainty of death seriously (CUP 1:86)?" (203–4).

25. See M. G. Piety, "The Dangers of Indirection: Plato, Kierkegaard, and Leo Strauss" in *Ethics, Love, and Faith in Kierkegaard*, ed. Edward F. Mooney (Bloomington: Indiana University Press, 2008), 172–73: "The obstacles to understanding the import of Kierkegaard's works are not ones designed to fell the dimwitted. They are ethical obstacles Kierkegaard clearly believes are built into any attempt to help others along the path to personality or authentic subjectivity in the sense of the self that is transparent before God. . . . The reason so many scholars have been confused, alienated, and even infuriated by Kierkegaard's works is not because they are intellectually impenetrable but because they are subjectively, or ethically, demanding. A proper interpretation of the content—at least in a general sense—of Kierkegaard's works is not difficult for a reader who is not offended by the question of whether he is living as he should." This may have been one of the reasons why Ludwig Wittgenstein (1889–1951) admired Kierkegaard. See Norman Malcolm, *Ludwig Wittgenstein: A Memoir*, 2nd ed. (New York: Oxford University Press, 1984), 93–94: "[What] is the use of studying philosophy if all that it does for you is enable you to talk with some plausibility about some abstruse questions of logic, etc., [and] if it does not improve your thinking about the important questions of everyday life. . . . [It] is . . . difficult to . . . *try* to think, really honestly about your life [and] other peoples lives. And the trouble is that thinking about these things is *not thrilling*, but often downright nasty." See also Fergus Kerr, *Work on Oneself: Wittgenstein's Philosophical Psychology* (Arlington, Virginia: The Institute for the Psychological Sciences, 2008), 25–26: "Right to the end, we may say, if one thing more than another lay at the center of [Wittgenstein's] writing, he sought to preserve ordinary everyday humanity, in a culture that threatened to lose it in a fog of metaphysical theorizing and scientific dogmatism."

26. Naomi Lebowitz, *Kierkegaard: A Life of Allegory*, 155, 197. Note also the need for edifying discourses to have "a kind of striptease" in them (JP 1:643).

Kierkegaard knew—in spite of his indirect methods—that "a selfish person even more selfishly can wish to be regarded as unselfish" (WL 276).[27]

There are many examples of the use of indirection through sarcasm and humor in Kierkegaard's authorship. For instance, in trying to explain the offensive view that sin entered into the world all of a sudden through the sin of Adam, no argument is given to discredit the opposing view that it happened gradually, "little by little." We instead are caught off guard by indirection—being reminded of "the counting rhyme in which children delight: one-nis-ball, two-nis-ball, three-nis-ball, etc., up to nine-nis-ball and tennis balls" (CA 32). This sarcastic ploy maligns the gradualist explanation of sin. The same sarcasm is applied to the gradualist view of faith—that it emerges "little by little" and not from a sudden rebirth of the spirit (PF 95). The gradualist view implies that we are "born with faith," which is as silly as supposing that one could be "born twenty-four years old" (PF 96). Such an inhuman occurrence of "a birth within a birth," is sarcastically called "a fabulous monstrosity" (PF 97). Or take the case of the rarity of repentance which threatens the forgiveness of sins (CA 114). To counter this malaise, spiritual trials are given to goad us on to repentance. But even so, we would still try to avoid them:

> The most effective means of escaping trial is to become spiritless, and the sooner the better. . . . In the old days, the road to perfection was narrow and solitary. The journey along it was always disturbed by aberrations, exposed to predatory attacks by sin, and pursued by the arrow of the past, which is as dangerous as that of the Scythian hordes. Now one travels to perfection by railroad in good company, and before he knows it, he has arrived. (CA 117)

By humorously contrasting this comfortable railroad trip with the dangerous footpath, we are inspired to embrace the very trials we would just as soon forget about. And on the matter of faith being the means by which we trust in Christ's message about life after death, an alternative grounding to that belief is ridiculed. It is the view that we should believe the message because it is profound and not simply because it comes from Christ.

On this alternative account we would believe because of our "cogitating and ruminating" (WA 103). But this would be as silly as believing in a sermon because of

> a pastor's affectation, . . . that he decks himself out and dolls himself up, or . . . speaks in a sentimental tone, or . . . rolls his r's like a Norwegian and wrinkles his brow, or . . . strains himself in energetic postures and revivalist leaps. (WA 104)

This comparison to the truly ridiculous case of rolling one's r's makes this alternative look silly—which on the face of it is a hard case to make since affectation looks

---

27. See also: "[False] self-denial is marked by this, that it looks like self-denial at first but turns out to be profitable in some other external way, so that basically it is sagacious calculation" (JFY 205).

like earnestness. And as for the point that baptism is nothing "without appropriation" (CUP 1:366), humor is again used to bolster the case for appropriation. Thinking the baptism of an infant is only "the piece of paper the parish clerk issues" is as silly as supposing that one could be "married in the cradle to someone" (CUP 1:368). And humor is again employed in order to show how far God is above all that is human. God, Kierkegaard writes, "is so alien to the natural man that with him it is as with a dog, which can indeed learn to walk upright for a moment but yet continually wants to walk on all fours" (WL 244).[28] This comic rendering of the vast difference between the human and the divine shows how foolish we are to try to bridge the yawning gap. Kierkegaard admits that it would be possible to try to bridge the gap since the dog can learn to walk upright, but in the end the dog prefers the lowly—and so should we, taking up the dog's life for ourselves.[29]

This indirect method, in addition to using humor, also assumes a problematic relationship between the speaker and the hearer.[30] This is because when we push away the Christian message we somehow also continue to remain interested in it. Kierkegaard's indirect method includes this double movement—back and forth—regarding the Christian message.[31] It combines apostolic speech with "worldling" talk. So added to the "composed" apostolic or faithful words, are expressions of "an imprisonment that . . . leaves the spirit sighing in the fragile earthen vessel, in the cramped space, in the status of an alien, because the home of the spirit is in the eternal and the infinite" (EUD 337). This combination of peaceful or composed words with alien ones—or "counter sentences" (JP 3:2906)—gives Kierkegaard's writings their compelling realism and religious complexity.[32] That combination also adds some uncertainty to our religious certainty (CD 211–12).[33] We see that mixture in the way Kierkegaard shows

---

28. See Steven Shakespeare, "A Word of Explanation: Transfiguring Language in Kierkegaard's *Eighteen Upbuilding Discourses*," IKC 5:92: "Commentators are increasingly compelled to point out how even Kierkegaard's most apparently direct authorial interventions are . . . intrinsically wayward and broken. The discourses are no exception. They are not . . . transparently declaring the truth of things."

29. See Psalm 131:1: "O Lord, my heart is not lifted up, my eyes are not raised too high; I do not occupy myself with things too great and too marvelous for me" (RSV).

30. Graeme Nicholson, "The Intense Communication of Kierkegaard's Discourses," IKC 15:352.

31. See Naomi Lebowitz, *Kierkegaard: A Life of Allegory*, 181: "[This] is the necessary maze of the literature, which reflects the ways we fall away from faith. It is a dangerous game, but it is in the service of the love that would offend the listener into disbelief. The literature must disappoint those who hunger to become themselves." Note also, that for Kierkegaard "the task of the religious poet is to repel disciples while stirring movements of faith" (97).

32. See Amy Laura Hall, *Kierkegaard and the Treachery of Love* (Cambridge: Cambridge University Press, 2002), 15: "Kierkegaard knows the contoured map of our unfaithful resistance to grace because he himself crawls along that path." Note also Kierkegaard's point: "A Christian discourse deals to a certain extent with doubt—a sermon operates absolutely and solely on the basis of authority, that of Scripture and of Christ's apostles. Therefore, it is neither more nor less than heresy to deal with doubt in a sermon, however well one might be able to deal with it" (JP 1:638).

33. See Mk 9:24: "I believe; help my unbelief!" (RSV).

that love does not seek its own (1 Cor 13:5)—while at the same time still having all things for itself (1 Cor 3:21):

> No, love does not seek its own, because to seek its own is simply self-love, selfishness, self-seeking, or whatever other names the unloving disposition has. And yet, . . . God . . . seeks his own, which is love; he seeks it by giving all things. . . . To be able to seek love and oneself to become the object of love, yet without seeking one's own, is reserved for God alone. . . . So, then, with love there is confusion; in this blissful confusion there is for the lovers no distinction between *mine* and *yours*. Wonderful! There are a *you* and an *I*, and there is no *mine* and *yours*! For without a you and an I, there is no love, and with mine and yours, there is no love; but "mine" and "your" (these possessive pronouns) are, of course, formed from a "you" and an "I" and as a consequence seem obliged to be present wherever there are a *you* and an *I*. This is indeed the case everywhere, but not in love, which is a revolution from the ground up. . . . Only for self-denying love does the specification "mine" disappear entirely and the distinction "*mine* and *yours*" become entirely canceled. . . . Then the wondrous thing occurs that is heaven's blessing upon self-denying love—in salvation's mysterious understanding all things become his, his who had no mine at all, his who in self-denial made yours all that was his. In other words, God is all things, and by having no mine at all self-denial's love won God and won all things. (WL 264, 265–66, 268)

In this passage, Kierkegaard goes from advocating self-denial to winning back everything for the self. By denying ourselves, we not only are able to love others, but also to love God—who then has all things ready to give back to us. It is a revolution, a mystery, and a wonder, he says, how we who give up on self-aggrandizement actually are fulfilled through self-denial (WL 302).[34] The key to this fulfillment is God—for "it is solely around him that everything revolves" (WL 383). God alone is able to enrich us without having us seek our own good when we love others selflessly. God has to be the determining factor because interpersonally the one who loves selflessly will[35] be injured by those loved[36]—and help for the injured cannot come from the injurers:

34. See Mt 6:33: "But seek first his kingdom and his righteousness, and all these things shall be yours as well" (RSV).

35. This necessity or certainty is softened into a possibility in M. Jamie Ferreira, *Love's Grateful Striving: A Commentary on Kierkegaard's Works of Love* (Oxford: Oxford University Press, 2001), 164. Against this softening see James M. Kittelson, *Luther the Reformer* (Minneapolis: Augsburg, 1986, 2003), 116: "'I know,' [Luther] added, 'that whoever wants to bring the Word of Christ into the world must, like the apostles, . . . expect death at any moment. If any other situation prevailed, it would not be the Word of Christ.'" See also Martin Luther, "Sermon on Luke 2:33–40" (1522), LW 52:117–18: "[Christ's] words must be condemned, banished, cursed as the worst heresy, error, and foolishness; wherever this happens, he has received his due. Where it does not happen, there is neither Christ, nor . . . the gospel. . . . For wherever Christ is and his faith, there must be opposition or it is not Christ."

36. See Amy Laura Hall, *Kierkegaard and the Treachery of Love*, 12, 13, 24: "Kierkegaard's description of love's task is outrageously strenuous and intentionally discouraging. Some scholars have read his provocations and subsequently sought to soften the blow, so to speak. I wish to retrieve his

The one who truly loves does not seek his own. With regard to his "own," he knows nothing about the claims of strict law or of justice, not even the claims of equity; neither does he know anything about an exchange that erotic love makes, which also knows how to watch out lest it be tricked (therefore knows how to watch out for its own). . . . The truly loving person becomes the unconditionally injured one—which he in a certain sense makes himself by self-denial. . . . [Only] true love loves every human being according to the person's distinctiveness. *The rigid, the domineering person* lacks flexibility, lacks the pliability to comprehend others; he demands his own from everybody, wants everyone to be transformed in his image, to be trimmed according to his pattern for human beings. . . . [The] one who loves also knows how to make himself unnoticed so that the person helped does not become dependent[37] upon him—by owing to him the greatest beneficence. (WL 269, 270, 274)

There is a recklessness in this selfless love since it cares so little about justice, equity and fair exchange for the lover. This love is enamored only with what is remarkable in the beloved. There is a consuming attention given to those personal details in the beloved—which makes for "a holy modesty."[38] That is why mutuality, reciprocity and exchange, which are basic to ordinary love, do not motivate the selfless lover—for love "does not love only as it is loved" (WL 35). These reciprocal concerns are important but not decisive—for when missing they can still hurt the selfless lover (WL 27, 314). But that pain is set aside for a greater good which is found elsewhere—in gratitude towards God:

Therefore, giving thanks to God, he declares: Now this individual is standing by himself—through my help. But there is no self-satisfaction in the last phrase, because the loving one has understood that essentially every human being indeed stands by himself—through God's help—and that the loving one's

---

intensity. . . . We are to be shocked and alienated by [*Works of Love*]. Kierkegaard intends to thwart our sense of progress and our presumption of clarity with the radical discontinuity between our love and the love commanded. *Works of Love* may be aptly read as Kierkegaard's sustained attempt to reinsert the indicting use of the law into a conversation over-confident in human effort and blithely reliant on God's corporate dispensation of grace. We may interpret *Works of Love* as Kierkegaard's attempt . . . to precipitate the awareness of sin indispensable for our repentance and to evoke the confession necessary for our reception of grace. . . . The rhetorical momentum of *Works of Love* is indeed to disorient the reader. We are turned topsy-turvy in at least two ways, one performative and the other epistemological. To the extent that we think we meet the law to love, we find that we fail. To the extent that we think we know the law of love, we find that we are ignorant. Simply put, we are both wicked and utterly confused, selfish and myopic." See also: "[Militant] piety . . . is Christianity or being a Christian" (PV 130).

37. This independence (WL 275, 278), however, must never degenerate into "proud self-esteem . . . . This independence depends only on love itself through eternity's *shall*; it does not depend on something else and therefore does not depend on the object of love as soon as this appears to be something else. . . . No, love abides; this is independence" (WL 39).

38. C. Stephen Evans, *Kierkegaard's Ethics of Love: Divine Commands and Moral Obligations* (New York: Oxford University Press, 2004), 152.

> self-annihilation is really only in order not to hinder the other person's God-relationship, so that all the loving one's help infinitely vanishes in the God-relationship. . . . In other words, if he had not been one who loves, he would have loudly and directly proclaimed the truth, less well thought through, and promptly had adherents who would have appropriated the truth—and hailed him as the master. Has, then, the life of the one who loves been wasted, has he lived entirely in vain, since there is nothing, nothing at all that witnesses to his activities and efforts? Answer: Is it wasting one's life not to seek one's own? No, in truth this life is not wasted. The one who loves is with blessed joy conscious of this and God is his confidant. In a certain sense his life is completely squandered on the existence of others. Unwilling to waste any time or energy on asserting himself, on being something for himself, in his self-sacrifice he is willing to perish, that is, he is completely and wholly transformed into simply being an active power in the hands of God. (WL 278, 279)

When we love another person selflessly we focus solely on helping that person—and not on any feelings of fulfillment we might long for in return. For love is not a feeling (WL 25, 99, 106, 175, 376)—contrary to popular opinion.[39] This shift away from feelings is as dramatic to Kierkegaard as annihilating oneself. This is because there can be no self-satisfaction in loving. While this will mean that the selfless lover's life is squandered, that will not also mean that it has been wasted. This is because even though there is little social acclaim for what one has done, one may still have the blessed, conscious joy that God approves of our selfless loving. And since God is the greatest of all—and so to depose of him would mean leaving his place "vacant" since no one else could fill it (WL 115; CD 292)—having his approval means everything.[40]

39. On Luther's similar critique of feelings, see his "Sermon on Mark 16:1–8" (1526), SML 8:244: "I have often said before that feelings and faith are two different things. It is the nature of faith not to feel, to lay aside reason and close the eyes, to submit absolutely to the Word, and to follow it in life and death. Feeling however does not extend beyond that which may be apprehended by reason and sense, which may be heard, seen, felt and known by the outward senses. For this cause feeling is opposed to faith and faith is opposed to feeling. . . . But since Christ died for our sins and was raised for our justification, we cannot see it nor feel it, neither can we comprehend it with our reason. Therefore we must disregard our feeling and accept only the Word, write it into our heart and cling to it, even though it seems as if my sins were not taken from me, and even though I still feel them within me. Our feelings must not be considered, but we must constantly insist that death, sin and hell have been conquered, although I feel that I am still under the power of death, sin and hell. For although we feel that sin is still in us, it is only permitted that our faith may be developed and strengthened, that in spite of all our feelings we accept the Word, and that we unite our hearts and consciences more and more in Christ. Thus faith leads us quietly, contrary to all feeling and comprehension of reason, through sin, through death and through hell."

40. But not for Kierkegaard's critics. See Sharon Krishek, "Two Forms of Love: The Problem of Preferential Love in Kierkegaard's *Works of Love*," *Journal of Religious Ethics* 36 (December 2008). She thinks we need to "amend Kierkegaard's understanding of love" (612) to include "an *unqualified* affirmation of self-concerned sensitivities and desires" (610). But if non-preferential love calls for a "setting aside" of oneself—as she believes Kierkegaard says it does (615)—then trying to get self-concern back into his view of love will take more than her argument provides. See also her *Kierkegaard on Faith and Love* (Cambridge: Cambridge University Press, 2009) where she argues that "non-preferentiality

But having everything after having annihilated oneself does not mean getting everything back as it was before one had annihilated oneself.[41] It instead means having something of more value than everything that one had before doing that – which is to have God himself.[42] This relationship to God is what eternalizes love and makes it selfless (WL 32, 113).

BE DOERS OF THE WORD

But indirection finally must give way to more direct forms of expression.[43] This, however, does not mean that indirection was a waste of time since the "tranquility

---

is not essential to this basic structure [of love] (but only to one of its manifestations, namely, to neighborly love), then we can see how neighborly love and preferential love can coexist" (160). But in order to maintain this view, Krishek would have to show how self-hatred in marriage has no legitimate place—contrary to Kierkegaard's own words (WL 307)! Unfortunately she gives no direct attention to these rousing words in defense of her thesis.

41. For a critique of this self-annihilation in Kierkegaard's thought, see Curtis L. Thompson, *Following the Cultured Public's Chosen One: Why Martensen Mattered to Kierkegaard* (Copenhagen: Museum Tusculanum, 2008), 167. Thompson stresses the beginning of JP 2:1399 which says Christians should guard against the "ascetic fanaticism" which wants to annihilate the self and the world. But he unfortunately leaves out the way that journal entry ends: "Yet God wants men to . . . make such a clean break with this world that the spirit really comes into existence. . . . [You] are to remember that there must be a striving . . . in order that the mind can be transformed away from the earthly. . . . Most people would perhaps completely lose their zest for life if they should ever understand to the degree I do how God at any second is able to transpose a person into a more rigorous spot." Note also that in Christianity we are not "to live pleasantly and comfortably" (JP 2:1354); that the "genuinely Lutheran way" is that "the whole world is . . . against us" (JP 2:1397); that our life with God makes us "unhappy in this life" (JP 2:1409); that "to die to the world . . . does not take place without frightful agonies" (JP 2:1410); that being involved with God is a "dreadful beating" (JP 2:1418); that "God's judgment of this . . . world is: it is a sinful, evil world; it is a vale of tears," even though it seems to be "a lovely, nice world" (JP 2:1439); and that assuming that God wants to use us as instruments "to influence" others is but an unjustifiable "alleviation" of the unconditioned in order to make it "less fatal" for us (JP 2:1449).

42. See Jn 14:27: "Peace I leave with you; . . . not as the world gives do I give to you" (RSV). And see Ps 23:1: "The Lord is my shepherd, I shall not want" (RSV). On this verse, see Martin Luther, "Commentary on Psalm 23" (1536), LW 12:159: "[If] you hold fast to [this Word, you] will . . . speak freely: 'Let the devil, the world, or my own conscience oppose me as violently as they may. I will not for that reason grieve myself to death. It must be so and it shall be so, that whoever is the Lord's sheep will surely be assailed by the wolves. Be it with me as it may, let them boil or roast me, it shall be my comfort that my Shepherd has given His life for me. Moreover, He has a sweet, kind voice, with which He comforts me and says that I shall never perish, neither shall any man snatch me out of His hand; I shall have eternal life (Jn 10:28). And He will keep this promise, no matter what happens to me. . . . [Therefore be] it with me as it may. This is still the comfort of my heart, that I have a gracious, merciful Lord, who is my Shepherd, whose Word and promise strengthen and comfort me. Therefore I shall not want.'"

43. See also C. Stephen Evans, *Kierkegaard: An Introduction* (Cambridge: Cambridge University Press, 2009), 45: "Kierkegaard is surely right to say that when one goes beyond ethical communication to religious communication, then indirect communication is no longer sufficient. At least this is true of Christianity, since Christianity is rooted in historical events, such as the life, death, and resurrection of Jesus, that not every person already knows. . . . However, Kierkegaard maintains that . . . the person in sin does not merely need information. Such a person also needs . . . faith, and although faith

and remoteness from life—and the thinker's composure" in indirection provides the needed perspective on the illusions that plague us (JP 6:6391). But since Kierkegaard's goal all along has been "to arrive at the simple, the communication in turn must sooner or later end in direct communication" (PV 7).[44] All of Kierkegaard's complicated elaborations in his indirect writings were in the service of the simple idea that we should not take the grace of God in vain (PV 16).[45] That is why his discussions of moral concepts, for instance, give "careful attention to motivational and epistemic conditions," and have "a mood of seriousness and personal exhortation that is foreign to moral theory."[46] Being serious about not taking the grace of God in vain is a large part of what it means to become a Christian according to the New Testament (PV 23, 41, 55; TM 39)—and to have more than mere inert aspirations but an actual "active idealism."[47] Kierkegaard labored to keep this higher view of Christianity from turning into "fantasticality and ludicrous exaggeration [and] to prevent people in 'Christendom' from existentially taking in vain Luther and the significance of Luther's life" (PV 17, 42–43). Kierkegaard did this by being a "religious author" under "great debt" to God (PV 12, 111, 122), first of all by having God shackle him to "a very restricted regimen" of writing (PV 86), and secondly by helping him "sniff out . . . malpractices and illusions and suspicious matters" (PV 87). As such his writings were a "devotion

includes beliefs, Kierkegaard describes it as a passion, a form of inwardness. Ultimately, one human cannot give faith to another; it is God's gift, freely offered. The direct testimony one offers to another can only be the occasion for this to happen; no merely human person can give faith to another."

44. But see: "[The] battle becomes a different one; up until now it has been between reflection and the immediate, simple Christianity—now it becomes a battle between reflection and *simplicity armed with reflection*" (JP 3:3704) (italics added).

45. See 2 Cor 6:1: "[We] entreat you not to accept the grace of God in vain" (RSV). See also Martin Luther, "Lectures on Isaiah 40–66" (1530), LW17:177–78: "2 Cor 6:1 . . . is an admonition. 'Make use of grace while you can.' Christ says (Jn 12:35): 'Walk while you have the light.' So here, 'beware that you do not despise this Word and the offered grace.' This is the most dangerous trial, sloth. Satan tempts us in various ways: first, by means of the oppression of tyrants, second through the fallacies of heretics. These cunning attacks we shall triumphantly overcome. Only sloth and smugness confound us so that we may lose the Word. To protect what has been acquired is no less a virtue than to acquire it. This calamity of becoming disgusted because of excessive neglect of the Word is very frequent, to such an extent that if one reads one chapter, he immediately wants to hear nothing more, so we get sick of the Word. . . . Therefore let us prayerfully keep busy with the Word. Excel in the way you live, as the apostles exhort, lest we become sluggish in this time of favor." Note also Ludwig Wittgenstein, *Philosophical Remarks*, trans. Raymond Hargreaves and Roger White, ed. Rush Rhees (New York: Barnes and Noble, 1975), 52: "Why is philosophy so complicated? It ought, after all, to be *completely* simple—Philosophy unties the knots in our thinking, which we have tangled up in an absurd way; but to do that, it must make movements which are just as complicated as the knots. Although the *result* of philosophy is simple, its methods for arriving there cannot be so."

46. Robert C. Roberts, "Kierkegaard and Ethical Theory" in Edward F. Mooney, ed., *Ethics, Love, and Faith in Kierkegaard*, 84. Note as well: "His conceptual remarks about the connection between divine command and the virtue of love [serve] his missionary intention of reawakening an awareness of what Christian existence is like—what its requirements and blessings are—and thus, if possible, fostering Christian love itself in himself and his readers" (87).

47. Ronald Grimsley, *Søren Kierkegaard and French Literature* (Cardiff: University of Wales Press, 1966), 141.

to God, . . . a divine worship" (PV 73).[48] By so doing God drove him to "discard all pomp and glory and wealth and worldly esteem and starred medals and emblems of honor," and run the risk of being "laughed to scorn, mocked, spat upon" (PV 68, 62, 20).[49] The key to all of this was to drive the reader by way of his writings into action—"to leave off all . . . concern for texts and interpretations and *act*."[50] This is how his writings became direct and why that directness is the "crucial" feature of his authorship (PV 53).[51] This directness made his books monumental, in that they were to take what is reflective and sedentary by nature—mere written words—and

48. On this point note as well: "I have basically lived like a scribe in his office. From the very beginning I have been as if under arrest and at every moment sensed that it was not I who played the master but that it was someone else who was the master, sensed it with fear and trembling when he let me perceive his omnipotence and my nothingness, sensed it with indescribable bliss when I related myself to him and the work in unconditional obedience" (PV 74). On writing as a vocation, see Martin Luther, "On Keeping Children in School" (1530), LW 46:249: "Some think that the office of writer is simple and easy, that real work is to ride in armor and suffer heat, cold, dust, thirst, and other discomforts. . . . True, it would be hard for me to ride in armor; but on the other hand, I would like to see the horseman who could sit still with me all day and look into a book. . . . The pen is light, that is true. . . . But in writing, the best part of the body (which is the head) . . . must lay hold and work as never before. . . . They say of writing that 'it only takes three fingers to do it;' but the whole body and soul work at it too." On Luther's writings, see Gerhard Ebeling, *Luther: An Introduction to His Thought*, trans. R. A. Wilson (1964; Philadelphia: Fortress, 1972), 46: "To undertake the study of his writings is to set sail upon an ocean. More than eighty years have already been spent upon what is at present time the standard edition of his works, the Weimar edition. Although almost all his writings are available in this edition, the end is scarcely in sight, since, besides additions, its deficient quality in some parts makes a revision in the form of supplements and corrections necessary, while the preparation of the index in particular presents great difficulties. The Weimar edition consists at the present time of a hundred folio volumes of approximately seven hundred pages each." I therefore disagree that Kierkegaard's "urge to write" was in part due to him being a *graphomanic*, suffering from *hypergraphia*. Joakim Garff, *Søren Kierkegaard: A Biography*, trans. Bruce H. Kirmmse (Princeton: Princeton University Press, 2005), 458. For an account of the storm around this biography, see C. Stephan Evans, "Kierkegaard Among the Biographers," *Books & Culture* 13 (July/August 2007): 12–13.

49. So when Kierkegaard says he writes "*without authority*" and that he is "a *reader* of the books, not . . . the *author*" of them (PV 12), that means God inspired his writings (PV 71–90) and that he did not have the authority of the church to preach and teach through the rite of ordination (PV 261). That disavowal does not mean that "Kierkegaard ... is but one voice in the Kierkegaardian cacophony, . . . too sly for his own good, outwitting even himself in the end . . . [having been] authored by another author in the Kierkegaardian authorship and, as that author is neither mentioned nor named within the authorship, that author must be considered anonymous." Joseph Westfall, *The Kierkegaardian Author*, 117. Kierkegaard believed that it is ordination that empowers the preacher to offend the public and say "You shall" instead of "I beseech the most honored, cultured public's lenient indulgence for these eternal truths" (JP 3:3477, 3146). Supposing, then, with the postmodernists, that Kierkegaard is an ironist "from first to last," creates the debilitating conundrum that one could never know what to take seriously—including whether or not he regarded himself as the author of his own writings. Sylvia Walsh, "Kierkegaard and Postmodernism," *International Journal for Philosophy of Religion* 29 (1991): 117.

50. George Pattison, "If Kierkegaard is Right About Reading, Why Read Kierkegaard?" 198.

51. See also: "The religious is decisively present already from the first moment, has decisive predominance, but for a little while waits patiently so that the poet is allowed to talk himself out" (PV 77).

have them become a platform from which to launch good deeds.[52] The desired action was to relate oneself "to the unconditional" or "eternity" (PV 20, 104)—or to imitate and "follow" Christ (JP 2:1905).[53] By so doing one would "carry out on Monday" the message heard in church on Sunday (PV 60)—by way of faithful obedience to God (PV 124; BA 5). By so doing one would take on "human frankness and openness" (JP 3:2608). In "unbroken evenness" then (PV 76), all his books were in some sense reaching forward to his 1851 discourse on James 1:22–27, "The Changelessness of God," which he subsequently published in 1855 (TM 263–81).

That discourse is about acting according to one's Christian beliefs and thoughts—being more than hearers of the word but also doers of it (FSE 25)—which commits the Christian to what is "not public but . . . objectively uncertain."[54] This discourse is about turning writing into action. Without this correlation between thought and action, the Christian life is inauthentic. That is because faith itself requires the believer to act in

52. See Martin Luther, "Sermon on Matthew 21:1–9" (1521), SML 1:44: "The church is a mouth-house [*mundhaus*], not a pen-house, for since Christ's advent, [the] Gospel is preached orally which before was hidden in written books. It is the way of the Gospel and of the New Testament that it is preached and discussed orally with a living voice. Christ himself wrote nothing, nor did he give the command to write, but to preach orally. Thus the apostles were sent out until Christ came to his mouth-house, that is, until the time had come to preach orally and to bring the Gospel from dead writing and pen-work to the living voice and mouth. From this time the church is rightly called Bethphage [Mt 21:1], since she has and hears the living voice of the Gospel." According to Origen (185–254), the etymology of the name Bethphage is "house of jaws." *Commentary on Matthew*, §16:17.

53. See 1 Pt 2:21: "Christ . . . suffered for you, leaving you an example, that you should follow in his steps" (RSV). See also: "The Christian requirement [includes] dying to the world, voluntary renunciation, crucifying the flesh, [and] suffering for the doctrine" (JP 6:6947). And finally, see Martin Luther, "A Meditation on Christ's Passion" (1519), LW 42:10, 13–14: "The real work of Christ's passion is to make man conformable to Christ, so that man's conscience is tormented in body and soul by our sins. This does not call for many words but for profound reflection and a great awe of sins. . . . After your heart has . . . become firm in Christ, and love, not fear of pain, has made you a foe of sin, then Christ's passion must from that day on become a pattern for your entire life. . . . If pain or sickness afflicts you, consider how paltry this is in comparison with the thorny crown and the nails of Christ. If you are obliged to do or to refrain from doing things against your wishes, ponder how Christ was bound and captured and led hither and yon. If you are beset by pride, see how your Lord was mocked and ridiculed along with criminals. If unchastity and lust assail you, remember how ruthlessly Christ's tender flesh was scourged, pierced, and beaten. If hatred, envy, and vindictiveness beset you recall that Christ, who indeed had more reason to avenge himself, interceded with tears and cries . . . for all his enemies. If sadness or any adversity, physical or spiritual, distresses you, strengthen your heart and say, 'Well, why should I not be willing to bear a little grief, when agonies and fears caused my Lord to sweat blood in the Garden of Gethsemane? He who lies abed while his master struggles in the throes of death is indeed a slothful and disgraceful servant.'"

54. Robert L. Perkins, *Søren Kierkegaard*, Makers of Contemporary Theology (Richmond: John Knox, 1969), 37. On this offense, see Martin Luther, "Sermon on Acts 2:1–13" (1534), LHP 2:163: "You see, it is in the nature and character of the gospel to be a foolish, offensive message, and almost universally rejected and condemned. If the gospel didn't upset citizens and peasants, bishops and princes, it would be a nice, sweet message, easy to proclaim, and the public would gladly accept it. But because it is a message that offends people, especially the high and mighty, therefore it takes great courage and the help of the Holy Spirit to proclaim it. The fact is [preachers must] dare to accuse all [the people] of being traitors and murderers, fully expecting to get their teeth knocked out [for their message]."

a corresponding way. So if you were to believe in helping the poor, for instance, you would be a phony if you did nothing to actually try to help them. But this obvious point is often contested by Christians. There have always been those who have said that if faith is based on grace, "then I must . . . be free from works—otherwise it surely is not grace" (FSE 17).[55] In his discourse on James 1:22–27, Kierkegaard counters this objection.[56] He begins with Luther—the great defender of grace and faith—whom Kierkegaard says affirms the correlation between faith and works by arguing for faith's restless yearning which is to correlate faith with good deeds (FSE 17).[57] Luther cannot be used then to defend the split between faith and works.

55. For a contemporary version of this view, see Gerhard O. Forde, "Luther's 'Ethics,'" in *A More Radical Gospel: Essays on Eschatology, Authority, Atonement, and Ecumenism*, ed. Mark C. Mattes and Steven D. Paulson (Grand Rapids: Eerdmans, 2004), 154: "Even in church publications we see all sorts of nonsense about how the gospel is supposed to have something to say about our ethical dilemmas. And the gospel just becomes synonymous with sloppy permissiveness. So sweet Jesus schlock reigns. The gospel does not have anything to say directly about such dilemmas. We must look to the proper use of the law, and particularly the first use. We have all we need there; we do not need a third use!" For Forde, the first use of the law is what "preserves order and restrains evil. It tells you to stop; you stop. . . . [But] it doesn't increase our faith. . . . But it does preserve us (first use), . . . it keeps the devil, the world, and the flesh from being the ruin of us" (152–53). And on the third use of the law he writes: "[The] law is said to be a 'guide for the believer.' The lion of the law may indeed have lost his teeth, but now you just get gummed to death! In other words, you may indeed have gotten saved without effort, but now comes payback time. There is no free lunch. Or as the contemporary favorite rejoinder has it, grace does not come cheap" (145).

56. This discourse has five sections. The first section (FSE 9–14), is about how the "true eloquence" that comes from one living out the Christian ideals on a daily basis, is more powerful than "all the eloquence of orators" (FSE 10–11). The second section (FSE 15–25), is about how faith—because of its restlessness—requires corresponding action. The third section (FSE 25–35), argues against a critical view of the Bible because it complicates the Bible to such a degree that one is unable to see oneself condemned and redeemed in it (FSE 25–26). The fourth section (FSE 35–44) is about taking the Bible personally so that when you read it will change you for the better. And the fifth section (FSE 44–51) shows how to keep from forgetting what you have learned about yourself in the mirror of God's Word. All five parts of this discourse show how one is to be changed by what one reads in the Bible—rather than trying to "defend oneself against God's Word" (FSE 32).

57. On this restlessness, see: "Faith expressly signifies the deep, strong, blessed restlessness that drives the believer, . . . and therefore the person who has settled down completely at rest has also ceased to be a believer, because . . . a believer travels forward" (UDVS 218). See also Martin Luther, "Preface to the Romans" (1546), LW 35:370–71: "Faith . . . is a divine work in us which changes us and makes us to be born anew of God. . . . O it is a living, busy, active, mighty thing, this faith. It is impossible for it not to be doing good works incessantly. . . . Whoever does not do such works . . . is an unbeliever. He . . . knows neither what faith is nor what good works are. Yet he talks and talks, with many words, about faith and good works. . . . Thus it is impossible to separate works from faith, quite as impossible as to separate heat and light from fire. Beware, therefore, of your own false notions and of the idle talkers who imagine themselves wise enough to make decisions about faith and good works, and yet are the greatest fools." See also his "Lectures on Romans" (1518), LW 25:251, 318: "[The] whole life of . . . faithful people . . . is nothing else but . . . seeking, and begging by the sighing of the heart, the voice of their works, and the labors of their bodies, always seeking and striving to be made righteous, even to the hour of death, never standing still. . . . [The] man who has Christ through true faith . . . stands firm on the solid rock, neither following after a soft life nor fleeing a hard life; not because he is not tempted to flee, . . . but in the end he does not consent, although it is with tremendous labor and sorrow that he barely resists and triumphs."

Kierkegaard imagines Luther coming back to life and saying:

> To what end has faith, which you say you have, made you restless, where have
> you witnessed for the truth, where against untruth, what sacrifices have you
> made, what persecution have you suffered for your Christianity, and at home
> in your domestic life where have your self-denial and renunciation been no-
> ticeable? (FSE 18)

Luther is the right one to ask this of us because as Kierkegaard's Climacus says,
"in every line" of any of his books there is "the strong pulse-beat of appropriation"—
or of faith manifesting itself in good works (CUP 1:366).[58] This is because Luther
struggled to practice what he preached. It was never an option for him to have his faith
float free from good works.[59] And since he believed that this conviction was grounded
in Christianity itself, he also expected the same from anyone claiming to be Christian.
Kierkegaard clarifies this appropriation, or what he calls in another discourse from
this same year—living "in accord with" God's will or being "on good terms" with him
(TM 276, 272):

> Ah, if you are living happily in a beloved home, if your wife is devoted to
> you with all her heart and all her strength, if your children give you joy, then
> consider what it means to go on living day after day in this peace and quiet,
> salutary for a person's soul, more salutary than the late afternoon softer light
> for one whose eyes hurt. . . . And if you are living . . . so that the work that takes
> your time . . . does it in such a way that there is sufficient rest from your work;
> . . . and if you are living . . . so that you have ample income; and if you have
> time for the many enjoyments that refreshingly fill out time and give life a new
> zest; and if . . . in happy obscurity you can rejoice in life, are permitted to walk

---

58. Contra Mark Dooley, *The Politics of Exodus: Kierkegaard's Ethics of Responsibility* (New York:
Fordham University Press, 2001), xv: "I see a real tension in Kierkegaard's work between, on the
one hand, his tendency to advance a strictly Lutheran idea that the individual's private salvation is
realized through an 'absolute relationship' to God, and on the other, his more radically liberating idea
of identifying the God-man as ethical prototype par excellence, the imitation of which engenders a
sensitivity toward the other qua neighbor. . . . In giving this message a contemporary application by
reading it from a Derridean perspective, we loosen the thread of *Kierkegaard's Lutheran straightjacket*,
thus making him more useful as a fellow traveler as we begin a new millennium" (italics added).

59. See Martin Luther, "Sermon on Titus 3:4–8" (1521), SML 6:145: "The entire Scriptures enforce
these two precepts [of believing and loving], and the practice of the one requires the practice of the
other. He who does not firmly believe in God's grace assuredly will not extend kindness to his neighbor, but will be tardy and indifferent in aiding him. In proportion to the strength of his faith will be
his willingness and industry in helping his neighbor. Thus faith incites love, and love increases faith."
Neither was it an option for Kierkegaard to separate faith from works: "Luther was completely right in
saying that if a man had to acquire his salvation by his own striving, it would end either in presumption or in despair, and therefore faith saves. But yet not in such a way that striving vanishes completely.
Faith should make striving possible, because the very fact that I am saved by faith and that nothing at
all is demanded from me should in itself make it possible that I begin to strive, that I do not collapse
under impossibility but am encouraged and refreshed, because it has been decided I am saved, I am
God's child by virtue of faith" (JP 2:1139).

about undisturbed and unnoticed and to be yourself; and if, precisely because you live in obscurity, you often have the opportunity to learn to know people from their better, their good, their lovable side; . . . and if, when you find occasion to do someone else a favor, a favor that is rewarded with so much joy that it is a question whether you are not actually doing yourself . . . a favor; and if you, easily understanding your own life, are easily in harmony with others and easily understood—[then think of the witness to the truth!][60] (FSE 22–23)

That witness to the truth is none other than Jesus himself[61]—who knew suffering and sacrifice, shame and loss—unlike his half-hearted followers who supposed they did not have to suffer like their master did.[62] Kierkegaard presses this matter regarding our pampered and cozy lives (FSE 11, 12, 23, 40) in order to prevent grace "from becoming a camouflage . . . for refined worldliness" (FSE 24). He criticizes our soft lives in order to drive us to renounce the world (FSE 36). And he does this with direct admonitions.

The first one is from Nathan to David—"Thou art the man" (FSE 38) and the other is from the parable of the Good Samaritan—"Go and do likewise" (FSE 41).[63]

60. See also: "And not until a man is unhappily tormented in the world to the degree that his suffering is like misanthropy, not until then does Christianity come into being for him. All this beer-hall enthusiasm about living *gemütligt* [pleasantly] and having such a good life in animal-human categories and then putting the name of Christ on top of the cake every Sunday—that this cowardice is Christianity is, of course, a pure lie" (JP 4:4964).On Kierkegaard's critique of economic affluence, see Eliseo Pérez-Álvarez, *A Vexing Gadfly: The Late Kierkegaard on Economic Matters*, Princeton Theological Monograph Series (Eugene, Oregon: Pickwick Publications, 2009), 173: "Kierkegaard's political love for the poor unmasked the ulterior motives in the preaching of Christianity as an accompaniment to the enjoyment of life. He criticized the 'teachers of Christianity,' i.e., the ones who had made preaching their career, for having transformed the glad news for the poor into the opposite." However, when addressing Kierkegaard's *Open Letter* of 1851, Pérez-Álvarez misses the priority Kierkegaard gives to inwardness (171). In that letter Kierkegaard writes: "There is nothing about which I have greater misgivings than about all that even slightly tastes of this disastrous confusion of politics and Christianity. . . . Christianity is inwardness, inward deepening. If at a given time the forms under which one has to live are not the most perfect, if they can be improved, in God's name, do so. But essentially Christianity is inwardness. Just as man's advantage over animals is to be able to live in any climate, so also Christianity's perfection, simply because it is inwardness, is to be able to live, according to its vigor, under the most imperfect conditions and forms, if such be the case. Politics is the external system, this Tantalus-like busyness about external change" (COR 53–54). This devaluation of externals—and good weather—would also play havoc with vacations: "It is still my unalterable opinion that travel is foolish" (LD 89)!

61. See Jn 18:37: "For this I . . . came into the world, to bear witness to the truth" (RSV).

62. See Mt 10:24–25: "A disciple is not above his teacher, nor a servant above his master; it is enough for the disciple to be like his teacher, and the servant like his master. If they have called the master of the house Beelzebul, how much more will they malign those of his household" (RSV).

63. See 2 Sm 12:7; Lk 10:37. In this regard, Kierkegaard, like Luther, was no pussy-footer [*leisetreter*] or one who steps "softly and quietly." Martin Luther, "Letter to Elector John" (May 15, 1530), LW 49:298. For a famous example of this, see Martin Luther, "Ninety-Five Theses" (1517), LW 31:29: "Thesis 40. A Christian who is truly contrite seeks and loves to pay penalties for his sins; the bounty of indulgences, however, relaxes penalties and causes men to hate them—at least it furnishes occasion for hating them."

These words, and others like them,[64] come from seeing oneself in the mirror of the Bible, which means taking what it says personally (FSE 25, 35, 36, 37, 40, 44).[65] This would be like reading the Bible the way they did in the ancient church—as the actual "terrifying voice of God" (FSE 39). Against this simple view of the Bible stands modern critical biblical scholarship. It raises questions about the Bible that fog over the mirror of God's word:

> Which books are authentic? Are they really by the apostles, and are the apostles really trustworthy? Have they personally seen everything, or have they perhaps only heard about various things from others? As for ways of reading, there are thirty thousand different ways.[66] (FSE 25)

This is to treat Holy Scriptures "the way Appius Pulcher treated the sacred hens. One consults them, and if they predict something bad, then like the general one says: If the sacred hens won't eat, then let them drink—and thereupon casts them overboard" (JP 3:3279). Kierkegaard is not swayed by this critical approach but believes it is nothing but "the full force of human craftiness" (FSE 26). Rather than clarifying the Bible, these critical comments only obscure the fact that the real problem is with the scholars who have "no desire to deny flesh and blood and . . . comply with God's Word" (FSE 32).[67] Because these critical, scholarly judgments are so disingenuous, they should be stopped from fogging over the mirror of the Bible which is there to show us our sin. Rather than trying to make the Bible unreliable, we should read it in a quiet place, all alone (FSE 49, 32), taking it personally, day by day, and then collecting

64. See Thaddée Matura, *Gospel Radicalism: The Hard Sayings of Jesus*, trans. Maggi Despost and Paul Lachance (Maryknoll, New York: Orbis, 1984), and Manfred T. Brauch, *Hard Sayings of Paul* (Downers Grove, Illinois: InterVarsity, 1989).

65. See also: "I doubt very much that there could be found among us one single person who in the old Christian or Jewish sense is able to have anything to do personally with a personal God. In relation to those heroes, we are a bunch of old rags, duplicates, a heap of bricks, mass-men, a school of herring, etc." (JP 2:1437).

66. See James Barr, *The Bible in the Modern World* (New York: Harper & Row, 1973), 10: "[Since the critical approach to the Bible holds that the] Bible is a limited set of books, chosen partly by accident and coming from a limited segment in the total history of the church; how can its insights be decisive for us in any way which is qualitatively different from that which attaches to other books and other times?"

67. For a good current example of this, see Peter Spitaler, "James 1:5–8: A Dispute With God," *Catholic Biblical Quarterly* 71 (July 2009): 575: "James's concern . . . is not that this person might be torn by intrapersonal doubts. Rather, contesting with God and fellow believers, this person does not submit to God (4:7–10) and foments warring factions within communities (4:1–3)." In his drive to break free from the condemnation of personal doubt in James 1, Spitaler misses how intrapersonal doubt fuels interpersonal turmoil, which discredits his forced option. On this same text see: "This is why the apostle says, 'Purify your hearts, you double-minded"; that is, cleanse your hearts of double-mindedness. . . . It is of this same purity of heart that the apostle is speaking when he says, 'If any of you lacks wisdom, let him ask God . . . but in faith, not as double-minded persons' (Jas 1:5, 6, 8), because purity of heart is precisely the wisdom that is gained by praying; a man of prayer does not pore over scholarly books but is the wise man 'whose eyes are opened—when he kneels down' (Nm 24:16)" (UDVS 25–26).

ourselves "in the impression of the divine" (FSE 50) so that God's Word gains "power over" us (FSE 47). The Bible, after all, is "an imperious book," which wants to change our entire lives "on a prodigious scale" (FSE 31).

If that massive change does not occur, it does not automatically spell our doom. We can still be "equally blessed" if we but have a "restlessness oriented toward inward deepening" (FSE 23–24). That deepening would include repentance and confession for our sins of laziness and cowardice—which would be "a humbling admission" and "shame" (FSE 31, 12, 17). This admission will come from reading the Bible as a mirror—by which we "read a fear and trembling" into our souls (FSE 43). As long as we do not try to cover up our failures, we can be blessed right along with the genuine witnesses to the truth.[68] Be that as it may, we will also concede that our obedience based on such inward deepening is "the least, the mildest, the lowliest form of godly piety" (FSE 24). This admission is important because it will keep us striving all our days to "grow up to salvation."[69]

A HUMBLE, PYTHAGOREAN CHRISTIANITY

The difficulty we have in reading Kierkegaard's writings serves the noble end of helping his readers become Christians. Because the appropriation of the Christian way is so difficult, he believed his books had to be tough if they were going to help us become Christians. This made his entire authorship a missionary tract, since he "considered himself a missionary whose task was to present the gospel . . . to a people gripped by the illusion . . . that being a Christian is simply to be a nice person, to conform to the established social norms."[70] The intensity and scope of this driving concern makes his authorship unique. Those who wonder about the expectations of the Christian life can do no better than read Kierkegaard's books, articles and journals. Those who are struggling to live the Christian life can find no greater human help regarding that narrow way than in his writings. Those who have been seduced by an overly intellectual approach to the Christian faith can find no deeper challenge to that prejudice than in his writings. Those who have grown weary in the struggle to follow the Christian way

---

68. Note as well: "Suppose that . . . all his officials . . . play him false. What do you suppose this omnipotent king will think of such a thing? I wonder if he would not say: That they do not obey the decree, I could forgive that. . . . But this I cannot forgive—that they shift the view of what earnestness is" (FSE 34). See also Mt 12:31: "Therefore I tell you, every sin and blasphemy will be forgiven men, but the blasphemy against the Spirit will not be forgiven" (RSV).

69. 1 Pt 2:2 (RSV). See also Martin Luther, "Sermons on 1 Peter" (1523), LW 30:47–48: "Therefore since the Lord Christ is now completely yours through faith, and you have received salvation, . . . you must henceforth let it be your concern . . . that no one should deal unfaithfully and falsely with the other person, . . . so that no one overreaches the other person in selling, buying, or promising, and the like."

70. C. Stephen Evans, "Kierkegaard: A Misunderstood Reformer," *Christianity Today* (September 21, 1984): 27.

can find no greater encouragement than what his authorship provides. So I share the excitement of Céline Léon when she writes about her experience reading Kierkegaard:

> Indeed, who better than Kierkegaard has voiced the passion for anguished self-examination, or more relentlessly thrown the reader back on his or her own resources. Ever since those early years, I have been dazzled by the uncanny soaring and diving of the thought, the despair and the pride, the anguish and the trust, the fear and the faith; I have savored the multivalent metaphors, the resplendent images, the daring similes, the poetic felicities with which the writings . . . are laced. Even now, I cannot think of any of these books without making mine the claim of the Young Man of *Repetition* (1843): "Every time I come to it, it is born anew as something original" (R 205). Although I have read many of these works over and over, each word remains enduringly and endearingly new to me, retaining most, if not all, of its original force, flavor, and freshness.[71]

The greatness in Kierkegaard's authorship is in large part due to his apt description of the Christian life (PV 138). In "Armed Neutrality," at the end of *The Point of View*, Kierkegaard displays in miniature "the traversed path" of his entire authorship (PV 7) in his analysis of the nature of Christian identity. He arrives at a simple affirmation of Christian identity, but only after a series of complex qualifications. In this last section I want to trace that path in order to explain what he calls a Pythagorean version of Christian identity.

He begins his discussion with the imitation of Christ. For Kierkegaard, what

> first and foremost must be brought into prominence . . . is the ideal picture of a Christian, so that it can appear as a task, beckoning, and on the other side, so that it can crush with all its weight the presumptuousness of wanting to go further than being a Christian. . . . It is the ideal picture that I have tried to present and will try to present. . . . From the very beginning my work has not been a rush job. . . . Therefore, to present in every way—dialectical, pathos-filled (in the various forms of pathos), psychological, modernized by continual reference to modern Christendom and to the fallacies of a science and scholarship—the ideal picture of being a Christian: this was and is the task. Jesus Christ, it is true, is himself the prototype and will continue to be that, unchanged, until the end. But Christ is also much more than the prototype; he is the object of faith. In Holy Scripture he is presented chiefly as such. (PV 130–31)

---

71. Céline Léon, *The Neither/Nor of the Second Sex: Kierkegaard on Women, Sexual Difference, and Sexual Relations* (Macon, Georgia: Mercer University Press, 2008), 1. Even so, Léon will not explain away Kierkegaard's apparent sexist lapses—placing "in his mouth the words we wish he had uttered" (260).

Unlike many modern Christian authors, Kierkegaard emphatically encourages the imitation of Christ as our Prototype who is to be followed,[72] but adds that Christ is most of all the Savior in whom we are to believe—apart from any good works.[73] This complex, dialectical treatment of Christ contributes to the greatness of his authorship. It also helps fill out his understanding of Christian identity:

> Let me take an imaginary situation. With a sword hanging over my head, I am ordered to say whether or not I am a Christian. My answer would be: I trust to God that I am a Christian; I believe that out of grace he will accept me as a Christian, and so on. If they are not satisfied with the answer but say, "You must say either that you are a Christian or not," then I would answer: No, that I will not do. If they persist—"Then we will put you to death because you will not answer as we demand"—my answer would be: Go ahead, . . . I accept this martyrdom. By this I mean that I am not afraid of being put to death – although I by no means flaunt a willingness for it nor am I eager for it. . . . [But] I do fear to say too much about myself. (PV 135)

Kierkegaard out of fear of saying too much about himself says that he both is and is not a Christian. First he says that he is a Christian provided that God in his mercy sees to it that he becomes one. But if he were forced to say more straightforwardly that he knew for sure he was a Christian, he would withdraw his previous avowal, say nothing more, and suffer the consequences.

This is because our Christian identity is not in our full control, and so what we say about ourselves must be sufficiently qualified to avoid making that impression:

> The question of whether I am a Christian (and thus for every individual, whether he is a Christian) is entirely a God-relationship. . . . I cannot speak of my being a Christian according to a merely human standard. . . . But then

72. See also: "Pay sharp attention to this matter of contemporaneity, because the crucial point is not the fuss you make over a dead person, no, but what you do in contemporaneity or that you make the past so present that you come to suffer as if you were contemporary with it—this decides what kind of person you are. . . . This thought is for me my life's thought. . . . Not that I have invented it, . . . it is an old invention, it is the New Testament's" (TM 289–90).

73. On the redemptive theme in Kierkegaard's writings, see: "No, apprehensive about myself as I have become, I will seek my refuge with him, the Crucified One. I will beseech him to save me from evil and to save me from myself" (CD 280). See also: "If the difference is infinite between God, who is in heaven, and you, who are on earth, the difference between the Holy One and the sinner is infinitely greater. Oh, but yet, also in this respect, even though in another way, he put himself completely in your place. If he, if the Redeemer's suffering and death is the satisfaction for your sin and guilt—if it is the satisfaction, then he does indeed step into your place for you, or he, the one who makes the satisfaction, steps into your place, suffering in your place the punishment of sin so that you might be saved. . . . Thus when punitive justice here in the world or in judgment in the next seeks the place where I, a sinner, stand with all my guilt, with my many sins—it does not find me. . . . I stand saved beside this other one, beside him, my Redeemer, who puts himself completely in my place—for this accept my gratitude, Lord Jesus Christ!" (WA 123). I agree, then, that "Kierkegaard was the most Christ-centered thinker in Christian history." Malcolm Diamond, *Contemporary Philosophy and Religious Thought: An Introduction to the Philosophy of Religion* (New York: McGraw-Hill, 1974), 145.

before God, would I dare say: I am—a Christian? No, I would not dare to do this—I least of all. But therefore neither would I dare to let the emphasis fall upon my being a Christian, so that I would be put to death because I was a Christian—for suppose God thought otherwise . . . [and] God is the judge. (PV 135–36)

Kierkegaard is emphatic that only God knows whether or not we are Christians.[74] Because of that, we cannot usurp his role and brashly declare—all by ourselves—that we are Christians. Furthermore it would be blasphemous of us to say we were Christian, and suffer martyrdom because of that confession, and then use that suffering to remove all doubt about our identity—because then we would be surreptitiously forcing God to judge us favorably. Kierkegaard explains this raid on heaven as a denial of a hypothetical, reverent confession of faith:

If I, then, were put to death because I, according to my own apodictic declaration, was a Christian, my life would be taken, . . . [but] I would by no means be through with it, because suppose I would run into trouble in eternity, that it was arrogance on my part to have said apodictically, instead of hypothetically because of reverence for God, that I was a Christian. I do indeed face judgment; therefore on Judgment Day I shall have to repeat that I was put to death because I, according to my own statement, was a Christian. But if I will say it, then by this I will be saying to God that I was a Christian. . . . But I would not dare say that to God under any circumstances. Face-to-face with God I would have to use a much humbler expression: I trust to God that in his mercy he will receive me as a Christian. (PV 136)

Nonhypothetical confessions of faith lack the humility that make them Christian. This humility is rooted in God's control of our faith in him—which keeps it from trying to manage our life with him.[75] Our boldness in confession, then, is not about our

74. See 1 Sm 16:7: "[The] Lord sees not as a man sees; man looks on the outward appearance, but the Lord looks on the heart" (RSV).

75. See Jn 3:8: "The wind blows where it wills, and you hear the sound of it, but you do not know whence it comes or whither it goes; so it is with every one who is born of the Spirit" (RSV). On this verse see: "The wind blows where it will; . . . [so] also with longing, the longing for God and the eternal, the longing for our Savior and Redeemer. Comprehend it you cannot, nor should you; indeed, you dare not even want to attempt it—but you are to use it. . . . Oh, it is piously said that one must not waste God's gifts, [and] what would better be called God's gifts than every prompting of the Spirit, every pull of the soul, every fervent stirring of the heart, every holy state of mind, every devout longing, which are indeed God's gifts in a far deeper sense than food and clothing. . . . A person can ignore its call; he can change it into an impulse of the moment, into a whim that vanishes without a trace the next moment. He can resist it; he can prevent its deeper generation within him; he can let it die unused as a barren mood. But if you accept it with gratitude as a gift of God, it will indeed become a blessing to you. . . . Even if it was inexplicable, inasmuch as it is indeed from God, . . . you still understood what was required of you. Truly, even though God gives everything, he also requires everything, that the person himself shall do everything to use rightly what God gives. Oh, in the customary pursuits of daily life, how easy it is, in the spiritual sense, to doze off, in the habitual routine of sameness, how difficult to find a break! . . . [Then, just] as longing has torn me away from what so easily entangles one

Christian identity, but about the certainty of God's judgment and mercy as revealed in the Holy Scriptures. That certainty stands regardless of the strength or certainty of our apprehension and implementation of the divine revelation. Kierkegaard draws out this point by way of contrasting external thinking with inward thinking:

> Externally oriented thinking is preoccupied with having the courage in relation to people to become a martyr; inwardly oriented thinking is preoccupied with having the courage in relation to God to be a martyr. This is martyrdom's proper fear and trembling. . . . But the ideality with regard to being a Christian is a continual inward deepening. The more ideal the conception of being a Christian, the more inward it becomes—and indeed the more difficult. Being a Christian then undergoes a change. (PV 137)

This change shifts our awareness more toward what God thinks of us than how others think of us.[76] This brings a deepening of our Christian identity because of the more difficult standards that God measures us by—to say nothing of greater fear and trembling. With the standards set so high, we can only approximate Christianity—or eat the crumbs from under the master's table, as it were.[77]

Imagining that we can master the Christian life and claim it for ourselves without remainder is not only arrogant but foolhardy. Kierkegaard reinforces this difference between approximation and mastery by way of the ancient Greek philosopher, Pythagoras:[78]

---

in a spell, so by earnest thoughts will I also cooperate so that I may tear myself completely away from what still might hold me back" (CD 253–54).

76. See also: "Therefore, it is a risk to preach, for as I go up into that holy place—whether the church is packed or as good as empty, whether I myself am aware of it or not, I have one listener more than can be seen, an invisible listener, God in heaven, whom I certainly cannot see but who truly can see me. This listener, he pays close attention to whether what I am saying is true, whether it is true in me, that is, he looks to see—and he can do that, because he is invisible, in a way that makes it impossible to be on one's guard against him—he looks to see whether my life expresses what I am saying. And although I do not have authority to commit anyone else, I have committed myself to every word I have said from the pulpit in the sermon—and God has heard it. Truly it is a risk to preach! . . . The proclaimer of the Christian truth . . . should be true, that is, that he himself should be what he proclaims, or at least strive to be that, or at least be honest enough to confess about himself that he is not that" (PC 234–35).

77. See Mt 15:27–28.

78. See Christoph Riedweg, *Pythagoras: His Life, Teaching, and Influence*, trans. Steven Rendall (Ithaca, New York: Cornell University Press, 2005), 97: "From the point of view of word formation, . . . *philó-sophos* in Greek does not denote a downgrading in comparison with *sophós*, but rather an intensification: A philosopher is a person who is engaged in particularly intensive dealings with *sophía* and who truly and exceedingly loves the latter." See also John Wild, "Kierkegaard and Classical Philosophy," *The Philosophical Review* 49 (September 1941): 547, 549: "It is here that his philosophic importance chiefly lies, as a critic of the false identification of being with thought. . . . Looking about him in the midst of a nation which took for granted that it was Christian, . . . [Kierkegaard also saw, in the same vein, no one] making an honest effort to apply Christian teaching to himself."

Formerly there were in Greece wise men. . . . Then came Pythagoras and with him the reflection-qualification . . . [regarding] being a wise man; therefore he did not even venture to call himself a wise man but instead called himself a . . . lover of wisdom. Was this a step backward or a step forward; or was it not because Pythagoras had more ideally apprehended what it would really mean, what would be required to call oneself a wise man; therefore there was wisdom in his not even having dared to call himself a wise man. (PV 137)

Through the example of Pythagoras, Kierkegaard argues for a more modest, humble and rigorous Christianity—a Pythagorean version of it, if you will.[79] A less rigorous Christianity can survive only because the Christian norms in Scripture and tradition have not been used to form it. And once those norms are fully used, Christianity is impossible to practice as we should—the mountain being too high for any of us to scale. But even when it cannot be mastered, it can be admired and loved and approximated. While this might seem like personal resignation and even rank unbelief to the simple-minded, the truth is that the entire life of a Christian is only a time of "willing to be righteous, but never achieving it."[80] The model, then, of the Christian life is not our witness to it, but the examples and instructions in the New Testament itself. Kierkegaard, in order to keep himself from mistakenly being turned into the model because of his authorship, says he is only a mediocre Christian like the rest:

If my relation were to pagans, . . . I would have to say that I am a Christian. But I am living in Christendom, among Christians, or among people who say they are Christians. It is not up to me, a human being, to judge others. . . . If I were now to insist that I am a Christian, what would this mean in the situation? It would mean that I am a Christian raised to the second power, the distinguished Christian. . . . [So I] declare forthrightly that I am a Christian in the sense that others are, but not in contrast to them. (PV 138–39)

Kierkegaard does not want to compete with other Christians over who is the best follower of Christ. His task is rather to present the most accurate and rigorous view of Christianity allowed for in the New Testament.[81] That ideal picture, and not any one individual person's faith and witness, is the standard by which all aspiring Christians

79. In an earlier journal version of this passage on Pythagoras, Kierkegaard says more about this rigorousness: "It is true than Christianity seems to be inimical to men, but that is because man, the natural man, is lazy and weak and sensate, and Christianity is the absolute. What the natural man understands by human love is nothing more or less than this: Be lenient with yourself and with us. If a man will cling to God, repent of his sloth as soon as it asserts itself, and not conceitedly delude himself that God has to be remodeled after him but just the opposite, then Christianity is in fact love. But it certainly is not this wretched silliness that human sympathy and stupidity have made it out to be" (JP 6:6237). A popular modern example of this leniency is I'm OK, You're OK (1969; repr.: New York: Galahad, 2004) by Thomas A. Harris.

80. Martin Luther, "Lectures on Romans" (1518), LW 25:268. See also Mt 5:6: "Blessed are those who hunger and thirst for righteousness, for they shall be satisfied" (RSV).

81. See Mt 5:48: "You . . . must be perfect, as your Father in heaven is perfect" (RSV).

will be judged. This method of verification avoids personal arrogance while still being able to discredit any self-declared Christians who disregard the norms of Christianity:

> The task, then, is to present the ideal of a Christian, and here I intend to do battle. . . . This is my idea of the judgment that I think will fall upon Christendom—not that I or any single individual should judge others, but the ideal picture of what it is to be a Christian will judge me and everyone who permits himself to be judged. . . . [For there have been] thousands of Christian [who] have known definitely that they were Christians but did not know definitely what it means to be a Christian. (PV 139–41)

By shifting the focus to this ideal picture of what it means to be a Christian, Kierkegaard not only directs attention away from himself as a magnificent author,[82] but also "jacks up" the price of being a Christian (PV 95, 138–39), which he could never do any other way. This combination of humility and strenuousness is what makes his many literary devices so effective and memorable.

This humble, Pythagorean version of Christianity is part of Kierkegaard's "enigmatic legacy."[83] Traversing a path that says one is both a Christian and not a Christian is a difficult path for some to walk.[84] Nevertheless, this complex path to religious

---

82. On the temptations in publishing, see *Willa Cather in Person: Interview, Speeches, and Letters*, ed. L. Brent Bohlke (Lincoln, Nebraska: University of Nebraska Press, 1986), 192–93: "The first time I was ever confronted by myself in print was one Sunday morning . . . when I opened the Sunday *Journal* and saw [my published article]. . . . That was the beginning of many troubles for me. . . . But what youthful vanity can be unaffected by the sight of itself in print! It had a kind of hypnotic effect."

83. On this legacy see Jack Mulder Jr., "Must All Be Saved? A Kierkegaardian Response to Theological Universalism," *International Journal for Philosophy of Religion* 59 (February 2006), 1: "Søren Kierkegaard has an enigmatic legacy. On the one hand, his rescue of 'New Testament Christianity,' as he so fondly called it, from the synthesizing clutches of Hegelian speculation often endears him to those who would seek to defend a traditional Christianity. Yet these are often turned away by his polemical attack on the Christianity of his day, which was so vociferous that he crept closely to direct criticism of the New Testament apostolic community itself. There are those who embrace his harsh critique of so-called Christendom but wish he had seen through to a rejection of Christianity, or at any rate, to a much more critical stance with regard to traditional Christianity. This mixed reception situates Kierkegaard's thought at an interesting place between fundamentalism and secularism, or perhaps, religious liberalism. I think that this interesting place is where Kierkegaard belongs."

84. See, for instance, the statement by William Heinesen (1900–91), quoted in Alastair Hannay, *Kierkegaard*, The Arguments of the Philosophers (London: Routledge & Kegan Paul, 1982), ix: "As a spiritual type . . . Kierkegaard belongs to the Mephistopheles category. . . . In fact, Kierkegaard goes one better than the devil. . . . While Mephistopheles simply dissolves in a smoke of brilliant conversation . . . Kierkegaard is the dire sufferer of his own Satanism. He is, one might say, the tragic satan." And from Kierkegaard's own time, Henrik Hertz (1797–1870) writes that Kierkegaard's books were "like tall trees in literature. High up in the treetops, his monkeys sit and eat from the trees. If you attack them, they throw large Kierkegaardian pieces down at you—rather like monkeys who sit up in coconut palms and thrown down nuts if you attack them with stones. If only the Kierkegaardian nuts were not so large and tough that you have a difficult time opening them to get to the relatively small kernel." *Encounters With Kierkegaard: A Life as Seen by His Contemporaries*, ed. Bruce H. Kirmmse, trans. Bruce H. Kirmmse and Virginia R. Laursen (Princeton: Princeton University Press, 1996), 220. It sounds like Hertz did not understand Kierkegaard's traversed path from complexity (the large and tough nuts) to simplicity (the relatively small kernels).

simplicity captures, in a compelling way, the heart of Christianity, which many more might come to see if "a favorable *Zeitgeist*, preferably the result of prolonged malaise culminating in a profound crisis on the person-spiritual level" and "the absence of any attitude of deliberate malice" were to prevail.[85] Since in our time "a slick campaign of propaganda . . . spreading an inane apologia of evil, . . . a mindless desire for transgression, a dishonest and frivolous freedom, exalting impulsiveness, immorality and selfishness as if they were new heights of sophistication,"[86] is prevailing, the conditions are right[87] for the coming of a humble, Pythagorean Christianity under the tutelage of Kierkegaard's authorship.

85. Habib C. Malik, *Receiving Søren Kierkegaard: The Early Impact and Transmission of His Thought* (Washington, DC: The Catholic University of America Press, 1997), 393–94.

86. Pope Benedict XVI, "Good Friday Prayers," *Newsweek* (April 24, 2006), "Perspectives." Note also Kierkegaard's prediction: "I find something sad in the fact that I . . . must always stand outside as a superfluity and impractical exaggeration. . . . But it will all end, as they say, with conditions getting so desperate that they must make use of desperate people like me" (JP 6:6709a).

87. For a cautionary note, see Sylvia Walsh, *Kierkegaard: Thinking Christianly in an Existential Mode* (Oxford: Oxford University Press, 2009), 205–6: "It is too early to determine how the theology of Kierkegaard will be received in the present century, although he is already being hailed in some quarters as a proto-postmodernist. . . . But if we are to think theologically or Christianly in an existential manner as Kierkegaard enjoins us to do, it is important to read his works first of all on their own terms, that is, as indirect communications to the reader, 'that single individual', for the sake of personal appropriation, rather than as theological fodder that must be translated into some other conceptual framework in order to have contemporary relevance."

2

On Sickness

EVEN THOUGH KIERKEGAARD WROTE extensively on topics in psychology, literature and philosophy, he said his whole authorship was "religious from first to last."[1] By this he meant he was concerned in his books with the matter of "becoming a Christian" (PV 6, 23). In this chapter I want to show how Kierkegaard, in his book *Christian Discourses*, believed illness helps in this matter of becoming a Christian—the overall theme of his authorship. I will do this first by defining illness in his book, *Christian Discourses*. Next I will show what this sickness teaches us about ourselves, especially through endangerment and nothingness. Third I will explain how and why he thinks illness does a better job at preaching than pastors in the pulpit do, by exploring the failure of preaching in his time. I will do this by stressing artistic distance, heterogeneity and earnestness in preaching. Then I will show how illness awakens faith in Christ. In this section I will study the place of reversals, Christ's crucifixion, and gracious unsureness in this awakening. And finally I will make a judgment on the sickbed preacher itself, showing that what Kierkegaard says about the positive role of sickness in Christianity is confirmed by a series of compelling contemporary cases.

DEFINING ILLNESS IN CHRISTIAN DISCOURSES

In this section I want to define what Kierkegaard meant by illness in *Christian Discourses*. In *Christian Discourses* he praises illness, calling it our best preacher. The "sickbed and the nighttime hour," he writes, "preach more powerfully than all the orators" (CD 164). His reason for this was that in illness we have "the terrors implicit

---

1. Even though this is Kierkegaard's avowal, it nevertheless remains hotly contested among the scholars. On this dispute see Ronald Goetz, "A Secularized Kierkegaard," *The Christian Century* 111 (March 9, 1994), 259–60. Goetz argues that a non-religious view of Kierkegaard does much damage to his authorship, reducing it to a "stylistic exercise in ironic indeterminism" (259). It also turns Kierkegaard himself into "a mere aesthetic, who plays with language in order to luxuriate in its potential for ambiguity" (260). But even as a religious author, Kierkegaard remains a "perplexing" one, situated somewhere between "C. S. Lewis and Heidegger." John C. Caputo, *How to Read Kierkegaard* (London: Granta, 2007), 5, 89. On Kierkegaard's religious strategy, see George Pattison, *Kierkegaard and the Crisis of Faith* (London: SPCK, 1997), 5: "Kierkegaard . . . begins by presenting in some detail the 'aesthetic' attitude which he regards as the typical attitude of modern bourgeois society in order to expose its inner contradictions and so lure the reader on to a confrontation with Christianity as an alternative stance towards life that is worth taking seriously."

in the power of circumstance" thrust upon us.[2] The power in illness to press these terrors on us is important because it produces the "ups and downs and ordeals and spiritual trials" which move us "in earnest for awakening" (CD 165). Illness engulfs us in these ordeals through the preacher of repentance that is "deep within every person's heart" (CD 192). From this we see that it is illness that helps us repent. This is highly significant because without repentance there can be no awaking, and without awakening, no one can become a Christian.

For Kierkegaard, the illness that drives us to repentance is simple physical sickness. This definition is quite different from the one he gives in his book, *Sickness Unto Death*. There, sickness is spiritual.[3] It has nothing to do with "earthly and temporal suffering: need, illness, misery, hardship, adversities, torments, mental sufferings, cares, grief" (SUD 8). Indeed, "no earthly, physical sickness is the sickness unto death, for death is indeed the end of sickness, but death is not the end" (SUD 17). This makes sickness unto death quite unlike ordinary physical illness. For indeed, not being spiritually sick or in despair "is not similar to not being sick, for not being sick cannot be the same as being sick, whereas not being in despair can be the very same as being in despair. It is not with despair as with sickness, where feeling indisposed is the sickness" (SUD 24–25). Sickness unto death is therefore more complex than simple physical illness. That's because it's a "sickness of the spirit" (SUD 22). And the human spirit, unlike the body, is "a relation that relates itself to itself," and is grounded "transparently in the power that established it" (SUD 13, 14, and 49, 79). These relations make the spirit more complex than the body, and so also, spiritual sickness more complex than physical illness.

Illness in *Christian Discourses*, therefore, is simpler than this Sickness unto Death. It is more straightforward. It cannot be disguised under its opposites, such as physical ailments like cancer or pneumonia, or being in bed due to a broken bone or the like. Physical illness is not the Sickness unto Death, but it is the contributions of such illness to the matter of becoming a Christian that I want to explicate in this chapter.[4]

2. I believe that this celebration of sickness contributes to the "very dark . . . mood" in *Christian Discourses*. Bruce Kirmmse, *Kierkegaard in Golden Age Denmark* (Bloomington: Indiana University Press, 1990), 358. I for one think that it's this mood that makes *Christian Discourses* one of Kierkegaard's "greatest works." Søren Kierkegaard, *Christian Discourses, Etc.*, trans. Walter Lowrie (1940; Princeton: Princeton University Press, 1971), xvi.

3. Kierkegaard also treats this spiritual sickness before the publication *Sickness Unto Death*. In 1844 he writes about "soul rot" which comes from "the monotony of self-concern" (EUD 207).

4. This does not mean that this more complex Sickness unto Death cannot also help one in becoming a Christian. "Only he whose being has been so shaken," Kierkegaard writes, "that he has become spirit by understanding that everything is possible, only he has anything to do with God" (SUD 40). Unfortunately "the majority of people" are "too sensate to have the courage to venture out and to endure being spirit" (SUD 43). They chafe at the proposition that "the self must be broken in order to become itself" (SUD 65). So while physical illness might well push one in the right direction—one who also suffers from this Sickness unto Death—that nudge alone will not keep one from retreating

Learning from Sickness

These physical ailments are important for Christianity because they have the potential to lead a person to faith in Christ.[5] In this section I will try to show how this is so. Illness can do this for Kierkegaard because it both endangers us and reduces us to nothing. Saint Paul experienced just this. After suffering his unrelenting "thorn in the flesh," he says of himself, "I am nothing" (2 Cor 12:7–11). Kierkegaard seems to have something like this in mind when he says that sickness can "grip a person" and "hurl him into the power of circumstances" (CD 165). This hurling is what endangers us. He elaborates this point in a journal entry the year right after *Christian Discourses* was published:

> Do you believe . . . that if you were thoroughly healthy you would easily or more easily achieve perfection? Just the opposite: then you would yield easily to your passions, to pride if not to others, to an intensified self-esteem and the like. In that way sufferings, even though a burden, are a beneficial burden, like braces used in the orthopedic institute.
>
> To be thoroughly healthy physically and mentally and then to lead a truly spiritual life—that no man can do. The sense of spontaneous well being immediately runs away with him. . . . This is why sufferings are a help. If a person suffers every day, if he is so infirm that the thought of death is simply right at hand, then he may be somewhat successful in being continually conscious of needing God.
>
> Physical health, the immediate sense of well being, is a far greater danger than riches, power, and esteem.
>
> Of course it has a deceptive appearance, as if it would still be a help to be physically, spontaneously strong. But if one is that, it is almost a superhuman task actually to live qua spirit. . . . Physical suffering, the infirm body, is a beneficial memento. (JP 4:4637)[6]

"again to the illusory sanctuary of their self-deception." Michael Watts, *Kierkegaard* (Oxford: Oneworld, 2003), 181.

5. This is so even if medical science one day succeeds in making us immortal. This is because such immortality is not "absolute. [It] cannot come with a guarantee . . . against accident or suicide. Even immortal life cannot be insured against new zoonotic viral epidemics or even against infectious diseases presently defying our best efforts at cure. All that can be reasonably expected of immortality is the permanent suspension of degenerative diseases that would otherwise accompany aging and senescence." Stanley Shostak, *Becoming Immortal: Combining Cloning and Stem-Cell Therapy* (Albany, New York: State University of New York Press, 2002), 42.

6. Some warn against seeing in Kierkegaard's *Journals* a clear interpretive tool for his published writings since they are "littered with so much incoherent material . . . [and] contain so many reading notes." Robert L. Perkins, "Introduction," IKC 6:7 n. 3. I, however, agree with Alexander Dru that Kierkegaard's *Journals* provide helpful "clarification." *The Soul of Kierkegaard: Selections from His Journals*, trans. ed. Alexander Dru (1959; Minoola, New York: Dover, 2003), 7. For the publication history of the *Journals*, see Niels Jørgen Cappelørn, Joakim Garff and Johnny Kondrup, *Written Images: Søren Kierkegaard's Journals, Notebooks, Booklets, Sheets, Scraps, and Slips of Paper*, trans. Bruce H. Kirmmse (Princeton: Princeton University Press, 2003).

This entry says the opposite of what we normally think, namely, that uninterrupted health, wealth and happiness are clear, unqualified benefits. Against this popular view, Kierkegaard dares to say that health and well being are very dangerous. This is because such blessedness intensifies our self-esteem which pulls us away from God.[7] So sickness is not a simple trauma, but actually a beneficial burden. It is so because it helps us realize our need for God. Without such a burden it would be quite unlikely for one ever to develop a need for God. This insight into physical illness is what gives it a silver lining for Kierkegaard. This benefit is often missed or defied by those burdened down by illness. What they long for is more than a silver lining. They would much prefer the security and comfort that only health can bring. Kierkegaard therefore rightly concludes that there is "danger in this security" (CD 163). For the security that good health brings leads to pride.[8] Good health and prosperity leave us in our selfishness and sin. Nothing in health and prosperity can rouse us from these.

But with sickness, the tables are turned. Sickness can be a cup of icy cold water thrown in our face. Kierkegaard does not distinguish between types of physical ailments, indexing them for their potential in spiritual renewal. He just lumps them altogether. He simply says that physical sickness can be arresting. It can teach us that we suffer because we sin.[9] We desperately need this realization because "most Christians

7. On this thought, see the chilling passage, Hos 13:4–6, "I am the Lord your God, . . . It was I who knew you in the wilderness, . . . but when they had fed to the full, . . . and their heart was lifted up; therefore they forgot me" (RSV).

8. On this judgment against self-esteem, see Martin Luther, "The Sermon on the Mount" (1532), LW 21:67: "Any self-esteem [eigen ehre] . . . is really a slander of [God's] honor and praise." See also Gerhard O. Forde, On Being a Theologian of the Cross: Reflections on Luther's Heidelberg Disputation, 1518 (Grand Rapids: Eerdmans, 1997), 27: "Self-esteem [is] the current circumlocution for pride." This is especially a problem for marriage. For my critique of self-esteem in marriage, see chapter 7 below.

9. Kierkegaard does not pull back from this highly contestable assertion. No doubt that is in large part due to his devotion to the Bible. On this see Jn 5:14: "Sin no more, that nothing worse befall you" (RSV). Note that this is not incompatible with Jn 9:3 which says: "It is not that this man sinned, or his parents, but that the works of God might be made manifest in him" (RSV). The first verse addresses personal culpability; the second divine mercy. Lk 13:2–3 is less complex: "Do you think that these Galileans were worse sinners than all the other Galileans, because they suffered thus? I tell you, No; but unless you repent you will likewise perish" (RSV). Against this view of suffering being caused by sin, see Fredrik Lindström, Suffering and Sin: Interpretations of Illness in the Individual Complaint Psalms, trans. Michael McLamb (Stockholm: Almquist & Wiksell, 1994). Lindström argues that "sickness can give rise to sin, rather than the other way around" (323) because any neat correlation which says sin causes sickness clouds over the telling "irrationality" in how sickness actually arises (464). Even so, Martin Luther incorporated this contentious correlation between sin and suffering into the way he visited the sick: "When Dr. Luther came to visit a sick man, he spoke to him in a very friendly manner . . . [asking] whether during this illness he had been patient towards God. And after he had discovered how the sick man had borne himself while sick, and that he wished to bear his affliction patiently, because God had sent it upon him out of his fatherly goodness and mercy, and that . . . by his sins he had deserved such visitation, and that he was willing to die if it pleased God to take him—then he began to praise this Christian disposition as the work of the Holy Ghost." Minister's Prayer Book: An Order of Prayers and Readings, ed. John W. Doberstein (1959; Philadelphia: Fortress, 1986), 367. For a historical study against this correlation between sin and suffering, see Peter Lewis Allen, The Wages

are spiritless mollycoddlers" that are incapable of knowing how sinful they are.[10] Sickness is therefore especially valuable. It drives us to repent—which is the labor required of those who are "burdened" by the guilt of their sin (CD 264). But normally we do not want to be "disturbed by hearing about or thinking about terrible things." We would rather settle "into meaninglessness" (UDVS 107). We would rather settle quickly for the ease of health. Sickness, on the other hand, charges ahead boldly, making us question ourselves. It strikes out against us. It attacks us in our complacency. And this is good, for by so doing we are drawn into a new life with God. So the truth is that salvation

> corresponds to being in danger; the one who is not in danger cannot be saved. . . . Just as the shipwrecked person who saved himself by means of a plank and now, tossed by the waves and hovering over the abyss between life and death, strains his eyes for land, so indeed should a person be concerned about his salvation. (CD 220)

Being shipwrecked is an apt image. This is what illness does to us. It is very dangerous and damaging to us. In a more abstract and later version, he says this is as appalling and "ethically dubious" as a "vivisection." For when the crisis hits, one is forced by circumstances to be "a man of will who no longer wills his own will but with the passion of his crushed will—radically changed—wills another's will," that is, God's will (JP 6:6966).

Endangerment. To be saved we need to realize that we are endangered by the terrors of sin—and these dangers are the "*conditio sine qua non* for all Christianity" (JP 1:452). Now there are dangers aplenty in the world, but what is even more terrible is the danger of sin, which makes all the other ones look like "child's play." It is just this danger of sin that illness presses upon us. So instead of "having sympathy for your earthly misery and busily remedying it, an even heavier weight is laid upon you—you are made a sinner" (CD 172–73). But the sin that truly terrifies us is neither the garden variety infraction nor some moral peccadillo. In a late journal entry Kierkegaard explains the seriousness of sin:

> What the world regards as sin and makes an uproar about is either stealing and anything related to the security of property and possessions, or it is sins of the flesh, indeed, precisely that which Christianity regards as most pardonable. A man who tricks and swindles day in and day out but otherwise is an extremely cultivated gentleman[11] belonging to the society of the cultivated—if

---

of Sin: Sex and Disease, Past and Present (Chicago: University of Chicago Press, 2000), 159: "[This correlation] reveals a failure of two qualities I believe are essential to civilized life, namely, charity and compassion."

10. John D. Caputo, *How to Read Kierkegaard*, 108.

11. See Martin Luther, "Large Catechism" (1529), BC 396: "[Gentlemen] swindlers or big operators . . . are the greatest thieves. . . . Far from being picklocks and sneak-thieves who loot a cash box,

he has the bad luck to get drunk once—heaven help him, it is an irreparable loss, and he himself condemns it so severely that he perhaps, as they say, never forgives himself, while it probably never occurs to him that he should need to be forgiven for all the tricks and frauds and dishonesty, for all the spiritually revolting passions[12] which make their home within him and are his life. (JP 4:4049)

These severe sins, these spiritually revolting passions, help us "find the terrifying and thus take the time . . . to understand . . . the most somber view of life" (CD 97). What is so sobering about these sins is that they are worse than we imagine. So if we refuse to repent of them, the consequences are great. Those sins will damn us to hell forever, no matter how much we try to cover them up.[13]

Nothingness. Since sickness opens up this salutary realization for us, it is God's gift.[14] For indeed, "no healthy person has ever been or can ever be saved by Christ" (CD 53). Sickness fashions a somber view of life which brings salvation. It creates penitents. And it is God who helps with this by sending "hard sufferings, by taking away his dearest possession, by wounding him in the tenderest spot, by denying him his one and only wish, by taking his final hope away from him" (CD 129).[15] All this reduces

---

they sit in office chairs and are called great lords and honorable, good citizens, and yet with a great show of legality they rob and steal."

12. See the distinction between minor and major sins in "The Apology to the Augsburg Confession" (1531), BC 102: "The major ones [are] . . . carnal security, contempt of God, hate of God, and similar faults that we are born with, . . . [which make up] the inner uncleanness of human nature." This hatred of God is easily concealed. For an exposure of it, see Martin Luther, "The Sermon on the Mount" (1532), LW 21:190: "A lover of money and property inevitably becomes an enemy of God. . . . [These false Christians] make a great show of serving Him, . . . but fundamentally all they are is genuine demonic saints, who hate God cordially and persecute Him, His Word, and His work. For hating the Word of God is really hating God."

13. See Martin Luther, "Small Catechism" (1529), BC 347–49: "[We] sin daily and deserve nothing but punishment," that our lives here are but a "world of sorrow," and that "the old Adam in us . . . should be drowned by daily sorrow and repentance and put to death." So *Christian Discourses* are rightly called "Christian" because they attack "smug churchianity . . . by the presentation of Christianity's severe demands." George E. Arbaugh and George B. Arbaugh, *Kierkegaard's Authorship: A Guide to the Writings of Kierkegaard* (Rock Island, Illinois: Augustana College, 1967), 275.

14. Others think that while God has good reasons for making us suffer, we cannot figure them out, and so we must reject all such explanations while maintaining our trust in God's goodness. On this see Marilyn McCord Adams, *Horrendous Evils and the Goodness of God* (Ithaca, New York: Cornell University Press, 1999), 156, 180. She knows God is good even though he lets us suffer so because in heaven "concrete ills are balanced off" (168). Kierkegaard would think we know more than this because of what the Bible teaches us about why we suffer so. But on her account, the Bible is far too "short on explanations of why God permits evils" to be of much help (137). Against such a judgment, Kierkegaard objects. For him the explanations in the Bible are long and they have to do with punishment and edification. And so he writes that "eternity disperses the crowd by giving each person separately an infinite weight by making him heavy—as the single individual. There the same thing that is the highest blessedness is the highest earnestness; there the same thing that is the most blissful comfort is also the most dreadful responsibility" (UDVS 134).

15. So true Christian belief definitely includes "vulnerability" before God, who ought not therefore

us to nothing[16]—which is what we need if we are going to be saved from our sins. When we are reduced to nothing, we realize our desperate need for God.[17] "Woe to the presumptuous who would dare to love God without needing him! . . . You are not to presume to love God for God's sake. You are humbly to understand that your own welfare eternally depends on this need" (CD 188).[18] It depends on God because in matters of our salvation, "God does everything, and that . . . is sheer grace" (CD 85).[19]

So when God, out of love for us, makes us "into something in relation to himself" so that we may have a "reciprocal relationship with him" (CD 127), he did not intend that transformation to make us independent, self-initiating and selfish. That is because there is "only one obstacle for God, a person's selfishness, which comes between him and God like the earth's shadow when it causes the eclipse of the moon" (CD 129).[20]

---

be thought of as "a very large bird, an elderly uncle, a fluffy marshmallow, or any other objective entity that can be imagined to exist on a cloud somewhere." Rick Anthony Furtak, *Wisdom in Love: Kierkegaard and the Ancient Quest for Emotional Integrity* (Notre Dame: University of Notre Dame Press, 2005), 111.

16. On this reduction to nothingness, see Leonard M. Hummel, *Clothed in Nothingness: Consolation for Suffering* (Minneapolis: Fortress, 2003). He argues that this reduction is necessary because it shows how God's help cannot be "stored up" in ourselves (143). That help rather comes only "in the history of address and response" (147). This is reminiscent of the manna from heaven in Ex 16:20–21 that would rot or melt if stored up. See also Martin Luther, "Commentary on Psalm 38" (1525), LW 14:163: "It is God's nature to make something out of nothing. . . . Therefore God accepts only the forsaken, cures only the sick, gives sight only to the blind, restores only the dead, sanctifies only the sinners, gives wisdom only to the unwise. In short he has mercy only on those who are wretched. . . . Therefore no proud saint, no wise or righteous person, can become God's material, and God's purpose cannot be fulfilled in him." Matt Frawley argues that this nothingness is "the basic ontological position" of Kierkegaard's anthropology, and that the struggle to accept it "is the essential, existential struggle raging within the inner being of every individual." "The Doctrine of *Creatio Ex Nihilo* in the Thought of Søren Kierkegaard," *Kierkegaardiana* 23 (2004), 8, 20.

17. See Gordon Marino, *Kierkegaard in the Present Age* (Milwaukee: Marquette University Press, 2001), 105: "It is . . . infinitely better to understand feelingly how badly you need God than it is to be psychologically well adjusted relative to a community that Kierkegaard literally saw as a madhouse."

18. Ever since the time of the church in Laodicea, Christians have suffered from presumptuousness. On this see Rv 3:17: "You say, I am rich, I have prospered, and I need nothing; not knowing that you are wretched, pitiable, poor, blind, and naked" (RSV).

19. "Kierkegaard has always insisted that when it comes to salvation collaboration from the person's side is out of the question." Gregor Malantschuk, *Kierkegaard's Concept of Existence*, ed. and trans. Howard V. Hong and Edna H. Hong (Milwaukee: Marquette University Press, 2003), 215.

20. Parallels between Kierkegaard and Ludwig Wittgenstein (1889–1951) are illuminating. On this see Stanley Cavell's judgment that they both share in the image of "the philosopher as a physician of the soul." *Themes Out of School* (Chicago: University of Chicago Press, 1988), 218. We can see this trait in Wittgenstein when he says that Christianity is "only for the one who needs infinite help, that is only for the one who suffers infinite distress. . . . Someone to whom it is given in such distress to open his heart instead of contracting it, absorbs the remedy into his heart. . . . If someone feels himself lost, that is the ultimate distress." Ludwig Wittgenstein, *Culture and Value*, Revised Edition, trans. Peter Winch (1994; Oxford: Blackwell, 1998), 52e. Note also: "Is being alone with oneself—or with God, not like being alone with a wild animal? It can attack you any moment.—But isn't that precisely why you shouldn't run away?! Isn't that, so to speak, what's glorious?! Doesn't it mean: grow fond of this wild animal!—And yet one must ask: Lead us not into temptation!" *Ludwig Wittgenstein: Public and Private*

So we are to take the personal power given to us by God and give it up. Yes indeed, the very "independence . . . that love gave" us (CD 129), we are to set aside. The "Christian gives up his self-will" (CD 91)—that is the proper use of our power and will before God. We are "always" to sacrifice our will to God (CD 84). And this obedience glorifies God, for one can become and be a Christian "only as or in the capacity of a lowly person" (CD 53). Indeed, in glorifying God through our lowliness, the "worshiper has lost himself, and [as a result] he has won God" (CD 132).[21] "Thus a human being is great and at his highest when he corresponds to God by being nothing at all himself" (EUD 311). Illness brings this nothingness and lowliness upon us. And that is glorious because it is the condition which makes our salvation possible.[22] Illness does this by increasing our dependence on God. When we are sick, we lose control. We are laid low. We cannot regain our health on our schedule. We must wait for it to return, if it is to return at all. At this moment, when we realize our helplessness, we start looking to God for healing. This is the principle benefit hidden in illness.

THE FAILURE OF PREACHING

Kierkegaard was struck by this overwhelming experience of being sick. And so he called the sickbed *the best preacher* (CD 164). In this section I want to examine the last part of that line—the preaching part. Why does he tie sickness in with preaching? This no doubt was largely due to the general failure of preaching in Kierkegaard's day.[23]

Occasions, eds. James C. Klagge and Alfred Nordmann (New York: Rowman & Littlefield, 2003), 247. Wittgenstein may well have learned this view of Christianity from reading Kierkegaard. Note his admiration for him: "Kierkegaard was by far the most profound thinker of the last century. Kierkegaard was a saint. . . . Mind you I don't believe what Kierkegaard believed, but of this I am certain, that we are not here in order to have a good time." *Recollections of Wittgenstein*, ed. Rush Rhees (Oxford: Oxford University Press, 1984), 87–88.

21. Paul Sponheim misses this salutary loss of self in the *Christian Discourses* due to his overly exuberant—and therefore undialectic—celebration of God making us "something in relation to himself" (CD 127). "Relational Transcendence in Divine Agency," IKC 20:52. Note the same mistake in Daphne Hampson, *Christian Contradictions: The Structures of Lutheran and Catholic Thought* (Cambridge: Cambridge University Press, 2001), 261. I do, however, agree with her that "Kierkegaard's way of conceptualizing the self is profoundly Lutheran" (281).

22. Kierkegaard also thought that death, like illness, can help us draw near to God. When the thought of our death strikes us, earnestness then "grasps the present this very day, disdains no task as too insignificant, rejects no time as too short, works with all its might even though it is willing to smile at itself if this effort is said to be merit before God, in weakness is willing to understand that a human being is nothing at all and that one who works with all one's might gains only the proper opportunity to wonder at God" (TDIO 83).

23. This failure was not unique but shared in the maladies of generations before and after. On this see Martin Luther, "Sermon on the Mount" (1532), LW 21:56–57: "Preachers no longer rebuke the people or show them their misery and incapacity or press for repentance. . . . They permit them to go along as if they were . . . all right. Thus they [destroy] . . . the true doctrine of faith." Kierkegaard agrees: "The clerical company that speculates in human numbers has . . . led [people] to think that they are Christians by duping them into something under the name of Christianity, something that appeals to them. Millions have then been very gratified to be, in addition, Christians in such a cheap

Without much coming from the church's pulpits, illness looked good by comparison. Since preaching was failing, illness could then step into the breach and proclaim Christianity as it should be proclaimed.[24]

Preachers in his time, Kierkegaard says, were "becoming more and more fastidious in craving the trumpery of eloquence."[25] He goes on to say that they "do not want to hear in earnest anything about the terror; they want to play at it, much as soldiers in peacetime, or rather nonsoldiers, play war; they demand everything artistic in the beauty of the surrounding" (CD 165)—"in the magnificent house of God" (CD 164). They want to keep all the tough issues at bay, and even, if possible, completely out of sight.[26] Unlike this pleasing, false preaching, illness is anything but. It rather is inexo-

---

and appealing way, in one half hour and with the turn of a hand to have the whole matter of eternity arranged in order then rightly to be able to enjoy this life" (TM 170–71). And Kai Munk (1898–1944), being influenced by Kierkegaard, gives memorable formulation to this same misgiving: "Do not trust too much in the preachers. . . . They are brought up as humanists. They have forgotten—or never learned—what Christianity is. They have imbibed lo-o-o-ve with the bottle milk in the cradle. . . . They preach peace at any price for the uplift of the devil, who rejoices to see evil develop in peace . . . . Do not trust the preachers until they wake up and remember that they are servants of the whole gospel, and of the Prince of Peace who came not to bring peace but a sword; of Him who forgave Peter and permitted Judas to hang himself; of Him who was meek and humble of heart and yet drove the sacrilegists from the temple courts." *Four Sermons*, trans. John M. Jensen (Blair, Nebraska: Lutheran House Publishing, 1944), 27.

24. The link between Christianity and sickness may even be tighter than this accidental correlation. See Mt 9:13, Mk 2:17 and Lk 5:32 where Jesus says he has come for the sick only. On this tighter connection Kierkegaard says: "If this were the case, then the Gospel . . . would exclude the happy people, . . . [those who] are healthy and do not need healing. . . . [But] the Gospel does not want to be an escape, a comfort and solace for a few troubled people" (CD 263). This Gospel is for all—but with the requirement "that the invited person labor and be burdened in the more profound sense. . . . [This burden does not] pertain to externals, not to your fortunes, past or future. . . . [Rather it pertains to] sin and the consciousness of sin. The one who bears this burden—alas, yes, he is burdened, extremely burdened, but . . . in the very way the Gospel's invitation requires it" (CD 264). Noting these biblical ideas in *Christians Discourses* is justified since the book is saturated with over 160 biblical references and allusions. L. Joseph Rosas III, *Scripture in the Thought of Søren Kierkegaard* (Nashville: Broadman & Holman, 1994), 179–183. But Jolita Pons cautions restraint, insisting that Kierkegaard's biblical allusions are more uncertain and delicate, being "blended" with his own ideas, on a Scriptural surface that is anything but "hard." Jolita Pons, *Stealing a Gift: Kierkegaard's Pseudonyms and the Bible* (New York: Fordham University Press, 2004), 141–47. She thinks the Bible floats throughout Kierkegaard's writings like his image of Napoleon's ghost unexplainably emerging in "an empty space" in the graveyard (CI 19). She further says that Kierkegaard's biblical references are playful and without authority (xiv, xix, 120–22, 140, 180). But this mild view belittles Kierkegaard's point that the Bible is "an extremely dangerous book" that wants to give us sinners a good "licking" (FSE 31, 35)! The truth is that for Kierkegaard the Bible is quite pushy—something altogether unlike an ethereal, graveyard apparition! For Kierkegaard, "all of scripture has a shingle hanging out saying, 'Follow Me!'" Timothy Houston Polk, *The Biblical Kierkegaard: Reading By the Rule of Faith* (Macon Georgia: Mercer University Press, 1997), 32.

25. They should have known better since 1 Cor 2:1–5 speaks against such eloquence. Kierkegaard also speaks against eloquence because it anesthetizes us with its glorious but "protracted deliberation" (EUD 113).

26. In Kierkegaard's time his critics ridiculed him with cartoons (COR 109–37). Guy & Rodd's cartoon, *Brevity* (August 30, 2005)—reprinted here on page 60—returns the favor, blasting preachers

rably upsetting. It pushes all the hard issues. It makes us think about the terrifying things we would just as soon ignore. Illness grabs us and makes us pay attention.

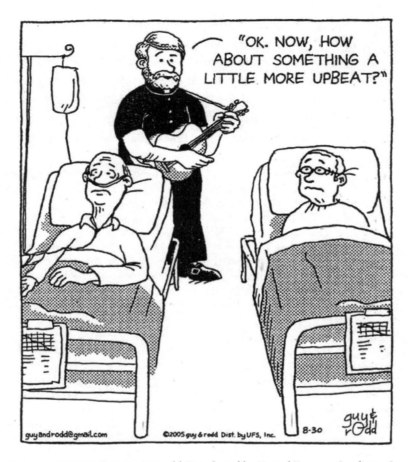

FIGURE 3: BREVITY © Guy & Rodd Distributed by United Features Syndicate, Inc.

Artistic Distance. In the same year *Christian Discourses* was published, Kierkegaard explains further in a journal entry this craving for the "trumpery of eloquence." Sermons, he writes, should be tough enough to expose the hypocrisy and corruption of our Christian lives, but on this score, the celebrated Bishop Mynster, for one, is "without a compass" (JP 6:6150). This is because Mynster wants—like most other preachers—

---

who sugar-coat what frightens the sick—for this pandering "aborts" their spirits (JP 4:4942)! For another word against these same spiritual abortions, see Dana Gioia, *Pity the Beautiful: Poems* (Minneapolis: Graywolf Press, 2012), 30: "No well-stitched words could suture shut these wounds." This conviction—note the contrasts drawn in it between words and wounds, stitched and sutured—needs to be in play when Is 50:4 is your tutor: "The Lord God has given me the tongue of those who are taught that I may know how to sustain with a word him that is weary" (RSV).

to protect himself and remain aloof. —It would be impossible, yes, most impossible of all, for Mynster to preach in the public square. And yet preaching in churches has practically become paganism and theatricality,[27] and Luther was right in declaring that preaching should really not be done in churches.

In paganism the theater was worship—in Christendom the churches have generally become the theater. How? In this way: it is pleasant, even enjoyable, to commune with the highest once a week by way of the imagination.[28] No more than that. And that actually has become the norm for sermons in Denmark. Hence the artistic distance—even in the most bungled sermons.

In a late journal entry he expands upon this corrupting, artistic distance. Preaching, he writes,

certainly . . . should not be done inside of churches. It is extremely damaging for Christianity and represents a changing (a modifying) of Christianity by placing it at an artistic distance from actuality instead of letting it be heard right in the middle of actuality—and precisely for the sake of conflict (collision), for all this talk about quiet and quiet places and quiet hours as the proper element for the essentially Christian is upside down.

Therefore preaching should not be done in churches but on the street, right in the middle of life, the actuality of the ordinary, weekday life. (JP 6:6957)

The point about preaching in the streets is to make sermons tough, confrontational and disruptive.[29] This is because the "essentially Christian . . . is the *attacker*" (CD 162). So instead of telling sweet little stories, sermons should go on the attack.

27. The church still suffers from theatricality. On this see Kennon L. Callahan, *Dynamic Worship* (New York: HarperCollins, 1994), 76, 22: "People are not helped by music that is mournful and . . . focuses solely on the experience of the cross. . . . The kingdom is not like a solemn, serious ceremony. Have fun, enjoy life." Or see Rick Warren, *The Purpose Driven Church* (Grand Rapids: Zondervan, 1995), 285: "[People] like bright, happy, cheerful music with a strong beat. Their ears are accustomed to music with a strong bass line and rhythm. . . . Within a year of deciding [to use this sort of music in our worship services, our church] *exploded* with growth." And finally see Walt Kallestad, *Entertainment Evangelism* (Nashville: Abingdon, 1996), 10, 12: "The three foundational principles Martin Luther believed were essential to making the Gospel relevant [were] . . . simplicity, . . . heartfelt relevancy, . . . and entertainment. . . . [So at our worship we] may have a stage band, a comedian, clowns, drama, mini-concerts, and other forms of entertainment." It must be noted in passing, however, that Martin Luther expressly admonishes in his "Large Catechism" (1529), BC 378, that worship should be free of all "entertainment"—contrary to what Kallestad thinks Luther believed.

28. Imagination is also taking over much of American preaching today. On this see Walter Brueggemann, *Texts Under Negotiation: The Bible and Postmodern Imagination* (Minneapolis: Fortress, 1993), 68–69: "Preaching . . . is not for instruction (doctrinal or moral) or even for advocacy, but it is for one more reenactment of the drama of the text, . . . [where] the listener is invited . . . to imagine the lines just beyond those voiced in the script. . . . Most, however, depends upon the freedom and courage with which the director [preacher] plays the script." See also his *Cadences of Home: Preaching Among Exiles* (Louisville: Westminster John Knox, 1997), 32, 33: "The work of preaching is an act of imagination [which] . . . requires a break with . . . doctrinal . . . preaching, . . . [thereby allowing] a good bit of room for maneuverability and idiosyncrasy."

29. I explore this interest of Kierkegaard's further in chapter 11 below, "On Walking."

But this "militant piety" (PV 130), if you will, was missing from the pulpits in Kierkegaard's day, and so he rightly lamented:

> Ah, there is so much in the ordinary course of life that will lull a person to sleep, teach him to say "peace and no danger." Therefore we go to God's house to be awakened from sleep and to be pulled out of the spell. But when in turn there is at times so much in God's house that will lull us to sleep! Even that which in itself is awakening—thoughts, reflection, ideas—can completely lose meaning through the force of habit and monotony, just as a spring can lose the tension by which alone it really is what it is. (CD 165)

Heterogeneity. This requisite tension is primarily found in the idea that Christianity is heterogeneous to society (JFY 191). Christians are therefore to strike a "polemical stance against the great human society" (JP 4:4175). Indeed followers of Christ must die to the world since their faith in Christ requires them to stand in opposition to the world. They must die to "finitude (to its pleasures, its preoccupations, its projects, its diversions), must go through this death to life, . . . and realize how empty is that with which busyness fills up life, how trivial is that which is the lust of the eye and the craving of the carnal heart" (CD 172).[30] This tension—this heterogeneity—cannot be expressed in the sermon in some blasé way. Reading a well-written essay from the pulpit cannot carry the load of Christian proclamation. The form must be wilder. Martin Luther thought sermons should be more like barroom yelling fits, filled with shouting and raving[31]—warning the sinner and trumpeting God's excessive mercy.[32]

Kierkegaard's version of this was a woman in labor. He says the voice of the preacher—or the "apostolic" voice—should be

> concerned, ardent, burning, inflamed, everywhere and always stirred by the forces of the new life, calling, shouting, beckoning, explosive in its outbursts, brief, disjointed, harrowing, itself violently shaken as much by fear and trembling as by longing and blessed expectancy, everywhere witnessing to the powerful unrest of the spirit and the profound impatience of the heart. . . .

30. Here we have an allusion to 1 Jn 2:15–16, "Do not love the world or the things of the world, . . . the lust of the flesh and the lust of the eyes and the pride of life" (RSV).

31. Martin Luther, "Lectures on Genesis 45–50" (1545), LW 8:260. On Kierkegaard's assessment of Luther, see Craig Hinkson, "Will the *Real* Martin Luther Please Stand Up! Kierkegaard's View of Luther versus the Evolving Perceptions of the Tradition," IKC 21:37–76 and Herman Deuser, "Kierkegaard and Luther: Kierkegaard's 'One Thesis,'" in *The Gift of Grace: The Future of Lutheran Theology*, eds. Niels Henrik Gregersen, et al (Minneapolis: Fortress, 2005), 205–12. Kierkegaard thought Luther was the truest Christian figure, second only to Jesus Christ himself (JP 3:2898). He said Luther was "extraordinary" (JP 2:2046) and "masterful" (JP 3:2422, 3:2465). But he also thought Luther could be too soft on sinners (JP 3:2556, 3:2682). I have tried to show how radically Lutheran Kierkegaard was in my review of Garff's biography in appendix 1, part 2, of this book. So I cannot agree with Viggo Mortensen that "Kierkegaard's understanding of Christianity, at least as it comes out in his last stage, comes in conflict with Luther—a conflict that borders on incompatibility." Quoted in Gregor Malantschuk, *Kierkegaard's Concept of Existence*, 296.

32. This image is most likely a gloss on the word "urgency" in 2 Tm 4:2.

If apostolic speech is always as impatient as that of a woman in labor, then two considerations in particular are likely to stir it up even more—on the one hand, the idea that the night has lasted long enough and the point is to use the day; on the other hand, the idea that the time is coming when one can no longer work, that the days are numbered, the end is near, that the end of all things is approaching. (EUD 69)

Such explosive sermons are well suited for the heterogeneity of Christianity. They can create collision and conflict in a way that a well-written essay, delivered with rhetorical poise, cannot. Without this exuberant form, the heterogeneous content of true Christian preaching is either blunted or lost. This is a catastrophe because a muffled warning protects no one, and an ambiguous declaration inspires no one.[33]

Earnestness. Without such harrowing and violently shaken sermons, the church wilts. It needs ardent, burning, inflamed sermons.[34] Without them, the church will mistake

the artistic for the Christian, human upbringing for Christian character, human cleverness for Christian recklessness, human superiority for Christian worth, the charming magnificence of appearance for the plain everyday dress of truth, a secular, not to say pagan, Sunday-Christianity for New Testament Monday-Christianity; it mistakes artistic seriousness in playing Christianity for the real earnestness of Christianity, the idyllic enjoyment of quiet hours for New Testament painful decision; it mistakes enjoyment for suffering, winning the world for renunciation of the world, heightening life's enjoyment for painfully dying to the world. (JP 1:825)

So attacks must be launched from the pulpits of the church.[35] Martin Luther also promoted militant preaching. He argued that sermons should "jab the soul," by taking away "every ground of trust" and ascribing redemption "solely to the blood of Christ."[36] They should suppress and cast out "the salvation, peace, life, and grace of the flesh."[37] By so doing they never are "discourses on paltry things, such as temporal

---

33. A possible biblical verse inspiring these thoughts is 1 Cor 14:8: "[If] the bugle gives an indistinct sound, who will get ready for battle?" (RSV). Martin J. Heinecken (1902–98), author of *The Moment Before God: An Interpretation of Kierkegaard* (Philadelphia: Muhlenberg, 1956), said this verse was his lifelong motto.

34. "What our age needs," Kierkegaard writes, "is *pathos* . . . (just as scurvy needs green vegetables) . . . . That is why there has to be a man who is able to short-suit reflectively all reflections" (JP 3:3129).

35. Once the preached word sinks in—with all of its shouting, yelling and explosive outbursts—then there can be meditative silence—after the dust settles, as it were: "Ah, but a woman who looks at herself in the mirror of the Word becomes silent! And if she becomes silent, this perhaps is the strongest indication that she is not a forgetful reader or hearer" (FSE 50–51).

36. Martin Luther, "Commentary on Psalm 45" (1532), LW 12:225.

37. Martin Luther, "Commentary on Psalm 2" (1519), LW 14:335.

riches, honor, might, and pleasures. For all these are nothing but sow dung and filth, dropped into the straw by swine."[38] So true, militant sermons are clearly not for gaining

> favor from men and from the world. For the world finds nothing more ir-
> ritating and intolerable than hearing its wisdom, righteousness, religion, and
> power condemned. To denounce these mighty and glorious gifts of the world
> is not to curry the world's favor but to go out looking for, and quickly to find,
> hatred and misfortune, as it is called.[39]

So Kierkegaard had it right, that "God intends Christianity to remain embattled to the end, oriented not to victory in time but to [triumph in] eternity" (JP 4:4856). If sermons are to remain faithful to the New Testament, they must have this orientation.[40] Without it we are quickly back to "craving the trumpery of eloquence" (CD 165). Seeing the sickbed, then, as the best preacher, as Kierkegaard does, makes good sense. For illness does not suffer from eloquence and artistic distance. It clearly trades in earnestness and heterogeneity. It attacks us and upsets us. Or as Kierkegaard says of the apostolic voice itself (EUD 69), illness shouts out and is explosive. It violently shakes us. Illness, in fact, does exactly what a sermon is supposed to do, but which rarely, if ever, is heard from the church's modern, well-adjusted pulpits.

---

38. Martin Luther, "Sermons on John 6–8" (1531), LW 23:402.

39. Martin Luther, "Lectures on Galatians 1–4" (1535), LW 26:58.

40. John Updike's character, the Rev. Fritz Kruppenbach, expresses this well in his harangue on death, misery and Christian preaching: "If [God] wants to end misery He'll declare the Kingdom now . . . . How big do you think your little friends look among the billions that God sees? In Bombay now they die in the streets every minute. . . . I say you don't know what your role is or you'd be home locked in prayer. *There* is your role: to make yourself an exemplar of faith. *There* is where comfort comes from: faith, not what little finagling a body can do here and there; stirring the bucket. In running back and forth you run from the duty given you by God, to make your faith powerful, so when the call comes you can go out and tell them, 'Yes, he is dead, but you will see him again in Heaven. Yes, you suffer, but you must love your pain, because it is *Christ's* pain.' When on Sunday morning then, when we go before their faces, we must walk up not worn out with misery but full of Christ, *hot* . . . with Christ, on *fire: burn* them with the force of our belief. That is why they come; why else would they pay us? Anything else we can do or say anyone else can do and say. They have doctors and lawyers for that. It's all in the Book—a thief with faith is worth all the Pharisees. Make no mistake. There is nothing but Christ for us. All the rest, all this decency and busyness, is nothing. It is Devil's work." *Rabbit, Run* (1960; New York: Knopf, 1994), 170–71. See also Updike's study on Kierkegaard entitled "The Fork," in *Kierkegaard*, ed. Josiah Thompson (New York: Doubleday, 1972), 164–82. Unfortunately this fine essay—originally published in 1966—ends in failure, quoting Kierkegaard saying we will all be saved (JP 6:6934)—supposing it to mean there will be no eternal damnation for anyone (182). Updike's failure is that he misses Kierkegaard's twist: "The N. T. clearly rests on the assumption that there is an eternal damnation and—perhaps not one in a million is saved. We who are brought up in Christianity live on the assumption that all of us surely will be saved. . . . O, but the N. T. is a terrifying book; for it takes into account this kind of a collision with true Christianity" (JP 6:6843, p. 484). Updike also errs in attributing to Kierkegaard the saying: "It is a fearful thing to fall into the hands of the living God" (175). That actually is Kierkegaard *quoting* Hebrews 10:31—a felicitous mistake on Updike's part, especially for those of us who see Kierkegaard as an advocate of Holy Scriptures!

AWAKENING FAITH

No one becomes a Christian naturally. Being a Christian goes against everything in us. So in order to be one, we must be radically transformed, that is, born again and made into a new creation, so we can actually believe in Jesus Christ. In this section I want to show how illness does not have to lead to despair and unmitigated ruin, but can actually awaken faith in us. Having faith in Christ is not as easy and simple "as pulling on one's socks" (PC 35). For belief to happen, God "grabs" us to make us his (JP 4:4532). He barges in through closed doors to wake us up (JP 5:5313). The Christian faith comes to a person only after much tribulation and soul-searching.[41]

So even though it is true[42] that the Sacrament of Baptism can draw a little infant into Christianity, Kierkegaard still insisted that we must all the more "vigorously see to it that rebirth becomes a decisive determinant" as the baptized child grows in years (JP 1:537). Baptism, as Mark 10:39 says, must also become a matter of suffering. The sickbed preacher works for just that rebirth, which brings about the awakening of faith. For many baptized children, the suffering caused from "out-living" (JP 2:1215) is needed *before* the lights go out and they come to "count it worthy to suffer dishonor for the name" of Jesus Christ (Acts 5:41).

Reversals. Illness and physical suffering, therefore, are what miraculously turn us around. In this reversal, faith is awakened. "When in adversity it seems impossible to move . . . a foot—then eternity makes adversity into prosperity, . . . so lightly does he walk. Eternity provides feet to walk on." With these new feet, faith makes the sufferer buoyant. For indeed,

> when eternity comforts, it makes one joyful; its comfort truly is joy, is the true joy. It is with the human grounds of comfort as it is when the sick person, who has already had many physicians, has a new one who thinks of something new that temporarily produces a little change, but soon it is the same old story again. No, when eternity is brought in to the sick person, it not only cures him completely but makes him healthier than the healthy. (CD 159)

This enhanced health comes from the awakening of faith in Jesus Christ. This faith sees life differently from that of an unbeliever. To unbelievers, "adversity is and remains adversity" (CD 158). But not for Christians. They have a bizarre view of the

41. The Bible verses informing this paragraph are, *seriatim*, Rom 11:24; Jn 3:5; 2 Cor 5:17; Jn 6:44, 20:19; Acts 14:22, 26:28. These verses explain why it is so that "the way to Christianity is long and difficult if one is going to take it seriously and not be satisfied with being a Christian in name only." Gregor Malantschuk, *Kierkegaard's Concept of Existence*, 256.

42. David Law misses this dialectic, erroneously supposing that Kierkegaard rejected infant baptism. "Kierkegaard on Baptism," *Theology* 91 (March 1988), 120. See JP 1:494 where Kierkegaard actually affirms infant baptism. It is true that at the end he questions infant baptism because it does not produce an "actual personality" which is needed for grasping the promises of Christianity (TM 244). But that personality, he also held, can actually come from the "rebirth" which is to follow upon baptism (JP 1:537). If that correlation holds, then infant baptism is not a problem.

world. It is marked with unexpected reversals.[43] For Christians, adversity is prosperity, and visa-versa. And what the world thinks of as sobering is actually intoxicating, and visa-versa (JFY 106). And furthermore, "precisely what worldliness regards as health is, Christianly, sickness, just as, inversely, Christian health is regarded by worldliness as sickness" (TM 158).[44]

Christ's Crucifixion. These reversals do not create instability but spiritual fortitude instead. One might think they would make us unstable because "from the worldly point of view Christian consolation is much more to despair over than the hardest earthly suffering and the greatest temporal misfortune" (CD 97). One would have to "look closely" for the consolation because of "the magnitude of the terror in the inwardness of guilt-consciousness" which overshadows everything else (CD 96). But even so, the upbuilding that follows upon these terrors is so sure,

> so reliable in itself. One must not be afraid of the terrifying, as if it hindered the upbuilding, must not timorously keep it away in the hope of making the upbuilding more pleasant, because the upbuilding itself leaves with the terrifying. But, on the other hand, the upbuilding is precisely in the terrifying. So triumphant is the upbuilding that whatever at first glance could seem to be its enemy is made a presupposition, a servant, a friend. If the art of medicine successfully performs the difficult task of turning poison into remedy, in the upbuilding the terrifying is far more gloriously transformed into the upbuilding. (CD 96–97)

The reason the upbuilding is so certainly there *in the terrifying moments* is because of Christ's presence. "*There* begins the upbuilding, the Christian upbuilding, which is named after him, our Lord and Savior, for he also suffered" (CD 97). Christ is the only true rest for the terrified sinner because in Christ

> there is forgiveness [which is built] on the one and only ground that can support a penitent, that atonement has been made. . . . That is what the exhausted laborer, the fatigued traveler, desires; and the sailor who is tossed about on the sea seeks . . . ; and the weary old man longs for . . . ; and the sick one who lies restless on his bed and does not find an alleviating position craves . . . ;

---

43. On these reversals see Sylvia Walsh, *Living Christianly: Kierkegaard's Dialectic of Christian Existence* (University Park, Pennsylvania: The Pennsylvania State University Press, 2005), 48: "True Christians . . . live without the ordinary human anxieties over wealth and station in life because their understanding of poverty, riches, lowliness, and highness are the opposite of the merely human, pagan, or natural understanding of them. One is able essentially to conquer temporal losses and misfortunes by inverting one's understanding of them." These reversals, Walsh points out, Kierkegaard "identifies as . . . 'the dialectic of inversion'" (7).

44. On these reversals see Martin Luther, "Lectures on Galatians 1–6" (1519), LW 27:403, "One who is really a Christian is uplifted in adversity, because he trusts in God; he is downcast in prosperity, because he fears God."

and the doubter who does not find a foothold in the ocean of thoughts craves. (CD 265)

The Savior Jesus Christ does not disappoint. So Kierkegaard says "I will seek my refuge with him, the Crucified One. I will beseech him to save me from evil and to save me from myself" (CD 280). Indeed Jesus is "not only your spiritual guide; he is also your Savior" (CD 266). And we need this Savior because we hide "from the truth as Adam hid among the trees." There is in our "innermost being a secret anxiety about and wariness of the truth." So we run from the truth which is our need to practice self-denial and we resist having it made "so clear that every excuse, every evasion, every extenuation, every refuge in the false but favorable opinion of others is cut off" (CD 170).

Christ saves us on the cross by winning "God's love" for us there (JP 3:2442). This is needed because "God is love, but not love to sinners. This he is first in Christ: i.e., the Atonement" (JP 2:1329). "By his holy suffering and death, . . . Christ has made full satisfaction for your sin" (JP 3:2442). This is the comfort of redemption, that Christ, "the substitute, . . . puts himself completely in your place and in mine!" (WA 123). This redemption happens between God and Christ, so that "Christianity is the divine combat of divine passion with itself, so that in a sense we human beings disappear like ants" (JP 1:532)![45] Because this redemption is found nowhere else, we "can be saved only by the blood of Christ" (JP 2:2300).[46] So we are to pray:

> Great are you, O God. . . . When under the arch of heaven I stand surrounded
> by the wonder of creation, I rapturously and adoringly praise your greatness,
> you who lightly hold the stars in the infinite and concern yourself fatherly
> with the sparrow. . . . You are indeed great, Creator and Sustainer of the world;

45. These five statements from Kierkegaard contrast with the judgment that there is no objective theory of atonement in the *Philosophical Fragments*. John D. Glenn Jr., "Kierkegaard and Anselm," IKC 7:242. While that may be true for the *Philosophical Fragments*, it is not necessarily so for his entire authorship. Closer to the truth is the view that in the entire authorship, Kierkegaard proposed "some sort of unified theory of the atonement which retains the objective and subjective elements of both." J. Preston Cole, "Kierkegaard's Doctrine of the Atonement," *Religion in Life* 33 (Autumn 1964), 600. On Anselm's objective view of the atonement, see Paul Tillich, *A History of Christian Thought: From Its Judaic and Hellenistic Origins to Existentialism*, ed. Carl E. Braaten (1967; New York: Touchstone, 1972), 166: "Behind its legalistic, quantitative thinking there is a profound idea, namely, that sin has produced a tension in God himself. This tension is felt. Anselm's theory became so popular because everyone felt that it is not simple for God to forgive sins. . . . The church has never dogmatized Anselm's theory, . . . but it is obvious that it liked Anselm's most, probably because it has the deepest psychological roots. This is the feeling that a price must be paid for our guilt, and since we cannot pay it, God must do it." Against traditional atonement theory, see S. Mark Heim, *Saved From Sacrifice: A Theology of the Cross* (Grand Rapids: Eerdmans, 2006), 27: "[Such theory is] a consistent fault line in the whole foundation [of Christianity] that runs from distorted views of God to spiritual guilt fixation to sacrificial bloodshed to anti-Semitic persecution to arrogant ignorance of world mythology."

46. On this see Gregor Malantschuk, *The Controversial Kierkegaard*, trans. Howard V. Hong and Edna H. Hong (1976; Waterloo, Ontario: Wilfrid Laurier University Press, 1980), 74: "Christianity alone is able to give a solution to all the existential problems."

but when you, O God, forgave the sin of the world and reconciled yourself with the fallen human race, then you were even greater in your incomprehensible compassion! (CD 289)

This reality of redemption awakens our faith in the Savior Jesus Christ—the One who both suffers and comforts, and comforts because he suffers. Our adversity ought not repel us for it did not repel Christ. Adversity rather is to awaken faith in Christ in us.

Gracious Unsureness. So redemption unexpectedly begins its work in our very unbelief.[47] In our uncertainty we are kept awake that we might "seek after certitude" (CD 194). For disbelief is not "spiritless ignorance; disbelief wants to deny God and is therefore in a way involved with God" (CD 67). The trauma and turmoil that sickness brings actually holds us close to God—instead of pushing us away as we would expect.[48] So "God's greatness in showing mercy is first an occasion *for offense* and then is *for faith*" (CD 291). Even so, the offense lingers in the heart of faith—and so Kierkegaard encourages us to pray:

Save me, O God, from ever becoming completely sure; keep me unsure until the end so that then, if I receive eternal blessedness, I might be completely sure that I have it by grace! It is empty shadowboxing to give assurances that one believes that it is by grace—and then to be completely sure. The true, the essential expressions of its being by grace is the very fear and trembling of unsureness. There lies faith—as far, just as far, from despair and from sureness. . . . Eternal God, therefore, . . . save me from deceiving any other person, because this deception lies all too close when one treats one's relationship with God as if it were a direct relationship with other human beings, so that one gets into comparisons and human sureness. If someone, regarded by many as extraordinarily noble and upright, were to continue in fear and trembling to work out his salvation, the others would become furious with him. In other words, they would want to have his sureness as an excuse for their own peace of mind, and they would want their own peace of mind to be his sureness. But, my God and Father, the question of my salvation indeed pertains to no other person, but only to me—and to you. . . . Should there not be, ought there not

47. For Luther's correlation of certainty and uncertainty, see "That These Words of Christ, 'This is My Body,' Etc., Still Stand Firm Against the Fanatics" (1527), LW 37:107: "All that interests [the fanatics] is to see if they can make the sayings of Scripture or of the fathers uncertain and bring them into doubt in the minds of the common people. When they have succeeded, they leave it at that. . . . But what kind of spirit is it who directs his ingenuity only to rendering Scripture passages uncertain and doubtful, and does not on the other hand render them certain and firm again, and thus builds on sand and boasts with certainty that he is making things uncertain—well, this is easy to see. Christ's Spirit it surely is not; he makes sure and certain all that he teaches, as St. Paul extols (Col 2:2)."

48. On this see Martin Luther, "Lectures on Isaiah 1–39" (1528), LW 16:232: "The more a . . . man falls outwardly and is wounded in his conscience, the more he lets go of himself and is driven to Christ [*agitatur ad Christum*]."

be, and must there not be fear and trembling until the end? Was this not the fault of the foolish bridesmaids, that they became sure and went to sleep—the sensible ones, however, stayed awake. But what is it to stay awake? It is unsureness in fear and trembling. And what is faith but an empty delusion if it is not awake? And if faith is not awake, what else is it but that pernicious sureness? (CD 211–12)[49]

In this magnificent prayer we see that just as illness upsets us with its unsureness, it awakens faith in us by fighting against all pernicious sureness. Illness plays the role of the five maidens that were ready for the bridegroom, Christ Jesus, because they remained uncertain—they remained awake (Mt 25:1–13). So the very thing that frightens us, miraculously becomes our friend. And so the fear and trembling of illness draws us to God. It does not defeat faith in God as it is usually supposed to do. This insight is Kierkegaard's great service to the promulgation of Christian faith.

JUDGING THE SICKBED PREACHER

But is Kierkegaard right about all of this? Can illness really awaken faith in Christ Jesus? Or does it not rather shut down Christianity altogether? Does not illness prove that Christianity's promises fail? Does not illness instead show that in Christ there is no health and victory, but only loss and shame? In this section I want to test Kierkegaard's claim that the sickbed is our best preacher. Does this claim have any compelling confirmations? William James notes in his famed Gifford Lectures the venerable place sickness has in Christianity. There it is viewed "as a visitation; something sent by God for our good, either as chastisement, as warning, or as opportunity for exercising virtue. . . . According to this view, disease should . . . be submissively accepted, and it might under certain circumstances even be blasphemous to wish it away."[50]

---

49. Kierkegaard is not saying, mind you, that we are to doubt, for instance, doctrine and the Bible and the divinity of Christ Jesus. No, "the doctrine . . . does not have to be reformed. . . . If anything has to be done—then it is penance on the part of all of us. . . . The doctrine . . . [is] very good. But the lives, our lives—believe me, they are mediocre. . . . Our lives are only slightly touched by the doctrine" (JP 6:6727). So what we are to be unsure about is that we are living up to Christian teachings as we should. Now it is also true that Kierkegaard cares that the "comprehensive view of the whole of Christianity" is properly presented (JP 3:2550). That would be the same concern as is in Acts 20:27 about preaching the "whole counsel of God" (RSV). But what he cares about most is the practice and exercise of those holy Words. On this same point see Martin Luther, "Sermons on 2 Peter" (1523), LW 30:159: "Your faith is [to be] well exercised [*trieben*] and applied [*üben*]." A wonderful summarization of this Kierkegaardian point is: "The Christian ideal has not been tried and found wanting. It has been found difficult; and left untried." G. K. Chesterton, *What's Wrong With the World* (1910; New York: Sheed & Ward, 1956), 29.

50. William James, *The Varieties of Religious Experience* (1902; New York: Penguin, 1982), 113n1. See also David G. Schoessow, "Sin, Sickness, and Salvation From Nazareth to Lake Wobegone," *Logia* 10 (Eastertide 2001), 5: "The sick and dying play an important role in our world, reminding the healthy not to lose sight of those matters that are of ultimate importance (Job; Hos 6:1–3; Jn 9:1–3; 11:4)."

Many, however, disagree.[51] When Rabbi Harold S. Kushner's son, Aaron, was stricken with progeria, or early aging disease, he did not see any visitation from God. It was offensive to suppose that misfortunes come from God. Aaron had nothing good to gain from being sick with progeria. God was not punishing or blessing him with this illness. Illnesses, Kushner concludes, are only "the painful consequences of being human"—nothing more, nothing less.[52]

On this view, Kierkegaard, in celebrating the sickbed preacher, appears to be peddling a "jaundiced view of life." Indeed "this strange man [appears to think] so poorly of our life in the temporal world[53] that he could characterize this life as a mere 'test' or 'examination.'"[54] And so Kierkegaard's Christianity looks "so extreme that no one could practice it."[55] Sickness is that hard on us. The famed comedian, Richard Pryor, would agree. Stricken with multiple sclerosis in 1986, it was no blessing for him in his illness. It "robbed him of his trademark physicality," leaving him "immobilized and imprisoned."[56] Many of the survivors of Hurricane Katrina in New Orleans feel the same way. Their misery "goes beyond 9/11, . . . the Oklahoma City bombing . . . and Hurricanes Andrew, Hugo and Ivan." New Orleans is experiencing "a near epidemic of depression, . . . of an intensity rarely seen in this country." And so the suicide rate has tripled. Because many have lost everything, they just want to die.[57] This sadness and despair, however, does not take away all silver linings. But to say even that, sounds criminal to some.[58]

51. This disagreement may be rooted in sin. On such a pervasive and devastating view of sin, see Martin Luther, "A Short Order of Confession" (1529), LW 53:117: "Miserable person that I am, I confess and lament to you before God that I am a sinful and weak creature. I do not keep God's commandments; I do not really believe the gospel; I do nothing good; I cannot bear ill."

52. Harold S. Kushner, *When Bad Things Happen to Good People* (New York: Schocken, 1981), 44, 76.

53. On this negativity see Martin Luther, "Lectures on Genesis 45–50" (1545), LW 8:114: "This life is horribly wretched, difficult, and troubled because of the various tribulations and vexations of all the devils and the whole world. . . . Therefore this life is not a life. No, it is a mortification and vexation of life." Luther could also rejoice in life—but only because of his faith in Christ Jesus. Therefore his negativity actually goes together with his joy.

54. Charles Hartshorne, *Insights and Oversights of Great Thinkers: An Evaluation of Western Philosophy* (Albany: State University of New York Press, 1983), 216.

55. Paul Ricoeur, "Two Encounters with Kierkegaard," in *Kierkegaard's Truth*, ed. Joseph H. Smith (New Haven, Connecticut: Yale University Press, 1981), 329.

56. Lynell George, "I Was Being Richard Pryor," *The Seattle Times* (December 11, 2005). Note also the flippant approach of Miriam Engelberg, *Cancer Made Me a Shallower Person: A Memoir in Comics* (New York: Harper, 2006), xiii: "Maybe nobility and courage aren't the only approaches to life with an illness; maybe the path of shallowness deserves more attention!"

57. Susan Saulny, "Suicide Rate Soars in Devastated New Orleans," *Seattle Post-Intelligencer* (June 21, 2006).

58. On this see the famous case of the Chamberlains who were accused of killing their daughter, Azaria, simply because they were "overcalm" regarding her death due to their belief in "Divine Purpose." See John Bryson, *Evil Angels: The Case of Lindy Chamberlain* (New York: Summit Books, 1985), 162. See also the report on their final vindication after thirty-two years of appeals in Kathy Marks,

Nevertheless, these contrary cases stand tall. Take forest fires, for instance. They create much suffering and loss. But they are not all bad. These fires in fact are "essential for the survival and reproduction of many species," and so fire is "not evil [but] often good. . . . Without it, our world would be a much poorer, less diverse, less interesting place. It is time for Smokey Bear to retire."[59] Another case is Pearl Harbor. At anniversary proceedings, Admiral Michael Mullen, the Navy's most senior sailor said "December 7, 1941, was not just a day of infamy. In many ways it was a day of discovery. . . . It changed us, it hurt us, it made us stronger."[60] The movie star, Michael J. Fox, says something similar about being inflicted with Parkinson's disease in the height of his career. "Despite appearances," he writes, "this disease has unquestionably directed me toward what is . . . good." So if his disease could miraculously be healed, he would unhesitatingly refuse taking back his previous good health. This is because he needed the disease to rescue him from his destructive "fun-house self."[61] Nothing else could have done it for him. National Public Radio correspondent, John Hockenberry, says the same. The car crash that left him a paraplegic provided the "leap" he needed to help him truly appreciate people and give up the illusion that we control our lives. So he writes, "[I am] grateful to have been a [cripple] for the past nineteen

---

"Coroner Rules Dingo Was Responsbile for Azaria Chamberlain's Death in Australian Outback," *The Independent* (June 12, 2012). A similar obtuseness is in Kierkegaard's praise for the sickbed preacher. But for some this makes him paradoxically attractive. On this see Dorothee Soelle, *The Window of Vulnerability*, trans. Linda M. Maloney (Minneapolis: Fortress, 1990), 117 118, 121: "Kierkegaard seduced me into religion. I devoured him. Today I could say that I fell in love with Søren. . . . I submerged myself in Kierkegaard. . . . Anxiety, according to Kierkegaard, . . . drives us to conversion. . . . Those who cannot get free of it . . . are hanging on God's hooks." See also Antje Jackelen, "Why is Søren So Popular?" *Dialog* 45 (Spring 2006). She says Kierkegaard is so popular because what he says makes life "more difficult" and thereby more meaningful (105).

59. Seth R. Reice, *The Silver Lining: The Benefits of Natural Disasters* (Princeton: Princeton University Press, 2001), 99. See also Randolph M. Nesse and George C. Williams, *Why We Get Sick: The New Science of Darwinian Medicine* (New York: Vintage, 1996), 11–12: "We would never argue that any disease is good, even though we will offer many examples in which pathology is associated with some unappreciated benefits."

60. Audrey McAvoy, "Pearl Harbor Made Us Stronger," *Seattle Post-Intelligencer* (December 8, 2005). President Clinton says something similar to this in his celebration of the Kansas State motto: *Ad astra per aspera*, "To the stars through difficulties." Bill Clinton, *My Life* (New York: Knopf, 2004), 741.

61. Michael J. Fox, *Lucky Man: A Memoir* (New York: Hyperion, 2002), 5–6, 135. The famed creative writer, Reynolds Price, says the same about his paralyzing spinal cancer in *A Whole New Life: An Illness and a Healing* (1982; New York: Plume, 1995), 189–90: "I know that this new life is better for me, and for most of my friends." He says this, having "tested that word *better* for the stench of sentimentality, narcissism, blind optimism or lunacy." His paraplegia made his life better by making him more patient and watchful. And secondly it forced "the slow migration of a sleepless and welcome sexuality from the center of my life to the cooler edge [which] contributed hugely to the increased speed and volume of my work, not to speak of the gradual resolution of hungers that—however precious to mind and body—had seemed past feeding." When he retells this story in *Letters to a Godchild Concerning Faith* (New York: Scribner, 2006), he no longer says he *knows* that his new life is better, but only that such a view is but one of a few "fragmentary guesses" on why he suffered so (62).

years; I may miss walking, running, or tree climbing from time to time, but I do not miss being a spectator."[62]

These reports on the benefits of illness and calamity reinforce Kierkegaard's praise of the sickbed preacher. They show that Kierkegaard has tapped into a rich vein of human well being. They show that Kierkegaard is not unjustifiably extreme[63] in his claims. His hope in the sickbed preacher is inspired by the truth that suffering builds character through endurance, as Romans 5 says.[64] This Kierkegaard calls "the best learning" ever taught (EUD 95). And that is so even if it might mean that fewer people will want to be Christian and the church, as it stands, will have to be relieved of some of its many "battalions" (PV 126). For the church

> in the next several decades is going to be a smaller, leaner, tougher company.
> . . . The way for the church now is to accept the shrinkage, to penetrate the
> meaning and the threat of the prevailing secularity, and to tighten its mind
> around the task given to the critical cadre.[65]

So rather than belittling Kierkegaard's sickbed preacher, we should take on a deeper appreciation of illness, and its darkness, considering

> how tremendous the spiritual change that it brings, how astonishing, when
> the lights of health go down, the undiscovered countries that are then dis-
> closed, what wastes and deserts of the soul a slight attack of influenza brings
> to view, what precipices and lawns sprinkled with bright flowers a little rise of

62. John Hockenberry, *Moving Violations: War Zones, Wheelchairs, and Declarations of Independence* (New York: Hyperion, 1995), 96, 101, 351. On this matter of control, Hockenberry writes: "Loss of control is a dark fear, particularly in America. Why we should so fear losing control in a world that we have no control over anymore is one of the central questions of American culture" (101). See also Eva Ensler, *In the Body of the World: A Memoir* (New York: Holt, 2013), 137, on how Ensler's cancer helped her get over the "almost homicidal competitiveness" that had torn apart her relationship with her sister.

63. On this option see Tolly Burkan, *Extreme Spirituality: Radical Approaches to Awakening* (San Francisco: Council Oak Books, 2001), 34: "The skin all over my body began to tingle, and the hair on the back of my neck stood up. I could barely catch my breath. The experience was not unlike an orgasm. I was in bliss! . . . More than any other challenge described in this book, pushing a needle through my hand has to stand out as the most difficult victory I've achieved. As a result, the lessons gleaned from this are more vital and valuable." The rest of the book is about firewalking, skydiving, smelling foul odors, sweating and walking on broken glass. Against this extremism see Martin Luther, "Sermons on 1 Peter" (1522), LW 30:110: "We should not [suffer] of our own accord. . . . If God inflicts [it] on you, then it is better."

64. This benefit, which "human flabbiness might wish [would come] without dangerous suffering" (EUD 329), Jacob Bøggild dismisses as self-contradictory. "Revocated Trials" in *The New Kierkegaard*, ed. Elsebet Jegstrup (Bloomington: Indiana University Press, 2004), 118, 125. But the possibility of interfering with the upbuilding (EUD 346) does not "nullify" the benefit as Bøggild alleges. All it does is separate the paths between the person who "fights the good fight of danger and terror; [and the one who] becomes sagacious and spiritlessly rejoices over the security of life" (EUD 346). This echoes 2 Cor 2:16 where it says that the same Savior can both have the odor of life and the odor of death.

65. This admonition is from the Lutheran doyen, Joseph A. Sittler (1904–87), in his *Grace Notes and Other Fragments*, eds. Robert M. Herhold and Linda M. Delloff (Philadelphia: Fortress, 1981), 99.

temperature reveals, [and] what ancient and obdurate oaks are uprooted in us by the act of sickness.[66]

This intensification of the importance of illness for Christianity will also help us see more clearly what Kierkegaard was about. Indeed his "originality and uniqueness" in describing Christian life is found "chiefly in his conception and use of inverse dialectic" whereby, for instance, adversity is prosperity and sickness is health.[67] Studying his praise of illness reveals this deep inversion in his Christian thought. So what might appear to be an embarrassing idea at the beginning, proves in the end to be nothing but profound.

A CRUMPLED AMEN

When Kierkegaard tells us that the sickbed is our best preacher, this claim all hinges on his inverse dialectic. Seeing the truth in that inversion enables us to experience illness as anything but the defeat of Christianity. When we are sick, we will have balance enough, as a result of this inverse dialectic, to fight the temptation to cry out to God, "Why me?" "This isn't fair!" "Please end it now!" In the place of this defiance and impatience, illness will teach us to pray to God with a resolved heart. Under the tutelage of our sickness, we will—pray differently. We will pray for help to endure the pain and fear brought on by our illness, so we might learn what God is teaching us. For this insight we are indebted to Kierkegaard, who

> . . . crawled
> To the monastery of his chaste thoughts
> To offer up his crumpled amen.[68]

Crumpled no doubt, difficult and chaste indeed, painful to say the least, but an amen all the same. And so we rejoice in our sickness because we finally see that it has value for us. In the face of suffering and sickness, then, "Christianity is collectively the great reassurance and the great protest, turned polemically against all human abjectness."[69]

66. Virginia Woolf, *On Being Ill* (1930; Ashfield, MA: Paris Press, 2002), 3.

67. Sylvia Walsh, *Living Christianly: Kierkegaard's Dialectic of Christian Existence*, 162. I have pursued this view of Kierkegaard in my parish, First Lutheran Church of West Seattle (Seattle, WA), since the beginning of our annual Kierkegaard celebrations in 1980. On this tradition, see Paul Sponheim, "America," *Bibliotheca Kierkegaardiana* 15, eds. Niels and Marie Thulstrup (Copenhagen: C. A. Reitzels, 1987), 36 and my "Søren Kierkegaard Comes to Seattle," *Lutheran Forum* 19 (Summer 1985), 15–16 and "Kierkegaard's Sesquicentennial," *Lutheran Forum* 40 (Summer 2006), 17–19.

68. *Poems of R. S. Thomas* (Fayetteville, Arkansas: University of Arkansas Press, 1985), 49. These last lines from the poem, "Kierkegaard," were originally published by Thomas in 1966 in a collection called *Pietà*. I think this poem measures up to what Robert Bly calls a great poem, namely, one that "helps us get rid of self-pity, and replaces self-pity with awe at the complicated misery of all living things." *The Rag and Bone Shop of the Heart*, eds. Robert Bly et al (New York: HarperPerennial, 1992), 198.

69. Johannes Sløk, *Kierkegaard's Universe: A New Guide to the Genius*, trans. Kenneth Tindall (Copenhagen: The Danish Cultural Institute, 1994), 119.

For in the face of illness we have learned from Christianity to say our crumpled, uncertain amen. Now we see how grateful we should be for the gains we can receive when we are sick. When we are ill we have a chance to "pierce the superficial optimism which claims that with . . . better health, a longer life, and more personal liberty, human beings can be made happy."[70] But even so we still would hope for a less painful way. We wish that faith could be awakened in us in some easier, more pleasant setting. We cannot help but want this. But that—lamentably—will never be. "Fantasies about alternative pain-free paths . . . are countered with talk of Jesus' divine authority, with its affirmation of the ultimate reliability of this suffering path to joy."[71] For indeed the message of Christianity in the New Testament and elaborated by Kierkegaard is this, and only this, that salvation comes through trauma, pain and suffering. And it is for that reason alone that the sickbed remains our best preacher.

70. Diogenes Allen, *Three Outsiders: Pascal, Kierkegaard, Simone Weil* (Cambridge, MA: Cowley, 193), 13. Kierkegaard, it would seem, is naturally drawn to such piercing, since he saw in Christianity "the subversion of the values of wealth and status." Steven Shakespeare, "Stirring the Waters of Language: Kierkegaard on the Dangers of Doing Theology," *The Heythrop Journal* 37 (October 1996): 435. For another critique of wealth and status in a Kierkegaardian vein, see Brett McCracken, *Hipster Christianity: When Church and Cool Collide* (Grand Rapids, Michigan: Baker Books, 2010), 247: "The desire to be cool, hip, fashionable, and recognized . . . it's all a vain pursuit and a waste of time. It comes from a very human place, but it's a distraction and a self-destructing futility . . . . As new creations [in Christ], saved by grace and guided by the Holy Spirit, we are called to lives of selflessness and love and renewal." For a wonderful cinematic presentation of this self-destructive futility—again in a decidedly Kierkegaardian vein—see the film, *Blue Jasmine* (2013) by Woody Allen—which has been described as a "tragedy without catharsis." Bruce Handy, "Woody Allen's *Blue Jasmine* Is Perhaps His Cruelest-Ever Movie," *Vanity Fair Daily*, August 25, 2013. On Woody Allen's interest in Kierkegaard, see David Dietmer, "Inauthenticity and Personal Identity in *Zelig*," in *Woody Allen and Philosophy: You Mean My Whole Fallacy is Wrong?* ed. Mark T. Conard and Aeon J. Skoble (Peru, Illinois: Open Court Press, 2004), 186, 193, 196.

71. Lee Barrett, "The Joy in the Cross: Kierkegaard's Appropriation of Lutheran Christology in 'The Gospel of Sufferings,'" IKC 15:283.

3

On Self-Hatred

KIERKEGAARD INSISTED THAT THE supreme test of love was not whether one could remain faithful to one's friends and loved ones or even love one's enemies. Rather it was whether one could take time to visit the cemetery and show respect for the dead. So in *Works of Love* he writes that "recollecting one who is dead is a work of the most unselfish love" (WL 349) and "the most faithful love" (WL 355). It is the supreme test of Christian love.

This test shows whether all improper self-love has been purged from one's love and continually fought back by an appropriate self-hatred. The test will disclose "what resides" in us and what our true "nature" is (WL 347). In this chapter I want to show the importance of this news from the graveyard for Kierkegaard's understanding of love.[1] I want to show that Kierkegaard thought proper self-hatred was what made Christian love great. In order to see this, Kierkegaard's understanding of appropriate self-hatred must be explicated.

DEFINING SELF-HATRED

Kierkegaard would agree that "the true disciple is able to say that 'I do not account my life of any value nor as precious to myself,' because the only thing significant about his life is his fidelity to 'the ministry which I received from the Lord Jesus, to testify to the gospel and grace of God' (Acts 20:24)."[2] He would like this because of the joining of self-deprecation (my life is not precious to me) and religious responsibility (I must testify to the gospel). This combination runs counter to what he called the "mark of inverted Christianity," namely that "in love of oneself to love God." Inverted Christianity eliminates the negative. He thought this elimination to be an "intrusion of Satan" which perverts the "only true relationship to Christianity: loving God to hate oneself." (JP 3:2685).[3] This self-deprecation or self-hatred simultaneously negates the Christian

1. I therefore agree that "one may most accurately summarize Kierkegaard's doctrine of love by saying that he demands that love behave towards all men as if they were dead." T. W. Adorno, "On Kierkegaard's Doctrine of Love," *Studies in Philosophy and Social Science* 8 (1939), 416–17 and reprinted in *Modern Critical Views: Søren Kierkegaard*, ed. Harold Bloom (New York: Chelsea House Publications, 1989), 19–34.

2. William H. Willimon, *Acts* (Atlanta: John Knox, 1988), 156.

3. Because this journal entry is from the year of Kierkegaard's severe illness and death, 1855, some

and affirms one's love for God. Because of this linkage, self-hatred—so defined—is not a perversion to be avoided. It rather is an authentication of one's love for God.[4]

Kierkegaard's most sustained treatment of self-hatred is in *Works of Love*. From beginning to end he indirectly explores various permutations of the topic while directly scrutinizing a Bible verse or concept having to do with love.[5] Because Kierkegaard's treatment of self-hatred in *Works of Love* is largely indirect, it is usually overshadowed by other themes.[6] This has eschewed the point of *Works of Love*, which I think is the overturning of this "inverted Christianity" (JP 3:2685).[7] Furthermore that point is the content of "the powerful polemic in *Works of Love*" (JP 5:6111).[8]

---

suppose it is nothing but "a passionate outburst" and of little substantive interest. James Collins, "Kierkegaard's Imagery of the Self," in *Kierkegaard's Truth: The Disclosure of the Self*, ed. Joseph H. Smith (New Haven: Yale University Press, 1981), 53. This criticism is not convincing, however, simply because similar journal entries appear earlier. Earlier examples would be from 1852 (JP 2:1432, 3:3772), from 1851 (JP 2:1799), from 1850 (JP 2:1789, 6:6645), from 1849 (JP 1:496, 6:6432, 6:6469), from 1848 (JP 1:491), and from 1845 (JP 2:2116).

4. Martin Luther would agree with Kierkegaard on this linkage. See "Lectures on Galatians 5–6" (1535), LW 27:65: "If we loved God truly and perfectly, . . . then poverty would be as pleasant for us as riches, sorrow the same as pleasure, death the same as life. Indeed, one who loved God truly and perfectly would not be able to live very long but would soon be devoured by his love." In opposition to this linkage in Luther, see Regin Prenter, "Luther and Lutheranism," 121–72, *Kierkegaard and Great Traditions*, Bibliotheca Kierkegaardiana, volume 6, eds. Niels Thulstrup and Marie Mikulova Thulstrup (Copenhagen: C.A. Reitzels Boghandel, 1981). Against Prenter, I find a "harmony" between Luther and Kierkegaard regarding the matter of self-hatred. For another congenial passage in Luther, see his "Lectures on Isaiah 40–66" (1529), LW 17:263: "To love the name of God is to hate our own name and seek the glory of God alone."

5.. For another commentary on *Works of Love* that goes against what I have to say here, see M. Jamie Ferreira, *Love's Grateful Striving: A Commentary on Kierkegaard's* Works of Love (New York: Oxford University, 2001).

6. One reason for this could be that the Danish term *Selvhad* (self-hate) does not appear in Kierkegaard's writings and is not "a key Kierkegaardian term." In the English translation self-hatred is used "as a short form of some phrase" meaning self-hatred in the Danish (Howard V. Hong, personal correspondence, December 18, 1998).

7. This attack on inverted Christianity is similar to what Robert C. Roberts thinks is critical in Kierkegaard's program of reintroducing Christianity into Christendom. Roberts sees him attacking "a covert proposal of a *new* usage" by way of "conceptual-grammatical discourse." Robert C. Roberts, "Kierkegaard, Wittgenstein, and a Method of 'Virtue Ethics,'" in *Kierkegaard in Post/Modernity*, eds. Martin J. Matustik and Merold Westphal (Bloomington: Indiana University Press, 1995), 153.

8. My reading of *Works of Love* also opposes the "new Kierkegaard" emerging "at the end of the twentieth century" designed to replace the classic portrait of "the implacable preacher of doom" with "an effervescent wit, . . . a mercurial ironist, . . . a seductive philosophical artist." *Kierkegaard: A Critical Reader*, ed. Jonathan Ree and Jane Chamberlain (Oxford: Blackwell, 1998), 1. I rather hold that Kierkegaard "philosophizes with a hammer," thereby ending up "in opposition to everything." But I disagree that his "harshness . . . emerges at the exact moment he transcends the ethical." Emmanuel Levinas, *Proper Names*, trans. Michael B. Smith (Stanford: Stanford University, 1996), 76. I think it rather most clearly emerges in his definition of Christian love. So in my analysis I want to develop the insight that in *Works of Love* "there is a continuous emphasis on the essential element of offense." Arnold B. Come, *Kierkegaard as Theologian: Recovering My Self* (Montreal: McGill-Queen's University, 1997), 212. I will try to show that this offense is rooted in self-hatred properly understood. What greater offense could there be than having the authoritative weight of Christianity tell you to hate

To show this, I will need to assemble something of a florilegium of many passages from Kierkegaard's writings. Only such a presentation will be able to show convincingly how the more obvious interpretation of *Works of Love*, namely that it presents the optimistic, "affirmative side of Kierkegaard's theology,"[9] is actually mistaken. Without mounting the raw data of text after text, this optimistic view will survive my examination unscathed.[10]

Kierkegaard understood self-hatred to be self-denial or self-renunciation (JP 3:3771).[11] It excludes all self-destructive impulses while including all self-effacing ones.[12] Rendering the person inert is not the goal of self-hatred. Self-hatred is instead supposed to straighten out the twisted person so that he or she only lives to love God and neighbor. It is this definition of self-hatred that Kierkegaard affirms.

My explication of Kierkegaard's analysis of Christian self-hatred will therefore show that there is a legitimate self-love, but it is not about liking oneself. Just so there is also a bad self-hatred, but it is not about disliking oneself. In keeping with

---

yourself? Just think of it: "God created this world of living beings, placed man in it, planted this enormous lust for life in him—and the meaning of life, the task of life—is to die, to die to the world!" This indeed seems to be "too hard!" (JP 3:3097).

9. Michael Plekon, "Kierkegaard the Theologian: The Roots of His Theology in *Works of Love*," in *Foundations of Kierkegaard's Vision of Community: Religion, Ethics and Politics in Kierkegaard*, ed. George B. Connell and C. Stephen Evans, (New York: Humanities, 1992), 5. Plekon argues that *Works of Love* and other similar writings of Kierkegaard's balance his "all too one-sided staring at Christ the prototype" (JP 2:1852). This journal entry, however, makes a christological point, not an anthropological one, and so does not support Plekon's claim. Christ's atoning sacrifice—the companion concept to Christ the prototype—does not imply a positive view of humanity. The fact that only the ignominious death of the second person of the Holy Trinity could rescue people from hell suggests rather a very negative view of people—one worse than "animal bloodthirstiness and savagery" (WL 169). I think Kierkegaard is best understood as one who presented "Christianity as a hard thing. It is hard to enter and hard to keep up; hard to understand and hard to explain; hard to believe and hard to live." William T. Riviere, *A Pastor Looks at Kierkegaard: The Man and His Philosophy* (Grand Rapids: Zondervan, 1941), 64.

10. I have chosen this more unconventional method after pondering Ludwig Wittgenstein's question: "Why, would it be *unthinkable* that I should stay in the saddle however much the facts bucked?" *On Certianty*, trans. Denis Paul and G. E. M. Anscombe (Oxford: Blackwell, 1974), § 616. My florilegium is also commended because the content of *Works of Love* is barely known since it is "seldom read." Peter Vardy, *Kierkegaard*, (Liguori, Missouri: Triumph, 1996), 85.

11. This 1852 journal entry casts "self-denial" and "hating oneself" in apposition. "Self-denial" and "renunciation" are also treated this way (JP 3:3781). Kierkegaard does not care to explore whatever nuances of difference there may be among these three terms.

12. So "in Kierkegaard, as in Luther, there is a Pauline theology in the treatment of the severe demands which Christianity imposes." George E. Arbaugh and George B. Arbaugh, *Kierkegaard's Authorship: A Guide to the Writings of Kierkegaard* (Rock Island, Illinois: Augustana College Library, 1967), 267. Christian love, according to Kierkegaard, therefore has "no humanistic base" (268). It instead builds on Saint Paul's fiery conviction in Gal 2:20: "I have been crucified with Christ; it is no longer I who live, but Christ who lives in me" (RSV). For a parallel in the field of athletics, see Bob Knight, *The Power of Negative Thinking: An Unconventional Approach to Achieving Positive Results* (Boston: Houghton Mifflin Harcourt, 2013), 36, 65: "Winning is the product of good leadership. Leadership is getting people out of their comfort zone. . . . It's a myth that people who are really cheerful tend to be healthier and live longer than those who view the world through a darker lens."

Kierkegaard's famous point that love is a work and not a feeling (WL 99), bad self-hatred is what impedes good works and legitimate self-love is what promotes good works.

The biblical warrant for sorting out what makes for good and bad self-hatred is life "in the Spirit."[13] This means Christians are to be spiritual rather than sensual. Charles Simic celebrates the sensual in an "old janitor on his death bed who demands to see the breasts of his wife for one last time."[14] More pervasively the sensuous is manifest attitudinally when we delight in good fortune and mourn its passing. To be spiritual, however, means "to become less" and know "how stupid . . . all this yelling about the positive" is (JP 4:4453).[15] Kierkegaard even insists that "no man can . . . lead a truly spiritual life" if he is "thoroughly healthy physically and mentally." Being healthy, "you would yield easily to your passions, to pride if not to others, to an intensified self-esteem and the like" (JP 4:4637)!

Living spiritually, then, means "to live as if dead (to die to the world)" (JP 4:4360). The "most suggestive symbol" for this life is "a human skull" (JP 4:2455). Consequently there must be an "infinite difference" between "the spiritual person and the sensate-psychical person" (WL 209). This is the appropriate context for explicating Christian self-hatred. Now we can see that "if a man's life is intended for the eternal, . . . how alienated he must become from that which binds him to the relationships of finitude. This alienation is indeed like hating the very relationships which are most important" (JP 2:1955)! A Christian, then, cannot be "a human being in the ordinary sense" (JP 6:6616). Heaven is "the one and only good and everything else" is nothing (JP 3:3754). To renounce everything and die to it means "to regard everything as one will see it at the moment of death," making everything "a matter of complete unconcern whether you enjoy it or not" (JP 1:724). This is spiritual living.[16] This is what

13. Rom 8:9. See also 1 Pt 2:11; 1 Cor 2:12–13; Galatians 5:16–17; and Jn 3:8, 6:63 and 14:17.

14. Charles Simic, *Selected Poems, 1963–1983*, (New York: George Braziller, 1985), 65. Simic won the Pulitzer Prize in 1990. Alan Bartlett also has this celebration of the sensual in his wholesale revision of Christianity. *Humane Christianity: Arguing With the Classic Christian Spiritual Disciplines in the Light of Jesus of Nazareth* (Cambridge: Cowley, 2005). He is against any and all attempts to "slip contempt for humanity . . . in under the guise of . . . sinfulness" (166). So he sings out: "God gave me my flesh, and I love it. When I no longer want to hear Bach or birdsong, no longer want to smell [wildflowers] or bonfires, no longer want to trudge through snow or sit by a blazing fire, drink wine, eat food, soak in a bath, read poetry or write it, then I'll promise I'll [quit loving my flesh]. But I don't expect to in this life or expect I'll [do so] in the next" (9–10).

15. See also Martin Luther, "Lectures on Galatians 1–6" (1519), LW 27.403: "A Christian is uplifted in adversity, because he trusts God; he is downcast in prosperity, because he fears God."

16. Kierkegaard's understanding of Christian spirituality is strikingly unlike modern popular versions that provide instead "techniques" to "achieve personal and professional success" Cynthia A. Jürisson, "Pop Spirituality: An Evangelical Response," *Word & World* 18 (Winter 1998): 16. Kierkegaard's is rather more like historic Lutheran spirituality which is "both a foul tasting potion and a powerful medicine." James M. Kittelson, "Contemporary Spirituality's Challenge to *Sola Gratia*," *Lutheran Quarterly* 9 (Winter 1995): 383.

Christian self-hatred strives to accomplish. This is the context in which my explication of Kierkegaard's analysis of self-hatred must be understood.

SELF-HATRED OUTSIDE WORKS OF LOVE

Kierkegaard was working on self-hatred years before he wrote *Works of Love*. His treatment of self-hatred in *Works of Love*, therefore, is not a dead-end road he tried once and then abandoned. The longest passage on self-hatred from his other writings is in Problema II of *Fear and Trembling*. There Kierkegaard's Johannes de silentio discusses Luke 14:26, "a remarkable teaching on the absolute duty to God," wherein the true Christian or knight of faith is expected to "hate . . . even his own life" (FT 72). That analysis, however, is only indirect. Rather than studying Abraham's hatred for himself, whereby "his life is like a book under divine confiscation" (FT 77), Johannes scrutinizes Abraham's alleged hatred for his only son Isaac:

> In the moment he is about to sacrifice Isaac, the ethical expression for what he is doing is: he hates Isaac. But if he actually hates Isaac, he can rest assured that God does not demand this of him, for Cain and Abraham are not identical. He must love Isaac with his whole soul. Since God claims Isaac, he must, if possible, love him even more, and only then can he *sacrifice* him, for it is indeed this love for Isaac that makes his act a sacrifice by its paradoxical contrast to his love for God. (FT 74)

This view of Abraham's hatred for Isaac may also illumine Abraham's self-hatred, as prescribed in general in Luke 14:26, by applying Abraham's treatment of Isaac imaginatively to himself. On this account, self-hatred would not be suicide. To think that would be to idealize Cain's murder of Abel, rather than Abraham's near sacrifice of Isaac. Self-hatred is instead the sacrifice of oneself to God, through one form of martyrdom or another, out of love for God and the claim he has on us. So even though self-hatred is not suicide, it will keep the terror of suicide. It will have to say before God, "not my will but thine be done" (Mt 26.39).[17] By practicing this proper form of

---

17. On this verse see Martin Luther, "An Exposition of the Lord's Prayer for Simple Laymen" (1519), LW 42:48: "Man must despair utterly of ever having or attaining a good will, opinion, or resolve. . . . A good will is found only where there is no will. Where there is no will, God's will, which is the very best, will be present. . . . You may say, 'Well, did God not endow us with a free will?' I reply: To be sure, he gave you a free will. But why do you want to make it your own will? . . . If you do with it whatever you will, it is not a free will, but your own will. God did not give you or anyone else a will of your own. Your own will comes from the devil . . . who transformed the free will received from God into its own. A free will does not want its own way, but looks only to God's will for direction." Similarly Kierkegaard thought a Christian is "a man of will who has acquired a new will. A Christian is a man of will who no longer wills his own will but with the passion of his crushed will—radically changed—wills another's will," *viz.*, God's (JP 6:6966). Both utterly despairing of one's will and crushing the will are equally Christian ways to hate oneself. Both cases damage the will. So Kierkegaard wrote magisterially regarding the meaning of losing oneself in Luke 9:25 that it "does not mean flatly to get rid of oneself, it means to retain oneself in damaged condition" (JP 4:3900).

self-hatred one may love God rightly and even thereby love oneself more because of all the good one does.[18] In fact, "in no other way can a human being love God. He must be in a state of agony so that if he were a pagan he would at no time hesitate to commit suicide. In this state he must—live. Only in this state can he love God" (JP 3:2454).

Two years after *Fear and Trembling* appeared, Kierkegaard elaborated this correlation between human deprecation and divine exaltation.[19] If we hate ourselves properly by letting our guilt before God crush us down to nothing, then we will be drawn closer to God. Furthermore he reinterprets the paradoxical nature of this correlation as a clash between worldly and religious viewpoints:

> The more profound the sorrow is, the more a person feels himself as a nothing, as less than nothing, and this diminishing self-esteem is a sign that the sorrower is the seeker who is beginning to become aware of God. In a worldly sense, it holds true that it is a poor soldier who does not hope to become commander. In a religious sense, it is the opposite; the less a person thinks of himself, not as humanity in general, and not with regard to his talents but with regard to his guilt, the more manifest God becomes to him. We do not want to increase the guilt in order that God might become greater but want to increase the acknowledgment of guilt. (TDIO 29)

This guilt which makes us feel like nothing is a prerequisite for properly loving God. It is guilt for dishonoring God and it is the right reason for hating ourselves. In the same year *Works of Love* was published, Kierkegaard defined this guilt by way of imagining how God will judge us in the end. God will not ask us about how great an influence we have had. Instead he will ask us about our self-hatred. He will want to

---

18. Saint Augustine also saw self-hatred as an enhancement of self-love. See his "Tractates on the Gospel According to St. John" §123.5: "In some inexplicable way, I know not what, every one that loveth himself, and not God, loveth not himself; and whoever loveth God, and not himself, he it is that loveth himself. For he that cannot live by himself will certainly die by loving himself; he therefore loveth not himself who loves himself to his own loss of life. But when he is loved by whom life is preserved, a man by not loving himself only loveth the more, when it is for this reason that he loveth not himself, namely that he may love Him by whom he lives." *Nicene and Post-Nicene Fathers of the Christian Church*, volume 7, ed. Philip Schaff (Grand Rapids: Eerdmans, 1974), 446. This self-love is clearly extraordinary. It does not dwell on itself. It rather affirms the exertion and accomplishment in a person's love for God and others. Only one's loving care for others is to be loved in self-love. The self itself is not to be loved in self-love. That means our ideas, dreams, needs, appearance, talents and feelings are not to receive love in self-love.

19. Kierkegaard gets this asymmetrical correlation by generalizing St. John the Baptist's comparison of himself with Jesus in Jn 3:30: "He must increase, but I must decrease" (RSV). On this he writes: "How elevating! No human sovereign is able to protect himself against indiscreet forwardness in this way. But God is protected, for the closer you come to him the lower you become—that is, the nearer you come to him the more infinite a concept you get of his infinite sublimity, but thereby you are lowered. 'He must increase, but I must decrease' is the law for all drawing near to God. . . . 'But then in a way I lose God.' How? Indeed, he increases! No, if I lose anything, I lose only my selfishness, myself, until I find complete blessedness in this adoration: He must increase, but I must decrease. . . . Indeed, it would surely be self-love if I wanted to increase along with God as he increases" (JP 2:1432). This asymmetry is indispensible for properly understanding Kierkegaard's analysis of Christian self-hatred.

know if we have denied ourselves. In those questions God defines our sin, disobedience and guilt. Those corruptions make us "slaves" to ourselves. Accordingly God will

> ask about what riches you have gathered in heaven, about how often you have conquered your own mind, about what control you have exercised over yourself or whether you have been a slave, about how often you have mastered yourself in self-denial or whether you have never done so, about how often you in self-denial have been willing to make a sacrifice for a good cause or whether you were never willing, about how often you in self-denial have forgiven your enemy, whether seven times or seventy times seven times, about how often you in self-denial endured insults patiently, about what you have suffered, not for your own sake, for your selfish interest's sake, but what you in self-denial have suffered for God's sake. (UDVS 223–24)

Not any self-hatred, however, will do, as I have already said.[20] Self-hatred that wastes time rather than increasing love for God and service to others is bad. There is "a hatred of oneself that wrongs the person himself so that he is merely inventive in increasing his own torment." Such self-hatred is "still also self-love, and all self-love is cowardliness" (EUD 374). Cowardliness is wrong because it, among other things, pulls us away from loving God and serving others. So in a letter to his frail sister-in-law, Henrietta Kierkegaard, written a couple months after *Works of Love* appeared, he warns against becoming melancholic. He intimates that self-hatred can lead to this unless it is correlated with an "infinite Godly diversion." This diversion reminds us that God can use us even when we are useless to the world. This is his point. In no way is he denying the call for Christians to hate themselves properly:[21]

> Ordinarily it is probably right to warn against self-love; still, I consider it *my duty to say to every sufferer* with whom I come into contact: *See to it that you love yourself.* When one is suffering and unable to do much for others, it is easy to fall prey to the melancholy thought that one is superfluous in this world, as others perhaps sometimes give one to understand. Then one must remember

---

20. I have argued that self-hatred is not self-destruction. Kierkegaard, after all, could wonder in 1849: "Just as sanguine men are required to hate themselves, perhaps it is necessary for me to love myself and renounce this gloomy self-hatred which can even become almost pleasurable" (JP 6:6432). He did not thereby think this gloom could be completely eliminated, however. In order to show that "Christ is not a savior for this life but for eternal life," Kierkegaard wrote in the same year, that Christians should expect to "slog along as if in a bog" (JP 6:6503). And close to the end of his life, Kierkegaard intensified this struggle all the more—calling it a "death penalty." So he writes that "when someone proclaims Christianity in such a way that the rejoinder replies, 'Remove this person from the earth; he does not deserve to live'—then know that this is the Christianity of the New Testament. Completely unchanged, as in the time of our Lord Jesus Christ, there is a death penalty for proclaiming what Christianity truly is, that it is: hating oneself, to love God; hating oneself, to hate everything in which a person has his life, everything that for him is life, hating that for the sake of which he selfishly wants to make use of God in attaining it or in being comforted if he does not attain it or loses it—the death penalty for proclaiming Christianity in character remains unchanged" (TM 334–35).

21. See footnote 31.

that *before God every person is equally important, without reservation equally important*; indeed, if there were any distinction, then one who suffers the most must be the closest object of God's care. And also in this lies infinite Godly diversion. (LD 236–37)

This same idea is pursued a year later in a letter to his invalid cousin, Hans Peter Kierkegaard. This time his consoling words are sharper. He warns against wasting time both by despairing of incapacities and by running around heedlessly. This shows that sufferers need just the right dose of self-hatred or they will come "to a standstill in the monotony of self-concern and self-preoccupation, . . . bordering on soul rot" (EUD 207):

> If I were to give you any advice about life, or taking into consideration your special circumstances, were to commend to you a rule for your life, then I would say: Above all do not forget your duty to love yourself; do not permit the fact that you have been set apart from life in a way, been prevented from participating actively in it, and that you are superfluous in the obtuse eyes of a busy world, above all do not permit this to deprive you of your idea of yourself, as if your life, if lived in inwardness, did not have just as much meaning and worth as that of any other human being in the loving eyes of an all-wise Governance, and considerably more than the busy, busier, busiest haste of busy-ness—busy with wasting life and losing oneself. (LD 280–81)

In both these letters Kierkegaard restores meaning to broken lives by showing how God can still use them. But unless one both values being used by God and devalues worldly rejection, this solution will not work. It will only work if one first purges all lingering, worldly ways from oneself. Complaining that God's help is too little, too late, or, even inversely, that it expects too much of the despairing soul, is no good. The latter ploy of despair is especially invidious. It becomes an excuse for not having to hate oneself properly. It makes the sufferer exempt from the demands of faith. It leaves us with "broken hearts and fine clothes (elegant and refined despair), without having rent hearts in the biblical sense" (JP 1:746). But this is a

> knavish trick, nothing but. It is just like females when they cunningly use fainting spells to get their way. And what does such a female need? She needs a man who calmly says, "Nonsense!"—then she does not swoon. In the same way Protestantism is in dire need of a hard man who, when man begins the tricky business of saying that otherwise he must despair, can say: Fine, go ahead, but do despair, then! (JP 3:3618)[22]

22. On this knavery see Martin Luther, "Appeal for Prayer Against the Turks" (1541), LW 43:228: "We cannot silence God's Word just because it does not please [us]. . . . As a matter of fact, true Christians willingly accept the rebuke and judgment that is in the preaching of God's word. But those who won't receive this judgment show plainly that they are really damnable knaves." Note also that men have their own version of this same female trait. See Kierkegaard's parable of the royal coachman (FSE 85–87) and chapter 6 in this book. Note as well John Lippitt, *Kierkegaard and the Problem of Self-Love*

Because self-hatred blocks these evasions, it is ennobling. There is a hidden strength in self-hatred. Kierkegaard makes this point in his analysis of the woman who loved much in Luke 7:47. Because God and humanity "are indeed opposites that are in mortal combat with each other," it is like "the most frightful annihilation to come near" to God. Consequently, inventive "in malingering excuses and evasions and deceits and glosses, the sinner flees, avoids this death march as long as he can, this encounter with the light." But not this woman. She "loved much. And what is the strongest expression for loving much? It is to hate oneself—*she went to the Holy One.* She, a sinner! Alas, a woman" (WA 137–38).

To do this required much strength. She got this from her self-hatred. In that hatred she developed a need for God which made her strong enough to go down that "death march" to God (WA 138):

> If someone were to say: Yet there was something self-loving in this woman's love; after all, in her need she basically still loved herself. If someone were to talk that way, I would answer: Naturally, and then add, God help us, there is no other way, and then add, God forbid that I would ever presume to want to love my God or my Savior in any other way, because if there were literally no self-love in my love, then I would no doubt be only imagining that I could love them without standing in need of them—and from this blasphemy may God preserve me! (WA 142)

SELF-HATRED IN WORKS OF LOVE

These scattered thoughts on self-hatred in Kierkegaard's writings receive sustained, methodical—albeit indirect—treatment in *Works of Love*. In this book he argues that Christianity redefines love to include self-hatred. This redefinition claims that Christian love is completely different from worldly, ordinary love, in that—among other things—the latter does not include self-hatred.[23] Self-hatred is what "drives out all

---

(Cambridge: Cambridge University Press, 2013), 135: "[I cannot love the good if I allow myself to be] a mere doormat in your interest." Lippitt's concern here seems to be nothing else than a case of Kierkegaard's fainting spells.

23. Against this stark incompatibility see David J. Gouwens, *Kierkegaard as a Religious Thinker*, (Cambridge: Cambridge University Press, 1996), 192: "Kierkegaard's vision of love is . . . open to a more 'holistic' interpretation; at least, the dialectic of unity tempers the undeniable dialectic of opposition in *Works of Love*. Divine love is the source of human love. *Agape* embraces *eros*. Again, the central theological vision underlying Kierkegaard's thought on Christian love is that all are created by God, and are invited to be on the way toward love of God and neighbor, in which natural loves are transformed but not eliminated." However since the catalyst for this transformation is self-hatred—something Gouwens does not consider—all his hoped for tempering and embracing is deflated. Christian love is too wild and too "dangerous" (WL 198, 277) to be so easily tamed. The "madness" that rightly marks Christian love (WL 108, 132, 185, 203, 238, 287, 290, 321) is a fatal omission in Gouwens' analysis. Missing this madness destroys the majesty of Christian love and renders *Works of Love* incoherent.

self-love" from Christian love (WL 55). Self-love can only "be dislodged by hating one's self" (JP 3:3771). Between these two conceptions of love is "the difference of infinity" (WL 113).[24] Christian love includes self-hatred where ordinary love does not. Because of this omission, ordinary love looks "very superficial" to the Christian (WL 364). Accordingly Kierkegaard rhetorically asks:

> See, worldly wisdom has a long list of various expressions for sacrifice and devotion. I wonder if among them this is also found: out of love to hate the beloved, out of love to hate the beloved and to that extent oneself, out of love to hate the contemporaries and to that extent one's own life? (WL 109)

In each chapter of *Works of Love* Kierkegaard defends the propriety of self-hatred. This defense, however, is not straightforward. Rather he addresses self-hatred as a consequence of pursuing the more general topic of Christian love.

At the beginning of the book in the preface we are to pray for sincere "self-renunciation" (WL 4). Self-renunciation is self-denial or self-hatred.[25] It puts an end to promoting and defending oneself.[26] In Christianity it is essential for every work of love. This is because Christians can only love rightly "by being in" God, and God is the one "who spared nothing but in love gave everything" (WL 3). If we are to be in

---

24. Kierkegaard's understanding of Christian love illustrates his overall view of Christianity. Therefore I agree with the early assessment of Kierkegaard's late writings by the philosopher Hans Brøchner (1820–75) that for him "Christianity was unconditionally incompatible with the world; it was absurd to the understanding; it could be embraced only in the passion of faith; its requirement was to die away [from the world]; its hallmark was suffering; its constant companion the possibility of offense. His polemics were therefore directed against everything that rested upon the fusion of Christianity and worldliness in an insipid security; against every notion that Christianity was something one came by easily, through birth or by means of ceremonies; against every attempt to falsify the inconceivable by wanting to conceive it, to falsify what must be the goal in the re-formation of life by wanting to relate oneself to that goal impersonally and merely intellectually or through some poetic notion." *Encounters With Kierkegaard: A Life as Seen by His Contemporaries*, ed. Bruce H. Kirmmse, trans. Bruce H. Kirmmse and Virginia R. Laursen (Princeton: Princeton University Press, 1996), 252.

25. Again, Kierkegaard puts self-denial and self-hatred in apposition to each other (JP 3:3771). This reflects the interchangeability between self-denial in Lk 9:23 and self-hatred in Lk 14:26. Kierkegaard defines self-denial as "self-sacrificing unselfishness" (WL 366).

26. It also puts an end to building self-esteem. Kierkegaard would agree with Martin Luther, "Commentary on the Sermon on the Mount" (1521), LW 21:67: "[Any] self-esteem [*eigen ehre*] . . . is really a slander of God's honor and praise." On this account, Cynthia Moe-Lobeda would be wrong to suppose that Luther "would be appalled" if self-love were not defended in his name. "Loving Your Neighbor & Casting Your Vote," *The Lutheran* (October 2004), 28. For the Christian debate on self-esteem see Joanna and Alister McGrath, *The Dilemma of Self-Esteem: The Cross and Christian Confidence*, (Wheaton: Crossway Books, 1992). Their claim that "Christians should not despise or hate" themselves (95) is asserted without any reference to the countervailing verses in Lk 14:26, Jn 12:25 and 2 Tm 3:2. For a working definition of self-esteem, see the one written in 1990 by the California Task Force to Promote Self-Esteem and Personal and Social Responsibility in Gloria Steinem, *Revolution From Within: A Book of Self-Esteem*, (Boston: Little, Brown & Company, 1992), 26: "Appreciating my own worth and importance and having the character to be accountable for myself and to act responsibly towards others." Note also Gerhard O. Forde, *On Being a Theologian of the Cross*, (Grand Rapids: Eerdmans, 1997), 27: "[Self-esteem is] the current circumlocution for pride."

God, then we too must give up everything. To do so is to practice self-renunciation. From this we see that self-renunciation or proper self-hatred does not come from some psychological perversion but from abiding in God.[27] According to this prayer in the preface, Christian self-hatred can only be rightly understood in relation to belief in God. This prayer sets the stage for every further discussion of self-hatred in *Works of Love*.[28]

In chapter 1 of the first series of deliberations, Kierkegaard argues not only that "the mysterious origin of love in God's love prevents you from seeing its ground," but also that "love, however quiet . . . in its concealment, is flowing nevertheless" and so is known "by its fruits" (WL 10). Our first lesson, then, is that love is both hidden and revealed. This dual point insists that love is more than a hidden feeling but must also be an action or work, and secondly that no work of love can ever fully reveal its depths.

One consequence of this dual point is that love requires the Christian "to deny oneself and to give up . . . self-love" (WL 7). As a work, love reaches out to the other and consequently away from itself through self-denial. The Christian also practices self-denial by admitting it cannot create love—its source rather is in God. So the self must be hated rather than admired and loved in order for the focus to stay on God and the neighbor. Otherwise Christianity, which is supposed to dwell on "divine egoity, is adroitly shifted into human egotism" (JP 3:3779).

In chapter 2 A, Kierkegaard begins his three-part study of Matthew 22:39, "You shall love your neighbor as yourself," by discussing both the phrase "as yourself" and the word "shall." Regarding the phrase "as yourself," "Christianity presupposes that a person loves himself and then adds . . . only the phrase about the neighbor *as yourself*. And yet there is the change of eternity between the former and the latter."[29] The change

27. Some, of course, would see this "abiding in God" to be all the more reason to imagine something perverse. On this see James T. Richardson, "Religiosity as Deviance: Negative Religious Bias in and Misuse of the DSM-III," *Deviant Behavior* 14 (1993): 1–14.

28. I therefore disagree that "love that would deny itself and endeavor to go without merit may be called the irony of love, for it takes the form of an incognito and is characterized by the maieutic method of loving another." Michael Strawser, *Both/And: Reading Kierkegaard From Irony to Edification* (New York: Fordam University Press, 1997), 210–11. This renunciation, however, marks the cost of love rather than "the irony of love"—as Strawser avers. Construing this as irony unnecessarily softens the pain in self-denial. So does Ferreira's fifteen page section on this prayer which only mentions the self-renunciation and its attending attack on meritoriousness but just to drop them. *Love's Grateful Striving*, 13–28.

29. Martin Luther also believed that the phrase "as yourself" was not a command to love ourselves. See his "Lectures on Romans" (1518), LW 25:513: "[With] this commandment 'as yourself' man is not commanded to love himself but rather is shown the sinful love with which he does in fact love himself, as if to say: 'You are completely curved in upon yourself and pointed toward love of yourself, a condition from which you will not be delivered unless you altogether cease loving yourself and, forgetting yourself, love your neighbor.'" John Lippitt does not take into account Luther's profound point in his analysis of Mt 22:39. *Kierkegaard and the Problem of Self-Love*, 2. Lippitt seems to think that Johannes Climacus refutes Luther's point (PF 39). But Lippitt does that only by skipping over the "collision" which offsets this imagined command to love in Climacus (PF 38–39). Unlike Luther, Erich Fromm sees an implication here: "The idea expressed in the Biblical 'Love thy neighbor as thyself!' implies that

is that self-love is "broken" without being eliminated. When it is broken it becomes "proper self-love" (WL 18).[30] Self-love is no longer "a prescriptive right" (WL 17). One should not suppose, however, that this change is minimal because self-love is not altogether eliminated. No, because the phrase ties this self-love to the neighbor; it is "a stipulation that is as perilous to self-love as possible" (WL 20). This break therefore amounts to a massive change in self-love.

The reason self-love is not eliminated altogether is because it preserves the self, "and by and in preserving yourself," love is preserved too (WL 43).[31] As a consequence of this correlation, Kierkegaard proposes six modifications to self-hatred:

> Whoever has any knowledge of people will certainly admit that just as he has often wished to be able to move them to relinquish self-love, he has also had to wish that it were possible to teach them to love themselves. When the bustler wastes his time and powers in the service of futile, inconsequential pursuits, is this not because he has not learned rightly to love himself? When the light-minded person throws himself almost like a nonentity into the folly of the moment and makes nothing of it, is this not because he does not know how to love himself rightly? When the depressed person desires to be rid of life, indeed, of himself, is this not because he is unwilling to learn earnestly and rigorously to love himself? When someone surrenders to despair because the world or another person has faithlessly left him betrayed, what then is his fault (his innocent suffering is not referred to here) except not loving himself in the right way? When someone tormentingly thinks to do God a service by torturing himself, what is his sin except not willing to love himself in the right way? And if, alas, a person presumptuously lays violent hands upon himself, is not his sin precisely this, that he does not rightly love himself in the sense in which a person *ought* to love himself? (WL 23)[32]

---

respect for one's own integrity and uniqueness, love for and understanding of one's own self, cannot be separated from respect and love and understanding for another individual. The love for my own self is inseparably connected with the love for any other being." *The Art of Loving*, Fiftieth Anniversary Edition (New York: HarperPerennial, 2006), 54–55. Against this implication, see footnote 45 below.

30. Martin Luther held a similar position in his "Lectures on Galatians 1–6" (1519), LW 27:356: "[Love] of oneself . . . is always wrong so long as it is in itself, and that it is not good unless it is outside itself in God; that is, that with my affection for myself and my love for myself completely dead, I look for nothing but that God's completely undefiled will be done in me."

31. When Kierkegaard uses self-love positively (WL 22, 114, 120, 127), he is not promoting self-esteem, self-respect, self-admiration or self-worth. He instead is celebrating earnestness. Self-love is supposed to make Christians serious and hard-working. Christians are supposed to apply great "care and concern" for their works of love (JP 3:2422). Christian self-love is not designed to protect our feelings. Its goal is to end sloppiness, laziness, dullness and error.

32. This combination of self-love and self-hate continues in Kierkegaard's last writings. A "person of character," he writes, knows "that to give in the slightest with regard to principles . . . is to give up oneself." By resisting this capitulation, life naturally becomes "sheer difficulty." So too with the truly Christian. By "dying to the world, hating oneself, [and] suffering for the doctrine," Christianity also makes life difficult (TM 319). In this passage Kierkegaard combines hating oneself with preserving oneself by maintaining that they both make life difficult.

The details in this remarkable passage are incontrovertible. They show that Christian self-hatred cannot be unqualified.[33] If it were not so, there would be nothing to prevent self-hatred from becoming a degenerate self-love all over again.[34] The self-love that is needed to combat this wasteful, foolish, depressed and violent living is a trust in God that "just marches ahead" when misfortunes occur.[35] This also is the goal of Christian self-hatred. On this view self-hatred and self-love are to work together. Self-hatred strips the person of selfishness and self-pity and self-love provides energy and concentration for the work at hand.[36]

Christian love therefore not only condemns the proud and arrogant but the depressed and morose as well. Both suffer from forms of self-love. Of these two the most difficult to accept is that the despondent are not innocent, pitiful victims. The depressed need to be stripped of pride and arrogance too. Their diffuseness and distractibility come from childish curiosity and avarice. Their cowering fear of others comes from liking only those they can control. Their irresponsibility comes from the

33. Saint Augustine makes a similar qualification in his "Tractates According to the Gospel of John" § 51.10: "But beware of harboring the notion that thou mayest court self-destruction by any such understanding of thy duty to hate thy life in this world. For on such grounds it is that certain wrong-minded and perverted people, who, with regard to themselves, are murderers of a specially cruel and impious character, commit themselves to the flames, suffocate themselves in water, dash themselves against a precipice, and perish. This was no teaching of Christ's. . . . He made it sufficiently plain that it is not by himself but by another that one must be slain who follows in the footsteps of Christ." *Nicene and Post-Nicene Fathers* 7:285. The attack on self-love, according to Kierkegaard, actually has more to do with the amelioration of its "enthusiasm for the finite" (JP 2:2086).

34. Good and bad self-hatred are both in the book of Job. Job 10:1 shows self-hatred leading to bitterness and inactivity, whereas Job 42:6 shows it leading to repentance and a restored life. Critics of Christian self-hatred refuse to ponder such helpful biblical distinctions.

35. Martin Luther, "Sermon on Luke 2:33–40" (1522), LW 52:143. This working definition of self-love is not the popular one of self-respect and self-esteem. Kierkegaard was against a self-love defined as "a proud flight that soars above the world." He rather favored a definition that included "self-denial's humble and difficult flight along the ground" (WL 84)! On the popular definition of self-love as self-esteem, see Suzanne E. Harrill, *Empowering You to Love Yourself* (Houston: Innerworks Publishing, 1995), 29.

36. This combination of self-love and self-hatred does not, however, require postulating some dignity or indelible human goodness, *contra* John R. Stott, "Am I Supposed to Love Myself or Hate Myself? The Cross Points the Way Between Self-Love and Self-Denial," *Christianity Today* (April 20, 1984): 28: "I'm a Jekyll and Hyde, a mixed-up kid, having both dignity, because I was created in God's image, and depravity, because I am fallen and rebellious." An alternative account of the origin of Christian self-love, which is free of this postulation, would be that it comes from Christ dwelling in us, according to Gal 2:20 and 2 Cor 3:5 and 5:17. Stott does not consider this alternative.

pleasure quietness and luxury bring.[37] Christian love therefore will neither tolerate the proud nor coddle the depressed.[38]

In chapter 2 B, Kierkegaard takes up the word "neighbor" in Matthew 22:39. He contrasts it to the lover and friend. In romance and friendship love is "preferential," marked by "love's most passionate boundlessness in excluding." But Christian love for the neighbor does not "exclude a single one" (WL 52). In romance and friendship "the essentially Christian is absent, the intoxication of self-esteem is at its peak, . . . the *I* intoxicated in the *other I*. The more securely one *I* and another *I* join to become one *I*, the more this united *I* selfishly cuts itself off from everyone else. At the peak . . . the two actually do become one self, one *I* . . . a new selfish self" (WL 56). So it is a "profound error" to suppose that "by falling in love or by finding a friend, a person has learned Christian love." Such love is only "self-deification" (WL 57)! Self-hatred and self-denial are what frees the Christian of this wretched self-deification. This self-renunciation alone "drives out all self-love" and roots out "self-willfulness" (WL 55).

In chapter 2 C, Kierkegaard goes on to complete his study of Matthew 22:39 by analyzing the word "you" at the beginning of the verse. According to Kierkegaard, that word is a subtle denial of the self as a valuable initiating subject. Consequently the goal is "to give up all claims on life, all claims on power and honor and advantage" and hold that it is "a mark of childishness to say: *Me wants, me—me*; a mark of adolescence to say: *I—and I—and I*; the sign of maturity and the devotion of the eternal . . . to will to

37. Therefore I disagree with Paul R. Sponheim, "On Being and Becoming a Person," *Word & World* 15 (Summer 1995):338–39: "[Both] forms of sin—self-elevation and self-denigration—[as being both] . . . caught up in the self, of being curved in upon the self, . . . will not work. . . . There may be some sense in which the *result* in both cases leaves the person stuck with her or himself. But it will not do to argue that the *intention* reveals a prideful self." This mistaken analysis resembles Kierkegaard's pseudonym, Anti-Climacus, and his description of "feminine" despair which results from failing "to be oneself" (SUD 49). But Anti-Climacus does not thereby imply that this failure evacuates the person of all pride and arrogance. In fact when we do not will to be ourselves it is due to too much self! "Like a father," writes Anti-Climacus, "who disinherits a son, the self does not want to acknowledge itself after having been so weak. In despair it cannot forget this weakness; it hates itself in a way, will not in faith humble itself under its weakness in order thereby to recover itself—no, in despair it does not wish, so to speak, to hear anything about itself, does not itself know anything to say. Nor is there any question of being helped by forgetting or of slipping, by means of forgetting, into the category of the spiritless and then to be a man and a Christian like other men and Christians—no, for that the self is too much self" (SUD 62). Having too much self includes the wanting, willing and wishing Sponheim refuses to attribute to the intentionality of the oppressed and depressed.

38. Therefore I agree with Kresten Nordentoft, *Kierkegaard's Psychology*, trans. Bruce H. Kirmmse (Pittsburgh: Duquesne University Press, 1978), 368: "[The] melancholic . . . loves himself, . . . and so does the nervously officious person, the reckless person, the self-torturer, and the suicide; in brief, the despairing person, who wastes his life, and who therefore, if possible, must learn to give up self-love and to love himself truly." Many today want to hold out and believe that "the brain and its chemistry" are the actual cause of much depression. Against this wishful thinking I side with Richard O'Connor, *Undoing Depression: What Therapy Doesn't Teach You and Medication Can't Give You* (New York: Berkley Books, 1997), 9: "The truth is that whether the roots of depression are in the past in childhood, or in the present in the brain, recovery can only come about through a continuous act of will, a self-discipline applied to emotions, behavior, and relationships in the here and now."

understand that this *I* has no significance unless it becomes the *you* to whom eternity incessantly speaks and says: *You* shall, *you* shall, *you* shall" (WL 90). When the I becomes a you, it is yanked away from itself and prepared for "humbly turning outward, embracing everyone, and yet loving each one individually but no one exceptionally" (WL 67). By so denying oneself it is then possible to lift "oneself up above the dissimilarities of earthly life" and truly love the neighbor (WL 72).

Kierkegaard studies Romans 13:10, that love is the fulfilling of the law, in chapter 3 A. Love, when defined as fulfilling God's law, is not a "hidden, private, mysterious feeling behind the lattice of the inexplicable," but "sheer action" (WL 99). Because these acts of love are prescribed by God rather than ourselves (WL 113), they make "every human being guilty" (WL 104). We are guilty because the law "starves out" all our pretensions to have adequately kept it (WL 105). Therefore standing before God's law reduces us to "nothing" (WL 102). This "annihilation" (WL 103) is what the lover needs to help others do.[39] This "help" equals loving God and oneself properly. But because of the guilt and nothingness involved, it will appear "as lovelessness" in the world (WL 107). In order to "tighten the relationship to that tension," the Christian will have "*to hate the beloved*" (WL 108). Since it is God who requires this, it makes him into "a burdensome encumbrance" (WL 115). His "intervention" into our lives is very "disturbing and inconvenient" (WL 112)! Loving such a God, in order to love ourselves, is therefore hating ourselves properly. So Kierkegaard wisely advises that "if your . . . highest goal is to have life made easy and sociable, then never become involved with Christianity" (WL 124)!

In chapter 3 B, Kierkegaard studies 1 Timothy 1:5 which says we should have a good conscience when we love. The conscience, for Kierkegaard, is "the infinite weight of God" on a person (WL 143). This weight stops love from being "the self-willfulness of drives and inclination" (WL 140). This turns Christian love into action—but only when accompanied by the right attitude. Christianity "does not want to make changes in externals; . . . it wants only to make infinity's change in the inner being" (WL 139).[40]

39. The radicality of Kierkegaard is revealed when his view that we are nothing is contrasted with the views of the popular civil rights leader, the Reverend Jesse L. Jackson. See his book, *Straight From the Heart* (Philadelphia: Fortress, 1987) for his famous "I Am Somebody" ritualized speech. Jackson holds that "if you don't feel that you're somebody, you won't act as if you're somebody, and you won't treat other people as if they are somebody" (205). While this viewpoint is based on social practicality, it is not Christian teaching according to Kierkegaard (see footnote 45 below). Arnold B. Come misses this point. He fails to draw the proper radicality from Kierkegaard's dialectic: "not become nothing," and yet "is nothing" (WL 272). *Kierkegaard as Theologian: Recovering My Self* (Montreal: McGill-Queen's University Press, 1997), 357. Pondering Kierkegaard's elaboration of this dialectic would have helped: "Inwardly he does not become self-important, since he is nothing, and outwardly he does not become self-important either, since he is nothing, he is nothing before God—and he does not forget that right where he is he is before God" (WL 365)!

40. Because *Works of Love* lacks a political platform, Adorno claims "Kierkegaard's religious rigorousness is not seriously meant." T. W. Adorno, "On Kierkegaard's Doctrine of Love," 422. But this judgment misses Kierkegaard's Archimedean point by which "you will move heaven and earth; yes, you will do something even more wonderful, you will move heaven and earth so quietly, so lightly, that

When we love properly we will be "weaned from the worldly point of view" that rests in action alone (WL 145). To be so weaned is like dying (WL 150). This dying is a denial and hatred for the self which enables us to love properly.

Kierkegaard explores 1 John 4:20 in chapter 4, which says we are to love those whom we can see. He says this verse means we are not to "bemoan humanity," supposing, because of our high standards, there are none "worth loving" (WL 157). Love is not "admiration's wide-open eye that is searching for excellences and perfections" (WL 161). Only an "inflated" self uses this definition (WL 162). Against it we should instead "bear patiently" the defects in others (WL 164). In order to do this we must "root out all . . . fastidiousness in loving" (WL 166). Self-denial and self-hatred root this out for us. This is what God wants. Therefore we "should begin with loving the unseen, God, because then" we will be able to love whomever we see, warts and all (WL 160). Kierkegaard clinches this point by saying if it were not so, "Christ would never have had a chance to love, for where would he have found the perfect person!" (WL 173).

In chapter 5 Kierkegaard examines Romans 13:8 which says we should remain in love's debt to one another. The verse denies that the people we love are actually the ones in debt to us. No, the truth is that when we love others we are not then free to stop loving them. Rather we continue to owe them love. This is because "God has truth's and infallibility's infinite conception of love; God is Love. Therefore the individual must remain in the debt—as surely as God judges it, or as surely as he remains in God, because only in the infinitude of the debt can God remain in him" (WL 190).

Christian love therefore ought not be some "fiery, snorting steed," but rather "incessantly in action" (WL 188). It "knows how to control love . . . so that this humbled love will learn that wanting to remain in debt is . . . no fanaticism but earnestness and truth" (WL 189). Love is humbled when we deny and hate ourselves properly. By so doing we "remove from love everything that is inflamed, everything that is momentary, everything that is giddy" (WL 188). When this is done, a person is stripped "in such a way that he possesses nothing, nothing, so that he himself admits that he possesses nothing, nothing, nothing" (WL 176).

In chapter 1 of the second series,[41] Kierkegaard studies 1 Corinthians 8:1 which says love builds up. This does not mean that one must tear down the person before love can build the person up. Rather it means love builds upon the love God "implants

---

no one notices it" (WL 136). On this critique of Adorno see M. Jamie Ferreira, "Other-Worldliness in Kierkegaard's *Works of Love*," *Philosophical Investigations* 22 (January 1999), 65–79, and "Other-Worldliness in Kierkegaard's *Works of Love*—A Response," *Philosophical Investigations* 22 (January 1999), 80–85.

41. I disagree with Bruce H. Kirmmse, *Kierkegaard in Golden Age Denmark*, (Bloomington: Indiana University Press, 1990), 312: "[The] two halves of *Works of Love* . . . relate to one another as 'theory' (the Law) and 'practice' (the Gospel)." I read equal amounts of theory and practice in each half. Both halves also equally address the matter of self-hatred. On Kirmmse's account, one might suppose that any discussion of self-hatred would only be in the first half, since the Law seems more welcoming to self-hatred than does the Gospel.

. . . in each human being." Therefore it is wrong to "arrogantly delude" ourselves into thinking we can "create love in another person" (WL 216). Therefore the goal of love is not "to transform the other person," but to "upbuildingly control" oneself (WL 217). When we control ourselves, we reduce ourselves to "absolutely nothing" and "conquer" ourselves (WL 218, 219). In this lies Christian self-denial and self-hatred. This is because love "is not a being-for-itself quality" (WL 223).

Kierkegaard begins a four part study of 1 Corinthians 13 in chapter 2. He looks first at verse 7 which says love believes all things. When love believes all things, it does not do so "in the same sense as light-mindedness . . . which believes everything on the basis of ignorance. . . . No, love is as knowledgeable as anyone, knows everything that mistrust knows, yet without being mistrustful" (WL 228). Because love is trusting, it does not however follow that it can be deceived into giving what is neither needed nor deserved. This is because "the one who loves preserves himself in love, remains in love, and hence in possession of the highest good and the greatest blessedness, and therefore is certainly not deceived" (WL 239). Even though "humanly speaking" a Christian may be deceived, it does not matter because "he breathes in God; he draws nourishment for his love from God, he is strengthened by God" (WL 244). Furthermore, the Christian "relinquishes his right to reciprocal love" and so deception is not destructive (WL 241). Love goes on even when it is not returned. Doing this requires self-denial and self-hatred. This, however, is "very difficult" because it requires one to "extricate oneself from the lower conceptual sphere and the pact of earthly passions with illusions" (WL 244).

In chapter 3, Kierkegaard takes up the part in verse 7 which says love hopes all things. This means that even in "the final moment" the Christian "hopes for the good for the worst reprobate" (WL 260). Love never gives up. It is not ashamed to never "give up on any human being" even though nothing comes of it (WL 254, 257). This persistence only happens when one's worldly wisdom is "conquered" and "scorned." This happens when we no longer want "to get ahead or further ahead in the world" (WL 261). Doing this requires self-denial and self-hatred. They prevent us from loving "others for the sake of one's own advantage" (WL 258).

In chapter 4, Kierkegaard examines verse 5 which says love does not seek it own. This means that even though "there is a *you* and an *I*, . . . there is no *mine* and *yours!*" (WL 266). But it is "only for self-denying love" that this cancellation occurs (WL 268). Love does this by making itself "unnoticed so that the person helped does not become dependent upon him—by owing . . . him the greatest beneficence." Indeed, true love "makes itself invisible" (WL 274). Self-hatred and self-denial do this for love.[42] There-

---

42. In 1629 Johann Gerhard (1582–1637) also correlated Christian self-hatred with self-annihilation in *The Daily Exercise of Piety*, trans. M.C.Harrison (Fort Wayne: Repristination, 1992), §3.10: "O Jesus Christ, . . . I beg You through Your most holy death and crucifixion, perfect in me the denial of self which You require. . . . May the sprout of self-love be rooted out of my heart that the sweetest plants of divine love may grow within me. . . . Only when we are brought to nothing and disappear do we truly exist in and live in God. . . . If all glory is owed to God alone, then honoring one's self is the

fore the lover "must be able to make himself anonymous, must magnanimously will to annihilate himself" (WL 276). This is not masochistic, however. It is only a matter of the Christian simply not wanting "to waste any time or energy on asserting himself, on being something for himself, in his self-sacrifice he is willing to perish, that is, he is completely and wholly transformed into simply being an active power in the hands of God" (WL 279).[43] By being simply God's tool, the lover is able to get out of the way of "the other person's God-relationship" (WL 278). By so doing the Christian has "won God and . . . all things" (WL 268).

Kierkegaard takes up 1 Peter 4:8 in chapter 5 about love hiding a multitude of sins. This means in true love there is a "kind of divine madness" which makes one "unable to see the evil that takes place right in front of one" (WL 287). This madness provides "sufficient dexterity to take away . . . sins by means of forgiveness." But if forgiveness is encumbered by reluctance or making oneself "important by being able to forgive," then "no miracle happens" (WL 295). Bitterness instead sets in (WL 288). This madness and dexterity is marked by self-denial and self-hatred. Through them "controlling surroundings" emerge that cover sins which were "waiting for an occasion" to erupt into greater evil (WL 299).

In chapter 6, Kierkegaard completes his four part analysis of 1 Corinthians 13 by studying verse 13 which says love abides. What abides in love is God's love which is "the third" in the relationship between the lover and the beloved (WL 301). This

---

greatest theft, for it ascribes to itself things which really belong to another. Extinguish this habitual desire for self-love and honor in me, O Christ, blessed for eternity, Amen." For Gerhard, annihilation does not mean destruction, inertia or suicide. Rather it means disappearance. This happens in our own consciousness by dwelling on God and others rather than ourselves. We disappear from our mind's eye, as it were. In praising God and serving our neighbor we rightly "forget" ourselves (JP 2:1409).

43. This passage, however, does not show that Christian love is "optimally" about how "one's life is 'completely squandered . . . on the existence of others' (WL 279)." Contra Sylvia Walsh, "Subjectivity Versus Objectivity: Kierkegaard's Postscript and Feminist Epistemology," in *Feminist Interpretations of Søren Kierkegaard*, ed. Celine Leon and Sylvia Walsh (University Park: The Pennsylvania State University Press, 1997), 272. Such squandering would not allow for the transformation of a person into an instrument for God—something which Christian love requires and this passage from *Works of Love* includes. Even so, M. Jamie Ferreira goes too far in thinking that this instrumentality includes being faithful to yourself and acknowledging the good in yourself (contrary to Rom 3:11–18, 7:18). "Rethinking Hatred of Self—A Kierkegaardian Exploration" in *Why Kierkegaard Matters: A Festschrift in Honor of Robert L. Perkins*, ed. Marc A. Jolley and Edmon L. Rowell Jr. (Macon, Georgia: Mercer University Press, 2010), 134, 142, 143, 145. Kierkegaard disagrees because "human nature cannot carry Christianity; it always reverses the relationship, evades the demand, avoids what Christianity really is" (JP 3:3779). Human nature wants instead "to enjoy and be gladdened by this life" (JP 3:3777)! Contrary to this pleasantry, the Christian, like a warrior, longs only to be with other "heroes where only wounds and battles and dangers and victories are talked about, . . . away from the confused opinions of the world to a place where all that is talked about is the suffering that is endured, misunderstanding, terror, mockery, and mortal danger—in short, the experiences of the one who takes up the cross and imitates Christ." By so doing one is practicing self-denial, which is to have "everything within one's power and then to give up all power, and to give it up in such a way that one cannot himself do the least thing, yes, cannot even do anything for his adherents, and to maintain it so rigorously that one even constrains creation, nature, which wants to supply something" (JP 3:3740).

triad—lover, beloved, love—changes the nature of broken relationships. When a wife, for instance, divorces her innocent husband, the marriage is not over as one would usually think.[44] This is because the third is "*love* itself, to which the innocent sufferer in the break can hold—then the break has no power over him" (WL 305). By so doing the husband "transforms what in and through the past is a break into a possible relationship in the future" (WL 305).

In order for the husband to do this, he must deny and hate himself. He must suffer the "chastening" of God's "rigorous" love (WL 303). This happens when his past is "drowned . . . in the oblivion of eternity." By drowning and denying himself, he "continually emancipates himself from his knowledge of the past" (WL 307). Once the husband is freed from himself, his love may abide, even if his wife hates him. He is able to be "the same at every moment," regardless of what happens to his marriage (WL 313). By loving constantly, "he absorbs the jolt" of his wife's rejection so that there is "no collision" (WL 314). Only a husband who hates himself and loves God does this.[45] Only the "powers of eternity" working in him can lead him down this path (WL 305).[46]

Kierkegaard takes up Luke 10:33–37, the parable of the Good Samaritan, in chapter 7. The key is that the Samaritan would still have been merciful even if he did not have enough money to rent the man a room. He, like the widow in Luke 21:1–4, could still "give out of . . . poverty." This is Christianity's "wonderful kind of arithmetic,"

44. This example of the divorced husband is partially designed to contest Adorno's charge that *Works of Love* resists "any real, non-symbolical, non-metaphorical case of human love," due to the "unyielding abstractness" of its argument. T. W. Adorno, "On Kierkegaard's Doctrine of Love," 418–19.

45. Critics say this is backwards. They say: "You get good at loving yourself, and suddenly you're able to love others." Wayne W. Dyer, *Your Erroneous Zones* (New York: Funk & Wagnalls, 1976), 30. But even though on the 1991 paperback edition of this book it says over 6 million copies have been sold, the book and its argument is still wrong for two reasons. First, when has one loved oneself enough to be "good at" it? Our need for self-adulation is limitless. We never will be good enough at it to move on to helping others. There will always be more we can do—and will want to do—for ourselves *first*. Secondly, how will the switch ever happen from caring for ourselves to caring for others, on the bet that we would one day get good enough at loving ourselves to have time to help someone else? Saying simply that it will happen "suddenly" is too glib. The fact is caring for ourselves cannot redirect our attention to others. There is nothing in it to turn us around, and Dr. Dyer shows us nothing that can do it either. Therefore I find it glib to say that if you "love yourself, you love everybody else as you do yourself." Erich Fromm, *The Art of Loving*, 58. The transition between the two seems far more bumpy to me—if not altogether blocked, as is probably the case. With Fromm's smooth transition between self-love and loving others, the "dangerous . . . art of depriving someone of his fatuities" is lost (WL 277).

46. These powers are missing from Susan Brison's otherwise pregnant notion of "outliving oneself." Susan J. Brison, "Outliving Oneself: Trauma, Memory, and Personal Identity," in *Feminists Rethink the Self*, ed. Diana Tietjens Meyers (Boulder: Westview, 1997). She defines outliving as staying "on a train, one stop past my destination" (19). For Brison—but not for Christians—there is no progress in this outliving. After a violent trauma, she believes the goal should be to "piece back together . . . one's lost self" (21, 30). For her it cannot be "to transcend the trauma." It must instead be "simply to endure" it (31). This, however, is too little for the Christian. Christians embrace what Brison denies—that misery is productive! So follow Rom 5:3 and "rejoice in your sufferings" (RSV), for when you have been "wrecked in the temporal, . . . the eternal accepts you" (JP 1:84)!

whereby something can come from nothing (WL 318). This is possible because it is "more important [that a person] has a heart [than] money in his pockets" (WL 316).

In order for the Christian to practice this new arithmetic, there must be self-denial and self-hatred. The Christian must become "ashamed in a God-pleasing way," of thinking money matters more than mercy (WL 316). We must become ashamed of the way we were "disciplined in the ungodly worship of money" (WL 320). This will only happen "by renouncing the illusions of worldliness and temporality" (WL 319). Then mercifulness is freed of all "glittering externality" (WL 328) and the rich are on a level playing field with "the poorest wretch" (WL 329).

In chapter 8, Kierkegaard explores the importance of loving one's enemies. If the first battle is "to overcome evil with victory," then "the most beautiful of all victories" is the "next battle, to win the one overcome" (WL 337). This second battle is so important because the first victory often leaves the victor "proud, conceited, arrogant, and self-satisfied and lost by having conquered!" (WL 332). In this battle one needs to "fight *for* the enemy" by fighting "against oneself" in order to show "the conciliatory spirit in love!" (WL 335). This attack uses self-denial and self-hatred. This makes it the "most difficult of all" battles because in it the victor "does not receive the honor of the first victory," but gives "God the honor" instead (WL 333).

This relinquishment of credit diminishes the victory but enhances love. It is "humiliating, which only love is able to endure, that one seems to be going backward as one goes forward, that it is inverted—when one has overcome everything, the one overcome has become more important" (WL 338). This inversion can only come from intense self-denial and self-hatred. "Thus the one who loves . . . hides something from the one overcome. But not in the way a weak indulgence does, which hides the truth—the one who loves hides himself" (WL 340). By so doing the truth, however, is not erased. No, for it is "part of love's work" that the one overcome "deeply feels his wrong" (WL 338).[47] The conciliation rather comes by accentuating God in the relationship between the victor and the vanquished. Indeed, "the one who loves introduces something higher between himself and the unloving one and in that way removes himself" (WL 339). God does this by making one "modest in relation to another person, because the presence of God makes the two essentially equal" (WL 342). Both victor and vanquished are subject to God and in that demotion is equality.

Kierkegaard describes "a very important" test for love in chapter 9, on recollecting the dead (WL 345). This is such an important test because "there is no one easier for the living to avoid" loving than the dead (WL 352). So if one loves the dead, love becomes genuine by being "truly unselfish." Now "every possibility of repayment" has been removed from love. All love is selfish and false that "aspires to . . . repayment,"

---

47. Criticism is appropriate only if there is no double standard: "The one who loves humbles himself before the good, whose lowly servant he is, and, as he himself admits, in frailty; and the one overcome does not humble himself before the loving one but before the good. But when in a relationship between two people both are humbled, then there of course is nothing humiliating for either of them" (WL 340)!

even in the form of "reciprocal love" (WL 349).[48] This is because the one who truly loves must remain faithful by maintaining "oneself unchanged in time" (WL 355). If the beloved grows colder or uglier with time, this should not change true love (WL 356). Self-denial and self-hatred alone make this changelessness possible. When changelessness abides, the lover can then "learn to loath the whole mass of excuses" that blames the divorce, for instance, on the other spouse's faithlessness (WL 358).[49]

This is the great news from the graveyard: Love should never be motivated by the hope of receiving love in return. In that sense true Christian love must be self-less. Its own interests never are important. Kierkegaard thought this point was most clearly shown in the graveyard. Apart from this example, Christian love will remain misunderstood. Making this point is one of the great achievements in *Works of Love*.

In chapter 10, Kierkegaard shows how love is properly praised and that it is a "work of love" to do so (WL 366). Unlike most wedding anniversaries, love should not be praised by honoring the husband and wife. Instead it is "only in self-denial" that one can "effectively praise love, because God is love, and only in self-denial can one hold fast to God." This is because it is only in self-denial that one can become "an instrument for God" (WL 364). Indeed it is only in self-denial that one can "discover that God is." In love this is both terrifying and blessed because an "omnipotent one cannot be your co-worker . . . without its signifying that you are able to do nothing at all; and on the other hand, if he is your co-worker, you are able to do everything" (WL 362).

So it is only "in self-denial" that one can "wonderfully . . . speak about love," for only then does one know "that he himself is capable of nothing" (WL 365). Self-denial and self-hatred finally enable one to tell the truth about love, namely that it is glorious

---

48. See Arnold B. Come, *Kierkegaard as Humanist: Discovering My Self* (Montreal: McGill-Queen's University Press, 1995), 348. There he argues that Kierkegaard does not adequately address our need to be loved by other people. This is a bad assessment, however, because it does not take into account this important test regarding loving the dead. Edward F. Mooney makes the same mistake when he says that "giving out our love is somehow linked . . . to getting back a love . . . if not directly [from the beloved] then from the source that empowers our own capacity for love." Mooney, "Review of Arnold B. Come, *Kierkegaard as Humanist*," *Søren Kierkegaard Newsletter*, Number 35 (January 1998): 9. For another example of this mistake, see Jeremy J. Allen, "The Soft Weeping of Desire's Loss: Recognition, Phenomenality, and One Who Is Dead in Kierkegaard's *Works of Love*," in *Kierkegaard and Death*, ed. Patrick Stokes and Adam Buben (Bloomington: Indiana University Press, 2011), 239, 248: "Although the relationship between the living and the dead is not mutual (at least in any verifiable sense of the word), it is possible to imagine the living subject looking forward to a time when conditions are such that the relation can be mutual once again. . . . [Therefore] the work of love in recollecting the dead is . . . most importantly . . . the cultivation of the attitude of faith . . . that the dead might one day be present again in such a way that mutuality is once more possible." This view, however, goes directly against Kierkegaard's major point about loving *without mutuality* and reciprocity (WL 349).

49. Indeed, it is so: "Judged by this criterion, many of us fail the test." Philip L. Quinn, "Kierkegaard's Christian Ethics," in *The Cambridge Companion to Kierkegaard*, ed. Alastair Hanny and Gordon D. Marino (Cambridge: Cambridge University Press, 1998), 357. This difficulty, however, is no reason to soften the criterion. Christianity, after all, brings us "to a halt" when we turn to it "for help" and discover that it "looks like torment" and that its relief seems more "like a burden" (PC 114)!

because it finds "the un-lovable object lovable." Nothing else does this. "Inclination and passion," will not even "gladly understand" this. So when love is properly praised, do not expect to be "honored and esteemed" (WL 374).

In the conclusion, Kierkegaard says he has been opposing a certain "sentimental, almost soft, form of love," lamentably common in Christian discussions.[50] In this soft form we "spare" ourselves and have "happy days without self-concern." All "rigorousness" is silenced; God's love becomes "fabulous and childish"; and Christ becomes "sickly-sweet" (WL 376). There is no self-denial and self-hatred in this popular view of love. Kierkegaard combats it by turning every relationship "into a God-relationship" (WL 376). Now "in everything the person must look at him. This is how God brings us up" (WL 377). And if God is always "present, he is also looking at you." Therefore when we relate to others we must not "forget that God is present." Otherwise we will become brazen, "pretend purity" and judge others recklessly (WL 383).

So when we turn "upward or inward" in our love for others, God is at work to "infinitize" our love for others. This is "the magnification of infinity." Now if we are mad at people who do us wrong, we actually are "indignant with God, since ultimately it is . . . God who permits" this to happen (WL 384). All our demands then for better treatment only bring us "punishment" from God (WL 385). But self-denial and self-hatred will prevent this. Without their "rigorousness," we will continue to be plagued with "fear and trembling," even though we rest in God's love (WL 386). With that dire warning, Kierkegaard ends *Works of Love*.

PRAYING FOR SELF-HATRED

Even though Kierkegaard insisted "Christianity must not be defended," we must still propose how best to inculcate the self-hatred he deems Christian (WL 200).[51] We rightly want to know how to teach what is learned in the graveyard about love.

Today Americans live in a therapeutic culture wherein the old "ascetic doctrines" which once had "spiritual perceptions of great depth, . . . now embarrass the churches, competing as they do for pride of place in a culture of affluence." Now it seems "absurd . . . to teach contented people how discontented they really are."[52] So for Kierkegaard

50. This is a principle reason why Christianity is offensive. So when "Christ resolves to become the Savior of the world, a lament goes through all humanity like a sigh: Why do you do this, you will make us all unhappy—simply because to become a Christian in truth is the greatest human suffering, because Christ as the absolute explodes all the relativity in which we human beings live—in order to make us spirit" (JP 6:6686).

51. Defenses are bad because they aim to make Christianity probable which in turn falsifies it. It is no surprise then that atheists know "if they can only get Christianity's qualitative extravagance tricked into the fussy officiousness of probability—then it is all over with Christianity." That will render it "completely cashiered" (BA 39). Softening this qualitative extravagance is "most dangerous" because it cuts at the heart of Christianity. Rightly understood, "Christianity is the attacker" (CD 162).

52. Philip Rieff, *The Triumph of the Therapeutic: Uses of Faith After Freud* (New York: Harper & Row, 1966, 1987), 253, 242.

to argue that self-hatred is an integral part of "historical Christianity [will] not meet the American situation."[53] It will either be ignored or deemed pathological.[54]

In opposition to these cultural norms, I have two proposals. The first one is that we must simply read Kierkegaard. Indeed, in order to celebrate "Kierkegaard spiritually, it is necessary to experience him literarily."[55] So he should be read and even "aloud, if possible" (FSE 3; JP 5:5981). Proposing, therefore, that Kierkegaard intentionally "'abated' up to 50 per cent of the 'height' of the Christian message,"[56] dilutes the impact of his powerfully crafted words, supposing that the positive half of Christianity can only be found elsewhere. What Kierkegaard actually confessed was that he had only managed to express half of the weight of the demands of historic Christianity:

> I witness before God that I am conscious, in relation to the Gospel's own presentation, of having scaled down 35 per cent, often 50 per cent, with regard to ideality. . . . See, what Christianity is has fallen into oblivion to such an extent that existences, which, if one would audit them, would be found to be essentially worldly with a little bit of an admixture of a little Christianity. . . . But my . . . belief is that there live among us some who will enter into Christianity in earnest when it is presented even somewhat as the power and as the ideal that it is. (Pap X 6 B 247)[57]

My second proposal is that we need to pray self-hatred back into Christianity. Kierkegaard knew that prayer puts God in "place of self."[58] This is what Christian self-

---

53. Harold Bloom, *The American Religion: The Emergence of the Post-Christian Nation* (New York: Simon & Schuster, 1992), 42.

54. See Karen Horney, *Neurosis and Human Growth: The Struggle Toward Self-Realization*, (New York: W. W. Norton & Company, 1950), 154, 147: "[Self-hatred is the] greatest tragedy of the human mind [and the] sole origin [for every] sadistic impulse." And see Robert H. Schuller, *Self-Esteem: The New Reformation*, (Waco: Word Books, 1982), 98: "[Contrary to Christian tradition, Christians must now hold that] sin is self-rejection." Se also Richard Taylor, *Restoring Pride: The Lost Virtue of Our Age* (Amherst: Prometheus Books, 1996), 108: "[Historic Christianity is responsible for unjustifiably] suffocating [human superiority]." Therefore I am grateful to Gordon Marino and Robert L. Perkins for their support. Marino calls my analysis of Christian self-hatred a "splendid treatment." *Kierkegaard in the Present Age* (Milwaukee: Marquette University, 2001), 98n25. Perkins calls it "one of the very best things I have ever read on Kierkegaard" (October 21, 2012 email).

55. Naomi Lebowitz, *Kierkegaard: A Life of Allegory* (Baton Rouge: Louisiana State University Press, 1985), xiii. One reason for this literary power is the similarity between Kierkegaard's words and those of apostolic speech. Such speech "is concerned, ardent, burning, inflamed, everywhere and always stirred by the forces of the new life, calling, shouting, beckoning, explosive in its outbursts, brief, disjointed, harrowing, itself violently shaken as much by fear and trembling as by longing and blessed expectancy, everywhere witnessing to the powerful unrest of the spirit and the profound impatience of the heart." This impatience, he says, is like that of a "woman in labor" (EUD 69).

56. Paul R. Sponheim, *Kierkegaard on Christ and Christian Coherence* (London: SCM Press, 1968), 239.

57. Translated by Edna H. and Howard V. Hong, in personal correspondence, dated November 1, 1997. Right after writing *Works of Love* Kierkegaard formulated his goal most clearly: "Christianity must be presented as the difficult thing it is" (JP 1:493).

58. Perry D. LeFevre, *The Prayers of Kierkegaard*, (Chicago: University of Chicago Press, 1976),

hatred does and so prayer has the same goal. Prayer's advantage, however, is that it is not abstract like the idea of self-hatred. It is a practice that even children can learn.[59] It is a practice like visiting the graveyard to see the true meaning of love. Kierkegaard wrote a prayer two years after *Works of Love* was published that teaches self-hatred. By studying it and memorizing it, all who long for Christian self-hatred will find it:

> My Lord and Savior, you whose love hides a multitude of sins, when I really am aware of my sin and the multitude of my sins, when before justice in heaven there is only wrath over me and over my life, when here on earth there is only one person I hate and detest, one person I would flee to the ends of the earth to avoid—myself—then I will not begin the futile attempt that only leads either more deeply into despair or to madness, but I will promptly flee to you, and you will not deny me the hiding place you have lovingly offered to all; you will shield me from the eyes of justice, rescue me from this person and from the recollection with which he tortures me; you will help me to dare—by becoming a changed, a different, a better person—to remain in my hiding place, forgotten by justice and by that person I detest. (WA 187)[60]

In this prayer self-hatred drives us to God. It threatens to drive us to despair, madness and even destruction, but God's hiding place saves us from that. We should run as fast as we can to hide there. Because this threat is real, we must quickly take up the shield of God, otherwise God's wrath and our sin will devour us. We hate ourselves because of our disobedience against God.[61] It is great and frequent. But God's love is greater. It gives us a savior, Christ Jesus, who is our hiding place. Once hidden, we begin changing. Our wickedness is broken. We start forgetting ourselves, and in the

---

213. I also agree with LeFevre that it is "strange indeed how little attention scholars have given to the place of prayer in Kierkegaard's life and thought" (196). Perhaps this is due to what Ronald Goetz has called the effort "to rescue Kierkegaard from his Christianity." Ronald Goetz, "A Secularized Kierkegaard," *The Christian Century* (March 9, 1994).

59. See Martin Luther, "Treatise on Good Works" (1520), LW 44:85: "[Parents are to train children to] neither fear death nor love this life." Kierkegaard would agree but not without this warning: "A certain outliving is necessary in order really to feel the need for Christianity. If it is forced on a person before that time, it makes him quite mad. There is something in a child and a youth which belongs to them so naturally that one must say that God himself has willed them to be that way. Essentially regarded, the child and the youth are only psychically qualified, neither more nor less. Christianity is spirit. To construe a child strictly under the qualification 'spirit' is an act of cruelty, in a way is like killing him, and has never been Christianity's intention" (JP 2:1215).

60. For my devotional elaboration of this prayer see "Praying Against the Storm," *The Rose* 5 (February 1998), 12.

61. So for Kierkegaard—as it was for Luther—"the I of the confession of sin is the only true I." Oswald Bayer, "The Modern Narcissus," trans. Christine Helmer, *Lutheran Quarterly* 9 (Autumn 1995): 307. Kierkegaard's reason for this was that even when one suffers innocently he must still "believe humbly that with God he is always in the wrong. . . . He is eternally guilty and therefore always guilty" (UDVS 286).

"room" this creates (WL 119), we pursue the glory of God, the love of neighbor, and those two alone.[62]

62. Therefore C. Stephen Evans errs when he says the pastor primarily helps others by developing "the kind of self-concern that will allow them to engage the Christian gospel." *Søren Kierkegaard's Christian Psychology: Insights for Counseling & Pastoral Care* (Grand Rapids: Zondervan, 1990), 119. Evans should have incorporated the inculcation of self-hatred through prayer into his account of self-concern. Seeing a greater affinity between Christian formation and "Marine basic training" would have furthered this inclusion into his account. Stanley Hauerwas and William H. Willimon, *Where Resident Aliens Live: Exercises for Christian Practice* (Nashville: Abingdon, 1996), 77.

4

On Divine Authority and Pastors

KIERKEGAARD IN HIS CRITIQUE of Adolph Peter Adler (1817–69), vicar of Bornholm, goes beyond scrutinizing his "confusions" (BA 3) to fashioning a profile of one who holds "divine authority" properly (BA 4). This is because Christianity is more than the "voluptuous shudders" of the numinous, flashing about "in the current" of divine encounters (BA 109). Such intense experiences, at least as they are understood in Christianity,[1] require refining, training and discipline. They require being held in check by submitting properly to divine authority. Wanting to go unbridled, having "a fling as . . . brothers and sisters of the free spirit" (BA 168), is deemed contrary to Christianity. "Lax concepts and indeterminately fluid relations do not shape a true extraordinary; they only pamper and corrupt him" (BA 156). In the place of these lax concepts, true Christianity insists upon obedience to divine authority to refine these intense experiences.[2] And this authority is found in a "deft drilling in individual dogmatic concepts" (BA 3). These binding concepts are to be used like our "northern fathers" did when "berserk fury" came upon them and "they had themselves constrained between shields" (BA 155).[3] Adler did not make use of any such shields and so he was not an ideal pastor—regardless of his position

---

1. Regarding the Sūfīs, or whirling dervishes in mystical Islam, see R. C. Zaehner, *Mysticism Sacred and Profane* (New York: Oxford, 1973), 51: "There is a definite connection between nature mysticism and lunacy."

2. This is similar to Saint Paul's point in 1 Cor 14:28 that one should not speak in tongues (*glossalaia*) unless it can be translated as it is being heard. Kierkegaard calls this motto of Saint Paul's a "requirement for composure" (BA 257).

3. For an example of the berserk in medieval Nordic literature, see *The Saga of King Hrolf Kraki*, trans. Jesse L. Byock (New York: Penguin, 1998). Kierkegaard's use of the Nordic image seems to refer to a warrior who has gone berserk on the battlefield and killed many enemies. Going berserk on the battlefield was of great military advantage since it gave the warrior going berserk extra strength which made him nearly undefeatable. But after the battle was over, the berserk warrior would become a serious threat to his own men if he could not calm down and become civilized again. In these cases the warrior would flail around, in blind rage behind the battle lines, unable to distinguish friend from foe, and end up killing one or more of his own fellow warriors. To stop this mayhem, the berserk warrior's friends would wedge him between two shields (using the two shields like the two slices of bread in a sandwich) in order to constrain the crazed warrior (the ham in the would-be sandwich). By so doing he then could no longer hurt any of his friends after the battle was over—his arms being pinned against him by the two shields simultaneously pressing against his front and back. Thus Kierkegaard says the berserk warrior is constrained "between" shields. This use of a warrior's shield is unlike the way shields are used on the battlefield. There the warrior stands "behind" one shield at a time to ward off incoming arrows and head-on assaults. In Kierkegaard's very different use, one berserk warrior is wedged between two shields by his friends, behind the battle lines, in order to force him to calm down and stop hurting them.

and passion. Kierkegaard therefore rightly says that his critique of him is only "in a certain sense" about him (BA 3). It is more about constraining the berserk between the shields of dogmatic concepts—which is what it means to hold divine authority properly. Theologically considered, the errors Adler makes concerning authority and revelation[4] matter more to Kierkegaard than the personal circumstances of his life—tragic and painful though they indeed were. But because Kierkegaard's analysis of these weightier conceptual matters is all intertwined with Adler himself, Kierkegaard would not publish his book on him during his lifetime. If he had, he would have run the risk of turning his analysis of Adler into a public "cockfight" between the two of them (JP 6:6079). Kierkegaard wanted more than that for his book on Adler. He wanted it to rise above the man[5] and his circumstances so that it might have lasting significance in "every age" (BA 27).[6]

In this chapter I want to show how Kierkegaard's critique of Adler does in fact achieve the lasting significance Kierkegaard hoped for. I want to show how this book offers valuable insights into what a faithful or ideal Christian pastor should be—one who obeys divine authority properly. Kierkegaard shows in his book on Adler how a pastor, in contradistinction to Adler, would look when clothed with the "full marching equipment of orthodoxy" (BA 93).[7] But before I lay out Kierkegaard's profile of this ideal, orthodox pastor, I will first describe the essential nature of Adler's mistake and show how Kierkegaard argued for increased obedience to God as the only way to

---

4. So Walter Lowrie's translation of *Bogen om Adler* is entitled *On Authority and Revelation* (1955; New York: Harper Torchbooks, 1966). Kierkegaard says in his preface that authority and revelation are the two concepts raised in the case of Adler (BA 3–4).

5. Neither was Kierkegaard writing surreptitiously about himself in this book. On this view see Joakim Garff, *Søren Kierkegaard: A Biography*, trans. Bruce H. Kirmmse (Princeton: Princeton University Press, 2005), 453: "May not Kierkegaard have recognized in Adler, if not his own self, then at any rate certain sides of himself which he did not wish to lay bare? Did Kierkegaard actually know from his own experience that Adler's revelation had nothing whatsoever to do with a revelation, but that something entirely different was involved, something about which Kierkegaard could not speak without revealing *his own* secret?" For my critique of Garff's biography, see appendix 1, part 2, in this book.

6. Peter A. Kwasniewski, for one, thinks Kierkegaard succeeded at this. See "A Review of *The Book on Adler*," *The Review of Metaphysics* 53 (September 1999), 173–75.

7. Kierkegaard's profile of a faithful Christian pastor is therefore not based on a liberal view of Christianity. For a liberal view, see Don Cupitt, *Radicals and the Future of the Church* (London: SCM, 1989), 124: "[Liberalism] called for a less realistic theism, an end to the supernaturalist world-view, a more experiential and symbolist view of doctrine and a more open and democratic church, purged of the old coercive ideology of hierarchized, spiritualized masculine power." See also John Shelby Spong, *A New Christianity for a New World: Why Traditional Faith Is Dying and How a New Faith Is Being Born* (New York: HarperCollins, 2001), 124–25: "The primal creedal doctrines of the Christian faith were built to address a human condition that is simply not true. There was no good creation followed by a fall into sin that required a divine rescue." And finally see Arthur J. Dewey, ed., *The Historical Jesus Goes to Church* (Santa Rosa, California: Polebridge, 2004), 120: "But what is the best way? Six central teachings of Christianity. [1] Our search for a safe world. [2] How your personality can change for the better. [3] The Spirit within needs to be nourished; then it nourishes everything. [4] Rehumanising a dehumanized society. [5] Our huge moral dilemmas. [6] Conventional religion! Who needs it? Five breakthroughs to a different Faith." Kierkegaard has little if anything in common with these views of Cupitt, Spong and Dewey.

resolve Adler's confusions. I will then take up this solution and show how it helps portray an ideal pastor. I will begin with what Kierkegaard construed as the foundational insights from Luther in his attempts to reform the church in sixteenth century Germany. With that in hand, I will go on to show how Kierkegaard saw pastors playing a key role in the proper functioning of the church. I will end by assessing Kierkegaard's ideas in light of what most are expecting from pastors in America today.

Throughout this chapter I will be quoting heavily from Kierkegaard's texts so that his powerful words may be heard—believing that in them there is uncanny reforming power.[8] Kierkegaard wanted to find a way to express himself powerfully, in addition to staking out a theological position. He longed for

> a voice as piercing as the glance of *Lynceus*,[9] as terrifying as the groan of the giants, as sustained as a sound of nature, extending in range from the deepest bass to the melting high notes, and modulated from the most solemn-silent whisper to the fire-spouting energy of rage. That is what I need in order to breathe, to give voice to what is on my mind, to make the *vicera* of both anger and sympathy tremble. (LD 54)

I therefore want to avoid paraphrasing Kierkegaard as much as possible so that his piercing and terrifying, groaning and whispering sounds may be heard.[10] In this way I will also try to attend to his celebrated literary style.[11]

8. On this approach see Reidar Thomte, *Kierkegaard's Philosophy of Religion* (Princeton: Princeton University Press, 1948), 204: "No student of Kierkegaard who is sympathetic to his great inward struggle to arrive at the Truth upon which he could live and die, who has a measure of appreciation for his tremendous dialectic powers and brilliant literary talents, could desire to furnish a critical estimate of his philosophy, for he finds himself standing under judgment."

9. In Greek mythology, Lynceus of Messenia was said to have had "such sharp eyes that he could see in the dark or divine the whereabouts of buried treasure." Robert Graves, *The Greek Myths*, Combined Edition (1960; New York: Penguin, 1992), 246.

10. I agree in large part that to "feel Kierkegaard spiritually, it is necessary to experience him literarily." Naomi Lebowitz, *Kierkegaard: A Life of Allegory* (Baton Rouge: Louisiana State University Press, 1985), xiii.

11. On Kierkegaard's literary style, see Brita K. Stendahl, *Søren Kierkegaard* (Boston: Twayne, 1976), 24: "His greatness as a poet does not depend on his style: at times it can be marvelous, poetic, witty, revealing an uncanny gift for the perfect metaphor, but at other times (and in the same paragraph), it may be as heavy, labored, and tortuous as any German philosopher's discourse." See also *The Kierkegaard Reader*, ed. Jane Chamberlain and Jonathan Rée (Oxford: Blackwell, 2001), 5: "His was an art not of the permanent and monological written word but of the ebbs and flows of intimate conversation, punctuated by occasional burst of hilarity." Note as well John D. Caputo, *How to Read Kierkegaard* (London: Granta Books, 2007), 7: "Kierkegaard's irony and humour represent a striking stylistic innovation in the history of philosophy, and they unmistakably mark off an author who is offering something different from the usual fare."

ADLER'S FAILURE

Adler's worst mistake was not *that he claimed* to have received a revelation straight from Jesus Christ or even *what he claimed* the revelation said. Neither of these—the revelatory experience nor the content of that revelation—mattered as much to Kierkegaard as *how* Adler understood what he thought had happened to him. Adler, after all, did not claim anything new in the revelation he received (BA 29, 59).[12] Kierkegaard believed that the "content" of a revelation matters less than the claim that it is "from heaven"—especially regarding its binding power (BA 32, 66, 179, 186). He even says that whether the content is "heretical or not . . . must be regarded as unimportant compared with what is qualitatively decisive"—namely, how Adler understood the revelation (BA 25–26). Therefore to dwell on Adler's claim that Jesus spoke to him would be to miss where he most seriously went wrong. And neither was Kierkegaard concerned that Adler might be delusional or insane (BA 16, 51, 89) because of the fact that he thought that Jesus had spoken to him.[13] Kierkegaard thought (BA 104) that Adler's claim that Jesus spoke to him was part of his excellence.[14] Kierkegaard says he "certainly will not begrudgingly disparage the worth of this excellence" (BA 108). This insight also leads Kierkegaard to find an "inciting significance . . . in Adler's style, . . . an almost audible lyrical seething" (BA 110). For in Adler's contentious assertion to have received a revelation from Jesus, Kierkegaard sees a passion that puts him high above the mass of Christians who are religious only in a civil sense, "but . . . not *had* by it" (BA 107). Thinking Jesus had talked to him was evidence that Adler believed he needed God "at every moment" (BA 106). It showed his seriousness. It showed that his religious consciousness was rooted "in inwardness, in being deeply moved" (BA 104). In that sense Adler was "had by" his religion or cared deeply about it.[15] Adler knows,

12. An example of a genuinely new view of Christianity is reported in "Reflections on Covenant and Mission," *Origins: Catholic News Service* 32 (September 5, 2002), 218–24. It comes from the U.S. Conference of Catholic Bishops. It is not a revelation as such, but rather a theological "invention" (BA 73), following Kierkegaard's categories. This proposal argues that out of respect for the Jews the church must change its teachings to include, for the first time, two ways of salvation: the one through Jesus Christ, as traditionally taught, and the other through Moses. If this proposal is adopted, which it has not yet been, the church would no longer call the Jews to baptism and faith in the name of God the Father, Son and Holy Spirit—for salvation through Moses would be sufficient. For a critique of this sort of view, see my "Luther's Alleged Anti-Semitism," *Logia* 21 (Reformation 2012): 5–8.

13. In our day, however, the Puerto Rican native, Jose Luis de Jesus Miranda, does seem to be delusional. He claims that Jesus appeared to him in 1973 and "integrated with" him. "As the second coming of Christ," de Jesus is also the Antichrist of 1 Jn 2:18, and so "he rejects the continued worship of Jesus of Nazareth." Arian Campo-Flores, "He Calls Himself God," *Newsweek*, February 5, 2007. Adler claimed nothing like this for himself.

14. Kierkegaard may have shown sympathy here because, although he never claimed a divine revelation for himself, he "nevertheless was conscious of a wonderful 'governance' by which God made use of his life." George E. Arbaugh and George B. Arbaugh, *Kierkegaard's Authorship: A Guide to the Writings of Kierkegaard* (Rock Island, Illinois: Augustana College Library, 1967), 231.

15. See Rv 3:15–16: "You are neither hot nor cold. Would that you were cold or hot! So, because you are lukewarm, . . . I will spew you out of my mouth" (RSV). On this theme Kierkegaard writes

unlike the vast majority, "what an enormous power the religious is" (BA 108). Adler is no casual believer.

But, in the end, none of Adler's inwardness matters. "Instead of being able to help the rest of us, he is more like the frightened . . . bird that with wing strokes of anxiety rushes ahead of the storm" (BA 50). Unfortunately his view of Christianity is like an "untrained rider" riding an unbroken horse. In such cases, "all is lost; the rider does not help the horse nor the horse the rider" (BA 115). This is because Adler terribly misunderstands his passionate experience. Therefore his revelation is of no benefit to the church of his time. He dissipates his great moment, reducing it to confusion and folly. "There is no concept that he has explained, no new categorical definition that he has provided, no older and accepted one that he has revived in renewed dialectical acuteness" (BA 239). If there had been, that would have been evidence that Adler had been doing some "deft drilling in individual dogmatic concepts" (BA 3). But as it is, this drilling is missing due to the way Adler misunderstood what happened to him. For he, after all, claimed that he could improve upon the revelation Jesus gave him by expressing it in a "more appropriate form" (BA 70). Saying Jesus' revelation needed to be improved upon was "blasphemy" because it arose from the "most dreadful presumptuousness," namely, that Jesus' first words to him needed correcting because they were like "a child's lisping babbling" (BA 69). Under this misguided view, Adler unwittingly demeans Jesus Christ, rendering "the Savior's form [of expression] . . . unsuitable" (BA 75). In this way, Adler goes berserk (BA 155). He flies off the handle. But he does so in humility and good faith, knowing that what *he* has written could always—and should always—be improved upon. That qualification, however, counts for nothing. For what "might seem to be praiseworthy author-modesty" is actually a case of over blown modesty and "being modest in the completely wrong place" (BA 68). Adler therefore is in a conceptual fog, so much so, in fact, that he cannot even be a "bona fide" blasphemer, but only a blasphemer "unconsciously" (BA 90, 114)! This is what he is because he in effect said that Jesus' words were in an "imperfect voice" (BA 61). Since Jesus was the very Son of God, with all the fullness of divinity dwelling in him (Col 2:9), his words could not possibly be imperfect, and to say so anyway is blasphemy.

But Adler is not burned at the stake for this blasphemy. He instead is officiously dismissed from his post and given an early pension. Unlike the fabled John Hus[16]

---

that "just as Christianity detests adultery, murder, theft, and everything else that can defile a person, it knows yet another defilement—cowardly sagacity and flabby sensibleness, despicable thralldom in probability, and probability, Christianly understood, is perhaps the most dangerous defilement" (JFY 102).

16. Luther thought he was Hus' rightful heir. On Luther's esteem for Hus, see his "Commentary on the Alleged Imperial Edict" (1531), LW 34:104: "St. John Hus prophesied of me when he wrote from his prison in Bohemia, 'They will roast a goose now (for "Hus" means "a goose"), but after a hundred years they will hear a swan sing, and him they will [have to listen to].'" See also Luther's "Concerning the Answer of the Goat in Leipzig" (1521), LW 39:134: "I would rather share Hus' disgrace than Aristotle's honor." Luther crowns these statements with his famous February 14, 1520, letter to his close friend, George Spalatin, LW 48:153: "We all are Hussites and did not know it."

(1369–1415) who was burned at the stake in Prague for challenging ecclesiastical authority,[17] Adler is simply dismissed from his post—even though he committed the far more egregious error of challenging *God's* authority. Hus argued that councils and popes could err and was executed for doing so. Adler said Jesus had revealed new words to him and only had to retire. Adler's bishop, Jacob P. Mynster (1775–1854), after reviewing his case, concluded that Adler should be suspended because he was suffering from a form of temporary insanity, "a state of so-called *idées fixes*."[18] But even so, his dismissal was lenient and he was retired early with a pension. Mynster's assistant, Dean F. L. Steenberg of Bornholm, interrogated Adler, asking him, among other things, whether he would admit that his works contained "many false propositions that deviated from Christian doctrine."[19] Because Adler's response to this and other similar questions was deemed unsatisfactory, he was suspended and later permanently dismissed, "albeit honorably," in August 1945.[20] This action conformed to the Lutheran Confessions which required Lutheran pastors to "pledge" that the "Old and New Testaments" are "the pure and clear fountain of Israel," and "the only true norm according to which all teachers and teachings are to be judged" (BC 503–4). Dismissing Adler honorably, however, veered away from these confessions. For they also say that if church leaders "teach, introduce, or institute anything contrary to the Gospel," they should be "cursed"[21] (BC 84). But Adler's superiors did not curse him. Because of that, he was able to get off with a lesser sentence. This was not surprising because at that time priests were considered to be

> elementary school teachers, not only as far as religion was concerned, but in general, and there was general agreement that a Church understood in this manner ought to liberate itself from Lutheran-orthodox dogmatics and be broadly tolerant. The biblical conceptions, and indeed the entire realm of biblical thought should be tailored . . . to fit the demands of the new age.[22]

---

17. See Matthew Spinka, *John Hus' Concept of the Church* (Princeton: Princeton University Press, 1966), 380–81: "Hus was declared an obstinate disciple of Wyclif, repeatedly disobedient to the ecclesiastical authorities, unlawfully appealing his case to Jesus Christ."

18. Carl Henrik Koch, *En flue på Hegels udødelige næse eller om Adolph Peter Adler og Søren Kierkegaards forhold til hom* (Copenhagen: C. A. Reitzel, 1990), 152. Quoted in Garff, *Søren Kierkegaard: A Biography*, 442.

19. Julia Watkin, *Nutidens Religieuse Forvirring. Bogen om Adler* (Copenhagen: C. A. Reitzel, 1984), 13. Quoted in Garff, *Søren Kierkegaard: A Biography*, 442–43.

20. Garff, *Søren Kierkegaard: A Biography*, 443.

21. See Gal 1:8.

22. Niels Thulstrup, *Kierkegaard and the Church in Denmark*, trans. Frederick H. Cryer, Bibliotheca Kierkegaardiana 13, ed. Niels and Marie Mikulová Thulstrup (Copenhagen: C. A. Reitzels, 1984), 113. On this reduction, see Bruce H. Kirmmse, *Kierkegaard in Golden Age Denmark* (Bloomington: Indiana University Press, 1990), 134: "Thus, Christianity is not the proclamation of a new being which is other than, and indeed radically different from, the earthly life, but is the imprimatur of the eternal upon it. Official Christianity is the perfume of the Spirit upon the body of flesh."

If anything, then, it is surprising that Adler was punished at all. The most likely explanation for this is that Bishop Mynster was quite rigid and opposed to "the general tendency of the age to challenge authority."[23]

OBEDIENCE AS THE CORRECTIVE

Kierkegaard also stood against this relaxation of standards, even though he did not favor a more severe punishment for Adler (BA 78–79). Nevertheless he believed that the only way out of Adler's muddle was to handle divine authority with greater seriousness. For when Adler tries to improve upon Jesus' actual words to him, he is not treating them in a properly authoritative way. If he had, he would have "bowed" down before them and taken them as they were dictated to him (BA 140). This is because, in the presence of a divine word, one "must . . . stand by it, argue on the basis of it, act in accordance with it, [and] transform [one's] whole existence in relation to it" (BA 85). If some set of words are to be treated with divine authority, they must be preeminent in just this way, for between human beings and God there is "an eternal essential qualitative difference" (BA 181).[24] This immense difference makes God our supreme "master" (BA 188) and shows that before him we have "no merit whatever" (WL 385).[25] This sort of "deft drilling" (BA 3) is missing in Adler's self-understanding. He should have known that all intellectual assessing, measuring, and judging are out of place when we are dealing with God's revelations to us. "In religious simplicity," one should instead see our time here on earth as "a time of work, in which at every moment there is to be a striving forward" (BA 130). We are to "imprison" our judgment "in obedience under . . . divine authority" (BA 26).[26] We are not therefore to test these

23. Niels Thulstrup, "Mynster," in *Kierkegaard's Teachers*, Bibliotheca Kierkegaardiana 10, ed. Niels and Marie Mikulová Thulstrup (Copenhagen: C. A. Reitzel, 1982), 29.

24. This disjunctive supposition inspired Karl Barth when he was crafting his grand revolution in twentieth century theology. See *The Epistle to the Romans*, 6th ed. (1928), trans. Edwyn C. Hoskyns (New York: Oxford, 1968), 10: "If I have a system, it is limited to a recognition of what Kierkegaard called the 'infinite qualitative distinction' between time and eternity, and to my regarding this as possessing negative as well as positive significance: 'God is in heaven, and thou art on earth.'"

25. On being diminished before God, see chapters 3 and 7 on self-hatred in this book. This line from *Works of Love* resembles the better known quote from Kierkegaard's country pastor: "In relation to God we are always in the wrong" (EO 2:353). It is not, however, as well known how this famous line ends: "this thought puts an end to doubt and calms the cares; it animates and inspires to action." Even so, it remains highly offensive. So James Wood has his fictional character, Thomas Bunting, attack Kierkegaard, saying: "Against *us* God is always in the wrong." *The Book Against God* (New York: Farrar, Straus and Giroux, 2003), 119. Samuel E. Balentine, in his commentary on the Book of Job, quotes approvingly Bunting's angry outburst. *Job* (Macon, Georgia: Smyth & Helwys, 2006), 556.

26. Putting such restraints on reason outrages many an intellectual. See, for instance, Brand Blanshard, *Reason and Belief* (New Haven: Yale University Press, 1975), 246: "It is useless to look for clearly stated theses [in Kierkegaard's books], still less for ordered arguments in support of them. He combined an undisciplined intellect with a remorseless, facile, unchecked, limitless, compulsive loquacity." Yet Mark C. Murphy has clearly shown that divine authority can only make demands on those who have first "surrendered their discretion about how to act on these principles to God's choice

revealed words for their reliability, but to offer ourselves up to "be tested" by them (BA 38, 101, 117, 128). Here there is "nothing at all for assistant professors . . . to do. The assistance of these gentlemen is needed here no more than a maiden needs a barber to shave her beard and no more than a bald man needs a hairdresser to 'style' his hair" (BA 34).[27] Adler therefore errs by assuming the role of a professor. Having taken that "wrong direction of reflection," he should see the error in his ways and "come back from it" (BA 131).[28]

This is a radical solution because normally obedience is only given "to the one whom people themselves have established, somewhat as the idol-worshiper idolizes and worships the god he himself has fashioned "(BA 319).[29] If this solution is to work, one must then be shocked into obedience, since humans do not naturally or automatically pursue obedience to God. Such a shock is needed because all religiousness "lies in subjectivity, in inwardness, in being deeply moved, in being jolted, in the qualitative pressure on the spring of subjectivity" (BA 104). An insult, a sting, a halt, a crisis, a blow—all these are just what is needed to bring about obedience (BA 20, 41, 129, 141, 165, 168). This is because in disobedience we fall asleep. Being shaken awake is the "universal basis of all religiousness" (BA 112).[30] On this point Kierkegaard

---

and command." *An Essay on Divine Authority* (Ithaca: Cornell University Press, 2002), 177. On how to surrender properly, see Nicholas Wolterstorff, *Divine Discourse: Philosophical Reflections on the Claim That God Speaks* (Cambridge: Cambridge University Press, 1995), 239: "[We can] interpret God's discourse more reliably [if we embrace] the features of the 'holy reading' (*lectio divina*) of monastic life: a leisurely approach to the text, the cultivation of a quiet receptiveness which allows the Holy Spirit to speak in a man's heart as it will, [and] patient reflection upon every detail of expression."

27. See Bradley R. Dewey, *The New Obedience: Kierkegaard on Imitating Christ*, foreword by Paul L. Holmer (Washington, DC: Corpus, 1968), 37: "No Christian ever arrived at faith on the magic carpet of blackboard proofs borne on the gentle zephyrs of dialectic." Note also Kierkegaard's wry humor in this regard: "When a lark wants to fart like an elephant, it has to blow up. And in the same way all scholarly theology must blow up, because it wanted to be the supreme wisdom instead of remaining what it is, an unassuming triviality" (JP 4:4780).

28. In this admonition, Kierkegaard sounds like Ez 33:11: "Turn back, turn back from your evil ways; for why will you die, O house of Israel?" (RSV).

29. On this misappropriation of authority, Kierkegaard argues: "Instead of keeping close to God and leaving the rest to him, we want—partly out of the stupid mediocrity which has never had a notion of the higher, partly out of fear of men, and finally for the sake of earthly profit—we want to stand in well with men and therefore incessantly change them into the authority which decides what truth is. Obviously Christianity would have a hard time of it in our age. That a man should . . . [have] his love of God . . . be so earnest that it actually means to hate the world—this, they would say, is revolting. Yes, . . . as soon as Christianity is set forth in its truth people will revolt against it" (JP 3:3508). Stephen N. Dunning misses the radicality of obedience, arguing instead that the "key to divine authority" is the concept of divine presence. "Who Sets the Task? Kierkegaard on Authority" in *Foundations of Kierkegaard's Vision of Community*, eds. George B. Connell and C. Stephen Evans (Atlantic Highlands, New Jersey: Humanities, 1992), 27.

30. Indeed, as Kierkegaard's pseudonym notes, "the self must be broken in order to become itself" (SUD 65). Furthermore he states that "the self whose criterion is man . . . takes on a new quality and qualification by being a self directly before God. This self is no longer the merely human self but... the theological self" (SUD 79).

follows Acts 14:22[31] which says we must "enter the kingdom of God . . . through many tribulations."[32] These tribulations are what put "pressure on the spring of subjectivity" which awakens us (BA 104).

Understanding obedience properly is essential for learning the right way to treat God's words. This is because disobedience is our bedeviling calamity. The calamity of our age, Kierkegaard writes,

> in religion and . . . in everything, is disobedience, not being willing to obey. One only deceives oneself and others by wanting to make us think that it is doubt that is to blame for the calamity and the cause of the calamity—no, it is insubordination—it is not doubt about the truth of the religious but insubordination to the authority of the religious. . . . Disobedience is the secret in the religious confusion of our age, . . . [and] also lies . . . at the base of what is the fundamental harm in modern speculation, that there has been a confusion of the spheres: profundity has been mistaken—for authority; the intellectual—for the ethical; being a genius—for being an apostle. (BA 5)

Defending the truth of Christianity on logical and evidential grounds, in order to make belief and discipleship possible, is therefore wrongheaded.[33] What keeps unbelievers from believing is their defiance, disobedience, and self-centeredness. They do not stay away because they have not yet heard a convincing argument for the truth of Christianity. What brings about faith is not a good argument but a subjective jolt. Suffering is such a jolt.[34] The matter is "very simple: will you obey or will you not obey; will you in faith submit to . . . divine authority or will you take offense" (BA 34)?[35]

31. This is no surprise since Kierkegaard thought Acts 14:22 expressed "the total and integral impression of Scripture's universal teaching" (UDVS 292).

32. Jaroslav Pelikan points out that in the early church this verse not only was construed as "words of reassurance," but also "as a saying of Jesus himself," being quoted later in the book of Acts. *Acts*, Brazos Theological Commentary on the Bible (Grand Rapids: Brazos, 2005), 167.

33. On this see Martin Luther, "Lectures on Romans" (1518), LW 25:177: "What is of God must be crucified in the world."

34. Kierkegaard explores this more fully in his 1847 discourse, *The Gospel of Sufferings*. There he writes that "just as we speak of a child's having to be weaned, . . . so also in the most profound sense a person must be weaned by sufferings, weaned from the world and the things of this world, from loving it and from being embittered by it, in order to learn eternity. Therefore the school of sufferings is a *dying to* and quiet lessons in *dying to*. . . . Only one thing is learned: obedience. Without suffering one cannot learn obedience, because suffering is the very guarantee that the attachment is not self-willfulness. . . . One learns . . . in the school of suffering . . . to let God be master, to let God rule. . . . If the fear of the Lord is the beginning of wisdom, then learning obedience is the consummation of wisdom. . . . At first the rigorous earnestness of suffering is like a discipline that increases . . . unrest, but if the sufferer will learn, then he is educated for the eternal" (UDVS 257–58).

35. This submission is at the root of Kierkegaard's orthodoxy (BA 93). It comes from his Lutheran heritage. On this note: "[We hold] fast and loyally to the doctrine that is contained in [these confessions], based solidly on the divine Scriptures, and that is also briefly summarized in the approved ancient symbols, recognizing the doctrine as the ancient consensus which the universal and orthodox church of Christ has believed, fought for against many heresies and errors, and repeatedly affirmed" (BC 3). The fact that some Lutherans today are anything but orthodox does not mean that these

No arguments are needed for this to happen.[36] Criticism, disruption and tribulation are what bring about faith. If we are to believe in God, we will have to be forced to move beyond where we feel comfortable. This is because our reflection has made us "ashamed of obeying, of submitting to authority. This rebelliousness even sneaks into the thought process of the better ones" (BA 184). Such submission is inappropriately regarded as a "cowardly . . . flight backwards" (P 33). And this deep seated rebelliousness can also make us "afraid of becoming so addicted to" God that we cannot imagine living without him (BA 107). If we are to believe, we will have to "humbly adapt" to God's word (BA 67).[37] Only bowing down before God brings about faith, for that alone brings about the required change "in the deepest ground" of our being (BA 101). Being drawn in by convincing arguments is not the way believers are made.

REFORMING THE CHURCH

Kierkegaard lamented that Adler was such a failure. He believed that Adler had the requisite emotional intensity but that he squandered it. This was because Adler lacked the needed "proficiency and schooling in . . . Christian conceptual definitions" (BA 114). He was not properly constrained by the conceptual foundations of Christianity. So what he was able to add by way of his passion was "only a drop in the bucket compared with confusing the all-important concepts upon which the whole of Christianity depends" (BA 238). The definitions he neglected were essential because "emotion that is Christian is controlled by" them. These definitions codify the "essentially Christian" which exists before any Christian exists. They

---

confessions are passé, but only that some Lutherans defy their confessional heritage. On this phenomenon, see David A. Gustafson, *Lutherans in Crisis: The Question of Identity in the American Republic* (Minneapolis: Fortress, 1993).

36. On this diminishment of reason, see Martin Luther, "The Bondage of the Will" (1525), LW 33:63: "If I could by any means comprehend how . . . God can be merciful and just who displays so much wrath and iniquity, there would be no need for faith. . . . Since that cannot be comprehended, there is room for the exercise of faith."

37. On this humility, see Martin Luther, "Sermons on John 6–8" (1531), LW 23:229–30: "You must not cavil at His Word, find fault with it, and dispute it. Just hear it. . . . But if you insist that you be heard, that your reason interpret Christ's Word; if you presume to play the master of the Word, to propound other doctrines; if you probe it, measure it, and twist the words to read as you want them to, brood over them, hesitate, doubt, and judge them according to your reason—that is not hearing the Word or being its pupil. Then you are setting yourself up as its schoolmaster. In this way you will never discover the meaning of Christ's Word or of His heavenly Father's will. . . . Therefore put your reason under lock and key, tread your wisdom underfoot, and do not permit it to grope, feel, or ponder in matters pertaining to salvation. Simply hear . . . His Word, and adhere to it. . . . To hear, to hear—that is the command, and thus we truly conform to God's will. . . . On the other hand, he who . . . listens to what he chooses and wants, has heaven closed and barred to him. He will never smell or taste a spark or a tittle of the true meaning of a passage or word of Scripture."

contain the qualification by which a test is made of whether someone has become a Christian; it maintains its objective continuance outside all believers,
while it is also the inwardness of the believer. (BA 117–18)

Going berserk, then, is clearly not enough—powerful and spectacular though it
may be. This is because without "rigorous and earnest schooling in concepts," Christian emotions easily lead us astray into "rash expression" (BA 119). Just as when "berserk fury came upon our northern fathers, they had themselves constrained between
shields" (BA 155), so all today who have moving religious experiences need the same
constraining. Schooling in Christian concepts—or shields, as it were—is what we
need to restrain our emotions.[38]

These concepts are the means by which the church is tested and reformed in any
and all ages. They test the church to see whether or not it is being governed by what
is essentially Christian.[39] As such these definitions can also "make the congregation
uneasy and concerned in regard to their salvation" (BA 48). But this uneasiness is
the required first move in any true reformation of the church.[40] For "in the course of

38. On this basic and persistent point in Kierkegaard's *The Book on Adler*, see BA 3, 94, 109, 111,
115, 117, 119, 121, 123, 126, 128, 133, 156, 157, 168, 174, 301! Kyle A. Roberts misses this essential
conceptual ingredient of Kierkegaard's when he argues that the quest for authenticity "begins with
genuine attention to the nature of the self as a dynamically evolving, integrated, and intrinsically
relational being." *Emerging Prophet: Kierkegaard and the Postmodern People of God* (Eugene, OR: Wipf
& Stock, 2013), 147.

39. On these concepts forming a kind of grammar, see Paul L. Holmer, *The Grammar of Faith*
(New York: Harper & Row, 1978), 12–13: "[The] theology of the Christian tradition has as one of
its principal tasks to instruct us in that art of living which will free us from slavery to fashion and
the danger of restlessly moving with the times. . . . [So every] theologian, like every good preacher,
must mediate always between the varying passions of men and the abiding verities of God. . . . [This
requires] that theology be stated in the vernacular rather than in language that is archaic, esoteric, or
even excessively learned. Theology, therefore, must have a cutting edge which addresses the age." See
also Paul L. Holmer, *Philosophy and the Common Life*, The Twelfth Annual Knoles Lectures (1960),
ed. William D. Nietmann (Eugene, Oregon: Wipf & Stock, 2008), 69: "Religion is learned. . . . The
Christian Scriptures make a point of this by differentiating between the first birth wherein we are
born into the natural environment and a second birth wherein we are born into grace and a new
set of motives. Whatever the merit of this circumlocution, the point is an acknowledgement of the
fact that the religious consciousness is not identical with naïveté and innocence." Note as well, Paul
L. Holmer, *Making Christian Sense* (Philadelphia: Westminster, 1984), 107, 109–10: "[Concepts] are
not just general words; they are abilities that enable us to use words correctly and with generality
. . . . There is a reproof in all this of thinking religiously at second hand, of collecting Christian ideas as
if they were idle artifacts, or of presuming that because we can put words on our lips or on the page,
we are entitled to the status of a Christian and a thinker. The priorities are clear once one sees what
Christianity is. There are hollow people in intellectual circles, people whose lives make no sense even
if they talk big. Christianity asks about the quality of one's life. This query is foremost. . . . Our point is
that Christianity is not only a request for integrity in thought; it is, in itself, the very means of realizing
that request. For there are Christian concepts. They do capacitate a person, but one must learn to let
them take root and grow. Nurture is essential."

40. So Kierkegaard proposes "that an annual Day of Penitence and Prayer ought to be introduced,
at which time we would bring into consciousness the fact that we permit ourselves to make Christianity into something far more lenient than it really is" (JP 3:3516).

time indolence and habit, lack of spirit or absence of spirit, and thoughtlessness have been allowed to dampen the coiled spring" of Christianity (BA 33–34).[41] A genuine reforming movement sets out to overcome that dampening. This is because supposing that "a changed uniform (an external change) was a true reformation" is completely untenable in Christianity (BA 157). To the contrary, the reformation Kierkegaard proposes is more orthodox, radical—and dreadful—one that hacks away at our rebellion against orthodox Christianity. In a journal entry from 1854, when his attack on the church was heating up, he writes more specifically about this disruption:

> Certainly there must be reforming, and it will be a dreadful reformation—by comparison the Lutheran Reformation will almost be a jest—a dreadful reformation . . . which will have as its watchword; "I wonder if faith is to be found on earth." It will be identified by people "falling away" from Christianity by the millions, a dreadful reformation, for the point is that Christianity actually does not exist at all, and it will be horrible when a generation pampered by a childish Christianity, enthralled in the delusion of being Christian, once again gets the deathblow of what it is to become Christian, to be Christian. (JP 3:3737)

This cleaning out of the church[42] is based on a commitment and fidelity to the norms of Christianity. It is a pushing of people to greater heights—to love God with "all" their heart, soul, strength and mind, and to suffer for the will and way of God on a "daily" basis.[43] Kierkegaard therefore rightly alludes to Luke 18:8 in this journal entry, "When the Son of man comes, will he find faith on earth?" (RSV). This is a legitimate concern given the rigorous and harrowing expectations inherent in genuine Christianity. We are told to "count the cost" before pursuing the Christian way.[44] And this is not some Herculean effort extending well beyond our abilities, so that if we were to push ahead in this direction we would fall into what Kierkegaard early-on called the

41. Two years later Kierkegaard similarly writes: "Ah, there is so much in the ordinary course of life that will lull a person to sleep, teach him to say 'peace and no danger.' Therefore we go to God's house to be awakened from sleep and to be pulled out of the spell. But when in turn there is at times so much in God's house that will lull us to sleep! Even that which in itself is awakening—thoughts, reflections, ideas—can completely lose meaning through the force of habit and monotony, just as a spring can lose the tension by which alone it really is what it is" (CD 165).

42. On this purging of the church, see Kierkegaard's more programmatic statement: "It is not my task . . . to create more nominal Christians . . . [but rather] the thankless . . . task of relieving Christianity of some of those battalions of Christians. . . . Therefore what first and foremost must be brought into prominence again is the ideal picture of a Christian, so that it can appear as a task, beckoning, and on the other side, so that it can crush with all its weight the presumptuousness of wanting to go further than being a Christian. . . . But to do this undauntedly in the service of the truth can easily expose me to the opposition of people, insofar as they generally take a dim view of jacking up the price or the requirement for being what they already think they are, the name of which they do not want to give up" (PV 125–26, 130–31, 138).

43. Lk 10:29, 9:23 (RSV).

44. Lk 14:28 (RSV).

depths of "a careless Pelagianism" (CI 61). Kierkegaard thought this intensification was rather only about willing "to do everything in one's power [and] to the utmost of one's capability" (EUD 361). Rightly understood, then, this reformation is not for the likes of Nietzsche's Übermensch,[45] but rather an attack on the lazy, ordinary person[46] who has given up on using his or her abilities and blessings. John 1:12 says that to all who believe in Christ, he gives "power to become children of God" (RSV). This is not a matter of self-reliance. It rather has to do with using what one already has. Not to do so would be sinful and lazy.[47]

All of this is grounded in a "militant piety" (PV 130). This piety is the struggle that brings genuine faith back into the church. It is "the good fight of faith."[48] Kierkegaard's Anti-Climacus puts it this way:

> What Christ said, "My kingdom is not of this world,"[49] was not said in a special sense about the connection with that age; it is eternally valid, for all times just as valid a statement about the relationship between Christ's kingdom and this world. As soon as Christ's kingdom makes a compromise with this world and becomes a kingdom of this world, Christianity is abolished. But if Christianity is in the truth, it is certainly a kingdom in this world, but not of this world, that is, it is militant. (PC 211)

Without this militancy, Christians, Kierkegaard writes, "fritter away their lives in the old rut that makes existence insipid because it is without salt, makes existence a

---

45. On Nietzsche's superman or Übermensch, see Karl Jaspers, *Nietzsche and Christianity* (1938), trans. E. B. Ashton (New York: Henry Regnery, 1961), 54–55: "Nietzsche arrives at [a] wholly un-Christian idea [when he] turns the direction of the total process [of world history] into a matter to be decided by the active human will [of a deliberately bred] superior type of man. The place of God the Creator as history's guiding spirit was to be taken by creative man who would plan and manage history as a whole." See also Peter Berkowitz, *Nietzsche: The Ethics of an Immoralist* (Cambridge: Harvard University Press, 1995), 104–8: "The attainment of human excellence, that is, of 'a higher type, which is, in relation to mankind as a whole, a kind of superman,' . . . faces, Nietzsche believes, an unprecedented peril in the form of modern Christianity [which teaches] men to consider the supreme values of [their natural] spirit as something sinful. . . . It commands the rejection of all versions of human perfection . . . because of the morality [Christianity] teaches, one in which 'all cowardices and wearinesses of the soul, find their sanction!'"

46. On the effort to remove sloth or laziness from the traditional list of vices, see Mel Levine, *The Myth of Laziness* (New York: Simon & Schuster, 2003), 1: "Laziness is not an innate trait. . . . Some individuals somehow, somewhere lose momentum; in the pursuit of accomplishments they fail to produce; they stall out. And often they face accusations of laziness. In truth, through no fault of their own, they suffer from hidden handicaps that disrupt and interrupt their output. They are not lazy; they have output failure."

47. On this neglect, see Martin Luther, "Sermons on John 1–4" (1537), LW 22:90: "The devil occasionally assails the pious Christian heart so hard with his fiery darts (Eph 6:16) that they not only become oblivious to the exuberant glory of their filial relationship to God but also give way to the opposite ideas. . . . Thus our faith is . . . very feeble and cold. If it were firm and stable as indeed it should be, we would almost die for sheer joy."

48. 1 Tm 6:16 (RSV).

49. See Jn 18:36.

confection because it is without earnestness" (UDVS 339). But with this militancy we can make gains against not being "conformed to this world."[50] For "to be a Christian in the Church militant means to express being Christian within an environment that is the opposite of being Christian" (PC 212). But without this militancy we are stuck in the rut of sleepiness, where we "scintillate with advantages gained without any effort [and] parade cravenly in the flabbiness of preferred treatment" (UDVS 249). Against these supposed advantages, we must fight since they rob us of a life with God—which is "inward" (UDVS 256). Indeed, "friendship with the world is enmity with God."[51] For these worldly advantages make us superficial—sinking us into a materialistic life—bereft of the Spirit. The militant church therefore knows what the triumphant church never can, namely that one cannot practice Christianity if one is receiving "glory from one another."[52] In order, then, to pursue a life with God, one must stand alone "like an alien" in the world, foregoing "the glad gospel that is proclaimed on the dance floor of youth" (BA 141).

TAKING LITTLE EXCEPTION TO LUTHER

Kierkegaard believed that Martin Luther was an ally in this struggle against the world. He honored Martin Luther, saying that next to Jesus Christ, he was "the truest figure" (JP 3:2898). And it rightly upset Kierkegaard to see Lutherans misrepresenting Luther. What they took from Luther was nothing but "an exegetical slave spirit, a hyperorthodox Lutheran coercion." What this did was make them think everything was settled if the doctrine is sound and corrupt leaders were toppled. But this is "*eo ipso* an illusion," for Kierkegaard believed that "every individual . . . must be reformed" as well (BA 158).[53] "Praise God for Luther," Kierkegaard writes, for he is "always a good help against the almost insanely inflated dogmatic and objective conceitedness which . . . abolishes Christianity" (JP 4:4549)! So while Luther rightly attacked as "dreadful spiritlessness" the medieval business which "sold the good works of others at fixed but cheap prices,"

> he did not therefore abolish imitation, nor did he do away with the voluntary,
> as pampered sentimentality[54] would like to have us think about Luther. He

50. Rom 12:2 (RSV).

51. Jas 4:4 (RSV).

52. Jn 5:44 (RSV).

53. Therefore the age of Luther "is past" (TA 89). For what the Reformation clarified for all time cannot change lives unless it is personally appropriated by succeeding generations, for "the trouble lies . . . in the listener himself" (JP 3:3468).

54. Kierkegaard notes that in this pampered sentimentality, "one's existence drifts with the current and one utilizes natural self-love to make life as cozy as possible for oneself" (JFY 196). Luther stands with Kierkegaard against such coziness. "We see so many people," Luther writes, "misusing the gospel, . . . as if now [since] they have been so liberated by the gospel, . . . there is no further need to do anything, give anything, or suffer anything. This kind of wickedness our God cannot check except

affirmed imitation in the direction of witnessing to the truth and voluntarily exposed himself . . . to dangers enough (yet without deluding himself that this was meritorious). Indeed, it was not the pope who attacked Luther, but it was Luther who attacked the pope; and although Luther was not put to death, his life was nevertheless, humanly speaking, a sacrificed life, a life sacrificed to witnessing to the truth. (JFY 192–93)[55]

By robbing Luther of his insistence on Christian imitation, the generation that followed him "slackened . . . [and] made the Lutheran position into doctrine, and in this way faith [itself[56] was] diminished in vital power" (JFY 193–94). This slackening completely misrepresents Luther. For he deeply believed that the best time of the church was "the time of the apostles and martyrs. . . . [For all] the quarrels and wars of the Old Testament . . . prefigured the preaching of the gospel, which must and should cause quarreling, disunity, dissension, and disturbance."[57] And it is this disturbance that contributes essentially to the imitation of Christ.

Luther worked hard to reform the Roman Catholic Church in Europe by trying to make Augustinian Christianity prominent in it once again.[58] He did this by

---

through suffering. Hence he must keep disciplining and driving us, that our faith may increase and grow stronger and thus bring the Savior more deeply into our hearts. For just as we cannot get along without eating and drinking so we cannot get along without affliction and suffering. Therefore we must necessarily be afflicted of the devil by persecution or else by a secret thorn which thrusts into the heart." Martin Luther, "Sermon at Coburg on Cross and Suffering" (1530), LW 51:207.

55. Luther believed that the blood of the martyrs "will drown . . . the devil . . . and preserve the Word of God in its truth and purity against the impure profaners of the Word. . . . [So] to die for God's Word and faith is a priceless, precious, and noble death, fit only for the Spirit and children of God . . . . For God, who [allows such suffering], surely has it in mind not only to punish the godless if they do not repent, but to use [such murders] for the benefit of many . . . and by [martyrdom] lead them to eternal life." Martin Luther, "The Burning of Brother Henry" (1525), LW 32:266–68. Kierkegaard could not possibly have had this treatise in mind when he said of Luther that he rejected the thought that it was "blessed to suffer" (JP 4:4695).

56. "The Lutheran emphasis on faith has now simply become a fig leaf for the most unchristian shirking" (JP 3:2481). On this point see Ernest B. Koenker, "Søren Kierkegaard on Luther," in *Interpreters of Luther*, ed. Jaroslav Pelikan (Philadelphia: Fortress, 1968), 249–50: "[In] the sterile and stultifying Lutheranism of Kierkegaard's Denmark, . . . Luther failed to offer the solution for Christianity's debility. He was a sensitive, suffering, articulate patient. He even diagnosed the malady quite well. But when it came to prescribing treatment he administered a sedative. Kierkegaard has no doubt but that the treatment was benevolent in Luther's own anxious condition, yet when as doctor of the church he prescribed such sedation for millions he drugged them into a state of spiritless torpor that marked Christendom in Kierkegaard's day. This was the doctor's marvelous cure: it was marvelous, but the patient died."

57. Martin Luther, "Concerning the Answer of the Goat in Leipzig" (1521), LW 39:133.

58. On this judgment, see Paul Johnson, *A History of Christianity* (1976; New York: Touchstone, 1995), 281–86, and to a lesser extent, Jaroslav Pelikan, *The Christian Tradition: A History of the Development of Doctrine*, 5 vols. (Chicago: University of Chicago Press, 1971–89), 4:17–18, 31–32, 126–27, 141–42. Note as well, Martin Luther, "Sermons on John 1–4" (1540), LW 22:512: "Augustine . . . lead me to Christ." And see also Michael A. Mullett, *Martin Luther* (London: Routledge, 2004), 56: "Luther cited St. Augustine with reverence and with massive frequency . . . because he . . . had emphases that were Luther's emphases and concerns that were Luther's: the pervasiveness of sin, the weakness of the

challenging the leaders and the rank-in-file alike to take up a more rigorous and faithful practice of true biblical Christianity, based on adherence to divine authority. A major result of his[59] success was an upheaval in the power and organization of the church. These changes were mostly external. His primary intention, however, extended far beyond the external. He also hoped that along with these external changes there would be a commensurate internal change in the hearts of individual believers.[60] Without this internal component, we cannot nurture our very religious structure. Kierkegaard describes this internal, religious structure in terms of confidentiality with God:

> Ostensibly it is an imperfection in earthly life that basically a person cannot entirely, cannot thoroughly make himself understandable to others; on closer inspection one will surely be convinced that it is perfection, since it suggests that every individual is religiously structured and is to strive to understand himself in confidentiality with God. Most people probably do not notice either this imperfection or that it is a perfection. (BA 92)

As part of the reformation of the church, Luther prayed[61] for Christians to be renewed and strengthened—*internally*—through an intensified apprehension of the truth of God in their daily lives.[62] External, objective change in the church is visible

---

human will and intellect and the utter need of sinners for God's grace. Thus Luther cited Augustine with the highest approval on such subjects as the realization that in the face of God we 'are nothing at all' and the fact that the gospel makes it known to us that we are children of wrath, helpless without the mercy of God, 'from whom you have whatever good you have and whose mercy forgives you whatever evil you have of your own'. Luther's intellectual polarities were, then . . . Aristotle with his confidence in human reason and human ethical capacity, *versus* Augustine with his despair at man's inherent capacity for good and his sole reliance for hope on God's mercy, evident in grace."

59. Against this attribution, Luther famously, modestly, and with some humor, said: "I simply taught, preached, and wrote God's Word; otherwise I did nothing. And while I . . . drank Wittenberg beer with my friends Philip and Amsdorf, the Word . . . did everything." Martin Luther, "Eight Sermons at Wittenberg" (1522), LW 51:77.

60. This coupling of internal and external changes in Luther's thought continues to be hotly debated. On this dispute see, *Union With Christ: The New Finnish Interpretation of Luther*, ed. Carl E. Braaten and Robert W. Jenson (Grand Rapids: Eerdmans, 1998), 166: "Do the Finns sometimes interpret Luther's idiomatic expressions too literally? For instance, 'Greta gives herself in love to Hans' would not normally be interpreted as 'Greta gives to Hans her being,' or 'Greta participates in the being of Hans.'"

61. See, for instance, *Luther's Prayers*, trans. Charles E. Kistler and ed. Herbert F. Brokering (Minneapolis: Augsburg, 1994), 97–98: "Almighty and everlasting God, we pray in the name of your dear Son, our Lord Jesus Christ, . . . give us thankful hearts that we may love your holy Word, prize it highly, hear it reverently, and improve our lives accordingly. And so may we not only understand your Word rightly but also meet its demands by our deeds. May we live in accordance with it and day by day increase in good works. Thereby may your name be hallowed, your kingdom come, and your will be done. Amen." In the same vein, Kierkegaard has Anti-Climacus pray for pastors: "Lord Jesus Christ, we pray . . . for those who are servants of the Word, those whose task it is, as far as a human being is capable of it, to draw people to you. We pray that you will bless their task, but also that in this task of theirs they themselves may be drawn to you, that in their zeal to draw others to you they themselves are not held back from you" (PC 260–62).

62. Luther was gripped by Lk 9:23: "And Jesus said to *all*, . . . 'Take up your cross *daily* and follow

and clear. The internal changes are far less certain and clear. Twelve years into the Reformation, Luther bemoaned how little internal change had taken place. The common people, he wrote, "like pigs and dogs . . . remember no more of the Gospel than [a] rotten, pernicious, shameful, carnal liberty. . . . [They] take the Gospel altogether too lightly, and . . . are sluggish and lazy."[63]

Kierkegaard thought there was more to this failure than confusion on the part of Luther's followers. He also thought that Luther himself shared some of the blame for this spiritual slovenliness. "Even the great reformer Luther," he writes, "cannot be entirely acquitted" (BA 158). Luther, he notes, gives in to our "cunning swindle," whereby we disingenuously whine and whimper about being "unable to accomplish anything," that we might justify our irresponsibility (JP 3:2682). But Christianity is seriously damaged when we believe that "Christ came to the world to soothe and reassure . . . anguished consciences. . . . But a sinful world really does not suffer from an anguished conscience. Here it is a question of arousing restlessness" (JP 3:2550). Where Luther goes wrong, Kierkegaard writes, is in expressing Christianity "in man's interest." But this is not the way of the true witness, who "expresses Christianity in God's interest, [who] comes with authority from God and in his interest" (JP 3:2556). This criticism does not take away any glory from Luther's wonderful emphasis on the category "for you," which is true "subjectivity." For indeed the dictum that "only the truth which builds up is truth for you" (EO 2:354) is "Luther's own," and on this "everything depends" (JP 3:2463). The only point is that "Luther probably did not take enough care. The norm is: for every higher degree of grace, law must also be made more rigorous in inwardness—otherwise the whole secular mentality rushes forward and takes 'grace' in vain.[64] And this is precisely what happened in the Reformation" (JP 2:1484). But Kierkegaard also says that he only takes "a little exception" to this in Luther since he knows that "every advance toward the ideal is a step backward." Nevertheless, this uneven advance must be "indicated and 'grace' all the more emphatically applied" (JP 2:1922). An "honest admission" would advance all of this. For

> subjects who cannot honestly pay the taxes are not rebellious subjects if they
> openly say to the monarch: We cannot pay the taxes. But on the other hand,

---

me" (emphases added) (RSV). See also Martin Luther, "Sermons on 2 Peter" (1523), LW 30:159: "Your faith is [to be] well exercised [*trieben*] and applied [*üben*]."

63. Martin Luther, "The Large Catechism" (1529), BC 358–59. See also Martin Luther, "Lectures on Galatians 5–6" (1535), LW 27:48: "The majority of men understand the teaching about faith in a fleshly way and transform the freedom of the spirit into the freedom of the flesh. This can be discerned today in all classes of society, both high and low. They all boast of being evangelicals and boast of Christian freedom. Meanwhile, however, they give in to their desires and turn to greed, sexual desire, pride, envy, etc. No one performs his duty faithfully; no one serves another by love. This misbehavior often makes me so impatient that I would want such 'swine that trample pearls underfoot' (Matthew 7:6) still to be under the tyranny of the pope. For it is impossible for this people of Gomorrah to be ruled by the Gospel of peace."

64. 2 Cor 6:1 (RSV).

they do not have the right to falsify the amount of taxes, quietly decrease them, and then honestly pay them. (JP 3:2551)

It is just this sort of chicanery that Kierkegaard opposes since he believes it unwittingly destroys the church by making Christianity too easy:[65]

> A reform which amounts to casting off burdens and making life easy is appreciated—and one can easily get friends to cooperate. True reforming always makes life difficult,[66] lays on burdens, and therefore the true reformer is always slain, as if it were enmity toward mankind. (JP 3:2481)[67]

This dialectical understanding of law and grace is founded on a "deft drilling" (BA 3) down into the conceptual foundations of Christianity—something which we see once again to be completely missing from Adler's self-understanding.

PROFILING THE IDEAL PASTOR

Because Kierkegaard believed that faithful pastors are essential for the well-being of the church,[68] Pastor Adler's failure was especially upsetting. In criticizing Adler, Kierkegaard was trying to edify the church. "Spiritually understood," he writes, faithless pastors are like "the busy housewife who herself, in order to prepare food for the many mouths, scarcely has time to eat" (BA 187). This means that these pastors are not practicing what they preach. Such disingenuousness is a disaster because those bringing the message of Christianity are not transformed themselves by what they commend to others. This pastoral failure is not inconsequential, for such abdication leaves the church rudderless and drifting. When pastors do not themselves eat the meal they

65. See the contrary call to rigorousness in Mt 7:13-14.

66. Such difficulty requires patience. On this see Martin Luther, *Lectures on Romans* (1518), *Luther's Works* 25:290: "The impatient man is not yet a Christian." And it is especially difficult to be patient today, living in a world where "a company is measured by its ability to accelerate everything from manufacturing to marketing, from hiring to distributing. If we can produce or process something faster, we can often do it for less money, serve our customers better, and get a jump on our competitors. For almost any business these days, speed is indeed life." Bob Davis, *Speed is Life* (New York: Doubleday, 2001), 17.

67. Kierkegaard uses the risky image of a band of criminals to express this enmity: "[They] must carefully watch out that no one comes into the [the church] . . . except the one whose mark is that he is polemic to the utmost toward society in the usual sense. This means that the Christian congregation is a society consisting of qualitative individuals and that the intimacy of the society is also conditioned by this polemical stance against the great human society" (JP, 4:4175).

68. On the primacy of pastors for the church, see Martin Luther, "Concerning the Ministry" (1523), LW 40:11: "The public ministry of the Word, I hold, by which the mysteries of God are made known, ought to be established by holy ordination as the highest and greatest of the functions of the church, on which the whole power of the church depends, since the church is nothing without the Word and everything in it exists by virtue of the Word alone." Against this view see Marva Dawn and Eugene Peterson, *The Unnecessary Pastor: Rediscovering the Call* (Grand Rapids: Eerdmans, 2000), 3: "[Pastors are unnecessary] as the linchpin holding a congregation together, . . . [as] the apex of ministry, . . . entrusted with the Word of God."

offer, they are being dishonest and irresponsible. It turns them into hypocrites. They tell the church one thing and then live an entirely different way. They give up on trying to be Christians—imagining they might try that later, "when some time has passed." Because of their unpracticed faith, these pastors have to "steal" any "solemnity" they might have at Holy Communion from the "fervor" of the "poor but pious" believers kneeling at the altar (BA 98). And this ruins the integrity of the church. This could all be solved by simply reintroducing obedience back into the lives of pastors—obedience to divine authority. The case of Adler shows how damaging it is to the church when this obedience is missing.

Kierkegaard takes up a specific case to show how pastors should be reformed. He asks us to consider writing an Easter sermon and how it would differ when obedience to divine authority is present. The chief difference, he argues, is that the sermon would have authority.[69] For to preach properly is "precisely to use authority, and that . . . has simply been altogether forgotten" (BA 180). Therefore a Christian pastor, when preaching on heaven,

> must simply say, "We have Christ's word that there is an eternal life, and with that the matter is decided. Here it is a matter neither of racking one's brains nor of speculating, but of its being Christ who, not in the capacity of profundity but with his divine authority, has said it." (BA 184)

A bad sermon on eternal life would say much more. It would spend time speculating on the mechanics of the phenomenon of immortality in order to prove the truth of this doctrine. But then the sermon would not be based on Christ's authority. It would instead be based on showing how the doctrine of eternal life is plausible and therefore worthy of one's full acceptance—based on what is intellectually compelling. Such speculations are designed to lessen the offense in the doctrine of eternal life and make it easier to accept. But this is the wrong way to go. The pastor instead should "use his divine authority to drive away all the impertinent people who are unwilling to obey but want to be loquacious" (BA 179). The pastor should burn so hot with divine authority that the impertinent are forced to say: "How can I get away from this man? His sermon catches up with me in every hiding place, and how can I get rid of him, since he is over me at every moment?" (BA 105). Rather than dazzling the congregation with one's intellectual prowess on social, historical and philosophical matters, all articulated "in plausible words of wisdom," the pastor should instead simply preach with the force "of the Spirit."[70] In a correlated journal entry, Kierkegaard writes that a pastor

> *must* use authority; he *must* say to men: *You shall*; that he must do even if they kill him, that he must do even if everybody falls away from Christianity. But

---

69. Note Mt 7:29 where it says that Jesus taught "as one who had authority," and Phil 2:8 where it says of him that he was "obedient unto death, even death on a cross."

70. 1 Cor 2:4 (RSV).

everyone will accept it if he were to say: I beseech the most honored, cultured public's lenient indulgence for these eternal truths. (JP 3:3477)

Kierkegaard further illustrates this point about pastoral authority in another journal entry by contrasting two sermons on the same theme—one in a blunted tone and the other in a more confrontational tone. In this regard Kierkegaard says the matter of authority must extend beyond what is actually said, to *how* it is said:

Take two preachers. Each proclaim—it is one and the same discourse—how truth must suffer in this world. It is a masterful lecture and also produces an enormous effect; the listeners are carried away in audible admiration—but the one preacher is in character according to the essentially Christian; he says: What a blunder I have made—and then directs his attack at the listeners themselves, and receives boos and catcalls etc. This is Christianity; the earnestness is not discourse, but what comes next.—The other preacher is a rhetorician, a cleric. He is delighted over the public's applause, bows and scrapes like those virtuosos who grant audience. More and more attention is directed to him because of his excellent discourse about how truth is derided in this world—he draws the attention of the government, becomes a Knight, ranking with the cabinet ministers, gets permission to have the velvet on the left arm, etc.—is this Christianity? No, this is playing at Christianity. (JP 3:3525)

Unreformed pastors are too soft[71] and therefore are a blight on the church because they do not lead the church into the way of truth, by the power of God's spirit.[72] Such pastors think the authoritative way is disrespectful, unreasonable and destructive of human responsibility. For those reasons they choose to be vague and confusing—circumventing the issues at hand. They hold an office with divine authority and yet, when speaking, act as if they were without authority. They "babble . . . Christianity down into something meaningless, into being spiritless impotence, suffocated in illusion" (JP 6:6943). As a result, the pastor becomes an

ecclesiastical-secular hermaphrodite, . . . [and] no one can definitely say what it is; it is an indefinable something, but someone who as such is present at all kinds of solemn occasions, . . . a sort of more elegant edition of an undertaker. (JP 3:3157)

What is missing in these churchly undertakers is the proclamation of Christianity itself—which is supposed to be their very *raison d'être*. But because "to proclaim

71. And on the proper training for a pastor, see Kierkegaard's advice: "It is no doubt pure drivel or, more correctly, it is hypocrisy as well, this rubbish about a teacher of religion having to be such a mild and kind-hearted and nice man. No, the best thing would be for him to make preliminary studies in a penitentiary—but even this is hardly adequate" (JP 4:4982). For indeed, "it is the most disastrous notion in the world that 'eloquence' has become the medium for the proclamation of Christianity. Sarcasm, irony, humor lie far closer to the existential in Christianity" (JP 1:818).

72. See 1 Tm 3:15; Jn 14:6, 10:4–5.

Christianity is to make sacrifices" (JFY 130), they shrink back from it. Christianity, truly conceived, is not what these makeshift pastors would want—which is only some sort of a "gentle, life-beautifying and ennobling ground of comfort" (JP 1:496). No, Christianity truly conceived and practiced, is rather a "dying to the world, voluntary renunciation, crucifying the flesh, [and] suffering for the doctrine" (JP 6:6947). But most pastors cannot bear this. Even so, the Christian is clear: you must suffer in precisely this way. And this may well mean for the pastor—due to the ill will in almost every congregation against a faithful pastor—that he or she will have to "endure proclaiming Christianity in poverty" (JFY 126). Thinking this is entirely unreasonable, pastors go the way of "cleverly pretending . . . to be nothing, living as pleasurably as any pagan, [and] possessing or aspiring to worldly goods as much as any pagan" (CD 363). No doubt, then, the proposition still holds, that

> for every person who in truth has willed the truth, there live—shudder!—there live one thousand pastors, who with families support themselves by hindering the sensate, the light-minded, the worldly-minded, the enormous crowd of mediocre people from receiving a truer impression of that one who in truth willed the truth. (TM 350–51)

Because of these problems, one might wonder if anticlericalism is the only solution to the problem. If pastors are so unreliable, maybe they should be eliminated altogether. But both 2 Timothy 4:1–5 and Titus 1:5–16 say that pastors are required for the church, so they cannot be done away with completely. What is instead needed are better pastors to replace these meager ministers. These better pastors are those who

> possessing the desirable scientific-scholarly education, yet in contrast to the scientific game of counting, are practiced in what could be called spiritual guerrilla skirmishing, in doing battle not so much with scientific-scholarly attacks and problems[73] as with the human passions; pastors who are able to split up "the crowd" and turn it into individuals; pastors who would not set up too great study-requirements and would want nothing less than to dominate; pastors who, if possible, are powerfully eloquent but are no less eloquent in keeping silent and enduring without complaining; pastors who, if possible, know the human heart but are no less learned in refraining from judging and denouncing; pastors who know how to use authority through the art of making sacrifices; pastors who are disciplined and educated and are prepared to obey and to suffer, so they would be able to mitigate, admonish, build up, move, but also to constrain—not with force, anything but, no, constrain by

---

73. For a contemporary example of this corrupt scholarship, see Thomas C. Oden, *The Rebirth of Orthodoxy: Signs of New Life in Christianity* (San Francisco: HarperSanFrancisco, 2003), 137: "The problem of unfaithful clergy extends to our seminaries. . . . These ordinands are . . . steered away from scripture toward tendentious gender studies, nihilistic deconstruction, uninhibited liturgical experimentation, the ubiquitous (and speculative) historical criticism, and counterproductive psychotherapies."

their own obedience, and above all patiently, to suffer all the rudeness of the sick without being disturbed, no more than the physician is disturbed by the patient's abusive language and kicks during the operation. For the generation is sick, spiritually, sick unto death. But just as a patient, when he himself is supposed to point to the area where he suffers, frequently points to an utterly wrong place, so also with the generation. (JP, 6:6256)

These pastors, in contrast to the pastoral charlatans who lust after popularity, are deeply formed by their persistent, disciplined efforts to obey God. This obedience enables them to understand the human heart and its unadmitted spiritual sickness. They learn how to combat this sickness even when the sick masquerade as healthy and unafraid. They refuse to turn the bruises they get from these battles into excuses for soliciting sympathy. They instead expect those whom they help to dislike them, since the aid they bring is too painful. Even so, they continue to warn the sick without belittling them and to call them to responsibility, without putting inordinate pressure on them. And they do all of this knowing that their greatest strength is not in being popular, but in the authority they bear for the sacrifices they make while serving as pastors—whether that authority is recognized and honored, or not. The authority they bear, and the obedience it requires, they do not claim for themselves, but testify to its—albeit contentious—divine origins.

These are the ideal pastors. And they can make the church flourish. They have what Adler lacked—"dialectical acuteness" (BA 239). Unlike Adler, their "whole existence" has been transformed by their faith in Christ (BA 85). They combine concepts with passion (BA 238). They are expert in the "deft drilling" (BA 3) of the conceptual foundations of Christianity. They do not go "berserk," due to an unbridled passion for God (BA 155). But while constrained by dogmatic concepts, they still yearn to be "addicted" to God (BA 107). They do not believe that "submitting" to divine authority (BA 184) is intellectually embarrassing. They take in the same message they serve (BA 187)—refusing to live by a double standard. They are not afraid if their message drives away the "impertinent" (BA 179). For they are convinced that "every individual . . . must be reformed" (BA 158).

The Very Reverend
Clarence Dimwitty

Courteously he chats; amiably he nods;
benignly he smiles. His blandness neither
clashes nor contradicts. Untroubled by
doubt or faith, he performs his churchly
duties well enough and nicely for the nice
people— whom he attends and who pay well
enough for this ornament of their nice
establishment. He threatens none,
he challenges none, he rouses none. Nothing
unseemly— nothing more. World without end.
Amen.

FIGURE 4: The Rev. Clarence Dimwitty cartoon (1990).

STANDING IN THE PILLORY OF SPECIAL SINGULARITY

The ideal pastor Kierkegaard imagines for the church—as stated in his book on Adler[74]—is exactly the opposite of what many are looking for in the church today. For them Kierkegaard's plan is much too strident and ethereal or other-worldly. This is because they want something less demanding and less spiritual. They are looking for simple, practical pastors who know how to get more young people into church, bring

---

74. See Arbaugh and Arbaugh, *Kierkegaard's Authorship*, 230: "This largely unnoticed book . . . is actually the beginning point of a great new authorship. It laid the foundations for most of the great concepts which followed."

in more money, and make the church more respected in society.[75] Imagining that increased personal obedience and enhanced pastoral authority could accomplish this, seems absurd. And in one sense they are right, for the pastors Kierkegaard describes are not of their dreams. Their dreams, however, are not Christian, and so this incompatibility should be a warning to them rather than a falsification of what Kierkegaard proposes. Rather than longing for some sort of non-Kierkegaardian pastor, they should encourage pastors to fight for what is godly—but always with humility and dedication. Most, however, will not follow this advice because they are so wrapped up in the times.[76] And their times are like Kierkegaard's were. "In our age," he writes, "it is impressive when someone receives an enormously big package in the mail" (BA 147). And so if the church is full on Sunday mornings, they falsely suppose that the church is doing well. For indeed, "how undermined our age is in a religious sense— while busy people hold general assemblies about trivialities, and while the thunder of cannons summons to amusements" (BA 169). Because the times are like this, the new patch of Christianity cannot be sewn onto the old garment of the world (BA 166).[77] For the Christian faith is not compatible with worldly affairs—but turns its adherents into "aliens" who are only passing through this world (BA 141). This is because God's ways are so far above and beyond our ways (BA 33).[78] Therefore faith cannot be based on the probable and evidential. For it "always pertains to what is not seen,[79] be it the *invisible* or the *improbable*" (UDVS 235). Therefore we need pastors committed to the militant church rather than some sort of flabby triumphant one.[80] We need pastors

75. This violates Luther's dictum that "size does not make the church." Martin Luther, "Lectures on Genesis 6–14" (1545), LW 2:101. And Kierkegaard is in agreement: "There are insects which protect themselves against attackers by raising a cloud of dust; likewise 'man' instinctively protects himself against ideas and spirit by raising a cloud of numbers. Numbers are the opposite of idea and spirit" (JP 2:1940). Note further his concise summarization on the matter: "The numerical is the very thing which tramples upon the unconditioned" (JP 2:2046).

76. An excellent survey of these many mistaken dreams is Philip D. Kenneson and James L. Street, *Selling Out the Church: The Dangers of Church Marketing* (Nashville: Abingdon, 1997). Kenneson and Street show how these false dreams fall into twelve types: The Entrepreneurial Church, The Instrumental Church, The Relevant Church, The Self-interested Church, The Full-service Church, The Therapeutic Church, The Forgetful Church, The Ephemeral Church, The Engineered Church, The Homogeneous Church, The Pragmatic Church and the Christendom Church.

77. See Lk 5:36–37. On this passage Kierkegaard writes: "In human weakness, this is the proper motto for my life: No one puts a new patch on an old garment.—The opposite is the wisdom of the prudent, who therefore are on good terms with the present moment, that is, they place their little smidge of improvement directly upon the established order" (JP 6:6184).

78. See Is 55:8.

79. See Heb 11:1.

80. I think such pastoral flabbiness is what Kierkegaard is attacking in *The Book on Adler*. Therefore I disagree with Julia Watkins that his target is leaders more like the esoteric pastors: Jim Jones, David Koresh, and Sun Myung Moon. See her *Kierkegaard* (London and New York: Continuum, 1997), 88, 93.

who do far more than help people "dance their own dance [and] sing their own song . . . without fear."[81]

But too many today are blinded by worldly preconceptions, and so they do not see the light of the world when they look at Jesus.[82] Nor do they see the paschal lamb who was slain to save believers from the wrath of God.[83] Instead they only see the carpenter's son—having been blinded by "the god of this world."[84] Kierkegaard surprisingly says this is because Jesus does not appear as he truly is. He instead appears as untruth. For all true communication of the truth must necessarily start "with an untruth." This is because, in part,

> the true communication of truth is circumspectly aware of the contingency that it was indeed possible that the recipients were in untruth, in which contingency the direct communication of the true would become untruth . . . [So] in relation to the extraordinary, to begin with an untruth is unavoidable, it is dialectically intrinsic to the matter itself. If this untruth is not included, then the extraordinary does not remain the extraordinary; it is then taken in vain, becomes a direct superlative in relation to the universal. (BA 170)

Without this appearance of untruth, there could be no faith in Christ Jesus. All we would instead have are pearls thrown before swine.[85] For to believe "in the eminent sense corresponds quite rightly to the marvelous, the absurd, the improbable, that which is foolishness to the understanding" (BA 47). We should not then commandeer Christianity so that it might conform to "the glad gospel that is proclaimed on the dance floor of youth" (BA 141). We must instead take a risk and present it to the wayward world as "an ideality that otherwise did not exist for it," and so dangerously arrange for ourselves many who will gladly oppose us (BA 337). In that sense we must be willing to pick a fight with the world—if the church is ever to abide by its true message. We must be willing to stand "alone, abandoned, in the designated pillory of special singularity" (BA 161).[86] And this is bound to happen if we work diligently to describe, dispatch, and defend pastors clothed with the "full marching equipment of orthodoxy" (BA 93)—as Kierkegaard beckons us to do in his critique of Pastor Adler, the berserk vicar of Bornholm.

---

81. Henri J. M. Nouwen, *The Wounded Healer: Ministry in Contemporary Society* (New York: Double Day, 1972), 91–92. For another study in this soft mode, see Gordon W. Lathrop, *The Pastor: A Spirituality* (Minneapolis: Fortress, 2006), 119: "[Pastors should confess the sin of] pretense at authority in God's name."

82. Jn 8:12 (RSV).

83. 1 Cor 5:7; Jn 3:36 (RSV).

84. Mt 15:55; 2 Cor 4:4 (RSV).

85. Mt 7:6 (RSV).

86. See also Kierkegaard's dire warning: "Anything that is to become popular must tend toward extensiveness and multiplicity; the intensive never becomes popular" (JP 3:2994).

5

On Worship—Hanging on God's Hook

KIERKEGAARD HAS NOT BEEN widely regarded as an important resource for reflecting on what makes Christian worship right. I think this is because he is not trusted. Therefore he is not thought to be worth the intellectual effort that a study of his writings on worship requires. And he is not trusted because of his well known contempt for the institutional church—especially in Denmark.[1] This contempt even led to the sad end of his life when he "declined to receive the Sacrament from the hands of an employee of the state," and so he died "without the viaticum."[2]

Because of this distrust, all that is usually taken from his vast writings is a little analogy comparing worship to a theatre. With that analogy Kierkegaard makes the good point that a worshipper is not like a theatre-goer—but being more than part of some listening audience—is actually "the actor, who in the true sense is acting before God" (UDVS 125). This is a worthwhile analogy, but it does not capture the richness of Kierkegaard's overall thought on Christian worship.

I want to suggest in this chapter that a better place to start would be his parable on the worshipping geese in his journals (JP 3:3067). This parable shares the qualities of his best parables, standing as an "enduring literary gem [with] explosive multicolored bursts of moral and spiritual illumination on the darkened skies of modernity," offering most "intriguing puzzles that invite the ordinary reader's most

---

1. On this point see John W. Elrod, *Kierkegaard and Christendom* (Princeton: Princeton University Press, 1981), 200: "From Kierkegaard's perspective, Danish Christianity, and Protestantism in particular, had become a cultural sedative that tranquilized the pains of misfortune and the fear of death and legitimated the human quest for power, authority, and comfort. Kierkegaard found it difficult to avoid drawing the conclusion that Danish Christianity had fallen victim to the natural egotistic impulses of the self in the new liberal order."

2. Walter Lowrie, *Kierkegaard* (New York: Oxford, 1938), 584. For an elaboration of this dark episode, see Michael Plekon's encyclopedic study, "Kierkegaard and the Eucharist," *Studia Liturgica* 22 (1992), 214–36. Plekon reports that "on October 19, 1855, Kierkegaard was asked if he wished to receive communion from his life-long friend, Pastor Emil Boesen. This was during his final sickness at Frederiks Hospital. Kierkegaard replied that he did, but only from a lay person, not from a priest. Boesen said this could probably not happen. 'So I will die without it,' Kierkegaard answered, and he did, much to Boesen's regret'" (222). It is Plekon's considered judgment, however, that "while there are some serious problems regarding Kierkegaard's own ecclesial and liturgical participation in the last years of his life, . . . Kierkegaard never fully excommunicated himself. His Eucharistic fasting and ecclesial critique were parts of a self-imposed asceticism, as he prayed and worked for the Church's renewal. Kierkegaard's perspective remains ecclesial and Eucharistic" (230).

intense reflection and extended contemplation."[3] My reflection on this parable will try to understand both the parable and how it connects and contributes to current studies on what makes worship right.

I hope that this chapter will encourage people to join Dorothee Soelle who "fell in love with Søren, . . . I submerged myself," she writes, "in Kierkegaard. . . . [He] was neither a poet nor a philosopher; he was a preacher in a secularized society. . . . What Kierkegaard has brought out is the anxiety that is concealed in the word need. . . . Need for God is the greatest perfection of a human person. . . . God baits us with anxiety; . . . those who cannot get free of it even with the finest cleansing agents—they are hanging on God's hook."[4] What I hope to show here is that this hanging keeps Christian worship right.

I have divided Kierkegaard's parable, for the purpose of my analysis, into what I take to be its seven natural units, commenting on each of them in sequence.[5]

OUR REAL HOMES

Kierkegaard begins his parable in a quiet, calm, unassuming manner:

> Imagine that geese could talk—and that they had planned things in such a way that they, too, had their divine worship service.
> The gist of the sermon was as follows: What a high destiny geese have, to what a high goal the creator—and every time this word was mentioned the geese curtsied and the ganders bowed their heads—had appointed geese. With

---

3. *Parables of Kierkegaard*, ed. Thomas C. Oden (Princeton: Princeton University Press, 1978), xviii. Since in this parable geese talk, it might be more correct to call it a beast-fable than a parable. *The Concise Oxford Dictionary of Literary Terms*, ed. Chris Baldick (New York: Oxford University Press, 1990), 80, 159. For another use of the image of geese in worship, see C. Michael Hawn, "The Wild Goose Sings: Themes in the Worship and Music of the Iona Community," *Worship* 74 (November 2000): 504–21. This article, which studies a remote Scottish Christian community, ends with the warning: "Finally, be open to the Spirit of the Wild Goose in liturgy which may alight at any time in unexpected and disturbing ways." As for Kierkegaard's use of parables, note that he thought such figures of speech can move us "as if through a secret door, indeed, as if by a magic stroke of the sudden, from the most common everyday conceptions [to standing] in the middle of the loftiest conceptions, so that while talking about the simple everyday things one suddenly discovers that one is also talking about the very highest things" (UDVS 306). And this sudden shift he likened to an "earthquake" (UDVS 330), because when it occurs, we can find ourselves believing in what we thought before was only boring or silly, incoherent or false.

4. Dorothee Soelle, *The Window of Vulnerability*, trans. Linda M. Maloney (Minneapolis: Fortress, 1990), 117, 118, 120–21.

5. One might suppose that because Kierkegaard never wrote as extended a commentary as I have on his parable of the worshipping geese, that my commentary is out of line. But I actually see it as in keeping with the spirit of his more extended commentary on another one of his parables, that of the seduced lily, as I would call it (UDVS 167–71). Thomas Oden calls it "The Liberation of the Lily." *Parables of Kierkegaard*, 170. I prefer the word "seduction" over that of liberation because of the word "untruthfully" (UDVS 167), which Kierkegaard uses in it.

the help of their wings they could fly to distant regions, blessed regions, where they really had their homes, for here they were but aliens.

But as Kierkegaard goes on in this first section of his parable, we soon see that worship is marked by turmoil. For at worship we are told that we are aliens in this world.[6] Our real home is not here—as much as we may like it here. With this announcement turmoil begins, for many like it here. But we are not to be satisfied here. We are to see that our real home is far from here, and only there will we be truly blessed. This is the startling message worship brings. It is a challenge based on a demotion of the here and now. We are challenged to see some distant region as our true home, no longer settle in here, and learn to long for the blessings to come from far away.

M. Francis Mannion also believes this is worship's proper message, and knows that it is badly damaged when in our worship our "personal energy is focused on the relentless pursuit of selfish needs."[7] Mannion laments that many today are saying that if worship does not meet our personal needs, here and now, then it has gone wrong.

Michael B. Aune, however, cannot share in Mannion's lament. He believes Mannion's lament is "needlessly inflammatory."[8] Rather than fiercely debunking the pursuit of selfish needs, Aune would rather defend "a more participant-centered perspective on the hermeneutically perplexing question of worship's meaning and value to and for someone."[9] By so shifting away from Mannion's inflammatory attack, dwelling on ourselves in worship will look more positive. By so doing, we will then be able to honor "our meaning-making efforts [to] seek some kind of . . . connection and involvement with another."[10] Aune believes this shift will actually challenge us and "reorient" our lives.[11]

---

6. On this alienation see Ps 119:19; 1 Pt 2:11 and Phil 3:20.

7. M. Francis Mannion, "Liturgy and the Present Crisis of Culture," *Worship* 62 (March 1988): 103.

8. Michael B. Aune, "Worship in the Age of Subjectivism Revisited," *Worship* 65 (May 1991): 224.

9. Ibid., 229. Aune seems to have backed off from this position in his "Liturgy and Theology: Rethinking the Relationship," *Worship* 81 (January 2007): 64: "The triumph of concepts such as 'celebration,' 'freedom,' and 'creativity' can be the result of an understanding of liturgy gone awry. The loss of awareness of God's activity in our worship can lead to 'autocelebration'—the church worshipping itself."

10. Michael B. Aune, "Worship in the Age of Subjectivism Revisited," 234.

11. Ibid., 227. For a better sense of the reorientation worship is supposed to bring, see Stephen Platten, "The Uses of Liturgy: Worship Nourishing Mission," *Worship* 83 (May 2009): 248: "It is by the liturgy that the Christian is unselfed. In other words, central to the moral life is the life of prayer and worship; the liturgy stands at the very heart of Christian patterns of discipleship and mission. Prayer, contemplation and regular attendance at the Eucharist form our moral lives and we proclaim the gospel to others through the way we live, which has been fashioned by our worship." See also Crina Gschwandtner, "Toward a Ricoeurian Hermeneutic of Liturgy," *Worship* 86 (November 2012): 504: "Liturgy opens a world to us, which it calls us to enter and to inhabit. . . . Its appropriation includes moments of confirmation or concordance, but also *many* aspects that critique and challenge, that produce conflict and discordance" (italics added).

True reorientation, however, requires greater personal upheaval than Aune allows for. Gordon W. Lathrop proposes just such upheavals in worship. This happens, according to Lathrop, through shocking "juxtapositions," "powerful shifts," and "accurate misnamings," where strangely "names [in worship] are inappropriate and yet they are inappropriate in the right direction."[12] Under these powerful shifts, Jesus becomes the true vine, God is called rock, and God's people are deemed holy. In these accurate misnamings, "revelatory twists occur."[13] Each of these twists is based on what I have called a *demotion*. Herein lies the upheaval. The demotion says people are not as good as they think. We instead have sinned, fallen from glory, and need rescuing. Now Aune's critique of Mannion misses this demotion of ourselves and so cannot offer true human reorientation for us. Aune's "participation-centered perspective" is too complimentary of worshippers to demote them and thereby prepare them for true reorientation.

EACH ONE WADDLED HOME

Kierkegaard continues his parable with a turn for the worst:

> It was the same every Sunday. Thereafter the assemblage dispersed and each one waddled home to his family. And so to church again the next Sunday, and then home again— and that was the end of it. They flourished and grew fat, became plump and delicate—were eaten on St. Martin's Eve—and that was the end of it.

This shocks us twice by the way the geese worship. First they do not heed the message of worship. Instead of loosening their grip on this world by flying off to their true home, they sink deeper into the things of this world.[14] But then the second, greater

---

12. Gordon W. Lathrop, "A Rebirth of Images: On the Use of the Bible in Liturgy," *Worship* 58 (July 1984): 299. See also his "*Ordo* and Coyote: Further Reflection on Order, Disorder and Meaning in Christian Worship," *Worship* 80 (May 2006): 210: "At best, the center of the meeting can be continually eccentric, the one at the center of the meeting, [Jesus Christ], encountered in word and sacrament, being the very one who identifies with the . . . disordered . . . and poor, who shares all still-hidden trauma, outside of this meeting, and whose story entails this diverse, wounded earth as holy ground. Furthermore, at best, the Spirit enlivening the meeting can be the very Spirit poured out from the cross, en-spiriting an unlikely people and still blowing where it will in the world [Jn 3:8]."

13. Lathrop, "Rebirth of Images," 294.

14. On worship defeating itself, all by itself, see David B. Batchelder, "Holy God, Dangerous Liturgy: Preparing the Assembly for Transforming Encounter," *Worship* 79 (July 2005): 293, 294–95: "So much of what is offered in our churches is worship carrying enough of the culture's toxins that it is no longer capable of disclosing the perils of the individualistic and narcissistic self. Instead, such worship cultivates a stronger 'self' as it researches and caters to individual preferences and appetites. . . . One Labor Day weekend our family attended worship at a Presbyterian church outside Columbus, Ohio. The worship space was a beautifully renovated barn. The liturgy began with a small girl singing a tribute to her dog with a song entitled, 'Blue Skies.' We were treated to a creed-less, font-less, (and perhaps even water-less) baptism that appeared to be simply plopped into a *Christian variety show* that featured a Bette Midler imitation, Sister Act announcement skit with actors in complete habits,

shock settles in. This disobedience is covered up with the blessings of this life![15] Even though they do not heed the message of worship, they still flourish in this life. And this flourishing even becomes an end in itself. Even though this flourishing only prepares them for death, it remains free of all anxiety. And nothing is wanted at all beyond this flourishing. Death is not a threat, but only a simple and fitting end to all of life.[16]

Mannion would agree with Kierkegaard. There is a sinking deeper into the things of this world, for "the majority of Americans now assume a personal rather than a social or ecclesiastical source for their religious beliefs."[17] When our *source* is personal we cannot but repeat ourselves. And that would preclude reorientation.

Aune is not nearly so negative about having personal sources in worship. He would rather see in them ways of connecting with others at worship. Indeed these connections produce "shared appreciations . . . [which give] a sense of 'being on the same wave length,' belonging, and therefore of sharing identity."[18] This restored life is indeed *extra me*, or beyond myself. It does not, however, move me *extra nos*, or beyond the concerns of humanity altogether. Remaining bound to our human sources restricts the scope of the venture and disserves the new life worship is supposed to bring.

Lathrop also recognizes this need for sources that are *extra nos*. "The central image-rebirth present in the liturgy," he writes, is that "this crucified man, [Jesus Christ], among the crucified ones of the world, among the little and suffering one, is the source of life created new by God, is himself the eschatological *basileus*—giving that old idea a radically new content—and is himself the word that gives new order to our disordered world."[19] God in Christ is the source of the new life given in worship. Our personal sources cannot produce this because new order cannot come from our

---

and an inspirational testimony (as sermon) by a former professional football player. Far from being 'common worship,' or even 'corporate worship,' what we experienced was, at best, 'Guidepost' worship, a homebrew of song, laughter, sentimentalism, and inspiration intended to give listeners the 'uplift' necessary to sustain them through another week. Missing, however, was any sign of the reign of God."

15. On the demonic nature of such self-defenses, see Martin Luther, "Sermons on John 1–4" (1538), LW 22:395: "To sin and err because of human weakness is understandable, especially if one's faith is still feeble; but to condone and try to justify a fall and not to acknowledge it as such, but to claim that it is perfectly proper—that is devilish." Kierkegaard, who thought Luther was the master of us all (JP 3:2422, 2465), says something similar to this at the end of his authorship: "Christianity is lenient [but only] in the form of an admission!—it can spare the single individual much when he humbly admits his own condition. . . . But the secular mentality in us does not let us be satisfied with this; it is never satisfied before it has managed to establish the error, the impiety, as an article of faith, as duty, as dogma, as true Christianity—so that it can renounce true Christianity as impiety" (JFY 101–2).

16. This goes against 1 Cor 15:26 and Heb 2:15.

17. M. Francis Mannion, "Liturgy and the Present Crisis of Culture," 104.

18. Michael B. Aune, "Worship in the Age of Subjectivism Revisited," 231. In his later article, "Liturgy and Theology: Rethinking the Relationship (Part II)," *Worship* 81 (March 2007): 141–69, Aune seems to have moved away from this view when he argues that the church must not be construed as a mere "association of religiously interested individuals or a religious club" (154).

19. Lathrop, "Rebirth of Images," 302.

present disorder. So Aune's trust in human resources is wrong. Indeed, to be *in Christ* and have the new life Christianity brings, we must be *extra nos*. Even the joint efforts of like-minded people cannot generate the human reorientation that we need. Saint Paul was right that we must first die to ourselves if we are truly to live in Christ.[20]

A SHREWD MUTUAL UNDERSTANDING

Kierkegaard goes on with this ominous and devious warning:

> That was the end of it. Although the Sunday discourse was very lofty, on Monday the geese would tell each other what had happened to one goose who had wanted to make serious use of the wings given by the creator and intended for the high goal set before it—what happened to it, what horrors it had to endure. The geese had a shrewd mutual understanding about this. But of course, they did not talk about it on Sunday; that, after all, was not appropriate, for then, so they said, it would be obvious that our Sunday worship actually makes a fool of God and ourselves.

Such an unspoken rationalization for our worship empties worship. It flattens it. By so doing we then are able to live comfortably with our disobedience. We can continue to go to church without changing anything in our daily routine.[21] And note why this flattening is done. Through it we avoid suffering and the horrors obedience brings.[22] Therefore we maintain the niceties of our rituals provided that their inherent message is not allowed to cut into our daily lives. This is the deal—and it is shrewd.

20. See Rom 6:3–4. Early and late, Kierkegaard affirmed the same. In his early discourses he writes: "This woman was granted the grace to weep herself out of herself, as it were, and to weep herself into the peacefulness of love" (EUD 76). And towards the end he writes: "The way certainly can be narrow when you are still allowed to use all your powers to push your way through when the opposition is outside yourself; but when you must use your powers to work against yourself, then it seems infinitely too little to say that the way is narrow—it is, instead, impassable, blocked, impossible, insane! And yet it is this way of which it holds true that Christ is the way; this is precisely how it is narrow" (FSE 61).

21. On this need for change, Kierkegaard writes: "Christianity's idea was: to want to change everything. . . . Christianity aims at a person's total transformation and wants, through renunciation and self-denial, to wrest away from him all that, precisely that, to which he immediately clings, in which he immediately has life. . . . To become a Christian in the New Testament sense is such a radical change that, from a purely human point of view, one must say it is the heaviest sorrow for a family if one of its members becomes a Christian" (TM 185, 248).

22. On this suffering in worship, see Angela Ashwin, "Spirituality and Corporate Worship: Separate Worlds or Vitally Connected?" *Worship* 75 (March 2001): 127: "Worldly wisdom expects instant gratification, easy answers, the quick removal of pain, and absolute security. But Christian discipleship offers none of these things. Just as the inner life is sometimes a movement of sheer faith in the middle of darkness, we may also be asked to go through a kind of *via negativa* in our experience of worship. Perhaps we come with our own personal agony, or with a deep anxiety about a conflict in our congregation or neighborhood. Or there may be a crisis of confidence in the church because many are drifting away. In these circumstances our job is to remain with God in the darkness. Wondering why God seems to have abandoned us we lay on the altar the pain of it all, and throw ourselves utterly on God's mercy, since we have nothing left of our own to offer."

It enables us to worship and not to worship at the same time without letting this dishonesty make us anxious. This dishonesty does not produce any anxiety for us because if it were to do so, God would be made out to be a fool. But since such divine ridicule cannot be defended, our anxiety-free dishonesty is allowed to float free of any critical broadside.

Therefore when Aune tries to move the discussion in the direction of "how the liturgical event can actually become an event for us," he looks naïve.[23] By stressing the *pro nos*, he unwittingly opens the liturgical gates to selfishness. If I think worship needs to recognize me, then I will determine what it offers me. But with this concession the game is over.[24] Worship is flattened out for good. It now has been reduced to personal aggrandizement.

Because of our shrewdness, we cannot be trusted. So we either must admit with Lathrop that "the needs and hopes we, out of our need and out of our religious tradition, sing toward the expected God are not nearly enough, not right at all when they encounter the unexpected one and the unexpected event, the possibility of God and God's grace."[25] Saying that our measurement of our needs is not right at all is to wage war on ourselves.[26] If this is not done, then worship goes wrong. Therefore David N. Power does not exaggerate when he says that those who would do battle with our liturgical traditions, "wrestling with God as Jacob wrestled, so that only those who are wounded can give testimony to the existence of angels"—this battle shows that "there is an extraordinary power of revelation latent in [our] liturgical traditions." Admitting that our measurement of our needs in worship is not right, is to suffer such a liturgical wound. And being wounded in precisely this way, is what keeps our worship right.

Insisting on the importance of such battle wounds helps us see Michael Warren's truth that "worship is a zone of contestation that puts the question of credibility to the lived commitments of worshippers," which in turn produces a "struggle for greater coherence between worship and life structure."[27] So Aune's naïve *pro nos* cannot pass

23. Michael B. Aune, "Worship in the Age of Subjectivism Revisited," 228.

24. And so Kierkegaard would agree with Luther in his "Lectures on Isaiah 40–66" (1529), LW 17:324: "Praise and thanksgiving and sacrifice of praise are nothing else than minimizing our own selves and confessing the grace of God alone."

25. Lathrop, "Rebirth of Images," 294.

26. In an early discourse Kierkegaard put it this way: "Only in this way is the struggle the truth, . . . when the single individual fights for himself with himself within himself" (EUD 143).

27. Michael Warren, "The Worshipping Assembly: Possible Zone of Cultural Contestation," *Worship* 63 (January 1989), 9. On this being easier said than done, see David B. Batchelder, "Baptismal Renunciations: Making Promises We Do Not Intend to Keep," *Worship* 81 (September 2007), 411–12: "I worry that our communities have learned to practice a way of speaking ritually that not only permits false witness at the font, but establishes it as the norm. We make claims concerning sin and evil but often live as if we have not really considered the implications. Sometimes I wonder whether the church believes there are any serious implications at all. . . . I fear that we are acquiescing to the larger culture's new *technology of speech* where we convincingly say to ourselves and others what we know we do not mean and never intended to mean. I am concerned that we have claimed permission to speak a strong truth without the ethical obligation to live [out] the strength of it as suggested by the language.

for liturgical wisdom. Instead, Warren's contest and battle zone are better indicators of what will keep worship on track. This may leave some feeling unwelcome, but they will only be the disingenuous.[28]

WANTING TO FLY

Kierkegaard then adds this myopic twist:

> There were a few individual geese among them who looked poorly and grew thin. The other geese said among themselves: There you see what happens when you take seriously this business of wanting to fly, they get thin, do not prosper, do not have God's grace as we have it and therefore become plump, fat, and delicate, for by the grace of God one becomes plump, fat, and delicate.

Here we have suffering being used to discredit obedience. This ploy plays on our fear of the pain and loss that suffering brings. It also builds upon a skewed or distorted picture of grace. Properly understood, grace does not safeguard us from suffering. It rather plunges us into it.[29] But our shrewd understanding of grace will have nothing to do with this proper rendering. Therefore we debunk the seriousness of wanting to fly and discredit the longings to be faithful. Sadly all but a few are taken in by these maneuvers. Therefore, once again, as we saw earlier in this parable, anxiety is overcome. We do not worry over being more than we are—we give up all thought about being

---

In such a practice, the potency of the ritual speech itself is sufficient to excuse weak practice. Even more dangerous still, the speech is accepted as a substitute for practice."

28. On the legitimacy of confronting worshippers, see 1 Cor 14:23–25. Note also Kierkegaard's commitment to thinning out the church: "It is not my task . . . to create more nominal Christians or to contribute to strengthening millions in the notion that they are Christians. No, the task is precisely to shed light upon this scoundrel trick that to the benefit of the princes of the Church, of the pastors, of mediocrity, . . . has procured these millions. [So mine is] the thankless . . . task of relieving Christianity of some of those battalions of Christians . . . by jacking up the price or the requirement for being what they already think they are, the name of which they do not want to give up" (PV 125–26, 138).

29. On this cohesion of Christianity with suffering, see Lk 9:23; Jn 16:33; Rom 5:3–5; 2 Cor 10:3–6; and 1 Pt 2:21, 4:13. See also Kierkegaard's *The Gospel of Sufferings*—especially this passage: "In order to grasp the thought of suffering and the joyous gospel of suffering, in order to endure the suffering and actually have benefit from it, in order to be able to choose suffering and in order to believe that this actually is wisdom leading to eternal happiness, a human being needs divine guidance. It can never occur to the natural man to wish for suffering. The most profound change must first take place before a person can believe this secret of sufferings. He must first be gripped by and then be willing to learn from the only one who went out into the world with the purpose of willing to suffer, with the choice of willing to suffer and with instance upon it. He went out into the world, but he did not go out the way a youth goes out from his paternal home. He went out from the Father in Heaven; he relinquished the glory he had before the foundation of the world was laid—yes, his choice was eternally free, and he came into the world—in order to suffer" (UDVS 250).

changed into the likeness of Christ Jesus.[30] And because all but a few have gone down this road, mediocrity has its way.[31]

Suffering, therefore, must be vigorously reintroduced into worship. With Lathrop we must also say that "it is a biblical, liturgical goal to let lament into the center of our assemblies [for] strong images are images of lament, of longing for what is not and what we need to be."[32] Lament has this importance because "the images in the Scriptures . . . have arisen in their greatest strength . . . at times of greatest disappointment."[33] So the suffering in lament and disappointment is actually salutary for worship and not a wet blanket thrown on it. Mannion is therefore ingenious to propose that "the image of the church as a city seems . . . more adequate than the images of church as family or community of friends," for the image of the city inspires a commitment that "is shot through with the ethos of praise, thanksgiving, and sacrifice." Keeping worship cozy—in a club-like fashion, through superficially shared delights—kills true worship.

It is therefore anemic of Aune to argue that the manner in which we "acquire and learn" the language of worship is "affectively."[34] The more full-blooded answer would be through lament with its loss, anxiety and suffering. Insisting that the church is a city wherein sacrifice, thanksgiving and praise abide does more for worship than Aune's model of a community of friends who share common values. Aune again misses the assault to ourselves[35] that makes worship thrive—but which is inherent in Mannion's image of the church as a city.

30. 2 Cor 3: 18 (RSV).

31. On this plight of mediocrity in the church, Kierkegaard writes: "Here in this earthly life there is the confusion that the unrighteous one can have the appearance of being righteous. . . . Thus righteousness seems to have the same character as everything else earthly, to be only to a certain degree, so that just as beauty requires being neither too large nor too small, likewise righteousness is a kind of middle way, so that it must not be sought after immoderately, and therefore it is justified when (as a consequence of the world's mediocrity) suffering and the opposition of people become the lot of the one who wants only righteousness, who loves righteousness more than his life. But the truth and perfection of eternal life are eternally to show the difference between right and wrong with the rigorousness of eternity, scrupulous as only eternity is, with a majesty that to the earthly-minded must seem pettiness and eccentricity. In eternity, therefore, it will be easy enough to distinguish between right and wrong, but the point is that you are not to do this first in eternity; you will be judged in eternity as to whether you in your earthly life have done this as eternity wants to have it done" (CD 207).

32. Lathrop, "Rebirth of Images," 298–99.

33. Ibid., 297.

34. Michael B. Aune, "Worship in the Age of Subjectivism Revisited," 232.

35. On this assault, see Louis-Marie Chauvet, "Are the Words of the Liturgy Worn Out? What Diagnosis? What Pastoral Approach?" *Worship* 84 (January 2010): 28: "To make the [Sunday orations] one's own requires an inner work of grieving, letting go of a God who would come to do our own will, the opposite of what we say in the Lord's Prayer. This spiritual work of conversion, a working on our inner resistances, is not undertaken joyfully or willingly. In what concerns us here, we should not forget that the real difficulty might well be the call to conversion that is at the heart of the Gospel. The same holds true for the readings from Scripture." In this same regard note also Martin Luther, "Lectures on Isaiah 40–66 and 1–39" (1529), LW 17:73, 98; 16:160: "We cannot praise God. We are all irritated by the idea, because it means getting rid of all our own things. All would be glad to sing, but they will not permit the annihilation of their own works. . . . There cannot be our praise and God's praise at the same time. One of them must be put away. . . . Because of images and idolatry human

THE OLD GANDER PREACHED

Kierkegaard continues with a dark note of denial and obfuscation, underscoring how the momentum of habit keeps us from waking up to the truth of Christianity—even though we might describe it accurately in our worship life—since we never take it to heart:

> Next Sunday they went again to the worship services, and the old gander preached about the high goal to which the creator (here the geese curtsied and the ganders bowed their heads) had appointed geese and for which their wings were intended.

When the high goals of worship and the suffering they entail are set aside, survival and longevity take their place. The curtsy and bow remain, but the obedience and suffering they require are left behind. Therefore the aged are venerated and long retirements are seen as rewards well deserved and long anticipated. With this shift the sacrificial is left out. Rather than risking losing our lives at a young age in service to the truth of the Christian faith, we scramble in any way we can to save our lives for retirement.

Mannion also sees "the progressive appearance of a lack of dignity, seriousness, and reverence in liturgical celebration."[36] When Christian sacrifice and suffering no longer have a serious place in worship, reverence also goes quickly out the window too. Or in Don E. Salier's words, when "our repertoire of song is reduced to the pleasant, the comfortable, the domesticated and the immediately accessible, so far is the emotional power of common prayer diminished." And when "the words we speak are dull, banal, self-serving or unctuous, . . . the style of presiding and the modes of participation are utilitarian and perfunctory, so far is liturgy's power to awaken us to awe, wonder and joy diminished."[37]

Again we see that Aune cannot trust the liturgy in this way. For him it is an egregious error to assume that there is "something called 'liturgy' which somehow floats above the living lives of congregations," and which "exists apart from those who worship."[38] We may hope for such a powerful liturgy, but it is not real.[39] Simply sup-

---

thinking is perverted; it fashions a god for itself and does so according to its own whim and the suggestion of Satan. A knowledge of God is implanted in all men [Rom 1:20], and therefore they think that God is to be worshipped. In this they certainly make no mistake, but they err in the manner of their worship if they worship Him not simply according to His Word and will but rather according to their own ideas."

36. M. Francis Mannion, "Liturgy and the Present Crisis of Culture," 106.

37. Don E. Saliers, "Liturgy as Art," *Liturgy* 8 (Spring 1990): 11.

38. Michael B. Aune, "Worship in the Age of Subjectivism Revisited," 234, 235.

39. To the contrary, see Louis-Marie Chauvet, "Are the Words of the Liturgy Worn Out?" 29: "Liturgy is not fiction. It remains, however, no less true that we cannot minimize the importance of the discrepancy between the forms of expression of the Christian liturgy and that of ordinary life. This discrepancy is of the same order as that which exists between an ordinary room and a church, an

posing that the liturgy holds such an objective power over us is not enough to free us from that fearful, "mindless subjectivity" with its "monstrous self-absorption."[40] All that this hoping and dreaming does is lamentably thwart "the desire to find a self . . . rooted in our inherent sociability."[41]

But if the liturgy is not able to elicit reverence by way of its objective power over the subjectivity of the worshippers, then worship will not inspire sacrifice in our daily living either. Then we, like Kierkegaard's geese, will also waddle home from Sunday morning worship unchanged. We too will have missed what Lawrence H. Davis has called "the automatic transition from perception . . . of the divine exaltedness to realization of the propriety of self-subordination to the divine."[42] That simple point of propriety will then go begging. With its elimination, worshippers will be able forever to maintain their favored place of repose in worship, against which "finding a self," in Aune's terms, will lamentably bring about nothing of importance.

STAY RIGHT WHERE YOU ARE

At this point Kierkegaard starts drawing tightly the correlation between his imagined worshipping geese and what goes on in our churches on Sunday mornings:

> So also with Christendom's worship services. Man, too, has wings, he has imagination, intended to help him actually rise aloft. But we play, allow our imagination to amuse itself in a quiet hour of Sunday daydreaming, and otherwise stay right where we are—and on Monday regard it as proof of God's grace to get plump, fat, delicate, get layered with fat—that is, accumulate money, get to be somebody in the world, beget many children, be successful, etc. And those who actually become involved with God and who therefore are obliged to suffer, appear concerned, and have torments, troubles, and grief (it cannot be otherwise, nor is it, according to the New Testament)—of these we say: There is proof that they do not have the grace of God.

---

ordinary drinking glass and the Eucharistic cup, ordinary clothing and the liturgical vestment of the priest. Is not all liturgy based on such a gap?"

40. Michael B. Aune, "Worship in the Age of Subjectivism Revisited," 236.

41. Ibid. Against this disregard for an objective liturgy, see Gerhard O. Forde, "The 'Old Synod': A Search for Objectivity" in *Striving for Ministry*, ed. W. A. Quanbeck, et al (Minneapolis: Augsburg, 1977), 77–78: "There was . . . the joy of living in the light of the truth of what God had done through the Gospel. . . . The truth was that sinners were accepted in baptism and forgiven through the means of grace, and that was that. . . . The liturgy was chanted by the pastor and responded to with gusto by the people. They were concerned to worship the Lord 'in the beauty of holiness' [Ps 29:2] without a lot of fussiness. . . . The only emotions which were genuinely sanctioned were the serious sorrow of repentance for sin (noticeable especially at Holy Communion) and the joy of praise to God for his gracious acts."

42. Lawrence H. Davis, "The Importance of Reverence," *Faith and Philosophy* 7 (April 1990): 143.

Here Kierkegaard shows how disaster ensues when daydreaming replaces discipline. For then we stay stuck in the world. Worship's high calling of the new life in Christ is thrown out and replaced with sheer worldly amusement. This spares us from the attack leveled against us by the Christian message in worship—freeing us to measure our worth by enhanced material well-being. Having freed ourselves from this liturgical discipline, we are also in a better position to distort the Holy Scriptures at will. No longer do we hear God's word call us to self-denial and cross-bearing—for we are no longer gripped by the regimen of following Christ. We instead hold that God's grace is all that matters and that he rewards the easy-going with more and more worldly comfort. But all of this is a fraud. The painful biblical truth is exactly the other way around.

Craig Douglas Erickson also affirms the importance of existential discipline in Christian worship. He argues that "immediate effectiveness can often be a misleading criterion by which to gauge the degree of participation, [since] it may take several exposures to some dimension of worship before a person begins to appropriate some spiritual gain."[43] This point captures the simple truth, that is easily lost, that the failure to appreciate the liturgy is not a sufficient reason for changing it. Because the richness of the liturgy is well beyond any one's use of it, we must first be tutored by it through repeated exposures before we can venture a judgment over against it.

So subjectivity has a place in the individual's struggle to learn and love the truth in the liturgy. A new creation in Christ is born of this struggle, and so with Mannion we do not reject the "concerns for subjective experience and interiority, but [seek] a conceptual and practical restoration of the liturgy as the origin and context of authentic subjectivity and spirituality."[44] So Aune errs when he insists that we "turn our full attention to the doer of liturgical 'doing,'" since it is the worshipper who "comprises meaning."[45] This is wrong because then we become the source for our new life rather than just the location of where it takes place.

It is because of our sinfulness that we cannot also become the source of our restoration. Sin distorts us and creates a disaster of our lives which makes it impossible for us to become a source of our salvation.[46] So we stand with Robert W. Hovda who argues that "growing up is difficult [because] straining for the Holy Who remains

---

43. Craig Douglas Erickson, "Liturgical Participation and the Renewal of the Church," *Worship* 59 (May 1985): 234, 322.

44. M. Francis Mannion, "Liturgy and the Present Crisis of Culture," 120–21.

45. Michael B. Aune, "Worship in the Age of Subjectivism Revisited," 226. Again, Aune seems to have gone beyond this position in his later article, "Liturgy and Theology: Rethinking the Relationship," 64: "[There is a need in the liturgy] to transcend much of culture's subjectivism and individualism." Note also in his Part II to this article: "Work needs to continue toward greater clarity about what *theology* is. And once that occurs, then the subjective side of theology as 'recognition' or 'acknowledgment' can begin to be worked out more fully—how the Christian expresses his or her response to God's gracious self-communication in the conditions of earthly life and history *and* worship—made possible by the ongoing revelation and action of God" (157).

46. On this point see Job 14:4; Ps 49:7–9; Eccl 9:18; Rom 7:24; Jas 4:14; and 1 Pt 1:23–25.

beyond our reach is somehow less attractive than reducing the Holy to dimensions we can handle."[47] Against this shameful dodge we are called to struggle. But we cannot do this alone. The liturgy, with its lessons and prayers, confession and sermon, music and sacraments, is our chief source and ally. So again with Hovda we see that the liturgy "moves us to use our brains and activate our imaginations, if we work at it with love and with dissatisfaction; if we adapt the language of the readings, songs and prayers to be not only inclusive but incisive and compelling; and if we open up the symbolic action until the gestures and the acts have no need of 'explanation.'" Then the "traditional, classic, slowly-evolving-through-countless-generations-of-believers liturgy [will keep] undermining our foundations [and keep] washing away the sand on which our castles are built."[48] Because we remain sinners this undermining and washing away must go on and on if there ever is to be new life among us.

THIS IS DELIGHTFUL

Kierkegaard brings his parable to a close in utter despair:

> And if someone reads this, he will say: This is delightful—and that's the end of it. He will waddle home to his family, will remain or will strive with all his might to become plump, delicate, fat—but on Sunday that pastor will preach and he will listen—just exactly like the geese.

So even though we give up on the central message of worship, that does not stop us from practicing our Sunday morning rituals—and even finding delight in them. This turns worship into an empty shell, but one that we find to be attractive nevertheless. Maybe it is still attractive precisely because we have made it into an empty shell. Then worship means nothing—and requires nothing of us. Then attending Sunday morning worship is all a sham—delightful though it may be. Because of this demise we see all the more clearly how paramount the content of worship is to keep it on the right path. We must not try to make worship easier by reducing its content just so visitors will be more inclined to like it. The problem is not that people are too weak to worship.[49] No, they have plenty of strength—just look at the way they struggle, scrape, sacrifice and toil to get more and more material wealth. No, the problem is that we are dissipating our power on the wrong things. That is why worship takes us in a different direction—smashing those false gods and idols and calling us to praise and adore the one true God with all of our might.

Mannion also mourns this emptying out of worship. "The loss or rejection of the integrity of ritual traditions," he writes, "ultimately involves the loss of the means by which religious conceptions and motivations are mediated and maintained," and so

---

47. Robert W. Hovda, "Liturgy's Sine Qua Non: A Sense of the Holy," *Worship* 64 (July 1990): 352.

48. Robert W. Hovda, "The Relevance of the Liturgy," *Worship* 64 (September 1990): 450.

49. On our residual strength, see 1 Jn 5:3.

leads "finally to a reduction of the religious sense to humanistic philanthropy."[50] And it is an amazing fact of our present situation that not all lament this empty shell of worship. Aune, for instance, rejoices in this change, seeing in it a surer way to make "personal sense of" worship. In this "shift away from a preoccupation with ritual as representative or epiphanic of some object or event, toward a focus on this action and activity as a transaction of consequence," he sees a way clear for the worshipper to make the Sunday morning experience more meaningful.[51] Without this shift we will mistakenly continue to long "for some 'objectivity' which perhaps never existed in the first place."[52]

Aune's joy is breathtaking! But in his exuberance he forgets to show the implications in dropping such liturgical objectivity. Don Cupitt, however, does not. With brisk clarity he shows that "in order to be God, he must be bound to a worshipper or group of worshippers as their own religious ideal, the goal of their lives, that toward which all their strivings are directed," and as such, "God must be the religious ideal and cannot be an objective being."[53] This implication makes Aune's attack on liturgical objectivity perilous because it demeans the Holy One glorified in Christian worship. That is because without this objectivity God has no existence or contribution to make apart from within the confines of human subjectivity. This renders God anemic.

But in the very logic of the divine Trinity itself there is enough conceptual freight to offset Aune's analysis. So "if Hellenic deity," as Robert W. Jenson argues, "is turning time's still center, in which we may ground ourselves, [then] the triune deity envelops time by racing ahead of it, to prevent all stagnation in an achieved present."[54] If this is indeed the case, then the triune God of Christian worship is independent of our subjectivity precisely so the demonic stagnations of the worshipper may be broken

---

50. M. Francis Mannion, "Liturgy and the Present Crisis of Culture," 107.

51. Michael B. Aune, "Worship in the Age of Subjectivism Revisited," 233.

52. Ibid., 238.

53. Don Cupitt, *Only Human* (London: SCM, 1985), 210. For a further elaboration on the logic of subjectivity, see Lewis S. Ford, "The Revised Subjectivist Principle Revisited," *Process Studies* 19 (Spring 1990), 28–48. Even though this is an exposition of the philosophy of Alfred North Whitehead (1886–1943), what Ford has to say extends beyond his primary focus. Aune, for instance, would do well to ponder this warning: "If all unification is subjective, then there can be no unified being somehow underlying the concrescent activity" (42), which is required by the unification itself. Kierkegaard holds a similar view—which surprises those who think he is the king of subjectivity. "The essentially Christian," he writes, "exists before any Christian exists; it must in order for one to become a Christian. It contains the qualification by which a test is made of whether someone has become a Christian; it maintains its objective continuance outside all believers, while it also is in the inwardness of the believer. In short, here there is no identity between the subjective and objective. . . . It is therefore a volatilization of the concept, a dislocation of all the essentially Christian, when one admits the wordplay that a revelation is a qualification belonging to subjectivity" (BA 117–18). See also Louis P. Pojman, *The Logic of Subjectivity: Kierkegaard's Philosophy of Religion* (Birmingham, Alabama: The University of Alabama Press, 1984), 144, 66: "Subjectivity, in a dialectical sense, is both truth and untruth [for Kierkegaard], but no substitute for objective, eternal truth. . . . The important thing in subjectivity is *appropriation*, the resolution and integration of an idea in one's life."

54. Robert W. Jenson, "The Logic of the Doctrine of the Trinity," *Dialog* 26 (Fall 1987): 247.

apart, and new life may arise. And only a God with power like this can save us. This is something a religious ideal, masquerading as God and without any salutary objectivity or arresting epiphany, could never do. But if God cannot save us from our stagnations, then our worship has been eviscerated. No anxiety for our sins remains. Reverence for God is gone. And worship has no impact on our daily lives after we've kept the Sabbath day holy. Without this power to bring us into a closer alignment with God, worship is only a vacuous delight at best.

IN THESE DESPERATE TIMES

What then shall we say is the overall impact of this gripping parable by Kierkegaard? Does it provide some profound truth to guide our worship life so that we may grow in faith and grace? Or must we say that all of the criticisms leveled against current liturgical trends in this analysis of Kierkegaard's parable have been made in vain?

I think that this parable is actually a theological gem and holds great promise for renewing Christian worship. In 1850 Kierkegaard wrote in his journal that he "must always stand outside as a superfluity and an impractical exaggeration," because the "conditions are still far from being confused enough for proper use to be made" of him, but that it will "all end . . . with conditions getting so desperate that they must make use of desperate people like" him (JP 6:6709a). In my judgment the times are now ripe for proper use to be made of Kierkegaard's parable on the worshipping geese.

But is there any corroborating evidence for my judgment? Thomas G. Long seems to offer some in an editorial for *Theology Today*, wherein he writes:

> Not long ago a minister, recently retired, decided to take advantage of his new Sunday freedom by sampling the worship in other parishes. Traveling around the country in his motor home, he dropped in on churches large and small, high and low, urban and rural. He visited congregations of many denominations and of a variety of ethnic compositions. He came away from his journeys shaken and discouraged over the state of worship in the church. There was the occasional liturgical oasis, of course, but mainly he wandered in dry and waterless places. Sermons, he reported, were mostly either rambling and ill-prepared lectures or frothy chants of pious positive thinking; prayers were often uttered without theological thought or a trace of sensitivity to language. Frequently the whole of worship was conducted with a bland nonchalance. Even in those settings where there was some sign of electricity and energy in worship, it often tended to be frenetic, disconnected from thought or substance. In sanctuary after sanctuary, he claimed to have slogged through a miry bog of liturgical distress.[55]

55. Thomas G. Long, "Liturgical Storm Clouds," *Theology Today* 68 (April 1991): 1. See also Thomas Day, *Why Catholics Can't Sing: The Culture of Catholicism and the Triumph of Bad Taste* (New York: Crossroads, 1992); D. G. Hart, *The Lost Soul of American Protestantism* (Lanham, Maryland: Rowman & Littlefield, 2002); Terry W. York, *America's Worship Wars* (Peabody, Maine: Hendrickson, 2003).

Kierkegaard would not be surprised in the least by these words. He would take them as confirmation of the desperate times he forecast.

And in addition to Long's gloomy findings, there are many other examples of our need for Kierkegaard's parable of the worshipping geese. The six I list here do their part in making Christian worship a "dry and waterless" place, as Long puts it. So we are told, in our first case, that the "prophetic monotheism" inherent in Christianity dictates that Christianity allows for it being "constructed by each believer."[56] And secondly we are told that "to call Jesus God . . . is misused when it is treated as a literal proposition."[57] Thirdly we are told that "Jesus was not an acceptable sacrifice for the sins of the whole world, because God does not need to be appeased and demands not sacrifice but justice."[58] Fourthly we are told that "using the Father/Son metaphor in the [baptismal] formula is not adequate to the task of summarizing Christina faith."[59] In a fifth case we are told that "the people themselves," rather than "where the sacrament of the Lord's Supper is consecrated," is a "better reminder of where God's presence is to be felt," since otherwise "other common experiences" with God would unjustifiably be deemed "less important."[60] And in my final example we are told that "the work of salvation is . . . the address not to a sinner but to the beloved; it assumes that the beloved is not evil but is loving wrongly."[61]

Kieran Flanagan has rightly exalted the Christian liturgy by arguing that "liturgical orders have a certain foolishness about them [in that] they invert 'correct' procedures; they dignify the slight; and brazenly bear witness to improbable messages."[62] Because of that, the liturgy has the power to stand against the half dozen aberrant proposals I have just listed above. Reasonable though they may appear to be to the worldly wise, the liturgy counters or inverts their varied points and puts in their place the ancient way of the Church. Because Kierkegaard's parable of the worshipping geese reinforces that ancient way, it is of great value in our time of liturgical distress.

As such it would be in good order to include Kierkegaard's parable as part of the catechesis of the Church—whereby the faithful work to reverse all that has gone astray in our Sunday morning worship. And under the tutelage of this parable let us hope and pray that the Church may once again sing with conviction and joy the holy words of God:

56. Scott Cowdell, *Atheist Priest? Con Cupitt and Christianity* (London: SCM, 1988), 84, 61.

57. John Hick, *The Second Christianity* (London: SCM, 1983), 32.

58. *Christianity, Patriarchy and Abuse*, ed. Joanne Carlson Brown and Carole R. Bohn (New York: Pilgrim, 1989), 27. I have also argued against this position in my "Preaching Against the Cross," *Lutheran Partners* 19 (September/October 2003): 24–29.

59. Ruth C. Duck, *Gender and the Name of God: The Trinitarian Baptismal Formula* (New York: Pilgrim, 1991), 5.

60. David Luecke, *Evangelical Style and Lutheran Substance* (Saint Louis: Concordia, 1988), 108.

61. Sallie McFague: *Models of God* (Philadelphia: Fortress, 1987), 144.

62. Kieran Flanagan, "Ritual Form," *Modern Theology* 2 (July 1986): 357.

The Lord reigns;
let the peoples tremble!
He sits enthroned upon the cherubim;
let the earth quake!
The Lord is great in Zion;
he is exalted over all the peoples.
Let them praise his great and terrible name!
Holy is he![63]

63. Ps 99:1–3 (RSV).

6

On Discipleship

KIERKEGAARD'S PARABLE OF THE royal coachman,[1] from his book *For Self-Examination*, was printed in the bulletin for the funeral of Edna H. Hong at Saint John's Lutheran Church in Northfield, Minnesota. This was because her family believed it showed "what was essential in her" as a Christian disciple and translator of Søren Kierkegaard's writings. The bulletin goes on to say that she

> first learned the discipline of the royal coachman, of the Lord Jesus Christ, in the home of her parents, Otto and Ida Hatlestad, and at Our Saviour's Lutheran Church in Taylor County, Wisconsin, and submitted to it for the rest of her life.[2]

In this chapter I want to honor the life and work of Edna Hong by analyzing this parable and the discipline which it champions.[3] I will do this by first laying out what Kierkegaard's parable says and then by showing how it can correct and enhance the way the Bible, baptism and hymn-singing are practiced in the church today. Using this parable to reform the church today is also a fitting tribute to Edna Hong. For in her 1992 lament over the Evangelical Lutheran Church in America (ELCA) she writes:

> May a grown-up daughter who loves her mother very much be permitted to share some concerns with her siblings, all children of the same Mother— namely, Mother Church, or more specifically, the . . . ELCA? . . . [Now] the doctrines that Mother Church teaches us are correct, . . . but where is what Kierkegaard calls "the existential"—*the existence*, the urgent call to *exist* in

---

1. In the *Parables of Kierkegaard*, ed. Thomas C. Oden (Princeton, NJ: Princeton University Press, 1978), this parable is called "The Rigorous Coachman: Of What is the Human Spirit Capable?" (59–60). And in *Kierkegaard the Christian: An Anthology of Quotations*, ed. Robert B. Scheidt (Enumclaw, Washington: WinePress, 2003), it is called "The Rich Man and His Team of Horses" (260). For a similar parable from the one whom Kierkegaard called "the master of us all" (JP, 3:2465), see Martin Luther, "The Bondage of the Will" (1525), LW 33:65–66: "The human will is placed between the two, . . . the god of this world . . . [and the] Spirit of the true God, . . . like a beast of burden. If God rides it, it wills and goes where God wills. . . . If Satan rides it, it wills and goes where Satan wills; nor can it choose to run to either of the two riders, . . . but the riders themselves contend for the possession and control of it."

2. This portion of the bulletin was reprinted in "Edna Hatlestad Hong, 1913–2007," *Søren Kierkegaard Newsletter* 51 (April 2007): 2–3.

3. For my other tribute to Edna H. Hong, see my poem, "The Thorough Kneading of Reflection," in the conclusion of this book.

the truths that are so rightly taught? . . . The Word of God comes through strongly in all its truth and purity from Mother Church until Pentecost, but in the long, long season that follows Pentecost, the Word of Response, the Word that calls me to the response in my existential life, my daily existence, calls me to respond in gratitude for the wonder of that grace—that Word from Mother Church has become weak and wobbly. Mother Church . . . seems to have become very unsure about . . . how to become the saints God has made us in Christ . . . Its task [should be] to teach you and me, who live in a world sapped of Christians ideals—indeed, mocks them—to believe in them, honor them, love them, teach them to our children. . . . Has Mother Church forgotten that Jesus Christ, who forgave without limit, also said, "Go and sin no more"?[4]

What I want to do in this chapter is use Kierkegaard's parable of the royal coachman to fight against this weak and wobbly practice Edna Hong identifies in the church today.[5] By so doing, I will further what she stood for—and by God's help—glorify the Holy Trinity she strove to serve all of her days.

KIERKEGAARD'S PARABLE

Kierkegaard's parable of the royal coachman is about the success, failure, and restored success of "a team of entirely flawless, splendid horses" (FSE 85–87). This beautiful team of horses—which stands for humanity—is purchased by a rich man for an exorbitant price. He buys them so he can enjoy their power and glory on a daily basis. But because of his preoccupation with their performance, he no longer runs them through the training regimen that made them the great team of horses they were in the first place. After a year or two of this luxurious living, they begin to wane and deteriorate in strength and performance. Their eyes become dull and drowsy and their gait lacks style and precision. They have no staying power. They even take on all sorts of quirks and bad habits.

In order to stop this downward spiral, the rich man hires a royal coachman to take over the care and keeping of his horses. And in just a month, the team turns around and regains its former glory. Once again their eyes are fiery and their gait beautiful. They can even now run for thirty miles in a stretch without stopping. Kierkegaard ends his parable with a question and an answer:

> How did this happen? It is easy to see: the owner, who without being a coachman meddled with being a coachman, drove the horses according to the

4. Edna H. Hong, "A Daughter's Lament," *FOCL Point: Quarterly Newsletter for the Fellowship of Confessional Lutherans*, 2 (Spring 1992), 1–2.

5. In this lament Edna Hong assumes that the church's teachings are secure. But with the advent of revisionists like John Shelby Spong, the situation has become even more grim with the teachings being undercut as well. *A New Christianity For a New World: Why Traditional Faith is Dying & How a New Faith is Being Born* (New York: HarperCollins, 2001).

horses' understanding of what it is to drive; the royal coachman drove them according to the coachman's understanding of what it is to drive. (FSE 85–86)

The fate of this team of horses mirrors exactly the human predicament. Kierkegaard therefore says that when he thinks of himself and the countless people he knows it looks like "the coachman is lacking." For generations, he says, we have been living according to our own wishes—without a royal coachman to train us. As a result we have become mediocre—being overly easy on ourselves.[6] We demand too little of ourselves. Because of this, we lack "elevation over the world" (FSE 87)[7] and

> it follows from this in turn that we are able to endure very little; we are impatient and promptly use the means of the moment and impatiently want to see instantly the reward for our work, which for that very reason is not very good. (FSE 86)

According to Kierkegaard, Christians have been taking poor care of themselves for a long time. We have been allowing ourselves to languish in the name of comfort and ease—expecting little of ourselves and idling our time away. This is the "stinging rebuke" Kierkegaard levels against modern Christian life.[8]

In the face of this turpitude, Kierkegaard says it does not have to be this way. At the time of the apostles, and shortly thereafter, it pleased the Deity himself to be our coachman. Because of that, he sings, "Oh, what a human being was capable of then!" Then we were able to proclaim and follow a word that aroused the hatred of the whole world against us.[9] This was because, as Edna Hong writes, "the spirit of truth does not seek comfort," but rather the "bath of self-severity."[10] And that severity is built upon "dying to the world, voluntary renunciation, crucifying the flesh [and] suffering for the doctrine" (JP 6:6947). This is what is required of us if we are to live according to the will of the royal coachman and not according to our own will.

DRIVEN BY GOD

This severity, coming from being driven by God to greater heights, runs throughout Kierkegaard's writings. His goal in those writings was to describe and further a "non-conformity . . . against churchly friendship with the world."[11] He wrote that the

---

6. This goes against Phil 4:8; 1 Cor 9:24–27.

7. This denial goes against Jn 15:18–19; Rom 12:2; 2 Cor 4:4; Gal 6:14; Col 3:2–3; 1 Jn 2:15, 5:4–5; Jas 1:27, 4:4.

8. C. Stephen Evans, *Kierkegaard on Faith and the Self* (Waco, Texas: Baylor University Press, 2006), 26.

9. See Jn 15:19: "If you were of the world, the world would love its own; but because you are not of the world, but I chose you out of the world, therefore the world hates you" (RVS).

10. Edna H. Hong, *The Downward Ascent* (Minneapolis: Augsburg, 1979), 70.

11. Vernard Eller, *Kierkegaard and Radical Discipleship* (Princeton: Princeton University Press, 1968), 33.

Christian is not "spiritlessly to prize the cozy and easygoing days of his life," but is to fight the good fight of faith in "danger and terror" (EUD 346).[12] This theme of struggle and severity extends into his last writings. Just a few weeks before his untimely death he wrote that Christianity is about dying in earnest "to the world, hating oneself, [and] suffering for the doctrine," so much so that life becomes "so difficult, yes, so agonizing" that even the toughest ones almost droop under these difficulties, writhe like worms, and even the most humble ones are "not far from despairing" (TM 319).

But this is what it takes if we are going to be ambassadors for Christ—having been changed into his likeness by his Spirit.[13] For indeed "the cross of suffering ennobles a person more than anything else" (EUD 305).[14] And that suffering is primarily manifest in "the colossal point of contention" between the love of God and the hatred of the world, for "the love of God is hatred of the world." And this "most terrible struggle . . . must be fought" nowhere else but "in a person's innermost being" (UDVS 205).[15] In all this suffering, struggling and severity, God is the educator—molding us into his disciples—just like those horses in Kierkegaard's parable are trained to run with power and precision. Therefore Edna Hong says we should pray:

> Father, . . . we pray that you not be gentle with us. Please send your Holy Prodder and have him push, shove, and pummel us onto Christ's new way, Christ's highway of living and loving and forgiving. In his name. Amen.[16]

Because the end is glorious, though the way is rugged, we need to pray this prayer. That is because we resist becoming what God would have us be.[17] So we must fight against ourselves with prayers like this. We resist God's training by clutching tightly to our own wills. So as our educator, God's concern for us is the

---

12. 1 Tm 6:12 (RSV).

13. 2 Cor 5:20, 3:18 (RSV).

14. Kierkegaard hastens to add that we should not demand the sufferer "to speak enthusiastically" of this benefit "too early, lest the believer's zealous words discourage us because this does not occur immediately" (EUD 305).

15. On this internal struggle see Mt 26:39: "Not as I will, but as thou wilt" (RSV). Kierkegaard thought this internal shift away from one's will to God's will resembled vivisection. On this existential fright, Kierkegaard writes: "A Christian is a man of will who no longer wills his own will but with the passion of his crushed will—radically changed—wills another's will [which is God's will]" (JP 6:6966). This journal entry from his last few weeks on earth could serve as a preamble to this parable of the royal coachman. On the "profound difference" in the shift from our will to God's will, see Clare Carlisle, *Kierkegaard's Philosophy of Becoming: Movements and Positions* (Albany: State University of New York Press, 2005), 114.

16. Edna H. Hong, *Forgiveness is a Work as Well as a Grace* (Minneapolis: Augsburg, 1984), 22.

17. This penchant for resistance may be a reason why Kierkegaard used the literary genre of the parable or metaphor. On this see Jamie Lorentzen, *Kierkegaard's Metaphors* (Macon, Georgia: Mercer University Press, 2001), 18: "It seems natural for readers to defend themselves from themselves with abstractions when envisioning the terrifying gap that metaphor cuts between what *is* and what *ought to be*" (emphasis in original).

greatest leniency and the greatest rigorousness. It is just as in nature, where heaviness is also lightness. The heavenly body soars lightly in the infinite—by gravity. But if it gets off its course, if it becomes much too light, then the lightness becomes heaviness, and it falls heavily—by lightness. In the same way God's rigorousness is leniency in the loving and the humble, but in the hardhearted his leniency is rigorousness. (WL 377)

Denying this divine adaptability gets us off the hook. If we insist that God's love toward us must always be lenient—even when we are hard-hearted—then we obstruct God's love which comes to drive us, push us, and force us back into faithfulness when we have gone astray. In these admonitions Kierkegaard echoes Saint Paul's words:

Put off your old nature . . . corrupted by deceitful lusts. . . .

Be renewed in the spirit of your minds. . . .

Be imitators of God. . . .

Let there be no filthiness, nor silly talk among you. . . .

Let no one deceive you with empty words. . . .

Learn what is pleasing to the Lord. . . .

Look carefully how you walk . . .

Do not be foolish but understand the will of the Lord . . .

Do not get drunk with wine for that is debauchery . . .

Give thanks always and for everything . . .

Put on the whole armor of God that you might stand . . .

Pray at all times in the Spirit. . . .[18]

It is this biblical rigorousness that Kierkegaard prizes and promotes. This is because through it God drives us to greater discipleship. But because we are slaves to sin,[19] we resist and defy God's care for us. We twist out of shape the word he has given us to train us.[20] But in Kierkegaard's writings we find resources for fighting against our resistance. Taking his parable of the royal coachman as our guide, we can then see in his other writings how, for instance, the Bible, along with baptism and hymnody, are ways God drives us to greater heights and more faithful or earnest discipleship. But even at these greater heights, all will still not go swimmingly for us. That is because

terror is the first aspect of the upbuilding from the perspective of the recipient because the upbuilding will treat him as sick, in spite of his (false) understanding of himself as healthy. To be upbuilt is at first to have one's self revealed in a new and unpleasant way.[21]

18. Ephesians 4:22, 23, 5:1, 4, 6, 10, 15, 17, 18, 20, 6:11, 18.

19. Jn 8:34 (RSV).

20. 2 Cor 4:2 (RSV).

21. Pia Søltoft, "To Let Oneself Be Upbuilt," *Kierkegaard Studies: Yearbook* 2000, eds. Niels Jørgen Cappelørn, Hermann Deuser and Jon Stewart (Berlin: Walter de Gruyter, 2000), 29.

We learn that our resistance to God's rigorousness makes us sick—and that this very sickness must itself be opposed. This diagnosis disorients and terrifies us. But if we can endure the treatment, spiritual health will come in some measure at the end.

In what follows I want to show how this treatment and ensuing health are manifest in the proper understanding of the Bible, baptism and hymn-singing. I believe that an analysis of these three topics helps to show how Kierkegaard's parable of the royal coachman is a powerful source for reforming the church today.

GOD'S HOLY WORD

Regarding Holy Scriptures, it is a mistake to suppose that Kierkegaard was "a champion of liberalism and postmodernism."[22] Therefore it would be wrong to suppose that he saw the Bible as a collection of puzzling metaphors to be interpreted imaginatively for our edification. As an orthodox Christian[23] he rather stressed the authorship of the Bible over its content and the interpretation of it. He believed that if we are driven to interpret the Bible, we then will never get to "the point of obeying" what the Bible commands—as he thought we must. And if the "main thing is the content of the teaching" of the Bible, and how to interpret it, then we will never be humbled by the "divine authority" of the Bible. When we skip over the divine authority of the Bible, "Scripture is treated so scientifically that it could just as well be by anonymities" (BA 34–35). Facing these matters about the Bible places the Christian squarely at the crossroads:

> Whether he will let go of what he learned first, chop down the bridge, and hold to what he learned later, or whether he will go back to his childhood and learn in reverse, because as a child he learned from adults, and now he himself as an adult is to learn from a child, learn from his childhood. . . . [If he were to learn in reverse, he would then be] in harmony with a strict Christian upbringing, with the Bible in hand. (BA 94–95)

Learning in reverse,[24] getting the Bible back in hand, and keeping the bridge up to our childhood training—all these restore the authority of Holy Scriptures.[25] And

22. David E. Mercer, *Kierkegaard's Living-Room* (Montreal & Kingston: McGill-Queen's University Press, 2001), 4.

23. On the orthodoxy of Lutheranism, see the introduction to the Lutheran Confessions, BC 3: "[Lutherans follow] the ancient consensus which the universal and *orthodox* church of Christ has believed, fought for against many heresies and errors, and repeatedly affirmed" (emphasis added).

24. For a contemporary example of this "learning in reverse," see R. R. Reno, *In the Ruins of the Church: Sustaining Faith in an Age of Diminished Christianity* (Grand Rapids: Brazos, 2002), 96: "If we are willing to accept the painfully unsophisticated tasks of spiritual childhood—to memorize the catechism as we once memorized multiplication tables, to hear with rapturous joy the literal sense of Scripture as we once listened to stories read at nighttime, to repeat again and again the ancient liturgies as we once repeated our favorite TV shows, word for word—then we will find our way toward a theological vocation proper to those who live in the ruins of the church."

25. And this orthodox view does not go uncontested. For a prominent critique of it, see B. A.

Kierkegaard could well have learned this from Luther, who taught the same. Luther wrote that it is "the will of the Father . . . that we listen to His Word." And he goes on to say:

> You must not cavil at His Word, find fault with it, and dispute it. Just hear it. Then the Holy Spirit will come and prepare your heart, that you may sincerely believe the preaching of the divine Word, even give up your life for it, and say: "This is God's Word and the pure truth." But if you insist that you be heard, that your reason interpret Christ's Word; if you presume to play master of the Word, to propound other doctrines; if you probe it, measure it, and twist the words to read as you want them to, brood over them, hesitate, doubt, and then judge them according to your reason—that is not hearing the Word or being a pupil. Then you are setting yourself up as its schoolmaster. In that way you will never discover the meaning of Christ's Word or of His heavenly Father's will.[26]

In full agreement with Luther, Kierkegaard says "*pereat* the commentators," that is, let them perish (JP 1:211). For they keep us from reading the Bible in a "primitive way" (JP 1:216), which is the way of obedience—something which research into the meaning of the Bible never upholds (JP 3:3021). Research thus is "hazardous" because by keeping us from following God's "will and wishes," the "vividly present" message of the Bible is lost (JP 1:210). Critical studies of Scripture discourage us from taking the Bible as we should. They block us from simply believing in it—"just as it is" (JP 3:2888). For such simple obedience is all that can open up the Bible for us.[27] All that "interpreting and scholarliness" does is soften the impact of God's word on us. In the "most cunning way," it removes God's word as far as possible from us, "infinitely further than it is from one who never saw God's Word, infinitely further than it is from one who became so anxious and afraid of God's Word that he cast it as far away as possible." So in this way scholarly research resembles the napkins a naughty boy puts "under his pants" before he gets his licking, to keep it from stinging him (FSE 35). But then the word of God is wasted—just as the spanking was on the bad boy. As a result we are not corrected and formed into a new and better person[28]—and so our discipleship wobbles and weakens. This is a travesty for Christians, because then we separate ourselves from Jesus Christ, "who for the joy that was set before him,

---

Gerrish, *Continuing the Reformation* (Chicago: University of Chicago Press, 1993), 55: "Luther's biblical theology was at the same time a theology of experience, and this is what justifies the *liberal* Protestant appeal to him" (emphasis added).

26. Martin Luther, "Sermons on John 6–8" (1531), LW 23:229.

27. This is how the Bible sees itself. For example, when Jas 2:23 quotes Gen 15:6 it only says, "The scripture was fulfilled which *says*, 'Abraham believed God, and it was reckoned to him as righteousness'" (emphasis added). Twenty more examples of such unencumbered citations—without any literary or historical analysis—are Lk 20:42; Acts 2:25, 34, 7:48–49, 13:35; Rom 9:15, 17, 25, 10:11, 16, 19, 21, 11:2, 9, 12:19; 14:11, 15:12; 1 Tm 5:18; Heb 5:6 and Jas 5:5–6.

28. See 2 Tm 1:7, 2:19, 3:5, 16.

endured the cross."[29] Looking into the mirror of God's word is a cross for us. When we do, our waywardness is condemned. And we need just this condemnation if we are to walk in newness of life—just like those horses in Kierkegaard's parable needed to be pushed if they were going to excel. And because the scholarly approach to the Bible thwarts this newness, it must be condemned and abandoned. Edna Hong therefore says we should pray:

> Our Father, we do not need a big dictionary and a dozen commentaries to understand your Word. Nor do you ask us to be interpreters. You desire only belief and obedience. . . . [Therefore] send us your Divine Firebrand to spark us! Kindle in us belief in your promises! Ignite us to action! In your Son's name. Amen.[30]

Rather than a scholarly approach to the Bible, wherein one regards the Bible as a literary object to be critically evaluated (FSE 33), Kierkegaard instead argued for a devotional approach to Holy Scriptures. For the Bible must not be read "calmly and coolly as you read newspaper advertising." One should instead let it "take hold" so that one no longer can defend oneself "against it" (FSE 32, 36). This approach will no doubt make us feel "awkward" (FSE 32) because it will lead us to "surrender" before God's word—without qualification (JP 2:1408). This is necessary if we are to make "the transition to the subjective," whereby we "incessantly" say, when reading the Bible, "it is I to whom it is speaking" (FSE 38, 40). It is just at this subjective turn that the Bible becomes the very "voice of God" for us (FSE 39). At just this point the Bible comes into its own—no longer being some "obsolete ancient book" with no binding power over us (FSE 33). Now the Bible becomes an "extremely dangerous book." For if one "gives it a finger, it takes the whole hand; if one gives it the whole hand, it takes the whole man and may suddenly and radically change my whole life on a prodigious scale" (FSE 31). This is because the Bible attacks us, thundering that the world is not a "lovely" place of prosperity, but "a lie and sin and a vale of tears" (JP 2:1439). When this negativity takes hold we are changed on a most prodigious scale. But this change is not depressing. For we see it as "superior to any human levelheadness." In it we see

> not an arid storm cloud that passes over and throws everything into disorder but an anxiety that clears the air and makes everyone gentler and more deeply inward, more loving and swifter to buy the opportune time, but also strong enough not to be exhausted by the thought that the hour of opportunity is past. (EUD 70)

The deepening that this devotional approach brings is born in obedience to the word of God and leads necessarily—to silence.

29. Heb 12:2 (RSV).
30. Edna H. Hong, *Forgiveness is a Work as Well as a Grace*, 50.

Obedience does not lead to debate, wrangling, yelling and academic shoving matches. No, it instead leads to silence—and only to silence—stopping all wordiness and "inept . . . thinking."[31] For if "one becomes talkative after looking at oneself in the mirror of the Word, this may be an indication of not having forgotten, perhaps, but the silence of the one who became silent is a sure sign" that God's voice has been remembered (FSE 51). For silence, "like the subdued lighting in a pleasant room, . . . exercises its beneficent power" in helping us remember what we have heard. It is "the fundamental tone" which is not talked about but which lies at the base of the appropriate response to God's word (FSE 49).[32] And it is just this silence, remembrance and obedience that mark the proper way to hear and read God's word so that it will drive us on to greater discipleship. Without God's Word driving us in just this way, the church will end up like Kierkegaard's dilapidated team of horses.

Therefore Kierkegaard hits the nail on the head for his time, as well as for ours, when he writes that

> the calamity of our age . . . in everything is disobedience, not being willing to obey. One only deceives oneself and others by wanting to make us think that it is doubt that is to blame for the calamity and the cause of the calamity—no, it is insubordination—it is not doubt about the truth of the religious but insubordination to the authority of the religious. . . . Disobedience is the secret in the religious confusion of our age. (BA 5)

This insubordination and disobedience is what ruined Kierkegaard's team of horses. When they lived according to their lazy desires, instead of according to the royal coachman's goals, they collapsed. The same is the fate of disobedient, careless, unrepentant and lazy Christians.

---

31. Edward F. Mooney, *On Søren Kierkegaard: Dialogue, Polemics, Lost Intimacy, and Time* (Burlington, Vermont: Ashgate, 2007), 230. See also the stopping of all mouths in Rom 3:19. For more on this inept thinking, see *Wittgenstein in Cambridge: Letters and Documents 1911–1951*, ed. Brian McGinness (Oxford: Wiley-Blackwell, 2012), 367: "Thinking is sometimes easy, often difficult but at the same time thrilling. But when it's most important it's just disagreeable, that is when it threatens to rob one of ones pet notions and to leave one all bewildered and with a feeling of worthlessness. In these cases I and others shrink from thinking or can only get ourselves to think after a long sort of struggle. I believe that you too know this situation and I wish you *lots of courage!* though I haven't got it myself. We are all *sick* people." On Wittgenstein's love for Kierkegaard, see above, p. 57, note 20.

32. For a contemporary example of Kierkegaard's view, see Thomas C. Oden, *The Rebirth of Orthodoxy: Signs of New Life in Christianity* (New York: HarperCollins, 2003), 88–91: "I reemerged out of the secularizing maze to once again delight in the holy mysteries of the faith. . . . Rather than interpreting the [biblical] texts, I found the texts interpreting me. . . . Once blown by every wind of doctrine and preoccupied with therapeutic fads amid the spirit of hypertoleration, I came to grasp the consensual reasoning that occurs so effortlessly within classic Christianity. . . . What changed the course of my life? A simple reversal that hung on a single pivot: attentiveness to the text of scripture, especially as viewed by its early consensual interpreters. . . . [They] taught me how to accept redemptive sacrifice, know through a worshipping community, refuse idolatries, and listen for intergenerational consensus. Collectively they lived through deeper crises and dilemmas than are imaginable within the narrow premises of modern living."

BEING BAPTIZED

And on the matter of holy baptism, it is important to note that Kierkegaard believed in "the possibility that one can be a Christian and yet not be a Christian" (BA 136). This is a serious problem because

> if a Jew is not a believing Jew, he is just as fully a Jew, but a Christian who is not a believing Christian is not a Christian at all. The qualification *Christian* is one of which it must be said absolutely: one is not *born* with the qualification; it is exactly the opposite; it is precisely what one is to *become*,[33] what one is to *come to be*. (BA 135)

Subsequently, when an infant is baptized—something which Kierkegaard did not oppose (JP 1:494)[34]—it is very important that rebirth follow on the heels of baptism as the child grows up. Otherwise baptism will ruin discipleship[35] and the church will end up like Kierkegaard's lazy team of horses. Those, then, who practice infant baptism must in fact "vigorously see to it that rebirth becomes a decisive determinant" when the baptized grow up (JP 1:537). In pursuit of that goal, Christians should pray:

> *Draw* [this baptized child] to yourself [O God]. And if the parents later influence the child in such a way that it is led to you, we pray you to bless this work of theirs; but if they have a disturbing influence upon the child, we pray that you will make up for it so that this disturbing influence will not draw the child away from you, that you will let this, too, serve the child in being drawn to you. (PC 260)

What the waters of baptism do for the infant, then, apart from guaranteeing rebirth, is to grant them atonement "for the past," even if not for the "later sins" they commit (JP 1:543). Those later sins they will have to repent of and fight against on their own. But baptism gets the child off on the right foot—washing away their *original* sin, with which they are born.[36] That advantage, however, does not imply that

---

33. In a similar vein, see Martin Luther, "Lectures on Romans" (1518), LW 25:251–52: "The whole life of . . . the spiritual person is nothing else but prayer, seeking, and begging by the sighing of the heart, the voice of their works, and the labor of their bodies, always seeking and striving to be made righteous, even to the hour of death, never standing still, never possessing, never in any work putting an end to the achievement of righteousness, but always awaiting it as something which still dwells beyond them." And like unto this, see his "Defense and Explanation of All the Articles" (1521), LW 32:24: "Life [with God] is not godliness but the process of becoming godly, not health but getting well, not being but becoming, not rest but exercise. We are not now what we shall be, but we are on the way. The process is not yet finished, but it is actively going on. This is not the goal but it is the right road. At present, everything does not gleam and sparkle, but everything is being cleansed."

34. Contra David Law, "Kierkegaard on Baptism," *Theology* 91 (March 1988), 120.

35. Note also Luther's chilling assertion in his "Lectures on Hebrews" (1918), LW 29:137–38: "[Whoever] fears death . . . is not a Christian to a sufficient degree, . . . since they love this life more than they love the life to come . . . and they have been baptized in vain."

36. See Ps 51:5; Eph 2:2.

"all difficulties are [now] over" (JP 3:3086). Mark 10:38 ties suffering to baptism (JP 1:368). And this suffering deepens baptism.[37] It brings "disruption," "pessimism," and "consciousness of sin," which is the very "*conditio sine qua non* for all Christianity" (JP 4:4344, 2:1448, 1:452). This suffering is an assault on the innocence of childhood. For indeed

> the truth of the matter is that Christianity as it is found in the New Testament, . . . is impossible for children, [for it propounds] a good which is identified by its hurting, a deliverance which is identified by its making me unhappy, a grace which is identified by suffering. . . . So it is with everything essentially Christian. Only man has from the hand of Governance the toughness to be able to endure the dialectical. Having to endure the dialectical is the most intense agony there is. A child, the little rascal, is completely safeguarded against it. . . . To have to endure the dialectical is the most intense agony possible. It is also easy to see that far more intense than, for example, becoming unhappy, is the suffering of becoming unhappy and in addition having to take this as one's very happiness—and in every respect. . . . But . . . Christendom has gotten everything transposed over into the immediate and direct—and therefore, quite right, "the child" has become the measure of what it is to be Christian! . . . And thus, quite logically, by means of the child Christianity was turned upside-down, became exactly the opposite of what it is in the New Testament, got to be sugar candy for children. (JP 4:5007)

When Jesus links Christianity to children,[38] he is not then endorsing immaturity, gullibility and naïveté.[39] No, he instead links Christianity to lowliness—saying thereby that "no eminent person as such can be saved" (CD 53). For only "a broken and contrite heart" is acceptable to God.[40] And he says in addition that being childlike is an openness to God—crying "Abba! Father!"[41]—which one must strive for all of one's life. Subsequently, in relation to God,

---

37. On this correlation between baptism and suffering, see Luther's "Large Catechism" (1529), BC 445: "Baptism . . . is simply the slaying of the old Adam . . . our whole life long. Thus a Christian life is nothing else than a daily Baptism, once begun and ever continued. For we must keep at it incessantly, always purging out whatever pertains to the old Adam. . . . And what is the old man? He is what is born in us from Adam, irascible, spiteful, envious, unchaste, greedy, lazy, proud, yes, and unbelieving. . . . Where this amendment of life does not take place but the old man is given free rein, . . . Baptism is not used but resisted. . . . The old man therefore follows unchecked the inclinations of his nature if he is not restrained and suppressed by the power of Baptism. . . . Here you see that Baptism . . . comprehends . . . the third sacrament, formally called Penance, which is really nothing else than Baptism. What is repentance but an earnest attack on the old man and an entering into new life?"

38. Mt 19:14.

39. Mt 10:16; 1 Cor 13:11.

40. Ps 51:17; Lk 15:17 (RSV).

41. Gal 4:6 (RSV).

there is an increasing openness. . . . But it is not like the relationship between adults and children, in which the openness comes after the child has grown up; here it is the reverse—one does not begin as a child but as a slave, and the openness increases as one becomes more and more a child. (JP 1:272)

This slows down the entire baptismal process—the task of having to become a child in later life rather than beginning as one. The long road of discipleship is now seen as an essential part of baptism—following the linkage between baptism and discipleship in Matthew 28:19. But this linkage is an offense to those who would want to avoid such lowliness and openness before God. For them

the way is easy; it goes faster than on a train; the whole thing is quickly decided in a minute, yes, without any inconvenience at all to ourselves. The whole thing consists of being sprinkled with a little water as an infant, and then say: Please move on—and Christ, who certainly is best informed, says of the few who go along the right path that they press on along the narrow way! (JP 1:540)

Kierkegaard shared with Luther this strident view of baptism. Luther believed that while baptism is "valid" for all times, even when administered to infants, it still can lose its "benefit" and become a "mere unfruitful sign"—just as those horses in Kierkegaard's parable became a phantom of their former greatness. This happens when the baptized refrain from "incessantly" purging themselves, on a "daily" basis, of the qualities in their old nature—namely, their "irascible, spiteful, envious, unchaste, greedy, lazy, proud, yes, and unbelieving" ways.[42] If these ways go unchecked for a lifetime, then one would have been "baptized in vain."[43] This is because "baptism has made the repose, ease, and prosperity of life a very poison and a hindrance to its work. For in the easy life no one learns to suffer, to die with gladness, to get rid of sin, and to live in harmony with baptism."[44] So to say "I am baptized,"

is not enough. It must [also] be your concern to believe, to conduct yourself as a Christian should, to be upright inwardly in your heart and outwardly in your life, and to be able to take pride in the Lord Christ and in your faith. Otherwise you are a false Christian, just as many Israelites were false. For if the heart does not believe, all is illusion and darkness; your life is not upright.[45]

Even so, one's baptism remains valid, according to Luther, even after it no longer benefits us. This is because if baptism is like a ship, then it "does not founder [when] we slip and fall out of the ship." Rather it stays afloat and waits for us to climb back

42. Martin Luther, "The Large Catechism" (1529), BC 441–45.

43. Martin Luther, "Lectures on Hebrews" (1518), LW 29:138.

44. Martin Luther, "The Holy and Blessed Sacrament of Baptism" (1519), LW 35:39. On this passage see my "Poisoning Baptism," *The Bride of Christ: The Journal of Lutheran Liturgical Renewal* 15 (Spring 1991), 9–14 and on the internet under "Baptism" at flcws.org.

45. Martin Luther, "Sermons on John 1–4" (1538), LW 22:197–98.

up into it "and sail on in it as . . . before."[46] This is because the word of God uttered at baptism is irrevocable. But the recovery of baptism is not automatic after a certain period of spiritual insubordination, but only happens as a result of intense personal struggle.[47] So Luther warned the parents of baptized infants: "Remember . . . that it is no joke to take sides against the devil and not only to drive him away from the little child, but to burden the child with such a mighty and lifelong enemy."[48]

This burden of Luther's understanding of baptism and rebirth coheres with Kierkegaard's view. For it was in that rebirth that the struggle against sin begins, which helps one live in harmony with one's baptism. Praying for the Holy Spirit is part of that rebirth. Edna Hong's stirring and demanding prayer for the Holy Spirit manifests this struggle to be born again:

> Come, Holy Spirit, into our dailyness. Refuse to lose track of us, pursue us in all our masks and masquerades. Come, God's Hound Dog, track us down in all our flights, escapes, and evasions. Come, Holy Provoker, push us, pull us, prompt us, tease us, please us, displease us. Come, Holy Tenacity, refuse to let go of us. If we shut the door, come in through the cracks.[49] Come, Holy Oddity, whimsical as the wind, surprise us at our most unexpecting moments as you surprised many a God-resister and brought him or her to faith in your Son Christ Jesus, as you surprised . . . that ruthless, cold-blooded iceberg Saul . . . on his way to Damascus to capture and kill Christians and turned him into Paul, the greatest missionary the world has known. Unplug us when we fill up with self-pity and misery. Rescue us when we drown in our dailyness. Restore in us the joy of our salvation in Jesus Christ. Pour your love and joy and power into us today as you poured it into the thousands on Pentecost Day. Come into our dailyness, O Holy Spirit, be our divine income, our holy, incorruptible income—and then, O Holy Spirit, help us to spend that income, spend it like the rich-in-spirit men and women you have made us to be! Amen.[50]

46. Martin Luther, "The Large Catechism" (1529), BC 446. Unfortunately some Lutheran scholars deny the need for climbing back into the ship of baptism, arguing that baptism, at its inception, is all we need and that all subsequent human activity is unnecessary. On this point of view, see Gerhard O. Forde, "Something to Believe: A Theological Perspective on Infant Baptism," *Interpretation* 47 (July 1993): 234. To say that all such activity is unnecessary is unfortunately a departure from Luther's catechism.

47. For a slightly different nuance, see Robert Kolb's translation from Luther's "Dritte Predigt uber die Taufe" (1538), in *Understanding Four Views on Baptism*, ed. John H. Armstrong (Grand Rapids: Zondervan, 2007), 99: "Baptism is an eternal covenant which does not lapse when we fall but raises us up again. If we fall out of the ship, God helps us on board once again. When Christians fall, they always remain in their baptisms, and God binds himself to them so that he will help . . . when the baptized call upon him."

48. Martin Luther, "The Order of Baptism" (1521), LW 53:102.

49. On this image, Kierkegaard adds: "If Christ is to come and live in me, it will have to be according to [John 20:19, 26, where] Christ enters through closed doors" (JP 5:5313). Note also his prayer: "O God, grab me, get hold of me—I beseech you to do it!" (JP 4:4532)!

50. Edna H. Hong, *Box 66, Sumac Lane: A Lively Correspondence on Sin and Sanctity* (New York:

Without the Spirit of God intruding in upon us—as this prayer passionately states—we will remain stuck in our wretchedness and in our love of self and pleasure.[51] This wretchedness, Edna Hong writes, is "a morbid crowd," grounded in self-love and made up of names with the prefix self—"self-abasement, self-abhorrence, self-accusation, self-annulment, self-conceit, self-congratulations, . . . self-contempt, self-defeat, self-depreciation, self-destruction, self-disparagement, self-hatred, self-loathing, self-mortification, self-pity, self-pride, self-scorn, self-torment, self-torture."[52] Only faith in Christ Jesus can rescue us from this foul crowd and our "recollection" of it which tortures us (WA 187).[53]

SINGING HYMNS

Regarding hymn singing, Kierkegaard also had deep concerns. He did not believe that hymns were of little consequence. So if God is driving us to greater discipleship, he believed that singing poor hymns will only stymie that endeavor. Singing poor hymns will drag us down just like those horses in Kierkegaard's parable were ruined by their lack of discipline. Now because proper hymns of praise are so important, they cannot be accompanied by "human understanding's toy tin trumpet but [only by] faith's celestial trombone":

> Thus the Christian in perfect obedience serves only one master. Just as the bird sings incessantly to the honor of the Creator, so also the Christian's life . . . ought to be. . . . Thus the Christian's life is like a hymn of praise to *the master's* honor, because this life obeys God even more willingly and in even more blessed harmony than the harmony of the spheres. This life is a hymn of praise, since a human being can praise God only by obedience. . . . But the tone of this hymn of praise is pitched so high and is so deeply gripping because this humble, cheerful obedience does not praise what one understands but what one does not understand. (CD 85)

But if the hymns we sing are not pitched high enough and are not sufficiently gripping, as Kierkegaard thought they should be, then they will end up weighing us down.[54] For the words and tunes in hymns are not automatically pleasing to God.

Harper & Row, 1989), 75–76, 86. Note also her inclusion (53–58) of Kierkegaard's parable of the royal coachman and his prayer at the end of it—which no doubt inspires this one of hers.

51. 2 Tm 3:2–4.

52. Edna H. Hong, *Forgiveness is a Work as Well as a Grace*, 91.

53. On this rescue, see chapter 3 on self-hatred.

54. In many American churches today, sacred music is being replaced with popular music. For a critique of this trend, see Jay R. Howard and John M. Streck, *Apostles of Rock: The Splintered World of Contemporary Christian Music* (Lexington: The University Press of Kentucky, 1999), 38: "Christian rock distorts the gospel by trying to show how groovy it is to be a Christian." See also Dan Lucarini, *Why I Left the Contemporary Christian Music Movement* (Darlington, England: Evangelical, 2002), 59: "Punk music is the ultimate statement of musical rebellion. Changing the words and the artists and

Indeed, if they are not properly formed, they will lead us astray.[55] The texts of hymns, in other words, should be combed over carefully—even down to the exact punctuation marks (JP 4:4763)—making sure every word glorifies God and leads us on into greater obedience.[56] "Therefore it is very important," writes Kierkegaard, "that everything that is said and sung in church should be true, not that it should be . . . ravishing, etc., not that I start to cry while my heart beats violently—no, the question is whether I am primarily related to all this in terms of acting accordingly" (JP 1:829). Affectation is thus out of place in worship (BA 185), for it distracts us from the true glorification of God and the proper transformation of our lives. Without such glorification and transformation, hymns are disastrous. They bring "in the spiritual sense, no airing out," for they leave us in the "toxic . . . old junk heap" of our sinful lives (TM 158). For hymns written and composed to "meet the needs of the times" are dangerous since they do nothing to strengthen our faith in Christ (TA 102). They only are for entertainment.[57]

Our faith in Christ is not only furthered by the words we sing but also by the tunes that carry those words. There is a problem here because musical tone can also breed affectation. So not only syrupy words, but also bad tunes—with their "trite rhythms, colorless melodic patterns, [and] lackluster harmonic progressions"[58]—can lead us astray. Kierkegaard was aware of this and wrote that the true tone of a hymn should display a deep "inward pain which in quiet sadness is reconciled to God" (JP 5:6097). He did not think that the popular Danish hymn writer, Nikolai F. S. Grundtvig (1783–1872), composed hymns like this. He thus disrespectfully called him a "jaunty yodeler" (JP 5:6097). Kierkegaard thought Grundtvig's hymns were stuck in the "enjoyment of life" (JP 6:6876, 2:1860) and not focused on Christ's sacrifice and our attending self-denial—which help us "grow up to salvation."[59] Grundtvig's hymns were too secular for that. They mimicked "the sounds of nature" (JP 1:784) and oozed with a "zest for life"—sounding like a "gallop" (JP 3:2788).

This is not surprising since Grundtvig's famous slogan was: "Man first and then Christian."[60] His hymns were rooted "in the people," like their "drinking songs" were

---

calling it Christian will never sanctify it. It has no place in a new Christian's life."

55. So Kierkegaard would probably agree with Plato that "our guardians must build their guardhouse and post a watch" when it comes to music (*Republic* IV:424d).

56. So Kierkegaard would have in large part endorsed the cynical saying: "Let me make the hymns of the people, and I care not who makes their creeds." June Hadden Hobbs, *I Sing for I Cannot Be Silent: The Feminization of American Hymnody, 1870–1920* (Pittsburgh: University of Pittsburgh Press, 1997), 1.

57. This goes against the Lutheran Confessions, BC 378: "[We would] desecrate the holy day . . . [if we were] to listen to God's Word as [one] would to any other entertainment."

58. Carl F. Schalk, "Some Thoughts on the Writing of Hymn Tunes," *Cross Accent: Journal of the Association of Lutheran Church Musicians*, No. 7 (January 1996): 10. A wonderful example of a tune that steers clear of these mistakes is Schalk's "Thankless for Favours from on High" on the internet at flcws.org. It is no mistake that Schalk gave this tune the name KIERKEGAARD.

59. 1 Pt 2:2 (RSV).

60. *N. F. S. Grundtvig: Selected Writings*, ed. and trans. Johannes Knudsen (Philadelphia: Fortress,

(JP 5:5136).[61] They lacked the "intolerance" that properly inspire saving the lost. For "Christianity has never been tolerant in such a way that it has let others be pagans or be lost. No, it has been so intolerant that the apostle would rather lose his life in order to proclaim Christianity" (JP 5:6122). Grundtvig's tolerance is especially horrible, then, because it breeds "indifferentism, the most extreme falling away from Christianity." And the tolerance from which this springs is worse than first supposed, since it comes from commercialism—the "mercenary concept." On this view, if the hymn is good for business, then it is used. For church music this means that we give people what they want, rather than what they need in their struggle to obey God. With this capitulation, the church at song sounds like the merchant who says: "Business and shipping and railways and the whole secular social amity—tolerance is an asset to all this. Long may it live!" (JP 4:4819).

It is not surprising then that Kierkegaard favored the hymns of Hans Adolph Brorson (1694–1764) over those of Grundtvig. For while Grundtvig's hymns stood for "the emerging democratic movement that later provided the political backing for the 'Danish People's Church,' . . . Brorson represented that part of the 'awakening' traditions that stressed the inwardness of the individual."[62]

1976), 141. This slogan clearly means more than that being human is the material perquisite for becoming Christian. No, Grundtvig's point is a religious one. "In contrast to Kierkegaard's strong demand for personal and ethical discipleship," writes Knudsen, "Grundtvig makes the claim that the only signs of Christian life are found in the fellowship of worship with its proclamation of the gospel, its confession of faith, and its songs of praise. The Christian life is not a separate, disciplined life; it is a true human life which is not a life different from the created life of mankind. The created life has been reborn and renewed through its participation with God in worship, particularly in the sacraments, but the new life is nonetheless a human life" (56). Kierkegaard would agree that we remain "earthen vessels" (2 Cor 4:7; Jas 4:14) even after conversion, alright, with our limitations of finitude, which cannot be denied. But we must not celebrate that condition, since we are to "groan" constantly for our release from it (Rom 8:23). And we need that because we, due to those same limitations, are "by nature" corrupt (Eph 2:3)—sinfully fighting against the spirit, as we do by nature (Gal 5:17; Acts 7:51; Mk 7:21-23; Jn 3:19; Rv 3:17). So when we convert to Christianity we are to become "new" creatures (2 Cor 5:17), rather than old remodeled ones. We should exclaim: "It is no longer I who live, but Christ who lives in me" (Gal 2:20, RSV). Even though Luther thinks this is a "peculiar phraseology," it is still true—albeit offensively so. On this point see his "Lectures on Galatians 1–4" (1535), LW 26:168.

61. One should not suppose that Grundtvig was merely following Luther at this point. On this distortion of Luther, see Joseph Herl, "Ten Myths About Hymn Singing Among Early Lutherans," *Cross Accent: Journal of the Association of Lutheran Church Musicians* 8 (Summer 2000): 40–41: "It is almost an axiom in the popular imagination that Luther, in order to further congregational singing and make his hymns more attractive to the people, used or adapted pre-existing secular melodies, even drinking songs. The well known question, 'Why should the devil have all the good tunes?'—said by English preacher Rowland Hill (1744–1833)—is frequently attributed to Luther. In truth, of all Luther's [thirty-seven] hymns, only one . . . is known to have had a secular origin. . . . Most often, when Luther wrote a hymn using a pre-existing melody, the melody was a Gregorian chant, . . . [or a] popular *religious* song (what would be akin to religious Christmas carols today), . . . many of [which] had already been sung in churches before Luther's time. . . . [So] there is . . . no justification for the argument that Luther attempted to promote congregational singing by catering to the tastes of the masses."

62. Andrew J. Burgess, "Kierkegaard, Brorson, and Moravian Music," IKC 20:219.

This inwardness was both strident and reassuring, as is seen in his hymn, "Children of God, Born of His Spirit":[63]

> Evil by nature, and dead in transgression,
> Cold as a statue, and hard as a stone,
> This was our state when Thou, mov'd by compassion,
> Chose in Thy wisdom to call us Thine own.
> Led by the Spirit, and call'd by Thy favor,
> Heard we the life-giving voice of our Savior.
>
> When we considered the tho'ts of our Father,
> As He elected us children by grace,
> Sending His Spirit with mercy to gather
> Us, who had fallen and turn'd from His face,
> How can we help to be mov'd by His favor,
> And to acclaim Him our Father forever.
>
> What can be charg'd to the Father's elected,
> Whom He made just in Christ Jesus, our Lord?
> Here is sweet balsam for all the afflicted,
> Grace for the lost in His life-giving Word.
> Faith, passing thro' ev'ry fear of damnation,
> Found in the Savior the pledge of salvation.

In this severe yet beautiful hymn,[64] we learn how to escape "ev'ry fear of damnation." This comes through faith in the Savior Jesus Christ.[65] This faith, however, does not come through one's rational discernment. That would not work because we are "dead in transgression." This spiritual death turns us "cold as a statue and hard as a stone." In that sense we are lost and fallen—and unable to think ourselves out of our misery. So our faith can only come as a result of God's compassionate and gracious selection of us. This does not offend us—even though it runs roughshod over us. For we know there is no other way to be rescued from sin. God's election of us, then, is only "sweet balsam." Rather than complaining and rebelling against it, we "acclaim

---

63. Hymn 295, verses 2–4, in *Hymnal for Church and Home: Revised and Enlarged*, Fourth Edition (1938; Blair, Nebraska: Danish Lutheran Publishing House, 1942).

64. Such substantial hymn texts are missing from among many new hymns today. On this bleak situation, see Madeleine Forell Marshall, *Common Hymnsense* (Chicago: GIA Publications, 1995), 202–3: "[Our] reluctance to analyze . . . what hymns mean is a result of the wonderful niceness of the Christian community. . . . [But this] has left us some texts and translations that are virtually unintelligible, some that are misleading, others that have been badly cut and altered, others that would benefit from simple correction. We also have wonderful hymns, worth singing over and over, worth memorization and lifelong reflection. But we [lamentably] won't let them set the standard or lead the way. We won't discriminate."

65. In Brorson's hymn, "Christians, Who With Sorrow" (Hymn 163, verse 3, *Hymnal for Church and Home*), he explains how faith in Jesus saves us: "When in death He gave His breath, to the cruel foe He yielded, that we should be shielded."

God our Father forever." We cannot help being "moved by his favor." But note that in all of this, there is no call in this hymn to love others as God first loved us.[66] Neither is there any call to pray for the sick[67] or bind up the wounded.[68] Instead, the focus is on God—pure and simple. We are to consider his thoughts and compassion. We are to acclaim his favor forever with our thanksgiving, honor and praise. This does not mean that these other concerns for the neighbor are not important, but only that they are of a lower priority. Here we see true Christian inwardness, undefiled.

This point is reinforced in Brorson's hymn, "I Walk in Danger All the Way":

My walk is heav'nward all the way,
Await, my soul, the morrow,
When thou shalt find release for aye
From all thy sin and sorrow;
All worldly pomp, be gone,
To heav'n I now press on;
For all the world I would not stay,
My walk is heav'nward all the way.

Such a hymn pulls us back from wallowing in earthly things[69] and points us toward the heavenly, eternal city[70] where our true commonwealth is found.[71] Being earthbound as we are, we cannot however easily ascend to these heights. And so in his hymn, "The Faith that God Believeth,"[72] Brorson attacks a weak, lazy, easy-going faith:

66. 1 Jn 4:19 (RSV).

67. Jas 5:14 (RSV).

68. Lk 10:34–37 (RSV).

69. Col 3:2 (RSV). Note also Luther's comments on not conforming to this world: "Sermon on Romans 12:1–6" (1525), SML 17:16–17: "We must be careful . . . to follow neither the customs of the world nor our own reason or plausible theories. We must constantly subdue our dispositions and control our wills, not obeying the dictates of reason or desire. Always we are to conduct ourselves in a manner unlike the way of the world. So shall we be daily changed [by] each day [placing] greater value on the things condemned by human reason—by the world. Daily we prefer to be poor, sick and despised, to be fools and sinners, until ultimately we regard death as better than life, foolishness as more precious than wisdom, shame nobler than honor, labor more blessed than wealth, and sin more glorious than human righteousness. Such a mind the world does not possess. The mind of the world is altogether unlike the Christian's. It not only continues unchanged and unrenewed in its old dispositions, but is obdurate and very old."

70. Heb 13:14 (RSV).

71. Phil 3:20 (RSV). Kierkegaard called this "being educated for the eternal," which comes through being "weaned from the world and the things of this world" (UDVS 258, 257). For a contemporary version of this point, see Peter K. Nelson, "Impractical Christianity," *Christianity Today* (September 2006), 80: "We can't get life to work; it never will until heaven. Instead of a better life, we're offered a better hope of intimacy with God—a relationship that carries us through and not around the pain and loss." Such earthly practicality, Kierkegaard writes, reduces Christianity to "an educational process . . . where it is not a matter of taking away [one's] nature but of improving it" (JP 5:6076). See also Martin Luther, "Lectures on Genesis 45–50" (1545), LW 8:114–15: "This life is no life. . . . [But those who believe] are sustained by the hope of a future and better life."

72. Hymn 298, verse 2, *Hymnal for Church and Home*.

> The faith that compromises
> And takes the easy way,
> The faith that never rises
> To fight and work and pray,
> That faith is dead and vile,
> Its holy name disgracing,
> And has no pow'r when facing
> The tempter's craft and guile.

This hymn vilifies a compromised faith by calling it vile and disgraceful.[73] In this hymn there is power to rise to the heights what so often eludes the believer. It is just this power which faith needs. And Brorson's hymn, "O Father, May Thy Word Prevail,"[74] connects this need with the sad state of baptism:

> Come, Jesus, come and contemplate
> Thy vineyard's sad estate:
> Baptized are millions in Thy name,
> But where is faith's pure flame?
> Of what avail that we
> Know of Thine agony,
> So long as we do not o'erthrow
> In faith the wicked foe?

Kierkegaard may well have been inspired by this hymn on the baptized millions when he wrote that his task was not "to create more nominal Christians," but to relieve Christianity "of some of those battalions of Christians" by "jacking up the price" for being a Christian (PV 125–26, 138). Such a winnowing—by way of the good hymns we sing in church—is just what we need if we are to be driven by God to greater discipleship. Without singing such rigorous, faithful hymns, we will languish—just like those horses did in Kierkegaard's parable of the royal coachman.

STAYING YOUNG

At the end of her book on the history of Saint John's Lutheran Church in Northfield, Minnesota, Edna Hong writes:

> The radical message of Christianity has not changed in the hundred years which we celebrate this centennial year of St. John's, but the Church which proclaims it has radically changed and will continue to change. Indeed, if it does not it is headed for disaster! There is a Revelation that is closed, but there

---

73. Brorson makes this same point in his hymn, "Stand Fast, My Soul, Stand Fast" (Hymn 348, verse 2, *Hymnal for Church and Home*): "But from the strife to run, when blows thy courage stun, is most disgracing."

74. Hymn 231, verse 2, *Hymnal for Church and Home*.

is also a Revelation that is forever open to a Church that believes that Christ is alive and present within human experience and human history today, in the year of our Lord, 1969. Believing this, St. John's congregation can boldly enter the second century with all the hope and joy and confidence of first-century Christians, knowing that in the power of His Spirit a Christian congregation does not grow old but is always a new creation, a new community of Christ.[75]

This is a stirring admonition to take up the new life in Christ each day of our lives and not to grow old spiritually. It is also a condemnation of those who would set aside the good fight of faith[76] and rest upon their spiritual laurels. The radical call of Jesus Christ to die to sin and rise to newness of life[77] must be heard and followed anew each and every day—regardless of our age. For as Luther said: "Faith takes no holidays."[78] Otherwise "spiritual rigor mortis" sets in.[79] So we cannot grow old in Christ, but must become new followers of him every day—making new sacrifices and enjoying new blessings day in and day out.

By hearing and reading the Bible as God's very voice to us, by taking up our baptismal battle against our flesh on a daily basis, and by singing hymns that elevate us beyond this "perverse generation,"[80] we can be driven by God into greater discipleship and newness of life in Christ. We can be like those horses in Kierkegaard's parable—performing at a high level under the training of the royal coachman. And as God gives us grace to enter into this disciplined life, we will be filled with gratitude, knowing full well that we have not achieved any of this by dint of our own efforts (JP 1:993). We will be thankful, knowing that we can do nothing without his help.[81] This is the lesson in Kierkegaard's parable of the royal coachman. May it ever be kept before us—just as Edna Hong labored all her life to do.

---

75. Edna H. Hong, *The Book of a Century: 1868–1969* (Northfield, Minnesota: Saint John's Lutheran Church, 1970), 129.

76. 1 Tm 6:12 (RSV). Due to the necessity of this battle, Kierkegaard would agree that "God has no grandchildren. He only has children" who have taken up for themselves this fight of faith. Richard John Neuhaus, "While We're At It," *First Things*, Number 130 (February 2003): 82. See also *Wittgenstein in Cambridge: Letters and Documents 1911–1951*, ed. Brian McGinness (Oxford: Wiley-Blackwell, 2012), 363: "Deciding to become a [Christian] is like deciding to give up walking on the ground and do tight-rope walking instead, where nothing is more easy than to slip and every slip can be fatal." On Wittgenstein's love for Kierkegaard, see above, p. 57, note 20.

77. Lk 9:23; 1 Pt 2:24 (RSV).

78. Martin Luther, "Preface to the Book of Romans" (1546), LW 35:378.

79. Edna H. Hong, *Forgiveness is a Work as Well as a Grace*, 17, 26.

80. Phil 2:15 (RSV).

81. Jn 15:5 (RSV).

7

On Divorce

In Gilbert Meilaender's sermon for his daughter Hannah's wedding, he sets out in part to show the relevance of Søren Kierkegaard's book, *Works of Love*, for Christian marriage.[1] This is because he thinks Kierkegaard helps explain the worthy thought that true "love never ends" (1 Cor 13:8).

This sermon also provides an alternative to all the sentimental slogans heard at Christian weddings.[2] Kierkegaard is well suited for this since he is harsh and philosophizes "with a hammer."[3] That trait gives him power to purge the drivel from wedding sermons. This power is Kierkegaard's relevance for weddings. So just because he broke off his engagement with the young Regine Olsen and never married after that[4] does not disqualify him in matters marital.[5] The preacher still should be able to fall "in love with Søren"[6] and use him confidently at weddings.

I want to present the gist of Meilaender's sermon in order to augment it with further material from *Works of Love* and then assess its overall commendability.

1. Gilbert Meilaender, "Love Abides," *Christian Century* 117 (October 11, 2000), 990–91. He makes a similar point in his essay, "The Task of Lutheran Ethics," *Lutheran Forum* 34 (Winter 2000): 20–21.

2. See, for instance, *Best Wedding Meditations: An Anthology*, revised edition, (Lima, Ohio: CSS, 1997): "Let there be spaces in your togetherness" (38, 53) and "Celebrate the staying power of love—so bright a flame nothing can put it out" (47). Note also *Wedding Readings: Centuries of Writing and Rituals on Love and Marriage*, ed. Eleanor Munro, (New York: Penguin, 1989): "You can transmute love, ignore it, muddle it, but you can never pull it out of you [because] love is eternal" (25) and marriage "is like a dance. . . . Now arm in arm, now face to face, now back to back—it does not matter which. Because they know they are partners moving to the same rhythm, creating a pattern together, and being invisibly nourished by it" (75). May Kierkegaard's thought save us from such "amatory banalities" as these. *The Book of Marriage: The Wisest Answers to the Toughest Questions*, ed. Mack & Blankenhorn (Grand Rapids: Eerdmans, 2001), 184.

3. Emmanuel Levinas, *Proper Names*, trans. Michael B. Smith (Palo Alto, California: Stanford University Press, 1996), 76. See also the aptly titled *Provocations: Spiritual Writings of Kierkegaard*, compiled and edited by Charles E. Moore, (Farmington, Pennsylvania: Plough, 1999), especially section V on "Christian Collisions."

4. See Susan Leigh Anderson, *On Kierkegaard* (Belmont, California: Wadsworth, 2000), 5–11, and Appendix 2 below.

5. See Carolyn Kizer's poem, "The Erotic Philosophers," in *The Best American Poetry* 1999, ed. Robert Bly (New York: Scribner, 1999). Kizer accuses Kierkegaard of supposing that what was "truly terrible" for him was "to be consoled by the love of another" because if one is to "suffer to love God, . . . he must tear himself away from earthly love" (102, 103).

6. Dorothee Soelle, *The Window of Vulnerability*, trans. Linda M. Maloney, (Minneapolis: Fortress, 1990), 117.

PATIENCE IN MARRIAGE

Meilaender rightly sees that Kierkegaard in *Works of Love* elaborates the theme of patience or what he calls "waiting for the beloved." Patience in marriage stops one from running off for a divorce at the first sight of trouble.[7] Patience enables one to wait for better times. Meilaender says that by being patient marital love reflects the "steadfastness and faithfulness" of God's love which is what "joins Father, Son and Spirit." By waiting, the husband or wife is able to "exercise just a little of God's own creative power" to determine that there will be "a future together." In that way they act like God. This makes the struggle to persevere in marriage noble.

Meilaender sees this point about patience in Kierkegaard's image of the broken hyphenated or compound word. That compound word is husband-wife or lover-beloved (WL 306). It depicts an intact, marital relationship. So if the wife leaves, she "cannot take the hyphen" with her. In this way the husband can still abide in his love for his upset wife—regardless of her behavior. He can wait with open arms. In fact what others might call "a break" is only "a relationship that has not yet been finished." This is because the husband cannot say he knows for sure "that nothing more is coming" (WL 306). Even after years elapse he still "continually emancipates" himself from the past sad years and waits "for the future" when her love for him may once again bloom (WL 307). So his love abides even though hers does not. He does not need her love to motivate himself to love her. He waits on his own because of his love for her. By so doing his love abides even when hers wanes.[8] On this account, the break between them is only apparent.

The other image from *Works of Love* that Meilaender uses is that of the dancer who remains on the floor even after her husband leaves in a huff.[9] Just because he runs off does not mean she must do so too. So "if the other remains standing in the position that expresses bowing toward the one who is not seen, and if you know nothing about the past, you will say, 'The dance will surely begin just as soon as the other one, who is awaited, comes'" (WL 307).

---

7. So we read in Pamela Paul's distressing book, *The Starter Marriage and the Future of Matrimony* (New York: Villard, 2002): "You're young and crazy and you just sort of go for it. . . . We never really talked about long-term goals." This quote comes from Mark D. Fefer's review, "The Young and Deluded: First-Marriage Survivors Tell All," *Seattle Weekly* (March 7, 2002). Acceptable reasons for divorce in the Church have been: "adultery, . . . political treason, planning of murder, disappearance for five years or more, unjustified accusation of adultery and . . . monastic vows of one of the partners." John Meyendorff, *Marriage: An Orthodox Perspective* (Crestwood, New York: Saint Vladimir's Seminary, 1975), 56.

8. This is no small matter if it is true that divorce by "mutual-consent . . . is rare [being that] over 80 percent of divorces are now . . . unilateral." Maggie Gallagher, *The Abolition of Marriage: How We Destroy Lasting Love* (Washington, DC: Regnery, 1996), 144. That statistic alone holds out the hope that many broken marriages could be restored simply by the persistence of one of the parties in the marriage.

9. Meilaender says that this passage, along with the one above on the broken, hyphenated word, are "two of the most unforgettable and powerful . . . I have ever read."

So love abides in the waiting wife on the dance floor. Meilaender astutely observes that this bowing posture could be "rather awkward. . . . One could get . . . lots of cramps. A stiff neck. One could tire," he says. But this failure to abide because of pain and impatience is warded off by the fact that "God gives us time, gives us marriage: that we may not tire, but, on the contrary, gain joy by abiding." So the time allotted in marriage is not only for enjoyment but also for putting the pieces of broken love back together.

SELF-HATRED IN MARRIAGE

This ends Meilaender's fine sermon. But he could have gone on. Kierkegaard's *Works of Love* has more to say. He could have said what Kierkegaard thought should be done with the time God graciously gives for the restoration of marriage.[10] In addition to having time to reconcile, an estranged couple also needs to learn how to fix their broken love. They should not use their time to sulk or play the blame game. That would be to misuse God's gift of time. They instead need to learn how to deal with their cramps and pain, disappointment and anger, stiff necks and fatigue.

Picking up where Meilaender leaves off in *Works of Love*, Kierkegaard makes this crucial, additional point:

> But perhaps the girl actually loved herself. She desired the union with the beloved for her own sake; it was her only desire, her soul was as one in this desire. In gratitude for this fulfillment, she would do everything possible to make her husband's life as beautiful as possible. Yes, this is true, but yet, yet it was for her own sake that she desired the union. If this is so, she is sure to become weary, she becomes attentive to the past, to the length of time—now she no longer sits at the window; she expresses that the break exists. (WL 307)

According to Kierkegaard, much more than time is needed to ward off fatigue, impatience and divorce. One also needs to use that time properly—specifically in three ways. First one must quit loving oneself. Second one must not want the marriage restored for one's own sake. And finally one must not look for fulfillment in marriage.

Well, it surely goes without saying that these are all highly contestable points—especially in our time when love has become "a consumptive item." In such a time "the only way to move one's spouse is to threaten to remove the object of his or her gratification—oneself. In this way . . . divorce permeates marriage." So "all talk of happiness

---

10. In personal correspondence, dated March 16, 2001, Meilaender says this additional point is "problematic" and so he excluded it. In his book, *Friendship: A Study is Theological Ethics* (Notre Dame: University of Notre Dame Press, 1981), he gives a reason for this. Any efforts, he writes, "to deny our neediness is to try to live a lie, and it must inevitably deny important features of our common nature" (45). But Kierkegaard is not guilty of this sin. He does not deny our neediness. All he does is prevent it from putting an end to love. He does not allow the tail (of need) to wag the dog (of marriage).

in marriage seems to be linked to a threat: Make me happy or I'll leave. . . . If the goal is the happiness of the individual partner, then the therapeutic love contract, or marriage, is inherently temporary."[11] No wonder, then, that *The New Yorker* published a cartoon that has the pastor telling the newlyweds: "OK, then. You may kiss, shake hands, and come out married."[12] Marriage looks like a boxing match today because threats and the specter of divorce permeate it.

Against this prevailing consumptive view of love and marriage Kierkegaard's point is particularly relevant—even if contested. Marriage is not about self-fulfillment and self-love.[13] But saying this does not make it so. Kierkegaard, however, does not leave it at that.

Earlier in *Works of Love* he argues that it is "foolish . . . to love others for . . . one's own advantage" (WL 258). If one therefore sets aside one's own advantage, love will "never give up" (WL 254). That is indeed the noble goal of marriage, *viz.*, to never give up loving. But how does one quit pursuing one's own advantage so that one may endure? How can we make love abide?

Kierkegaard's answer is simple. We give up pursuing our own advantage in marriage by hating ourselves. Love that truly abides must be purged of all self-love and selfishness if it is to endure what Martin Luther called the "thorns and thistles in marriage."[14] Such love is "self-denial's love [that] drives out all . . . self-love" (WL 55). Indeed one must hate "one's own life" in order for love to abide (WL 109). Self-hatred has the power to enrich marriage. By hating oneself in marriage we no longer yearn to be at the center of our marriage. We fight against being selfish and thinking that marriage is for our "own sake" (WL 307).

Surely we would prefer not hearing such tough words amidst all the finery and festivity of a church wedding. Having three children myself I can imagine wishing

---

11. Maggie Gallagher, *The Abolition of Marriage*, 231.

12. *The New Yorker* (March 15, 1999), 50. For perhaps the seminal study on fighting in marriage, see G. Bach & P. Wyden, *The Intimate Enemy: How to Fight Fair in Love and Marriage* (New York: Avon Books, 1968, 1983). Note especially that "making a person angry is the surest way to find out what he cares about and how deeply he cares. Since intimates keep measuring and re-measuring how much they care for one another ('Are you getting bored with me?'), they can make each other angry in normal but usually unconscious tests of the depth of their involvement. . . . These fight games can be informative [and lovers] find out by this process that affection grows deeper when it is mixed with aggression" (27). Whew!

13. For a confirmation of this point, see the *Catechism of the Catholic Church*, Revised Edition, (London: Geoffrey Chapman, 1999), §1609: "After the fall, marriage helps to overcome self-absorption, egoism, pursuit of one's own pleasure, and to open oneself to the other, to mutual aid and to self-giving." This confirmation is an example of how "extremely close to Catholicism" Kierkegaard actually is. H. Roos, *Søren Kierkegaard and Catholicism*, trans. Richard M. Brackett (Westminster, Maryland: Newman, 1954), 19.

14. Martin Luther, "Lectures on Genesis 26–30" (1545), LW 5:195–96. Against self-hatred in marriage, see: "'I, Janet Downes, take myself with all of my strengths and faults...' Vows that Janet Downes of Bellevue, Nebraska, plans to exchange with herself in front of a mirror and two hundred friends and relatives at a ceremony where she will marry herself, in celebration of the fact that she is 'happy with herself.'" *Newsweek* (June 29, 1998), 19.

for something better. But Kierkegaard warns against making love something "sentimental" (WL 376). The Christian goal after all is not an "easy and . . . sociable" life (WL 124). Luther was right that Christian living rightly brings with it "danger and difficulty."[15]

Because of the bitterness and despondency self-hatred can bring, its value is less than clear. In order to combat these pitfalls, Kierkegaard steers clear of inappropriate self-hatred. Self-hatred is wrong if it is wasteful, foolish, depressing or violent (WL 23). Properly construed self-hatred "removes from love everything that is inflamed, everything that is momentary, everything that is giddy" (WL 188). This alone is the value of self-hatred. With it love can truly reach out to the beloved and abide.[16] When both husband and wife practice self-hatred, a marriage lasts. This is because they are able to help each other battle back selfishness.

So the indelible mark of love is that it diminishes and devalues reciprocity. Marital love does not live because it is returned—that would be selfish. Self-hatred enables one to let go of a dependence on reciprocity in marriage. All Christians should hear this point shouted from the rooftops at weddings. It is wrong to love only if we are loved in return. If love is returned, it is sweet—but that does not control whether or not we ourselves love. In this sense love is free of the burdens of reciprocity. That is what it means to devalue and diminish it. According to Kierkegaard, love is selfish and false when it "aspires to . . . repayment"—even in the form of "reciprocal love" (WL 349). Reciprocity is defanged when it no longer controls whether or not we love. When allowed to roam unchecked, reciprocity destroys true, unselfish love.

This, however, does not turn husbands and wives into automatons. They must still rejoice in being "loved" (WL 39) whenever it happens.[17] For whether or not we are loved is not "a matter of indifference" (WL 27). Abandonment hurts. Devaluing reciprocity does not eliminate that pain or the desire to be loved. But neither will withdrawal, rejection or attack sway us from loving.[18] This determination surfaces only after reciprocity has been devalued. According to Kierkegaard, this makes love wild and "dangerous" (WL 198, 277). It will show itself when the prudent have given up. Looking around we know how people can display "animal bloodthirstiness and savagery" (WL 169). But we are to be ready for that and not be surprised when it happens—even when it appears in its softer forms of carping and sulking. In the face of

---

15. Martin Luther, "Sermons on John 14–16" (1538), LW 24:162.

16. I have explored this thesis in chapter three of this book.

17. So "to rebuild marriage, we must recognize that grimly hanging in there 'for the sake of the children' will not work, that it has never been enough." Sober, self-sufficient endurance by one of the parties will not restore a marriage. For marriage is "the incarnation of eros, the body of love. It is the psalms and the Song of Songs and it is the Crucifixion, or at least it is our aspiration to all of these things." Gallagher, *The Abolition of Marriage*, 263–64. Endurance can lead to restoration but is too grim to amount to restoration itself.

18. This would be an extension of the teaching that we should lend money "expecting nothing in return" (Lk 6:35), and an appeal to the hope of being "repaid at the resurrection of the just" (Lk 14:14).

this we are to abide even if it makes us look foolish and a bit "mad" (WL 108, 132, 185, 203, 238, 287, 290, 321). So in some sense you have to be a little crazy to stay married and hold onto your wedding vows.[19] The church, Kierkegaard is saying, should push for such craziness in marriage. Going the extra mile has its place in marriage.

One way to promote this teaching on self-hatred and disregard for reciprocity in wedding sermons would be to base them on Ephesians 5:21–33[20] rather than on 1 Corinthians 13:8. This classic marriage text from Ephesians is about "sacrifice."[21] It says husbands and wives should mutually subject themselves to each other out of reverence for Christ. Within that rubric of sacrifice, Kierkegaard's criticism of reciprocity fits nicely. So a wedding sermon based on Ephesians 5 could wonderfully reflect Kierkegaard's point, that self-hatred is what makes marriage last. It is what wards off divorce.

Another verse would be John 12:25. Even though this verse is not explicitly about marriage, it also can help. It says that if we hate ourselves we will be saved from hell. Now if we were to extend that thought into the realm of marriage, we could say that self-hatred also saves us from divorce—what many know to be a living, earthly hell, anyway. So if self-hatred can save us from going to hell, it surely can save us from getting divorced. Conquering hell, after all, is much more difficult than conquering divorce. Seeing that pivotal role for self-hatred in marriage is precisely Kierkegaard's cure for divorce.

CONFESSION IN MARRIAGE

Criticisms of this cure are many and intense. But far be it from Kierkegaard to make a proposal that would be anything less than contentious.

So there are questions. How, for instance, can it be that a loving husband should wait indefinitely for his errant wife to return? And is it always wrong to cut the ties that bind and look for another spouse? Or how can it be that a battered wife should keep loving her abusive husband without regard for her own safety? Should she not leave in order to protect herself? And how can it be that a husband should stay with

---

19. Researchers have now mounted sizable scientific evidence against keeping one's marital vows. They try to show that just as "infants have their infancy," so adults naturally have their adultery. David P. Barash and Judith Eve Lipton, *The Myth of Monogamy: Fidelity and Infidelity in Animals and People* (New York: W. H. Freeman, 2001), 2.

20. Meilaender explores Ephesians 5 in *Things That Count: Essays Moral and Theological* (Wilmington, Delaware: ISI Books, 2000), 44–57. The importance of sacrifice in marriage, however, is missing from his account. Elizabeth Achtemeier has a better understanding of Ephesians 5 as the call to husbands and wives to imitate "Christ's faithfulness and yearning and sacrifice." *The Committed Marriage* (Philadelphia: Westminster, 1976), 86.

21. See *Galatians, Ephesians, Philippians*, ed. Mark J. Edwards, Ancient Christian Commentary on Scripture: New Testament, vol. 7 (Downers Grove, IL: InterVarsity, 1999), 195.

his wife when he gets absolutely nothing out of the marriage? And is it always wrong to expect fulfillment in marriage?[22]

How would Kierkegaard respond to these questions? I think he would say we need to learn how to live under the weight of the ideal of this "higher" (WL 45) form of love and marriage.[23]

Kierkegaard knows that up against this exalted ideal of love we look "shabby" indeed (WL 284). Our efforts at approximating it are "superficial" (WL 364). These failures render us "unworthy servants" (WL 365) of the God who calls us to this exalted life of suffering love.

In the face of these failures, our temptation is to settle for some "medium grade" of love (WL 45) that is less demanding. With it we could master love and erase our guilt for failing to live up to this more exalted ideal. No longer would we have to appear in "an unfavorable light" (WL 370). But Kierkegaard resists this temptation. That medium grade of love must be "thrust down," he says (WL 45). We must not "slacken" the higher form of love (WL 50). We cannot expect to "spinelessly whimper" our way into righteousness (WL 379).

Watering down the higher form of love is not the way to go. We instead must continue to aspire to this exalted ideal while admitting that we have not reached it. And we must say that we are "always only . . . on the way" (WL 48). Even though we may never arrive, we must always hope we will.

Kierkegaard explains this dialectical relation to the exalted ideal of Christianity in his book *Judge For Yourself!* In the face of the "difficult and complex" problems foisted on us by this ideal, the faithful Christian should with "a purity like that of a virgin and a blushing modesty like that of an adolescent," refuse to act "sagaciously" (JFY 103). We should dump "flabby sensibleness" and the "despicable thralldom in probability" (JFY 102).

His reason for this is that those maneuvers constitute a "mean slandering of all . . . the martyrs" in the past who died for true, rigorous Christianity (JFY 101). Their deaths, for all time, show that Christianity is "sheer agony" and that Christians are nothing but "worms" (TM 189). Backing off from this severe judgment only defames the centrality of martyrdom in Christianity.

So we should let the ideal "stand firm" and declare that the "only way to be exempted" from the rigors of the ideal is by "humbling oneself and making an admission" (JFY 102). We must humbly admit that we are afraid to live by the ideal because it is

22. For a helpful discussion of these questions, see "Appendix: Hard Questions" in Kalbach & Kopp, *Because I Said Forever: Embracing Hope in a Not-So-Perfect Marriage* (Sisters, Oregon: Multnomah, 2001), 235–46.

23. M. Jamie Ferreira has a different solution. She uses the "category of responsiveness" to balance out Kierkegaard's account. This in turn eliminates the "extreme" elements in Kierkegaard's view of Christian love. *Love's Grateful Striving: A Commentary on Kierkegaard's Works of Love* (Oxford: Oxford University Press, 2001), 226, 224. I prefer a less creative solution which stays closer to Kierkegaard's actual textual formulations.

too hard for us. Miraculously this confession does not exclude us from God. When we confess our failure and our hope for doing better, we are "eternally saved" (JFY 207). Then we "come . . . to . . . grace" (JFY 142). God grants us forgiveness and the hope of living righteously through him.

This confession is monumental. It shows that our weak faith, straining under the weight of these lofty ideals, is really not "Christianity at all" (JFY 142). True Christianity is too high for us. It would leave us unfulfilled, battered and alone. But that is "treason against us!" (JFY 141). We cannot sacrifice "everything for Christianity" (JFY 134). We are too weak for that.[24] So we live with less. We live with a "mitigation" of true Christianity (JFY 142). The only faithfulness we have left is to refuse to "establish the error" as the true, redefined Christian faith (JFY 102). To do so would be to turn Christianity into something else. Here Kierkegaard stands with Luther. "This entire life," Luther wrote, "is a time of willing to be righteous, but never achieving it, for this happens only in the future life."[25] This admission humbles us. With it we know we are too weak to live the pure Christian life and must depend on God to carry us along.

With this confession we develop "some respect for Christianity" (JFY 209). We refuse to water it down in order to make it easily achievable. We know we would like to change Christianity—but we refuse to do it. "Moreover, just as suspicious characters must register with the police," so we will report to God on the "dubiousness" of our Christian identity—knowing full well that God is "sheer love and grace and compassion" and will welcome us while still expecting us to "be honest in the relationship" with him (JFY 207).

Once we have learned to live under the weight of this ideal, Christian love will remain as extreme as ever. The picture of love in *Works of Love* will be allowed to stand

---

24. On this admission see the need for confession in true love in Amy Laura Hall's *Kierkegaard and the Treachery of Love* (Cambridge: Cambridge University Press, 2002), 106: "The love to which Kierkegaard calls us requires us actively to acknowledge that true love itself is necessarily precarious—requiring prayers of confession and forgiveness." And this precariousness is grounded in our inability to understand each other thoroughly. On this predicament, see *Wittgenstein in Cambridge: Letters and Documents 1911–1951*, ed. Brian McGinness (Oxford: Wiley-Blackwell, 2012), 450: "The older I grow the more I realize how terribly difficult it is for people to understand each other, and I think that what misleads one is the fact that they all look so much like each other. If some people looked like elephants and others like cats, or fish, one wouldn't *expect* them to understand each other and things would look much more like what they really are." On this incommensurability, see BA 92 on p. 116 above. And on Wittgenstein's love for Kierkegaard, see above, p. 57, note 20.

25. Martin Luther, "Lectures on Romans" (1518), LW 25:268. See also Luther's "Defense and Explanation of All the Articles" (1521), LW 32:22: "[The Christian life] is not godliness but the process of becoming godly." See also his "Lectures on First John" (1527), LW 30:272–73: "Christ destroys the works of the devil; the devil destroys the works of Christ. Christ builds love, humility, chastity, etc., in us; the devil builds uncleanness, fornication, strife, and pride. Therefore if you realize that you are affected in such a way that you do not want to sin, to commit fornication; or, if you feel this way and yet resist; or if you feel that you are inclined to have compassion, Christ already has His work in you. But if you feel the opposite, namely, an inclination to adultery, to fornication, etc.; if you see that your brother is in need and do not want to come to his assistance if you are able to do so, the devil already has his work in you. Therefore one can easily know under whom you are."

in all of its fierce boldness. It will stand even though we will not be able to live up to much of it. We will not be able to sacrifice the way it wants us to. But we will be able to lament our failure. We will not explain it away. We will continue to let the pressure of this ideal bear down upon us—pushing us to greater faithfulness. With our sadness, however, we will also have hope. With our sorrow there will be rejoicing (2 Cor 6:10). For through God's abiding mercy we will be saved while we are yet sinners: "For our sake God made Christ to be sin who knew no sin, so that in him we might become the righteousness of God" (2 Cor 5:21).[26]

26. I am grateful to Gordon D. Marino for his criticisms of earlier drafts of this essay. I would also like to dedicate this essay to my dear wife, Jane L. Harty, on the occasion of our 30th wedding anniversary (1972–2002).

8

On God and Dialectics

THE PREVAILING VIEW REGARDING Kierkegaard's last published discourse, *The Change-lessness of God*, is that it is an unqualified celebration of God's love for us and that he published it with his writings against Christendom in order to offset their negativity.[1] But a closer reading of this discourse shows us something different. The two dominant images in the discourse—that of an impassable mountain and a refreshing desert stream (TM 273, 280)—play off against each other in a dialectical way, complicating God's un-changing love for us. As a result, we do not have in *The Changelessness of God*, a simple paean to God's infinite love. What we have is a dialectical rendering of that changeless love which is anything but a "nice, cozy, pleasant . . . love" (JP 3:3475).[2] By way of this dialectical treatment, the "sheer joy" in this unchanging love (TM 269, 271) "quivers with pain," so that it can "resound in the heart" (JP 2:2183; EUD 122). This quiver-ing necessarily combines our joy with the suffering and pain inherent in trying to be obedient to God. It is what complicates Kierkegaard's account of what is positive and consoling in God's unchanging love. It is this quivering in pain that prevents us from regarding God's changeless love "so positively that the positiveness itself is a kind of swindle" (JP 4:4890).[3] In Kierkegaard's book, *For Self-Examination*, published the same

---

1. See, for example, David J. Gouwens, *Kierkegaard as Religious Thinker* (Cambridge: Cambridge University Press, 1996), 228: "[It] is significant that in August of 1855, in the midst of the final phase of his attack, Kierkegaard published the little discourse, . . . "The Unchangeableness of God" [on the] infinite love . . . of God. . . . [So] at the end, despite the undoubted extremity of his attack, Kierkegaard does not abandon God's love as the 'fundament.'"

2. On Kierkegaard's dialectical approach of conjoining opposing ideas, see David F. Swenson, *Something About Kierkegaard*, ed. Lillian Marvins Swenson (1945; Macon, Georgia: Mercer University Press, 1983), 117: "The existential dialectic bears . . . a mutual confrontation of opposites." See also David R. Law, *Kierkegaard as Negative Theologian* (Oxford: Oxford University Press, 1993), 53: "[Existential] dialectics does not proceed by negating the negative but by holding the positive in con-junction with the negative." Kierkegaard believed his dialectical approach guarded his inquiries from "glossing-over" what was most significant (PV 9).

3. For a similar view on Christian joy, see Martin Luther, whom Kierkegaard regarded as "the master of us all" (JP 3:2465). See his "Sermons on John 14–16" (1538), LW 24:399–401: "Although Christ . . . promised His disciples that they would rejoice, . . . He also knows that their joy will . . . be mingled to such an extent with sadness that the sadness will be felt far more intensely than the joy. . . . [For] our joy cannot be full until we see Christ's name hallowed perfectly, all false doctrine and sects abolished, all tyrants and persecutors of Christ's kingdom subdued; not until we see the will and designs of all godless people and of the devil checked and God's will alone prevailing; not until the cares of the belly or hunger and thirst no longer assail us, sin no longer oppresses us, temptation no longer weakens the heart, and death no longer holds us captive. But this will not take place until the life to come. . . . In this life . . . we have only a droplet of this joy. . . . [In this life] progress is slow and

year that Kierkegaard wrote his discourse on God unchanging, he likens this swindle to a quack doctor:

> Harder sufferings! Who is so cruel as to dare say something like that? My friend, it is Christianity, the doctrine that is sold under the name of the gentle comfort, whereas it is eternity's comfort, yes, truly, and for all eternity—but it certainly must deal rather severely.[4] Christianity is not what we human beings, both you and I, are all too eager to make it; it is not a quack doctor. A quack doctor is promptly at your service and immediately applies the remedy and bungles everything. Christianity waits before it applies the remedy; it does not cure every brief little indisposition with the help of eternity—indeed, this is surely an impossibility just as it is self-contradictory! It cures with the help of eternity and for eternity when the sickness is such that eternity can be applied, it is at the point, that is, where you must die to. Therefore Christianity's severity—lest it become nonsense itself (something we human beings are all too willing to make it), lest it confirm you in nonsense. (FSE 80)

This dialectical relation between severity and comfort in the eternal is the key to any proper understanding of Kierkegaard's discourse on *The Changelessness of God*.[5] This is because the eternal in Christianity is more than pure comfort. It also includes severity[6]—held in a dialectical relationship with its comfort. If we rid that eternal comfort of all severity, it would turn it into a quack doctor who is quick to help but does us no good.[7] Soon we would find out that the therapy we received is actually harmful and the medicines administered are either ineffectual or poisonous.

---

cannot be perfect either in faith or in life. Again and again we fall into the mire and are weighed down with sadness and a heavy conscience, which prevent our joy from being perfect or make it so slight that we can hardly feel this incipient joy."

4. Kierkegaard conjoins, without comment, the eternality of God with his changelessness (JP 4:4890; TM 270, 272, 273, 274, 275, 276, 277). For a contemporary statement of the same, see Paul Helm, *The Eternal God: A Study of God Without Time* (1988; Oxford: Oxford University Press, 1997), 90: "God's immutability would appear to . . . entail timeless eternity." Against this correlation, see Robert Cummings Neville, *Eternity and Time's Flow* (Albany: State University of New York Press, 1993), 119: "Eternity is not something static, . . . but something inclusive of the changing dates of the present. Only in eternity is the dynamism of change significant."

5. For a definition of Christianity in terms of the eternal, Kierkegaard writes: "Christianity is the predominance of the outlook of eternity over everything temporal; Christianity grips a man in such a way that because of the eternal he forgets everything of this earth, considers everything of this earth to be 'loss,' exposes himself even to suffering all possible persecution for the sake of the eternal" (JP 6:6958).

6. On severity in Christianity, see Martin Luther, "Lectures on Galatians 1–4" (1535), LW 26:118: "[In Gal 2:14] Paul is acting with a serious and sincere heart and is not pretending to rebuke Peter. But the text makes it obvious that Peter was pretending, and that it was for this that Paul rebuked him. In Paul there is no pretense, but there is pure and Christian severity [*saeveritas*] and a holy pride, which would have been a fault if Peter had committed some trivial sin and had not sinned against the chief doctrine of Christianity."

7. On divine sublimity—which is the opposite of divine quackery—Kierkegaard writes: "Alas, we humans have no conception of divine sublimity! If we can just live on the fat of the land and God

This is precisely what happens when we force eternity to help us too soon. That quick treatment is quackery. It is a distortion of God's changelessness. It skips over our dying to the world which is required if God's changelessness is to bless us.[8] This dying is what enables us to obey God, which in turn sends us God's blessings.[9] Without dying to the world we continue in our rebellion against God. In that case God's changelessness becomes a horror, even though "ordinarily" this is overlooked (TM 272–73).[10] But this correlation between God's changelessness and our response to it is essential. This is because the blessings inherent in God's changelessness are withheld from us if we are not obedient—"in unconditional obedience, . . . completely obedient in unchanged obedience" (TM 268, 279). This correlation is at the heart of the dialectic in

---

does not crack down on us—then we completely forget that his very calmness, just this, can signify his disfavor. We drag God down to the pettiness of someone who stingily watches out for himself and promptly makes a fuss if he does not get what he wants—but the very fact that he lets us get drunk on a life of ease and frothy gratitude can be an expression of his contempt and disfavor, whereas the lives of his beloved ones express that they must suffer, that they are willing to suffer, because they have understood this to be God's will which he has proclaimed clearly enough to us and which we know, but which we harden ourselves against, and clubbing together with others we fortify ourselves in this state—for in solitariness you will become aware" (JP 3:2442). Note also Kierkegaard's warning: "But we must not do what Christendom has done—reduce the majesty of God in order to maintain the conception of God as love" (JP 2:1449).

8. On dying to the world, Kierkegaard writes: "Not until you have died to the selfishness in you and thereby to the world so that you do not love the world or anything in the world, do not selfishly love even one single person—not until you in love of God have learned to hate yourself, not until then can there be talk of the love that is Christian love" (FSE 83–84). On self-hatred in Kierkegaard's thought, see chapters 3 and 7 in this book.

9. This is not works righteousness or Pelagianism, but the necessary compliment to grace and faith. On this correlation see Martin Luther, "Lectures on Romans" (1518), LW 25:235: "[When] St. James [in Jas 2:24] and the apostle [in Rom 2:13] say that a man is justified by works, they are contending against the erroneous notion of those who thought that faith suffices without works, although the apostle does not say that faith justifies without its own works (because then there would be no faith . . .), but that it justifies without the works of the Law. Therefore justification does not demand the works of the Law but a living faith which produces its own works." See also his "Sermon at Coburg on Cross and Suffering" (1530), LW 51:207: "[It is] highly necessary that we suffer not only that God may prove his honor, power, and strength against the devil, but also in order that when we are not in trouble and suffering this excellent treasure which we have may not merely make us sleepy and secure. We see so many people, unfortunately it is all too common, so misusing the gospel that it is a sin and a shame, as if now of course they have been so liberated by the gospel that there is no further need to do anything, give anything, or suffer anything."

10. On this change in how we receive God, see Martin Luther, "Lectures on Romans" (1518), LW 25:219: "God is as changeable as possible. . . . For as each person is in himself, so God is to him as an object. If he is righteous, God is righteous; if he is pure, so is God; if he is wicked, God is wicked, etc. Hence to the damned He will forever seem evil, but to the righteous, righteous, [which is] as He actually is in Himself. But this changeableness is external." On this same point Kierkegaard writes: "The primary effect of anger that is not righteous before God is that a person is made hard of hearing in attending to the admonition [to be slow to anger]. . . . But the person who is quick to pay attention to what does not incite . . . rash words is . . . slow to anger; he will not let the sun go down on his anger [Eph 4:26], and he will fear an even more alarming eclipse, that he might never more be able to see the Father of lights, who is hidden by the shadows of wrath that changed the unchanging" (EUD 138).

Kierkegaard's 1855 discourse. It says that we should match God's changelessness with our unchanging obedience to him.

In this chapter I want to show how this dialectical understanding of the changelessness of God works itself out in Kierkegaard's last discourse on James 1:17–21. I will do this by first showing how the two images of the impassable mountain and the refreshing desert stream are developed in his discourse. Then, I will compare this discourse to his earlier ones on James 1:17–21, to show how his last one builds on them. Finally, I will argue that this discourse on the changelessness of God is included in his late writings from the *Fatherland* and *The Moment*, to show how they are integral to his overall authorship and not a departure from it.

THE DISCOURSE ON THE CHANGELESSNESS OF GOD

This discourse on the changelessness of God is about God's resolute will to love us and our need to conform to it. It is based on his favorite Scriptural text, James 1:17–21,[11] in which God is described as "the Father of lights, with whom there is no change or shadow of variation." This reference to the changelessness of God is the basis for the title of the discourse.[12] Even though this text in James is not untroubled due to the *hapax legomena* in it, its basic meaning is clear. Kierkegaard would agree with the best of modern scholarship that its point is that the steadfastness of God is opposed "to the changeableness of creation."[13] This text "removes God completely from the realm of human passion and destructiveness," and links him with "stability and consistency rather than with change and alteration."[14] Kierkegaard would also follow the ancient church that just as surely as God is unchanging in his love for us, so we who obey him should also be steadfast and free of all "double-mindedness."[15] Because God remains firm and unchanging, "those who have been formed by the gospel . . . which comes

11. See Kierkegaard's remark on Jas 1:17–21: "If a person were permitted to distinguish among biblical texts, I could call . . . [Jas 1:17–21] my first love, . . . my only love—to which one returns again and again and again and *always*" (JP 6:6965). Kierkegaard's love for Jas 1:17–21 is duly noted in Luke Timothy Johnson, *The Letter of James*, The Anchor Bible 37A (New York: Doubleday, 1995), 152: "In the sermon entitled 'The Unchangeableness of God,' . . . Kierkegaard placed himself in the tradition of patristic and medieval interpretation by invoking as his text James 1:17 in support of God's immutability and, therefore, God's constancy in giving." Johnson also notes that this theme of God's changelessness in Jas 1:17 is "one of the noblest *theologoumena* in the New Testament" and "in the *Liturgy of St. John Chrysostom*, . . . James 1:17 is the last citation from Scripture heard by the worshipers before leaving the liturgical assembly" (204–5).

12. The Danish title, *Guds Uforanderlighed*, has also been translated as "The Unchangeableness of God" by David F. Swenson in *A Kierkegaard Anthology*, ed. Robert Bretall (Princeton: Princeton University Press, 1946), 469 and Alastair Hannay in *Søren Kierkegaard: Papers and Journals: A Selection* (New York: Penguin, 1996), 527. Another translation is "The Unchangingness of God" by Bruce H. Kirmmse in *Kierkegaard in Golden Age Denmark* (Bloomington: Indiana University Press, 1990), 521.

13. L. T. Johnson, *The Letter of James*, 196–97.

14. Ibid., 204.

15. Jas 1:8 (RSV).

from above, are called to persevere in these precepts . . . and not . . . be swept away by the times in which we live."[16]

Kierkegaard takes this dialectical text from James, with its opposing ideas of divine stability and the flux of creation, and develops it in his discourse. He juxtaposes the faithfulness of God with the inconstancy and disobedience of humans in order to show what is at the heart of God's changelessness. This means that his discourse cannot be seen as an unadulterated celebration of the joy that is there in the changelessness of God—for that would turn it into a quack doctor. This discourse is a troubled, strained treatment of the two opposing ideas of God's faithfulness and our disobedience. Kierkegaard certainly believed that God's faithfulness is "simply and solely sheer consolation, peace, joy, [and] blessedness" (TM 271). But because we cannot live in strict harmony with that divine purity, as the apostle James could, being ourselves "only beginners under instruction" (TM 271), we cannot have such a full celebration of that joy. We instead must approach the matter dialectically, understanding it "both in terror and for assurance" (TM 271). This is Kierkegaard's boldly printed programmatic statement at the beginning of his discourse: both in terror and for assurance.[17] Any proper understanding of this discourse will have to account for the connection between terror and assurance in that opening declaration. By combining the two, Kierkegaard prevents the majesty of God's changelessness from degenerating into spiritual quackery. Kierkegaard therefore

> warns that there is sheer fear and trembling for frivolous men in the thought of God's unchangeableness. . . . However, when a man has wearied of earthly mutability and is willing to be disciplined by God's unchangeable will, then such horror is replaced by joy. When man himself is willing to renounce inconsistency and caprice, then he can find peace and repose in the God who is dependably and steadfastly the same. This duality of a God who is immovably stern yet unchangeably gracious reflects the sin-grace duality in S. K.'s attack on the church, which recognized divine forgiveness and compassion but only after the sinner came to penitence.[18]

---

16. Severus of Antioch (488–538) as quoted in *James, 1–2 Peter, 1–3 John, Jude*, ed. Gerald Bray (Downers Grove, Illinois: InterVarsity, 2000), 15. In this regard see also Eph 4:14: "No longer be children, tossed to and fro and carried about with every wind of doctrine, by the cunning of men, by their craftiness in deceitful wiles" (RSV). On this verse Kierkegaard notes that "in the motley, teeming crowd, in the noise of the world, little attention is paid from day to day and year to year to whether a person completely wills the good if only he has influence and power, is in a big enterprise, is somebody to himself and to others" (UDVS 65).

17. Even though this discourse does not have any clearly defined sections (such as the six sections in EUD 31–48), two italicized lines seem to divide the discourse into two main parts. The first is: "This thought is *terrifying, sheer fear and trembling*" (TM 272). The second is: "But then it is also the case *that there is reassurance and blessedness in this thought*" (TM 278). If these lines truly are dividers, then the first section on terror is twice as long as the second one on assurance.

18. George E. Arbaugh and George B. Arbaugh, *Kierkegaard's Authorship: A Guide to the Writings of Kierkegaard* (Rock Island, Illinois: Augustana College Library, 1967), 376–77.

Kierkegaard notes this essential duality of renunciation and repose in order to ward off any lesser accounts of God's changelessness. This duality does not allow his exuberance for the joy he finds in God's changelessness to displace, through an undialectical understanding, the terror that is also there in that changelessness.

In the short preface to the 1855 publication of this same discourse, Kierkegaard reports that it was first delivered in the Citadel Church on May 18, 1851 and only published some four years later on September 3, 1855 (TM 267). He also notes that he has three other discourses on the same text—published in two separate collections from 1843 (EUD 31–48, 125–39, 141–58). But unlike these first three discourses, he actually preached his last one in church on a Sunday morning.[19] Pastor Peter Zahle[20] (1825–98) was there in the Citadel Church when Kierkegaard delivered his discourse on the changelessness of God and reported that no one could "forget that extremely weak, but wonderfully expressive voice. Never have I heard a voice," he says, "that was so capable of inflecting even the most delicate nuances of expression."[21] The fact that he preached this discourse on a Sunday morning with such earnestness and that he had three earlier ones on the same text, all gives this 1855 discourse a unique place in his authorship. This reference to his earlier discourses also complicates our understanding of his last one on the same text. It tells us that this discourse on the changelessness of God is not straightforward but must be read in light of his earlier work. It tells us that its meaning is somehow tied to what he had to say at the beginning of his authorship. And this joining of his earlier discourses with his last one is yet another dialectical feature in the 1855 discourse.

The opening prayer to this 1855 discourse is also dialectical. In it Kierkegaard says that God is "changeless in love" (TM 268). This is based on the conviction that while God can be "moved" by our pleas to him, he nevertheless remains unchanged:

19. See Niels-Jørgen Cappelørn, "Die ursprüngliche Unterbrechung: Søren Kierkegaard beim Abendmahl im Freitagsgottesdienst der Kopenhagener Frauenkirke," *Kierkegaard Studies: Yearbook* 1996: 315–88 as quoted in Michael Plekon, "Kierkegaard at the End: His 'Last' Sermon, Eschatology and the Attack on the Church," *Faith and Philosophy* 17 (January 2000): 83n5. See also K. Brian Söderquist's translation of the Cappelørn essay, "Søren Kierkegaard at Friday Communion in the Church of Our Lady," IKC 18:255–94.

20. On Peter Zahle, see *Encounters With Kierkegaard: A Life Seen by His Contemporaries*, ed. and trans. Bruce H. Kirmmse with Virginia R. Laursen (Princeton: Princeton University Press, 1996), 301.

21. Quoted in Joakim Garff, *Søren Kierkegaard: A Biography* (2000), trans. Bruce H. Kirmmse (Princeton: Princeton University Press, 2005), 675. Zahle's description sounds similar to what Kierkegaard's pseudonym Hilarius Bookbinder said about the wonders of the Danish language: "I feel fortunate to be bound to . . . a mother tongue that is rich in intrinsic originality when it stretches the soul and with its sweet tones sounds voluptuously in the ear; a mother tongue that does not groan, obstructed by difficult thought, and perhaps the reason some believe it cannot express it is that it makes the difficulty easy by articulating it; . . . a language that is not without expressions for the great, the crucial, the eminent, yet has a lovely, a winsome, a genial partiality for intermediate thoughts and subordinate ideas and adjectives, and the small talk of moods and the humming of transitions and the cordiality of inflections and the secret exuberance of concealed well-being; . . . a mother tongue that captivates its children with a chain that 'is easy to carry—yes, but hard to break'" (SLW 489–90).

[O God, you] are not like a human being. If [a human being] is to maintain a mere measure of changelessness, he must not have too much that can move him and must not let himself be moved too much. But everything moves you, and in infinite love. Even what we human beings call a trifle and unmoved pass by, the sparrow's need, that moves you; what we so often scarcely pay attention to, a human sigh, that moves you, Infinite Love. But nothing changes you, you Changeless One![22] O you who in infinite love let yourself be moved, may this prayer also move you to bless it so that the prayer may change the one who is praying into conformity with your changeless will, you Changeless One! (TM 268)

From this prayer we could easily conclude that God is both moved and unmoved.[23] Kierkegaard seems, however, to be saying instead that the fact that God is infinitely moveable is what shows the very majesty of his changelessness. But this is not obvious since our experience of constancy or changelessness differs radically from God's changelessness. Unlike God, our changelessness is jeopardized when we feel the influence of others. Under their sway we change. This makes it difficult for us to see how God could be both changeless and moved at the same time.[24] Kierkegaard explains that if we were to allow ourselves to be moved by others, we would have

22. Further into this discourse, Kierkegaard explains how God is moved yet unchanging: "God is changeless. . . . He puts on the visible world as a garment; he changes it as one changes a garment—himself unchanged. . . . In the world of events, he is everywhere present at every moment, . . . when a sparrow dies and when the Savior of the human race is born. At every moment he . . . changes everything in an instant, the opinion of people, judgments, human loftiness and lowliness; he changes everything—himself unchanged. . . . In unchanged clarity—indeed, that is precisely why he is unchanged, because he is pure clarity, . . . no darkness can come close. . . . We are not clarity in this way, and that is why we are changeful—at times something becomes clearer to us, and at times darker, and we are changed. Now change takes place around us [and] we ourselves in all this are in turn changed within us. But God is changeless" (TM 271–72).

23. On this conundrum, see Brian Leftow, *Time and Eternity* (Ithaca: Cornell University Press, 1991), 302, 361: "A timeless God . . . can interact with creatures without undergoing real change—for such a God can create a universe with His responses in a certain sense 'built in' . . . [Therefore] God is beyond and in a sense above time. But . . . this does not diminish His efficacy within it. [He] can have the greatness both of the philosophers' transcendent source of all and the believers' living Lord."

24. On this difficulty, see William Hasker, "Does God Change?" in *Questions About God: Today's Philosophers Ponder the Divine*, ed. Steven M. Cahn and David Shatz (New York: Oxford, 2002), 140–41: "[On the one hand, if] the majestic and supremely admirable Lord of all is 'without passion'—if he views the world and all its sorrows and sufferings with serene, imperturbable bliss—then should not this be our aim as well? Conversely, if it is fitting and good that we humans should care deeply for one another, should love one another in a way that makes us vulnerable to suffering and loss, then should not a love like this be attributed to God also? Perhaps the two ideals, of human and divine love, could be pried apart—but only at the cost of voiding the scriptural injunction to be 'imitators of God' (Eph 5:1). . . . [However, if] God were to change, so the argument goes, then he would change either for the better or for the worse. But God cannot change for the better, since he is already perfect. And he cannot change for the worse, for this would mean that he would no longer be perfect. So God cannot change." Regarding prying the two ideals apart, see Is 55:8–9; Lk 18:27; Rom 8:3–4 and Heb 4:15. On that score, the call to imitate God would not be in every case—like loving the world, for instance (Jn 3:16 vs. 1 Jn 2:15–17).

to be very circumspect about it. We could not let it happen too often, and when it did, we could not allow ourselves to be moved too deeply. This is because individual constancy and interpersonal empathy are at odds in us. Our constancy or changelessness conflicts with our empathy—and vice versa. When constancy holds sway in our lives, our empathy fades away due to that constancy or changelessness holding us back from showing any empathy. The two cannot be combined without one or the other giving way—for in us constancy and empathy very often are mutually exclusive. But not so with God. His majesty is precisely that he can always be both unchanging and moved at the same time.[25] He can be perfectly changeless and perfectly open to the needs of others without compromising either one.[26]

In this prayer Kierkegaard is keeping us from supposing that God's changelessness makes him distant or remote—without any interest in moving us, let alone being moved by us. But this lack of interaction is not what Christianity teaches. In order to make that point, he shows how God can still be moved by us even while remaining unchanged.[27] Knowing this, we would have to concede that we should also be moved by God. The point is that God's changelessness does not slam the doors shut on our interactions with him. God's very changelessness is supposed to change us, by changing our inconstancy into an approximation of his changeless fidelity. At the beginning of this opening prayer we read: "Would that we . . . let ourselves be brought up, in unconditional obedience, by your changelessness" (TM 268). God's changelessness is supposed to breed steadfastness in us. And at the end of the prayer it says: "May this prayer also . . . change the one who is praying[28] into conformity with your change-

---

25. For another argument on this same point, see Keith Ward, "God as Creator," in *The Philosophy in Christianity*, ed. Godfrey Vesey (Cambridge: Cambridge University Press, 1989), 118: "If we are to follow the Christian Fathers in affirming the ineffability of God, perhaps we should say, not that he is wholly immutable, but simply that he does not change as we do, by loss and decay. It glorifies God more to say that he is both changeless in wisdom and bliss and endlessly creative in loving response than to say that there is nothing more he can be than what he already is. At least, that is what we might expect a faith founded on belief in the incarnation of the eternal in time to say."

26. On this duality, Kierkegaard adds these twists: "O, in grace they have touched him, moved him deeply, him who is infinite love. But it does not follow from this that your desire is fulfilled. He has *so infinitely much* to take care of, and *one thought is to be maintained* throughout the whole, and thus it may well be that he must deny you this. But it touches and moves him, both your prayer *and that he must deny it*—for nothing changes him" (emphasis added) (JP 4:4891).

27. Kierkegaard even argues that the more unchanging God is, the more moved he is by our pleas and concerns: "Be assured that [God] suffers much more than you—for he cannot change" (JP 4:4892). This is because his changelessness restrains his countervailing yearning to gladden us.

28. On this appropriate sort of change ensuing from prayer, Kierkegaard writes: "The true prayer-relationship does not exist when God hears what is being prayed about but when the *pray-er* continues to pray until he is the *one who hears*, who hears what God wills. . . . The true pray-er is simply *obedient*" (JP 3:3403). In this regard see, *The Prayers of Kierkegaard*, ed. Perry D. LeFevre (1956; Chicago: University of Chicago Press, 1976), 221–22: "Kierkegaard's view of true prayer implies a concept of false prayer. . . . False prayer falsely conceives of God. It thinks God is changeable; it tempts God, but God neither tempts nor can be tempted. It thinks God operates in terms of human conceptions of good and evil, pleasant and unpleasant. It turns God into man writ large, as if he could be persuaded, cajoled, bargained with. . . . The individual who prays truly is humble and finds the experience of

less will." God's changelessness is not meant to leave us alone in our self-enclosed independence and isolation from him. That again would be spiritual quackery. To the contrary, God's changelessness is meant to make us obedient to him by bringing us into unchanging compliance with his changeless will. Kierkegaard believed that when we rebel against God—suffering from what he calls "ungodly unawareness"—we become "pirated editions." (CD 64).[29] By rebelling, we deny that God, "the infinitely lofty one, is very close" to us (CD 166). Kierkegaard warns that "if a person can lose his composure when he is placed before His Royal Majesty and can forget what he wanted to say, how terrible[30] to be placed before God, because His Royal Majesty is neither as lofty as God nor can he come as close to you" (CD 167). This loftiness and terror should dissuade us from rebelling. They should also show us the futility in trying to make a quack doctor out of this divine majesty (FSE 80).

The Images of the Mountain and the Stream. A few pages into the discourse, Kierkegaard compares God to an unchanging, impassable mountain (TM 273) in order to make the point that we need to obey God's unchanging will, rather than

---

prayer humbling. The individual who prays falsely bolsters his own self-esteem and is presumptuous in his prayer. True prayer accepts everything and refers everything to God. . . . True prayer maintains the dialectical tension in man's sense of the distance and the nearness of God; false prayer either volatilizes the God-relationship in a fantastically elevated conception of God or so likens God to man that it treats God as a fellow human being. The man who prays truly strips himself of all cleverness, while false prayer is often an attempt at clever conversation. . . . The man who truly prays listens to God; the man who prays falsely wants God to listen to him."

29. In the words of Kierkegaard's Anti-Climacus, we then no longer rest "transparently in the power" that establishes us (SUD 14, 30). Obeying God allows us to rest transparently in God. Disobeying God obscures this fact of our dependence on him. That dependence, however, is not cancelled when we disobey. On the meaning of transparency, see John D. Glenn Jr., "The Definition of the Self and the Structure of Kierkegaard's Work," IKC 19:17: "The more 'transparent' a self is in its God-relation, . . . the greater its conception or consciousness of God."

30. On this divine majesty, Kierkegaard adds: "Who really comprehends the eminence and the elevation of the divine? Suppose that God's cause were almost lost, humanly speaking. Now someone comes along and humanly, yet honestly, wants to help. And God, who has been waiting in heaven, answers: Well, now, so you want to be examined? . . . [For] the closer you come to God the more rigorous he becomes. He does not make the mistake of rejoicing over this help—no, it becomes your examination. But no clubbing with God, no fraternizing" (JP 2:1422)! But, as Kierkegaard notes, this does not totally remove God from us: "God does not naïvely become involved with a man as friend with friend. . . . Yet we have come closer to God; but just as in relation to the ideal every step forward is a step backward, so it is in relation to God: approach, withdrawal, and yet, *actual* approach" (JP 2:1425). This oddity Kierkegaard calls "the law of inversion"—"To come closer is to get farther away: infinite majesty!" (JP 2:1432). Therefore in summarization, Kierkegaard writes: "God is at one and the same time infinitely close to man and infinitely far away. To come into relation to God is a voyage of discovery somewhat comparable to an expedition to the North Pole, so rarely does a man ever actually press forward on this way, to discovery." (JP 2:1415)! On this law of inversion, see Sylvia Walsh, *Living Christianly: Kierkegaard's Dialectic of Christian Existence* (University Park, Pennsylvania: Pennsylvania State University Press, 2005), 162: Kierkegaard's "originality and uniqueness" in describing Christian life is found "chiefly in his conception and use of inverse dialectic."

to make it coincide with our own likings.[31] This image[32] introduces "fear and trembling" (TM 272, 276) into this discourse,[33] making it lose "some of the gentleness" of his earlier ones.[34] This frightfulness comes from the contrast drawn between the changelessness of God and the "changefulness of human beings," which is depressing and exhausting because of its corruptibility (TM 269). This contrast between God's changelessness and our corruptibility is part of the dialectic in this discourse and is integral to any proper analysis of the changelessness of God. This contrast shows the changelessness of God—"from another side" (TM 271). What is supposed to be "sheer joy and gladness" (TM 269) can actually frighten us. This fear comes from our imperfect reception of the good news of God's changelessness. There is a "spirit of gloom" in this failure, but it is not part of James 1:17–21, which speaks only about "the changelessness of God, not about anything else" (TM 269). Nevertheless, that failure on our part must be included in any adequate analysis of God's changelessness—even if it is not in James 1:17–21 itself. For when we "come in conflict with this changeless will," as we inevitably will, due to our rebellion, we learn that what is so lovely can actually "crush" us (TM 272). Our rebellion, then, is not extraneous to God's changelessness, but integral to it, in that it reveals its terrifying nature which otherwise would go unnoticed.[35] This happens because God will not change just so we can escape from his

31. On this image, see Psalm 76:4: "Glorious art thou, O God, more majestic than the everlasting mountains" (RSV).

32. Kierkegaard's writings are filled with images, metaphors and analogies. In Section VII of the *Cumulative Index to Kierkegaard's Writings* (Princeton: Princeton University Press, 2000), over 600 analogies are listed (449–57). On this feature of Kierkegaard's writings, see Jamie Lorentzen, *Kierkegaard's Metaphors* (Macon, Georgia: Mercer University Press, 2001), 166: "Metaphor appropriated religiously becomes a signpost of grace by illuminating the possibility of faith, redemption, and an ideal life after death through the contrasts of opposites."

33. This reference to fear and trembling, as well as to that imposing mountain, reminds one of *Fear and Trembling* by Kierkegaard's pseudonym, Johannes de Silentio. In *Fear and Trembling*, Abraham goes "up the mountain [of Moriah] alone with Isaac" (FT, 9) to sacrifice him at God's command, "in fear and trembling" (FT 75). Even though Abraham is not mentioned in this 1855 discourse on God's changelessness, his specter floats throughout it. Abraham was "the first to feel and to bear witness to that prodigious passion that disdains the terrifying battle with the raging elements and the forces of creation in order to contend with God" (FT 23)! That same terror is felt before God's changelessness, which demands that we sacrifice our "self-will, . . . caprice and willfulness" (TM 278). And when we do, we finally come to rest in an "overwhelming security" (TM 280) and share in Abraham's greatness, which is "great by that power whose strength is powerlessness, great by that wisdom whose secret is foolishness, great by that hope whose form is madness, great by the love that is hatred to oneself" (FT 16–17)! These veiled references to Abraham's trial and triumph, are another way in which this discourse is dialectical. Just so, Johannes de Silento insists that there is no way to share in Abraham's blessing without going through the same "anxiety and distress" he had to suffer (FT 53, 64, 66, 74, 113). And so too in our life experiences we cannot skip over the journey to Mt. Moriah (FT 52).

34. Arbaugh, *Kierkegaard's Authorship*, 377.

35. On the intrinsic wrath of God, see Jim McGuiggan, *Celebrating the Wrath of God* (Colorado Springs, Colorado: Water Brook, 2001). See also Martin Luther, "Lectures on 1 Timothy" (1528), LW 28:264: "Christ . . . has become the Price by which satisfaction is made for divine justice and wrath on our behalf. . . . The wrath of God is real, not imaginary. It is no joke. Were it false, mercy would be false. You see, as wrath is, so is the mercy which forgives. May God avert that joke from us. When genuine

punishments (TM 273).[36] That determinedness is part of what is unchanging in God's changelessness. If he were to change, then our waywardness would cease being bad. But that would turn God into a quack doctor—healing us without requiring of us any effort on our part.[37]

Such a divine alteration is impossible because God is an enormous, unchanging, and impassable mountain. All that we can do when faced with such a God is "stop at the foot" of the mountain and surrender (TM 273). That would resolve our conflict with God, if we were to do so. In this conflict with God, we are the only one who can make a change for the better. We must forswear our rebellion and obey God. But if we refuse to do that, God will crush us. That is the point in the image of the impassable mountain. But Kierkegaard goes on to say that God can also remain "absolutely still, . . . almost as if he did not exist." In this case, we are not crushed by that mountain for failing to be "in accord with" God's will (TM 276). God refrains from that because he is "eternally sure of himself"[38] and can take his time since he "has eternity" (TM 274).[39] In this case, eternity is neither sheer joy nor religious quackery. Now the eternal

---

wrath is at its highest, so is genuine mercy."

36. So I disagree with Arbaugh, *Kierkegaard's Authorship*, 376: "How frightening that the silent, changeless God cannot even be moved into striking back at those who mock him!" The point actually goes in the opposite direction—that the One who "crushes" the disobedient (TM 272) can also ignore them (TM 274), for God can show either "gentleness or severity" (TM 276). The surprise is that if God is gentle, our plight becomes "even more terrible" (TM 274), since by delaying our punishment, our disobedience becomes "more malignant" (TM 275). With this increase in our disobedience, there is necessarily a commensurate increase in punishment. Arbaugh misses how that ostensibly kind delay in our punishment actually makes things worse. See also Martin Luther, "Commentary on 1 Corinthians 15" (1534), LW 28:159–60: "Even though many are now going their own way unconcerned, do you not suppose that God may be postponing His punishment until a time when they have long forgotten the sin? Then they regard themselves as pious, lament and cry as though they did not deserve this. For God does not let punishment follow immediately on the heels of sin but lets people go on long enough and restrains Himself to see if they will reform. However, in the end and when least expected He comes with real terror."

37. On healing too quickly, Kierkegaard writes: "As a rule Christianity is dismaying rather than consoling. Even I, who have been brought so far out, can scarcely bear Christianity's consolation—and then the average man! But if I am a Christian clergyman, I am obligated to bring consolation in the Christian way. The question remains whether I would have the courage to be Christianly cruel. The thing is: momentary relief is always human sympathy. A whimpering mother who coddles her child has the most sympathy, but we find fault with that. She has the most sympathy, always helps at the moment, therefore cannot educate. . . . But Christianity . . . educates with the help of eternity and to eternity. Therein lies the dismaying aspect of Christianity's help, for when a person suffers, Christianity's help begins by turning the whole temporal life into suffering. The more quickly help comes, the more inferior and meaningless the education" (JP 6:6262).

38. See 2 Tm 2:13.

39. Against this basic assertion of Kierkegaard's, which he inherited from Christian doctrine, see Nicholas Wolterstorff, "God Everlasting" in *Contemporary Philosophy of Religion*, ed. Steven M. Cahn and David Shatz (New York: Oxford, 1982), 97: "God is everlasting rather than eternal. God is indeed without beginning and end. But at least some of his aspects stand in temporal order-relations to each other. Thus . . . his life and existence is itself temporal." See also his "Suffering Love" in *Philosophy and the Christian Faith*, ed. Thomas V. Morris (Notre Dame: University of Notre Dame Press, 1988), 230:

unchanging God uses his immutability to leave us twisting in the wind indefinitely. The impassable mountain does not crush us in some cascading avalanche, but just sits there silently—and that itself is our punishment. This confident, divine stillness leads to the accounting of eternity on judgment day. On that day there will be a final punishment which, Kierkegaard says, will be worse than any partial, earthly one.[40] But before it comes, there is mercy and time for "turning around and reformation" (TM 274). That is another dialectical element in this analysis. But sinners will not act in their best interest. They will not jump at the chance because "the longer the time between the guilt and the punishment, . . . the more tempting it is to be light-minded," and suppose that God will not follow through on his punishments (TM 275). This hope, however, is futile because God is unchanging. The truth is that "you will never escape him," since he is that enormous, impassable mountain—unchanging and not at all forgetful of our failures. Because of that divine relentlessness, "there is sheer fear and trembling in this thought of God's changelessness" (TM 276). No quackery here. Our failure to be "in accord with" the will of God (TM 276) has a negative impact on us. It turns the sheer joy of God's changelessness into sheer fear for us. That possible negative outcome is an essential feature of any proper analysis of God's changelessness. Finding such trembling in what is intrinsically "sheer consolation" (TM 271) is the central dialectic in Kierkegaard's last discourse on God's changelessness. It shows us how God's changelessness can boomerang on us—while still remaining the sheer consolation that it is, in and of itself.

But this boomerang effect is not emphasized as it should be (TM 272).[41] As a result, the "fear and trembling" (TM 272, 276) in this discourse is not given its due as

---

"Our hearts will not find their full rest [in God] until the heart of the Lord is itself fully at rest in his perfected Kingdom."

40. Kierkegaard writes that in that day you will be asked by Christ, who was self-denial himself, about "how often you in self-denial endured insults patiently, about what you have suffered, not for your own sake, for your own selfish interests' sake, but what you in self-denial have suffered for God's sake" (UDVS 224). Note also, however, Kierkegaard's conviction that "temporal life is the critical time, the crisis, when the decision is made whether you are a Christian or not and thereby, again, your situation for an eternity is determined" (JP 4:4815).

41. On this oversight, see Michael Plekon, "Kierkegaard at the End," 71, 75: "If his work in this last conflict with the Church is a corrective, then this sermon is that corrective's corrective. . . . Kierkegaard's sermon neither begins nor concludes with the dread seemingly attached to being always in the wrong before God. . . . Throughout 'God's Unchangingness' human fluctuations and confusion, weakness and duplicity are met with divine forgiveness and refreshment, a theophany of divine compassion." Missing from this account is that God can and will "crush" the disobedient (TM 272). Without this dialectical element, the "sentimental flirtation [and] brashness with which we generally speak of the consolation in the thought of God's unchangeableness is an illusion" (JP 2:1428). Kierkegaard rightly attacks this sentimental illusion by dialectically joining the peace and joy in God's changeless love (TM 269, 271), with the "sheer fear and trembling in this thought of God's changelessness" (TM 276, 278), which happens when our will is not "unconditionally" his will (TM 272). Similarly, it would be misleading to say that in his discourse on God's changelessness Kierkegaard was enclosing his late polemical writings in "parentheses of comfort." M. Jamie Ferreire, Kierkegaard (West Sussex, United Kingdom: Wiley-Blackwell, 2009), 187.

Kierkegaard's bold opening declaration called for (TM 271). Kierkegaard wanted both the terror and assurance included in our understanding of God's changelessness (TM 271). We are not to truncate his changelessness—reducing it to just a celebration of the joy that is rightly in it. Samuel Barber (1910–81), in his famous choral arrangement of the opening prayer to this discourse, expresses musically the fear and trembling in Kierkegaard's 1855 discourse.[42] In his piece, called *Prayers of Kierkegaard*,[43] the enormity of the terror that can come from God's changelessness is powerfully presented—with its pounding *fortissimo* sections in measures 22–32, and again in measures 54–60. These harsh sections are preceded by extended *pianissimo* sections—depicting the peace and joy that are also there in God's changelessness—which provide a stark contrast to the crushing punishment that comes when we disobey God. When the pounding sections on God's wrath come, "the orchestra hammers percussively on D minor [while] the chorus decreases in volume but remains 'unchanging' in its major tonality."[44] In this anthem, Barber understands the dialectical nature of Kierkegaard's discourse—playing off against each other, as it were, the *pianissimo* and *fortissimo* sections. In this dialectic, Barber gives full sway to both God's unfailing love for us and our sinfulness, to both the comfort his changelessness brings and also the wrath it can inflict on us when we disobey God.

Near the end of this discourse, Kierkegaard introduces his second image for the changelessness of God—that of a refreshing, cool stream in the middle of a hot, burning desert (TM 280). In this image the positive side of the changelessness of God is given full and lasting expression. Languishing in the desert of our rebellion, we are not without hope—even though standing before that imposing mountain, God's changelessness seemed too "far, far beyond human powers to . . . be involved with" (TM 278). But now a stream of refreshment and gladness beckons to us—and in that, the sheer consolation that is at the heart of God's changelessness, gladdens us. But this "gladness" is not cast in stark contrast to the terror in that impassable mountain. This comforting image of God's unchanging love for us, does not come through as unbridled pleasantness. It rather is haunted by 2 Corinthians 6:1: "We entreat you not

42. "Program Notes" on *Prayers of Kierkegaard*, Oregon Symphony, Portland, Oregon, March 31, 2007: "The orchestra enters, followed by full chorus, crying out an indictment: 'But nothing changes Thee, O Thou Unchanging!'" This frightful element is also noted in Hidetomo Yamashita's study of Kierkegaard's last discourse, "The Conquest of Impermanence," *Kierkegard Studies: The Kierkegaard Society of Japan* 1 (November 2001): 1–23.

43. Samuel Barber, *Prayers of Kierkegaard: For Mixed Chorus, Soprano Solo and Orchestra with Incidental Tenor Solo; Alto Solo Ad Libitum, Opus* 30 (New York: G. Schirmer, 1954). *Prayers of Kierkegaard* was first performed by the Boston Symphony, December 3, 1954, with Charles Munch conducting, Leontyne Price, soprano, and the Cecelia Society. For a recording see *Barber, Bartók, Vaughan Williams*, TELARC 20 BIT (1998), CD-80479. For other musical settings of other words of Kierkegaard's, see *Kierkegaard Set to Music*, Danica Records (1998), DCD-8184.

44. William A. Dailey, *Techniques of Composition Used in Contemporary Works for Chorus and Orchestra on Religious Texts* (PhD dissertation, Catholic University of America, 1965), 8. See also Barbara B. Heyman, *Samuel Barber: The Composer and His Music* (New York: Oxford, 1992), 348–59.

to accept the grace of God in vain."[45] In the spirit of this verse, Kierkegaard peppers the lines following the introduction of this second image with six conditional clauses and six other equivalent expressions. Together they restrain the image and limit the refreshment this stream brings. This stream—God's unfailing love for us—surely will refresh us, but not as quackery. It is far more pleasant than that dialectical, opposing image of the crushing mountain! But that cool desert stream can only refresh us *if we obey God*. This obedience requires us to "renounce . . . caprice and willfulness" (TM 278). While this renunciation means loss and weakness on our part, as compared with our prior willfulness, it also brings great happiness and abiding joy:

> Never, never did any lover become as happy, never, never did the parched and drought-stricken earth sense the rain's refreshment as deliciously as the worshipper in his weakness blessedly senses God's strength. Now these two suit each other, God and worshipper, happily and blissfully as lovers have never suited each other. Now the worshiper's only wish is to become weaker and weaker, because that would mean all the more worship; worship's only desire is that God will become stronger and stronger. The worshiper has lost himself, and in such a way that this is the only thing he wishes to be rid of, the only thing from which he flees; he has won God—so it is directly his concern that God will become stronger and stronger. (CD 132)

That promised refreshment, which hinges on our increasing weakness and God's increasing strength, is "always only good news," in its own right (TM 269). Our disobedience has not dried up all of the streams in the wastelands of our rebellions! There is still hope for us, even in the aftermath of our failures. But if we refuse to obey God, not even these remaining desert streams can quench our thirst. That impassable mountain still waits there alongside the desert stream to crush us, if need be (TM 272). *The desert stream cannot wash away that threatening mountain.* Kierkegaard therefore warns:

> When you allow yourself to be brought up by his changelessness so that you renounce instability and changefulness and caprice and willfulness—then you rest ever more blessedly in this changelessness of God. That the thought of

45. (RSV). On this verse Kierkegaard writes from the same time of his last discourse: "The error from which Luther turned was an exaggeration with regard to works. And he was entirely right; he did not make a mistake—a person is justified solely and only by faith. That is the way he talked and taught—and believed. And that this was not taking grace in vain [2 Cor 6:1]—to that his life witnessed. Splendid! But already the next generation slackened. . . . It made the Lutheran position into doctrine, and in this way faith also diminished in vital power. . . . Works—well, God knows there was no longer any question about that; it would be a shame to accuse this later age of exaggeration with regard to works, and neither were people so silly that they presumed to want to have merit for what they exempted themselves from doing. . . . [But this has] very little resemblance to Luther's way—from the horror, through having tortured himself in a monastery for a number of years without finding rest for his soul or rest from this horror, finally to find faith's blessed way out, so that it was no wonder that this much-tried man witnessed so powerfully against building one's salvation upon works, not against works—it was only the sly world that heard wrong" (JFY 193–94).

God's changelessness is blessed, indeed, who doubts that; just see to it that you become like that so that you can blessedly rest in this changelessness! . . . No one but you yourself can disturb this rest. . . . There will . . . come times when you will . . . say: Change is not pleasing. . . . When that happens, you will be especially prompted to seek . . . the Changeless One. . . . [But] if you yourself want it otherwise, this thought about the changelessness of God will . . . be soon forgotten in changefulness. Yet this fault is not due to him, the Changeless One! (TM 278–79)

In this passage the blessings of God clearly hinge on our obedience and willingness to ask for his help.[46] If we refuse to renounce our willfulness then we will obstruct God's blessings and lose those refreshing waters.[47] And this is not the fault of the stream—or of that changeless One of infinite love. The stream remains there, beckoning us with its refreshment.[48] It is our fault that we have not been refreshed since we are the ones who have refused to conform to God's will.[49] While it is true that "from *above* there is always only good news" (TM 269), we can still ruin it through our disobedience.[50] Even so, the good news still remains good—just not for us. This puts a

46. For an example of such an admission, see Paul Tillich, "On the Transitoriness of Life," in *The Shaking of the Foundations* (New York: Scribner's, 1948), 69: "So short is our life—and it seems so long. . . . [This] shortness of our life . . . makes a real fulfillment impossible. Although very few want to repeat their lives, we often hear people say: 'If only I could start my life again, with all its experiences, I could live it in the right way. It would be more than this broken piece, this fragment, this frustrated attempt which I call my life.' But life does not allow us to begin again. And even if we could begin again, or even if our life were among the most perfect and happy and successful ones, would we not . . . feel that the most valuable things in it, the good, the creative, and the joyful hours, were based on endless toil and followed by disappointment? Would we not feel that what we thought to be important was not?" On this point Kierkegaard notes: "Christianity continually speaks about eternity, constantly thinks about the eternal—and then Christendom repeats the same thing and [erroneously] thinks about this earthly life" (JP 4:4799). On this same thought, see Col 3:2: "Set your minds on things that are above, not on things that are on earth" (RSV).

47. But this spring does not dry up due to our disobedience. It, rather, unlike actual water springs, is "always to be found unchanged" (TM 280). This is reminiscent of Luther's image of the baptismal boat in his "Large Catechism" (1529), BC 446. There he argues that if we abandon our baptism and live contrary to its principles, then we have gone overboard—but the boat itself has not sunk because of that. Instead we can always swim back to the boat—living once again in harmony with our baptism and benefiting once again from its graciousness. After we go overboard, the boat keeps floating on the high seas, ever waiting for us to return—much like Kierkegaard's desert stream that does not dry up but flows on into the future, ever waiting for us to repent and drink from its waters of refreshment. "Ah, delicious coolness! . . . your faithful coolness, O beloved spring, is not subject to change" (TM 280)!

48. Therefore it would be right to say here, as it was said of Abraham, that we have "no dirge of sorrow" (FT 17).

49. On this breathtaking turpitude, Kierkegaard adds: "The unconditional joy is simply joy over God, over whom and in whom you can always unconditionally rejoice. If you do not become unconditionally joyful in this relationship, then the fault lies unconditionally in you, in your ineptitude in casting all your sorrows upon him, in your unwillingness to do so, in your conceitedness, in your self-willingness" (WA 43).

50. See Martin Luther, "Lectures on Genesis 21–25" (1545), LW 4:49: "It is correct . . . to say that

huge qualification on the joy that is there in God's changelessness. God's unchanging love does not wash away all human willfulness. How we behave affects whether or not we will receive God's love—for we can disturb and disrupt it (TM 279).[51]

But if we obey God's will, loving him with all our heart, then his changelessness refreshes us (TM 272). Then the stability that is inherent in God's changeless love, gives rest for our souls.[52] Now we are, "God be praised, provided for," as Kierkegaard rightly says (TM 280). We will not be disappointed by having God let us down. The fact that we have rebelled in the past does not disqualify us when we turn over a new leaf and follow God. Whenever a person comes to God, "at whatever age, at whatever time of day, in whatever condition—if he comes honestly, he will always find" God's love (TM 281). That is the basis for the sheer joy that we have in the changelessness of God. He will not renege on his promises because we have repeatedly rebelled over the years. All that matters for us is that we are honest about our failure and our need for God's help.[53] Insincerity, or the lack of earnestness, is all that God will not tolerate

---

people should be buoyed up and comforted; but a definition should be added—a definition stating *who such people are*, namely, that they are those who are wasting away from hunger and thirst in the desert after they have been cast out of their home and country, who sigh and cry to the Lord and are now at the point of despair. People of this kind are *fit hearers of the Gospel*. But those who feel that they are in a state of grace because of some physical prerogative, who vaunt their own righteousness and sanctity, do not think they are in the desert. . . . They do not know what it means to wander in the desert. They are not humbled. They are not killed. They must be struck with the hammer of the Law and broken to pieces. *Yes, they must be reduced to nothing*" (emphasis added). On this same nothingness in Kierkegaard's thought, see EUD 226; UDVS 193, 339; WL 102–3, 218, 267–68, 272, 347, 365–66; CD 58, 81, 128, 223, 298, 299; WA 10, 157; JFY 106, 115, 167; TM 10, 189, 257, 307; BA 108. Kierkegaard believed that "[culture] and education and sensibleness and social life" all work against the realization of the importance of this nothingness and self-annihilation, for they make "people, in the religious sense, absentminded [and] spiritually abstracted" (BA 109). That is because culture, education, sensibleness, and social life keep us from thinking "lowly" of ourselves (CD 186). For an example of this abstraction, see M. Jamie Ferreira, "Rethinking Hatred of Self—A Kierkegaardian Exploration" in *Why Kierkegaard Matters: A Festschrift in Honor of Robert L. Perkins* (Macon, Georgia: Mercer University Press, 2010), 143: "True, Kierkegaard asks for self-denial and dying to the self, but these are a 'transformation' of the self—not a petulant, childish rejection of the good in us."

51. See Martin Luther, "Lectures on Romans" (1518), LW 25:204: "[We must] become nothing, . . . we [must] empty ourselves of everything [and] humble ourselves. . . . For . . . no sheep is sought except the one who is lost (Lk 15:4), . . . no one is exalted except the man who has been humbled, nothing is filled except that which is empty. . . . Therefore . . . it cannot happen that he who is filled with his own righteousness can be filled with the righteousness of God, who fills none but the hungry and the thirsty. Therefore he who is sated with his own truth and wisdom is incapable of receiving the truth and wisdom of God, which can be received only in an empty and destitute heart."

52. On this rest, see Saint Augustine, *Confessions* (400), trans. Henry Chadwick (1991; New York: Oxford, 1998), 3: "You are great, Lord, . . . and our heart is restless [*inquietum est cor nostrum*] until it rests in you." On this classic line, see George P. Lawless, "Interior Peace in the *Confessions* of St. Augustine," *Revue des Études Augustiniennes* 26 (1980): 55: "God's rest is beyond time in the manner of His vision and immutability. Nevertheless, He creates the realities which are seen in time, time itself and everything that exists with time. God, meanwhile, is ever at rest because he is rest Himself. This truth, Augustine concludes, is beyond the grasp of men and angels. Such knowledge is a gift of the Holy Spirit available only to the person who prays."

53. Because of this need for honesty, Robert Bretall is mistaken that Kierkegaard's 1855 discourse

(FSE 34). Such earnestness, however, does not require us to be morally or spiritually perfect. We can still rebel, provided that it is done "straightforwardly, honestly, candidly, openly, directly," since "an honest rebellion against Christianity can be made only if one honestly acknowledges what Christianity is and how one relates oneself to it" (TM 48). That provision shows just how deep the waters run in this refreshing stream. What is required of us is only the admission that Christianity is difficult and that we have failed to practice it as we should. This means that we cannot pretend, for instance, that self-hatred is unimportant to Christianity.[54] Nor can we suppose that repentance does not matter (TM 297). We have to admit that the conditions for our salvation still stand, even though we violate them. But if we live within these conditions, we will have "overwhelming security" for we will "rest ever more blessedly in [the] changelessness of God" (TM 278, 280). Even so, it remains the case that this image of the desert spring has much in common with the first one of the impassable mountain. Just as that mountain warned against entering into conflict with God (TM 272), so does this image of the desert spring. This makes this discourse on the changelessness of God as much about our rebellion and obedience as it is about God's unchanging love for us.

THE 1843 DISCOURSES ON JAMES 1:17–21

Kierkegaard wrote three discourses at the beginning of his authorship in 1843 on James 1:17–21—the same text he used for his 1855 discourse on the changelessness of God. All three of these discourses have the title "Every Good and Perfect Gift is From Above"—which comes from James 1:17. In the first of these three discourses, Kierkegaard begins with a dialectical prayer. It contrasts God's opposing mighty hand with his gentle hand, and his opposing open hand with his closed hand (EUD 31). His mighty hand catches the wise in their foolishness, and his gentle hand satisfies everything that lives. The first is for punishment and the second sends blessings. His closed hand makes us suffer by denying us our wishes, and his open hand again sends blessings. This prayer internally differentiates God—having him respond favorably if we are obedient and unfavorably if we are not—creating both weal and woe, depending on how we think and act in relation to him.[55] This prayer prepares the way for

ends on a note of mildness. *A Kierkegaard Anthology*, ed. Robert Bretall (Princeton: Princeton University Press, 1946), 469. For Kierkegaard's dire warning based on the unforgivable sin in Mt 12:31–32, see: "If God does not require of us that we leave everything, he still does require honesty of us. . . . [In fact] God cannot be involved with a dishonest person. . . . [For] there is one sin that makes grace impossible, that is dishonesty; and there is one thing God unconditionally must require, that is honesty" (CD 186–87).

54. See Jn 12:25; Lk 14:26. For references to self-hatred in Kierkegaard's last writings, see TM 4, 47, 52, 168, 177, 184, 189, 206, 213, 240, 248, 319, 335, 346.

55. See Is 45:7, Jn 5:28–29, Rom 2:6–11 and Martin Luther, "Lectures on Genesis 21–25" (1545), LW 4:131: "[It] is God's nature to do contradictory things when things are contradictory."

Kierkegaard to say that it is the troubled and grieving ones who have been weaned early from "the milk of success," who "penetrate through the changing to the lasting" in obedience to God (EUD 34). The meekness that comes from being weaned makes us receptive to his unchanging ways with us (EUD 45). Without that meekness we rail against heaven, complaining that God is not answering our prayers. But if you are meek, you instead will confess

> in all humility that God surely did not deceive you when he accepted your earthly wishes and foolish desires, exchanged them for you and instead gave you divine comfort and holy thoughts; that he did not treat you unfairly when he denied you a wish but in compensation created this faith in your heart, when instead of a wish, which, even if it would bring everything, at most was able to give you the whole world, he gave you a faith by which you won God and overcame the whole world. (EUD 36)

At the beginning of his 1855 discourse, Kierkegaard condenses this point saying that everything moves God according to infinite love but nothing actually changes him (TM 268). In the first of these three 1843 discourses on James 1:17–21, Kierkegaard shows how God is moved by exchanging our prayers for better ones—all the while remaining unchanged in his plans for us. This angular answer to our prayers is the best, since by it God marvelously creates from our "impatient and inconstant" hearts, "the imperishable substance of a quiet spirit" (EUD 36). Such a quiet spirit is good because it enables us "always to thank God, and thereby to learn to understand one thing: that all things serve for good those who love God" (EUD 42). By so doing, we "gain God in constancy and rescue our soul in patience," thereby becoming like God "who remains the same"—whether we received what we originally asked for or not (EUD 40). In the 1855 discourse Kierkegaard challenges us to match God's changelessness with our "unchanged obedience" (TM 279). The dialectical association of God's changelessness with our unchanging obedience to him is also in this 1843 discourse when it links our patience with God's constancy. What both of these discourses are saying is, "you must be either with the good or with the evil" (TM 278). If we are with the evil in disobedience, then we distort the eternal (EUD 37) and it will not bless us. But if we repent and stand with the good (EUD 45), then the eternal returns with "overwhelming security" for us (TM 280).

In his second 1843 discourse on James 1:17–21, Kierkegaard begins by saying that because we no longer live in paradise, we cannot be fully "absorbed in joy and glory." In our paradisiacal absorption, we had no "questions about the giver" who sent us goodness from on high (EUD 126). But with the Garden of Eden closed, "everything was changed" (EUD 127). Then questions about the giver crept in. This was because of the "terrible upheaval" that came upon us when God said we were "evil." On that account the good could only come from God—since we were evil (EUD 133). But then those original words of comfort that all good comes from God became "the seed of doubt" for us, even though "the words remained unchanged" (EUD 130–31). This doubt bred rebellion against God for banning us from bestowing the good (EUD 134). We refused to accept that "the way to the good" was closed off to us (EUD 135). In this rebellion we were "fettered . . . in distress and contradiction" (EUD 127). The only way out was "to doubt that which in itself is transitory, which will more and more vanish" and to doubt ourselves as well (EUD 137). In his 1855 discourse, Kierkegaard further clarifies this predicament saying that we must "renounce instability and changeful-ness and caprice and willfulness" in order to rest blessedly in the changelessness of God (TM 278). In this 1855 discourse, the fall in paradise is missing, but Kierkegaard draws out the implications of it. We must, he writes in that discourse, "at some time, sooner or later, come into conflict with" God's changeless will for us (TM 272). Be-cause of that inevitability, we no longer can enjoy the euphoria of being fully absorbed "in joy and glory" (EUD 126). This means that God's goodness and changeless love can now become "frightful" (TM 277). This makes God's changelessness a source of terror if we do not repent (TM 271). And to repent means to be "honestly striving to understand" God's loving will for us, and to have our self-will "expire" (TM 272, 278). This dialectical correlation between God's changelessness and our obedience or rebel-lion runs through both of these discourses.

In the third discourse from 1843 on James 1:17–21, Kierkegaard says that if every good and perfect gift comes down from God, then "every externality" must be dis-carded, and "the thralldom of the world abolished" (EUD 142). This thralldom is to be replaced by "the divine equality that opens the soul to the perfect," by which God "is able to perfect every difference in equality" before him (EUD 143, 145). Without this perfecting, we will not be able to see the perfection and goodness in what God gives. This is because in the world

> the differences work frantically to embellish and to embitter life, as beckoning goals, as rewards of victory, as oppressive burdens, as attendants of loss; in the world, external life takes arrogant pride in differences—or cravenly and worriedly sighs under them. (EUD 142)

Seeing the truth in God's goodness hinges on how we perceive the world and the differences which are "so numerous and so variable . . . that it is difficult to speak of them" (EUD 143–44). If they are allowed to embitter life, then God's invariable goodness is clouded over, since we will have failed "to pierce through" the differences by means of God's word (EUD 145).[56] Only if we pierce through those differences will we be able to love everyone equally as God commands us to (EUD 142). This "equality in love . . . is the only thing that lasts" (EUD 158). In his 1855 discourse, Kierkegaard builds upon this attack by pursuing what lifts us "above all the changefulness of earthly

---

56. On this failure, see Robert C. Neville, *Eternity and Time's Flow*, 17: "One of the deepest errors of the modern world is its obsessive passion for time." See also Jan-Olav Henriksen, "Postmodernism and the Unchangeability of God," *Studia Theologica* 57 (2003): 99: "Radical affirmation of the contin-gencies of this world can . . . be seen as the presupposition for saying that God's otherness expresses itself in his unchangeability."

life" (TM 269). What lasts in this 1855 discourse is the changelessness of God manifest in his infinite love for us which sustains us for all of eternity (TM 268, 279). We will reach out to that wonderful love only when we have grown "weary from . . . earthly changefulness and alteration" and our own "instability" (TM 278).[57] That description is an elaboration of the sinister differences noted in the 1843 discourse and ties the two discourses together.

These three discourses on James 1:17–21 from 1843, feed into Kierkegaard's 1855 discourse on the changelessness of God. He focuses more clearly the content of the earlier ones by changing the title of the 1855 discourse to *The Changelessness of God*. The first three discourses drive toward this change of title by what they say regarding divine constancy, paradisiacal perfection and lasting love, based on divine equality. But without this change of focus to the changelessness of God, those three points are not as sharply drawn as they could have been. The other major development in the 1855 discourse is the addition of the images of the mountain (i.e., severity) and the stream (i.e., mildness). These images contrast in such a way as to accentuate the dialectic in Kierkegaard's understanding of God's changelessness—something which he says is often missed (TM 272). This is because the terrifying in the dialectic is what drops out, since "severity is the dialectical factor, . . . men have completely done away with it and have made Christianity out to be mildness." It is cut because it is what "is to be resolved" through admission, repentance and amendment of life (JP 3:2873). But by so doing, any chance for further repenting is lost because the dialectical tension that severity brings to mildness is removed—and this is wrong since at its core, Christianity has mildness dialectically related to severity.

THE LATE WRITINGS

Kierkegaard's last discourse on the changelessness of God is not opposed to his other writings which were published with it in 1855. That discourse is not a positive antidote to the negative writings against Christendom, but rather trades on the deeper "contrast between the tumult of the times and the serenity of the divine."[58] Because of that, this

---

57. As long as we think that change is pleasing, we will not be "prompted to seek . . . the Changeless One" (TM 279). For an example of this, see George Allan, "Ultimate Value," *Process Studies* 33 (Fall-Winter, 2004): 300: "One of my deepest intuitions is the sense that all things perish—not some things, not a lot of things, but absolutely all things, from flashes of lightning to cosmic epochs, from passing fancies to metaphysical principles—and that this is good. . . . Its obverse . . . seems a misguided yearning to be plucked out of the world of Creative Advance, and to be set down in that new heaven and new earth where there is no adventure but endless rest."

58. Robert L. Perkins, "Upbuilding as a Propaedeutic for Justice," IKC 5:333. See also Robert L. Perkins, "The Authoritarian Symbiosis of Church and Crown in Søren Kierkegaard's 'Attack Upon Christendom,'" in *Anthropology and Authority: Essays on Søren Kierkegaard*, ed. Poul Houe, Gordon D. Marino and Sven Hakon Rossel (Amsterdam: Rodopi, 2000), 139: "The contrast between making a career and being called as a minister is central to Kierkegaard's argument [in his attack on the church], and he returns to the issue time and again [TM 107; 5, 133–35, 150, etc.]." I take this second contrast

1855 discourse reinforces the themes[59] in those late writings from 1854–55 against the Church. This discourse on God's changelessness buttresses the late writings by expressing the same ideas in a different genre—that of a preached discourse.[60] And since it also ties in with the three 1843 discourses on James 1:17–21, this 1855 discourse also links by extension the late writings against the church with the beginning of Kierkegaard's authorship. This shows that his late writings are not an aberration but an integral part of his entire authorship. Making the name of his 1855 discourse on James 1:17–21, *The Changelessness of God*, rather than "Every Good and Perfect Gift is From Above," like the first three discourses on James 1:17–21 were named, was Kierkegaard's way of intimating that he himself was also unchanged throughout his authorship.[61]

At the core of those late writings is the attack on the church for compromising God's changelessness. In a journal entry from 1854, Kierkegaard explains this attack as a defense of God's changelessness:

> When we hear that someone is supposed to be a loving person, very kind and loving, this means that we no doubt will have our way with him—for, after all, he is such a kind, loving person. . . . But this is not the way the New Testament puts it. In the New Testament God is love, infinite love; yes, this is a certainty. He knows best of all what an agony it is if a man is to become spirit, is to love God in truth. To that end he is willing enough to suffer with the beloved in infinite love, he will hear your every sigh, sorrow with you, weep with you, count your tears—but change him—no, that you cannot do. Be assured that he suffers much more than you do—but change him—no, that you cannot do.

---

to be subservient to the first one Perkins notes between time and eternity.

59. On the themes in the late writings, see Alastair McKinnon, "The Relative Importance of God and Christ in Kierkegaard's Writings," *Kierkegaard Studies: Yearbook* 1996, ed. Niels Jørgen Cappelørn and Hermann Deuser (Berlin: Walter de Gruyter, 1996), 415: "The two main theses of the attack [are that] Christendom is totally different from the Christianity of the New Testament and the other that it is an offense against the majesty of God." See also Robert L. Perkin's Julia Watkin Memorial Kierkegaard Lecture, "At His Lutheran and Evangelical Best—Kierkegaard's Critique of Christendom 'With the Help of the Ideals—Against Illusions: For Eternity!'" *Søren Kierkegaard Newsletter* 51 (April 2007): 12: "The three nouns, . . . ideality, illusions, and eternity (TM 486), encompass the generative concerns of Kierkegaard's authorship."

60. On this genre, see George Pattison, *Kierkegaard, Religion and the Nineteenth-Century Crisis of Culture* (Cambridge: Cambridge University Press, 2002), 159–60: "Kierkegaard's religious discourses offer a way forward that acknowledges the negative power of time with regard to all things worldly, including—and indeed emphasizing—the way in which time brings to nothing all collective and, indeed, individual attempts to realize a 'new world' on the plane of phenomenal history, . . . but that also, in the struggle with time, finds that which is more-than-temporal: the eternal that gives meaning and value to our being-in-time." If this is the case, then Kierkegaard's last discourse on God unchanging is his quintessential discourse. Note also Kierkegaard's chilling characterization: "True upbuilding consists in being spoken to rigorously" (WL 42).

61. For a similar point, but which goes beyond mine, see *The Essential Kierkegaard*, ed. Howard V. Hong and Edna H. Hong (Princeton: Princeton University Press, 2000), 482: "*The Changelessness of God* is representative of the *total Anlæg* (comprehensive plan) at its core and in its intent."

> Be assured that he suffers much more than you—for he cannot change. . . . If
> he could be changed, . . . then on other grounds it would be impossible for
> you to love him—for if he could be changed in this way, then he would not be
> God but a phantom, an unreality. Thus it is easy to see that Christendom has
> fallen away from Christianity, for Christendom is: God changed according to
> mankind's will. (JP 4:4892)

Kierkegaard's attack on Christendom is therefore waged because it attacks the
changelessness of God.[62] In our stubborn disobedience against God we want to have
our way with him—changing him so he will change his plans to go along with ours.
This makes our chief problem disobedience, for indeed "the calamity . . . in religion,
. . . as in everything, is disobedience" (BA 5). We do not want to suffer with Christ
in obedience to God, but would rather go the way of least resistance. By so doing, we
turn God into a phantom, and instead of ending up with a likeable, palatable God, as
we had planned, we end up with no God at all.[63] This decimates Christianity—turning
it into a naturalistic humanism, which is nothing but a "secular" version of what it
is supposed to be (JP 4:4343).[64] This is because we do not want to be dialectical, but
would have God loving us without it hinging, in any way, on us having to love him
in return. "Christendom," Kierkegaard again writes in 1854, "has agreeably wanted
to play the game of taking God by the nose: God is love, meaning that he loves me—
Amen!" (JP 2:1446)—which means we owe him nothing in return. When we take God
by the nose like that, we make him out to be a quack doctor (FSE 80).

In these writings Kierkegaard attacks the church for "hypocritically and knav-
ishly . . . falsifying the definition of what it is to be a Christian. . . . All the strenuousness, struggle, and anguish associated with what is required to die to the world, to
hate oneself," has been thrown out in favor of turning Christianity into worldliness
and the enjoyment of life (TM 168, 42–44). These changes are made because "the
wretched, miserable, ordinary populace are . . . unable to bear the divineness that is
the Christianity of the New Testament" (TM 33). As such, "everything is changed to
the very opposite" (TM 123). Then "the most profound, the most incurable break with
this world" is lost (TM 17). This amounts to "the assassination of Christianity" (TM
48). "Then *the Way* has . . . become something else, not the one in the New Testament:

62. For a recent version of this assault, see John Shelby Spong, *Why Christianity Must Change or
Die* (New York: HarperCollins, 1999), 39: "Einstein . . . introduced relativity as something present
in all things, including that which religious human beings had once called 'eternal and unchanging
truth.'"

63. On our false worship, Kierkegaard adds: "What 'Christendom' is guilty of is the most dreadful
kind of blasphemy: to transform the God of spirit into—ludicrous blather. And the most spiritless
kind of worship, more . . . spiritless than worshipping a stone, an ox, an insect as God, more spiritless
than anything, is: to worship under the name of God—a blatherplate!" (TM 122).

64. On the secularization, Kierkegaard adds: "By conforming to the age I would not have benefited
the age but instead would have promoted the sickness of the age; it was plainly my task to remain heterogeneous. The basic evil of the age is that . . . it secularizes and finitizes every higher endeavor—that
is, it denies that a higher endeavor truly exists" (JP 6:6859).

in abasement, hated, abandoned, persecuted, and cursed to suffer in the world—no, the Way is: admired, applauded, honored, and knighted to make a brilliant career!" (TM 22). In these late writings, Kierkegaard attacks these changes—in the name of the changelessness of God. So it makes good sense for him to add to these writings his discourse on the changelessness of God. For that divine changelessness exposes the waywardness of our changefulness. "The words in God's Word that deafeningly witness against" all these wretched changes to Christianity in Christendom are at the heart of Kierkegaard's critique (TM 132). For these words "strike a blow at . . . the actual world in which we live" (TM 119).

What drives these questionable changes is the desire to be "on good terms with people, . . . out of fear of people" (TM 137). But this yearning is deeply flawed because God, and not our fellow human beings, is our "most appalling . . . mortal enemy" who must be appeased (TM 177).[65] God is that impassable mountain who will crush us if we disobey him (TM 272). Because of God's majesty, he is to be honored first,[66] but we switch this around—calling our interpretation an actual "perfecting"—and instead say: "first everything else and last the kingdom of God; . . . first a consideration for what fear of people bids or forbids, and then God's kingdom" (TM 235). This reversal must be turned around so that we trust "only in God" (TM 153). Only then will we be able to tell the truth about Christianity—that it is "the doctrine of renunciation, of suffering, of heterogeneity to this world, the doctrine that issues no checks except on another world"[67]—and this we must do even though it "wins nobody, . . . but instead frightens everyone away" (TM 125).[68] We must do this because we mistakenly think that

---

65. On this point see Mt 10:28: "Do not fear those who kill the body but cannot kill the soul; rather fear him who can destroy both soul and body in hell" (RSV). For an answer to this verse, see Mt 25:31, 41. Kierkegaard calls this "a still greater fear" (TM 211). This is because Christianity "took away the fear of death and replaced it with the fear of judgment" (JP 1:727).

66. See Mt 6:33.

67. On these four claims, see Lk 14:33, 1 Pt 2:21; Jn 15:19; Rom 8:18.

68. The reason we cannot trust in ourselves is because we are unreliable and sinful. We are desperately corrupt and defiled (Jer 17:9; Mk 7:21–23). We love ourselves and pursue pleasure rather than honoring God (2 Tm 3:2–4). And we refuse to admit that we are "wretched, pitiable, poor, blind, and naked" (Rv. 3:17) (RSV). As a consequence, we will not "hold firmly to the truth" if it upsets us (TM 170). On this disconcertedness, see M. Jamie Ferreire, "Rethinking Hatred of Self—A Kierkegaardian Exploration," 122: "I find it worrisome that Kierkegaard is ever used to support an appeal to self-hatred or self-denial that is equated with self-depreciation." On her account, we would then have to give up on being a Christian, which according to Kierkegaard, "surely ought to correspond to the prototype—a worm, not a human being [Ps 22:6]" (TM 189)! Kierkegaard may have picked up this emphasis on self-depreciation from The Lutheran Confessions which call humans "recalcitrant" donkeys because of their corrupt nature which is "deep, wicked, abominable, bottomless, inscrutable and inexpressible" (BC 568, 510). Or he may have learned it from one of Luther's sermons. See, for example, "Sermon on John 1:19–28" (1533), LHP 1:91: "What all Christians should do and say with Paul is this: My holiness is plain filth and dung; and with John: My holiness is a rag when I compare it with Christ's holiness and deed."

the point is merely to be able to slip happily and well through this world; and Christianity thinks [in contrast] that all terrors actually come from the other world, that the terrors of this world are childish compared with the terrors of eternity, and that the point is therefore not to slip happily and well through this life, but rightly to relate oneself to eternity through suffering. (TM 294)

We suffer when we stand up for Christianity—which says we must die to the world[69] because God "hates specifically that in which you naturally have your life, to which you cling with all your zest for life" (TM 177).[70] If we refuse to stand up for this teaching, we will be condemned—suffering "the terrors of eternity" (TM 294)—because there are no exceptions and "eternity does not change" (TM 293). Christianity is seriously distorted when it is turned into something easy. Preventing that from happening will be difficult. But since there are no short cuts in Christianity, we must oppose all such distortions of it. But there are hazards everywhere we turn. Kierkegaard therefore warns:

Be yourself watchful, because the earnestness of existence is precisely this, that you are placed in a world where the voice that calls you to the right way speaks very softly, while thousands of voices outside and inside you speak ever so loudly about exactly the opposite—precisely this is the earnestness: that this voice speaks softly because it wants to test you to see if you will obey even this faintest whisper. Consider, it is not eternity that needs you and then for its own sake raises its voice when the other voices become strident; no, it is you who need eternity, and it wants to test you—what earnestness!—your attentiveness, and therefore it becomes softer to the same degree that the others

---

69. Gal 6:14 (RSV). On this dying to the world, Kierkegaard also writes: "The apostles were indeed dead, dead to every merely earthly hope, to every human confidence in their own powers or in human assistance. Therefore . . . you must first die to every merely earthly hope, to every merely human confidence; you must die to your selfishness, . . . because it is only through your selfishness that the world has power over you; if you are dead to your selfishness, you are also dead to the world. But naturally there is nothing a human being hangs on to so firmly—indeed with his whole self! —as to his selfishness!" (FSE 77).

70. For the charge that Kierkegaard is pompous because of his supposed exaggerations—like this one on the zest for life—see Peter J. Mehl, *Thinking Through Kierkegaard: Existential Identity in a Pluralistic World* (Urbana, Illinois: University of Illinois Press, 2005), 160–61: "The Kierkegaardian ideal of personhood is . . . concerned with . . . flourishing as a self-transcending spiritual self. . . . But take it too far [as Kierkegaard does] and a degree of spiritual dis-ease can infect all one's finite relations. . . . The *modest* spiritual evaluator [in contrast to Kierkegaard] retains moral seriousness, . . . but always restraining moral self-righteousness and pomposity." Mehl may have been less distressed over this problem if he had followed R. R. Reno, *In the Ruins of the Church: Sustaining Faith in an Age of Diminished Christianity* (Grand Rapids: Brazos, 2002), 37: "The contemporary allergy to authority and flight from truth are certainly familiar to any one who has sampled the air of American culture. . . . Enforced uniformity of belief and practice [it is supposed] requires violent assaults upon conscience, intellect, and will. Therefore we must reject all authoritative claims as acts of violence. Of course, Christianity is inevitably caught up in the postmodern flight from authority. . . . [Therefore] the authority of tradition must be overthrown, the sacred bonds of loyalty to what has been passed on must be broken, so that we can be released from the oppressive burdens of present power."

become louder—something that cannot happen except through your fault. Nothing is easier than to shout down the voice of eternity, which speaks about suffering for the truth. (TM 299–300)

This warning makes three crucial points. First, it says that the voice of eternity can easily be missed. One might suppose that God's almighty power would drown out all other voices. But Kierkegaard favors the "still small voice" in 1 Kings 19:12.[71] Like God's invisibility, his voice does not overpower finitude. Wanting his voice to win all earthly contests[72] would err by making the church too quickly triumphant (PC 211–24). Secondly, it says that this faint voice of eternity is not just some metaphysical fact. It is actually a deliberate test of our willingness to attend to and obey God's voice. The test is if we will obey God when the reasons for doing so are not conclusive or very compelling. And thirdly, it says that God does not need us.[73] If he did, he would have made the test easier for us to pass so that we would not be repelled by his severity. But as it is, God has not eased up on us and we can do nothing without him—not vice versa.[74]

These three points all are consistent with Kierkegaard's discourse on the changelessness of God. The small divine voice is there in the image of the impassable mountain. We remember that this mountain does not always crush us but sometimes, in silent condemnation, God simply shows no "sign of noticing" our faults at all (TM 273). This silent divine neglect is close to that nondomineering, small divine voice. And regarding being tested, in the 1855 discourse there are repeated conditional statements made which say that if we do not obey God we will find no rest. These statements are veiled tests to see whether or not we will strive to get "on good terms with God" (TM 272). And finally, regarding God having no need for us, this is expressed in God's changelessness itself. That changelessness is "unchanged clarity, . . . to which no darkness can come close. . . . We are not clarity in this way, and that is why we are changeful. . . . But God is changeless" (TM 272). If God needed us, he would change according to our wishes and concerns. But God's changelessness makes that sort of interaction with us impossible.

---

71. Against this standard translation, see J. Lust, "A Gentle Breeze or a Roaring Thunderous Sound?" *Vetus Testamentum* 25 (January 1975): 110–15.

72. Such domination would go against 1 Jn 5:19 and Rv 12:7–12.

73. This tilt towards divine aseity, goes against Paul R. Sponheim, "Relational Transcendence in Divine Agency," IKC 20: 49n9: "Tim Rose [writes] that 'Kierkegaard's God is wholly consistent with the God of traditional Christianity.' . . . I could not agree [since] traditional formulations of the divine involve no real relation."

74. See Jn 15:5. On this verse see Martin Luther, "Sermons on John 14–16" (1538), LW 24:230: "[Let] others carve and make whatever they can without Him, until they have fashioned a new birth out of their works and a tree from the fruit. What they will do, please God, is to verify this verse, and it will all amount to a big zero."

AT LAST

Kierkegaard published his 1855 discourse a month before he ended up in the hospital with what he knew was a fatal illness (LD 28). As it turned out, he never left the Royal Frederick's Hospital, dying there a little over a month later.[75] This close correlation between his death and the publication of his last discourse on the changelessness of God makes it reasonable to suppose that he thought of it as something of a last will and testament.[76] In the discourse he twice mentions hastening toward eternity (TM 271, 278). And in the last sentence of his book on his authorship, he speaks of dying of a disease but also "of a longing for eternity in order unceasingly to do nothing else than to thank God" (PV 97). He had been holding on to this last discourse since he first preached it in 1851. Now that his death was imminent, it was time to bequeath his last will and testament to the world. With his hour of death looming large in his mind, he no doubt was extending his life-long interest in dying to the world, to the hour of his death when "every good work . . . will be of the utmost urgency" (JP 1:724). Having his discourse on God's changelessness published, would be a last good work. In that discourse, God's changelessness requires unchanging obedience from us (TM 279–80). Dialectically they work together—God's unchanging love for us blesses us with "overwhelming security" when we are "on good terms" with him (TM 280, 272). Kierkegaard had no better final word for the world than this discourse which he had preached in church in 1851, for in it he expressed the center of Christianity as stated in his journals from 1851—"infinite humiliation and grace, and then a striving born of gratitude" (JP 1:993). His coming demise furnished the needed impetus to get him to act and publish his discourse on the changelessness of God. On needing such a goad he wrote in 1846:

> A penetrating religious renunciation of the world and what is of the world, adhered to in daily self-denial, would be inconceivable to the youth of our day. . . . The age of great and good actions is past; the present age is the age of anticipation. . . . Action and decision are just as scarce these days as is the fun of swimming dangerously for those who swim in shallow water. Just as an adult, himself reveling in the tossing waters, calls to those younger: "Come on out, just jump in quickly"—just so does decision lie in existence. (TA 71)

Just so death called out to him to jump quickly and publish the discourse on God's changelessness. The time was right and he could wait no longer, for his death was at hand. While in the hospital under the care of doctors, the situation was right to

---

75. Joakim Garff, *Søren Kierkegaard: A Biography*, 782–83.

76. On Kierkegaard's deliberate use of his last discourse, see Michael Plekon, "Kierkegaard at the End," 82: "While there are significant passages in the later writings to warrant the interpretation that there was more to his thinking than the negativity of the attack literature, I am arguing that his fully deliberate location of the sermon on God's unchangingness should be taken as an important expression of his theological understanding."

recall how Christendom had turned the eternal God into a quack doctor (FSE 80)—circumventing the need for grace to work together dialectically with our righteous deeds. In his discourse on God's changelessness, he joins grace and good works together as well as he ever did in his twelve-year-long authorship.[77]

So now, at last, it was time to obtain eternal salvation—and he was not grasping for it "too early" (EUD 346), since his death was so close at hand. It was now reasonable for him to suppose that he would not continue much longer slogging along in the bog of life (JP 6:6503).[78] That little phrase, "at last," from the end of the old prayers of the church, which Kierkegaard had recollected at the beginning of his authorship,

77. Other examples from Kierkegaard's authorship regarding the proper understanding of time and eternity would be: "Father in heaven! . . . the restless mind . . . may find rest . . . that in relation to you we are always in the wrong" (EO 2:341); "three cheers for the dance in the vortex of the infinite, . . . for the cresting waves that fling me above the stars" (R 222); "he sins who lives in the moment as abstracted from the eternal" (CA 93); "the sailor . . . looks up at the stars . . . because they are faithful; they have the same location . . . [and he conquers] the changeable . . . by the eternal" (EUD 19); "God has become changed . . . [because] the one who prays understands him differently and demands no explanation" (EUD 400); "the decision of eternity [makes us] dead to temporality" (UDVS 114); "This awareness [of eternity] . . . will transfigure and illuminate your conduct in the relationships of life, . . . while concern for your eternal responsibility will keep you from . . . busily taking part in everything possible—an activity that can be called a waste of time" (UDVS 137); "Everything that a human knows about the eternal is contained in this: it is God who rules" (UDVS 258); "gabbily to gush about the glory of eternal happiness is empty and foolish talk, but with closed lips, as it were, instead of speaking directly about eternal happiness, [to speak about that happiness by way of] speaking . . . about one's hardships in life, . . . is the language of the royal court" (UDVS 316); "[Christian perfection is to be] able to live in any climate, [to live] according to its vigor, under the most imperfect conditions and forms" (COR 54); "[Christian love] is not dependent on this or that; it is dependent only on that alone which liberates—therefore it is eternally independent. . . . But the love that has undergone this change of eternity by becoming duty certainly feels a need to be loved, . . . but it can do without [being loved in return]. . . . Unchangingness is the true independence" (WL 39); "The infinite, the eternal, hence the true, is so alien to the natural man that with him it is as with a dog, which can indeed learn to walk upright for a moment but yet continually wants to walk on all fours" (WL 244); "the more perfect is the love, . . . the more justice shudders" (WL 266); "No one longs to be away from [the] noise and clamor of the moment in order to find the stillness in which God dwells" (WL 369); "The more he attempts to will to dispense with the eternal, the further away he is from living today" (CD 78); "Every 'loss' is temporal, but what you lose temporally you gain eternally" (CD 143); "Eternity provides feet to walk on" (CD 159); "But the difference between right and wrong remains eternally, just as he remains, the Eternal One" (CD 208); "The misfortune of our age is precisely that it has become merely *time* by itself, temporality, which impatiently wants to hear nothing about eternity" (PV 104); "[Wanting the finite and the infinite blended together is like wanting] to have one's mouth full of cake and wanting also to whistle [which is nothing but] pure-and-simple rubbish" (JFY 133). These passages all illustrate well Kierkegaard's overall concern: "To live only in the unconditional [or eternal], to breathe only the unconditional—the human being cannot do this; he perishes like the fish that must live in air. But on the other hand, a human being cannot in the deeper sense *live* without relating himself to the unconditional; he expires, that is, perhaps goes on living, but spiritlessly. . . . This is what I to the best of my ability and with maximum effort and much sacrifice have fought for, fighting against every tyranny, also the tyranny of the numerical. This endeavor of mine has incurred opprobrium as enormous pride and arrogance" (PV 20).

78. For a similar view on the arduousness of life, see Martin Luther, "Commentary on 1 Corinthians 15" (1533), LW 28:122: "[When we die, we] shall be led from this vale of tears by [Christ] and abide where He is." On this vale of tears, see also TM 178; JP 2:1439, 3:2622, 4:5031.

was now, at the end,[79] dialectically stirring him with its "calm" and with its "longing" as well:

> The older person among us, who is almost within reach of the goal, gazes back in thought over the road he has traveled. He recollects the course of events, and the faded figures become vivid again. He is overwhelmed by the abundant content of his experience; he is weary and says: and then at last obtain eternal salvation. The younger person, who still stands at the beginning of the road, gazes in thought out over the long course, experiences in thought what is to come: the painful privations, the secret troubles, the sad longings, the fearful spiritual trials. He is weary of mind and says: and then at last obtain eternal salvation. (EUD 28)

79. Luther has a similar passage for the equivalent phrase, "at the last." Martin Luther, "The Three Symbols or Creeds of the Christian Faith" (1538), LW 34:207: "I have . . . noted in all histories of all of Christendom that all those who have correctly had and kept the chief article of Jesus Christ have remained safe and secure in the right Christian faith. Although they may have sinned or erred in other matters, they have nevertheless been preserved at the last. For whoever stands correctly and firmly in the belief that Jesus Christ is true God and man, that he died and has risen again for us, such a person has all other articles added to him and they firmly stand by him. Therefore, what Saint Paul says is quite certain, that Christ is 'capital wealth,' base, ground, and the whole sum, around and under which everything is gathered and found, and in him are hidden all the treasures of wisdom and understanding (Col 2:3) . . . . If you believe this, then good for you; if not, then have your own way, but your lack of belief will change nothing herein. And Christ will indeed remain in spite of you, together with all his believers, as he has remained heretofore, against all the power of the devil and the world."

9

On Self-Forgetfulness

ONE OF THE ENDURING contributions to Christian theology that Kierkegaard makes is his understanding of sin and salvation. Nothing that he writes about "goes deeper into the mystery of life, or reveals a more profound psychological insight," than what he has to say about these loci in Christian theology.[1] His analysis of them coincides with the historical norms of Christianity and so provides an antidote to the liberal creed that a "God without wrath brought man without sin into a kingdom without judgment through the ministrations of Christ without a cross."[2]

Because this creed still influences large sections of Christianity today,[3] Kierkegaard's words on sin and salvation continue to be of help to those who contend[4] for the truth of the historical Christian teachings. At the heart of his analysis of these concepts is self-denial. This remains to be true today, even though self-denial has been widely contested as an essential ingredient in key Christian concepts.[5] Nevertheless,

> Kierkegaard has insisted that theology . . . must neither be formed nor receive its content from philosophical positions alien to its own nature. It is not the business of theology to become intellectually respectable to any time; because when properly understood, theology will be a scandal and a stumbling block to the philosophy, the rationalism and the idolatry of any age.[6]

In this chapter I want to lay out what Kierkegaard has to say about sin and salvation, and their attending concepts of confession and judgment, in order to show how

1. David F. Swenson, *Something About Kierkegaard*, ed. Lillian Marvin Swenson (1945; Macon GA: Mercer University Press, 1983), 178.

2. H. Richard Niebuhr, *The Kingdom of God in America* (1937; Middletown, Connecticut: Wesleyan University Press, 1988), 193.

3. On the continuing minimization of sin in Christian theology, see Marsha G. Witten, *All Is Forgiven: The Secular Message in American Protestantism* (Princeton: Princeton University Press, 1993), 127: "Conversion is portrayed far less as the need to grapple with sin-nature than as a reorientation of one's psychology toward the creation of a close interpersonal relationship with God."

4. On this contention, see Jude 1:3. Even though Kierkegaard disfavored defending Christianity (CD 162, PV 80), he did believe in laying out a clear roadmap to the truth (JP 6:6283).

5. See Harold Bloom, *The American Religion: The Emergence of the Post-Christian Nation* (New York: Simon & Schuster, 1992), 53: "American religion [is based on] the faith of and in the American self." Note also that "American Religion [is a] religion of the self" (265).

6. Robert L. Perkins, *Søren Kierkegaard*, Makers of Contemporary Theology (Richmond, Virginia: John Knox, 1969), 41.

compelling the rationale is for these historical Christian concepts in a time when they are widely contested.

SIN

Kierkegaard writes that we are all under the scrutinizing eye of eternity—and that we do not stand before God "only during specific hours" of the day (WL 366). This puts us under extreme pressure to measure up to the exalted standards or ideals of eternity that tower over us (UDVS 285). It is "frightful" to be under "eternity's inspection," and this "accounting" by God of what we do and who we are, necessarily plunges us "into anxiety and unrest to the point of despair" (TM 29, 278). This is because

> God's thoughts are eternally higher than the thoughts of a human being, and therefore every human conception of happiness and unhappiness, of what is joyful and what is sorrowful, is faulty thinking. By remaining in this circle of conceptions, a person remains continually in the wrong with God. . . . [So the] fundamental relation between God and a human being is that a human being is a sinner and God is the Holy One. Directly before God a human being is not a sinner in this or in that, but is essentially a sinner, is . . . unconditionally guilty. But if he is essentially guilty, then he is *always* guilty, because the debt of essential guilt is so extreme as to make every direct accounting impossible. (UDVS, 284–85)

If this guilt is not removed through forgiveness, then God's condemnation of us is "more terrible than any human revenge" (EUD 56)—which is made all the worse since no one can escape it either (CD 207). Imagining that God would never "crush" us in this way (TM 272, 274) is to suppose we can "remodel" him (EUD 331) into someone less terrifying, less demanding, and less exacting.[7] But Kierkegaard opposes such remodeling because Christianity would then be cut off from the norms of the New Testament from which it arises (TM 212, 58, 44, 17). Therefore we "must always be on watch" lest we forget God, because his ways are "so alien" to us (WL 130, 244).[8] His ways are so alien because of "the lofty earnestness of the eternal," which neither wants "the recommendation . . . of the majority nor of eloquence,"

---

7. For more on this remodeling, Kierkegaard notes: "If Christianity is to be proclaimed as it essentially is in the gospels, proclaimed as and being: imitation, sheer suffering, misery and wailing, sharpened by a background of judgment where every word must be accounted for—then it is fearful suffering, anxiety, quaking, and trembling. Quite right. But where in the gospels does it actually say that God intends this earthly life to be anything else? . . . [But still] we want Christianity to leave us in peace. So we turn Christianity around and get an insipid optimism out of the dreadful pessimism which Christianity is in the New Testament. . . . [With] this we shove Christianity out completely and now things are beginning to hum with all the jobs, begetting children, and finite busyness and enjoyment of life, etc., etc." (JP 6:6863).

8. On this difficulty, Kierkegaard succinctly says: "I have to concentrate all my earnestness solely on this—that I am a sinner" (JP 4:4038).

does not dare to promise you earthly advantages if you accept and in appropriation adhere to this conviction. On the contrary, if adhered to, it will make your life strenuous, many a time perhaps burdensome; if adhered to, it will perhaps expose you to ridicule by others, not to mention that adherence might ask even greater sacrifices from you. (UDVS 136)

When we adhere to God in this way, we are led into self-denial—which requires us to "renounce instability and changefulness and caprice and willfulness" (TM 278). This means dying to "every merely earthly hope, to every merely human confidence; . . . to your selfishness, or to the world" (FSE 77).[9] Enduring ridicule, burdens, sacrifices, and strenuousness, all contribute to this denial of self. These traumas are invaluable because through them alone are we able to discover "that God is" (WL 362).[10] Kierkegaard calls these tears blessed because through them we forget ourselves, deny ourselves, discover God and his salvation, and quit endlessly stewing over our sins.[11]

But because self-denial is so strenuous, we rebel against it. This resistance shows that disobedience or "insubordination" is the "calamity of our age" (BA 5). Consequently "every sin is disobedience and every disobedience is sin" (WA 35). Kierkegaard links sin to "anxiety" (CA 56–60) and "despair" (SUD 68)[12] as well, which helps him show all the more how defiance (CA 144) and disobedience (SUD 81) are at the heart of sin. Sin, then, cannot be overcome through some life improvement plan.[13] It runs so deeply in us that it is beyond sheer ignorance of the right (SUD 95)—being

9. Kierkegaard adds that this dying is like a plague: "Humanly speaking, Christianity must make a person unhappy if he is earnest about Christianity. It immediately directs his whole mind and effort toward the eternal; he thereby becomes heterogeneous with the whole secular mentality and must collide. . . . [This] doctrine . . . is like a plague to the natural man" (JP 3:2711).

10. And so Kierkegaard notes how dismaying Christianity actually is: "I do know how to console. . . . I also know that . . . the sufferer will feel relieved and will take a great liking to me. But the trouble is that I know that this is not Christianity. I take it from another flask. It is poetry with an invigorating addition of the ethical. But Christianity it is not. As a rule Christianity is dismaying rather than consoling" (JP 6:6262). And so Kierkegaard notes the importance of anguish: "Only the struggle and distress of the anguished conscience can help one venture to will to have anything to do with Christianity" (JP 4:4018).

11. On these tears of self-forgetfulness, Kierkegaard sings out—albeit in a minor key: "O blessed tears—that in weeping there is also this blessing: forgetting! She has forgotten herself completely, forgotten the setting with all its disturbing elements. A setting like this is impossible to forget unless one forgets oneself. Indeed, it was a setting frightfully and agonizingly designed to remind her of herself—but she weeps, and as she weeps she forgets herself. *O blessed tears of self-forgetfulness*, when her weeping does not once remind her anymore of what she is weeping over; in this way she has forgotten herself completely" (WA 140) (emphasis added).

12. For an exposition of these linkages, see Sylvia Walsh, *Kierkegaard: Thinking Christianly in an Existential Mode* (Oxford: Oxford University Press, 2009), 80–110.

13. Against this reduction, Kierkegaard says as well: "Christ is not a savior for this life but for eternal life. Yes, what is more, . . . he is the very opposite of a savior for this life" (JP 6:6503). On this point see also Alexander Schmemann, *Celebration of Faith*, 3 vols, trans. John A. Jillions (Crestwood, New York: Saint Vladimir's Seminary, 1991–95), 1:68: "Christianity is a religion of salvation. This means that it is not merely a 'life improvement' plan."

instead "the most dreadful thing" possible (JP 4:4027).[14] As sinners, we are dealing with the "one enemy" we cannot conquer by ourselves (EUD 18). If sin were only ignorance, we could chip away at it through education. But because it is rooted in defiance and disobedience, we cannot stop it by simply modifying our behavior.

CONFESSION

Once the intensity and gravity of our sin is fixed in our minds, it can petrify us. In that case the blessings of self-forgetfulness do not mark the tears we shed over our sins (WA 140). Our sins instead leave us "to sit and brood and stare" at them (JP 4:4036). But Kierkegaard wants to move sinners beyond such spiritual stagnation. He thought we could do that simply by asking "about what lasts," for in that question we pass over "from temporality into eternity" (UDVS 77). In inquiring about what lasts, we see that recalcitrance is the last thing we need when facing our sin, for it deprives us of the "medication" that can heal us. Without that medication we are stuck—forever "indisposed" by our sin (JP 4:4048). This questioning about what lasts is the medication we need. It gives us a chance to see that "the object of all faith's work is to get rid of egotism and selfishness in order that God" may "rule in everything." For when we suffer over this questioning about what lasts, the discomfort it brings becomes "the receptive soil in which the eternal can take root" and replace selfishness with obedience (UDVS 259). This brings us to the brink of confession. This makes the tears we shed over our sins a blessing by ushering in self-forgetfulness.

This leads to a confession of our sins which makes us "alone with the Holy One." In this solitude the sinner sees that

> he is the greatest of sinners, because directly before the Holy One he [sees] the essential magnitude of the sin within himself. . . . Anyone who thinks of his sin in this way and wishes in this stillness to learn . . . the art of sorrowing over his sins—will certainly discover that the confession of sin is not merely a counting of all the particular sins but is a comprehending before God that sin has a coherence in itself. (TDIO 30–32)

This coherence is monumental because it blocks the "perpetual enumerating" of one's sins by "a petty arithmetician in the service of faintheartedness." Counting

14. On this underestimation of sin, Kierkegaard adds: "[It] is part of sin to have only a shallow notion of sin and also because only God, the Holy One, has the truly divine idea" (JP 4:4035). Note further C. Stephen Evans, *Kierkegaard: An Introduction* (Cambridge: Cambridge University Press, 2009), 180–81: "It is a consistent theme in Kierkegaard's writings that human sin is not something humans can understand through their own philosophical resources. . . . However, . . . there is still something in the Greek perspective which modern Christendom needs. . . . When Socrates sees someone who does not act in accordance with what he says is true, he concludes that he must not genuinely understand what he claims to know. . . . This echoes the Kierkegaardian distinction between understanding that is purely verbal, and the kind of 'subjective understanding' that links what is understood to a person's existence."

our sins keeps our repentance from being "before God," and turns it into some corrupt form of "self-love in depression." This "religious debauchery," or debasement of repentance, is "the most dreadful of all" (TDIO 34–35).[15] But this alone does not cure us because we still want to go over our specific sins before God. We fear that gathering our sins together into one general confession will ruin repentance—for we think that it "is nauseated by the empty generality" and its "superficiality" (TDIO 34–35). But this desire for more detail is "fraudulent" and is rather about usurping what rightfully belongs "solely to God" (TDIO 39, 36). God is fully able to keep track of all our many and varied sins. He does not need us to enumerate them before him in our confession. We could compose a long speech about our many and varied sins, but we would never be able to use it in confession. That is because going to confession is like being "out to sea . . . in a storm," Kierkegaard writes, where the knowledge we had on land regarding our many sins, fails us once we are at sea—due to the terror, darkness, and powerlessness that disrupts us at sea (TDIO 36). In the storm we are tongue-tied by the terror of it all, and so we are not able to deliver our speech on our many sins. This desire for "much knowledge" deceives us (TDIO 36). It makes us think that we can orchestrate our own confession when we in fact cannot, for the stillness in confession "belongs to God" (TDIO 39). Knowing that we are guilty and that we are sinners is enough—anything else is deceptive, fraudulent, and religious debauchery (TDIO 40).[16]

In this vein, Kierkegaard provides through Anti-Climacus, a prayer for confessing our sins which combines generality and specificity—yet without the illegitimate enumeration of personal sins:

> Lord Jesus Christ, our foolish minds are weak; they are more than willing to be drawn—and there is so much that wants to draw us to itself. There is pleasure with its seductive power, the multiplicity with its bewildering distractions, the moment with its infatuating importance and the conceited laboriousness of busyness and the careless time-wasting of light-mindedness and the gloomy brooding of heavy-mindedness—all this will draw us away from ourselves to itself in order to deceive us. (PC 157)

15. On this corruption of repentance, see Martin Luther, "The Smalcald Articles" (1537), BC 309: "Repentance is not partial like repentance for actual sins, nor is it uncertain like that. It does not debate what is sin and what is not sin, but lumps everything together and says, 'We are wholly and altogether sinful.' We need not spend our time weighing, distinguishing, differentiating. On this account there is no uncertainty in such repentance, for nothing is left that we might imagine to be good enough to pay for our sin. One thing is sure: We cannot pin our hope on anything that we are, think, say or do. And so our repentance cannot be false, uncertain, or partial, for a person who confesses that he is altogether sinful embraces all sins in his confession without omitting or forgetting a single one." Since Kierkegaard thought that Luther was "the master of us all" (JP 3:2465), his attack on weighing, distinguishing and differentiating sin, could well be an illumination of Luther's attack on enumerating sin.

16. This is what is behind Martin Luther's famous dictum *pecca fortiter* or "sin boldly." Martin Luther, "Letter to Philip Melanchthon" (August 1, 1521), LW 48:282. To sin boldly does not mean to sin all the more, but to admit that you are a terrible sinner—*fortissimus peccator*. Luther's *pecca fortiter* might well have shaped Kierkegaard's emphasis on the "admission" of one's sinfulness (JFY 102).

This prayer cautions us about the temptations we have in pleasure, distractions, busyness, light-mindedness and heavy-mindedness. No specific personal sins are listed in this prayer, but this does not detract from its power to guide any and all repentance.

First, it warns us that pleasure is seductive and not simply a matter of us satisfying our cherished goals. This is based on the conviction that sin has its fleeting pleasures.[17] From this we confess how appealing sin is—which is why it is so seductive. As a result we will not be eager to discard it, nor will we be able to get rid of it easily when we try to. Second, distractions are sinful. They build on the bewildering multiplicity of stimuli that bombards us. This variety is not always the spice of life, but can also drain us. Under the barrage of these many distractions, we become diffuse—losing all focus and the ability to get things done.[18]

Third, there is busyness. This rush of tasks makes us feel important—long before we ever are worn out with fatigue. Kierkegaard calls this busyness "conceited laboriousness." This is because this sinful busyness would have us think we are important because of our work. Faith says the opposite—that we are valuable because we glorify and serve the creator and redeemer of us all.[19]

Fourth, there is the superficiality of light-mindedness. Under its sway, the big questions of life are covered over by the trivial concerns of popular culture. The sin of light-mindedness keeps us from pondering and pursuing matters of truth and goodness. It makes us waste our time on the insubstantial.[20]

Fifth, there is heavy-mindedness—the very opposite of light-mindedness. This sin takes seriousness and earnestness and ruins them by turning them into gloom and brooding depression. As a result we despair over our self-control and diligence, which leaves us to wallow in self-indulgence and egotism. But if we divert our attention from ourselves and focus on God and our neighbor, then our seriousness is saved from this gloomy, brooding, heavy-mindedness.

Gathering up all five of these considerations into a confession, restores the blessedness of self-forgetfulness for the tears that we shed for our many and varied sins (WA 140).

JUDGMENT

Even though Kierkegaard was against scaring people to death with the threats and punishments of hell (UDVS 44), he still thought the impending judgment of God could provide "a helping hand" when it came to confessing our sins (UDVS 51).[21] At

17. See Heb 11:25 (RSV).
18. On this problem of getting things done, see Gal 3:3 and Phil 1:6.
19. Mt 22:37–40 calls this the summation of all the law and the prophets.
20. See Prv 9:6: "Leave simpleness and live and walk in the way of insight" (RSV).
21. On this tension, see Jack Mulder Jr., "On Being Afraid of Hell: Kierkegaard and Catholicism

the beginning of *The Gospel of Sufferings*, Kierkegaard imagines this final judgment day. He offers it as an incentive for following Christ "in the crisscrossing busyness of life," when it seems more than we can handle. In those moments, Kierkegaard warns, we are not to

> forget that it is eternity that will judge how the task was accomplished and that the earnestness of eternity will call for the silence of a sense of shame with regard to everything of the world, about which there was perpetual talk in the world. (UDVS 223)

If then we have pulled back from following Christ for fear of what the world thinks of us, we must remember that this ploy will only hurt us on judgment day. It is not a good defense then, to say that we did not follow Christ as we should have because we were afraid of being unpopular.[22] Kierkegaard says all such arguments must be silenced at the end, and so we should not depend on them now.

In addition to being stripped of this defense, Kierkegaard argues that the criterion by which we will be judged is especially stringent. This criterion will also be separate from all earthly values and accomplishments.[23] It will be based instead on self-denial. When Christ uses this criterion on judgment day, he will do so with the intensified twist that he

> does not merely know what self-denial is, he does not merely know how to judge in such a way that no malpractice can hide itself—no, his presence is the judging that makes everything that looked so good, which was heard and seen with admiration in the world, become silent and turn pale; his presence is the judging, because he was self-denial. He who was equal with God took the form of a lowly servant, he who could command legions of angels, indeed, could command the world's creation and its destruction, he walked about defenseless; . . . he who was the lord of creation constrained nature itself to keep quiet, for it was not until he had given up his spirit that the curtain tore and the graves opened and the powers of nature betrayed who he was: if this is not self-denial, what then is self-denial! (UDVS 224)

Kierkegaard enhances this criterion in order to terrify us. If Christ, who embodied self-denial, will judge how well we denied ourselves, then we cannot hope

---

on Imperfect Contrition," *Kierkegaard Studies: Yearbook* 2007, ed. Niels Jørgen Cappelørn, Herman Deuser and K. Brian Söderquist (Berlin: Walter de Gruyter, 2007), 96–122, and its revision in his *Kierkegaard and the Catholic Tradition: Conflict and Dialogue* (Bloomington: Indiana University Press, 2010), 153–77.

22. This is inspired by Mk 8:38: "Whoever is ashamed of me and of my words in this adulterous and sinful generation, of him will the Son of man also be ashamed, when he comes in the glory of his Father with the holy angels" (RSV).

23. On this point see Lk 16:15: "What is exalted among men is an abomination in the sight of God" (RSV).

somehow to fool him on judgment day.[24] This will be impossible because Christ will judge us in the most penetrating, thorough and unrelenting way—for he himself will have the most exacting standard, being self-denial himself. On judgment day he will ask

> about how often you have conquered your own mind, about what control you have exercised over yourself or whether you have been a slave, about how often you have mastered yourself in self-denial or whether you have never done so, about how often you in self-denial have been willing to make a sacrifice for a good cause or whether you were never willing, about how often you in self-denial have forgiven your enemy, whether seven times or seventy times seven times, about how often you in self-denial endured insults patiently, about what you have suffered, not for your own sake, for your selfish interests' sake, but what you in self-denial have suffered for God's sake. (UDVS 223–24)

The detail and relentlessness in this examination is terrifying. In self-defense we can imagine ourselves saying, "Well, I know I did not, but wait a minute! Give me a chance to explain! This is not fair. You are taking my life in the wrong way!" But such maneuverings will not finesse Christ—for he embodies self-denial in himself. These divine, rapid-fire interrogations cannot be stopped by any side-stepping on our part. Christ forces us to answer: Did you conquer your mind, control and master yourself, or were you a slave to your own base desires? Did you sacrifice your time and money for a good cause or use it for your own plans and pleasures? Did you forgive your enemies over and over again, or block them, hate them, trip them up and stop them by any means necessary? Did you take the insults hurled at you as if you deserved them, or did you squeal and complain that you deserve more respect? Were you ashamed of God when reasonable, good people pointed out to you how immoral and intellectually disrespectful his ways and will actually are—or did you love and honor him all the more in spite of their arguments?

This description of judgment day is designed to drive us to repent of our sins and to follow Christ all the more diligently. Its point is to keep us from holding back—stressing instead "unconditionally relating oneself to the unconditioned" (JP 4:4906). But it does this without appealing to the fires of hell and the threats of everlasting punishment and condemnation in hell. For Kierkegaard, it is enough for us to know what is expected of us—with no need to explore in detail the excruciating punishments awaiting all those who disobey, do not repent and squander forgiveness. In his day[25] that wretched scenario had already been described:

24. And not even right now, Kierkegaard would say: "Alas, many think that judgment is something reserved for the far side of the grave, and so it is also, but they forget that judgment is much closer than that, that it is taking place at all times, because at every moment you live, existence is judging you, since to live is to judge oneself, to become disclosed" (WL 227–28).

25. For a contemporary version, see Jack Handey, "My First Day in Hell," *The New Yorker* (October 30, 2006), 52: "My first day in Hell is drawing to a close. . . . Most of the demons are asleep now. . . .

The punishments of Hell . . . are the most exquisite pains of soul and body, . . . arising from the fear and sense of the most just wrath and vengeance of God against sins, the most sad consciousness of which they carry about with them, the baseness of which is manifest, and of which, likewise, no remission, . . . no mitigation or end can be hoped for. Whence, in misery, [the damned] will execrate, with horrible lamentation and wailing, their former impiety, by which they carelessly neglected the commandments of the Lord, the admonitions of their brethren, and all means of attaining salvation—but in vain. For in perpetual anguish, with dreadful trembling, in shame, confusion, and ignominy, in inextinguishable fire, in weeping and gnashing of teeth, amidst that which is eternal and terrible, torn away from the grace and favor of God, they must quake among devils, and . . . be tortured without end to eternity.[26]

Kierkegaard assumes this dire end[27]—which may be why he is so emphatic about stressing the great sacrifices we must make now, in order to ward off going to that terrible place of torment at the end, for all of eternity.

SALVATION

But all of this confession, condemnation, and judgment can leave our tears without the blessing of self-forgetfulness (WA 140). We can cry over our failures and be "crushed, almost despairing" (JFY 147). We do not live as we should, and our repentance for these sins is all too meager. In fact, our very will to follow Christ is contorted by our rebellion—corrupted by the disobedience itself. As a result, our "ability to receive is . . . simply not . . . in order" (PV 54). Burdened down by this incapacity, Kierkegaard cries out:

They look so innocent, it's hard to believe that just a few hours ago there were raping and torturing us. . . . The food here turns out to be surprisingly good. The trouble is, just about all of it is poisoned. So a few minutes after you finish eating, you're doubled over in agony. The weird thing is, as soon as you recover, you're ready to dig in again. . . . It's odd, but Hell can be a lonely place, even with so many people around. They all seem caught up in their own little worlds, running to and fro, wailing and tearing at their hair. . . . I thought getting a job might help. . . . I became the assistant to a demon who pulls people's teeth out. . . . I decided I had to get away—the endless lines, the senseless whipping, the forced sing-alongs. You get tired of trying to explain that you've already been branded, or that something that big won't fit in your ear, even with a hammer. . . . I had better get some rest. They say the bees will be out soon and that it's hard to sleep with the constant stinging. . . . Tomorrow we're supposed to build a huge monolith, then take picks and shovels and tear it down, then beat each other to death. It sounds pointless to me, but what do I know. I'm new here."

26. Matthew Hafenreffer (1561–1619), "Loci Theologici," *The Doctrinal Theology of the Evangelical Lutheran Church*, 3rd edition (1899), ed. Heinrich Schmid, trans. Charles A. Hay, Henry E. Jacobs (Minneapolis, MN: Augsburg, 1961), 658. "[Hafenreffer's Loci] was especially esteemed in . . . Denmark, where it was generally used as a text-book" (666). Kierkegaard, however, did not have a copy of this book in his personal library. *Auktionsprotokol over Søren Kierkegaards bogsamling*, ed. Herman P. Rohde (Copenhagen: Det Kongelige Bibliotek, 1967).

27. See UDVS 47, 58; CD 294; TM 121; 211, 294; JP 3:3589.

> From this moment I will no longer believe in myself; I will not let myself
> be deceived. . . . No, apprehensive about myself, . . . I will seek my refuge
> with him, the Crucified One. I will beseech him . . . to save me from myself."
> (CD 280)

These passionate, desperate words push us beyond confession and judgment. For
when the judgment in the next world "seeks the place where I, a sinner, stand, . . . it
does not find me" (WA 123). So when we recall "the lust of the eye that infatuated,
the sweetness of revenge that seduced, the anger that made us unrelenting, [and] the
cold heart" that ran away from God—it is our refuge, Christ, who keeps our "minds
free," our "courage uncrushed, and heaven open" (EUD 7). Christ does that by being
our "high priest" who steps into our place, and suffers "the punishment of sin," that we
"might be saved" (WA 123).[28] This sacrifice gives us confidence when before we were
almost despairing (JFY 147). It bolsters our efforts to follow Christ—without leaving
us to fend for ourselves before God. For this sacrifice in fact draws God closer to us,
for "the satisfaction of the Atonement" means that we "step aside" (WA 123). Christ
satisfies God's need for justice when he dies in our place. This satisfaction overcomes
the wrath of God that separates us from him and would damn to hell for all eternity.[29]
By enhancing God's mercy toward us, we are helped along in our life with him. Just
enough of the pressure is lifted from our backs so that we can take up our discipleship
again—being "kept in the striving" (JFY 147). This is what the "recourse to grace" is
for (TM 292).

STRIVING BORN OF GRATITUDE

All these burdens of sin, confession and judgment are for salvation. They are not
meant to end in despair as some may think. Instead they are preparations for salvation. These burdens are to humble us so that we will want to reach out to the grace of
God. Learning about sin and judgment shows us our need for a salvation which can
only be fulfilled from outside of ourselves. It helps us see that we lack the resources

---

28. See Sylvia Walsh, *Kierkegaard: Thinking Christianly in an Existential Mode*, 137: "[The] substitutionary perspective is clearly dominant in [Kierkegaard's] soteriology." This soteriological perspective shows the influence of Luther. See his "Sermon on Matthew 2:1–12" (1522), LW 52:253: "Why
else did [Christ] die, except to pay for our sins and to purchase grace for us so that we might despair
of ourselves and our works, placing no trust in them, so that we might, with courageous defiance, look
only to Christ, and firmly believe that he is the man whom God beholds in our stead and for the sake
of his sole merits forgives us our sins, deigns to look upon us with favor, and grants us eternal life.
That is the Christian faith."

29. See Mt 3:12; Mk 9:47–48; Lk 16:19–31; Jn 3:36, 5:28–29; Rom 5:9; 2 Thes 1:5–10. On Kierkegaard's opposition to universalism, or the view that hell must have no one in it, see Jack Mulder Jr.,
"Must All Be Saved? A Kierkegaardian Response to Theological Universalism," *International Journal
for Philosophy of Religion* 59 (February 2006): 1–24. Note Mulder's caveat: "[In] much of Kierkegaard's
writing, [he] in effect says, 'Stop working on metaphysical questions and start working on yourself!'"
(2). See also his *Kierkegaard and the Catholic Tradition*, 127.

from within to heal ourselves. So we have to resist the tendency to attenuate the strictness of Christianity in order that we may be relieved from the burden of sin and judgment. For if we were to do that, we would lose the necessary preparation for Christian salvation. But that would be to cut off our nose to spite our face. Kierkegaard resists this temptation and so his authorship is for us a treasure trove of Christian wisdom.

As long as we are plagued by the temptation to cut back on the hard truths of Christianity, what Kierkegaard has to say about sin, confession, judgment and salvation will be of help. For he is able to show us in a myriad of ways, that "infinite humiliation and grace, and then a striving born of gratitude," is what Christianity truly is (JP 1:993).

10

On Prayer

> Father in heaven! … we call upon your Spirit to … bring courage and life
> and power and strength, … but might it first of all make us sober.
> (JFY 95)

> O eternally secure, O blessedly safeguarded hiding place! … If justice … were to fly
> into a rage, what more does it want than the death penalty; but that penalty
> has been paid [by] Jesus Christ [and] his atoning death.
> (WA 186)

> Loving Father, I am a total failure–and yet you are love. I even fail to cling to this,
> that you are love…. [But] I believe that … it is still out of love
> that you permit it to happen, O infinite love.
> (JP 3:3450)

THESE THREE SHORT PRAYERS[1] by Kierkegaard can easily be taken up in a Christian's daily devotions—using the first one for the beginning of the day, the second one around midday, and the last for the close of the day. I will try to show the value in doing this by first pointing out how they reinforce basic Christian themes.[2] Second, I will show how they provoke us with their words to increase their power over us to make us better. Third, I will show how faith fits into these provocations, by building upon the disruptions and upheavals in life. Fourth, I will show how our faith must be militant if it is

---

1. Or fragments of prayers—which I have used for easier use on a daily basis. For a selection of Kierkegaard's better known prayers, see *Two Thousand Years of Prayer*, ed. Michael Counsell (Harrisburg, Pennsylvania: Morehouse, 1999), 363–64. The second of my three opening prayers is the most fragmented. Nevertheless, I still think it is of value as it stands, and that it can also be of use as a segment for a longer prayer.

2. On demurring from such a project, see Robert L. Perkins, "Kierkegaard's Prayers as Art, Theology, and Prayer," *Christian Scholar's Review* 19 (Winter 1989): 121: "I thought many times as I wrote this paper that I would comment on Kierkegaard's prayers. But, finally that cannot be; they are too personal, too exalted, too childlike, too contrite, too desperate, too joyful, too confessional to be lectured about. Finally, then, I join with those who object to the analysis, be it aesthetic or philosophical, of actual prayers. Kierkegaard's prayers must finally be prayed, and if we pray them, we find in them that Kierkegaard secured that 'second immediacy' of Christianity." I, however, will try to do both— pray these prayers and also think about them. 1 Corinthians 14:14 encourages me in this project: "I will pray with the spirit and I will pray with the mind also."

going to survive. Fifth, I conclude with the category of struggle as the key component in all Christian prayer. And sixth, I will explain how this struggle eventually leads to a blessed silence wherein we listen more to God's Word, when we pray, than to our own thoughts and words.

THREE DAILY PRAYERS

So I first want to survey our opening three prayers, to show how they, and prayer in general for Kierkegaard, are integral to his understanding of Christianity. According to him, "prayer maintains in its God-relationship what it is striving for itself in its authentic form—such joy in the presence of God and in conformity with him as is won by the one who prays, illuminated by God and transfigured in him."[3] This transfiguration can be seen in the first of our three little prayers in its war against spiritual intoxication. But this battle is different than you might think—since the intoxication to which it refers is not just some form of "enthusiasm . . . and venturing in such a way that one relinquishes probability" (JFY 98). That is because "the entire relation in the distinction, spiritually understood, between being sober and being intoxicated is turned around" (JFY 103)! This reversal[4] pits us against the safe life of reasonableness and probability—resulting in a veritable existential explosion!

> [For] when Christ resolves to become the Savior of the world, a lament goes through all humanity like a sigh: Why do you do this, you will make us all unhappy—simply because to become a Christian in truth is the greatest human suffering, because Christ as the absolute explodes all the relativity in which we human beings live—in order to make us spirit. But in order to become spirit one must go through crises which make us, from a human point of view, as unhappy as possible.(JP 6:6686)[5]

3. J. Pedersen, "Kierkegaard on Prayer," trans. Howard V. Hong, Bibliotheca Kierkegaardiana, vol. 2: *The Sources and Depths of Faith in Kierkegaard*, ed. Niels Thulstrup and Marie Mikulová Thulstrup (Copenhagen: C. A. Reitzels, 1978), 64. For a similar point on the importance of prayer, see Martin Luther, "Sermon on Luke 18:31–43" (1534), LHP 1:310: "[As] soon as trouble presses [on the Christian], he should go directly into the church or his closet, fall on his knees, and say, 'Lord, here I am; I have need of this or that, although I am unworthy; however, look upon my misery and need, and help me for thy honor's sake.' So, I learn to petition boldly and do not doubt that God will for Christ's sake give you *what is for your good*" (italics added).

4. We must not think that Kierkegaard believes that we can settle in easily with this reversal: "But we see that 'man' is clever; he quickly turned the whole thing around and said: Well, fine, but it is confoundedly strenuous to be an apostle or disciple, so I, as far as I am concerned, would rather be exempted from that great distinction. But in addition to being clever, man is also cowardly and hypocritical; therefore he did not say it aloud, no, he adulterated what it is to be an apostle and a disciple to being a genius, etc.—and so we are happily rid of Christianity in a nice way. And when things really got rolling, this whole business of millions and millions of Christians began in earnest" (JP 3:2907).

5. In an extended journal entry, Kierkegaard explores this explosion in more detail: "This is the thesis—as soon as one single true Christian in the most rigorous sense exists, Christianity exists; and on the other hand, if there were 7 billion, 5 million, 696,734 or 35 Christians of the up-to-a-certain-point kind—Christianity for that reason does not exist. . . . Seen from the other side, very

So the intoxication against which Christians are to fight is "sensibleness, lev-elheadedness and sagacity" (JFY 103). No wonder then, that if you do this, you will look "crazy," "reckless," and like a most ridiculous "exaggeration" (JFY 155, 118, 123), or explosion—"just as [when] the graves burst" open at the crucifixion of Jesus (Mt 27:52)[6] (JP 2:1645)! In his book, *Works of Love*, Kierkegaard explains further this dif-ficulty with the help of an image of a dog walking on his hind legs:

> It is very difficult to extricate oneself from the lower conceptual sphere and the pact of earthly passions with the illusions. Just when one has understood the truth best, the old suddenly crops up again. The infinite, the eternal, hence the true, is so alien to the natural man that with him it is as with the dog, which can indeed learn to walk upright for a moment but yet continually wants to walk on all fours. (WL 244)

So trying to live spiritually sober lives will be as unpleasant as biting into a "sour apple" (JFY 131)![7] And if we manage somehow to do it anyway, we will quickly learn that our family and friends (JFY 116) will think we are "unbearable" (JFY 113)—which will only discourage us all the more from fighting against this debilitation. Praying this prayer by Kierkegaard every morning will help offset these drawbacks. It will set the agenda for the day—to sober up spiritually.

The second prayer is about Jesus our savior—the one who rescues us from our-selves (CD 280). This prayer is especially important because of the pressure the first prayer puts on us to live spiritually sober lives. In our spiritual exhaustion, we need assurances from outside of ourselves that we can still be righteous, even though we re-peatedly get drunk spiritually—gorging ourselves on reasonableness and probability.[8] We need to know that there is still a way for us to sober up, even though we fail to do it on our own. And that way, the New Testament says, is found in Christ:

---

likely we are fortunate that there is not, in the strictest sense, one true Christian, for one true Christian would explode existence and presumably have the effect that all the rest of us desert completely" (JP 3:2958–59).

6. And so indeed the resurrection did not end the power of death, but—paradoxically—the very death of Jesus did that (Col 1:22; Heb 2:14). What his resurrection did was demonstrate or prove—not cause—the defeat of death, by making Jesus the "first fruits" of eternal life (Rom 6:5; 1 Cor 6:14; 15:20–23; 2 Cor 4:14; Jn 14:19; Heb 6:20).

7. Here Kierkegaard is following the Lutheran Confessions: "We for our part preach the foolish-ness of the Gospel, which reveals another righteousness, namely, that because of Christ, the propiti-ator, we are accounted righteous when we believe that for Christ's sake God is gracious to us. We know how repulsive [*abhorreat*] this teaching is to the judgment of reason . . . and that the teaching of the law about love is more plausible; for this is human wisdom" (BC 139).

8. On the dangers of probability, Kierkegaard writes that corrupt, institutional Christianity "re-moves from the essentially Christian the offense, the paradox, etc. and replaces it with: probability, the direct" (TM 184). And since this corrupt view is prevalent, the majority of people "do not really *live*; they are only repetitious, center their lives within the security of probability, and therefore are not superstitious—that is, they are not aware that this, their faith in probability and their security within probability, is in another sense a prodigious superstition" (JP 4:4741).

> [His] death infinitely changes everything. It is not as if his death abolishes
> the importance of his also being the prototype. No, but his death becomes
> the infinite comfort, the infinite headstart with which the striver begins, that
> satisfaction has been made infinitely, that the doubter, the discouraged one is
> offered the ultimate pledge—it is impossible to find anyone more reliable!—
> that Christ died to save him, that Christ's death is the Atonement, is the satis-
> faction. (WA 159)

On the cross Jesus becomes our substitute, who stands in our place and is punished for our sins (WA 123), so that all who believe in him might be saved from the
wrath of God (JP 1:532),[9] and given the hope of eternal life. We need this assurance
every day so that we can avoid being crushed by our failures. This is only found in
Christ's crucifixion.[10] Kierkegaard calls it the "ultimate pledge," "the infinite headstart"
that "infinitely changes everything."[11] Entrusting our lives to the satisfaction Christ's
death earns before God, gives us the peace of mind we so desperately need, and makes
us "indescribably happy" (JFY 198). Only faith in Christ can do this for us (JFY 193).
So when God flies into a rage, as Kierkegaard puts it in this second prayer, due to our
disobedience, rebellion, weakness and ignorance of his way, we are saved from his
wrath by our faith in Christ. And when we have this peace, we can finally heed with
great joy Christ's command: "Venture a decisive act; . . . become heterogeneous with
the life of the world" (JFY 191)! At this point Christians are able to move on from
Christ the redeemer and go on to imitate him. But even here we have to be cautious.
Even in our venturing out boldly in the name of Christ, we must "fear most of all"
our pride in our spiritual diligence (JFY 197). So even in our bona fide imitation of
Christ there must be leniency! Therefore, Kierkegaard confesses: "I do not dare to assert imitation any further than an onerous possibility that can press doubt into silence
and press in the direction of humility" (JYF 198).

9. See also JP 2:1329, 2:1425, TM 121, 211.

10. And so William Shakespeare's Lady Macbeth was wrong (*Macbeth*, II.ii.66–67): "A little water
clears us of this deed: How easy is it, then!" For more on this difficulty, see Martin Luther, "Lectures
on Galatians 5–6" (1535), LW 27:5: "The words 'freedom from the wrath of God' . . . are easy to say;
but to feel the greatness of this freedom [through faith in Christ] and to apply its results to oneself
in a struggle, in the agony of conscience, and in practice—this is more difficult than anyone can say."

11. And so even now our praying has to be done only in the name of Jesus—for "I do not dare
approach God except through an intermediary"; Kierkegaard argues, "if my prayer is to be heard, it
must be in the name of Jesus. . . . The name of Jesus is not a casual endorsement but the decisive factor.
. . . [For] Jesus takes upon himself the responsibility and all the consequences; he steps forward for
us, steps forward in place of the one who is praying" (JP 3:3441). On this condition, see also Martin
Luther, "Sermon on John 16:23–30" (1525), SML 3:171, which may have inspired Kierkegaard: "Christ
. . . is our Mediator, through whom all things are given to us. . . . It is praying aright in Christ's name,
when we thus trust in him that we will be received and heard for his sake, and not for our own sake.
Those, however, who . . . presume that God will hear or regard them, because they say . . . such godly
prayers, will merit and obtain nothing but wrath and disgrace; for they wish to be people whom God
should regard without a mediator." See also my "Praying in Jesus' Name," *The Bride of Christ: The
Journal of Lutheran Liturgical Renewal* 22 (Lent and Easter, 1998): 3–7.

And so in the third prayer, for the close of the day, we reinforce this humility by admitting that when it comes to imitating Christ by fighting against spiritual intoxication, we are nothing but abject failures. For indeed, even our most gallant efforts and our greatest accomplishments are but filthy rags in God's eyes.[12] They never measure up to the Christian ideal. So Kierkegaard encourages us to join him in saying: "That I fail or turn out to be the dunce of the class—I humbly resign myself to that" (JFY 199)! This third prayer, wherein we say that we are total failures, helps us admit that we are all dunces. By so doing, we nurture in ourselves the humility that is expected of all Christians at all times—taking up the view that we are not to think more highly of ourselves than we ought to.[13] This humility, however, does not mean being "humbly satisfied with mediocrity"—which is only to "humbly—shirk Christianity" (JP 2:1438, 3:2725)![14] No, rather it means "gladly, adoringly letting yourself be totally shattered by God in order that he can unconditionally advance his will" in you (JP 2:2098). And this shattering humiliation is exactly what makes "infinitely nothing" out of us (JP 3:2721).[15] And to be nothing before God is glorious, even though in this world it is widely disparaged:

> The life of the true Christian is therefore always double. Over against God he must humbly confess that he is very far indeed from being sufficiently gentle and meek; he must thank God for the suffering, that it might help him to become meeker. But if over against men he were to say the same thing—that the reason he is persecuted is that he is not sufficiently gentle and meek—then this is nonsense, for if he were more so, he would simply be persecuted more.

12. See Is 64:6 (KJV) and Rom 7:18: "I know that nothing good dwells within me" (RSV). On the "existential neediness" that comes from this humble awareness of our waywardness, see David Roberts, *Kierkegaard's Analysis of Radical Evil* (New York: Continuum, 2006), 150: "Kierkegaard's authorship is an attempt to confront the single individual with the limitations of existence, and the weakness of the self in overcoming these limitations, in hopes of awakening the need for God. All pursuit and love of wisdom must remain within this existential neediness."

13. See Rom 12:3.

14. Countering this false humility, Kierkegaard proffers: "That true humility and pride are one can . . . be seen in this that there is something very proud in saying: I fear only God—otherwise nothing. And yet only this is fear of God, for to fear God and then also something else is not genuine fear of God" (JP 2:1388).

15. And because of this stridency, worldly ridicule will also be an essential part of true humility: "The world ridicules the humble person" (JP 3:2482). Added to this will also be disdain: "If a person really gets serious about the humility which abases unconditionally, you will see that it will be condemned as the most frightful arrogance" (JP 3:2679). On passing on this most difficult lesson to children, see Marietta McCarty, *Little Big Minds: Sharing Philosophy with Kids* (New York: Tarcher/ Penguin, 2006), 230, 231: "[Kierkegaard's writings] lead children most often to an exploration of the clearly *human* capacity for the rejection of others that kids recognize with dismay in themselves. . . . Each time I talk to kids about Kierkegaard, . . . they tell me that the experience of being isolated from the crowd is 'brutal.' Cliques can make you feel that who you are is inferior and that you need to be like someone else. . . . It's puzzling, a few tell me, to 'feel like an outsider for being left out of something that you don't really care about anyway' . . . [On the other hand, many] have begun already the painful, lifelong effort to resist the pressure to conform and go along with the crowd."

> O, what frightful strenuousness to have two such thoughts in one's head at the same time without confusing them and being rendered powerless. Before God it can be true that one suffers because he is not humble enough, and in respect to the world it is true that he suffers because he has some humility and would suffer more if he had more humility. (JP 4:4623)

So when it comes to being humble before God, we must not follow worldly sentiments regarding humility, which would mislead us. We instead must always be aware of our nothingness and our failure to live soberly. This in large part is what the New Testament means when it calls us to hate ourselves[16]—thereby underscoring our insignificance in this life. And so this last prayer, offered at the end of each day, promotes "the Christian view," as one lays down to sleep, which is "one of suffering, of enthusiasm for death, [and] belonging to another world," which also knows that "one can love only by hating this world and one's own life in this world" (TM 206).[17]

PROVOCATIVE LANGUAGE

So for all of Kierkegaard's literary sophistication, he was not adverse to writing prayers and including them in some of his books. He knew this could appear to be a malapropism because praying can look like "a cowardly and fainthearted business" (EUD 378)[18]—which would go counter to his overall concern for, and pursuit of, Christian rigorousness (JFY 120).[19] But he did not think that all prayers had to be fainthearted. He knew that prayers should actually be anything but cowardly. Such intellectually and ethically challenging prayers—like the three that we have begun with—were the kind he believed in.[20] He called them "real" prayers (JP 3:3435).[21] These prayers were

16. See Jn 12:25; Lk 14:26; 2 Tm 3:2–5.

17. For other passages on self-hatred in this same work, see TM 47, 52,168, 184, 189, 238, 240, 312, 319, 335, 346.

18. There are also other, more serious problems with prayer. On this Kierkegaard writes: "A hasty explanation can suppose that to pray is a futile act because a person's prayer does not, of course, change the changeless; but in the long run would this be desirable, could not the changing person easily come to repent that he had managed to get God changed! Thus the true explanation is also the one and only one desired: the prayer does not change God, but it changes the one who prays" (UDVS 22).

19. See also *Fear and Trembling* on the requirement of agony and distress (FT 53, 64, 65, 66, 74, 113).

20. On the sophistication of prayers like Kierkegaard's, see Robert L. Perkins, "Kierkegaard's Prayers as Art, Theology, and Prayer," 109: "To be sure, there is nothing obviously artistic or composed, there is no aesthetic distance or aesthetic objectivity in the prayer of the thief on the cross, 'Lord, remember me when thou comest into thy kingdom' (Lk 23:42). Yet there are a considerable number of qualities of this statement that could be aesthetically analyzed: its terseness, its immediacy, its audacity, its subtle combination of religious respect for the divine with the existential and undeniable demand of the human, and the confrontation of the immediacy of death with the hope of life, etc."

21. On Kierkegaard's distinction between true and false prayers, see *The Prayers of Kierkegaard*, ed. Perry D. LeFevre (Chicago: University of Chicago Press, 1956), 221–22: "Kierkegaard's view of true prayer implies a concept of false prayer. . . . False prayer falsely conceives of God. It thinks God

like Jacob wrestling with God at the river Jabbok (Gn 32:22–32), where God "judges, chastises, and scourges [us] until we learn [to follow his] perfect will."[22] Sometimes Kierkegaard put these prayers at the beginning of his discourses where one might expect to see them (EUD 7, TM 268). At other times, without any warning, he puts them in the middle of an argument (JFY 166–67, 174) or at the end of a long discourse (PC 260–62, FSE 87). Over fifty of his prayers are in his journals (JP 3:3366–3466). But wherever and whenever we find them, more often than not, they are provocative—as we have seen in the third of our opening prayers on being total failures. That same demanding quality is in Kierkegaard's prayer for the church, which closes by saying: "Our Lord Jesus Christ was a nobody—remember that, Christendom!" (JP 3:3449).[23]

A couple of years before he died, Kierkegaard wrote in a journal entry from 1853 that he did not always favor provocative prayers, but more sedate ones (JP 6:6837). "How rash my soul was," he confesses, in daring to pray for "earthly gifts, happiness, [and] prosperity. . . . I thought something like this: One should not himself make an almighty being stingy and petty." And so, when everything turned out fine after he prayed, "how full of gratitude my soul . . . was to give thanks—for my belief that God expresses his love by sending earthly goods was unshaken." But then gradually he started changing his prayers. Slowly but surely a desire awakened within him to offer different kinds of prayers. This change was based on the deeply disturbing view— a new "conception of God," he calls it—that "to be loved by God" cannot be combined with "worldly enjoyment and temporal victory." And so he came to realize that if he

---

is changeable. . . . It thinks God operates in terms of human conceptions of good and evil, pleasant and unpleasant. It turns God into man writ large, as if he could be persuaded, cajoled, bargained with . . . . The one who prays falsely complains and then gives thanks only for what he himself thinks is good. . . . The man who truly prays listens to God; the man who prays falsely wants God to listen to him." On this correlation between a false conception of God and bad prayers, Kierkegaard further notes in his journals, that there shall be "no dreaming, for God is pure act, and therefore a mere dreamy loitering over the thought of him is not true prayer" (JP 2:2008).

22. Martin Luther, "Lectures on Genesis 31–37" (1545), LW 6:152. Kierkegaard's prayers are also in keeping with the ancient church. On this view see *Unseen Warfare*, trans. E. Kadloubovsky and G. E. H. Palmer (Crestwood, New York: Saint Vladimir's Seminary, 1987), 200: "[By way of] prayer you put your battle-axe into God's hand, that He should fight your enemies and overcome them."

23. As a possible reason for the sharpness of this reminder, Kierkegaard writes against this reduction of Christianity to education: "Mynster's [mistaken] view [holds that] Christianity is an educational process, being Christian is approximately what the natural man in his most blissful happy moment could wish to be at his best: poised, harmonious perfection in itself and in himself consummately prepared virtuosity. But such talk is 100,000 miles removed from the Redeemer who must suffer in the world and who requires the crucifixion of the flesh, all that agony as the birth pangs of salvation, because under the circumstances there is in fact an infinite, a qualitative difference between God and man, and the terror of Christianity is also its blessedness: that God wants to be the teacher and wants the disciple to resemble him. If God is to be the teacher, then the instruction must begin with disrupting the learner (man). For the sake of quality it cannot be otherwise. There is not much use in speaking of God as the teacher and then have the instruction be only a purely human improvement program. . . . If there is not to be any conflict between Christianity and the world, if the insignia of battle are not to be carried, if there is to be peace of that sort, then it is really something great to have a figure such as Mynster" (JP 5:6076).

were to go on praying his old reckless prayers—with his former "burning fervor"—he would be cutting off his nose to spite his face! He would, in effect, be praying: "O God, will you stop loving me and let me stop loving you"? And then it started dawning on him that God was answering back: "My little friend, consider what you are doing; do you really want me not to love you and do you want to be released from loving me"? And so his prayers were stopped, dead in their tracks, and he was at "a standstill." "To pray outright for suffering, however, seemed to me to be . . . presumptuous," he writes, "so that God might, as it were, become angry about it, as if I perhaps wanted to provoke him." He was not strong enough to pray himself "into suffering." So Kierkegaard's prayers rather became "a calm leaving of everything to God." Gradually he came to see, as he says, "that God speaks . . . a different language than I do." And that different language is what we find expressed in Kierkegaard's provocative prayers.[24] None of them ask God directly to make us suffer, but they all pray for things that will bring it upon us indirectly.[25]

BECOMING A CHRISTIAN

We first see the function of this provocative language by noting that Kierkegaard's prayers are strident because they "corroborate" the overall purpose of his authorship, which is to help a person with the difficult and harrowing task of becoming a Christian (PV 6, 23).[26] Kierkegaard believed one could pray even if one were not yet a devout Christian. That is because all that is needed to start praying is the desire to want to become a Christian. A good example of this struggle to be a Christian is his prayer on divine discrimination:

24. Kierkegaard's provocative prayers are in the prophetic tradition of Jer 4:3 and Hos 10:12—calling us to break up our "fallow ground."

25. Mt 4:5–7 says that we are not to recklessly endanger ourselves because that would be to tempt God—which is prohibited (Dt 6:16). This does not mean, however, that we should flee from all suffering. On this complication, see Martin Luther, "The Blessed Sacrament of the Body of Christ" (1519), LW 35:56: "Now if one will make the afflictions of Christ and of all Christians his own, defend the truth, oppose unrighteousness, and help bear the needs of the innocent and the sufferings of all Christians, then he will find affliction and adversity enough, over and above that which his evil nature, the world, the devil, and sin daily inflict upon him."

26. *Søren Kierkegaard: The Mystique of Prayer and Pray-er*, trans. and ed. Lois S. Bowers and George K. Bowers (Lima, Ohio: CSS Publishing, 1994), 11. Note also: "By means of prayer we do not win out over God. In prayer God conquers our minds and our attitudes and vanquishes our rebel, errant ways. God's victory over us in prayer gives us the victory over life!" (24). On this arduous transformation, see also JP 1:731, 2:1409, 3:3101, 6:6503, 6:6947, 6:6966. So Kierkegaard rejoices: "[Because God seems to be] so infinitely sublime that one does not dare think of him at all, [it would seem that] he must become disgusted and tired of listening to one's nonsense and nauseated with one's sins. But a person is not to give in; he is to fight against it, [and] thank God that God has *commanded* that one *ought* to pray to him, for otherwise it is hardly possible to force one's way through the spiritual trial" (JP 2:2008). Luther also makes a similar point on the necessity of prayer in his "Sermons on John 14–16" (1537), LW 24:89: "A Christian without prayer is just as impossible as a living person without a pulse."

Lord Jesus Christ, you who loved us first,[27] you who until the last loved those who you had loved from the beginning, you who until the end of time continue to love everyone who wants to belong to you[28]—your faithfulness cannot deny itself.[29] Alas, only when a person denies you can he force you,[30] so to speak, you the loving one, also to deny him. May this be our comfort when we must indict ourselves for the offense we have committed, for what we have left undone, for our weakness in temptation, for our slow progress in the good, that is, for our unfaithfulness to you, to whom we once in our early youth and repeatedly thereafter promised faithfulness—may it be our comfort that even if we are unfaithful you still remain faithful; you cannot deny yourself. (CD 282)

This prayer is interrupted by the word "alas." Up to that point the prayer is mesmerizing in its repeated affirmations of God's love for us. But then, abruptly, we learn—by way of that interjected "alas"—that we can drive God away from us. For if we stand against him, deny him, reject his goodness and mercy, then he will give up on us and quit loving us. So those repeated assurances about God's love are limited and must be treated dialectically.[31] We can indeed stop God's love cold when we defy him—which is what we do when we refuse to indict ourselves because of our sins. But this prayer does not end on that sour note. It goes on to include the word "may" twice, assuring us of the comfort that we can receive even if we have enraged God in the past. Now we learn that we can be comforted in our faithlessness—since unlike our denial of God—our faithlessness does not enrage him. For when we indict ourselves for our sins, God will love us to the end, even if we have behaved badly and have been unfaithful. That is because God can put up with our weakness and our sin, just as long as we repent and confess our sins before him by indicting ourselves—"for the offense we have committed," as Kierkegaard puts it in this prayer. The comfort in this is that God will not abandon us on a whim, but only in reaction to our repeated, hardened, defiance of him, which is what provokes him to abandon us.[32] Otherwise he will roll with

---

27. See 1 Jn 4:19.

28. See Jn 14:21 and Jas 4:4.

29. See 2 Tm 2:13.

30. On provoking God to anger, see Gn 6:5–7, Jgs 2:12, Ez 16:23–29, Mt 21:33–41, Acts 13:23, and Gal 6:7–8.

31. On this dialectical analysis, see Julia Watkin, *The A to Z of Kierkegaard's Philosophy* (Lanham: The Scarecrow Press, 2010), 65: "Kierkegaard's use of dialectic . . . is different from that of Georg W. F. Hegel [1770–1831], who conceives dialectic to be the ongoing and opposing movements in the world-historical process. For Kierkegaard, there is still a sense of something opposing something else, but in this case it is in terms of one's taking a questioning and critical stance, striving to see all possible angles in a situation or with a problem, especially seeing what counts against one's own view. Kierkegaard also uses the word dialectic to indicate what is doubtful or ambiguous or presents contrasting perspectives to one. . . . Dialectic may also mean that one is required to hold two at least apparently contradictory thoughts together."

32. But if our prayers cannot change God's mind, then how do our evil deeds provoke him to

the punches, so to speak.[33] This prayer, then, is rigorous because of the way it moves back and forth between comfort and threats, confidence and offense, not settling for simple unqualified platitudes.[34]

This prayer on divine discrimination is therefore a good elaboration of our three opening prayers. Regarding the first one, it encourages sobriety. Regarding the second one, it reinforces the hope we have in God's abiding love for us in Christ Jesus. And regarding the last one, it specifies how we are complete failures in our faithlessness.

PRAYING FOR FAITH

This comfort, however, that is dialectically linked to those divine threats, will not come our way until we first believe in God through Christ Jesus. That is because only by this faith can we repent, be forgiven and then find the comfort we so desperately long for. Without such faith, we will never indict ourselves, and God will remain enraged with us and cut off all comfort.[35] Therefore Kierkegaard prays to God to bless us with faith:

> Father in heaven! What is all man's knowledge but a chipped fragment if he does not know you, what is all his achievement but half-finished work if you do not share the work, what are all his labors but sheer vanity if he does not seek you.[36] We pray, then, that you will form the hearts of those who live without God in the world, so that they might seek you; the hearts of those who seek you that they might wait upon you; the hearts of those that wait upon you that they might find you; and the hearts of those that find you that they might give away everything in order to buy what they possess[37] and that nothing might

---

anger? If we are unable to affect God with our prayers, how do our misdeeds get through to him? Kierkegaard does not see any inconsistency here. For him the operative distinction is to move God but without changing him (TM 268). So both our prayers and evil actions move God, but neither change him. Therefore when we provoke God to anger, that does not mean that we have changed him into a malevolent God.

33. On this divine congeniality, see 1 Jn 1:8–9: "If we say we have no sin, we deceive ourselves, and the truth is not in us. [But] if we confess our sins, God is faithful and just, and will forgive our sins and cleanse us from all unrighteousness" (RSV).

34. Kierkegaard's Constantin Constantinus clarifies the perils of this dialectical rigorousness with the shocking analogy of killing a man and then, at the same time, keeping him alive: "Above all, it is asking too much of an ordinary reviewer to be interested in the dialectical battle in which the exception arises in the midst of the universal, the protracted and very complicated procedure in which the exception battles his way through and affirms himself as justified, for that unjustified exception is recognized precisely by his wanting to bypass the universal. This battle is very dialectical and infinitely nuanced; it presupposes as a condition an absolute promptitude in the dialectic of the universal, demands speed in imitating the movements—in a word, it is just as difficult as to kill a man and let him live" (R 226).

35. On this condition see Heb 11:6: "Without faith it is impossible to please God" (RSV).

36. On these opening lines, see also UDVS 153–54.

37. See Mt 13:45–46.

tear you from them or them from you until their final blessed end.[38] And if, alas, though seeking, they did not find you as the years went by, if they did not find you when they were told in their youth to rejoice in the delights of the world and not to seek what will come in time,[39] if they did not find you when they were cast down and were told to forget God and let the world heal them, and if they did not find you when they were told in their old age that they had lived in vain—Lord God, if he did not find you until the hour of death,[40] if he had continually sought you, then he also found what we all seek: a final blessed end. (JP 3:3399)

This prayer is complex in both of its two major parts. In the first half it makes the point that life without God is incomplete and also vain, precisely because it is incomplete. This implies that the significance of what we do is not established simply by finishing up the work. No, some grand over-arching scheme is also needed if our labors are to fit in, make a difference and matter. And our work is given that scheme in God's kingdom—which is the overarching structure that we need for our labors to matter. But for our work to fit into that kingdom, we need to believe in God. This rationale for faith justifies the long third sentence of this prayer when faith is finally prayed for. This is also a complex part of the first part of this prayer, and for two reasons.[41] First, it complicates faith by saying that it can only arise in us if God properly forms our hearts so that we can believe in him. Without this formation, our will to believe is too disordered (PV 54) to reach out to God in faith, trust and hope.

DISRUPTION

Kierkegaard, however, does not explain in this prayer how that formation takes place and how it brings about faith in us. Elsewhere he does say that an "upheaval" (EUD 136)[42] is needed in our lives if we are to come to faith in God. And, in as much as God sends us these disruptions, he forms our hearts so that we can believe and trust in him. The Lutheran Confessions even daringly say that we need to be "coerced into the

---

38. See Jn 10:29.

39. See Lk 12:19.

40. See Lk 23:40–43.

41. The second reason is taken up below on p. 228.

42. On this precondition for faith, Kierkegaard also says: "[Imagine] someone living in Christendom [saying] he would very much like to believe if only he could get settled definitely what he is to believe. This sounds quite acceptable, and yet there is deceit in it. He is unwilling to venture out into the dangers and decisions where faith comes into existence; he is unwilling to become alone, alone in the life-perils of the spirit, and therefore he speaks about this difficulty; in the anxiety of his soul he is not willing to risk everything. . . . The nearest way [to God] is the way of life-perils; the most comfortable way, which, however, does not lead to faith, is to begin to get busy about not being able to make historically definite what it is one is to believe. The most reliable information is received in life-peril, where one hears (what one basically knows) with a clarity that only life-peril provides, because in life-peril one becomes infinitely ready to hear and is infinitely close to what one is to hear" (CD 245).

obedience of Christ," by being clubbed with "punishments and miseries" throughout the days of our lives (BC 568). Those calamities are what prime the pump of our will, so to speak, so that we might trust in and follow God through Christ our Lord. These disruptions are what "drive us to Christ"—*agitatur ad Christum*—as Luther put it.[43] Troubles, then, more than rational proofs or irrefutable evidence, are what lead us to faith in Christ. Therefore Kierkegaard prays for these upheavals to save us:

> O Holy Spirit—we pray for ourselves and for all people—O Holy Spirit, you who give life, here there is no want of capabilities, nor of education, nor of sagacity—indeed, there may rather be too much.[44] But what is wanting is that you take away whatever is corrupting us, that you take power away from us and give life. Certainly a person experiences a shudder like death's shudder when you, in order to become the power in us, take power away from him. (FSE 87)

One is glad to have Kierkegaard admit that when praying for these upheavals we "shudder"—since the likely impact of these upheavals on us will be awful.[45] Nevertheless these assaults are needed since we cannot think our way into faith. On that score, Kierkegaard is right, that we might already have too much information, gathered from too much thinking, over whether or not we should believe. And the only way for us to learn that more information will not do the trick, is to become weak. But that will only happen when God takes away our strength since none of us will give it up gladly. Therefore it is only

> when all confidence in yourself or in human support, and also in God in an immediate way, is extinct, when every probability is extinct, when it is dark as on a dark night—it is indeed death we are describing—then comes the life-giving Spirit and brings faith. This faith is stronger than the whole world; it has the power of eternity. (FSE 82)

But this is also a description of how we come to need God—and that is equally essential because without any need for him, no one will trust in him. Kierkegaard emphasizes this point by saying that our need for God is our "perfection," since through it

43. Martin Luther, "Lectures on Isaiah 1–39" (1534), LW 16:232. See also Luther's *Small Catechism* (1529): "I believe that by my own reason or strength I cannot believe in Jesus Christ, my Lord, or come to him. But the Holy Spirit has called me through the Gospel, enlightened me with his gifts, and . . . preserved me in true faith" (BC 345). See also Luther's "Lectures on Galatians 1–4" (1535), LW 26:310: "The presumption of righteousness [within us] is a huge and a horrible monster. To break and crush it, God needs a large and powerful hammer, that is, the Law, which is the hammer of death, the thunder of hell, and the lightning of divine wrath."

44. See Mt 11:25–26: "Jesus declared, 'I thank you, Father, Lord of heaven and earth, that you have hidden these things from the wise and understanding and revealed them to babes; yes, Father, for such was your gracious will'" (RSV).

45. Luther shows this same empathy in his "Lectures on Genesis 21–25" (1545), LW 4:340, 361: "To pray [properly] is a most difficult work. Therefore it is also very rare. . . . [So] it is a sacrifice pleasing to God when we pray in such a way that the prayer surpasses our comprehension and understanding."

we are "saved from the presumptuousness that could be called ungodly unawareness" (CD 64).

FIGHTING AGAINST OURSELVES

And so Kierkegaard adds that "faith sees best in the dark" (UDVS 238)—which is what we experience when we need God. One would not think that such need and darkness help us believe—preferring reasonability and hard evidence over need, as we like to do.[46] But if we are going to believe in God, he will have to help us fight against our self-reliance that springs from our yearning for intellectual respectability. That is because we are the one enemy that we have that we cannot conquer on our own (EUD 18). But with God's help, each one of us can fight "for himself with himself within himself" (EUD 143). And we must do this because "everyone's heart is . . . indulgent enough to want to decide for itself what is the good" (EUD 25).[47] This personal control over defining what is good for ourselves, will only lead to faithlessness and disobedience. For on the matter of faith itself, we will surely fashion a counterfeit version of it whereby faith is "only a fleeting emotion, mirroring . . . earthly happiness" (EUD 25). So we must fight against that mirroring, that we might come to

> doubt in the right way, not to doubt what stands firm and will stand firm forever in its eternal clarity, but to doubt that which in itself is transitory, which will more and more vanish, to doubt himself, his own capacity and competence, so that it becomes an incapacity that is discarded more and more. False doubt doubts everything except itself; with the help of faith, the doubt that saves doubts only itself. (EUD 137)

This undermining of the transitory, by doubting it, opens up the way to faith. With that opening, good doubt falls into place, and we can exclaim with Kierkegaard that we will seek "refuge with . . . the Crucified One . . . to save" us from ourselves (CD 280)! We need this rescuing because we are sinners who cannot save ourselves.[48] That

---

46. Those sinful longings of ours go against Heb 11:1: "Faith is the assurance of things hoped for, the conviction of things not seen" (RSV).

47. On what this freedom brings, see Is 5:20: "Woe to those who call evil good and good evil, who put darkness for light and light for darkness, who put bitter for sweet and sweet for bitter!"

48. On this negative assessment of Christians, Kierkegaard is in sync with the Lutheran Confessions: "Christians . . . continue in a constant conflict against the Old Adam. For the Old Adam, like an unmanageable and recalcitrant donkey, is still a part of them" (BC 567–68). This is one reason why we will have to die to ourselves if we are ever to believe in and follow Christ (Gal 2:20, 6:14). On this dying, see Adam Buben, "Christian Hate: Death, Dying, and Reason in Pascal and Kierkegaard" in *Kierkegaard and Death*, ed. Patrick Stokes and Adam J. Buben (Bloomington: Indiana University Press, 2011), 75: "While most Christian thinkers speak of the pitfalls of worldliness, and therefore of *some degree* of dying to the world, it is [the] issue of dying to reason that really exposes whether one is *merely wary* of the world or interested in the possibility of a *thoroughgoing eschewal* of it. To be dead to reason is really to lose one's last shreds of comfort and security in worldly existence; it is a switching off of life support in the hopes that God will sustain one's being in some form or another. Kierkegaard

is because our battle with ourselves is over confessing our sinful identity. That is what these upheavals help us to do. Without the realization of our sinfulness, we will never have any need for faith. So what matters most for faith is that you are a sinner, that

> before God you are a sinner, that in fear and trembling before this thought you are to forget your earthly need. An odd way to comfort, is it not? Instead of solicitously asking how you feel, instead of giving you advice and suggestions . . . instead of having sympathy for your earthly misery and busily remedying it, an even heavier weight is laid upon you—you are made a sinner. (CD 172–73)

Because sin is fundamentally not trusting in God,[49] "the first condition [then] . . . for my arriving at faith is that I become aware of whether I have it or not" (EUD 27). And because upheavals in life help me find this out, they too are a condition for coming to faith.

HAZARDS TO FAITH

And the second way that his prayer for faith (JP 3:3399) is complex, is in its component parts. In this prayer Kierkegaard implies that faith is made up of seeking, waiting, finding, giving, buying and preserving, and that they build upon each other—seriatim. These inter-relationships turn faith into something more than simple assent and trust. Furthermore they present internal obstacles to faith since we could, on this account, find, and then never get around to, buying what was found.[50] It fits, then, with these complications, that Kierkegaard would also pray this additional, extraordinary prayer:

> Lord, my God, I really have nothing at all for which to pray to you; even if you would promise to grant my every wish, I really cannot think of anything— except that I may remain with you, as near as possible in this time of separation in which you and I are living, and entirely with you in all of eternity. (EUD 392)

---

has shown that he is focused, at least in his description of Christianity, on precisely this *extreme sort* of dying to the world." (italics added)

49. See Rom 14:23. Luther elaborates upon our sinfulness in his "Lectures on Romans" (1518), LW 25:191–92: "Our nature, unless helped from above, remains captive to evil lusts, opposed to the Law and is full of evil desires, no matter how much it may produce works when it is prompted externally by fear of punishment or drawn by the love of things secular. . . . [So] the whole task of the apostle and of the Lord is to humiliate the proud and to bring them to realization of this condition, to teach them that they need grace, to destroy their own righteousness so that in humility they will seek Christ and confess that they are sinners and thus receive grace and be saved. . . . [However, we do] not want to hear this and take it to heart."

50. In this regard, Kierkegaard also prays: "Father in heaven, how well we know that seeking always has its promises. . . . But we also know that seeking always has its toil and its spiritual trial—how much more, then, the terror in seeking you, you Mighty One!" (TDIO 9).

This is Kierkegaard's best prayer.[51] It nicely links his doubt of the transitory with his principle that prayer changes us rather than God. "The true prayer-relationship," he explains, "does not exist when God hears what is being prayed about but when the *pray-er* continues to pray until he is the one who hears, who hears what God wills" (JP 3:3403).[52] Kierkegaard knows this is not the common[53] view of prayer and that it

51. Another one of Kierkegaard's wonderful prayers is this one: "Lord, give me weak eyes for things of little worth, and eyes clear-sighted in all of your truth" (SUD 3). The strength of this prayer is in its brevity, elegance and powerful contrast. But what it lacks is the specification of what is, and what is not, of particular worth—which my first choice includes (EUD 392).

52. See also this late prayer of Kierkegaard's: "Even what we human beings call a trifle and un-moved pass by, the sparrow's need, . . . that moves you, Infinite Love. But nothing changes you, you Changeless One! O you who in infinite love let yourself be moved, may this our prayer also move you to bless it so that the prayer may change the one who is praying into conformity with your changeless will, you Changeless One!" (TM 268). Note a similar view in Ellen Michaud's simple little article, "Wrapped in Love: Prayer Shawl Groups Weave Faith and Hope Together," *The Saturday Evening Post* 282 (September/October 2010): 34: "The purpose of prayer is not to change the situation. . . . It's to change the person in the situation." Luther elaborates this point in his "Lectures on Genesis 38–44" (1545), LW 7:175–76: "God does not act according to our wish when He governs according to His . . . wisdom, goodness, mercy and power. Then we do not understand; for we think that God does not know us and does not want to concern Himself with or think about the outcome of our trial. This is the way reason judges. But this is not in accordance with the doctrine of Christians or with the knowledge of God in the Spirit. . . . This teaches us that the goodness, mercy, and power of God cannot be grasped by speculation. . . . [So] just endure and wait for the Lord. Hold fast. Be content with His Word. . . . Learn . . . that God is merciful, wise, and good, and that for this reason He can, and wants to, give more than I understand and ask. His mercy is far too great for me to be able to fathom its magnitude by re-flection." Kierkegaard also argues that deep down it is actually unpleasant to want to change God with our prayers (UDVS 22). However, there is the prayer of King Hezekiah which appears to move God in Isaiah 38:5 to reverse Hezekiah's illness that God inflicted upon him, and save his life. Nevertheless, see Luther's mitigation of this imagined effect upon God in his "Lectures on Isaiah 1–39" (1534), LW 16:336: "Know . . . that the Sacred Scriptures exalt the fact that always more is granted than was requested. However, we must leave the time, the place, and the circumstance to God. Let us place only the matter itself before God." On this account, Kierkegaard would say that our prayers should then not try to change some historical situation—illness or calamity—for that would be to blasphemously narrow down God and prayer to "finite categories." So what we should instead pray for is "the strength to endure—and therefore every time he prays to God he confirms and establishes all the more firmly the impossibility of the suffering being taken away" (JP 3:3461). This, however, raises the burning question: "Do you have the courage to pray this way?" (JP 3:3462). If we do, it is only because God has given it to us (2 Tm 1:7; Jas 4:15).

53. It also seems to conflict with Lk 18:5 where God is construed as an unjust judge, who after being pestered by a widow, says: "*Because* this widow bothers me, I will vindicate her, *or she will wear me out* by her continue coming" (italics added). In drawing a comparison between this case and that of parents coming to the aid of their *crying* children, Kierkegaard writes: "[The child] seemingly extorts love from the parents—*seemingly* extorts, because it actually extorts love only from the parents who are not what they ought to be. . . . If the child could not cry—well, despite this there would probably be many a father and mother who would tend to it with much love; oh, but there would probably also be many a father and mother who then would, at least many times, forget the child. It is not our intention to declare outright that such a father and mother are therefore unloving; but the love in them would still be so weak, so self-loving, that they would need this reminder, this compelling" (WL 351–52). Luther sees a different point in this pestering of God, as he writes in his "Lectures on Galatians 1–4" (1535), LW 26:382–84: "This faint sigh [or pestering] of ours does not seem to penetrate the clouds . . . . In fact, we suppose, especially as long as the trial continues, that the devil is roaring at us terribly,

takes courage to pray in this unusual way (JP 3:3462). But what matters most is that we quit trying to be cunning little children who only give thanks when we get what we want (JP 3:3413). The point of prayer, is instead to focus us on God and on what he cares about, rather than on our hopes and dreams. Kierkegaard therefore asks us quite pointedly:

> Are you . . . conscious of who it is you call upon for help, what it means to invoke his help, what it commits you to? . . . [Would] you dare have the nerve to think that it is God who should serve you, that he, the Most Exalted, should promptly . . . listen to your petitions and fulfill your wishes? . . . Yes, he certainly is the Omnipotent One and can do everything he wills, and it does look almost tempting, as if you needed only to wish.[54] But take care. No thoughtless word is avenged as is a thoughtless petition to God, and no word commits one as does the petition that calls upon God for help, because it now commits you unconditionally to let God help you as he wills. You may ask a human being for help, . . . and if he is unwilling to help you as you wish, you may say, "That is not what I asked for." But if you have asked God for help, then you are bound, bound to accept the help as he sees fit. (CD 168–69)

So in our prayers we must ask for help to hold onto God "over the world's allurements, the mind's unrest, the anxieties over the future, the horrors of the past, the needs of the moment" (JP 3:3394)—and obey him alone.[55] These five hazards are what we fight against when we fight against ourselves in our prayers to God—for they come from nothing but "busy self-induced cares" (JP 3:3382). Fighting against them brings us to faith in God. With that faith our lives fit into God's grand scheme, which is his kingdom, and not into our limited and corrupted vision of what is best for us. Then our lives are not futile but are established in the wisdom from above.[56]

And the second part of this prayer on faith (JP 3:3399) is also complex because it combines failure and fulfillment. With a forlorn tone it asks what will happen if we diligently seek after God and do not find him because we have been tripped up along the way. This part begins with the word "alas" as well—and then adds, "though seeking" we fail to find God. We fail because early on we were duped into rejoicing "in the delights of the world." And in old age we fail because we come to think that we have "lived in vain." But when this happens, we are not lost, as long as we are seeking

---

that heaven is bellowing, that the earth is quaking, that everything is about to collapse, that all the creatures are threatening us with evil, and that hell is opening up in order to swallow us. This feeling is in our hearts. . . . [But] Paul says in 2 Corinthians 12:9 that the power of Christ is made perfect in our weakness. For then Christ is truly almighty, and then He truly reigns and triumphs in us when we are, so to speak, so 'all-weak' [omni-infirmi] that we can scarcely emit a groan. . . . Likewise in Luke 18:1–8, in the parable of the unjust judge. . . . Therefore we have the greatest need for the aid and comfort of the Holy Spirit, and he is . . . nearest to us when we are at our weakest and nearest to despair."

54. See, for instance, Jn 14:14—"If you ask anything in my name, I will do it" (RSV).

55. See Mt 4:10.

56. See 1 Cor 2:7.

after God continually. Then time does not run out for us. And the good news in this is that we can find God even up to the hour of our death and end up having a blessed final end, even if during our whole life we missed out on God. And nothing is lost in this late finding, for this blessed end is "what we all seek." Getting this break at the end could be seen as undercutting faith, but nothing like that is mentioned. The point made at the end of this prayer is only that it is never too late to find God—for what God has for us comes to fruition primarily at the hour of death. For believing in God through Christ Jesus turns death into a sleep from which we will awake when we enter into the eternal glories of heaven.[57]

This wonderful prayer on faith also enriches our three opening prayers. So it can be used to amplify all three of those shorter prayers. Regarding the first one, this prayer enlarges our understanding on how spiritual intoxication erodes faith. Regarding the second one, it helps us see how difficult it is to grasp in faith Christ's sacrifice. And regarding the last one, this prayer intensifies our failure to trust in Christ as we should—by delighting in the world instead of Christ and trusting in the world that it will heal us.

MILITANT CHRISTIANITY

In this prayer on the formation of faith, we have seen a warning against turning God's kingdom into some sort of worldly kingdom based on earthly triumphs—being that faith actually stands against a righteousness based on the accumulation of knowledge and the enjoyment of worldly delights (JP 3:3399). Since entry into this kingdom comes by way of upheavals, earthly triumphs are fundamentally opposed to it. Kierkegaard therefore leads us in another one of his provocative prayers, to pursue a militant and godly kingdom:

> Lord Jesus Christ, it is indeed from on high that you draw a person to yourself, and it is to victory that you call him, but this of course means that you call him to struggle and promise him victory in the struggle to which you from on high call him, you, the great victor. Just as you keep us from all other error, keep us also from this, that we delude ourselves into thinking ourselves to be members of a Church already triumphant here in this world. Your kingdom certainly was not and is not of this world.[58] The place of your Church is not here in the world; there is room for it only if it will struggle and by struggling make room for itself to exist. But if it will struggle, it will never be displaced by the world either; that you will guarantee.[59] But if it deludes itself into thinking it is to be triumphant here in this world, then, alas, it does indeed have itself to blame that you withdrew your support, then it has succumbed, then it has

57. See Mt 9:24; Jn 11:13; 1 Cor 15:18; Eph 5:14.

58. See Jn 18:36.

59. See Mt 16:18.

confused itself with the world.[60] Be, then, with your militant Church so that this might never happen—would be obliterated from the earth by becoming a triumphant Church. (PC 201)

This prayer also moves back and forth between the positive and the negative, as we have seen in other prayers by Kierkegaard. It gives us a guarantee, and then circumscribes it with possible obliteration. It promises victory, but not without struggle. It contrasts being drawn to Christ with being deluded by success. It contrasts having a place in the world with having only a small room in the world. Three times this prayer pivots on the word "but." First, it does so in order to include struggling as a component part of the sought after victory. Second, it does so to add a guarantee to the instability of our struggle. And third, it does so to contrast divine withdrawal with the promise of God's unending support. This zigzagging could drive a person crazy—or at least make the person praying it a bit confused. So in an effort to head that off, this prayer ends with a fiery request based on a simple distinction. It does this by asking God to help us remain militant so that we might prevail.[61]

Kierkegaard lived out this prayer in his attack on the state church in Denmark at the end of his life—just a couple of years after he wrote it down through a favored pseudonym of his, Anti-Climacus. In that attack Kierkegaard accused the church of trying to make the world "as pleasurable as possible," when according to the New Testament, it is nothing but a "vale of tears and prison," designed to be a "time of testing related to an accounting and judgment" (TM 178–79). And so the church did "not uncompromisingly make clear the Christian requirement" that "hating one's own life in this world" is the only way we have of saving it for eternity (TM 47). By not helping us fulfill this requirement, the church, in breach of its trust, sends us all to judgment day unprepared. Now if our salvation truly hinges on hating ourselves in this world, then we are in for trouble, because self-hatred is "unacceptable to the human being," for indeed "there perhaps is not one single person in millions who is sufficiently honest and honorable to accept this." And that is because if we were to practice self-hatred as we should, then this life would become "unconditionally the very opposite of . . . a human being's taste and disposition," having become "sheer suffering, agony, wretchedness" (TM 253). Because we find what the New Testament offers to be so foul, the church maliciously helps us sinners out by championing "the assassination of Christianity"

---

60. See Rom 1:25. See also Charles Taylor, *The Secular Age* (Cambridge: Harvard University Press, 2007), 774: "[Secularism is the] culturally hegemonic notion of a closed immanent order."

61. See my prayer for the church, "Not to Us"—based on Ps 115:1—written in 2008, in what I believe is this same sort of Kierkegaardian spirit: "O God, we thank you for your church, which is the very body of your dear Son, Jesus Christ, our Lord. Keep us from turning this mystical and mysterious union with Christ into one more human organization—made by people, run by people and preserved by people. Let it instead be the very bulwark of the truth—standing against all our ungodly teachings and deceitful wiles. May it rest now and forever on your Holy Word—both in the severity of the law and in the compassion of the gospel. And may the many members of your church, with their various spiritual gifts, live in harmony and under the watchful eye of your life-giving discipline. Amen."

(TM 48). This, however, must stop! And to do that, we will have no choice but to let the "incendiarism" of New Testament Christianity burn it up!

> And it is already burning; indeed, it will no doubt become a spreading con-
> flagration, best compared to a forest fire, because it is 'Christendom' that has
> been set afire. It is the prolixities that must go, this enormously prolix illusion
> involved in the—well-intentioned or knavish—scholarliness in the Christian
> sphere, the enormously prolix delusion involved in the millions of Christians
> (something that no doubt suits the princes of the Church, both for pecuniary
> advantage and for the sake of material power, and something that becomes
> the most select and most delicate sophistication by—scoffing at God and the
> New Testament!—by passing as Christian fervor and zeal for the propagation
> of the doctrine). (TM 51)

Here we see how important it is for the church to regain its "militant relation to this world" (TM 334) by taking on churchly scholarship, large congregations, pecuniary advantage, material power, and misplaced fervor and zeal.

First, scholarship has to be refashioned because it scoffs at God and the Bible— intentionally skewing the "essential significance" of the Bible.[62] Through a critical ap- proach to the divine revelation, intellectual analysis does away with the impact of the Bible upon us. And so we critically scrutinize the claims in the Bible for the sole purpose of defending ourselves "against God's Word" (FSE 34). One would think that

> all this research and pondering and scrutinizing would draw God's Word very
> close to me; the truth is that this is the very way, this is the most cunning way,
> to remove God's Word as far as possible from me, infinitely further than it is
> from one who never saw God's Word, infinitely further than it is from one
> who became so anxious and afraid of God's Word that he cast it as far away as
> possible. (FSE 35)

Therefore modern, critical biblical scholarship is deceptive and disingenuous. While this intellectual pursuit advertises itself as the best possible understanding of the divine revelation, it actually knows nothing about it at all! This is because biblical

---

62. Endel Kallas, "Kierkegaard's Understanding of the Bible With Respect to His Age," *Dialog* 26 (Winter 1987), 33. Kallas also says that this was because the scholars in Kierkegaard's time, as in ours, were "so confused about, so bewildered by, [and] so indifferent toward the sacred biblical tradition" (30). Note also John P. Milton (1897–1972), "How My Mind Has Been Changed Regarding the Bible (1966)," *Word & World* 32 (Fall 2012), 400: "I cannot believe that in response to Elisha's curse, God sent forth a couple of she-bears to kill some mean little boys! [2 Kgs 2:24]. . . . What then shall we say of these things that on their face seem contrary to the mind of Christ? What can we say but this, that the Scriptures record accurately not only the will of God but the imperfect comprehension of that will by people, and that everything in Scripture must ultimately be tested as to its truth or falsehood by its conformity to the norm which is Jesus Christ?" But what perfect person shall do that testing to make sure we get the Bible in its pure form? Milton skips that quintessential question which leads the wary reader to suspect that his whole complex analysis of the Bible is either naïve or disingenuous.

scholars have an antipathy for the Bible—the very text they are studying. Kierkegaard explains this by imagining a scholar with the Bible in hand:

> To be alone with Holy Scripture! I dare not! If I open it—any passage—it traps me at once; it asks me (indeed, it is as if it were God himself[63] who asked me): Have you done what you read there? And then, then—yes, then I am trapped. Then either straightway into action—or immediately a humbling admission. (FSE 31)

But the biblical critic can tolerate neither of these options. That is because they force the critic into "the awkward position, . . . either to have to comply with the Word immediately or at least to be obliged to make a humbling confession" (FSE 32). So instead of that, they make up this academic alternative, saying:

> "There is no problem as far as I am concerned; I certainly intend to comply— as soon as the discrepancies are ironed out and the interpreters agree fairly well." Aha! That certainly will not be for a long time yet. The man succeeded, however, in obscuring the fact that the error is in him.[64] (FSE 32)

And because these scholars are so resolute,[65] Kierkegaard thinks any modification to the scholarly method will not be of any help. Therefore he somewhat puckishly proposes that we give the Bible back to God (JP 1:216)! And if climbing up to Mt. Sinai to do so would be too much for us, then all we need to do is just quit reading it (JP 1:209)! So he was ready to admit that another "famine of the word"[66] was well on its way.

63. In this same vein note: "Oh, what depth of cunning! One makes God's Word into something impersonal, objective, a doctrine—instead of its being the voice of God that you shall hear. This is the way the fathers heard it, this terrifying voice of God; now it sounds as objective as calico" (FSE 39).

64. And so instead of having "a holy fear and a sense of shame before the good," we wrong-headedly "fear financial loss, loss of reputation, lack of appreciation, disregard, the judgment of the world, the mockery of fools, the laughter of light-mindedness, the cowardly whining of obeisance, the inflated insignificance of the moment, the delusive, misty apparitions of miasma. Indeed, for many people these high-minded thoughts are only too much like gold-plating, which comes off in the double-mindedness of life, which gnaws and gnaws" (UDVS 58).

65. On this recalcitrance, see Walter Brueggemann, "Biblical Authority," *The Christian Century* (January 3, 2001), 16: "As eyewitnesses created texts out of observed and remembered miracles, texted miracles in turn become materials for imagination that pushed well beyond what was given or intended even in the text. This is an inescapable process for those of us who insist that the Bible is a contemporary word to us. We transport ourselves out of the 21st century back to the ancient world of the text or, conversely, we transpose ancient voices into contemporary voices of authority." Brueggemann needs to concede, however, that there is more peril in going beyond what the text intends than he is willing to say. For a view opposite to that of Brueggemann's, see Robert W. Jenson, "Can a Text Defend Itself? An Essay *De Inspiratione Scripturae*," *Dialog* 28 (Autumn 1989), 255: "When scripture is communally read and interpreted by the church, the Holy Spirit which God gives to the church is the spirit of the text, in which the text lives as a personal reality to assert itself over against even the individuals who read and interpret [it]."

66. See Amos 8:11.

And second, regarding large congregations, money and power—we need to fight for the small and humble in the church, for the single individual. Kierkegaard celebrated the individual person—not because we are right in our own eyes[67]—but because each one of us needs to be transformed into the likeness of Christ our Lord.[68] For "Christianity's idea was: to want to change everything" for the better, which includes each one of us (TM 185). So this militancy is needed in order to draw us closer to God that we may follow Christ more diligently. What is big and powerful distracts us from this task by reinforcing our individual responsibility. The more we have and the more attention we receive, the more we are inclined to stay as we are because everything is going so well for us. Therefore

> God's idea with Christianity was, if I may put it this way, to get really tough with us human beings. To that end, he put "individual" and "race," the single individual and the many, together inversely, set them at odds, introduced the category of discord, because, according to his thought, to be a Christian was precisely the category of discord, the discord of "the single individual" with "the race," with millions, with family, with father and mother, etc. (TM 188)

And we also see this militancy in our opening three prayers. The first prayer fuels our fight against spiritual intoxication. The second prayer fights against our delusion that we can save ourselves. And the third prayer fights against the false view that we are not total failures in God's eyes, but actually have quite a bit going for us of intrinsic worth.

PRAYING AS STRUGGLING

So we see that to pray with Kierkegaard means to pray for a militant church which is marked by the struggle to fight against our sinfulness and hold tight to God through faith in Christ Jesus. On Kierkegaard's view, "the one who prays" must yield "himself in the inner being, because otherwise he is not praying to God" (EUD 383). That is because it is perfectly "atrocious" to pray in order to "advance [one's own] will" (EUD 384).[69] So the key struggle in praying is to come before God in faith and trust, knowing full well that both what we call good and evil must give way and be "ascribed to him," and his definitions (EUD 386). As long as we fight against that attribution—that God

---

67. See Num 15:39; Dt 12:8; Jgs 17:6, 21:25; Prv 3:7; 1 Cor 2:13. That being said, the truth "is always found only in the minority, but it does not necessarily follow that the minority is always in the truth" (JP 4:4850).

68. See 2 Cor 3:18 and Rom 12:2. Therefore in prayer, it is not a matter of "changing God's will to ours but discovering God's will for us." Grace Adolphsen Brame, "The Forgotten Side of Prayer," *The Lutheran* (March 2006), 24.

69. Kierkegaard elaborates this point by drawing an analogy between prayer and breathing: "The Church Fathers were right in observing that to pray is to breathe. [And just as I do not] intend to change the world through my breathing—I simply intend to replenish my vitality and be *renewed*— [the same holds] with prayer in relation to God" (JP 3:3432).

brings both weal and woe, good and bad, gathering and burning, life and wrath[70]—we cannot faithfully reflect God's likeness in our lives, as we are supposed to do. For just as "when the ocean is exerting all its power, that is precisely the time when it cannot reflect the image of heaven, and even the slightest motion blurs the image; but when it becomes still and deep, then the image of heaven sinks into its nothingness" (EUD 399).

In prayer, then, we are to struggle to calm down and stop forcing our way upon God and yearn instead to become nothing before him.[71] Kierkegaard believed that these struggles were unavoidable and essential for genuine prayer. Even though they make our prayers strident and hard on us, that is exactly what we need if they are to draw us closer to God. And so Kierkegaard's intense call to prayer, echoes the words of Martin Luther when he says that prayer "is a constant violent action of the spirit as it is lifted up to God, as a ship is driven upward against the power of the storm."[72] In Kierkegaard's call to pray, he challenges us to contend with God but also to love him—to see that our identity is all wrapped up in him, and humbly to admit[73] that we are not going to understand him, nor thank him, as we should, when we are praying:

> So the struggle goes; the struggler contends with God in prayer, or he struggles with himself and in his prayer calls on God for help against himself. But if the struggler still does not give up his inwardness and consequently stop praying, if he loves God greatly, if he longs for God humbly as one longs for someone without whom one is nothing, fervently as one longs for someone by whom one becomes everything; if he deals honestly with his debt of thanksgiving and adoration to God, which constantly increases because as yet he cannot give thanks aright, cannot understand aright; if he deals with it as a good entrusted to him for better times—then, then he is struggling in prayer. (EUD 397–98)

70. Is 45:7; Job 2:10; Mt 3:12; Rom 2:6–8.

71. See also CD 129–32, 298, WL 103. Note as well 2 Cor 12:11 where Saint Paul says "I am nothing"—without a whiff of despair or resignation, implying that this realization is a blessing.

72. Martin Luther, "Lectures on Romans" (1518), LW 25:460.

73. On this humility, Kierkegaard further says: "We are not related to you, O God, as to a man from whom we buy—you must first of all give and only then can there be mention of our duty to buy from you—what you have given: faith, hope, love, longing, the opportune moment. You give all things and without payment. . . . Here is the whole mistake in paganism—namely, that man relates directly to God as to another person, a more powerful man, instead of man's first relating to God secondarily: after God has given everything for nothing. . . . Thus do you condescend to become involved with us men; you are not ashamed to be our God. . . . And yet it is, indeed, as when we give to a child and then, to delight the child, pretend as if he were giving to us—what we, in fact, gave the child, what really belongs to us. Yes, the relation to God is not even of this nature, for God is also the one who gives in order to make perfect. It must then be like that of a father or mother helping the child write the birthday letter which is then accepted on the birthday as a gift [from the child who only pretends to have written it all by himself]" (JP 3:3415).

And in this struggle God shows us a most strange mercy—whereby he exchanges our prayers for better ones. Coming to see that is also part of our struggle to pray as we should. When that happens, we end up confessing, in all humility, that

> God surely does not deceive you when he accepted your earthly wishes and foolish desires, exchanged them for you and instead gave you divine comfort and holy thoughts; that he did not treat you unfairly when he denied you a wish but in compensation created this faith in your heart, when instead of a wish, which, even if it would bring everything, at most was able to give you the whole world, he gave you a faith by which you won God and overcame the whole world.[74] Then you acknowledged with humble joy that God was still the almighty Creator of heaven and earth,[75] who not only created the world from nothing but did something even more marvelous—from your impatient and inconstant heart he created the imperishable substance of a quiet spirit.[76] (EUD 36)

SILENCE

So we see that this struggle to pray, results in a "quiet spirit" that desires to stand simply and silently before God. This is odd since speaking is what distinguishes us from the other animals and usually is what we think of when we pray. But Kierkegaard notes that "in relation to God, wanting to speak can easily become the corruption of the human being, who is able to speak." That is because

> God is in heaven and the human being is on earth and therefore they can hardly converse. God is infinite wisdom; what the human being knows is idle chatter; therefore they can hardly converse. God is love and the human being, as we say to a child, is a little ninny[77] even in regard to his own welfare, and therefore they can hardly converse. Only in much fear and trembling is a human being able to speak with God . . . [but] much fear and trembling makes speech fall into silence. (WA 11)

---

74. See 1 Jn 5:4.

75. So because of God's great power, it is foolish for you to want "God's ideas about what [is] best for you to coincide with your ideas" (EUD 37).

76. See 1 Pt 3:4. Note also Phil 4:11–13: "I have learned, in whatever state I am, to be content. I know how to be abased, and I know how to abound; in any and all circumstances I have learned the secret of facing plenty and hunger, abundance and want. I can do all things in him who strengthens me" (RSV). And this strange adaptability, mind you, is not belittled here, but favored over cases like Elijah when he was miraculously fed by the ravens (1 Kgs 17:6).

77. On this depreciated view of people, see Isaiah 40:22 and its comparison of people to grasshoppers. Note also Michael Pollan, *The Botany of Desire: A Plant's-Eye View of the World* (New York: Random, 2001), 222: "I asked Heath about the NewLeaf potato. He had no doubt that resistance would come—'Face it,' he said, 'the bugs are always going to be smarter than we are.'"

This movement toward silence is the last great goal in this struggle to pray aright. In it we learn that to pray is to have "less and less to say," and finally to become "completely silent" (WA 12).[78] This does not mean, however, that all we are left with is listening to ourselves:

> Contrary to the anthropocentric turn in modern philosophy, Kierkegaard argued for a dialogical conception of theology. In the law God addressed humankind; in the prophets God addressed humankind; and finally in the person of his Son, God addressed humankind. Given revelation, dialogue between God and humanity is possible. Persons are not alone. Persons are addressed, and the meaning of prayer is that persons can hear, respond and speak back.[79]

So, we are to be dialogical—and that will eventually mean "to become silent and to remain silent, to wait until the one praying hears God" (WA 12). This thesis turns the tables. Now, rather than God listening to our prayers, we wait until we hear God speaking to us.[80] We are just ninnies, after all, who do not have our best interest at heart—therefore God has no reason to pay attention to our idle chat. When we are told to pray constantly,[81] what that means is that we are always to be listening to God's voice as given to us in his Holy Scriptures. That attentiveness will guide us and bless us more than any rescue from earthly calamity will.[82] In that regard, it is "good to agree that one drop [of] ocean water holds all of Kierkegaard's prayers."[83]

Going back to our three beginning prayers, then, we note that keeping them short helps remind us of the goal of silence—the fewer words we have, the more silence there is. In the first one, the struggle to combat spiritual intoxication yearns

78. And filled with gratitude. On this see E. Skjoldager, "His Personal Prayers," revised by Howard V. Hong, Bibliotheca Kierkegaardiana, vol. 12: *Kierkegaard as a Person*, ed. Niels Thulstrup and Marie Mikulová Thulstrup (Copenhagen: C. A. Reitzels, 1983), 158: "For [Kierkegaard], giving thanks is the consummating moment in prayer."

79. Robert L. Perkins, "Kierkegaard's Prayers as Art, Theology, and Prayer," 117.

80. For an example of this Kierkegaardian shift, see *Lutheran Book of Worship* (Minneapolis: Augsburg, 1978), 26 (prayer 89): "O God, your ears are open always to the prayers of your servants. Open our hearts and minds to you, that we may live in harmony with your will and receive the gifts of your Spirit; through your Son, Jesus Christ our Lord." Note the movement from God being open to us, to the one praying being open to him. The fact that God is open to us does not mean that he will give us what we want. It instead means that we should be open to him and obey his will, even if it conflicts with what we want. In this way this shift is based on the logic in the "nevertheless" in Mt 26:39: "Jesus fell on his face and prayed: 'My Father, if it be possible, let this cup pass from me; nevertheless, not as I will, but as thou wilt'" (RSV). This prayer 89 comes from the 1952 *Les Oraisons du Missel Romain*. See Philip H. Pfatteicher and Carlos R. Messerli, *Manual on the Liturgy: Lutheran Book of Worship* (Minneapolis: Augsburg, 1979), 404–6.

81. 1 Thes 5:17.

82. This, however, would not apply to being rescued from the eternal calamity of the infernal punishments of hell.

83. Robert Bly, *My Sentence Was a Thousand Years of Joy: Poems* (New York: HarperCollins, 2005), 53.

for the silence found in upending reasonableness and probability. In the second one, we look to Christ for our redemption. Seeing his sacrifice on the cross, which brings about our salvation, renders us all silent.[84] And in the third prayer, there is the silence that comes from admitting that we are total failures.

And because our attention to matters that are divine regularly eludes us, and, more often than not, "frightens every one away" (TM 125) by their stringent ideality, I close with this small list of six goals as reminders of the ideals that I have tried to show are inherent to Kierkegaard's way of praying:

1. Use Christ's cross as your only accreditation.

2. Favor provocative words over sedate ones.

3. Look for value in pain, loss and confusion.

4. Give up dreaming for worldly successes.

5. Listen to God instead of compiling requests.

6. May your many words give way to silence.

These principles all work together to help us fight against bad prayers, which in their worst form, stress "the absolutizing of the person's values, the affirming of one's own private feelings, [and] the assertion that our feelings are absolute."[85]

---

84. See Rom 3:19.

85. Robert L. Perkins, "Kierkegaard's Prayers as Art, Theology, and Prayer," 115. Even though this is a quotation from Ludwig Feuerbach (1804–72), regarding his attack in general on prayer, it can still be helpful in ferreting out good prayers from bad ones.

11

On Walking

KIERKEGAARD WAS NOTORIOUS FOR walking the streets of Copenhagen and talking to strangers wherever he went. Because of his biting criticism of Danish life, this habit puzzled his fellow citizens. They thought he would rather stay to himself. But he baffled them and walked among them, talking hours on end. Kierkegaard knew this behavior was confusing, so he tried to explain it in both his published and unpublished writings.

On the one hand, he said he liked to walk because it was healthy:

> [Every] day I walk myself into a state of well-being and walk away from every illness; I have walked myself into my best thoughts, and I know of no thought so burdensome that one can not walk away from it. . . . [By] sitting still, and the more one sits still, the closer one comes to feeling ill. Health and salvation can only be found in motion. . . . If one just keeps on walking, everything will be all right. (JP 5:6063)

Commenting on these word in *Lutheran Women Today*, Kate Sprutta Elliott wrote that if "you're under stress about a decision, walking can help you gain clarity and well-being. And on a practical level, it can help you sleep better at night."[1]

While it is true that walking can do this for us, Elliott misses Kierkegaard's basic point. He goes on to say in that same journal entry from which Elliott quotes, that such jaunts also run the "risk" of being "intercepted" by the "sufferings" of others who stop to talk. When that happens, all is "lost," Kierkegaard says. Confusion and agitation set in. Peace of mind slips away. But Elliott ignores this complicating factor of inter-ruption. It conflicts with the serenity she is peddling—as well as the anti-theological agenda of her magazine, *Lutheran Women Today*.[2] But in fairness to Kierkegaard, the risky part in walking should have been included. It fills out his overall point about well-being. It is supposed to include more than clarity of mind and a good night's rest.

---

1. Kate Sprutta Elliott, "A Wonderful Plan for Your Life," *Lutheran Women Today* 14 (January–February, 2001): 17.

2. On this point see James Kittelson, "Contemporary Spirituality's Challenge to *Sola Gratia*," *Lutheran Quarterly* 9 (Winter 1995): 380.

FIGURE 5: Kierkegaard Walking by Paul D. Turnbaugh (1986).

I wrote to *Lutheran Women Today* about this mistake and Beth McBride answered by saying that my correction did not "meet their needs."[3] Maybe so. But could it be that the truth of the matter might pre-empt McBride's assessment of what is needed? Kierkegaard thought pursuing the truth mattered even if it meant being stripped of the "interior attire" of our opinions (JP 4:4889)!

So what was the truth? Kierkegaard's reasons for walking were not as simple as Elliott would have us believe. His contemporary, Georg Brandes (1842–1927), said that when he walked the streets of Copenhagen, Kierkegaard was "as accessible to everyone . . . as he was inaccessible in his home, just as profligate with his person here as he was protective of it elsewhere."[4] Did this mean his walks were really insincere?

3. In an undated form letter received April 29, 2001.

4. *Encounters With Kierkegaard: A Life as Seen by His Contemporaries*, ed. Bruce H. Kirmmse,

Was he a misanthrope in disguise? Were his conversations phony and his walks a "sheer hoax"?[5]

Kierkegaard walked the streets chatting as he went in order to do more than get his exercise and put his mind at rest. He was trying to "renounce" himself by becoming so familiar that no one would expect him to be a profound thinker and give his publications the benefit of the doubt. No, he wanted to come off as "a street-corner loafer, an idler," so that if his ideas were to catch on they would do so on their own without any benefit from that "bestial flattery of the crowd." By discrediting himself, he hoped to establish a "pure idea-relationship" between his writings and the world. He did not want his ideas enjoying the advantages authorial esteem bestows (PV 58–61).

This renunciation also carried its fair share of pain. When he walked the streets, he was criticized and ridiculed for what he wrote. He said that was like being "trampled to death by geese" (JP 5:5998) or like "being cast to the insects" after first being "smeared with honey to whet the insects' appetite" (JP 6:6906). But he knew a Christian should not long for "an effeminate life, snobbishly aloof in aristocratic circles." Christians should instead "insist on getting out into the streets, among men, where there is danger and opposition." Christians must not want "to live cowardly and effeminately at a fashionable distance in select groups, guarded by illusion" (JP 5:5941).[6] The Christian goal, after all, is to become "a thorn in the eye of the world" (JP 6:6492). To forswear this danger would be to turn the Christian into "a sissy swimmer, the kind who does not want to go out into the water, a society of such swimmers who on dry land make each other believe they are swimmers" when they are only make-believe ones (JP 5:5049).[7]

---

trans. Bruce H. Kirmmse and Virginia R. Laursen (Princeton: Princeton University Press, 1996), 98.

5. Ibid., 94.

6. On Kierkegaard's anti-elitism, see Jørgen Bukdahl, *Søren Kierkegaard and the Common Man*, ed. and trans. Bruce H. Kirmmse (1961; Grand Rapids: Eerdmans, 2001), 30: "In his father he encountered, almost palpably, a 'common man' for whom education was neither a crutch nor a mask and for whom dialectics were not speculative fencing but expressions of existential conflicts and contradictions, saturated with the passion that made them into absolutes. Søren's relation to his father shattered any possible respect he might have had for the sort of education he saw among the upper-class elite, and the categories of the common man and the simple person became absolutely fundamental both to his philosophy and to his final action. For Kierkegaard, of course, 'simplicity' is not to be understood in the intellectual-psychological sense, but evangelically, concerning the pure of heart who shall see God through sin, doubt, and repentance." And this is true even though Kierkegaard also "admired [the] aristocracy of intellect all his life [and] could manage the tenor of the times as few others could" (56). And for what Bob Dylan calls "a musical accompaniment to your perambulation," see his *Theme Time Radio Hour*, Episode 63 (January 19, 2008) on "Walking"—especially cuts ten and twelve on walking as a stranger and walking with your cross.

7. Luther called these sissy swimmers, amateurs. See his "Lectures on Zechariah" (1526), LW 20:151: "Each of us has his own divinely imposed cross to bear so that we complete that which is lacking in Christ's afflictions, as we have it in Colossians 1:24. This [is what Zechariah 13:9] calls being led through fire. [It takes] the place of a test for you so that you are proved by the cross, as silver is proved by the fire. Today there are many who deal with the Gospel to our great disgrace. These are the amateurs [*neophyti*] whom the cross has never trained . . . . Should any danger threaten them, should

So walking the streets of Copenhagen was important to Kierkegaard because it helped him clarify the Christian faith.[8] He believed his rough-and-tumble times on the streets enabled him "to illuminate Christianity" (JP 5:6105). On the streets he learned how to starve "the life out of all the illusions in which Christendom" had run aground (JP 6:6228). Chief among them was that Christianity was being "related to the natural man in the same way as horsemanship is related to the horse, as the trained horse to the untrained horse, where it is not a matter of taking away its nature but of improving it." This mistake reduced Christianity to "an educational process" (JP 5:6076). This illusion robbed Christianity of its "radical cure" (JP 3:3247). That cure is about "crucifying the flesh, hating oneself, suffering for the doctrine, about weeping and wailing while the world rejoices, about the most heartrending sufferings caused by hating father, mother, wife, one's own child, about being what Scripture says of [Christ, being] a worm, not a human being" (TM 189). Indeed, one who has taken this cure is no longer "a human being in the ordinary sense" (JP 6:6616).[9]

This Christianity, illuminated in the hurly-burly of the streets, is also where it should be preached. Preaching Christianity

> should not be done inside churches. It is extremely damaging for Christianity and represents a changing (a modifying) of Christianity by placing it at an artistic distance from actuality instead of letting it be heard right in the middle of actuality—and precisely for the sake of conflict (collision), for all this talk about quiet and quiet places and quiet hours as the proper element for the essentially Christian is upside down. Therefore preaching should not be done in churches but on the street, right in the middle of life. (JP 6:6957)

So when Kierkegaard walked the streets, he had something more in mind than exercise and a good night's rest. He was not vying to promote jogging suits. Nike, after all,

---

evils and the cross oppress them; they then would learn to cling solely to the goodness of God, they would despair of their own counsel and imagination, which otherwise are the wellspring of many heresies. You see, while they are not preoccupied with very serious business, their minds meanwhile are free for leisurely thinking, and they cannot help but dream up new dogma [which is anathema]."

8. See Niels Jørgen Cappelørn, Joakim Garff, Johnny Kondrup, *Written Images: Søren Kierkegaard's Journals, Notebooks, Booklets, Sheets, Scraps, and Slips of Paper* (1996), trans. Bruce H. Kirmmse (Princeton: Princeton University Press, 2003), 138: "Even if Kierkegaard's 'gadding about in the streets' could give the impression that his daily life was haphazard, the opposite was in fact the case, at least with respect to his work. He wrote at set hours every day, and he had great self-discipline. If he was not in the mood to work when he sat down, the mood promptly presented itself after he got under way. He reported this to the literary scholar, Frederik L. Liebenberg, in the course of one of their many walks, a walk that was in fact cut short by Kierkegaard's remark: 'Now I must go home and write.'"

9. On Kierkegaard's loving critique of the rank and file, see *Kierkegaard and the Common Man*, 101–2: "Behind all of his secondary attributes such as talent and genius, we see the . . . lineaments of Kierkegaard's true greatness. Here, in the hell of his suffering, he triumphed over disdain and held fast to love, and above all, love for the common man, who knew not what he did, misled as he was by the pastors and by the press."

is not likely to replace their famous swoosh with his profile—hat and all—to sell their merchandise.

Woody Allen is closer to the truth. In reflecting on his Oscar winning movie, *Annie Hall* (1977), he tells of a scene cut from it:

> It was a fantasy scene that we staged at Madison Square Garden, with the then Knicks, like Bill Bradley and Earl Monroe. We had the Knicks playing against five great philosophers. One was Kierkegaard, I remember. One was Nietzsche. Kierkegaard was a hunchback, so the actor who played him was either a hunchback or we made him one. And the thing that we were showing was the awkwardness of those great thinkers in real life and how graceless the cerebral act is compared to the beauty of physical acts.[10]

It is precisely this awkwardness within Christianity itself, that Kierkegaard learned to write about, more clearly and profoundly, as a result of taking his walks down the streets of Copenhagen. On the whole, then,

> Christianity is suspicious of being honored and esteemed in one's lifetime. Far be it from Christianity to be so foolish as to say that everyone who was mocked while he lived was on the right road. It only says: The true Christian must normally be found among those who were mocked while they lived. This is Christianity's view: what is eternal, what is true, cannot possibly win the approval of the moment,[11] must inevitably win its disapproval. (CD 227)

---

10. *Newsweek*, June 28, 1999. Kierkegaard knew that philosophers would come up short when trying to comprehend Christianity. And so he wrote that if "someone who was going to run a race [1 Cor 9:24] came rolling up dressed in seven overcoats, five pairs of trousers, and enormous boots and an open umbrella, everyone would find it ridiculous, but scientific scholarship and professors and reasons which are supposed to help men into the unconditioned are fundamentally just as ridiculous" (JP 4:4904).

11. On this moment, Kierkegaard further says: "Indeed, to have faith, which is held in such profound contempt by worldly sagacity or at best is a Sunday ceremony all prinked up with borrowed platitudes—to have faith, this and only this relates itself as possibility to the moment. Worldly sagacity is forever excluded, disdained, and detested, as it is in heaven, more than all vices and crimes, since by nature it of all things belongs to this wretched world, it of all things is furthest removed from having anything to do with heaven and eternity" (TM 339).

12

Sermons—Not for Itching Ears

KIERKEGAARD WOULD AGREE THAT sermons "yield the cash value of a person's theology."[1] In this collection of sermons, I want to show how his insights, many of which I have already discussed in essay form, can also take flight in the preached word, the living word, or the *viva vox* of the sermon. So these Kierkegaardian sermons are designed to show how his thoughts can be preached in church—giving sermonic flight to what I have discussed at length in my chapters. Some of these sermons are almost completely controlled in thought and form by Kierkegaard's words themselves. Others only use a quotation here and there to illumine a point in the sermon. But I think a sermon can be Kierkegaardian, or imbued with his view of Christianity, even if it is not replete with his words. I even think that a sermon can be Kierkegaardian that doesn't have any quotations from him at all, or mention his name.

All the sermons in this chapter are expositions of biblical passages.[2] In that sense they are all expository, didactic sermons. They are not very imaginative in thought or form.[3] They stay close to the text, believing that what is written is what God wants to

---

1. Carl E. Braaten, *Because of Christ: Memoirs of a Lutheran Theologian* (Grand Rapids: Eerdmans, 2010), 179.

2. On reasons for not doing this, see Elizabeth Achtemeier, *Creative Preaching: Finding the Words* (Nashville: Abingdon, 1980), 76: "Many feel that it is much too difficult to try always to preach from a biblical text. The Bible is so foreign to our secularized congregations that it takes too much time to explain a text and to bridge the gap between the Bible's world and that of the congregation. Or even when the bridge is constructed, the Bible's message, from a primitive and agricultural age, may remain irrelevant to our modern technological time."

3. For a critique of various kinds of sermonic innovations, see Elizabeth Achtemeier, *Creative Preaching*, 11: "Creativity in the pulpit is not a matter of continually coming up with new and different sermon ideas or preaching from obscure texts never heard before by the congregation. It does not consist of surprising one's people with a striking sermon form or of scandalizing them with coarse or colloquial language. . . . No preacher can show forth simultaneously his or her own cleverness and the lordship of Jesus Christ. No, a preacher may deal with a well-known text within a standard three-point outline, deliver the sermon in the most quiet and unspectacular fashion, and still be creative. For creative preaching is the fashioning of a sermon into such an artistic and effective whole that the Word of God, spoken through the text, is allowed to create that reality of which it speaks within the individual and corporate lives of the gathered congregation. Creative preaching is the release of the active Word of God to do its judging and saving work. . . . Its effectiveness comes not from itself but from the Lord whom it serves. Its power is not that of its own words, but of the lively Word of the Lord." So what matters more for one's preaching than innovation in form and theme is using language in logical, varied, simple, energetic, profound, honest, joyous, fitting, convicted and beautiful ways (87–96). An example of going too far afield would be Jennifer M. Phillips, *Preaching Creation Throughout the Church Year* (Boston: Cowley, 2000), 32: "[The] image of Christ as a sacrificial animal does not take us far into the

say to us directly today.[4] I try to do this in a distinctly Kierkegaardian way—by asking how these biblical words, once believed, will change our lives in the present time. The structure of each sermon follows the format prescribed in the Lutheran Confessions[5]—going from condemning sin to proclaiming Christ and finally to advocating

---

mystery of the incarnation. [So I suggest] topsoil. It is very Christ-like in its passivity and beneficence, and the penetrating energy that issues out of its peacableness. . . . It is enriched by all things that die and enter in to it. . . . Its fertility is always building up out of death into promise. Death is the bridge or the tunnel by which its past enters its future." Phillips could benefit from reading Dietrich Bonhoeffer, *Worldly Preaching: Lectures on Homiletics*, trans. Clyde Fant (New York: Crossroads, 1991), 106–7, 11, 112, 116: "Every sermon fights a battle. But this does not occur through the dramatic efforts of the preacher. It happens only through the proclamation of the One who has trodden upon the head of the devil [Gn 3:15; 1 Jn 3:8]. . . . If our preaching is to be testimony to the biblical witness, then we must have a reverence for the biblical word. . . . The word does not belong to us, it is Christ's, . . . therefore we should not make the text a springboard for our own thoughts. . . . True witnesses wish to stand behind their testimony. They do not want to add anything with human words to Christ's words. . . . The authority of my particular worldview and the force of its inspiration is not sufficient. . . . [The] dealings of God with humanity as they are testified to in the Bible and made known through the teachings of the church are sufficient. . . . It is scarcely the right situation when applause is handed out for a sermon according to the mental agility of the speaker. When the sermon is regarded as an interpretation, then the involvement of the preacher is that of someone whose self is put to death for the sake of the Word, who dies to his or her own will and only wishes to be a handservant of God. The preacher must want what the Word itself wants. . . . Preachers do not bring the Scripture into the pulpit for their use; they must allow themselves to be used by it for the congregation. They must entrust everything to the scriptural word. The preacher should want this Word to enter into the congregation in order that the members might become mature in its use. That is the pastor's task as an evangel."

4. On the Bible as direct divine address, see Timothy Houston Polk, *The Biblical Kierkegaard: Reading by the Rule of Faith* (Macon, Georgia: Mercer University Press, 1997), 149, 120: "[We are to read the Bible] with infinite suspicion of self and utter confidence in God, and the faith to be not just a reader but a doer, since it will be in reading as in life [for] to lose the stomach for scripture is to lose the heart of Christian living." Kierkegaard's reading of the book of James illustrates this approach quite well. On his reading of James, see Richard Bauckham, *James: Wisdom of James, Disciple of Jesus the Sage* (London and New York: Routledge, 1999), 161: "Kierkegaard is not an exegete, at least in the modern sense. He makes his contribution at the stage of interpretation and appropriation of the biblical texts. . . . It makes no sense to ask where his reading of James ends and his own creative thinking begins. But this is the way . . . the exemplary followers of Christ, known and unknown, . . . have lived creatively with the texts they loved. . . . By contrast with [critical] commentaries that seem to tie the text up safely in a protective package of learning, Kierkegaard's biblical interpretation . . . lets the power of the biblical texts loose in his own life and in the lives of his sympathetic readers." Bauckham, however, is mistaken when he says that Kierkegaard's "antithesis between 'objective' study of the texts and 'subjective' appropriation of them as God's word is too sharply drawn" (8). This sharpness is especially important in light of the revisionist positions of notables like John Shelby Spong. See his *The Sins of the Scripture: Exposing the Bible's Texts of Hate to Reveal the God of Love* (New York: HarperCollins, 2006), 288: "[The revised heart of the Bible shows that] there is no superhuman parent God above the clouds who watches over us, guards and protects us, keeping the tides inside their boundaries and the rains timely and moderate."

5. Luther himself was more free-wheeling. On this see Fred W. Meuser, *Luther the Preacher* (Minneapolis: Augsburg, 1983), 57: "Johann Gerhard described Luther's preaching as 'heroic disorder.' The main point of the text came first. From then on there was often a verse-by-verse exposition, but with the main point never far away. . . . Luther did have a plan for the sermon, his so-called *Konzept*. But Paul Althaus puts it just right when he says, 'Luther's sermons were born in the pulpit.' They were conceived in the study and born in the pulpit. 'The whole is not undisciplined, but it is unregulated,

specific good deeds to do (BC 185–86)—which, of course is Lutheran, but also Kierkegaardian, since for him the Christian faith leads directly to good works.[6] These sermons also frequently quote[7] Luther himself—often from the Lutheran Confessions—because Kierkegaard's thought runs parallel to his and builds upon it.

The spirit of these sermons is also somewhat aggressive and confrontational. That is because it was Kierkegaard's intent that we should preach as if we had enemies[8]—stinging the soul (PC 242). This in large part means that there should be a vein of low-intensity warfare running through a sermon—rather than soothing, grassy Elysium fields.[9] This agitation or turmoil is warranted because Christians have been called to a

uncalculated, alive, like a free-flowing stream.' . . . Often Luther let himself be led to and fro by some particular scripture verse. . . . If, after having left the thought in one verse, he remembered something he wanted to say, he just went back to it. . . . In the good sense of the word, he just let himself go. Not that he was verbose—he scorned preachers who just spouted words. But in him there was fullness of faith, insight, experience, love, and personal dynamic whose inherent extemporaneity could never be harnessed."

6. This was a major concern of Kierkegaard's—that we practice what we preach. On the biblical warrant for this, see Mt 7:21; Gal 5:25; Eph 4:1; Phil 1:27; Col 1:10; 1 Thes 2:12. Another major concern of his was the sacrament of the Lord's Supper (Mt 26:17–29; 1 Cor 11:20–30). He noted that this sacrament was a central focus or "fulcrum" of his entire authorship (JP 6:6519; WA 165). So each of my sermons also give the Lord's Supper a central place. On the importance of this sacrament for Kierkegaard's authorship, see Sylvia Walsh's introduction to Søren Kierkegaard, *Discourses at the Communion on Fridays*, trans. Sylvia Walsh (Bloomington, Indiana: Indiana University Press, 2011), 1–33.

7. Because these quotations are often numerous, complex, and fairly long, I always provide the congregation with a texts of the sermon—either before or after I preach the sermon. So sometimes the text of the sermon is actually included in the bulletin so that the congregation can read along, if they wish, while I am preaching. Otherwise they can read over the sermon text later. This practice is partially in keeping with Kierkegaard's thought that the hymn texts by Thomas Hansen Kingo (1634–1703) were too difficult to sing, but great to read over at home as devotions (JP 5:6097).

8. See Stanley Hauerwas, "Preaching As Though We Had Enemies," 53 *First Things* (May 1995), 48: "Preaching . . . is an affront to the ethos of freedom. As a Church, we stand under the word because we know we are told what we otherwise could not know. We stand under the word because we know we need to be told what to do. We stand under the word because we do not believe we have minds worth making up on our own. . . . Ironically, in the world in which we live if you preach with such humility you will more than likely be accused of being arrogant and authoritarian. To be so accused is a sign that the enemy has been engaged. After all, the enemy (who is often enough ourselves) does not like to be reminded that the narratives that constitute our lives are false. Moreover, you had better be ready for a fierce counteroffensive as well as be prepared to take some casualties. God has not promised us safety, but participation in an adventure called the Kingdom. That seems to me to be great good news in a world that is literally dying of boredom." And it also is an echo of Martin Luther's "Lectures on Galatians" (1535), LW 27:44–45, 26:58: "There is nothing that vexes the devil more than the proclamation of the Gospel. . . . Therefore it is unavoidable that when the Gospel flourishes, . . .the cross will follow; otherwise it is sure that the devil has not really been attacked but has only been gently caressed. If he is really attacked, he does not remain quiet but begins to raise a terrible disturbance and to create havoc everywhere. . . . For we teach that all men are wicked; we condemn the free will of man, his natural powers, wisdom, righteousness, and all self-invented religion, and whatever is best in the world. . . . This is not preaching that gains favor from men and from the world. For the world finds nothing more irritating and intolerable than hearing its wisdom, righteousness, religion, and power condemned. To denounce these mighty and glorious gifts of the world is not to curry the world's favor but to go out looking for, and quickly to find, hatred and misfortune, as it is called."

9. Vergil, *Aeneid* 6:542, 638–44, 744.

life of faith that is called a good fight (1 Tm 6:12). That struggle is chiefly against our waywardness and unbelief.[10] It pushes for the implementation of what Luther called a "daily" baptism in his *Large Catechism* (BC 445). In his Isaiah commentary, written around the same time, Luther says our business is "to be converted day by day" [*quottidie converti*][11] (LW 17:117). This is another version of our daily baptism. According to this conception, we must be constantly fighting against unbelief so that we can keep on believing all the days of our lives. Kierkegaard also expresses this same idea a third way. He said his writings themselves were like a map that was "so accurate a characterization of Christianity and its relationships in the world that an enthusiastic, noble-minded young person" could become a Christian by following its directions (JP 6:6283). Kierkegaard thought such a map was needed to regain "a comprehensive view of the whole of Christianity" (JP 3:2550) by restoring the "difficulty" of its original message (JP 3:3086). While the image of a map is less upsetting than the waters of baptism and the strains of conversion, it still carries within it the fear of dislocation, disorientation, and getting lost, which ties into the first two themes of baptism and conversion.

All of these sermons were preached at First Lutheran Church of West Seattle between 2005 and 2012.[12] In the pulpit I have affixed this statement from Kierkegaard's

10. On this personal struggle, see Joseph Sittler, *The Anguish of Preaching* (Philadelphia: Fortress, 1966), 29, 31–33: "[The] anguish . . . in Jesus . . . constitutes . . . a hard and unloosened knot in the spirit of any man who would listen to him, think and feel and imagine himself into understanding of Jesus. Participation in Jesus transfers what was an anguish for him into a bequest from him. That he was straitened [Lk 12:50] haunts forever; and the same tautness characterizes [his preachers]. . . . A part of the malaise, the endemic flatness that from all quarters is reported to infect seminary students is certainly related to this anguish. . . . The acceptance in faith and joy of precisely this tautness is the way of the Christian. . . . The preacher in a special posture stands between the 'It is finished' [John 19:30] and the tremendous word of the Apostle, 'The whole creation waits with eager longing' [Rom 8:19]. Every Christian is indeed called to fill up what remains of the sufferings of Christ [Col 1:24]; it is the Christological anguish of the preacher that he must speak of it!—speak from behind, forward into the actuality of the day and situation that now is. . . . The preacher by the burden of his office can have no authentic selfhood if he repudiates this way. . . . The institution and the world wants adjustment, not anguish. And one may even understand his theological education as tutelage toward acquiescence in non-anguish. . . . Martin Luther once wrote [that] he searched deep, and the searching-place was pointed out to him by his temptations. . . . Here we stress what Luther stressed—the driving into the center of Christ and the gospel with all the anguish, pathos, and imperious personal questioning that each of us knows as he sees older meanings and inheritances die, beholds the personal damnation that occurs when the formally correct is unattended by that personally re-enacted passion which comes from probing prodded by temptation."

11. I periodically use Latin words and phrases in these sermons. On this practice see Brian McGuinness, *Wittgenstein: A Life: Young Ludwig, 1889–1921* (Berkeley, California: University of California Press, 1988), 255: "[With] his Olmutz friends . . . he read the Bible—chiefly the New Testament. . . . Wittgenstein thought it best read in Latin. The great building blocks of that language always appealed to him, but there was also the remoteness, the hieratic quality that Latin lent to the text, quite the opposite of that familiarity with the sacred which he so much disliked."

12. The one exception is my last sermon, "Don't Try to Save Yourself," which I wrote on October 8, 2005, and is to be read at my funeral. Now lest you think it is too macabre to preach, in effect, at your own funeral, recall Kierkegaard's words—*periissem, nisi periissem,* "I would have perished, had I not

Anti-Climacus about how God judges our sermons, which helps me stay on the straight and narrow when I am in the pulpit preaching. This passage was on my mind when I was preparing and preaching all of these sermons:

> It is a risk to preach, for as I go up into that holy place—whether the church is packed or as good as empty, whether I myself am aware of it or not, I have one listener more than can be seen, an invisible listener, God in heaven, whom I certainly cannot see but who truly can see me. This listener, he pays close attention to whether what I am saying is true, whether it is true in me, that is, he looks to see—and he can do that, because he is invisible, in a way that makes it impossible to be on one's guard against him—he looks to see whether my life expresses what I am saying. And although I do not have authority to commit anyone else, I have committed myself to every word I have said from the pulpit in the sermon—and God has heard it. Truly it is a risk to preach! . . . The proclaimer of the Christian truth . . . should be . . . true, that is, he himself should be what he proclaims, or at least strive to be that, or at least be honest enough to confess about himself that he is not that. (PC 234–35)

Finally, I call this collection, "Sermons Not For Itching Ears." This phrase comes from 2 Timothy 4:2–5 which is about those who wander away after myths and refuse to endure the demands of "sound teaching" because of their itch or hankering for novelties instead of the historical Christian teachings. These sermons are designed to stay the course—and so they are not for folks with itching ears. Kierkegaard was not looking for any new doctrine or theory of life (JP 6:6727), and neither was Luther (LW 41:127, 51:61)—and so my sermons are not characterized by any novelties in thought and theology. The only newness Kierkegaard was looking for was the newness inherent in a deeper appropriation of the Christian message by each and every believer

---

perished." On this slogan Kierkegaard writes in 1848 that it "still is and will be my life motto. This is why I have been able to endure what long since would have killed someone else who was not dead" (JP 6:6154; SLW 194). On this he also notes at the end of his life: "But to be a Christian means to be a dying man in the state of dying (you must die to yourself, hate yourself)—and then to live, perhaps 40 years in this state!. . . . We shrink from reading about what an animal used for vivisection has to suffer; yet this is only a short-lived picture of the suffering of being a Christian: to be kept alive in the state of death" (JP 1:731). And the year before he adds: "What is 'spirit'? (And Christ is indeed spirit, his religion is of the spirit). Spirit is: to live as if dead (to die to the world). So far removed is this mode of existence from the natural man that it is quite literally worse for him than simply dying." And so Kierkegaard warns anyone who would champion this motto: "The natural man," he goes on to say in this same journal entry, "can tolerate it for an hour when it is introduced very guardedly at the distance of imagination—yes, then it even pleases him. But if it is moved any closer to him, so close that it is presented in dead earnestness as a demand upon him, then the self-preservation instinct of the natural man is aroused to such an extent that it becomes a regular fury, as happens through drinking, or as they say, a *furor uterinus* [nymphomania]. In this state of derangement he demands the death of the man of spirit or rushes in upon him to slay him" (JP 4:4360). And so Kierkegaard would have agreed with Martin Luther in his "Lectures on Genesis 6–14" (1545), LW 2:20: "Every preacher or minister of the Word is a man of strife [*vir rixorum*] and of judgment, and because of his office he is compelled to reprove whatever is wrong, without regard for either person or office among his hearers."

who listens to sermons.[13] That is also what my sermons try to accomplish. And I have struggled to do that in thanksgiving to God for Kierkegaard's abiding witness to the often offensive, unpopular, and cantankerous truth in Christianity.

EXCURSUS: WITHOUT AUTHORITY

But Kierkegaard is elusive when it comes to sermons.[14] On the one hand, he says that he is "without authority" (EUD 5, WA 99) to write or preach them in church[15] because

---

13. And this appropriation of the Christian message was even more important for Kierkegaard than who was preaching the sermon. So he writes: "The secular mind asks, 'Who preached today?' In a godly spirit one would not ask about such things. For here, in God's house, whether the pastor preaches or the sexton, the most renowned pastor or the least-known student, there is always One who preaches, always one and the same—God in heaven. That God is present, this is the sermon; and that you are before God, this is the content of the sermon" (JP 1:591). This presence—standing before God—drives us to appropriate the message, "to strive toward likeness," because it wipes out all trying to "fraternize with God . . . childishly," by coming before him "chummily" (JP 2:1873). See also Martin Luther, "Sermon on Matthew 21:1–9" (1521), SML 1:27: "This is what is meant by 'Thy king cometh.' You do not seek him, but he seeks you. You do not find him, he finds you. For the preachers come from him, not from you; their sermons come from him, not from you; your faith comes from him, not from you. . . . Therefore you should not ask, where to begin to be godly; there is no beginning, except where the king enters and is proclaimed."

14. This does not mean, however, that he thought they were unimportant—"No, what I do want," he wrote in his journals, "is truth in our speaking and above all in our preaching" (JP 6:6685). In this regard, note Paul L. Holmer, *On Kierkegaard and the Truth*, ed. David J. Gouwens and Lee C. Barrett III (Eugene, Oregon: Cascade, 2012), 261: "Kierkegaard was a constant listener to, and reader of, sermons. He went to the downtown churches and heard the reputable preachers. His many personal papers record an almost continuous give-and-take with sundry sermons. He was a sharply critical, yet worshipful, listener. He was never slow to spot difficulties, the lapse of thought, the drop of sweat trickling down his Reverence's nose as his voice quavered and arms flailed the air. But he knows also on the occasion of a preached sermon, seriousness, joy, and even the dread and sense of guilt which belongs to a man in the presence of God."

15. This is a notoriously ironic admission, since Kierkegaard's discourses far exceed the quality of almost all the sermons ever preached by ordained ministers. On the paltry state of preaching in America, see, for instance, John Wilson, "The Hunt for a Good Sermon," *The Wall Street Journal* (May 31, 2012). On bad sermons, Kierkegaard writes: "The proclamation of the doctrine is done at too great a distance, Christianity is not a power in actuality, our lives are only slightly touched by the doctrine. But this can be forgiven if it only is acknowledged. But do not incur new guilt by wanting to reform the Church when Christianity is no more" (JP 6:6727).

he was not ordained.[16] On the other hand, he actually wrote many discourses,[17] from the beginning of his authorship to its end, that were written in the form of the Danish sermons of his day,[18] and which actually looked like "genuine Christian sermons."[19] And some of them he even preached in church (PC 151; CD 249, 392; JP 6:6769).[20] So when it comes to assembling a collection of Kierkegaardian sermons, as I have done here, an eyebrow or two may well be raised regarding the propriety of it all.[21] Even

16. In our day of mail-order ordinations—see The Universal Life Church at themonastery.org, where it reports on having sent out over twenty million ordination certificates—Kierkegaard's concern seems over-wrought. But he respected the church and its ordinances even though he was critical of its morals and worship—which he famously thought made a fool of God (TM 21–23, 30–32, 307–8) by not remaining faithful to its own historical norms—including "all the strenuousness, struggle, and anguish associated with what is required, to die to the world, to hate oneself" (TM 168). Ordination, in and of it self, is a contested matter within the church—since it confers special powers and privileges on sinners for reasons that strain credulity. On the contemporary discussion, see *Called and Ordained: Lutheran Perspectives on the Office of the Ministry*, ed. Todd Nichol and Marc Kolden (Minneapolis: Fortress, 1990). And on the trend of using lay ministers instead of seminary educated, ordained ones, see Lawrence Wood, "Called But Not Ordained," *The Christian Century* 127 (July 13, 2010), 26: "Increasingly, we are saying that ordination does not matter." Note also that "an overwhelming majority of [them] are serving part-time, as the sole pastor of one congregation or more. They receive hardly any benefits; only 8 percent get health insurance, and still fewer receive a pension. They are usually paid much less than ordained clergy. Most are serving in places where ministers of Word and Sacrament are not willing to serve" (23). Finally, on the failure of seminary training and Christian ordination, see John Updike, *Roger's Version* (New York: Fawcett, 1986), 114: "My ears shut as his words droned upward, in that voice we hear all the time over at the Divinity School, the singsong voice of homegrown Christian piety: believing souls are tucked in like muddy, fragrant cabbages from the rural hinterland and in three years of fine distinctions and exegetical quibbling we have chopped them into cole slaw salable at any suburban supermarket. We take in saints and send out ministers, workers in the vineyard of inevitable anxiety and discontent. The death of Christianity has been long foreseen but there will always be churches to serve as storehouses for the perennial harvest of human unhappiness."

17. See Søren Kierkegaard, *Discourses at the Communion on Fridays*, 7: "Kierkegaard distinguished between several types of discourses in his authorship: upbuilding or edifying discourses; . . . occasional discourses; . . . devotional discourses; . . . Christian discourses; . . . Christian deliberations in the form of discourses; . . . Christian discourses and expositions for upbuilding, awakening, inward deepening, and self-examination; . . . and communion discourses."

18. See George Pattison, *Kierkegaard's Upbuilding Discourses: Philosophy, Literature and Theology* (London: Routledge, 2002), 13: "Formally, each of them—following the conventions of contemporary Danish sermons—has an extended prelude leading up to and introducing the text or topic of the discourse and then proceeds to develop this through the remainder, although some repeat the text or its key words, offering a series of variations on it. Many are expositions of texts prescribed for preaching in the liturgical calendar of the Danish Church. Some, but not all, begin and end with prayer."

19. Ibid., 32.

20. See Niels Jørgen Cappelørn, "Søren Kierkegaard at Friday Communion in the Church of Our Lady," IKC 18:282n83: "There was a long tradition for allowing students or theology graduates to preach. . . . [But] Kierkegaard preached at Friday communion at a time when his former faculty was against it."

21. One could also object that my sermons are not as tentative as Kierkegaard's discourses are—and so technically they are not Kierkegaardian at all. On this see George Pattison, *Kierkegaard's Upbuilding Discourses*, 165: "[It] seems as if Kierkegaard cannot finally escape a highly damaging dilemma. Despite aiming at what I have called a 'whole game-plan' for the moral life, he seemingly fails to

so, Kierkegaard's concerns actually had far more to do with the morality of preaching than with the formalities of ordination and what sermons had to say.[22] Sermons, rightly conceived, he thought, should be marked by "Christian restlessness," instead of by "artistic serenity," because only then can they provide the required "impetus to action" (JP 6:6717). Kierkegaard's favorite[23] pseudonym, Anti-Climacus, makes this same point by contrasting admiration with resembling. He favors resembling, in this contrast, because only the imitator of Christ, or the one who struggles to resemble him, is "the true Christian" (PC 256). Therefore the preaching moment is lost or "abolished" altogether, unless the preacher "is himself[24] personally in motion, a

---

deliver anything that could finally ground or justify such a life rationally. Worse still, not only does he conspicuously deny himself the possibility of appealing to idealist or to ultilitarian principles or of grounding his moral thought in any kind of descriptive anthropology or worldview, he also declines the assistances of divine revelation or ecclesiastical authority, so that he ends up by falling between philosophy and religion, being too suspicious of reason for the one, and sitting too lightly to authority for the other. What, then, is the meaning of non-authoritative religious discourse—as opposed both to autonomous philosophical discourse and to authoritative religious discourse—if not simply making up our values for ourselves? And does this not mean that . . . Kierkegaard is a kind of Nietzschean without really knowing it?"

22. On this point Kierkegaard has the parable of the two preachers: "Imagine two preachers. Each delivering one and the same discourse . . . about renunciation [Luke 14:33]. It is masterful [and] makes . . . an almost overwhelming impression on the listeners. . . . How can we thank him, these honest, simple men wonder. One decides to send him 50 dollars; . . . another, a pair of silver candlesticks; a third, according to his humble best, a goose, etc. Imagine that one of the two preachers was, for example, an ascetic, living in character according to the essentially Christian—what then? Yes, here comes the earnestness—when the worthy gentlemen come with their presents, he cannot accept them, has no use for them. 'If you want to thank me,' he declares, 'then do what I have proclaimed to you; for example, give this to the poor, and more yet.' This is Christianity. It is quite true that the earnestness is greatest and truest at another point; the earnestness is not the discourse, but that which comes next.—The second preacher is a rhetorician, a cleric—he is pleased as punch over the presents; a few days later he goes around and thanks each one individually. Then, prompted by all of these big gifts, he gives a great banquet with ten courses—this is playing at Christianity. This proclamation produces an actuality just the opposite of the essentially Christian actuality" (JP 3:3525).

23. See JP 6:6501, 6:6786.

24. So the quality of the sermon is at least in part correlated with the preacher's faithfulness: "Then the preacher begins. But naturally he is not at all afraid of God; for him God is infinitely far, far away. What the preacher fears is—men, so he is careful to preach Christianity in such a way that they do not deny him his career, offerings, and incidentals. Thus the art of preaching consists of seeing how the wind blows, how men really want to be talked to—this he studies, and then he preaches Christianity. This is Christianity!" (JP 4:4904).

striver,"[25] and likewise the congregation "whom he . . . stirs up,[26] encourages, admonishes, and warns, but all with respect to a striving, a life" (PC 234).[27] So the one "who preaches Christianity shall . . . himself be just as polemical as that which he preaches" (JP 2:1846). For the sermon is to make Christ's way of life "a requirement upon my life, like a sting in my soul that propels me forward,[28] like an arrow that wounds me" (PC 242): "According to God's stipulation, the one who is called should use his divine

25. So the sermon "must not contentiously confirm the distinction between the gifted and the ungifted; in the unity of the Holy Spirit, it must simply and solely fix attention upon acting according to what is said" (FSE 11). Christianity, then, "wants to be proclaimed by witnesses—that is, by men who proclaim the teaching and also existentially express it" (JP 6:6521)! Therefore Kierkegaard believed we should say to the preachers: "Shut up, and let us see what your life expresses, for once let this be the speaker who says who you are" (JP 3:2334)! Kierkegaard goes on to say that "the ability to speak" is as dangerous to us as "the sins of flesh and blood." And that is because by way of language, we "use the highest expressions, to inflate them and thus to make it appear as if one himself were such a person or as if one's life really were related to them." On this score, Kierkegaard sides with Pythagoras against Luther. "There was . . . something very true in that ancient view that character training begins with silence (Pythagoras). . . . [So] if . . . I compare Luther with Pythagoras from this point of view, the comparison is not to the advantage of Luther with his insistence that the important thing is that the doctrine be proclaimed unadulterated—that is, objectively." Luther, however, would fully agree with Kierkegaard on this point. See "Sermons on Matthew 5–7" (1532), LW 21:63: "[Shepherds (Acts 20:29), who have become wolves], sitting in the ministry, [are] scared off by threats and danger and persecution, [and] fooled by friendship, acceptance, popularity and wealth. Thus they do not step forward and open their mouths, but they sneak off into a corner, hide behind a hill, and put their whistles into their pockets. . . . All they really want is to be famous, and they preach only so long as they have a following, and need fear no danger."

26. Kierkegaard knew this stirring up would be rare: "A modern clergyman is . . . an active, adroit, quick person who knows how to introduce a little Christianity very mildly, attractively, and in beautiful language, etc.—but as mildly as possible. In the New Testament Christianity is the deepest wound that can be dealt a man, designed to collide with everything on the most appalling scale and now the clergyman is perfectly trained to introduce Christianity in such a way that it means nothing. . . . How disgusting! It would be fine if a barber could become so perfect he could shave off beards so lightly one would not notice it—but with respect to what is explicitly designed to deal a wound, to become so skilled in introducing it that it is as far as possible unnoticeable—this is nauseating" (JP 6:6860)!

27. And so Kierkegaard warns that we have wanted to make Matthew 7:14—"'the way is narrow' and [other verses] like it into an objective teaching—so objective that it does not apply to one single person, not even to the one proclaiming it—no, it is purely objective. Utter rubbish! . . . On the whole it is impossible to preach objectively, for to preach is gassing neither with the mouth nor with the r---, but is essentially one's existing; what my existing says is my sermon. But my existing is my subjectivity . . . . Either all the existential statements in Scripture become historical, so that all tenses in the New Testament must be changed to perfect or pluperfect, or they are eternal statements and existentially are just as valid as at the time Christianity entered the world. This nonsense about an objective doctrine is hypocrisy [since it is] indifferent to personal existing" (JP 4:4566).

28. See also BA 41. And Kierkegaard also uses cognates for this stinging—such as insult, jolt, halt, crisis, and blow (BA 20, 104, 129, 141, 165, 168). Because of the monumental nature of this stinging, Kierkegaard adds: "Moreover no man can bring himself this close to the unconditioned, he cannot do it, and no man dares venture it since this blow, this sunstroke, is like the deadliest danger, something every man must shrink from as more horrible than death. It is Governance itself which brings a man so close to the unconditioned or strikes him this way with the sunstroke of the unconditioned. This being the case, it is the greatest favor which can be shown to a man" (JP 4:4903).

authority to drive away all the impertinent people who are unwilling to obey[29] but want to be loquacious" (CD 179). Kierkegaard called this driving away of impertinent people, preaching "men to bits so that they turn to grace" (JP 2:1857).

And ordination, lamentably, presents a problem for this "driving away," this braking up of people into "bits," because it keeps the minister from stinging the soul of everyone who comes to worship. That is because "it is to the interest of his trade that there be as many Christians as possible"—no matter if they are "useless in war" against the flesh.[30] Under such watered down conditions, Kierkegaard goes on to say, anyone "who can pay is a Christian, that is if he is willing to pay—otherwise he is pagan. If he is willing to pay—fine, then he is an earnest Christian. If the household pets[31] could pay for themselves, I am certain that 'the clergymen' would make them Christians as well" (JP 6:6919).

This of course is deplorable, because by so doing, the preacher completely guts the requirement to believe in Christ and imitate him. Here we see how ministers have "discovered how to relax the requirement, [and] abolish the ideal" (JP 6:6521). But the point of the sermon is not to relieve the congregation of these obligations,[32] but to sting the soul—so that I then "immediately begin my effort" at imitating Christ (PC 242). So once the grace of God has been announced in the sermon (JP 1:993), the

29. For indeed, to "preach is precisely to use authority"—which is the making of demands that must be obeyed (BA 180). To this Kierkegaard adds: "A Christian pastor, if he is to speak properly, must quite simply say, 'We have Christ's word that there is an eternal life, and with that the matter is decided. Here it is a matter neither of racking one's brains nor of speculating, but of its being Christ who, not in the capacity of profundity but with his divine authority, has said it' . . . [So if a listener] is willing to obey on the basis of the [pastor's] profundity and brilliance, . . . on that basis [this listener] simply cannot obey [Christ], because his critical attitude with regard to whether the command is profound and brilliant undermines the obedience. . . . [So] it is corrupting when the thought process of the sermon address is affected, when its orthodoxy is achieved by placing the emphasis on an entirely wrong place, when basically it exhorts believing in Christ, preaches faith in him on the basis of what cannot at all be the object of faith" (BA 184–85). And so Kierkegaard concludes, with amazingly prescient words: "Yet rarely, very rarely, does one hear or read these days a religious address that is entirely correct. The better ones still usually dabble a bit in what could be called unconscious or well-intended rebellion as they defend and uphold Christianity with all their might—in the wrong categories" (BA 183).

30. See Gal 5:16–26, Lk 12:15, 14:33, 16:15. These verses certainly throw us into a fierce battle with ourselves (EUD 143; FSE 77, 83). Kierkegaard therefore concludes: "A thoroughly Christian Christian I have not seen. The highest examples I have seen are some few of what I call human-lovable Christianity. But here the authentic qualification of the absolute is missing. It is more a quiet human kindliness, sympathetic concern, and the like, which of course was also found in paganism. The Christian requirement of sacrifice stops at no point. One gives up everything, unconditionally everything, chooses God, holds to God. Enormous task, how rarely, how rarely does it happen. . . . A Christian pastor I have never known" (JP 6:6252).

31. Kierkegaard is even more pointed than this in his condemnation of our lack of earnestness: "Yes, if [the slovenly] could cut a three-month old fetus from a dead mother, I believe 'the preacher' would gladly baptize it and declare it a true Christian; the more, the better; the earlier, the better" (JP 1:547)!

32. See 2 Cor 6:1—"We entreat you not to accept the grace of God in vain" (RSV).

preacher must say to the congregation—"you must" begin striving to follow Christ.[33] And the sad fact is that "the relevance of ordination," for getting all of this said, is far from clear (JP 6:6670)![34] So for Kierkegaard to say he writes without authority is actually not a liability.[35] It opens up the whole process of conforming to Christ as being "not a matter which only duly authorized persons are entitled to talk about. The one who is without authority writes as one on the same level as his readers and what he can do for them, they can do for him [which leads to] actualizing both the individual's self-responsibility as regards the God-relationship, and the building up of spiritual community."[36]

33. And so "rigorousness and gentleness" go together (JP 6:6535), in that the "prototype must be presented so ideally that you are humbled by it and learn to flee to the prototype, but in an entirely different sense—namely, as to the merciful one" (JP 6:6521).

34. On the need for rigorousness in the ministry—especially when it comes to preaching law and gospel—Kierkegaard adds: "There is a shameful abuse fostered by the division: the law terrifies—the gospel reassures. No, the gospel itself is and must be terrifying at first. If this had not been the case, why in the world did it go with Christ as it did when he said: Come to me [Mt 11:28]—and they all went away, they fled from him [Mt 26:56]. It becomes more and more clear to me that only an apostle can in the stricter sense proclaim Christianity, for only he has the authority to be rigorous in this way. A man does not have this authority and therefore must compromise. Only a person who in the more rigorous sense is himself transformed to 'spirit,' only he can no longer understand, does not want to understand the confounded nonsense, the infirmity in which the rest of us are trapped, with the result that we coddle ourselves much too much and *rest* in grace too soon, and rest in it apart from striving instead of resting in it to be renewed for renewed striving" (JP 4:4333).

35. But ordination and being ensconced as a parish pastor can certainly be a liability: "When being a pastor means to have every possible earthly and secular security, to be along in all the pleasures of life, plus the enjoyment of honor and esteem—in return for orating eloquently, beautifully, and soulfully once a week in a quiet hour (in that splendid edifice called a church where everything is arranged esthetically)—then I maintain that this is as far as possible from Christianity, is the most refined life-enjoyment, a titillation of the senses, so subtly intensified that paganism could not have thought of anything so refined" (JP 6:6807)! All these pastors are mere admirers: "The admirer will make no sacrifices, renounce nothing, give up nothing earthly, will not transform his life, will not be what is admired, will not let his life express it—but in words, phrases, assurances he is inexhaustible about how highly he prizes Christianity—[while being] exasperated with [the] imitator" (PC 252).

36. George Pattison, *Kierkegaard's Upbuilding Discourses*, 143–44.

So inasmuch as this collection of sermons aims to put pressure on those who read[37] them, to believe in Christ and follow him,[38] they make good use of Kierkegaard's thoughts and words. In that sense they are Kierkegaardian sermons:

> If . . . the discourse makes us as imperfect as we are, then it helps us to be kept
> in a continuous striving, neither makes us, intoxicated in dreams, imagine that
> everything was decided by this one time, nor, in quiet despondency, give up

37. Even though Kierkegaard wrote his discourses to be read quietly alone—he also knew how important the *viva vox* of the *preached* sermon was. And he thought this was so important that they should be preached with passion. The preacher must always be "as impatient as that of a woman in labor," he wrote, "inflamed, . . . calling, shouting, beckoning, explosive in outbursts, brief, disjointed, harrowing" (EUD 69). His written discourses, however, are anything but that—sitting there dead on the page, as it were. To offset this morbidity, in some small measure, Kierkegaard advised that his discourses be read aloud by his readers (UDVS 5; FSE 3, JFY 92). And I would make the same suggestion with my collection—but only in order to better catch the *viva vox* of *Kierkegaard's* quotations that I use in them. On this matter, see also George Pattison, *Kierkegaard's Upbuilding Discourses*, 147–49, while noting that with my collection, the sermons are in fact records of real talks: "[Kierkegaard's discourses] are not 'talks' in any literal sense nor even stenographic records of talks, but written texts, written as written texts. Although some of the discourses that Kierkegaard composed specifically for the Friday communion services were in fact spoken by him in the context of the liturgy, that is not the case with any of the discourses we are considering here. . . . The status of the written text in relation to an actual sermon is thus, on the one hand, preparatory, and, on the other, mnemonic. It is to assist the preacher in saying what he wants to say, and to assist the listener to recall it. It is from the beginning a substitute for a spoken word delivered once, and only once. . . . [So] Kierkegaard's readers would know from the beginning that these were not the transcripts of live sermons but were simply written addresses, printed words, books (or, more precisely, booklets). There is no empirical actuality to which the discourses correspond. Their reality is exclusively literary. . . . [But note that at] the heart of Kierkegaard's rhetorical stylistics [is] the absence of 'I', the first person singular personal pronoun. . . . Rarely in the discourses themselves does Kierkegaard speak simply and directly in his own voice. . . . This is not in itself a departure from the precedent of printed sermons. . . . [But what] is the significance of this reticence? In one respect it would seem to follow from Kierkegaard's disclaiming of authority . . . . No less importantly (and, at the same time, in close connection with the disclaiming of authority), this reticence reflects the self-consciously literary nature of Kierkegaard's discourses. The discourses are not mnemonic in the same sense as printed sermons, not a reminder of a concrete occasion when 'I' spoke to 'you', but are themselves, as literary works, the sole site on which the communicative event they are 'about' can occur. But because this site is precisely that of a literary text, a piece of writing that is paradoxically figured as a 'talk', that communicative event is not, primarily, between real life flesh-and-blood Søren Kierkegaard and ourselves, but between ourselves and the particular manifold of possibilities represented in the text. . . . This concealing of the authorial 'I' is complemented by two important and, perhaps, more obvious elements. The first is the explicit emphasis on the role of the reader, the second is the invention of a succession of subordinate voices, that represent the various points of view that engage the attention of the reader in her journey through the texts. These subordinate voices [do] not merely conceal, they displace the voice (as it were) of the author and give definition to the communicative space opened up by the discourses." On Kierkegaard vacating his own discourses, see EUD 295—"And although the trail always leads ahead to *my* reader, not back, and although the previous messenger never returns home, and although the one who sends him never discovers anything about his fate, the next messenger nevertheless goes intrepidly through death to life, cheerfully goes its way in order to disappear, happy never to return home again—and this is precisely the joy of him who sends it, who continually comes to his reader only to bid him farewell, and now bids him farewell for the last time."

38. See Jn 14:1, 15:12, 19, 20:27.

because this time we did not succeed according to our wish, because things did not turn out as we had prayed and desired. (WA 170–71)

So while Kierkegaard was not himself an ordained preacher, what he wrote can still be viewed as a treasure trove for those who are—as I have tried to show in this collection of my sermons. And that is because Kierkegaard's "calling" was actually to depict, as accurately as possible, "what Christianity is" (JP 6:6497)—which should be of help to any serious Christian preacher. He did this by being an "auditor"[39] of Christian concepts, by which "all transaction are conducted" in Christian matters. This is because Kierkegaard found that "it all too easily happens that the concepts are gradually distorted, become entirely different from what they were originally, come to mean something entirely different, come to be like counterfeit money."[40] And Kierkegaard believed this was his calling because, given the details of his life and his inborn talents, he was, for some reason, "extremely familiar with all possible kinds of swindling." So he uniquely knew how to "penetrate the counterfeits and lead back to God" (JP 6:6912).

By way of his auditing, Kierkegaard finds that "in Protestantism, especially in Denmark, the point has been reached of having the very opposite of what the New Testament understands to be Christianity": "The situation in the Church is not that the clergy are sunken in dissoluteness and wild debauchery, by no means; no, it is sunken in inanity, in trivial philistinism, and they drag the parishioners down into this flat mediocrity and absence of spirit" (JP 6:6943).

The solution to this problem is nothing less than a strong dose of the New Testament[41]—wherein we are confronted with a new way of life that transforms us into the likeness of Christ.[42] As this happens to us, we are gradually marked by "dying to the world, voluntary renunciation, crucifying the flesh, [and] suffering for the doctrine"[43] (JP 6:6947). Kierkegaard did not believe, however, that true imitation of

39. Like unto this role, Kierkegaard also thought of himself as "a secret agent" (JP 6:6922), "a vexing gadfly, a quickening whip" (JP 6:6943), "a bird called a 'rain-warner' [*Regnspaaer*; curlews]" (JP 5:5842), and "the vanguard . . . on the mountain" (JP 6:6727).

40. Kierkegaard's bishop, Jakob Peter Mynster (1775–1854), played a big part in this counterfeiting: "He substitutes the artistic for decisive Christianity; for Christian dignity he substitutes the most beautiful and spellbinding edition of human distinction; he substitutes the most refined prudential concerns and considerations for Christian venturesomeness, the most tasteful worldly culture for Christian heterogeneity with this world, a rare, uniquely refined enjoyment of this world and this life for renunciation and self-denial" (JP 6:6844).

41. And note well: "O, but the N. T. is a terrifying book [for it] clearly rests on the assumption that there is an eternal damnation and—perhaps not one in a million is saved" (JP 6:6843)! And in this same vein, Kierkegaard goes on to say: "Just as Luther stepped forward with only the Bible at the Diet of Worms, so I would like to step forward with only the New Testament, take the simplest Christian maxim, and ask each individual: Have you fulfilled this even approximately?" (JP 6:6727).

42. See 2 Cor 3:18, 5:17; 2 Pt 1:4; Rom 11:24; Phil 2:5; Col 3:9.

43. Lest we think doctrine is anemic, Kierkegaard notes: "There is a man I love with all my heart—but I know that if I present what Christianity is essentially he will be furious, will become my enemy. And Christianity commits me to it" (JP 6:6831). For indeed, the true follower of Christ is "[frightfully]

Christ comes about solely "by preaching." No, it only happens if "a man really comprehends and feels profoundly and truly how infinitely much" Christianity is—then, and only then, is imitation "sure to follow" (JP 2:1883). Nor did Kierkegaard believe that this massive transformation required him to "bring down the established order, but [only] constantly to infuse inwardness into it" (JP 6:6531). And so he regularly made use of "the comic . . . to show the incongruity between [the] Sunday ceremony and daily life" (JP 6:6694). With that humor in hand, Kierkegaard says "[I now can] begin my task along the lines of stripping the costumes and disguises of illusions from Christian ideas and concepts [and] work toward an awakening" (JP 6:6943). That awakening is what gives the church a good auditing. That awakening is also what makes sermons faithful, truthful, and good. But the truth "must essentially be regarded as struggling in this world." And this is the struggle Kierkegaard hoped all Christian sermons should take up:

> The world has never been so good, and so good it will never become, that the majority want the truth or have the true conception of it so that its proclamation would therefore immediately win the approval of all.[44] No, the person who wants truly to proclaim some truth must prepare himself in another way than with the aid of such a beguiling expectancy; he must essentially be willing to renounce the moment. (WL 366)

My hope is that my collection of sermons, peppered with diverse quotations from Kierkegaard, will renounce the moment, tell the truth about human unrighteousness and God's righteousness in Christ, contribute to the restoration of Christian concepts, and further the transformation of all who read and hear them—into the very likeness of Christ! And that would be a mighty blessing, because the situation now is that for

> the average man Christianity has shriveled to sheer meaninglessness, a burlesque edition of the doctrine of grace. . . . They have the whole thing in an infinitely empty abstract summary. . . . [For nothing] can be taken in vain as easily as grace; and as soon as imitation is completely omitted, grace is taken in vain. But that is the kind of preaching men like. (JP 2:1878)

---

tough and hardy as one who has died to the world, unmoved and immovable, he quotes the price of being a Christian to you and me, to all of us, a price as high as 'spirit' is high; he abolishes all boundaries; he hastens with longing after his own martyrdom, and therefore he cannot save the rest of us" (JP 6:6727).

44. Toward the end of his life, Kierkegaard adds this to his point about immediate approval: "But to entrust the proclaiming of Christianity to speech experts is *eo ipso* to do away with Christianity; and the fact that the proclaiming of Christianity at a given time is simply and solely represented by speech experts is sufficient proof that Christianity does not exist. A speech expert is just as suitable for proclaiming Christianity as a deaf-mute for being a musician. In order for it to become a theme for the speech experts, the characteristic aspects of essential Christianity (the dialectical, the sign of spirit) must be removed. But of course when that which makes Christianity Christianity is taken away, it goes swimmingly, enchantingly, convincingly—but it is not Christianity" (JP 3:3535).

Sermon 1

Practice Your Faith

JESUS IS MEAN TO the Pharisees in Matthew 23:3—our Gospel reading for today. He says "do not do as they do, for they do not practice what they teach." And those same condemning words are aimed at us too. You don't have to be a Pharisee to be Jesus' target. All you have to be is a lazy Christian, one who doesn't practice what you say you believe; that is, a Christian who fails to take daily prayer seriously as well as not getting to the reading of the Bible, fasting, repenting, tithing, warning of the coming Judgment Day, witnessing to Christ, teaching the baptized the tough words of the Catechism, cleaning up the earth, helping the poor, keeping the Sabbath holy, fighting against the wicked, defending the oppressed and waiting eagerly for Christ's return.

That's all it takes for Christ Jesus to take aim at you. That's all it takes—just kicking-back and not doing what you're supposed to do. And that includes all of us. For we like sheep have all gone astray, says Isaiah 53:6. All have fallen from the glory of God, says Romans 3:23. We are all weak, even when we actually follow Jesus, says Matthew 26:41, for we cannot follow up on our good intentions: "The spirit is willing," says the Lord, "but the flesh is weak."

OUR WEAKNESS

Now why are we this way? Why are we weak and lazy? Why are we faithless, asks Malachi 2:10, from our first reading for today. In 1848, Søren Kierkegaard wrote *Christian Discourses*, whose Sesquicentennial we honor today. There he explains our weakness. "There is only one obstacle," he writes, and that is "a person's selfishness, which comes between him and God like the earth's shadow when it causes the eclipse of the moon. If there is this selfishness, then he is strong, but his strength is God's weakness; if this selfishness is gone, then he is weak and God is strong; the weaker he becomes, the stronger God becomes in him" (CD 129). Oh most wonderful explanation!—that our weakness comes from thinking we are strong when we are weak because of our sinfulness! Putting things off and going with the flow, we say, can't be all that bad. Why label it laziness, we say? Isn't it just mellowness? And isn't that good for the heart and one's longevity? Doesn't it give balance and avoid extremes?

Oh what crafty shrewdness! Oh what clever evasion! And it can only be learned about in church! So if you "fled into God's house," Kierkegaard writes, "from the horror on the outside, from the most terrible thing in the world that can happen to a person, you are coming to something still more terrible. Here in God's house there is essentially discourse about a danger that the world does not know, a danger in comparison with which everything the world calls danger is child's play—the danger of sin" (CD 172). Kierkegaard calls this danger being sagacious—a word dripping with deceit. Sagacity, he says, is the most loathsome of all sins because it "has the world's approval." It covers up our weakness and laziness with "mitigating and euphemistic names." God says it's laziness, dishonesty and selfishness, but we say it's relaxing, being balanced and healthy. So Kierkegaard concludes that the "sin of sagacity is to sin in such a way that one ingeniously knows how to avoid punishment" by giving "the appearance of the good" (CD 180).

OUR HOPE

So what shall we do? Are we hopelessly lost? Are we so consumed with selfishness and dishonesty that we'll never practice what we say we believe? Are we lost because as Isaiah 5:20 says, we think good is evil, and evil is good? No, we are not hopeless. Exaltation is possible, says our Gospel in Matthew 23:12, if we but humble ourselves. Repent and God will forgive you. But can we muster it? Isn't it nigh unto impossible for a selfish ol' boy to become humble and repent? Again, Kierkegaard's *Christian Discourses* sees through this spiritual dodge. "Disbelief," he writes, "is not spiritless ignorance; disbelief wants to deny God and is therefore in a way involved with God" (CD 67). This is enough to get us started. If you can believe it, our sin actually ties us, albeit tenuously, to God! It turns us, Matthew 23:10 says, so we can look to Christ Jesus, our master, and be blessed. As the old Latin Bible has it, *magister vester unus est Christus*. Yes, indeed, *magister vester unus*, Christ is your only help. No one else can pull you up and out of your moral degradation and sinful lusts and selfish weakness. Look to him and you'll repent—and you'll be blessed. No wonder, then, as Kierkegaard notes, the only guilt that God cannot forgive "is to refuse to believe in his greatness" (CD 294).

But how does this blessing come about? What's in Jesus that pulls us to him? John 12:32 says it's his death on the cross that does it. And so Kierkegaard writes: "I will seek my refuge with . . . the Crucified One . . . to save me from myself." Well, in what way does he do that? Kierkegaard goes on: "Only when he holds me fast, do I know that I will not betray him. The anxiety that wants to frighten me away from him, so that I, too, could betray him, is precisely what will attach me to him; then I dare to hope that I will hold fast to him—how would I not dare to hope this when that which wants to frighten me away is what binds me to him! I will not and I cannot do it, because he moves me irresistibly; I will not inclose myself in myself with this anxiety for myself, . . . with this guilt . . . that I, too, have betrayed him—I would rather, as a guilty one, belong to him redeemed. Oh, when he walked about Judea, he moved many by his beneficial miracles; but nailed to the cross he performs an even greater miracle" (CD 280). I should say! Yes, I should say. Oh, the depth of our sin and Christ's mercy. Oh, the profundity of their intermingling. Who has ever seen into these depths so clearly before? Maybe Saint Augustine? Maybe Luther? Maybe Oscar Romero (1917–80)?

But how does this daring, this holding, this attaching, this binding, this hoping, this moving, this belonging to Christ, happen through his death on the cross, of all things? How? Kierkegaard continues: "Truly, Christ did not come into the world to be served without making repayment. . . . Yes, he makes repayment for what they do against him! They crucify him—in repayment his death on the cross is the sacrifice of Atonement for the sin of the world, also for this, that they crucified him!" (CD 280). Oh what abounding mercy. Oh what joy that knows no telling! It is this sacrificial love that unravels my guilt and binds me to Christ. He bears my sin, says 2 Corinthians 5:21, that I might not be punished by God for it. So my master saves me by being my substitute before the very wrath of God. He was smitten, says Isaiah 53:4-5, stricken by God and afflicted—and through his wounds we are healed. Or in Kierkegaard's words: "In order to express God's sovereignty he chooses a very simple man as . . . his ambassador. . . . And in order to do a thorough job of it, . . . God joins in beating up his own ambassador—yet out of love, yes, out of love. O you infinite love!" (JP 3:2976). So praise Christ Jesus—the ambassador of God, his only Son. Honor him, our substitute. Believe in him. Come to the Altar this day and receive him—in, with, and under the bread and wine of the Lord's Supper—that your faith might be strengthened in his sacrifice for you sins.

OUR OFFENSE

And also honor him in your good deeds. Do good works in his name, for James 2:26 says that faith without works is dead. In 1 Thessalonians 2:13, our second reading for today, we have a good work to do. Say *verbum Dei*, as the old Latin Bible has it, and not *verbum hominum*. With that verse, take a stand that the Bible is not some human invention or worldly theory or culture-bound artifact or *verbum hominum*, but God's own precious word to us from on high: *verbum Dei*. Declare the biblical truth loudly and boldly. Do not cower under the assaults of the worldly wise. These assaults are not insightful—they are doomed as 1 Corinthians 2:6 says. Do not waver. Hold fast to God's only revelation. Know that it is "first an occasion for offense," as Kierkegaard writes, again in *Christian Discourses*, and only later does it become an occasion for faith (CD 291). Know this. Expect this. But also pray for mercy that offense may give way to faith—that all who call on the good and merciful name of the Lord may be saved. Amen.

Sermon 2

Do Just a Bit

Second Kings 5 is about the prophet Elisha healing the Syrian army commander, Naaman, of his deadly leprosy. I suppose we could mine this passage for a biblical defense of the reality of miracles in a time when many think they're foolish.[1] But that would be to blur the focus of our text. For it dwells on the advice Naaman's servants give to him to heal him. Let us then dwell on that counsel as well.

KICKING A GIFT HORSE

And when we do, we're surprised to find that Naaman's servants come down on him like a ton of bricks—talking to him like a proverbial Dutch uncle! They aren't afraid of him. And so they shove him around—and with intellectual sophistication at that!

For they present him with a counter-factual hypothetical. They say that he shouldn't balk at Elisha's request—to wash himself in the Jordan river seven times—simply because it's too simple for him to do (2 Kgs 5:10–13). He shouldn't think it's beneath him and disrespectful! And that's because if Elisha had asked him to do something very difficult [גדל, *gathal*]—like climbing a high and rugged mountain or traversing miles of scorching desert—he would have gladly done so! And that's because military commanders are tough, and rarely if ever cower before what's harrowing! So, Naaman's servants add, that if he would be willing to do the difficult thing, then why not also do what's less demanding—that little bit asked of him—that he may be healed?! After all, it's not that he doesn't have the energy and will to get it done!

Basically Naaman's servants rebuke him for being foolish—and kicking a gift horse in the mouth (John Heywood, 1497–1580). For he has a wonderful offer—but wants to pick at it anyway!

BEING LIKE NAAMAN

Now we sinners certainly can understand that! Naaman doesn't mystify us. For we know what it's like to take the grace of God in vain (2 Cor 6:1)! We know what it's like to drift away from so great a salvation (Heb 2:1–3). We know what it's like to get started on the right foot and then blow it (Gal 3:3). And that's because we're not willing to settle for the little bit of faith that's required of us, but would rather try to save

---

1. See my "Misconstruing Miracles," *Dialog* 39 (Winter 2000), 297–98.

ourselves by doing the mightier [גדל] works of the law (Rom 3:28)—by not offending anyone and by not being morally awry in any way.

Martin Luther, our "most eminent teacher" (BC 576), helps us understand our waywardness. Jesus tells us that it's our faith that heals us (Mk 5:34, 10:52), and yet we still balk at it. And so does Naaman—refusing to believe that simply by washing himself in the Jordan River he would be healed! Luther explains:

> [We are] like a man who has fallen into the middle of a stream. He catches the branch of a tree somehow to support himself above the water and be saved. So in the midst of sins, death, and anxieties we, too, lay hold of Christ with a weak faith. Yet this faith, tiny though it may be, still preserves us and rules over death and treads the devil . . . under foot. (LW 12:262)

And so Lutherans confess that faith "is not an idle thought, but frees us from death [and] brings forth . . . new life" (BC 116)! This is the case since "it makes everything easy, good and sweet, even if you were in prison or in death, as the martyrs prove. And without faith all things are difficult, evil and bitter, although you possessed the pleasure and joy of the whole world, as all the great lords and wealthy prove, who at all times lead the most wretched lives" (SML 1:248).

Even though our faith, then, be small, it can still do great things. And so we must not "think too lightly of faith," but regard it as the "valiant hero" which it is (LW 36:62; 28:73)! For when the disciples cried to the Lord, "Increase our faith!"—he assures them that if they only had a bit of faith—the size of a tiny grain of mustard seed—it could still root up a huge mulberry tree and plant it in the sea (Lk 17:5–6). Just think of it! And so we too pray for increased faith—that we might believe that just a little bit of it will do. We, like that famous Danish Lutheran of old, Søren Kierkegaard—whose bicentennial next year is already beckoning us—cries out to the Lord in prayer: "O lazy human discernment, O deceitful mortal wisdom, O dull, dead thoughts of slumbering faith, O wretched forgetfulness of a cold heart—no, Lord, preserve every believer . . . and deliver him from evil!" (JP 3:3409).

We pray, then, that we might come to see that faith isn't puny but a "mighty [and] daring confidence in God's grace" (LW 35:370)! We pray that we might realize that "he who doesn't think he believes, but is in despair, has the greatest faith" (LW 40:241)! And that even though "the world would not give a penny for it"—"no matter how feeble it is, . . . [faith] is still . . . so mighty that it tears heaven and earth apart and opens all graves" (LW 28:73)!

GOD'S TINY BITS

Even so, we must not let faith run wild and gobble up all of what's valuable in our life with God. No, says Luther. "Not that faith does the reconciling in and of itself," he writes, "but it lays hold on and obtains the reconciliation which Christ has performed for us" (LW 36:177). So when Jesus is asked to heal the lepers he says, "I do choose. Be made clean" (Mk 1:41). These six little words are condensed into just two in the old Latin Bible—*volo mundare!* There you have it—God's powerful little bit which saves us! That's what we're to hold on to—*volo mundare.* Let those two little good Latin words ring in your ears—*volo mundare!* For in them God makes it known that he has come to help sinners. And he does that on the cross. For that is where we see, as the Lutheran confessions say, that "only Christ, the mediator, can be pitted against God's wrath and judgment" (BC 136). For by shedding his blood, Christ saves us from the wrath of God (Rom 5:9).

So on the cross, Jesus cries out as he is dying, "It is finished" (Jn 19:30)—which again, in the old Latin Bible, is just two words—*consummatum est!* Yes, God's wrath has come to an end in the crucifixion of Christ—*consummatum est.* On the cross he is punished in our place (LW 26:284) and so we are saved from everlasting condemnation in hell—if we just believe in him (Jn 3:16; Rom 3:25; LW 32:76). For it is that cutting word (Heb 4:12) from the cross, that makes him our Savior (Jn 10:17).

So receive him today in a tiny bit of bread and a few drops of wine at the Sacrament of the Lord's Supper. We don't need a huge spread of food to fill us, and, by being stuffed, show us that our sins have been forgiven. No, if anything, being stuffed may well close our eyes to the wonders of salvation in Christ (Hos 13:6; Jn 6:26)! So excess—gluttony and drunkenness—has no place at this "most venerable" sacrament (1 Cor 13:21; BC 577)! That's because this food isn't for temporal gains, like some "belly sermon" (LW 23:5), but for our faith, as Luther explains: "The Lord's Supper is given as a daily food and sustenance so that our faith may refresh and strengthen itself and not weaken in the struggle but grow continually stronger" (BC 449).

And see also this salvation in the little bit of water that we'll sprinkle on Shirley Woods today in her baptism. I'm not going to dowse her with a bucket full of water to heal her—and she no doubt is glad to hear that! No! Just a little bit of water will do it—for we believe that it is the word that gives power to the water, and "not the water" itself or the amount of it (BC 349)! No, that little bit of water will be her Jordan River in which Shirley is dipped, as it were—and cleansed from her sin, from her "spiritual leprosy" (Titus 3:5; SML 1:152)!

MORTIFYING THE FLESH

This doesn't mean, however, that all difficulties are wiped away! Jesus, after all, says that the way is narrow and hard (Mt 7:14), and Saint Paul calls faith a fight (1 Tm 6:12) and Luther says faith is "exceedingly arduous" (LW 29:149; 28:73)! So where does this difficulty properly lie? The Bible is able to proclaim both ease along with difficulty (Mt 7:14, 11:30)—but can we?

Because faith includes more than trusting in God, but obedience as well (Lk 11:28; LW 25:238), difficulties arise. That's because faith is also "the mortification of the flesh [and] the reviving of the spirit" which helps us bring "the Savior more deeply into our hearts" (LW 14:329, 51:207). So Saint Paul famously charges us to pummel our bodies in order to aid this deepening of our faith (1 Cor 9:27)! And it's just this battle that makes faith so difficult and so "easily obscured and lost" (LW 26:114)!

When I graduated from high school in 1967, it was called the summer of love.[2] Many rushed off to California for free sex and drugs. Their creed was, "if it feels good, do it!" But words like these fuel the battle of faith! For it's in the face of such temptations and "the agonies of death" that we learn how difficult it is to "adhere to God's Word" (LW 23:179). May God then help us in the battle that follows, when we've joined Christ by doing our little bit to believe in him. Amen.

2. See Terry H. Anderson, *The Movement and the Sixties* (New York: Oxford, 1996), 321; and Bernard von Bothmer, *Framing the Sixties: The Use and Abuse of a Decade from Ronald Reagan to George W. Bush* (Boston: University of Massachusetts Press, 2010), 200. See also Joel Selvin, *Summer of Love* (New York: Cooper Square. 1999).

SERMON 3

Rejoice in the Intercessor

TODAY WE HEAR THAT Jesus Christ is our everlasting intercessor (Heb 7:25) who appears before God the Father, on our behalf, to save us from our sins. Søren Kierkegaard, whom we commemorate today, explains how Jesus does this for us.

BEING BUFFERED

Kierkegaard believes this intercession hinges on our need for a mediator between God and us—just like 1 Timothy 2:5–6 says—that "there is one mediator between God and men, the man Jesus Christ, who gave himself as a ransom for all." This mediation needs to be given the highest regard, because without it, none of us will ever have any peace with God (Rom 5:1; Col 1:20). So while large numbers of American Christians today think that getting along with one another is what it's all about,[3] that can't be true! For without peace with God, all eternal blessedness in the life to come, gives way to excruciating misery (Lk 16:23, 28)! And without this eternal blessedness, we won't even be able to get along with one another now (Eph 2:13–16). So Martin Luther—who was Kierkegaard's mentor, even though he was only able to learn from Luther at a distance, across the centuries, through what he wrote—Luther says, if you have Christ, then you have it all, but if you don't believe in Christ, then "all is lost" (LW 23:55). That's how important this mediation is for us! For "our whole concern is to be eternally in Christ; to have our earthly existence culminate in yonder life when Christ shall come and change this life into another, altogether new" one (SML 8:356)!

And Kierkegaard adds to Luther by writing in his journal that

> a mediator is necessary . . . simply to make me aware that it is God with whom
> . . . I have the honor of speaking; otherwise a man can easily live in the indolent
> conceit that he is talking with God, whereas he is only talking with himself.

---

3. See D. G. Hart, *The Lost Soul of American Protestantism* (Lanham, Maryland: Rowman & Littlefield, 2002), xxiv: "[Revivalism] did not respect but in fact undermined the importance of creedal subscription, ordination, and liturgical order. In a word, confessionalists opposed revivalism because it spoke a different religious idiom, one that was individualistic, experiential, and perfectionistic, as opposed to the corporate, doctrinal, and liturgical idiom of historic Protestantism. Confessionalism is the lost soul of American Protestantism, then, in the sense that pietism, through revivalism, has largely routed it over the course of two and a half centuries. One way to measure this defeat is to ask any American Protestant if the Apostles' Creed, the real presence of Christ in the Lord's Supper or the ministry of the local pastor is as important as personal times of prayer and Bible study, meeting with other Christians in small groups, witnessing to non-Christians, or volunteering at the local shelter for the homeless."

. . . Seen from this aspect, the Mediator in a certain sense means the buffer; he is like the courtier who informs us that we cannot get to talk directly to the king lest we stupidly and thoughtlessly go in and talk to the king as if we were peers. What consistency there always is in the divine! Always a redoubling—when he subtracts he also adds. He subtracts, involves himself with us human beings, sends a mediator—yes, but in another sense the mediator expresses aloofness, that God does not naïvely become involved with men as friend to friend—no, now there is a mediator. Yet we have come closer to God; but just as in relation to the ideal every step forward is a step backward, so it is in relation to God: approach, withdrawal, and yet, *actual* approach. (JP 2:1424, 1425)

So while Kierkegaard assumes that Christ's mediation overcomes the wrath of God (Rom 5:9) by allowing us to approach him with peace and joy (CD 299), he also values this distance between God and us, that keeps God distinct from his creation (Rom 1:25). This distancing humbles us—and is what's required if we ever are going to be exalted with God (Lk 18:14; Jas 4:10)! So even though God draws close to us in Christ's glorious incarnation at Christmas, he doesn't completely close the gap! No, enough distance remains to humble us. Kierkegaard underscores this humility by redoubling God, as he puts it—by keeping him distant, so we don't think of him as just one of us; by putting up a buffer to keep us in our place; by eliminating all familiar speech with him, our great ideal, so that we bow down before him; and by emphasizing his righteous and holy aloofness.

BEING UNABLE

But how can we believe in such an aloof, elusive One—who dodges and weaves like this—pulling back right when he steps forward? Now you see him; now you don't! (Lk 4:30; Jn 14:19, 21:4; 1 Tm 6:14–16; LW 24:59–60). If we're really going to trust in a God like that, we'll have to be humbled—eating off the floor the crumbs left there by our master, and only them (Mt 15:27). But when we hear that, our pride recoils and we leave dejected—or *contristatus*, as the old Latin Bible puts it in the case of that rich man of old (Mk 10:22). And this *contristatus* is just what stymies us before God. It is so bad that Luther, in his *Small Catechism*, blurts out—"I believe that . . . I cannot believe" (BC 345)!

Kierkegaard goes on to think more about this volitional impediment, if you will. Our choices, he writes, are "cramped by . . . the multitude of considerations" (UDVS 248). And so our will ends up being disordered (PV 54). *Contristatus!* We can't believe! We are unable to breath deeply enough, and stretch out our wings widely enough, to soar up high enough to trust in the Lord.

BEING GRIPPED

And so Luther famously adds—being that we cannot believe on our own—that it is God, through his spirit and by the hearing of his word, who calls, enlightens, and sanctifies us, preserving us in the one true faith (BC 345). So if we believe, it's because God has facilitated it—and so all the thanks has to go to him for making it happen! Therefore we can never take any credit for our faith! It's a gift—something which "only God can give" (CD 194)! And if, conversely, we don't believe in Jesus, then we need God's mercy to open our eyes and soften our hearts so we can believe in and follow him (Lk 11:13). Kierkegaard calls that being "gripped" (UDVS 250). Without God doing this, we will never believe. So "no one can come to me unless the Father who sent me draws him," Jesus said (Jn 6:44)! And Kierkegaard writes that it can "never occur to the natural man to wish" to believe in and suffer with Christ (UDVS 250). "Good night, Ole!" (JP 4:4175).

What is it like, then, to be gripped by God so we can believe in Christ? Kierkegaard thinks that we can learn this from the believers in the Bible—noting their "quiet, deep, God-fearing sorrow that is silent before God"—and his word, which is "the one thing needful" (WA 149). Such moments are well worth utilizing—by calling on God for help (Acts 2:21)! And that sorrow, which is deep and silent before God, is precisely over our sin. And because this silent, deep sorrow is the breakthrough, Kierkegaard praises it:

> Happy is the one in whom there is true sorrow over his sins, so that the extreme unimportance to him of everything else is only the negative expression of the confirmation that one thing is unconditionally important to him. . . . [This is a sickness unto life] because the life is in this, one thing is unconditionally important to him: to find forgiveness. (UDVS 152)

BEING FORGIVEN

And—glory be to God!—this forgiveness is here for us today. It's all taken care of for us—indeed, "it is finished" (Jn 19:30)! We do not have to search high and low for it. For through faith in Christ, we have the forgiveness of sins (Col 1:14–20), since on the cross he was punished so we could be forgiven (Mt 6:14, 12:31, 18:35). This is Christ's mediation, and in it we rejoice! He bore our sins on the cross, that we might be freed from all eternal punishments for those sins. As Luther put it, Christ's "truly priestly sacrifice for us . . . has the power of reconciling God and of removing our sins from us [by way of the] cross [which] was the altar on which He presented the living and holy sacrifice of His body and blood to the Father" (LW 13:321, 319). So at the altar today, we will receive the Lord's Supper "for the forgiveness of sins" (Mt 26:28). And about this Kierkegaard exclaims:

At the Communion table you are capable of less than nothing. At the Communion table it is you who are in debt of sin, you who are separated from God by sin, you who are infinitely far away, you who forfeited everything, you who dared not step forward; it is someone else who paid the debt, someone else who accomplished the reconciliation, someone else who brought you close to God, someone else who suffered and died in order to restore everything, someone else who steps forward for you. . . . Everything depends on someone else's being present at whom God looks instead of looking at you, someone else you count on because you yourself only subtract. . . . You cannot be Christ's co-worker in connection with [this] reconciliation, not in the remotest way. You are totally in debt; he is totally satisfaction. (CD 299)

BEING WISE

So let us who believe in Jesus, share then in his wisdom (1 Cor 1:30). Let us become "wise as serpents"—as Jesus urges us to be (Mt 10:16)! Kierkegaard expands upon this, saying: "If the fear of the Lord is the beginning of wisdom, then learning obedience is the consummation of wisdom, it is to be promoted in wisdom by being educated for the eternal" (UDVS 258).

Psalm 90:12 does just that by saying wisdom comes by learning to measure our days. Luther says we do this by going about our daily tasks "in full awareness of God's wrath" (LW 13:130)—which includes both constant thanksgiving (Eph 5:20) and laboring tirelessly (Gal 6:9).[4] Amen.

4. See also Jer 31:25; 2 Thes 3:13; Heb 12:3.

Sermon 4

Rejoice in Christ's Victory

Easter is for us the best day of the year! Alleluia! Χριστος ανεστη, Αληθως ανεστη! —"Christ is Risen! He is Risen indeed!" That greeting has been exchanged by Christians for generations from all over the world, because Easter is our grand and glorious feast of Christ's victory over "sin, death, God's wrath, the devil, hell, and eternal damnation" (LW 23:404)—as our blessed Martin Luther rightly puts it.[5] Alleluia!

But if that is the case, then why do we have those upsetting words in Mark 16:8— that seem to rain on our Easter parade!—saying, in no uncertain terms, that the first disciples to discover the empty tomb of our crucified Savior, Jesus Christ, which was to be proof-perfect that Jesus was alive and well—that they, instead of being merry and jubilant and sharing the good news with everyone they saw, instead "fled from the tomb, for terror and amazement had seized them, and they said nothing, . . . for they were afraid"? Unbelievable! They were afraid—or *timebant*, as the Old Latin Bible has it! *Timebant!* Can you believe it? And so we're tempted to say, "Shame on you Mark 16:8! Why are you so sheepish?!"

THREE REASONS

And there's more. We're also shocked to discover that we're not told why they were afraid and didn't tell anyone about the empty tomb! So what we have here is actually a double conundrum—they not only didn't [1] celebrate the first Easter, but we don't know [2] why they were afraid to. So what shall we make of that? Are we left to languish in bewilderment? Well, not quite, for there are still a few biblical pieces we can put together. For even though we don't have any straight-forward answers to our questions, we do have scattered insights of considerable worth. And the first of those has to do with fearing that the resurrection of Jesus might lead to some sort of indiscriminate resurrection—with dead people popping back to life all over the place, since death now has been defeated (Heb 2:14; 1 Cor 15:54–55). This has happened before, you know, but in small measure (Mk 5:42, 9:4), and the fear now is that resurrections will start cropping up all over. So the resurrection cat is out of the bag and we're scared!

Threatened. First, we're afraid because maybe now murderers from the past will come back to hunt us down. Maybe Jezebel of old, who tried to kill Elijah (1 Kgs 19:2), will come back to life and come after us! And also King Herod, who tried to kill the baby

5. Edgar M. Carlson, *The Reinterpretation of Luther* (Philadelphia: Westminster, 1948), 68–73.

Jesus (Mt 2:13), maybe he'll spare nothing in trying to kill us! And what of all those modern day murderers like Mao Zedong (1893–1976), Josef Stalin (1879–1953) and Adolf Hitler (1889–1945)?—who wants them running around again! Now if that's what Easter is about—even in small measure—no wonder those first disciples fled in fear! Wouldn't you have done the same?!

Prodded. Or maybe just the good guys from the past will come back to life, like Jeremiah, Amos, Hosea and John the Baptist. But even that wouldn't be much fun, for they pushed and prodded their people to live better lives back then—lambasting them when they felt they needed to! And they would do the same to us! "Everyone is greedy for unjust gain" (Jer 6:13)! "I will punish you for all of your iniquities" (Am 3:2)! "My people have left their God to play the whore" (Hos 4:12)! "You brood of vipers! Who warned you to flee from the wrath that is to come" (Mt 3:7)! Now who would want to put up with harangues like those?

Embarrassed. Finally, what about Judas (Lk 22:47)? What if he comes back to life and embarrasses us all the more with his faithless thoughts, words and antics? Who wants to put up with his ongoing betrayals of our Lord? And what's more, wouldn't his influence finally overtake us, turning us into him? That's enough to scare any Christian—and make us run in the opposite direction!

ONE MORE REASON

But maybe the real answer lies elsewhere. Those first witnesses of the grand resurrection of Christ, maybe they were afraid because they were expecting the risen Jesus–to get even with them! They saw how Jesus blew up at the scribes!—saying they looked great on the outside, but in their hearts were rotten, nothing but "dead men's bones" (Mt 23:27)! They knew they broke their promise to defend Jesus to the end (Mk 14:31) when they all fled after he was seized and taken to the cross (Mk 14:50)! And so they feared his anger against them, if he were to come back to life! For Christ is judge (John 5:22), as the creeds say! At the end of his life, that great Lutheran writer from Copenhagen, Søren Kierkegaard wrote a pamphlet on this scary matter, called, *What Christ Judges of Official Christianity*. There he says that

> if a comfortable, pleasurable life is to be achieved by proclaiming and teaching Christianity, then the Christ-picture must be changed somewhat. Adornment, no, there will be no sparing of gold and diamonds and rubies [and the pastor's mummery will] make people think that this is Christianity. But rigorousness, the rigorousness that is inseparable from the earnestness of eternity, that must go. So Christ becomes a sentimental figure, pure Mr. Goodman. . . . Above all it is connected with wanting, out of fear of people, to be on good terms with people, whereas the Christianity of the New Testament is: in fear of God to suffer for the doctrine at the hands of people. (TM 136–37, 132)

YOU ARE DELIVERED

What then are we to do to get out from under this damning indictment against us? Kierkegaard has nailed us—or, rather Christ has done it through this Danish author's writings! So what then are we to do? Well, let us cry out to the Lord in our shame— "O wretched man that I am! Who will deliver me from this body of death?" (Rom 7:24). And God will hear us! For we're told, with bold confidence, that Jesus "was put to death for our sins and raised for our justification" (Rom 4:25)! So believe in him (Rom 3:25)—rejoice and be glad! For God has set us free from all of our sins and all the flaming punishments they bring us (Gal 5:1)!

And in addition to this confession of faith, receive Jesus, your Lord and Savior, today. For he is here in the Lord's Supper. Come and bow down before him, eat and drink, that you may be confident that your sins truly have been forgiven you (Mt 26:28).

CONSOLE OTHERS

But there's even more to our faith than believing in Jesus and receiving the sacrament today! We're also expected to do good works (Eph 2:10). Luther explains why this is the case:

> God . . . gives us His Son, who is very God. He gives us the very dearest thing He has and is. . . . And what are we to give God in return for this love? Nothing. You shall not . . . perform this or that good work. Only believe in Christ, cast off your old nature, and cleave to Him. Your faith, however, must be of the sort that abounds in good works. . . . [For] when this Gift enters your heart and you sincerely believe in Christ, you do not remain your former self, as, for instance, a thief, an adulterer, or a murderer; but you become a new man. . . . Such a faith will no longer permit you to be arrogant and proud; for if the heart is cleansed, then hands, eyes, feet, and all other members are also pure, and their works are also different. (LW 22:374)

And so "we receive fire and light, by which we are made new and different," Luther adds, "and by which a new judgment, new sensations, and new drives arise in us" (LW 26:375).

Let us today agree on showing this newness (Rom 6:4) by comforting "those who are in any affliction, with the comfort with which we ourselves are comforted by God" (2 Cor 1:4). Does that mean we'll say that everything is just fine? No, for in this life we have tribulations (Jn 16:33) and sufferings (1 Pt 4:13)! And so, as Kierkegaard points out, the help that Christianity gives "looks like torment, the relief like a burden" (PC 114)! Nevertheless, we do not consider the sufferings "of this present time" worth "comparing with the glory that is to be revealed" (Rom 8:18). And believers have that glory in Jesus' words—"Because I live, you will live also" (Jn 14:19)! Death, therefore, has no dominion over any believer in Christ! So when we die, we will be raised again to live for eternity in heaven with God. When we die, the eternal Christ will meet us to take us with him into heaven (Jn 14:3; Rom 8:39; 1 Thes 4:18). Share these great words with all who will listen. But as Kierkegaard warned, this good news, by way of the resurrection from the dead,

> is not learned by rote, it is not learned by reading about it, it is acquired slowly, and it is acquired only by the person who worked himself weary in the good work, who walked himself tired on the right road, who bore the concern for a just cause, who was misunderstood in a noble striving, and not until it is well gained in this way is it in the right place and a legitimate discourse in the mouth of the Very Reverend [and any one else who wants to witness to it]! (TDIO 101)

With that caveat in mind, move ahead!—"knowing that he who raised the Lord Jesus will raise us also" (2 Cor 4:14)—so we can now confidently rejoice forever in Christ's victory. Amen!

SERMON 5

Be Confident

TODAY WE CONTEMPLATE THE confidence or boldness in 1 John 4:17, based on the fact that "as [Jesus] is, so are we in this world."

THE BLOOD OF LOVE

But earlier in that verse, it says that through this confidence God's love has been perfected in us. And 1 John 4:10 further says that his love is seen in sending Jesus to be "the atoning sacrifice for our sins." Now it is Martin Luther, that great reformer of the church, who takes up these three themes: (1) God's love, (2) Christ's sacrifice on the cross, and (3) his sharing of our life in the world—and shows how they together contribute to our confidence:

> [The] love of God is so great that we are able to have confidence on the Day of Judgment, [when] the whole world will tremble. . . . [And] through . . . knowledge of this love we also have faith, so that we can pass muster at the judgment. . . . This is what the blood of love which was shed for us does. . . . [But] we do not fittingly value [it, even though] no human religion can hold its own in the face of the judgment, but it is solely in the blood of Christ that we have confidence on the Day of Judgment. . . . [For] in this life we are surrounded by all evils. [And] so was [Christ]. But we have Christ, who frees us from all these evils. And this life is an embodiment of all evils. But the flesh does not permit us to pay close attention to them. . . . If we weighed this carefully, we would also weigh the preciousness of the blood of Christ carefully. . . . [So the fanatics] make Christ a spirit without flesh and blood [a Cosmic Christ] in order that they may belittle the worth of His blood for us. But the flesh and blood of Christ still profits us. (LW 30:301–2)

And they do, provided that we don't follow suit and also belittle the worth of the blood of Jesus for us! For our confidence in God's love for us, comes "solely in the blood of Christ," as Luther says, even though we may fail to appreciate and value it as we should!

CONFESSING OUR DEFIANCE

Therefore repent! Don't pass over your sin lightly! See to it that your waywardness becomes "sinful beyond measure" (Rom 7:13). Otherwise, as Luther pointed out long ago (LW 10:368), you'll never feel compelled to tell God you're ashamed of yourself (Ps 83:16, Ez 16:54; Jer 3:3; Mk 8:38) for what you have done—by belittling the blood sacrifice of Christ! Now Søren Kierkegaard, that profound Danish Lutheran advocate of the proposition that "Christianity is unique,"[6] helps us to take our sin seriously![7] Through a late pseudonym of his, he explains that

> if sin is being ignorant of what is right and therefore doing wrong, then sin does not exist. . . . [For in this account, what is missing] is the will, defiance. [For] the intellectuality of the Greeks was too happy, too naïve, too esthetic, too ironic, too witty—too sinful—to grasp that anyone could knowingly not do the good, or knowingly, knowing what is right, do wrong. . . . [And] the truth of this should not be disregarded, . . . in a time like this, which is running wild in its profusion of empty, pompous, and fruitless knowledge. (SUD 89–90)

Yes, and that same pomposity infects us to this day, and so we'll also have to come to terms with our defiance! Thank God, then, for Kierkegaard!—and the "eddying, unpredictable waters of his sentences, with their deadly undertow of logic, [which] sweep away the fashionable clichés we use to hide the poverty of our ideas."[8]

FAITH IN HIS BLOOD

And do not balk at Kierkegaard's deadly logic, but take it to heart, confessing your sins boldly (LW 48:282), instead of slighting them. And agree with Luther, from the depths of your hearts, that

> no faith is sufficient but . . . the faith that believes in Christ and accepts solely through him the two principles—satisfaction of divine justice, and the gracious bestowal of eternal salvation. . . . [For Christ was] not only . . . given to put away sin and fulfill the commandments of God, but also to render us worthy, through him. . . . [So] it is not just "faith" but "faith in his blood." [For] with his blood . . . he has rendered full satisfaction and become for us a throne of grace. (SML 7:163)

And so being a kind, sensitive man doesn't make Jesus our savior! Neither do his miracles or teachings. And his bloody crucifixion can't be just about exposing our vicious hopes for his demise. No, that sacrificial death is mostly about the satisfaction of divine justice by the blood of his cross (Rom 5:9)—which comes by way of the giving up of his life as a fragrant offering and sacrifice to his Father in heaven (Eph 5:2; Heb 9:14; SML 7:152)! And so Luther rightly sounds forth his theological alarm, saying:

6. Walter W. Sikes, *On Becoming the Truth: An Introduction to the Life and Thought of Søren Kierkegaard* (Saint Louis: The Bethany Press, 1968), 153.

7. Contra Wayne W. Dyer, *Your Erroneous Zones* (1976; New York: HarperPerennial, 1991), 90.

8. Kenneth Hamilton, *The Promise of Kierkegaard* (Philadelphia: Lippincott, 1969), 11.

> For this is what God insists on and nothing else, that no one shall stand before him except by that innocent blood alone. And if anyone undertakes some other method, . . . he shall belong to the devil much more than anyone else. For it is a very serious matter with God and he will have no jest made of it, because for this purpose he gave his Son to die. . . . We have preached this and reiterated it so often that everyone can know it well and can conclude from it that all our own works undertaken to expiate sin and escape from death are necessarily blasphemous. They deny God and insult the sacrifice that Christ has made and disgrace his blood, because they try thereby to do what only Christ's blood can do! (LW 36:313)

And so Jesus says that it is only by his death that we are drawn to him through faith (Jn 12:32). And Luther adds that this death is even what makes the believer "grow sweet and disposed toward God" (LW 44:38). And to this Kierkegaard adds that it's only in the "Crucified One" that sinners can find "refuge" (CD 280)!

REAL CONFIDENCE

So hold on to this good news—for it is the reason for our confidence. And note well that this firmness of faith doesn't come from any epistemological sureness that might dwell within us—for that would be, as Kierkegaard warns, only a "pernicious sureness" (CD 211)! No, what is certain is what Christ did for us on the cross when he died for our sins to reconcile God to us (LW 8:210, 274)![9] And if you believe in this settled fact (Jn 19:30), show your confidence today, by bowing down at the altar and receiving the Lord's Supper as a guarantee of the forgiveness of sins—for Christ's sake (Mt 26:28)! For indeed, "the mass was not instituted for its own worthiness, but to make us worthy and to remind us of the passion of Christ" (LW 42:8)!

OUR INVERTED GREATNESS

But how does this sacramental worthiness go with the negativities in Christ's passion and our sinfulness? Aren't they more than we can bear—"the stern wrath and the unchanging earnestness with which God looks upon sin and sinners, so much so that he was unwilling to release sinners even for his . . . dearest Son without his payment of the severest penalty for them" (LW 42:8–9)? Well, Kierkegaard, for one, thinks not, and holds that our likeness to God (Gn 1:27), where our greatness comes from (Ps 100:3), is inverted:

> The upright gait is the sign of distinction, but to be able to prostrate oneself in adoration and worship is even more glorious. . . . This is what is expected, . . . that worshipping, [the human being] shall praise the Creator, something

9. See also LW 12:377; 24:163; 30:280.

nature cannot do. . . . [So] the human being and God do not resemble each other directly but inversely; only when God has infinitely become the eternal . . . object of worship, only then do they resemble each other. (UDVS 193)

So our greatness is inverted and made perfect in the lowliness of worship—just as our "power is made perfect in weakness" (2 Cor 12:9)! So when Hannah and Seth are baptized today, be confident and worshipful—and don't let your attention be "fixed upon the visible baptizer, but rather upon the unseen Baptizer, who instituted . . . baptism; to him [we] must look . . . if [we are] to be certain of [our baptisms]" (LW 51:324)! Be confident in this good Lord alone—and not in the vain hope of an easy life for them because they're baptized (Mark 10:39)—since "the politics of moderation depends on a balance between a core certainty and many possibilities of action, none of which has the quality of certainty."[10] So stay focused, and praise the God of baptism—with certainty and confidence! Amen.

---

10. Peter Berger and Anton Zijderveld, *In Praise of Doubt: How to Have Convictions Without Becoming a Fanatic* (New York: HarperOne, 2009), 150.

SERMON 6

Don't Preach Yourself

TODAY WE'RE WARNED IN 2 Corinthians 4:5 that preaching Christ must never involve promoting ourselves, because the transcendent or extraordinary power of this message "belongs to God" and not to us (2 Cor 4:7)! So if we were to say that Jesus is for real and the best there ever was simply because we think so, that would be to preach ourselves rather than the Lord we're called to serve!

THE COLOSSAL CONTENTION

The New Testament is emphatic about this warning. And so in 1 Corinthians 2:4–5 we're told also that our sermons must never be preached in "plausible words of wisdom, but in demonstration of the Spirit and power," for otherwise they will look like they're resting on "the wisdom of men" instead of on "the power of God."

But this boost doesn't make it any easier to heed this warning against building our sermons on ourselves! And Søren Kierkegaard, that profound Danish Lutheran writer, would agree. "The struggle is terrible," he writes, "the struggle in a person's inner being between God and the world"—since our life "is fused with the visible" (UDVS 208)! And it's that way because we "dwell on all the defectiveness and mediocrity and instability and small-mindedness" of the world around us (UDVS 328). Therefore "a human being can achieve amazing things, encompass a multifariousness of knowledge without . . . understanding himself." "Despite all this knowledge he can be and continue to be a riddle to himself, an unknown" (UDVS 256). "Therefore love of God is hatred of the world and love of the world hatred of God; therefore this is the colossal point of contention, either love or hate; therefore this is the place where the most terrible struggle carried on in the world must be fought, and where is this place? In a person's inward being" (UDVS 205). And so the Holy Scriptures challenge us all by saying: "Work out your salvation with fear and trembling" (Phil 2:12)!

DAMNING SINNERS TO HELL

And work it is!—since following Christ and preaching of him properly isn't easy (Mt 7:14; 2 Tm 4:2–5). And it doesn't help that God is also set against us sinners, to trip us up at every turn (Mi 1:2; 1 Pt 2:8)! So God indeed hates sinners (Pss 5:5, 95:10) and wants to kill them (Is 13:9; Lk 13:3)—this is the intimidating, "bare voice of God," *nudam vocem* (LW 29:238), that resists all interpretation to tone it down! So Luther rightly rejects the saying about hating the sin but loving the sinner. No, we are to hate both!—sin and the sinner—by preaching that "our Lord God will . . . cast a sinner away" who refuses to repent in the name of Jesus! And so "if you do not believe in Christ, you will go to hell," Luther thunders from the pulpit, "be damned for all eternity, and death will be an eternal and inescapable prison for you" (LHP 2:256, 139)! Wow!

OUR INDISCREET FORWARDNESS

Now what this adds up to is that we're in deep trouble! "Wretched man that I am! Who will deliver me from this body of death?" (Rom 7:24). Wretched indeed! For when an unforgiven sinner meets the Almighty, Holy God, he doesn't see a loving heavenly father but only a fierce bear (Am 5:19; Hos 13:8) or a fire-breathing crocodile, with a heart of stone (Job 41:8–34)! So we see that the horrors of sin "must be indescribably great" (LW 7:280). Kierkegaard is then right to say that if we were to try to cozy up for mercy with a God such as this, it would be a most severe case of "indiscreet forwardness" (JP 2:1432)!

PUNISHED IN OUR PLACE

But this brashness need not abide! It can give way to the humble repentance of faith in Christ Jesus—who bridges the gap between the one Holy God and all of us abject sinners! "And so He is not the Mediator of one; He is the Mediator of two who were in the utmost disagreement!" For the offense is such, that "God cannot forgive it and we cannot remove it" (LW 26:325). So Christ is our one mediator (1 Tm 2:5). By his death he makes us righteous (1 Cor 1:30) and overcomes God's wrath (Rom 5:9)—giving us a reconciled God, *deus reconciliatus* (LW 12:377), and a placated God, *deus placatus* (LW 30:280, 26:355)!

And only Christ can do this because he is "the one and only Victim with which satisfaction has been made to the wrath of God" (LW 7:227). And this comes from being punished "for our person" (LW 26:284)—for sin can only be "purged away by the blood of the Son of God and that ineffable sacrifice" (LW 7:280). For we "cannot pay God" (LW 51:280; Psalm 49:7) in order to escape from his wrathful indignation for the sins which we have committed. Therefore we must "pay God with Christ"—*Gott mit Christum bezahlen* (LW 30:12)—as Luther aptly puts it. *Gott mit Christum bezahlen!* Pay God with Christ because only he can "step between you and God, so that no wrath or displeasure can touch you" (LW 51:280). And when he does, as Luther notes,

> it cost him much and was achieved with hard work and bitter sweat since he paid for it most dearly with his own blood and life. For it was not possible to overcome God's wrath, judgment, conscience, hell, death, and all evil

> things, and indeed to gain all benefits, unless God's righteousness received satisfaction, sin was given its due reward, and death was overcome by justice. (LW 52:280)

So Kierkegaard rightly concludes, with searing clarity, that "God is love, but not love to sinners. That he is first in Christ" (JP 2:1329)—for it is only in Christ, as Luther argues, that God is "moved . . . to grace" for repentant sinners (LW 51:277)! Therefore Kierkegaard goes on to say, with the same striking precision, that God "becomes my Father in the Mediator" (JP 2:1432).

CONVERSE ON HIGH

And just how does Jesus do that? Well, he moves God to mercy by being our "intercessor" (Heb 7:25) and "advocate" (1 Jn 2:1). By so doing, Jesus shields us from God's wrath and gives us "access" to his grace (Rom 5:2). This is not a pretty picture because it seems to compromise God's goodness and mercy by making it conditional on Christ's intercessions. No wonder then, that Luther preached that you shouldn't become a Christian to gain "great . . . pleasure and fame here on earth, but rather to get the world as enemy" (LHP 2:149)! Even so, how does Jesus move God to love us? What does he say to him to bring that about? As far as we know, those conversations on high are private! But Luther ventures out to imagine what one might sound like anyway. So he writes:

> Christ came and stepped between the Father and us, and prays for us: Beloved Father, be gracious unto them and forgive them their sins. I will take upon me their transgressions and bear them; I love thee with my whole heart, and in addition the entire human race, and this I will prove by shedding my blood for mankind. Moreover, I have fulfilled the law and I did it for their welfare in order that they may partake of my fulfilling of the law and thereby come to grace. (SML 5:188)

BUILDING UP OTHERS

So is that it? Is our belief in Christ the Mediator all we need (Eph 2:8)? Or is there more? Romans 12:18 says there is. "If possible," it says, "live peaceably with all." So while faith in Christ's death draws us to God, we still need to work on overcoming our separation with each other. And God cares about this, for "he who loves God should love his brother also" (1 Jn 4:21)! So if we dwell on grace all by itself, "the majority of men," Kierkegaard argues, will do this only "to hide their own inner squalor" (JP 3:3531)! So love we must—but it surely won't be easy!

For 1 Corinthians 8:1 says it is love that builds up—so love is the key to breaking down our separation. Love is the way that we can build up our lives with others—overcoming our separation with them. But as Kierkegaard points out in his book, *Works of Love*, that doesn't imply that we plant love in others when we build up love in them—for only God can do that (WL 216, 219, 224). No, all that we can do is "draw out the good, [or love] forth" and "praise" the love, that's already in them (WL 217, 222, 223). And that will take great self-control and much "self-denial" (WL 217–18)—since we think we have to "tear down" (WL 219) what's bad in a person before we can build up any love in them. Because of that "it is more difficult to build up the way love does than to complete the most amazing undertaking" (WL 218). And that's because we have to presuppose love in people, although it's "never completely present in any human being, inasmuch as it is indeed possible to . . . discover some fault or weakness in it" (WL 218), for they may well strike back at us with ingratitude and anger (WL 220). And so we'll have to be willing to draw "nourishment out of what seems to be least nourishing" (WL 220)—much in the way that a mother "puts up with all her child's naughtiness" (WL 221). But that's what true Christian love is! It's what weaves us into "the great common life," and wins us for "the great fellowship of existence" (UDVS 183). By overcoming our separation with one another in this way, we'll also be honoring Christ's mediation on the cross, and preaching him aright. Amen.

SERMON 7

Don't Try to Save Yourself

WITHOUT CHRIST AND FAITH in him, we end up with Job 14:12, "So man lies down and rises not again." When death strikes, that's what remains: sheer hopelessness. Nothing more than that. Death has done its dirty work—nothing and no one can stop it. Indeed, Hebrews 9:27 has it right: "It is appointed for men to die once, and after that comes judgment." So death is clearly relentless. It flattens out us all.

This is because of Saint Paul's explanation in 1 Corinthians 15, "flesh and blood cannot inherit the kingdom of heaven, nor does the perishable inherit the imperishable." It's beyond us, you see. We are stuck with this life and its deadly aftermath. All must die. None save Enoch (Gn 5:24), Elijah (2 Kgs 2:11–12) and maybe Saint Mary, get out alive. We die and can't break free into something better afterwards. All we have is the transient, material, ordinary flow of things. And then they end—many sooner and only a few later. And we can't muster anything better afterwards on our own either. Death defeats us—one and all.

DEATH'S DARKNESS

This is no doubt due to our creaturely limitations. But there's more to it than that. It's not just because we're weak and unable to fend off dying. It's also because we are sinners. Just think of it. Imagine the horror of it all! We have gone against (Rom 1:18) the source of our being (Acts 17:28) and the font of human kindness (Jas 1:17)! We are a "stiff-necked people" (Acts 7:51), "children of wrath" (Eph 2:3). And so we die because of our rebellion—because of our sin (Rom 6:23). We are left low in our death. Nothing good follows. So the Welsh poet, Dylan Thomas (1914–53), should actually have pushed his wonderful line further saying that we in fact *can't* go "gentle into that good night."[11] We can't because there isn't one! Only gloom, made up of privation and punishment, is awaiting us. We are stuck in loss, shame, meaninglessness and pain. Death's darkness completely envelops us.

FEARING PUNISHMENT

But this is not simply because of the loneliness death brings—cutting us off from our loved ones as it does. No, fear also comes with dying. It strikes us too. The fear of being punished for all of eternity for what we have done and failed to do in this dreary

---

11. *The Collected Poems of Dylan Thomas* (New York: New Directions, 1957), 128.

life—this "vale of tears" as Luther called it (LW 28:122). Fear!—that's what makes death dark, dank and gloomy. And this failure and doom are not to be passed over once lightly. Oh no! Their horrors are to be impressed upon us diligently and even "beyond measure" (Rom 7:13)! Have your noses rubbed in it! It'll wake you up to your need for the Savior. The horror of it all will actually "drive you to Christ" (LW 16:232). So under the rightfully unpleasant "screeching" of the Law's condemnation (LW 2:161), your sin—now painfully exposed—should make you squirm. Nothing less. Nothing less. Take it with all its force—you deserve it and it's for your good.

THE SILVER LINING

So when that gloom and doom hit home as they should and make you "hurt" (LW 8:6), there is still something better awaiting. This cloud has a silver lining. And the "darkness cannot overcome the light" (Jn 1:5). Thanks be to God for that silver lining! Thanks be to God for those blessed words from the Gospel according to John, "Whoever believes in the only Son of God, Christ Jesus, will not perish but have eternal life." Now that's far better than doom and gloom. In those words we have hope. In them is eternal life and salvation. So you need not perish! But without this salvation—as that same Gospel reading has it at its bitter end—only the wrath of God is mercilessly awaiting you! (John 3:36).

JESUS OUR SUBSTITUTE

So thanks be to God for those words about belief and salvation in Christ Jesus! He can save you from the aftermath of death. He can save us from our sins (1 Tm 1.15). And he is the only one who can do this. There is salvation under "no other name" (Acts 4:12). Therefore Luther rightly preached in 1530, that if I have Jesus, I have everything, and if I don't, I have nothing—I've "lost all" (LW 23:55). For he is the only savior (1 Tm 2:5). He is our only advocate (1 Jn 2:1–2). In him is hope because in his death he saves us from the eternal punishments we had coming for our sin. "Not with silver and gold," as Luther said in the catechism, "but with his own precious blood." By suffering and dying on the Cross, Jesus pays "what I owed," makes satisfaction, and thereby saves all believers, restoring them to the "Father's favor and grace" (BC 414). This is because God punishes Christ in our place. He is our "substitute" (LW 22:167). He was stricken, smitten by God and afflicted, and "by his wounds we are healed" (Is 53:4–5). This was endured by no one else—only Jesus came to die for us—not Buddha, not Arjuna in *The Bhagavad Gita* (Hinduism), not Mohammad, not Moses, not even your most loving friend. Believing in the sacrificial death of Jesus Christ (Heb 9:26) and him alone is precisely what saves us.

And thanks be to God that Ron Marshall was baptized into that hope expressed in those wonderful words of Holy Scriptures. Thanks be to God that his heart hankered after that hope—albeit in fits and starts—right up to the end. Thanks be to God that his faith was nurtured at the Altar of the Lord and through God's Holy Word. Thanks be to God that his good deeds were grounded in that same hope. Thanks be to God that his life is now in the hands of him who brought us that hope, Christ Jesus himself.

So honor the Father for the gift of his Son, Christ Jesus, the Savior of the world. Come to the Altar and eat of the bread and drink from the cup. In, with and under the bread and the wine, Christ Jesus himself will be truly present by the power of his Word which consecrates this sacrament for us. Eat and drink and have your faith in the Savior strengthened—for Jesus has promised to abide in us if we abide in him (Jn 6:56). Eat and drink and be in communion with believers, the saints, who have died in Christ and are now at rest.

SIMUL

But make no mistake. Ron Marshall didn't make this fine future for himself. Oh no. For he is and was a sinner—albeit a redeemed and forgiven one. But still a sinner. So he could not save himself. Not even with the faith of Christ in him, and the good works done in Christ's blessed name, could he save himself. Indeed, "no man can ransom himself," for it's too "costly" (Ps 49:7–8)! Besides, in our hearts remains what Luther called that "devil's yeast" (LW 7:233). So along with the Spirit of God in Ron Marshall's heart remained that ol' sinful Adam. He like all Christians was a mixed bag: some good, not of his own making, and much evil. Ron Marshall was as Luther notoriously asserted in that apt Latin phrase, *simul iustus et peccator* (LW 25:260, 434; 26:232)—at the same time both rotten and good, sinful and saintly. Jesus therefore had it right in Mark 7:21–22 that within us remain "evil thoughts, fornication, theft, murder, adultery, coveting, wickedness, deceit, licentiousness, envy, slander, pride, [and] foolishness." This is the bone-chilling Gospel truth. So Saint Paul rightfully erupts in Romans 7:24, "Who will deliver me from this body of death?" Yes, indeed! Who can save us?—for we surely can't do it ourselves!

LOVE FORTH THE LOVE

So be warned. We cannot save ourselves. All of us need the savior, Jesus Christ. Look not to your own thinly veiled goodness for help. Forget your assets, accolades and accomplishments. Saint Paul after all says they're all rubbish anyway (Phil 3:7; 1 Cor 4:13). Our righteousness is only "filthy rags" (Is 64:6, KJV). So look only to Christ (Heb 12:2). And pray as Kierkegaard did in 1849: "Lord Jesus Christ, . . . help us . . . that we might love you much, . . . inflame [our love], purify it, . . . mercifully . . . love forth the love that loves you" (WA 137). Yes, "love forth" that love because none of us can "love Christ with an undying love" (Eph 6:24) as we should. Yes, mercifully love forth in us that love for Christ, O Lord!

And then pray those same words of thanksgiving we have offered up for Ron Marshall this day. Pray that when you're dead and gone, Christ will meet you with mercy too, because of your faith in him and in him alone. Amen.

APPENDIX 1

PART 1

A Dangerous Man

WHY WOULD ANYONE SAY that Kierkegaard was "a dangerous man?"[1] Could it be because he said that Christianity was dangerous and then went on to show us in his writings just how dangerous it was—and then pushed that danger upon his readers in compelling ways and in great detail throughout his many writings? Yes, that is probably it—and here is an example of him pushing some of that danger on us:[2]

> Is there anything more terrible than to be at a distance from one's salvation? To be at a distance from one's salvation, to be in this condition, this, after all, means to distance oneself more and more. Salvation corresponds to being in danger; the one who is not in danger cannot be saved either. Therefore if you are in danger and you do not come closer to your salvation[3]—then you are of course sinking deeper and deeper into danger. (CD 220)

1. Frederick Sontag, *A Kierkegaard Handbook* (Atlanta: John Knox, 1979), 147. See also Hugh Pyper, *The Joy of Kierkegaard: Essays on Kierkegaard as a Biblical Reader* (Sheffield, England & Oakville, Connecticut: Equinox, 2011), 43, 49: "Reading Kierkegaard frightens me. . . . Reading either the Bible or Kierkegaard faithfully might well frighten me, because it shows me that I do not love enough, and that to love more will increase rather than diminish the painful scandal of the text."

2. See also this journal entry from 1854: "It is very strenuous to have anything to do with God— and it is natural that under the name of Christianity men have gotten Christianity made over into its very opposite: amiable mediocrity, instead of the most excruciating strenuousness toward ideality . . . . The more you are involved with him, the wilder it gets and the more he cudgels you. He is just as infinitely concerned with one person of intensity, yes, one, as he is infinitely indifferent to millions and trillions. God is always the inverse of man. Man believes numbers mean something; for God it is precisely numbers which mean nothing, nothing at all" (JP 2:1807). And add to this entry, one from 1851: "Essential Christianity is always this *quid nimis* [or extreme position]. . . . [But] cannot the proclamation of Christianity be mediated so as to become an inoffensive, good, safe position for a man and his family. O how the extraordinary one must still suffer! It always seems to be verging on madness. . . . Mediation is mob rebellion against the sovereignty of Christianity. We boast that mediation is the only thing that unites men; we also boast that mediation has 'the crowd' on its side—and thus we dethrone Christianity" (JP 2:1617)!

3. See Rom 13:11. Kierkegaard also expounds further upon this verse: "This discourse [on Rom 13:11] quite properly is constructed in such a way that it could almost just as well be a discourse about what has been interwoven as a commentary: Woe to you if everybody speaks well of you [Lk 6:26]. Its polemical aim, therefore, must also be at such an existence. . . . Anyone who has any kind of

Appendix 1

After Kierkegaard died, Hans Brøchner expanded upon this danger in a letter to C. K. F. Molbeck on February 17, 1856. For Kierkegaard, Brøchner writes,

> Christianity was unconditionally incompatible with the world; it was absurd to the understanding; it could be embraced only in the passion of faith; its requirement was to die away [from the world]; its hallmark was suffering; its constant companion was the possibility of offense. His polemics were therefore directed against everything that rested upon the fusion of . . . Christianity and worldliness in an insipid security; against every notion that Christianity was something one came by easily.[4]

Kierkegaard's polemical approach attacked Christians living in the "haze of uncertainty" about their Christian identity (CD 217)—and who had never before been "probed . . . to the core" (CD 219) by God's word and the spirit.[5]

It is not surprising, then, that from the beginning Kierkegaard's life was troubled in various ways.[6] He was born in Copenhagen on May 5, 1813 and died there at the

---

prominence must expose himself to something—but the numerical, gloating numbers, the crowd, is in the difficult position of being able to avoid all spiritual trials" (JP 5:6118).

4. *Encounters With Kierkegaard: A Life as Seen by His Contemporaries*, ed. and trans. Bruce H. Kirmmse (Princeton: Princeton University Press, 1996), 252.

5. See Heb 4:12: "The word of God is living and active, sharper than any two-edged sword, piercing to the division of soul and spirit, of joints and marrow, and discerning the thoughts and intentions of the heart" (RSV). See also Gregor Malantschuk, *Kierkegaard's Way to the Truth: An Introduction to the Authorship of Søren Kierkegaard*, Foreword by Howard V. Hong, trans. Mary Michelsen (Minneapolis: Augsburg, 1963), 13–14, 16, 17: "The outstanding characteristic of the age of disintegration, says Kierkegaard, is that in such an age nothing is absolutely solid. No longer does man have an absolute standard by which he may order his life. Belief in eternal values is replaced by the leveling of all values. But without belief in something eternal, man gives himself over to annihilation. . . . Christianity stood unshakably firm, but gradually influences developed that turned man away from Christian truth and advanced modern paganism. Christianity pointed out to man his limitations and his sin. It demanded obedience and belief. But modern man wants to be his own master and would rather not acknowledge a limit to his knowledge and powers. . . . Kierkegaard stands squarely in the middle of this dangerous situation. He describes graphically how he feels after having discovered the peril. He feels 'like a spider who after the last house-cleaning manages to live his wretched life in a hidden corner while in anguish he feels within himself the impending storm' [CUP 1:63]. . . . After he himself has been captured and conquered by Christianity, he regards it as his particular calling to draw the attention of men to Christianity as the only way out of the anxiety and hopelessness of the modern age." Note in conjunction with Malantschuk's point, Anoop Gupta, *Kierkegaard's Romantic Legacy: Two Theories of the Self* (Ottawa, Ontario: University of Ottawa Press, 2005), 107: "For Kierkegaard, . . . relativism is ruled out; not all ways of being are as good as any other."

6. For this biographical sketch I draw from Walter Lowrie, *A Short Life of Kierkegaard* (Princeton: Princeton University Press, 1942); Julia Watkin, *Kierkegaard* (London: Continuum, 1997, 2000); Susan Leigh Anderson, *On Kierkegaard* (Belmont, California: Wadsworth, 2000); Jørgen Bukdahl, *Søren Kierkegaard and the Common Man* (1960), trans. Bruce H. Kirmmse (Grand Rapids: Eerdmans, 2001); Alastair Hannay, *Kierkegaard: A Biography* (Cambridge: Cambridge University Press, 2003); and Joakim Garff, *Søren Kierkegaard: A Biography* (2000), trans. Bruce H. Kirmmse (Princeton: Princeton University Press, 2005), with a corrected paperback edition published by Princeton University in 2007. And to guard against any hagiography, one would do well to take to heart Kierkegaard's warning: "Do not look at my life—and yet, do look at my life only to see what a mediocre Christian

age of 42 on November 11, 1855. He was the youngest of seven children born to Michael (1756–1838) and Ane Lund Kierkegaard (1768–1834). Kierkegaard's father's first wife, Kirstine Røyen (1758–1796), who was the sister of his business partner, died just two years after they were married. His second wife, Ane, had been his father's housemaid before they were married. The family name means church (*Kierke*) yard (*gaard*) or cemetery—and *gaard* is pronounced *gor*. Therefore the following jingle rhymes:

> Kierkegaard
> Said it before.[7]

The name Søren is a Danish version of the fifth century monk's name—Saint Severinus (d. 482). He came to Italy from the East to help fight off the barbarians—not with armaments but by his cunning. He has been extolled for his bravery and wisdom. But after Kierkegaard took on that name, it became a taunt word in Denmark because of their general disdain for him (JP 6:6738). He got his name from his maternal grandfather, Søren Lund. His middle name, Aabye, is a distant family name.

Kierkegaard's siblings were Maren (1797–1822), Nicoline (1799–1832), Petrea (1801–34), Peter (1803–88), Søren Michael (1807–19), and Niels (1809–33). Maren died from a kidney disease; Nicoline and Petrea both died in giving birth; Søren Michael died from a head injury on the playfield; and Niels died in Pittsburgh, Pennsylvania, from respiratory problems. So between 1832 and 1834, Kierkegaard's father lost his second wife and three of his children. After those *anni horribiles*, all he had left were Kierkegaard and his brother Peter.[8]

HIS FATHER: THE FIRST CRISIS[9]

Kierkegaard's father was strict and sober. He was born in the harsh back country of Denmark, out on the Jutland and only moved into Copenhagen as a young adult. Even

---

I am, something you will see best when you listen to what I say about the ideal. Listen to that and never mind about my trifling person. . . . The Church does not have to be transformed, nor does the doctrine. If anything has to be done—then it is penance on the part of all us. That is what my life expresses" (JP 6:6727)!

7. William T. Riviere, *A Pastor Looks at Kierkegaard: The Man and His Philosophy* (Grand Rapids, Michigan: Zondervan, 1941), 22.

8. On the risks inherent to biographical analyses of Kierkegaard, see Howard V. Hong, "Foreword," in Gregor Malantschuk, *Kierkegaard's Way to the Truth*, 7: "It is particularly easy to commit the genetic fallacy with regard to an existential thinker and thereby to present biographical, psychological, and personal studies rather than to point to the thought and the works. Such approaches may at times illuminate the thought; nevertheless, although they are not the thought and cannot 'explain' or give grounds of evaluation, they tend to eliminate the thought. Biography is a legitimate sphere of interest, but it ought not be equated with that which reminds us that the individual, the author, ever lived at all."

9. On the four crises in Kierkegaard's life, see Brita K. Stendahl, *Søren Kierkegaard* (Boston: Twayne, 1976), chapter 3.

though he was a loving father, he never lost the harshness of his childhood. He was raised a devout Moravian, but later in life worshipped in the Lutheran state church as well. He stressed the problem of sin, the need for personal conversion, and how Christ was a man of sorrows. He pressed his spiritual melancholy on his family—especially on Kierkegaard, who in many ways took after his father spiritually. Therefore it was a sure and certain trauma when Kierkegaard learned that his father had cursed God when so many of his family members had died—and also that his sister Maren had been born just six months or so after his father had married Ane, his housemaid. These moral and spiritual lapses weighed heavily upon Kierkegaard. So he rebelled against his father. But when his father died in 1838, Kierkegaard restored his admiration for him and his harsh brand of Christianity—and saw in his death a sacrifice that enabled him to start living his own life. He therefore fought in all of his writings to set Christianity straight—adding terror to its blessings (CD 175), and severity to its mildness (JP 3:2873). Kierkegaard also received a considerable fortune from the estate of his father ($400,000 U. S. dollars by 2001 standards)—who had become a successful business man after moving to Copenhagen.

Kierkegaard excelled at the University of Copenhagen—receiving his doctorate in 1841. He defended his dissertation in Latin and then published it under the title, *The Concept of Irony, With Continual Reference to Socrates*. He also studied to become a Lutheran pastor but never was ordained. He wrote many sermons or "upbuilding discourses" as he liked to call them, but preached few of them in church—believing he was "without authority" to do so (WA 99). In preparation for his theological exams, he memorized all twenty eight articles of the 1530 revered Lutheran document, the *Augsburg Confession* (LD 447). So even though he never was ordained, he was still very serious about the ordained ministry.

HIS FIANCÉE: THE SECOND CRISIS[10]

During this time he was also engaged to Regine Olsen (1822–1904), who was but seventeen years old. Their engagement lasted a year, with Kierkegaard breaking it off on August 11, 1841. He never got over his love for her and in the end bequeathed all that was left of his estate to her. Their breaking up was traumatic for a number of reasons—not the least of which was that engagements at that time were usually only broken due to infidelity, which was not the reason in their case. Kierkegaard never gave an unambiguous reason for breaking off his engagement with Regine, but it most likely was due to his fear that his intense personality would destroy her.[11]

---

10. See also Appendix 2 below, "On Regine Olsen."

11. On Regine's guilt for the broken engagement, see Walter W. Sikes, *On Becoming the Truth: An Introduction to the Life and Thought of Søren Kierkegaard* (Saint Louis, Missouri: The Bethany Press, 1968), 37–38: "She rebuked herself in her old age, . . . because she had not taken the initiative in arriving at a full understanding with him. She wrote: 'Since his death, it has seemed to me as if it were

After this painful separation his writing career began in earnest—producing some twenty-eight books and a three thousand page journal within a short fifteen year period. His books were written in many difference styles with many of them being published under pseudonyms with his own name appearing on the title page as the publisher—which left no question that Kierkegaard was the author of the pseudonyms. But he liked the pseudonyms for the freedom they gave him to explore challenging ideas—even though they, on purpose, gave him no anonymity. His pseudonyms were odd, suggestive and sometimes funny: Victor Eremita, Johannes Climacus, Anti-Climacus, Vigilius Haufniensis, Constantin Constantius, Johannes de silento, Hilarius Bookbinder, Frater Taciturnis, William Afham, Nicolaus Notabene, Inter et Inter, and A Married Man.[12] Only the last half of his books were taken up by a publisher. Kierkegaard paid for the publication of his first books—noting that

> to be an author—unless one is . . . in connection with a public office—is about the poorest paid, the least secure, and just about the most thankless job there is. If there is some individual who has the capacity of being an author and if he is also fortunate enough to have private means, then he becomes an author more or less at his own expense. This, however, is quite appropriate; there is nothing more to be said about it. In that way the individual in his work will love . . . the cause he serves. (PV 5)

During these busy years of writing, his servant Anders C. Westergaard kept his home set at an exact 57° F, just as Kierkegaard wanted. Kierkegaard did not hole up in his fairly luxurious home as was his inclination, but walked about town for hours, talking to anyone who passed by—and then writing by night alone at home. Wiling away his daylight hours on the streets and in the cafes made him look like anything but a serious author. So when his complicated, dense books on weighty topics were published, they caught the public off guard—wounding them indirectly "from behind," as he would say (CD 223–33). He thought this stealth tactic was the only way to get through to his readers and crack their encrusted indifference to what he had to say.

---

a duty I had neglected from cowardice; a duty not only towards him, but towards God, to whom he sacrificed me, whether he did it from an innate tendency to self-torment . . . or whether, as I think time and the results of his work will show, from a higher call from God." Regine later married Privy Councilor, Johan Frederik Schlegel (1817–96). Even so, Regine remembered all her life Kierkegaard's words to her: "Look, Regine, there is no such thing as marriage in eternity [Matthew 22:30]; there both Schlegel and I will be able to rejoice in being together with you." George Pattison, *Anxious Angels: A Retrospective View of Religious Existentialism* (New York: Saint Martin's, 1999), 29.

12. On Kierkegaard's dual authorship, see M. Jamie Ferreira, *Kierkegaard*, Blackwell Great Minds (London: Wiley-Blackwell, 2009), 4: "[Kierkegaard] wrote from [the] beginning to end of his career two parallel sets of quit different kinds of writings . . . . [One] set of texts was written under a variety of ingenious pseudonyms, and a second set, . . . written in his own name."

Appendix 1

JOURNALISTS: THE THIRD CRISIS

In the midst of this flurry of publications, Kierkegaard entered into a controversy on the pages of the satirical Copenhagen tabloid, *The Corsair*. After receiving good reviews in *The Corsair*—especially for his books *Either/Or* and *Stages on Life's Way*—Kierkegaard decided in 1845 to end his most favored status and attack the editor, Meir Aaron Goldschmidt, and *The Corsair's* chief writer, Peder Ludvig Møller, so that he would be pilloried[13] in the same way that the other victims of *The Corsair* had unfairly been in his eyes. In Kierkegaard's shot across the bow, he wrote that "*The Corsair's* corrupt cleverness, along with its hidden helpers—producers and peddlers of pandering witticisms—must and should be ignored literarily just as public prostitutes should be ignored civically" (COR 47). With the aid of the biting caricaturist, Klaestrup, Goldschmidt and Møller returned the insults—and the war of words was on. Kierkegaard fought back and in the end got what he wanted—an embattled social image for himself and the ruin of his two opponents, Goldschmidt and Møller.

HIS CHURCH: THE FOURTH CRISIS

After the death of his father's friend, Bishop Jacob Peter Mynster (1775–1854), on January 30, 1854, Kierkegaard unleashed a merciless attack on the state church of Denmark during the last eighteen months of his life. It was spurred on by the praise bestowed upon Mynster at his funeral for being one, in a long line of courageous Christians, who had "witnessed to the truth" (TM 3–15).[14] Kierkegaard was outraged by this honor claiming that it defamed the memory of all the great martyrs of the Church down through the centuries. They, after all, were the true witnesses, against which all subsequent Christians were to be judged. And if Bishop Mynster was to be evaluated in that way, no one in their right mind would praise him as a witness to the truth—since he lived such a soft life of plenty and ease (FSE 22–23, 80, JFY 200–1, TM 110–11). But this did not happen because those martyrs were not respected as

13. On this mistreatment, Kierkegaard notes: "What I as a public person am suffering is best described as a slow death, like being trampled to death by geese, or like pettiness's painful method of execution used in distant lands: being cast to the insects, and the offender is first smeared with honey to whet the insects' appetite—and in the same way my reputation is the honey which really whets the insects' appetite" (JP 6:6906).

14. Unlike Bishop Mynster, a true Christian witness "is a person whose life from first to last is unfamiliar with everything called enjoyment, . . . on the contrary, from first to last it was initiated into everything called suffering [and] into spiritual trials, into anxieties of soul, into torments of spirit; . . . in poverty witnesses for the truth, in poverty, in lowliness and abasement, is so unappreciated, hated [Jn 15:19], detested, so mocked, insulted, laughed to scorn. . . . For him there was never advancement and promotion except in reverse, step by step downward. . . . A truth-witness . . . is flogged [Heb 11:35–38], mistreated, dragged from one prison to another, . . . then finally is crucified or beheaded [Mt 14:10] or burned or broiled on a grill, his lifeless body thrown away . . . into a remote place, unburied . . . or burned to ashes and cast to the winds so that every trace of this 'refuse' [1 Cor 4:13] . . . might be obliterated" (TM 5–6).

Kierkegaard had hoped for. This cut him to the heart. So he fought back vehemently, publishing sharp brief articles in the newspapers, *The Moment* and *The Fatherland*. For this he was hated throughout Denmark because Bishop Mynster was such a beloved prelate.[15] From this confrontation we learn that when

> the Christian witness ceases to astonish the world, it will be a sign the church has lost its mission. The church is not established to make it easier to become a Christian, but harder. Beware, then, when the church appears to triumph in the world and it is fashionable again to be a Christian. That will be the sign the church has lost its militancy, which is to say its proper mode of existence.[16]

DYING WITHOUT HOLY COMMUNION

On October 2, 1855, shortly after he finished writing his tenth article for *The Moment*, Kierkegaard "was struck down in the street with paralysis of his legs. He was taken by carriage first to his home, where he then asked to be transported to Frederik's Hospital. Two weeks prior to this, he had fainted at a party and again the following day whilst getting dressed at home."[17] On October 19, his brother Peter, now a bishop in the church, came to see him after traveling quite a distance. But Kierkegaard turned him away—despising pastors as he did, believing that most of them, including his brother, did not "care a fig for [the] imitation" of the Savior Jesus Christ (TM 323). He believed that pastors were guilty of performing millions of spiritual "abortions" on the very people they were to care for and protect spiritually (JP 4:4942). He believed

---

15. Kierkegaard was also hated because he blew the whistle on the state church. For a study on how whistleblowers are abused, see C. Fred Alford, *Whistleblowers: Broken Lives and Organized Power* (Ithaca: Cornell University Press, 2001). Note especially how the strategy of "nuts and sluts" is used to discredit them so that "their claims [might be] ignored by finding them to be emotionally disturbed or morally suspect" (104–5).

16. *The Witness of Kierkegaard: Selected Writings From Kierkegaard on How to Become a Christian*, ed. Carl Michalson (New York: Association, 1960), 126–27. On this struggle, see also Murray Rae, *Kierkegaard and Theology* (London and New York: T. & T. Clark, 2010), 180: "Kierkegaard speaks . . . of the cost to be borne by those who follow Christ—the cost in venturing out beyond the security of objective certainties, worldly possessions, finite aspirations and society's approval. These must be let go in order to become contemporary with Christ. The biggest obstacle to such discipleship, the greatest hindrance to communion with Christ and with one's neighbor, is simply sin. That concept does not enjoy the popularity that Kierkegaard himself does. But Kierkegaard would not be surprised." And that is because, as Kierkegaard notes in his journals, "I have to concentrate all my earnestness solely on this—that I am a sinner" (JP 4:4038)! And regarding this divestment, see Philippians 3:8. Kierkegaard laments, regarding this verse: "[How] many have the capacity to think the triumphant reverseness of bold confidence that is implied in this statement" (UDVS 332)? He also, however, exclaims: "Who has more: the one who has God and also something else, or the one who, deprived of everything else, has God alone? Surely the latter, since 'all else is loss' [Phil 3:8]. . . . [So praise] be all the persecution, the scorn, the mockery that taught him, that compelled him, to be alone with God, to have God only—how blessed to suffer mockery for a good cause!" (CD 225).

17. Michael Watts, *Kierkegaard* (Oxford: Oneworld, 2003), 53.

pastors were sly soul-sellers (TM 169–71).They were more concerned with feathering their own nests than with proclaiming the unpopular truth about God in Christ Jesus—which demands dying to the world and the slaying of ones will (JP 4:4384). Later he even refused Holy Communion from his pastor and friend, Emil Boesen (1812–81), saying that he would only receive the sacrament from a layman. Since that was banned by church law, he died without Holy Communion on November 11, 1855 in Frederik's Hospital. The cause of death was probably tuberculosis of the spine marrow.[18] His refusal to receive the sacrament, however, does not mean that he died a crushed man—despondent and forlorn. For despite his circumstances, the joy of Christ (JP 2:2183; UDVS 229; TM 271) never departed from him. One of Kierkegaard's nephews makes this point in his report on a visit to him shortly before Kierkegaard died:

> When I extended my hand to him, the others [who were visiting him with me] already turned toward the door [to leave], so it was as though we were alone. He took my hand in both of his own—how small, thin, and transparently white they were—and said only: "Thank you for coming to see me, Troels! And now live well!" But these ordinary words were accompanied by a look of which I have never since seen the equal. It radiated with an elevated, transfigured, blessed brilliance, so that it seemed to me to illuminate the entire room. Everything was concentrated in the flood of light from these eyes: profound love, beatifically dissolved sadness, an all-penetrating clarity, and a playful smile. For me it was like a heavenly revelation, an emanation from one soul to another, a blessing, which infused me with new courage, strength, and responsibility. . . . [For me, this was] an encounter with a spirit which was transfigured and ready to depart . . . into the peace for which he had so deeply longed.[19]

At his funeral his brother Peter gave the eulogy and implied that Kierkegaard was not of sound mind toward the end of his life and so his attack on the church should not be taken seriously. On the way to the grave, the funeral procession was abruptly stopped by another one of Kierkegaard's nephews, Henrik Lund (1825–89). He cried out that the funeral was a sham and that it proved that Kierkegaard's attack on the church was exactly on target. Perhaps because of Henrik's outburst,

> Peter felt deep guilt concerning his behavior towards Søren, and it haunted him until his death. He had inherited Kierkegaard's estate, which Regine had

---

18. See Jens Staubrand, *Søren Kierkegaard's Illness and Death* (1989), trans. Gwyn Hodgson (Søren Kierkegaard Cultural Production, 2009), 56: "Kierkegaard's illness [was] pulmonary tuberculosis which spread to the spinal canal. In other words, it was a case of spondylitis tuberculosa: a tuberculous inflammation in the lumbar vertebra, a collapse of this and thereby a compression of the spinal cord."

19. The nephew was Troels Frederik Troels-Lund (1840–1921). See *Encounters With Kierkegaard: A Life as Seen by His Contemporaries*, ed. trans. Bruce H. Kirmmse, with Virginia R. Laursen (Princeton: Princeton University Press, 1996), 190.

declined, but later he donated to charity the money that had accumulated from the royalties inherited from the sales of new editions of Søren's books, of which two were published by Peter. He decided finally that he no longer deserved to be a Bishop and that perhaps he never had, . . . and resigned in 1875. In 1879 he returned all his royal decorations to the government and in 1883 he sent a letter to the Probate Court [which] began with the text of 1 John 3:15, "Anyone who hates his brother is a murderer, and you know that no murderer has eternal life abiding in him." Finally, in 1884, he renounced his legal right to take care of his own affairs, thus assuming the legal status of a child, and died a ward of the State on February 24, 1888, age eighty-two, in the darkness of insanity.[20]

THE WRITTEN KIERKEGAARD

Some hope that "in our day there will arise another Kierkegaard to point the way."[21] But he is already here among us—"in an almost eerie way"[22]—through his profound, unsettling and always relevant writings—that somehow remain "inexhaustibly rewarding."[23] For they not only continue to "knock the conceit" out of us,[24] but they also clearly and passionately point us in the direction of the Savior Jesus Christ— through whom we alone are "delivered from the obsession with [our] own worthiness or unworthiness."[25]

20. Michael Watts, *Kierkegaard*, 55.

21. Walter Sundberg, "The Therapy of Adversity and Penitence," in *Limning the Psyche*, ed. Robert C. Roberts and Mark R. Talbot (Grand Rapids: Eerdmans, 1997), 293.

22. Lee C. Barrett, III, *Kierkegaard* (Nashville: Abingdon, 2010), 73.

23. Howard V. Hong, "Three Score Years with Kierkegaard's Writings," *Kierkegaard Studies*, ed. Niels Jørgen Cappelørn and Hermann Deuser (Berlin and New York: Walter de Gruyter, 1997), 7.

24. Humphrey Carpenter, *W. H. Auden: A Biography* (Boston: Houghton Mifflin, 1981), 285.

25. Walter W. Sikes, *On Becoming the Truth*, 179.

FIGURE 6: Anders Stengaard (1990),
one of Kierkegaard's last known living relatives.

Appendix 1

Part 2

A Critique of Garff's Biography

Kierkegaard, in a fit of disgust, once imagined pulling his bishop, Jacob Mynster, from the pulpit and replacing him with something like a music box.[1] This machine would then play the words of the sermon without the bishop having to be there.

The advantage for Kierkegaard in this was that he did not have to wonder any more whether Bishop Mynster practiced what he preached. The music box sermon would put an end to that. It's just a machine, after all, and cannot be expected to follow Christ. So the music box gets Mynster off the hook. Also Kierkegaard would not have to be infuriated by all the bishop's phoniness any more for he would not be there.

But this cannot be! No such solution is really possible. This reverie then, is nothing but pure sarcasm. Music box preachers cannot be Christian. Christians are expected to practice what they preach—as best as they can—painful though it may be. "Count the cost,"[2] the Lord Jesus warned all who would follow him or preach in his name. A music box in the pulpit cannot circumvent that responsibility so easily. Christians are expected to "share Christ's sufferings."[3] And so an easy life freed of suffering is doomed.[4]

Kierkegaard makes this point well. If Christians do not struggle to practice their faith in Christ "in the middle of the daily hustle and bustle of the workday,"[5] then they are good for nothing. People can still call themselves Christian, but it is only a delusion—or even a deception. For indeed "it is very easy to know what Christianity is, but exceedingly difficult to become a Christian."[6]

---

1. Joakim Garff, *Søren Kierkegaard: A Biography* (2000), trans. Bruce H. Kirmmse (Princeton: Princeton University Press, 2005), 655. Note that in the 2007 paperback edition of this translation it says "as a result of various suggestions . . . a number of minor changes and corrections" have been made (xxiv).

2. Lk 14:28 (RSV).

3. 1 Pt 4:13 (RSV).

4. See Mt 7:13.

5. Joakim Garff, *Søren Kierkegaard: A Biography*, 658, 693.

6. Walter Lowrie, *Kierkegaard* (New York: Oxford, 1938), 293.

Appendix 1

KIERKEGAARD'S BOSWELL

In Joakim Garff's new monumental 867 page biography on Kierkegaard, *Søren Kierkegaard: A Biography*, he recounts this episode with charm. Of the music box image Garff says, "Kierkegaard was simply beside himself with delight. . . . The noncommittal chattiness of a music box was a perfect parody of Mynster's art of preaching."[7]

In Garff—it has already been said—Kierkegaard has finally found "his Boswell."[8] This is a biography rich in detail, beautiful in its expanse, suspenseful in its narration, and amply sprinkled with fresh insights to old historical problems. For instance, Kierkegaard is actually closer to his pseudonyms than he admits.[9] Kierkegaard actually is not an introvert.[10] Kierkegaard's prodigious output was probably due in part to suffering from hypergraphia.[11] His delight in his famous convoluted writing style may have had erotic overtones.[12] His ill health and early death may have stemmed from epilepsy.[13] And he broke off his engagement with Regine Olsen because he feared his "excesses" would hurt her.[14]

In addition, Bruce H. Kirmmse has rendered the original Danish edition of this biography into beautiful English. One of my favorite passages is Kirmmse's translation of the stunning section from *Stages on Life's Way* in praise of the Danish language.[15] This page says as much about thinking in any language as it does about the glories of Danish. It deserves to be read aloud to a favorite fellow traveler.

But all does not go swimmingly for Kierkegaard's Boswell. Already Garff has drawn fire for his deconstructive bent.[16] Deconstructionists insist that there is no "overarching scheme" in Kierkegaard's writings.[17] So Garff will not take Kierkegaard at his word—supposing him to be a cagey fellow[18]—filled with irony, wit and even personal pique at times.[19] On this account, Kierkegaard is an "effervescent wit, . . . a mercurial ironist, . . . a seductive philosophical artist."[20] This view turns ostensibly

7. Joakim Garff, *Søren Kierkegaard: A Biography*, 656.

8. Gordon Marino, "The Anxiety of His Influence," *The Wall Street Journal* (February 3, 2005), D8.

9. Joakim Garff, *Søren Kierkegaard: A Biography*, 268, 363, 633.

10. Ibid., 312, 323, 576.

11. Ibid., 458.

12. Ibid., 138, 190, 350, 456, 556, 601.

13. Ibid., 784.

14. Ibid., 250.

15. Ibid., 337.

16. See Sylvia Walsh, "Reading Kierkegaard With Kierkegaard Against Garff," *Søren Kierkegaard Newsletter* 38 (July 1999), 4–8; Jonathan Lear, "Other Names for Kierkegaard: The Problematic Lives of Søren Kierkegaard," *The Times Literary Supplement* (January 28, 2005): 4; Gregory R. Beabout, "Kierkegaard's Voices," *First Things*, No. 154 (June/July 2005): 48.

17. *The New Kierkegaard*, ed. E. Jegstrup (Bloomington: Indiana University Press, 2003), 9.

18. Joakim Garff, *Søren Kierkegaard: A Biography*, 532.

19. Ibid., 394, 498, 515.

20. *Kierkegaard: A Critical Reader*, ed. J. Rée & J. Chamberlain (Oxford: Blackwell, 1998), 1.

clear sentences into suspicious ploys. Kierkegaard at times may then even be seen to mean the opposite of what he says. So in his criticism of Adler, for instance, he is really taking aim at himself.[21] Or when he says that he has been a religious author all along, he has not been.[22] Kierkegaard is much more of a *literati* than a Christian preacher or theologian—regardless of his own avowals.

GARFF'S MISTAKEN CRITIQUE

These and other biographical points will no doubt receive continued lively debate.[23] For me, however, what matters most is Garff's critique of Kierkegaard's theology. For Garff, Kierkegaard's view of Christianity is marked by an "*odium generis humani*, a hatred of everything human."[24] This view of "the later Kierkegaard," "this abnormally developed 'egoity,' has emerged out of an extreme intensification of the thesis that subjectivity is truth. What has been lost is the dialectical dynamic that had issued from the *antithesis*—in which subjectivity is *un*truth. It is not Kierkegaard who is mad, it is his theology, and this is attributable precisely to the loss of this dialectical dimension."[25] According to Garff, this theological madness is rooted in Kierkegaard's "one-sidedness."[26] In Kierkegaard there is much pain, sorrow and outrage, but little joy, confidence and community.

But surely this cannot be so. This is not a compelling explanation for Kierkegaard's supposed lopsidedness. For there could just as well be a subjectivity that delights in the human—as with certain forms of humanists and Epicureans, for instance. No, this hard view on humans comes from the New Testament itself. Here Kierkegaard's contemporary and critic, Nikolai Grundtvig (1783–1872) hits the nail on the head. Kierkegaard's extremism, Grundtvig argues, is rooted in his "backward way of thinking, according to which *the book*, 'the New Testament,' is supposedly the true source of *Christianity*, its *foundation*, or its *rule of faith*."[27] Not surprisingly then, Kierkegaard writes: "To live such a way that one works more strenuously than any compulsory laborer and in the process puts money into the project; to amount to nothing; to be ridiculed, and so forth. For the great mass of people, living like this must seem to be a kind of madness; in any case, most people will feel that this is alien

---

21. Joakim Garff, *Søren Kierkegaard: A Biography*, 453, 557.

22. Ibid., 552, 558.

23. See Jonathan Lear, "Other Names for Kierkegaard," 3; Beabout, "Kierkegaard's Voices," 48–49; and C. Stephen Evans, "Kierkegaard Among the Biographers," *Books & Culture* 13 (July/August 2007): 12–13.

24. Joakim Garff, *Søren Kierkegaard: A Biography*, 714 and 766, 779, 796.

25. Ibid., 715.

26. Ibid., 794. Contra Søren Kierkegaard, *Spiritual Writings: Gift, Creation, Love*, trans. George Pattison (New York: HarperCollins, 2010), xviii.

27. Ibid., 768.

and will look upon such a way of living as alien. The truth, however, is that this sort of life is a life lived in relation to the Christianity of the New Testament" (TM 257).[28]

This high, exalted, demanding view of Christianity[29] comes not from some crazy, rampant subjectivity, but rather from the pages of the New Testament itself—viewed as "biblical simplicity."[30] But not everybody reads the Bible in this extreme way. Whence cometh then Kierkegaard's reading? Was he *sui generis*?

KIERKEGAARD AS A LUTHERAN

No, his reading came from Lutheranism—with its ties to "the classic Christian tradition."[31] Kierkegaard was a Lutheran. Garff makes too little of the fact[32] that Kierkegaard committed to memory all twenty-eight articles of the *Augustana* (LD 447)—the chief document in the Lutheran Confessions. In those confessions it says that the Bible is "the pure and clear fountain of Israel, which is the only true norm according to which all teachers and teachings are to be judged" (BC 503–4). And in the Bible there is nothing but law and gospel, which are designed "to terrify and to justify and quicken the terrified" (BC 189). This terrifying, exclusive view of Holy Scripture makes the Christian faith "difficult" (BC 161) having been born of "a great battle in the human heart" (BC 154). Therefore Christians should not hope to "live a nice, soft life" (BC 392). Fasting and other bodily disciplines are to "be practiced continually" (BC 69). Realizing that we "deserve nothing but punishment" also follows quickly (BC 347). This makes life nothing but "a world of sorrow" (BC 348).

Furthermore, these confessions say that Martin Luther is our "most eminent teacher" (BC 576). Kierkegaard drives that point home by saying that "Luther is the truest figure," second only to Jesus himself (JP 3:2898)—a stunning line Garff does not share with his readers. So when Luther says "the world is one big whorehouse,"[33] Kierkegaard would agree. When Luther says "all bishops nowadays are of the devil,"[34] Kierkegaard would agree. And when Luther says "faith takes no holidays,"[35] "what is of God must be crucified in the world,"[36] "preference must be given to truth" over friends,[37] "we have no greater enemy than ourselves,"[38] Kierkegaard would agree again.

---

28. Ibid., 755.
29. Ibid., 740, 770.
30. Ibid., 403.
31. Beabout, "Kierkegaard's Voices," 48.
32. Joakim Garff, *Søren Kierkegaard: A Biography*, 153.
33. Martin Luther, "The Sermon on the Mount" (1532), LW 21:180.
34. Martin Luther, "Lectures on Titus" (1527), LW 29:17.
35. Martin Luther, "Preface to Romans" (1546), LW 35:378.
36. Martin Luther, "Lectures on Romans" (1518), LW 25:177.
37. Martin Luther, "Lectures on Genesis 1–5" (1535), LW 1:122.
38. Martin Luther, "An Exposition of the Lord's Prayer" (1519), LW 42:48.

And when Luther also says that "this life is not a life . . . but a mortification and vexation of life,"[39] that we should "neither fear death nor love this life,"[40] "love of oneself . . . is always wrong,"[41] "the majority remains blind,"[42] the gospel makes Christians "sleepy and secure" when they wrongfully suppose "there is no further need to do anything, give anything, or suffer anything,"[43] "Christians are few and far between,"[44] "reason is the devil's prostitute,"[45] the believer "hangs between heaven and earth, . . . suspended in the air and crucified,"[46] and is "lonely in the faith,"[47] Kierkegaard would also agree. And when Luther says that "the life of a Christian is as hard as if he were walking on . . . nothing but razors,"[48] "there is no life . . . on earth more wretched than that of a Christian,"[49] "a counterfeit faith . . . does not produce a new man, but leaves him in his former opinion and way of life,"[50] Christians who mock God "have been baptized in vain,"[51] the clarity of the Bible "ensures the victory over all evasive subtleties,"[52] those who reject God's attack on sin "show plainly that they are really damnable knaves,"[53] "baptism has made the repose, ease, and prosperity of this life a very poison . . . to its work,"[54] "a Christian is uplifted in adversity, because he trusts God; he is downcast in prosperity, because he fears God,"[55] and that martyrdom helps Christians "receive salvation"[56]—to all these and many more like them, Kierkegaard would say yes, yes, and yes. For indeed "Luther is . . . the master of us all" (JP 3:2465)—another remarkable line Garff leaves out.

39. Martin Luther, "Lectures on Genesis 45–50" (1545), LW 8:114.

40. Martin Luther, "Treatise on Good Works" (1520), LW 44:85.

41. Martin Luther, "Lectures on Galatians 1–6" (1519), LW 27:356.

42. Martin Luther, "Lectures on Genesis 6–14" (1536), LW 2:354.

43. Martin Luther, "Sermon at Coburg on the Cross and Suffering" (1530), LW 51:207.

44. Martin Luther, "Temporal Authority" (1523), LW 45:91.

45. Martin Luther, "Against the Heavenly Prophets" (1525), LW 40:175.

46. Martin Luther, "Lectures on Hebrews" (1518), LW 29:185.

47. Martin Luther, "Commentary on Seven Penitential Psalms" (1525), LW 14:181. And because Luther also preached this, Kierkegaard could further say of him: "[What] a relief to read Luther. There is a man who can really stay by a person and preach him farther out instead of backwards" (JP 3:2464).

48. Martin Luther, "Sermon on the Mount" (1532), LW 21:245.

49. Martin Luther, "Commentary on 1 Corinthians 15" (1534), LW 28:106.

50. Martin Luther, "Lectures on Galatians 1–6" (1535), LW 26:269.

51. Martin Luther, "Lectures on Hebrews" (1518), LW 29:138.

52. Martin Luther, "The Bondage of the Will" (1526), LW 33:186.

53. Martin Luther, "Appeal for Prayer Against the Turks" (1541), LW 43:228.

54. Martin Luther, "The Holy and Blessed Sacrament of Baptism" (1519), LW 35:39.

55. Martin Luther, "Lectures on Galatians 1–6" (1519), LW 27:403.

56. Martin Luther, "Sermon for Epiphany on Matthew 2:1–12" (1522), LW 52:277.

Appendix 1

KIERKEGAARD'S HEAVENLY WHORES[57]

No wonder then that Kierkegaard so viciously attacked bishops and pastors. No wonder he imagined replacing Bishop Mynster with a music box, of all things![58] By pulling back on the hard lines of the New Testament and Lutheranism, church leaders were falsifying Christianity and depriving the world of salvation. As such, they were performing millions of spiritual "abortions" (JP 4:4942), blabbering Christianity "down into something meaningless, into being spiritless impotence, suffocated in illusion" (JP 6:6943)! So he bitterly—and rightly so—says that pastors "are from the point of view of eternity what public prostitutes are in temporality" (JP 6:6254). Nothing but heavenly whores! Pastors are "perfectly trained to introduce Christianity in such a way that it means nothing. . . . How disgusting! It would be fine if a barber could become so perfect he could shave off beards so lightly one would not notice it—but with respect to what is explicitly designed to deal a wound, to become so skilled in introducing it that it is as far as possible unnoticeable—this is nauseating" (JP 6:6860).

And what is that wound? It is that part of the New Testament message about "dying to the world, voluntary renunciation, crucifying the flesh, [and] suffering for the doctrine" (JP 6:6947).

This stridency does not make Kierkegaard's theology crazy or "irrational"[59] as Garff supposes. It only brings it into touch with the genuine sources of Christianity which have been obscured by the enculturation of Christianity—in what Kierkegaard contemptuously called Christendom or "mild Christianity" (JP 2:1882).

Neither does it make it anti-clerical.[60] Nor does it call for the end of the Church![61] Kierkegaard's "entire witness," after all, makes it plain that even his "leaving of the church was motivated not by the search for a *churchless Christianity* but for a truly *Christian church.*"[62]

KIERKEGAARD'S MILITANT CHURCH

What Kierkegaard wanted was for the phony church triumphant of Christendom to be replaced with a genuine militant church. "The Church triumphant and established Christendom are untruth, are the worst tragedy that can befall the Church, are its downfall and also its punishment, since, after all, this can happen only through its

57. This section is based on my "Kierkegaard's Heavenly Whores," *Dialog* 31 (Summer 1992): 227–30.

58. Joakim Garff, *Søren Kierkegaard: A Biography*, 655.

59. Beabout, "Kierkegaard's Voices," 48.

60. Joakim Garff, *Søren Kierkegaard: A Biography*, 329, 788.

61. Ibid., 623, 759, 791. For this same premature ecclesiastical obituary, see Alastair Hannay, *Kierkegaard: A Biography* (New York: Cambridge University Press, 2001), 425.

62. Vernard Eller, *Kierkegaard and Radical Christianity: A New Perspective* (Princeton: Princeton University Press, 1968), 31.

own fault" (PC 232). Christ wants a smaller, leaner, tougher church that fights the good fight of faith (1 Tm 6:12). The "only . . . possible rescue" for Christianity is "rigorousness" (PC 228). For Christendom "swelled up in unhealthy fat, almost nauseatingly expanded in carnal obesity" (PC 230). The narrow way of Matthew 7:14 must return and with it the enmity with the world in James 4:4 (PC 224). The Church can only be triumphant after the world ends.

Kierkegaard's arresting image for the true church in this life is that of a band of criminals. In this church, "each Christian . . . by staking his life on the absurd has said farewell to the world, has broken with the world. The society of those who have voluntarily placed themselves outside society in the usual sense of the word is all the more intimate precisely because each one individually feels isolated in 'the world.' But just as the company of criminals must carefully watch out that no one comes into the society who is not branded as they are, so also in the society of Christians: they must watch out that no one comes into this society except the one whose mark is that he is polemical to the utmost toward society in the usual sense. This means that the Christian congregation is a society consisting of qualitative individuals and that the intimacy of the society is also conditioned by this polemical stance against the great human society" (JP 4:4175).

And who will lead such a militant, polemical church? Surely not pastors who say: I depend "artistically on what gifts of eloquence I have, . . . on whether I have a good voice, how my clerical gown fits, how much of the most recent philosophy I have studied" (PC 216). No, it will need pastors "who possessing the desirable scientific-scholarly education, yet in contrast to the scientific game of counting, are practiced in what could be called spiritual guerrilla skirmishing, in doing battle not so much with scientific-scholarly attacks and problems as with the human passions; pastors who are able to split up 'the crowd' and turn it into individuals; . . . pastors who are disciplined and educated and are prepared to obey and to suffer, so they would be able to mitigate, admonish, build up, move, but also to constrain—not with force, anything but, no, constrain by their own obedience, and above all patiently, to suffer all the rudeness of the sick without being disturbed, no more than the physician is disturbed by the patient's abusive language and kicks during the operation. For the generation is sick, spiritually, sick unto death" (JP 6:6256). This is the best elaboration of the suffering pastor in 2 Timothy 4:5 I have every read.

These genuine pastors will also practice consolation differently. "Contemporary American culture," for instance, "says, 'Let guilt be forgotten.' 'Let grief be short.' and 'Let suffering be avoided.' By contrast, to the guilty, Kierkegaard says, 'Do not run from your guilt. Gather it up into yourself and carry it with you.' To the grieving he says, 'Weep softly, but grieve long. Remember the dead, for it is a work of the freest, most unselfish, most faithful love (WL 355).' To those who suffer he says, '*Will* your suffering, accept it unto yourself, for suffering is the way of those who follow Christ.'"[63]

63. William Langsworth, "Kierkegaard and Pastoral Ministry," *Perkins Theological Journal* 36 (Fall 1983): 4.

Appendix 1

BLIND PROFESSORS

It has been said that Garff's very long biography needs yet another chapter on Kierkegaard's influence on the generations that followed him.[64] I would think instead that something of an epilogue is needed to explore Kierkegaard's disgust for professors—especially those who would study him after his death (JP 6:6872, 2:2232)—of which Garff is one. Kierkegaard said they don't have lives of their own, but "live off" their subject matter (JP 3:3583). This writing makes them "stupid" about life—having not struggled to make a way for themselves (JP 3:3594). They hide behind "big books" (JP 3:3597). Worst of all, scholars can't possibly understand a Christian subject, since "the essentially Christian thing to do is not to write but to exist" (JP 6:6840).

So when Kierkegaard says that God inspired his writing or lead and "governed" him, making him into a "ghostwriter" for God,[65] this is deemed an "imposition."[66] Garff thinks Kierkegaard's concern could easily—and more simply—be reduced to "language itself, which . . . always extends beyond the person who writes in it, and . . . by means of grammatical rules—can keep a writer within certain channels and perhaps even point him in a quite specific direction"[67]—thereby effectively replacing God with grammatical rules!

Garff clearly will not allow his religious subject to be religious. Kierkegaard's faith does not make sense to him and needs a good shave with Occam's razor. But it is difficult to read this without thinking that "Garff has become impatient with his subject and has started to patronize him."[68] If Garff had paid more attention to Kierkegaard's critique of academics, his biography would have been better on matters religious. He might even then have concluded that Kierkegaard is "overwhelmingly Christian."[69]

But as it stands, Christianity is ironically this biography's weakest link. Garff seems to use his literary and historical acumen to buffer himself from Christianity. This is not at all surprising, especially if critical thinking wants any way it can to "dislodge the contingent, de facto supports that our daily life depends upon."[70]

Kierkegaard attacked this intellectual ploy with the image of a naughty boy about to get a good whipping. In order to cunningly defend himself against the licking, he puts "a napkin or more under his pants" to pad his rear from the sting of the whip. Just so, the scholar shoves in "one layer after another" of scholarly research to keep the

64. John Updike, "Incommensurability: A New Biography of Kierkegaard," *The New Yorker* (March 28, 2005): 76.

65. Joakim Garff, *Søren Kierkegaard: A Biography*, 556.

66. Ibid., 557.

67. Ibid., 557.

68. Jonathan Lear, "Other Names for Kierkegaard," 4.

69. Robert B. Scheidt, *Kierkegaard the Christian: An Anthology of Quotations* (Enumclaw Washington: WinePress, 2003), 17.

70. Robert Fogelin, *Walking the Tightrope of Reason: The Precarious Life of a Rational Animal* (New York: Oxford, 2003), 67.

claims of Christianity as far away as possible (FSE 35). Garff, as you would imagine, finds no place for this arresting image in his biography of the one he calls an aristocratic radical.[71]

GARFF'S FAILURE

But from beginning to the end, Kierkegaard knew what he wanted to say—even if the scholars doubt it—supposing such certainty comes from indefensible "blunt readings" of what Kierkegaard wrote.[72] Kierkegaard clearly wanted to show how Christianity is "hard to enter and hard to keep up; hard to understand and hard to explain; hard to believe and hard to live."[73] That is why it is only "in a paroxysm of terror that one confronts the essential truth of Christianity."[74]

And so Kierkegaard early on warned Christians not to be "captivated . . . by the joys of life or by its afflictions," so that at last one may "obtain eternal salvation," in spite of "the painful privations, the secret troubles, the sad longings, [and] the fearful trials" of this life (EUD 28). We suffer so because Christ truly is "not a savior for this life but for eternal life" (JP 6:6503). So we need God to "strengthen the weary, hearten the disheartened, lead back the straying, [and] give solace to the struggling" (UDVS 217).

At the end, Kierkegaard intensified Matthew 5:44 which says we are to love our enemies. Yes, we better love our enemies, he writes, because God, "humanly speaking," is our enemy and we surely are to love him anyway. So this verse is more about being reconciled to our contrarian God than settling human tribal animosities. God is indeed "our most appalling enemy" because he wants you "to die, to die to the world; he hates specifically that in which you naturally have your life, to which you cling with all your zest for life. . . . So terrible . . . is God in his love, so terrible . . . is it to be loved by God and to love God." Unable to stand this intensity, Christians turn God's love into "syrupy sweets." This bastardization is like turning a funeral march into "a vigorous gallop" on the basis of "poetic license" alone. Then this "vale of tears and prison" in which we live, is made into phony "delight and merriment." But this counterfeit, "glorious world" is nothing of the sort. In all seriousness it is only "the time of testing related to an accounting and judgment" (TM 177–79).

Because Garff's biography—for all its intriguing historical detail—lacks this seriousness, it is a blind guide to the one it rightly calls a "freelance prophet."[75]

---

71. Joakim Garff, *Søren Kierkegaard: A Biography*, 318.

72. Roger Poole, "The Unknown Kierkegaard" in *The Cambridge Companion to Kierkegaard*, ed. Alastair Hannay & Gordon D. Marino (New York: Cambridge University Press, 1998), 60.

73. William T. Riviere, *A Pastor Looks at Kierkegaard* (Grand Rapids: Zondervan, 1941), 64.

74. Josiah Thompson, *Kierkegaard* (New York: Knopf, 1973), 201.

75. Joakim Garff, *Søren Kierkegaard: A Biography*, 427.

APPENDIX 1

PART 3

A Lutheran Heritage

BARNETT'S BOOK ON THE influence of pietism on Kierkegaard,[1] joins those studies that go beyond the philosophical in his writings to the explicitly Christian. By so doing Barnett not only plunges into what Carter Lindberg calls "the vast swamp of Pietism studies,"[2] but also replaces Marie Thulstrup's monograph as the standard book in the field.[3]

Barnett's dense but well written book has six chapters, equally divided in two. The first part is a study of Danish pietism and the writers who influenced Kierkegaard—including Arndt, Spener, Francke, Zinzendorf, Tersteegen, Brorson and Hamann—as well as Tauler, Bernard of Clairvaux and Thomas à Kempis. In these discussions, Barnett deftly addresses difficulties in sanctification, holiness, separatism, humility,[4] mystical union,[5] rationalism,[6] imperceptibleness,[7] and legalism.[8]

In the second half, Barnett shows how Kierkegaard's writings have a pietistic context[9]—even though he opposes pietistic separatism.[10] He does this by examining sections of the *Postscript, Stages on Life's Way, Two Ages, Upbuilding Discourses in Various Spirits, Without Authority, Practice in Christianity* and *Judge For Yourself!* He argues for Kierkegaard's version of pietism driving him to the *imitatio Christi*, albeit

---

1. Christopher B. Barrett, *Kierkegaard, Pietism, and Holiness* (Farnham, Surry: Ashgate, 2011).

2. Jonathan Strom, "Review of *The Pietist Theologians*, ed. Carter Lindberg," *Lutheran Quarterly* 20 (Summer 2006), 215.

3. Marie Mikulová Thulstrup, *Kierkegaard og Pietismen* (Copenhagen: C. A. Reitzels Forlag, 1967).

4. Barrett, *Kierkegaard, Pietism, and Holiness*, 67, 69, 71n51, 85, 180–89.

5. Ibid., 82, 199.

6. Ibid., 92, 98–100.

7. Ibid., 82n129, 83, 157–67.

8. Ibid., 4, 42, 89–90. This judgment opposes the view that it is Hegel's philosophy that provides the context for what Kierkegaard wrote. On this alternative, see Jon Stewart, *Kierkegaard's Relation to Hegel Reconsidered* (Cambridge: Cambridge University Press, 2003), 32: "[There] are many more points of comparison and similarity between [Kierkegaard and Hegel] than are generally recognized."

9. Barrett, *Kierkegaard, Pietism, and Holiness*, 208.

10. Ibid., 90, 111.

in an inverted form, as "a likeness that does not presume identity with the beloved, but resembles the beloved in its absolute respect for alterity."[11]

It is hard to see, however, how this "absolute respect" is possible, given our deep incapacities. The same can also be said for our need for "absolute reliance on God's grace."[12] Barnett could have explained these stringent requirements better by going back to *The Gospel of Sufferings* and applying its notion of being "gripped" by Christ as a precondition for any following of him (UDVS 250).

I highly recommend Barnett's book, but I think he goes too far when he says that Kierkegaard's famous attack on Christendom was the "outcome" of the "corrective movement of Pietism"[13]—rather than coming from Martin Luther. I think he says this because he makes too much of Kierkegaard's point in *Two Ages* about the age of Luther, or of the hero, having come to an end (TA 89).[14] By making Kierkegaard so unlike Luther, he forgets that Kierkegaard thought Luther was, next to Jesus Christ, the truest Christian (JP 3:2898, 4:4549). He also forgets that Kierkegaard was a diligent student of Luther's sermons—even to the extent of reading them to himself aloud (JP 2:2416, 2:2485, 2:2492, 2:2516, 2530, 3:3496). And he did that because, as the *Postscript* says, "the strong pulse-beat of appropriation" is on every page of Luther (CUP 1:366).

So Luther had a large impact on Kierkegaard through his sermons.[15] This is true even though the influence of Socrates[16] and Hegel[17] on Kierkegaard is far better known and researched. But there is no doubt that Kierkegaard was adamant about Luther's sermons—reading his favorites ones out loud, to himself, "again and again" (JP 3:2485)."[18] And he also believed it would be good for church renewal "to take Luther's

---

11. Ibid., 199.

12. Ibid., 195.

13. Ibid., 206.

14. Ibid., 156.

15. On the general influence of Luther on Kierkegaard, see Craig Q. Hinkson, "Will the Real Luther Please Stand Up! Kierkegaard's View of Luther vs. the Evolving Perceptions of the Tradition," IKC 21:37–76; Hermann Deuser, "Kierkegaard and Luther: Kierkegaard's 'One Thesis,'" 205–14, *The Gift of Grace: The Future of Lutheran Theology*, ed. Niels Henrik Gregersen, Bo Helm, Ted Peters and Peter Widman (Minneapolis: Fortress, 2005); and David Yoon-Jung Kim and Joel D. S. Rasmussen, "Martin Luther: Reform, Secularization, and the Question of His 'True Successor,'" 173–217, *Kierkegaard and the Renaissance and Modern Tradition*, Tome II: Theology, ed. Jon Stewart (Surrey, England: Ashgate, 2009). See also the imaginative dialogue between Luther and Kierkegaard in Edna H. Hong, *Gayety of Grace* (Minneapolis: Augsburg, 1972).

16. See Benjamin Daise, *Kierkegaard's Socratic Art* (Macon, Georgia: Mercer University Press, 1999), Jacob Howland, *Kierkegaard and Socrates: A Study in Philosophy and Faith* (Cambridge: Cambridge University Press, 2006), and Peter Kreft, *Socrates Meets Kierkegaard: The Father of Philosophy Meets the Father of Christian Existentialism* (South Bend, Indiana: Saint Augustine's Press, 2013).

17. See Niels Thulstrup, *Kierkegaard's Relation to Hegel*, trans. George L. Stengren (Princeton: Princeton University Press, 1980); Mark C. Taylor, *Journeys to Selfhood: Hegel and Kierkegaard*, Second Edition (New York: Fordham University Press, 2000), and Jon Stewart, *Kierkegaard's Relations to Hegel Reconsidered*.

18. Luther also held his sermons, or *Postil*, in the highest regard. See his "That These Words of Christ, 'This Is My Body,' etc., Still Stand Firm Against the Fanatics" (1527), LW 37:147: "[The] best book I ever wrote [is] the *Postil*."

book of sermons and extract a great many sentences and ideas, . . . and publish them in order to show how far the preaching nowadays is from Christianity," so that his "exaggerations" could be seen as coming from Luther (JP 3:2516)![19]

Kierkegaard especially liked Luther's sermon on I Corinthians 15.[20] In his comments on it, Kierkegaard says that Luther "quite rightly, as usual, characterizes faith [as being] dialectically opposed to feeling (the qualification of immediacy)." This is important because without this dialectical treatment "the entire sphere of faith vanishes and with it Christianity" (JP 3:2532). Luther makes four points in this sermon about the dialectical relationship between faith and feelings that are foundational to Kierkegaard's understanding of Christianity.[21]

The first point is that faith cannot be sustained unless it makes its decisions "contrary to" what human wisdom "sees and feels [and] comprehends with the senses." This is because what we see around us does not confirm what we believe in. So when we believe against what we experience, we turn the wisdom of the world into "foolishness" for thinking that Christianity is "a stupid message." What Luther has in mind here is the belief in the resurrection of the dead in light of the fact that when we die we perish "more wretchedly than any beast or carcass."[22] This contentiousness of Luther's is also a hallmark of Kierkegaard's thought.

Luther's next point is that we cannot quietly slip away satisfied with this trumping of experience by faith. No, we must instead let these "two facts . . . stand side by side"—dialectically—namely, that we are "lords over devil and death and that we at the same time lie prostrate at their feet. The one must be believed, the other felt." This tension between the two cannot be ignored or wished away—and so we must "believe contrary to our experience what cannot be believed humanly, and . . . feel what we do not feel. Accordingly, in the very thing in which the devil, with respect to feeling, is my lord, he must be my servant." And when that happens, "experience must come along" to support our faith,[23] however, it "must follow later, and faith must precede it,

19. To a lesser extent, Kierkegaard also states: "Instead of preaching himself every Sunday, why does it never occur to a pastor to read a sermon aloud, one by Luther, for example!" (JP 3:3496). In this regard, Kierkegaard further notes: "Yes, one can easily eulogize Luther—but read Luther aloud!" (JP 2:2530).

20. The sermon is found in SML 8:221. The sermon refers to "Commentary on 1 Corinthians 15" (1534), LW 28:59–213. Kierkegaard dwells on the first part of this sermon, LW 28:69–75. His Danish source for this sermon was En christelig Postille, sammendragen af Dr. Morten Luthers Kierke- og Huuspostiller . . . i Oversættsle Jørgen Thisted [I–II] (København, 1828) vol. II, pp. 406ff., where it is included as a sermon from the Postils, rather than as a separate commentary as it is now referred to in LW 28.

21. I believe this is so even though Kierkegaard never lists them anywhere as such. For his dialectical understanding of Christianity, see JP 1:993; 3:2873. And on specifically the matter of faith and feelings in Christianity, see UDVS 71–72; BA 104–32. For other more broadly dialectical characterizations of Christianity, see WL 375–86; WA 169–77; JFY 123–43; PV 91–97; TM 267–81.

22. "Commentary on 1 Corinthians 15" (1534), LW 28:69, 71.

23. See Ps 30:5: "joy comes with the morning," and Jn 16:20: "your sorrow will turn into joy" (RSV).

working without and beyond" any experiential or affective support.[24] This spiritual tentativeness and vulnerability in Luther is also central to Kierkegaard's thought.

Luther's third point is that even when we are in this dialectical stew, there is still power "to fend off all questioning, subtle arguing, and disputing, and not to give way to the devil's suggestions, whether these be from without by his factions or from within by our own heart." But because we can only "believe . . . feebly that we through Christ are lords over world and devil; we feel the direct opposite much more." Nevertheless we still "console ourselves as much as we can with the fact that we have the Word, which excels all might and wisdom." But to hang on in this way will not be easy for "to adhere to faith in the face of seeing and feeling calls for an arduous battle."[25] This conviction that faith is always engaged in a lopsided struggle is a major contribution that Luther makes to Kierkegaard's thought.

And Luther's last point is that the Word of God continues to call us to faith since the devil "has never been able to detract from it or to invalidate it. Indeed, he slinks around us on all sides in order to lure us away from it; but he does not attack the Word itself. And so long as you have it in your heart, he does not face you squarely. He may make you writhe, but he will not overcome you." So even though we may "feel differently and be weak; that does not matter, so long as we cling to the Word."[26] Kierkegaard also has this same confidence in the power of God's Word to ward off all temptations in the end.

So contrary to what Barnett says, Kierkegaard is "a footnote to Luther"[27]—whom Kierkegaard thought was the master of us all (JP 3:2422, 3:2465). Whatever criticisms, then, Kierkegaard had of Luther, they were only "little exceptions" (JP 2:1922) to his otherwise compelling argument against Christendom.

Another mistake is Barnett's naming of mysticism, along with the nature of the church, as topics for further study on the relation of Kierkegaard to pietism.[28] Further study is actually more needed on Kierkegaard's reverence for the Bible—which, in *For Self Examination*, we are told, is based on it being the very "voice of God" for us (*FSE* 39). Kierkegaard pushes this reverence furthest in his late writing, *What Christ Judges of Official Christianity* (July 1855). There he dares the hypothetical that the preacher "ascends the pulpit, picks up the New Testament, pronounces God's name, and then reads before the congregation the specified passage loudly and clearly—after that he must be silent and remain standing silent in the pulpit for five minutes, and then he may go." Kierkegaard then adds: "This I regard as extremely beneficial" (TM 132). This antidote for poor preaching follows up on *For Self-Examination*, where Kierkegaard rejects the historical-critical interpretation of the Bible for intentionally keeping the

---

24. "Commentary on 1 Corinthians 15" (1534), LW 28:71.

25. Ibid., 72, 73.

26. Ibid., 74.

27. Ibid., 202.

28. Ibid., 206–12.

Bible from having a life changing impact on us. This high regard for the Bible is also found in pietism, as Barnett notes, without making much of it.[29] We must remember that all of Kierkegaard's many upbuilding discourses begin with Bible verses.

Kierkegaard remains in the news, with the outrageous pop singer, Lady Gaga, being called "a Kierkegaard in fishnet stockings," for, of all things, her witness to Jesus as a cultural misfit in her "Judas" video.[30] Barnett's book—unbeknownst to him—helps us put that comment in the context of Kierkegaard's pietism. It helps us understand Lady Gaga as a Kierkegaardian figure, not for her theological sophistication but for her cultural criticism—in the style of Kierkegaard's pietism.

29. Ibid., 16, 36, 34, 112.

30. Rodney Clapp, "From Shame to Fame," *The Christian Century* (July 26, 2011), 45. Go to You-Tube to see her Judas video. As of June 2013, it has received 167 million hits. At the end of it she sings: "Jesus is my virtue and Judas is the demon I cling to." For a more direct, recent reference to Kierkegaard in popular culture, see Kim Kardashian's twitter feed, KimKierkegaardashian@KimKierkegaard, which she started on June 28, 2012. In her October 4, 2012 entry, she refers to Kierkegaard explicitly. And in her July 13, 2012 entry she supplies this commentary on EUD 143: "Each individual fights for himself, with himself, within himself, in order to free himself before God. I'm gonna be sooo sore tomorrow." And then she has this ironic entry for December 24, 2012: "Why does it occur to no one that what the world truly needs this Christmas is more subtle yet sexy peek-a-boo flashes of midriff?" She makes a more direct hit in her December 18, 2012 entry: "This year we went for a Christmassy all white wardrobe, to cover up the dark, insatiable void we feel within." Not bad for a supposedly superficial glamour girl.

APPENDIX 2

On Regine Olsen

KIERKEGAARD ARGUED THAT THE Christian life is "sheer agony, an agony compared with which all other human sufferings are almost only childish pranks" (TM 189)![1] This troubling idea is explored in *Loving Søren*, a novel by Caroline Coleman O'Neill about the love affair between Kierkegaard and his fiancée, Regine Olsen (1822–1904).[2] It draws the reader into Kierkegaard's reasons for breaking off his engagement with Regine and foregoing earthly pleasures and worldly happiness—something which has baffled scholars for generations.[3] Kierkegaard's contentious romance has been compared to the more famous ones between "Pyramus and Thisbe, Dante and Beatrice, Abelard and Heloise, Petrarch and Laura, Romeo and Juliet, Werther and Lotte."[4] The complexities in Kierkegaard's relation with Regine come to life in O'Neill's novel—making it "a real page-turner" for an historical novel![5] Some have compared it to an Oscar Wilde play, with its deft depictions of "argumentative disposition and drastic mood swings."[6] O'Neill delves deeply into these matters, refusing to "deify her subject,"[7] or cover-up in any other way the difficulties between Kierkegaard and his fiancée.

1. In this same vein Kierkegaard notes: "The truth is: to become a Christian is to become, humanly speaking, unhappy for this life; the proportion is: the more you involve yourself with God and the more he loves you, the more you will become, humanly speaking, unhappy for this life, the more you will come to suffer in this life" (TM 212).

2. Caroline Coleman O'Neill, *Loving Søren: A Novel* (Nashville: Broadman & Holman, 2005).

3. See Peter Thielst, *Søren og Regine: Kierkegaard, kærlighed og kønspolitik* (Copenhagen: Gyldendal, 1980), Finn Jor, *Sören und Regine. Kierkegaard und Seine unerfüllte Liebe* (Munich: Piper Verlag, 2003), and Joakim Garff, *Regines Gåde: Historien om Kierkegaards forlovede og Schlegels hustru* (Copenhagen: Gads Forlag, 2013).

4. Joakim Garff, *Søren Kierkegaard: A Biography*, trans. Bruce H. Kirmmse (Princeton: Princeton University Press, 2005), 176.

5. Alyce Wilson's review in *Wild Violet—Live Steel*, Vol. VI, No. 1, online.

6. See the *Christian Fiction Review*, online. For a study on Oscar Wilde (1854–1900), see Richard Ellmann, *Oscar Wilde: A Biography* (New York: Random House, 1984).

7. Cynthia Lott Vogel's review in *Treasures From Darkness* (August 13, 2012), online.

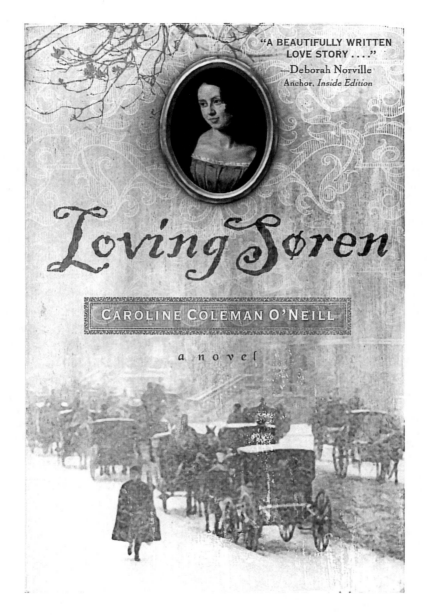

FIGURE 7: *Loving Søren* book cover (2005).

O'Neill does all of this with literary flare. Søren and Regine were engaged on September 10, 1840 and ended it a year later on October 11, 1841.[8] They first met at the widow Rordam's stately home. This is how O'Neill describes the moment Regine first sees Søren:

8. Note also their age differential. O'Neill, *Loving* Søren, 4: "Regina guessed he was about twenty-five—ten years older than she was." This difference is accentuated by Kierkegaard thinking of himself as an old man (8). At the time of their engagement Kierkegaard was twenty-seven and Regine was eighteen.

The maid mumbled a name, and a thin young man strode into the room. His blue eyes, defiant and questing, had one of the most intelligent expressions that Regina[9] had ever seen. He held his lips in a tight, compressed smirk that quivered slightly at the edges. A knee-length black coat that he wore over a black waistcoat and cravat had a shiny, threadbare look at the elbows. The huge collar of his starched white shirt nearly buried him, and his blond hair seemed to leap from his head. The man's face had the nervous intensity and delicate beauty of an artist. His whole body, Regina decided, radiated an inner zeal.[10]

And much later, after Regine gets the bad news about Kierkegaard ending their engagement, she languishes at her parents' home. O'Neill describes her sorrow in this way:

The next morning, Regina lay fully clothed on her bed. The morning light seemed to mock her with its ordinary texture. It had the clean freshness that proclaims a new day is here, new beginnings are upon us, there is a chance to start over.

Regina's back felt sore from lying in the same spot. She rolled on her side. The waistband of her skirt pinched her stomach and her corset[11] prickled her skin. There didn't seem to be any air in the room at all.[12]

These two passages nicely show O'Neill's literary artistry, and so I agree that she may well have done something quite unique in *Loving Søren*—combining "a romance novel with a learned and thoughtful presentation of religious and philosophical ideas."[13]

---

9. On the different versions of Regine's name, see O'Neill, *Loving Søren*, 45: "[Søren] pinned her hand against his side. 'Miss Regine Olsen,' he said. 'Please, call me Regina. Everybody does,' she said . . . 'Not everybody, Miss Olsen. Not everybody.'"

10. O'Neill, *Loving Søren*, 2.

11. O'Neill refers to her uncomfortable corset throughout the book (142, 167, 189, 220, 230, 273). It seems to be a metaphor for Kierkegaard's adverse effects on her!

12. O'Neill, *Loving Søren*, 214–15.

13. See the review at *brothersjudd*, online.

HAPPINESS

The two reasons usually given for Kierkegaard's break-up with Regine are that his personality quirks would have driven her crazy (JP 6:6488)[14] and his writing career would have left him little time[15] to be with her (PV 331)—and so out of compassion, the reasonable thing to do was not to get married. "I was perfectly right," Kierkegaard notes in his journal, "and acted most nobly toward her" (JP 5:5664).[16] He knew he could never be a good husband to anyone, let alone to Regine (LD 120)![17] But that

14. Even their estranged relationship and broken engagement hurt her—well ahead of their coming marriage. So Kierkegaard compares her to a withered rose in one of his letters: "I send you a rose with this. Unlike your present, it has not blossomed in my hands in all its splendor but has withered in my hands; unlike you I have not been a happy witness to all its unfolding; I have been a sad witness to its gradual decay, I have seen it suffer; it lost its fragrance, it hung its head, its leaves drooped in its struggle with death, its blush faded, and its fresh stem dried. It forgot its magnificence, thought itself forgotten, and did not know that I always had it in mind, nor did it know that together we both preserved its recollection" (LD 85). But none of those little things were any good for Regine. All she wanted was to be Kierkegaard's wife—and only that would keep her from withering away in despair. On the harm done to Regine by the break-up, see Alastair Hannay, *Kierkegaard: A Biography* (New York: Cambridge University Press, 2001), 155: "Instead of inspiring stoic fortitude [as Kierkegaard had desired, the break-up] energized her into a frenzied defense of the engagement."

15. See O'Neill, *Loving Søren*, 200: "'Do you think that there is room for a wife in the life of this impassioned writer?' she asked him." On this being an occupational hazard, see Andrew Shaffer, *Great Philosophers Who Failed at Love* (New York: HarperCollins, 2011), 2: "The great Western philosophers . . . have consistently sabotaged their own relationships with their neurotic tendencies. In or out of love, philosophers are overly critical, condescending, and holier-than-thou. Their theories are impenetrable, their positions contradictory, their probing questions are a nuisance. Such temperamental behavior has made philosophers unsuitable candidates for marriage. It is not surprising that so many philosophers simply opted out of the love game altogether."

16. On September 7, 1849, he writes in his journal: "Suppose I had married her. Let us assume it. What then? In the course of a half year or less she would have been unhinged. . . . She probably would have bungled my life as well, for I always was overstraining myself with her because in reality she was in a sense too light for me. I was too heavy for her and she was too light for me, but both factors can very well lead to overstrain. . . . [She] would have been a torment to me simply because I would see that she was altogether wrongly situated through her being married to me" (JP 6:6488).

17. On the willfully unmarried—including himself—Kierkegaard has these damning words to say through his pseudonym: "[Marriage frees a person] from stagnating in habit by maintaining a fresh current; it frees him from people precisely by binding him to one human being. I have often noticed that people who are unmarried drudge just like slaves. In the first place, they are slaves to their whims; in their daily lives they dare indulge themselves in everything, owe no one an accounting, but then they are also dependent on, in fact, slaves of, other people. What a role a servant, a housekeeper, etc. often plays. . . . [Even so] such unmarried people often are not satisfied. After all, they are able to buy the satisfaction of every wish. On occasion, they are ill-tempered and petulant, afterward weak and good-natured. Indeed, a couple rix-dollars makes everything all right" (EO 2:67*). And this critique even applies to the current use of robotic companions. See Sherry Turkle, *Alone Together: Why We Expect More From Technology and Less From Each Other* (New York: Basic Books, 2011), 66: "Dependence on a robot presents itself as risk free. But when one becomes accustomed to 'companionship' without demands, life with people may seem overwhelming. Dependence on a person is risky—but it also opens us to deeply knowing another. Robotic companionship may seem a sweet deal, but it consigns us to a closed world—the lovable as made safe and made to measure."

does not mean that she was not dear to him. No, he actually loved her very much.[18] This is quite vividly portrayed in one of his early love letters to her:

> The little window is open, the moon swells, outdoing itself in the splendor so as to eclipse the mirror image in the sea, which seems to outshine it, almost audibly—it is that wonderful. The moon flushes with rage and conceals itself in a cloud, the sea shivers—You sit on the sofa, your thoughts float far afield, your eye is fixed on nothing, infinite thoughts fade away only in the infinity of the wide heavens, everything in between is gone, it is as though you sailed in the air. And you summon the fleeting thoughts that show you an object, and if a sigh had propulsive force, if a human being were so light, so ethereal that the compressed air released by a sigh could carry him away, and indeed the more quickly the deeper the sigh—then you would be with me in that very instant. (LD 61–62)

In fact, Kierkegaard never quit loving her.[19] In his last will and testimony he stated that he felt married to her, even though they never were married and she ended up marrying someone else (LD 33). But Kierkegaard hoped that in heaven he could finally be with her and her earthly husband, Johan Frederik Schlegel (1817–96),[20] in some sort of celestial threesome![21]

O'Neill, however, does not settle for these standard explanations and goes on to explore other reasons for their break-up. One of them was that Kierkegaard would

---

18. With nostalgia, Kierkegaard notes in his journals a couple of years before he died: "Today it is twelve years since I became engaged" (JP 6:6826). Even so, Kierkegaard was no hopeless romantic. He believed that the best marriages were the difficult ones—like that of his hero Socrates to his fiery wife, Xanthippe: "To be married the way Socrates was is something quite different from what is generally understood by marriage. Socrates saw in marriage a hindrance and for that reason—married, and for that reason was *happy* with Xanthippe, or counted himself fortunate—namely, because of the difficulty" (JP 2:1824)! "In stark contrast to the submissive lives that woman were expected to lead in ancient Greece, Xanthippe publicly berated her elderly husband. According to one legend, after a heated verbal exchange between the couple, Xanthippe poured dirty water from a pail on to her husband's head. Socrates knew that he had it coming to him, joking that 'it generally rains after thunder.'" Andrew Shaffer, *Great Philosophers Who Failed at Love*, 153. See also Benjamin Daise, *Kierkegaard's Socratic Art* (Macon, Georgia: Mercer University Press, 1999), and Jacob Howland, *Kierkegaard and Socrates: A Study in Philosophy and Faith* (New York: Cambridge University Press, 2006).

19. In a 1849 journal entry, Kierkegaard tells how he felt after the break-up: "I spent the nights crying in my bed. But in the daytime I was my usual self, more flippant and witty than even necessary. My brother told me he would go to the family and prove to them that I was not a scoundrel. I said: If you do, I'll blow your brains out. The best proof of how deeply concerned I was" (JP 6:6472, p. 196).

20. They were married on November 3, 1847. It ended when Schlegel died on June 8, 1896. On Regine's continued love for Kierkegaard, even after five years into her marriage to Schlegel, see Andrew J. Burgess, "Kierkegaard's Discourses on 'Every . . . Perfect Gift' as Love Letters to Regine," IKC 5:21.

21. This comes from Regine's memoirs. See *Encounters With Kierkegaard: A Life as Seen by His Contemporaries*, ed. and trans. Bruce H. Kirmmse with Virginia R. Laursen (Princeton: Princeton University Press, 1996), 42: "[In old age, Regine] repeated with sincere conviction Kierkegaard's words to her: 'You see, Regine, in eternity there is no marriage [Mt 22:30]; there both Schlegel [her husband] and I will happily be together with you.'"

have been too happy if he had married Regine. Regine thought this was ridiculous—as did the widow Rordam, who upon hearing Kierkegaard mention it, retorts, "Oh, for heaven's sake. . . . Nonsense. . . . Why would God create man in order [for him] to die out?"[22] Most readers no doubt side with Regine and the widow Rordam.[23] O'Neill builds on that sympathy and mulls over Kierkegaard's reason in various settings. At one point he confesses, "I trust only in the finite, . . . but this life is despair." But Regine thinks this is all wrong. O'Neill has her contemplate Kierkegaard's mistakes for thinking this way:

> There was a leap involved, a fanatical leap, a leap too far. He had leapt from longing for the eternal to completely rejecting everything else. Why couldn't the things God created be good? Why did they have to be renounced, scowled at? All you have to do was recognize that created things—created people weren't God. All you had to do was make sure you didn't make a false idol out of another person. It was easy.[24]

But according to Kierkegaard, Regine was the one who was wrong. He knew that the New Testament taught the very opposite—and that it was true even if she went against it.[25] For according to the New Testament, we cannot love both God and the world.[26] We must also renounce everything if we are going to follow Jesus.[27] And we will also have to hate our lives in this world if we are going to be saved for eternity.[28] So Kierkegaard felt he had to give Regine a hefty, leather-bound copy of the New Testament—as if to say that she needed to pay closer attention to what it taught! She, of course, takes this in the wrong way, criticizing him by saying, "I was humiliated when you sent me a copy of the New Testament."[29] Kierkegaard should have known this would happen, since as a piano student, her teacher chided her, saying, "'Stop focusing on that sticking key. Focus on the entirety of the music.' Regina tried, but she couldn't ignore the sticking key. She just couldn't."[30] And so she similarly takes up God's love and glosses over the self-denial and renunciation expected of us, hanging like a banner over the pages of the New Testament, calling us sinners to repent and

---

22. O'Neill, *Loving Søren*, 7, 6.

23. Because of that, it is helpful to remember that Christ, after whom Christians are to model their lives (Lk 9:23; Heb 12:2; 1 Pt 2:21, 4:13), was a man of sorrows (Is 53:3). On this see Martin Luther, "Sermon on Matthew 2:1–12" (1532), LHP 1:198: "[As Christ's] birth is poor and wretched, so his entire life is likewise nothing but poverty, privation, suffering, misery, shame, and disgrace. The one who loses the Word and merely with human eyes regards him lying in the manger, in the stable, and so on, has already lost him."

24. O'Neill, *Loving Søren*, 149.

25. Ibid., 175, 93.

26. See Mt 6:24; Jas 4:4; 1 Jn 2:15.

27. See Lk 14:33.

28. See Jn 12:25.

29. O'Neill, *Loving Søren*, 168.

30. Ibid., 27.

live a life contrary to the ways of the world. Kierkegaard fears that Regine wants to use their engagement to avoid "the dark night of the soul, . . . the howling of the wolves, the eternal power appearing."[31] Kierkegaard feared this, knowing that "man is always happiest in a herd,"[32] even when it is just the two in a marriage![33]

Still Regine imagined being married to Kierkegaard and all the happiness it would bring:

> She threw herself, fully clothed, on her bed. Her body was still trembling. A husband, babies, happiness—all of this was within her grasp. She could hardly stand herself. Would her children look like Søren? Would they have wild blond hair? Piercing blue eyes? Would they be sharp as tacks? Gadflies? Her sons might be, but not her daughters. They would be kind and thoughtful, brown-haired and brown-eyed.[34]

Later, after Kierkegaard dies, Regine even admits that he was "more important to [her] than anything else. Even God."[35] And that was because she believed that she "wasn't complete without him."[36] Kierkegaard knew about this and was critical of Regine because of it:

> His face closed in on itself, giving him the hooded look of a lizard.

31. Ibid., 197.

32. Ibid., 155.

33. On the fast-growing American trend of never marrying, see Eric Klinenberg, *Going Solo: The Extraordinary Rise and Surprising Appeal of Living Alone* (New York: Penguin, 2011), 231: "The lack of time for oneself is one of the great complaints of men and women in today's harried marriages and that those who feel lonely actually spend no more time alone than do those who feel more connected . . . . [Living] alone has given people a way to achieve restorative solitude as well as the freedom to engage in intensely social experiences." See also Robert D. Putnam, *Bowling Alone: The Collapse and Revival of American Community* (New York: Simon & Schuster, 2000).

34. O'Neill, *Loving Søren*, 102.

35. Ibid., 280.

36. Ibid., 231. This could be construed as demeaning women. On Kierkegaard's alleged misogynist tendencies, see Céline Léon, *The Neither/Nor of the Second Sex: Kierkegaard on Women, Sexual Difference, and Sexual Relations* (Macon, Georgia: Mercer University Press, 2008), 147–59, 185–87. For a more positive view of Kierkegaard's understanding of women—through his highlighting of particulars in geocentric theory—see Jane Duran, "The Kierkegaardian Feminist" in *Feminist Interpretations of Søren Kierkegaard*, ed. Céline Léon and Sylvia Walsh (University Park, Pennsylvania: The Pennsylvania State University Press, 1997), 263: "Failing to meet an individual in his or her specificity appears to be conceptually foreign to Kierkegaard, and for good reason. His philosophical thinking asks us to come to grips with our own lives, and to think about, as he might phrase it, the bungling in which we are enmeshed." Duran understands this tendency as showing sensitivity on Kierkegaard's part toward women's issues. This sensitivity would be especially valuable in a time like ours, with the magnification of "the absolute centrality of thinness, beauty, fashion, sexual objectification, and boyfriends to teen girl happiness." Susan J. Douglas, *The Rise of Enlightened Sexism: How Pop Culture Took Us From Girl Power to Girls Gone Wild* (New York: Saint Martin's Griffin, 2010), 31. See also, Ariel Levy, *Female Chauvinist Pigs: Women and the Rise of Raunch Culture* (New York: Free Press, 2005), and Deborah Siegel, *Sisterhood, Interrupted: From Radical Women to Grrls Gone Wild* (New York: Palgrave MacMillan, 2007).

"Søren! Why are you doing this?"

"Well," he said, pursing his lips, "the problem is, you love me too much. Don't you?"

"Kiss me," she said.[37]

So while Regine had earlier said it would be "easy" to fall in love and keep everything in its proper perspective,[38] in its proper perspective, it did not prove to be so, even for her.[39]

Kierkegaard knew that marriage was not the sole purpose to life because birth was not the supreme good. In his dark humor he joked [40] about insects dying after having coitus (JP 1:805)! That was not to say, however, that marriage was evil.[41] O'Neill has Kierkegaard saying, "I love marriage."[42] The problem rather was in making too

37. O'Neill, *Loving Søren*, 222. For a study of this phenomenon, see Robin Norwood, *Women Who Love Too Much: When You Keep Wishing and Hoping He'll Change*, Tenth Anniversary Paperback Edition (New York: Pocket Books, 1997), xix–xx: "[In] spite of what amounts to virtually global recognition of the problem, many, many women of all ages are nevertheless just as dependent, just as needy and even desperate in their relationships with men as women were before the condition of loving too much was ever defined. This continues to be the case even though women are now enjoying greater freedom than at any time in history: societal restrictions have relaxed in the areas of personal choice and expression; there is more equal opportunity in education and business as well as more options regarding pregnancy and childbearing; the physical strength and economic support of a man are no longer necessary to our survival. But still the problem of loving too much persists." See also Janet Fishburn, *Confronting the Idolatry of Family: A New Vision for the Household of God* (Nashville: Abingdon, 1991), 86: "Membership in a family may presuppose little more in common than biological kinship. There is no sociological entity that can accurately be called *the Christian home*. The family is not essential to the Christian life. People can become Christian through participation in a congregation of Christians whether they were born into a Christian family or not. Only the church is essential to the Christian life."

38. O'Neill, *Loving Søren*, 149.

39. On the best reason for Christians to get married, see Elizabeth Achtemeier, *The Committed Marriage* (Philadelphia: Westminster, 1976), 33: "The question of whether or not to marry is finally a question about the vocation to which God has called us. It is to ask oneself, Can I better trust and obey my Lord in partnership with this other?"

40. Two years later he includes it in *Either/Or* (EO 1:20).

41. See 1 Tm 4:3.

42. O'Neill, *Loving Søren*, 69. Note also Kierkegaard's confession: "I do not claim and never have claimed that I did not get married because doing so is contrary to Christianity, as if my being unmarried were, from a Christian point of view, a perfection in me. . . . I have not rejected marriage out of vanity, far from it; it has its warmest advocate in me" (JP 6:6500). Kierkegaard believed that his books showed that he had mounted "one of the most substantial and inspired defenses of marriage" (JP 3, p. 809; Pap X 6 B 115). Through his pseudonyms, Kierkegaard praises marriage in the most glowing of terms. About two years after his break-up with Regine, we have these words: "[How] true it is that marriage does educate—that is, if one does not feel superior to it but, as always when it is a question of education, subordinates oneself to that by which one is to be educated. It matures the whole soul by simultaneously giving a sense of meaning and also the weight of a responsibility that cannot be sophistically argued away, because one loves. It ennobles the whole man by the blush of modesty that belongs to the woman but is the man's disciplinarian, for woman is man's conscience. It brings melody into man's eccentric movement; it gives strength and meaning to the woman's quiet life, but only insofar as she seeks this in the man and thus this strength does not become an unfeminine masculinity.

much of marriage—by saying that it is the very point of being alive. But marriage and procreation are not "the great benefaction," because at birth we are all plunged into "a miserable, wretched, anguished existence. . . . Thanks [a lot]!"[43] And so it is nonsense

His proud ebullience is dampened by his constant returning to her; her weakness is strengthened by her leaning on him. . . . Marital love . . . has its enemy in time, its victory in time, its eternity in time—therefore, even if I were to imagine away all its so-called outer and inner trials, it would always have its task. Ordinarily its does have them, but if one is to view them properly one must pay attention to two things: that they are always inner qualifications and that they always have in them the qualification of time. For this reason, too, it is obvious that this love cannot be portrayed. It always moves inward and spends itself (in the good sense) in time, but that which is to be portrayed by reproduction must be lured forth, and its time must be foreshortened. You will be further persuaded of this by pondering the adjectives used to describe marital love. It is faithful, constant, humble, patient, long-suffering, tolerant, honest, content with little, alert, persevering, willing, happy. All these virtues have the characteristic that they are qualifications within the individual. The individual is not fighting against external enemies but is struggling with himself, struggling to bring his love out of himself. And these virtues have the qualification of time, for their veracity consists not in this, that they are once and for all, but that they are continually" (EO 2:67, 139). And from some two years later we have this: "The movement of falling in love is light, like dancing in the meadow, but the resolution catches hold of the weary one until the dance begins again. This is what marriage is like. It is happy like a child, and yet solemn, for it continually has the wonder before its eyes. It is modest and concealed, yet festivity lives within it, but just as the storekeeper's door to the street is locked during a divine service, so is marriage's door always shut, because a divine service is going on continually. It is concerned, but this concern is not unbeautiful, since it rests in understanding of and feeling for the deep pain of all life. . . . It is content with little, it also knows how to use much; but it knows how to be beautiful in scarcity and knows how to be no less beautiful in abundance! It is satisfied and yet full of expectancy; the lovers are sufficient unto themselves and yet exist only for the sake of others. It is plain and everyday—indeed, what is plain and everyday as marriage; it is totally temporal, and yet the recollection of eternity listens and forgets nothing" (SLW 118). And finally from the same year we have this: "Do I dare to say that all . . . married people [do] not at one time begin with what is called 'really being in love with each other,' so that they felt the sweetness of surprise when love awakened, felt the restlessness of longing, found time to disappear when they were together and time to be so long when they were apart, found themselves glowing at the thought of wanting to be everything for each other. Let [such a one] put [this other] question to himself: Do I dare to deny that the sorry outcome may also have its basis in this, that in the time of youth and hope and surprise and rashness one lacked the direction or earnestness to renounce sentimentality and the lure of the moment and the illusion of fancy in order to subject oneself to the rigorous upbringing of resolution. . . . [Through such a] resolution marriage will take away the romantic fancies and illusions and provide a secure abode for erotic love within the impregnable fortress of duty and give the resolved one new enthusiasm and in the course of time daily wonder over his happiness" (TDIO 55–56).

43. "We want Christianity to leave us in peace. So we turn [it] around and get an insipid optimism out of a dreadful pessimism which Christianity is in the New Testament" (JP 6:6863). And this corrupted Christianity is about "as authentic as tea made from a piece of paper in which a few dried tea leaves had been kept, leaves which had already been used three times" (JP 4:4722)! On this negativity, see Jacques Ellul, "On Christian Pessimism" (1954), in *Sources & Trajectories: Eight Early Articles by Jacques Ellul That Set the Stage*, trans. Marva J. Dawn (Grand Rapids: Eerdmans, 1997), 94, 99: "Christians, especially the Reformed, are in general very bothered when they are told that they are pessimists. In our times that is a defect—a sort of betrayal of humankind. . . . [But] the book of Revelation teaches us that all human history is made by the gallop of four horsemen [Rv 6:8]. They represent the constants of history, which are War, Famine, Disease, and the Word of God. Human beings can do nothing to change these constants. All that they can do (and must do) is to brake this or that formidable consequence and labor to conserve the world, knowing that this task is truly the boulder of Sisyphus and that every breach closed announces the opening of another." See also Carl Zimmer,

to continually "attempt to make a fine world out of" our actual wretched one (JP 4:5032)![44] It is wrong to join in with "the majority of people" who feel that the "one thing" that matters is "having children" (JP 6:6155)![45] If, then, we imagine that at birth we all automatically came forth as "eternal, eternally blessed creatures," then the "most Christian thing we could do" would be to have sex "all day long, if that were possible" (JP 4:3966)! No, the goal of life is rather to be reborn (BA 135; JP 1:537; 3:3101) children of God by baptism, faith and discipleship[46]—long after our first, physical birth has happened. Otherwise all we are doing is making babies to be sent off to hell.[47]

FAITH

O'Neill also explores Kierkegaard's lack of faith as another reason for his break-up with Regine. On a walk together, Regine figures him out to herself in her own mind:

> He was afraid. He was afraid to be vulnerable, afraid of intimacy. All this blustering about irony and subjectivity was to cover over his doubt.

Parasite Rex: Inside the Bizarre World of Nature's Most Dangerous Creatures (New York: Touchstone, 2001), 203: "The [malaria] parasite that had taken so many lives (by some counts, half of all the people who were ever born) was on the verge [in 1955] of succumbing to the power of modern medicine . . . . [But as] I write these words, forty-four years later, . . . a person dies of malaria every twelve seconds. In the time [in between then and now], scientists have unbraided the mystery of DNA; they have stared closely at the face of cells; they have climbed some of the chains, link by link, from genes to action. And yet, malaria still romps through the human race." Note as well Andrew Spielman and Michael D'Antonio, *Mosquito: The Story of Man's Deadliest Foe* (New York: Hyperion, 2001), 223–24: "Posed against an enormously dangerous environment, this seemingly simple organism thrives . . . . And though it is incapable of thought, it manages to meet great challenges, adapting to our use of pesticides, the loss of habitat, even climate change. . . . With their glassy wings, delicate legs, and seemingly fragile bodies, mosquitoes are nevertheless a powerful, even fatal presence, in our lives." And on the persistence of our moral corruption, see Peter Unger, *Living High & Letting Die: Our Illusion of Innocence* (New York: Oxford University Press, 1996).

44. This is the test: "God has a very good understanding of what examining means. He does not place man in a world which forces him in every way to recognize that it is a vale of tears—and then declare in his Word that it is a vale of tears in order to see whether man will believe him. No, this would be a stupid examination, and it would never be believed. No, the world seems a lovely, nice world, unequalled—and now God says in his Word: The whole thing is a lie and sin and a vale of tears; now let us see if you will believe me" (JP 2:1439).

45. On the raging economic debate over whether or not happiness comes from increased wealth and the good fortune of improved social conditions, or "the inherited capacity to live with and overcome life's hardships," see *Economics and Happiness: Framing the Analysis*, ed. Luigino Bruni and Pier Luigi Porta (New York: Oxford University Press, 2005), 10. See also Deirdre N. McCloskey, "Happyism: The Creepy New Economics of Pleasure," *The New Republic* (June 28, 2012).

46. See Jn 3:3–6, 1:12–13, 6:63; Mt 16:17, 26:41. On this need for our rebirth to tear us out of our original "conceptual setting [of] the facility of a child," Kierkegaard adds: "If you are to become blessed in your relationship to [God], your conception must be transformed, and this transformation, this rebirth, is a very painful operation, and in the process there comes the moment when it seems to you as if God were like a superior sort of seducer" (JP 2:1409).

47. See Mt 7:13–14; Mk 13:13; Jn 15:18–20; Rom 8:17, 10:8–9; Phil 2:12; Heb 12:4; Rv 2:10. Kierkegaard does not deny "how dreadful eternal perdition is" (JP 4:5032)!

Søren must doubt that God was really strong enough to heal him of his depression. He must doubt that God could bind up the wounds left by the loss of all but one of his beloved family. He must doubt that God could forgive his doubt.

Yet God is at work healing him this very moment. If only he knew. The depth and certainty of her perception gave Regina a feeling of superiority—the kind of superiority that every woman likes to feel over the man she loves.[48]

Later when they actually discuss Regine's ideas about him, Kierkegaard counters her by saying, "But what if depression is the thorn in my flesh[49]—the thing God refuses to take away so I can learn that His power is made perfect in weakness?"[50] His biblical rejoinder catches Regine off guard. Nevertheless, Kierkegaard does admit in his journal: "If I had faith, I would have stayed with Regine. . . . My sin is that I did not have faith, faith that for God all things are possible,[51] but where is the borderline between that and tempting God; but my sin has never been that I did not love her" (JP 5:5664, 5521).

In these entries, Kierkegaard encounters a biblical conflict within himself between God making all things possible and yet retaining the thorn of suffering in him. Even so, after he endures this trauma and others similar to it, he concludes: "Yet my faith is unshaken that I will remain standing on the spot" (JP 6:6105)! In the case of Regine, then, "one thing is sure, my relationship to her has been a very personal contemporaneous course in getting to understand what faith is" (JP 6:6470).[52] And this is what he learned:

Thus it is actually frightful to become involved with God, who cannot and will not provide positive assurance or a contractual relation—and yet it is blessed, blessed to be a nothing in his hands, he who nevertheless eternally is and continues to be love, however things turn out. Only this do I have for sure

48. O'Neill, *Loving Søren*, 124.

49. See 2 Cor 12:7–10.

50. O'Neill, *Loving Søren*, 148.

51. See Lk 18:19. Over five yeaers after their break-up, Kierkegaard finally confesses in his journal: "For God all things are possible. This thought is now in the deepest sense my watchword and has gained a meaning for me which I had never envisioned. Just because I see no way out, I must never have the audacity to say that therefore there is none for God. For it is despair and blasphemy to confuse one's own little crumb of imagination and the like with the possibilities God has at his disposal" (JP 5:6135).

52. Kierkegaard notes how internal conflict added to his understanding of faith: "[God] used her to capture me. . . . I was meant to be captured. And I had to be captured in such a manner that, in the deepest sense, I had to come into conflict with myself. For that reason the other party had to be someone who in a sense was nobody, an object and yet not an object, an inexplicable something who by capitulating brought me to do battle with myself. It took a woman to do that, a woman who femininely uses weakness as a weapon. And she had to be lovely in order to be able to affect me all the more—thus all the more assuredly bringing me to do battle with myself. She had to be young so that the father, regarding her practically as a child, felt all the more called upon to put the whole responsibility on me" (JP 6:6488).

... this I believe. . . . If I have made a mistake, it will surely become clear to me; then I repent—and God *is* love. (JP 6:6623)

Given this account of certainty, it is also then appropriate for Kierkegaard to ask of himself, and of all the rest of us who also thirst for righteousness,[53] "Are you a Christian now?" (JP 6:6725). And Kierkegaard's answer is: "I myself manage to be only a very simple Christian" (JP 6:6431). For Kierkegaard this means he is always on the road to becoming one. O'Neill turns this answer into a dispute between the two of them:

> She had to find the truth out now. . . . "Søren, are you a Christian?" . . .
> He drew his lips together, and in a flash, she knew she wasn't going to get the truth. "I like to think of myself as *becoming* a Christian." He emphasized the word *becoming* like a challenge.
> Father would have a fit. She narrowed her eyes. "You mean becoming a *better* Christian?"
> "I choose my words carefully, Regina," he said, leaning further forward . . .
> She sprang off the sofa. If she sat in the sofa any longer, it would swallow her up. . . . "I mean, of course you must have been saved, felt the joy and peace of the Holy Spirit flood your heart, and all that."
> "Joy," he said staring at her. . . . "Yes. I have felt indescribable joy. Just before my father died." The church bell across the pier pealed at that very moment . . .
> "So you believe." Regina said . . .
> "No," he said. . . . "I don't believe Christianity is objectively true. . . . You can't prove Christianity objectively. . . . My faith . . . has everything to do with passion." He advanced on her. "And decision."
> "I—" She had a thousand questions, a thousand complaints. Before she could voice any of them, he was at her side, pinning her to the softness of the sofa, kissing her.[54]

Kierkegaard could "declare forthrightly that I am a Christian in the sense that others are" (PV 139). But he was more concerned with the deeper point that only God is the judge of whether any of us are Christians or not, and so the best thing to say, when asked, would be: "I trust to God that in his mercy he will receive me as a Christian" (PV 136).

This faithful modesty is infuriating to those looking for simple answers—like Regine was in O'Neill's novel. But this was Kierkegaard's task, "to disabuse men of the illusion that they are Christians," with the intent of "serving Christianity" and not tearing it down (JP 6:6918).[55] He knew this project would make trouble for him by

---

53. See Mt 5:6.

54. O'Neill, *Loving Søren*, 112–14.

55. Note also Kierkegaard's other explanation for his trouble: "[Just] because I do not call myself a Christian, it is impossible to get rid of me, having as I do the confounded capacity of being able, also

putting him "at variance with what commonly preoccupies men" (JP 6:6585, 6531, 6916). But he still had to do it because "being a Christian nowadays . . . is just as strange as someone's being a violinist by virtue of not being able to play the violin" (JP 6:6850)! And so he argued for "a more radical characterization of the concept of 'faith'" than had been known before (JP 6:6698). This came from the New Testament, which provides a "completely different concept (and also sheer pathos) of faith" than was current at his time. What he has in mind are those biblical "signs which should accompany those who believe" (JP 2:1153).[56] The faith went awry when it was cut loose from this Scriptural mooring and championed instead being "pampered by grace, so that the genuinely earnest expression of respect for God [was] lost," as it had been received "during the flood, when God scrapped a whole generation" (JP 6:6834)! This pampering produced a terrible "spiritual retardation [due to] the many happy years of immediacy" in which it wallowed (JP 2:1123). And because this more radical approach to faith "requires so much self-denial . . . it cannot be particularly inviting to the world" (JP 1:516). While keeping this ethical pressure on one's faith, Kierkegaard also knew that what Christ does for us still matters the most: "[This] motto . . . is an authentic [one] for my endeavor—I do not feel strong enough to imitate you to the point where I die for you or your cause; I am content to do something else, in adoration to thank you that you would die for me" (JP 6:6419).

LIBIDO

O'Neill also intimates that there may have been some sort of physical infirmity which kept Kierkegaard from marrying Regine and consummating their marriage. She says he always thought in ways "very different" from other people[57] and that he one time coughed up blood at a social gathering.[58] Céline Léon develops this thesis in greater detail, showing that Kierkegaard suffered from some sort of sexual impotency, which kept him from marrying Regine.[59] She builds her case on suggestive comments by Kierkegaard. He says he wanted to marry Regine "but was incapable of it" (JP 5:5663). He speaks metaphorically about a "major leak" in his life that needs repairing, but

---

by means of not calling myself a Christian, to make it manifest that the others are even less so" (TM 342)!

56. See Mk 16:17–18 about healing the sick, casting out demons, speaking in new tongues, handling deadly serpents, and drinking poison. On this passage, see my "Taking Up Snakes in Worship," *The Bride of Christ: The Journal of Lutheran Liturgical Renewal* 20 (Christ the King, 1996), 20–23, 41.

57. O'Neill, *Loving Søren*, 39.

58. Ibid., 155.

59. Céline Léon, *The Neither/Nor of the Second Sex*, 239–53. See also SLW 100. For further speculation on Kierkegaard's alleged sexual dysfunction, see Joakim Garff, *Søren Kierkegaard: A Biography*, 105: "[Other] researchers take a firm grasp on the very root of the matter, speculating on the size and shape of Kierkegaard's generative organ, including the possibility that he might have been equipped with a curved penis, whose vaginal maneuverability would in all probability have been somewhat limited."

which his physician tells him would have a "doubtful" outcome. This private matter is largely unknown and so Kierkegaard says of it: "I am like the lord whom the poor day laborers envied—until he saw that he had no legs" (JP 5:6021). This "misrelation between my mind and my body," he writes, "does not inflate me, *for I am crushed*; my desire has become a daily bitter pain and humiliation for me." But he concludes this entry by saying "that I bear the agony with which God keeps me in check and thus perhaps performs the extraordinary" (JP 5:5913). And that genius is rooted in his unusual "composite of melancholy, reflection, and piety." It, however, takes from him "the animal-attribute." That makes him "the only one of my kind, and with whom, therefore, no one feels a bond of affinity." And against this isolation he blurts out: "Give me a body [and] I would not have been this way" (JP 6:6626)! So while he wanted to marry Regine, God stopped him from doing so. "To be loved by a woman, to live in a happy marriage, enjoying life," he confesses, "this is denied me. . . . To be healthy and strong, a complete man with the expectation of a long life—this was never granted me." But rather than lamenting this, he sees in it God's infinite love for him. "I now realize," he concludes in this entry, "how everything that went wrong, even the most trifling matters, was designed to wound me in just the necessary way if God was going to use me" (JP 6:6837). And so rather than complaining about this wound, he says that "one thing remains: that I can never adequately thank God for the indescribable good he has done for me, far more than I expected" (JP 6:6603)!

While Léon's thesis has some basis in fact, most of it is fueled by speculation beyond the facts. Kierkegaard did say, after all, that he could have "easily" secured for himself "a very comfortable life," but that he felt something greater was being demanded of him (JP 6:6810). This confidence works squarely against any concern there might be over any sort of imagined sexual dysfunction on Kierkegaard's part.

FAME

For whatever reasons Kierkegaard broke off his engagement to Regine, his goal was clearly to set her free (JP 5:6135). He wanted to honor her in this way because he felt he owed his best to her—that she was the "occasion" for his most creative endeavors (JP 6:6144). And so he dedicated all his writings to her and his father—"an old man's wisdom and a woman's lovable lack of understanding, . . . the lovable tears of her misunderstanding."[60] By so doing he honored her more than he ever could have

---

60. Joakim Garff, *Søren Kierkegaard: A Biography*, 191. See also JP 6:6409. Those tears may also have turned the physical act of writing for Kierkegaard into an indirect relation with Regine herself. On his actual writing pen—albeit regarding the matter of letter-writing—he confesses in a 1847 letter to his cousin, Julie Thomsen: "I am actually in love with the company of my pen. It might be said that this is a poor object on which to cast one's affection. Perhaps! But it is not as though I were always content with it. Occasionally I hurl it away in anger. Alas, this very anger shows me once more that I am indeed in love with it, for the quarrel ends as lovers' quarrels do. I confide completely in my pen, whether I become angry when it sometimes seems to me that it cannot do what I can do, cannot follow the thought that I am thinking—or whether I am surprised when it seems as if it can do what I cannot.

done by marrying her—by making her Mrs. Kierkegaard, which she so desperately wanted. No, by breaking off the engagement in his tumultuous way, he notes that "my whole author-existence will accent her" (JP 6:6488). This is the great honor he wanted for her for being his inspiration. And Regine lived long enough to enjoy "the fame [Kierkegaard] conferred upon her and was especially delighted by the interest his works excited in Germany."[61]

FIGURE 8: Kierkegaard's Fiancée (2013)

I cannot tear myself away from the company of my pen; indeed, it even prevents me from seeking the company of anybody else" (LD 209). For a pictorial rendering of this passage, see FIGURE 8 above.

61. Walter Lowrie, *Kierkegaard* (New York: Oxford University Press, 1938), 194. One wonders, however, if Kierkegaard could ever have dedicated any of his books to Regine in the following way: "For [Regine], who even through dark valleys kept me from becoming lost in the hospitality of this beautiful world." *Notes From a Wayfarer: The Autobiography of Helmut Thielicke* (1984), trans. David R. Law (New York: Paragon House, 1995), v.

O'Neill develops this fame through the character of the English woman, Eleanor Fielding—a friend Regine makes on the Danish island of Saint Croix, where Regine's husband, Fritz Schlegel's job takes them. Upon seeing the letter from Kierkegaard's brother, telling them that they were the beneficiaries of his will, Eleanor says she is interested in hearing about their time with him:

> "I've read everything Søren Kierkegaard has ever written—and I can tell you, that's no small accomplishment. Especially for an uneducated old woman like me. What is it—fifteen or so books, not counting the sermons? What a genius he is! Such an original thinker!" . . .
>
> "I didn't realize Søren's work was so well-known outside of Denmark," Fritz said. He glanced at Regina.[62]

When Eleanor learns that Regine is the one referred to in Kierkegaard's books, she is shocked. She is so excited to know who Regine is, that she wants to hear all about everything that happened between the two of them.[63] As they grow in their relationship, Regine confides in Eleanor that she is having trouble forgiving Søren for breaking up with her. Eleanor then gives her a profound lesson in Christian forgiveness:

> "You poor dear child," Eleanor said, taking Regina's slender hand in her own large, soft, wrinkled one. . . . "You don't just forgive once and it's done. You have to forgive over and over again, every time a memory pops into your head. . . . And this wretched Søren Kierkegaard has just tormented you from the grave—God rest his soul—and so you have to start all over again on the forgiving. . . . It's hard—oh, yes—it's hard. You have to admit that someone who loved you actually chose to hurt you—deliberately.[64] You have to open yourself

62. O'Neill, *Loving Søren*, 245.

63. This is just what Regine needs to brighten up her dismal life—just as Kierkegaard imagined and planned for. On her gloomy life, see O'Neill, *Loving Søren*, 266: "She was a failure. Her life had been nothing but a string of failures: a broken engagement, a dead father, a sick mother, a dead baby, a dead marriage. And now a dead fiancé."

64. Kierkegaard could indeed be unkind: "My service through literature is and will always be that I have set forth the decisive qualifications of the whole existential arena with a dialectical acuteness and primitivity not to be found in any other literature. . . . But at present no one has the time to read seriously and to study; this being the case, until a later time my productivity is wasted, like delicacies served to yokels" (JP 5:5914). On the difficulties in marriage, see James O. Wilson, *The Marriage Problem: How Our Culture Has Weakened Families* (New York: HarperCollins, 2002), 187–88: "Men and women think somewhat differently, a matter that probably reflects some complex interaction between nature and nurture. Women are much more accurate than men in interpreting all of the unspoken messages that make up so much of human communication—the gestures, facial expressions, and tones of voice by which people convey their subtler meanings. Men and women have roughly the same intelligence but not the same talent at finding meaning in posture, photograph, or glance; in these matters, women are more skillful. The latter have more expressive faces, gaze and smile more, and are less restless. Some of this may result from how their brains are wired, some from coping with being a subordinate person, and some from having babies. Watching an infant means being acutely alert to nonverbal cues. When a husband and a wife disagree, the man is more likely to stonewall, whereas the woman is more likely to criticize. Men like to avoid arguments (though they are likely to explode after

up to the pain. To suffering. It's the only way forward. The way of the cross. You have to throw yourself on God's mercy, and say, 'Lord, help me to forgive. Help me to give up my desire for revenge. Help me to release this person into Your justice system, not try him according to mine.'"[65]

Regine is moved by Eleanor and resolves to take up the hard work of forgiving Søren all over again. After Regine goes through a long private litany of things to forgive Søren for, the book ends with the line: "But there was a more excellent way. A way of pain."[66] This is largely derived from Eleanor's earlier assessment of Kierkegaard's books:

"I read Søren Kierkegaard," Eleanor said, pursing her lips, "when I feel depressed about being stuck out here in this dreadful heat. I've never met a man who understood doom and gloom so perfectly."

"That's Søren Kierkegaard all right," Fritz said. He looked at Regina. "Doom and gloom."

Eleanor threw up her fleshy arms. "Just as I've decided he must be the most narcissistic, vacillating, self-centered man who ever walked the planet, just then—almost as if he knows he's gone too far—he says something so profound and beautiful that I feel sympathy for him and keep going. Do you know what I mean?"[67]

"Well—er—yes," Fritz said. He cast another worried glance at Regina.[68]

So even though Regine and Eleanor pretty well rake Søren over the coals at the end of this novel, it nevertheless ends on a decidedly Kierkegaardian note about the salutary nature of pain[69]—without ever directly vindicating Kierkegaard himself. But that oblique way of showing respect for what he wrote is just as it should be for Kierkegaard—or for any Kierkegaardian for that matter! And that is because Kierkegaard knew if any one were to "make a big fuss" over him with accolades, honors and undying praise, his "cause would be ruined" (JP6:6263).[70] For his plan was never to "get

---

an argument begins), women think arguments will help solve problems (though they will get upset when the man does not respond appropriately). Given these differences, marriages almost always involve disputes, and so if divorces are readily available, marriages will end more frequently."

65. O'Neill, *Loving Søren*, 276–77.

66. Ibid., 287.

67. This is close to Kierkegaard's own self-assessment: "I live constantly on the border between felicitous Arabia and desert Arabia. . . . The only consoling thought I have is [to] confess the love which makes me just as unhappy as it makes me happy" (JP 5:5503, 5490).

68. O'Neill, *Loving Søren*, 246.

69. On the Kierkegaardian nature of this point, see Alastair Hannay, *Kierkegaard: A Biography*, 154: "Helplessly pinned down under the weight of melancholy and sadness, it was in these that [Kierkegaard] had to find anything infinite in his life, not in the yea-saying, world-affirming experience of love."

70. This was because Kierkegaard believed that "Christianity has been harmed incalculably by being given a deep bow and meaningless respect" (JP 3:2379).

ahead" in this world, but rather to be "as insignificant as possible" (JP 5:5947)! "The proper motto for my life," Kierkegaard adds, would then be this: "No one puts a new patch on an old garment.[71]—The opposite is the wisdom of the prudent, who therefore are on good terms with the present moment, that is, they place their little smidge[72] of improvement directly upon the established order" (JP 6:6184).

This novel by O'Neill is a fine presentation of Kierkegaard's life and thought, and an engrossing read as well. Taking it up in a parish book club would be a great way to introduce Kierkegaard's writings to a congregation.[73]

71. See Mt 9:17.

72. That same "little smidge" is all that Kierkegaard sees in book reviews: "I reject all reviews, for to me a reviewer is just as loathsome as a street barber's assistant who comes running with his shaving water, which is used for all customers, and fumbles about my face with his clammy fingers" (JP 5:5698).

73. O'Neill dedicates her novel to her father "for bringing us up on Søren Kierkegaard [and to] my mother, for not." See also the online interview with Caroline Coleman O'Neill—"I was raised on Søren Kierkegaard's philosophy. My father became a born again Christian in his early forties by reading Søren Kierkegaard, and he was quoted in our home as often as the Bible. But I found Søren's renunciation of the world far too extreme, and I resisted reading him. . . . [Later when spending seven years writing *Loving Søren*] I traveled to Copenhagen. I went to the Danish West Indies, which is now the U. S. Virgin Islands. I read extensively. I read biographies. I read contemporary accounts. . . . I read over two-thirds of Kierkegaard's works."

Conclusion

The Thorough Kneading of Reflection

I CAN IMAGINE SOMEONE finishing this book and saying that it is too intellectual,[1] that it has too many long, complex footnotes, and that it is not practical enough to be a book about how to carry on a Kierkegaardian ministry in a local congregation. I will grant that in Kierkegaard we see a certain verbal sophistication and conceptual depth that makes for anything but light and breezy reading, and that this book could rightly be charged with some of the same since it aims to saturate itself in what Kierkegaard had to say.[2] But I have still tried to show how a pastor could make constructive use of Kierkegaard's writings in the church—*pro ecclesia*. Throughout the writing of this book, I have made constant reference in my mind to the parish. And in the sermons, I have constantly addressed faith and morals, which are a constant concern of any parish minister. So while this is not an easy book to read—I grant you that—I still think that careful attention to its many quotations from Kierkegaard will repay any pastor seeking to fashion a Kierkegaardian ministry in a local congregation.[3]

---

1. On being an intellectual pastor, see William H. Willimon, *Clergy and Laity Burnout* (Nashville: Abingdon, 1989), 86: "[Some] of the most effective pastors possess strong intellectual appetites. They may not think of themselves as intellectuals, but they are. They are at home in the world of ideas, are not threatened by the novel and the unconventional, are forever trying to figure out what's going on. Few congregations will admit to desiring an 'intellectual pastor.' None of them need an armchair academic as pastor. But all of us need help with making sense out of life as Christians. Pastors who enjoy that task, who are always on the prowl for handles, insights, concepts, and models for thinking life through, will never be bored in the parish."

2. In this regard, it is worth noting that Kierkegaard never aimed at writing easy-to-read journalism: "[The] very beginning of the test to become and to be a Christian is to become so turned inward . . . that one is quite literally alone in the whole world, alone before God, alone with Holy Scripture as a guide, alone with the prototype [Christ] before one's eyes. But the language [we speak is] of outward turning; it very much resembles the way a journalist expresses himself" (PC 225).

3. Let me note here—*caveat lector*—that by implementing Kierkegaard's jarring ideas, you will also throw your ministry into jeopardy! Carroll Hinderlie (1913–92), confided in me, on November 17, 1986, after being the featured speaker at our annual Kierkegaard commemoration, that he was fired—because of Kierkegaard—from every position he ever held in the church. It was because of Kierkegaard's idea of inwardness (JP 6:6531)—*viz.*, that believers have to be constantly deepening their faith in life and practice—that he was forced from his positions as parish pastor, seminary professor and church administrator. See Lee Moriwaki, "Rev. Carroll Hinderlie, 78, Always a Leader of Diversity and Debate," *The Seattle Times* (March 28, 1992). On this matter of inwardness, Kierkegaard writes that there is "a cowardly, soft religiousness that does not itself want to be out upon the deep in decisions. . . . But just because there are religious people like that, and all too many of them, it is important, especially in our sensible and soft sagaciously refined Christendom, that the one who has been deeply moved should not in his inwardness give up, that in holy anger he should know how to

Kierkegaard thought that it was just such demanding Christian ideas which are difficult to read about and think about—as I have explored in this book—that actually hold the promise of church renewal and the invigoration of parish ministry. In *Christian Discourses* Kierkegaard explains how these ideas figure in:

> Ah, there is so much in the ordinary course of life that will lull a person to sleep, teach him to say "peace and no danger." Therefore we go to God's house to be awakened from sleep and to be pulled out of the spell. But when in turn there is at times so much in God's house that will lull us to sleep! Even that which in itself is awakening—thoughts, reflections, ideas—can completely lose meaning through force of habit and monotony, just as a spring can lose the tension by which alone it really is what it is. (CD 165)

This is an apt image, dialectically[4] treated by a great Christian writer, to explain how the church both dies and rises to newness of life, over and over again, by way of its foundational ideas and thoughts. It dies by letting those ideas drop to the side, and it comes back to life by plumbing their depths and putting them into practice, day in and day out. My book is designed to help us understand how and why the church periodically dies, and then to provide concrete suggestions on how it may once again come back to life. Kierkegaard cared deeply about the Christian sermon, and so I have provided some sermons inspired by his writings—designed to bring life back into worship and Christian living. This is the most specific guidance provided in my book for the renewal of the church. That is because I agree with Luther that the sermon is "the highest and chief" part of everything that the pastor does.[5] And so the church will lose out on any and all renewal if it does not have persistent, faithful, and robust preaching. So my collection of sermons has received the lion's share of what I have to offer for the improvement[6] of the church in this book—something new in Kierkegaard studies.

I have also proposed—in a very practical vein—a few prayers of Kierkegaard's to pray on a daily basis. I have also outlined a way to read the Bible in an edifying or upbuilding way—as well as how best to regard baptism and hymn singing. I have thought through in this book the matter of ministering to the ill, injured, and those with marital difficulties—all in Kierkegaardian terms—something that every parish

---

get behind these cowardly soft ones in order to force them out in the current, instead of abandoning himself to them for entertainment and drama" (BA 108–9). And Kierkegaard goes on to add—in confirmation of Hinderlie's point—that "people . . . take a dim view of jacking up the price or the requirement for being what they already think they are, the name of which they do not want to give up" (PV 138).

4. For Kierkegaard, a dialectical treatment brings "contrasting" thoughts into conversation with one another (JP 2:1852)—as in this case between the church sleeping and awakening.

5. Martin Luther, "A Sermon on Keeping Children in School" (1530), LW 46:221. Kierkegaard, in keeping with Luther's sentiment, also devoted a large amount of his writings to the discourse form.

6. On this call to improve, see 2 Cor 13:9. And on the hope for spiritual "progress," see Martin Luther, "The Large Catechism" (1529), BC 449.

minister wrestles with on a regular basis. In addition, I have explored what makes for a good parish pastor—noting specifically what are the key traits that every pastor should have. I have also discussed—albeit in less practical ways—the nature of Christian spirituality, in terms of self-hatred and Pythagorean simplicity, as well as repentance and judgment, worship, prophetic disruption, and demanding, rigorous discipleship.

Throughout I have tried to implement Kierkegaard's dictum regarding the "thorough kneading of reflection" (TA 111). This thorough kneading has made for some extended quotations, prolix commentary and complex footnotes. But all of this has been in the service of those challenging Christian ideas. In honor of one of Kierkegaard's great English translators, Edna H. Hong (1913–2007), I have elaborated this dictum poetically, with the hope of drawing greater attention to it:

> The board is barely dusted.
> Patting and molding follow.
> Then the pushing down—back and forth.
> Some flour's in the air.
> Clumps get folded in for rising.
> Beautiful arcs take shape.
> My elbows and wrists start aching.
> I'm thinking too soon of the oven
> and how it will taste.[7]

Many such clumps, or awkward considerations, have been folded into the dough of this book—and I hope all of them have somehow, by God's grace, contributed to the rising of greater understanding of Christianity and enhanced Christian living. And this is indeed needed, since we who consider these awkward Christian ideas are but fearful, sanctimonious people, as Kierkegaard once put it so passionately:

> O, you sanctimonious people with your love which does not set you apart from life—no, your love of self would prevent that! O, you sanctimonious people with your practicality that takes an active part in life—or hastily takes hold of the advantages! O, you sanctimonious people with your earnestness which does not have the imagination to withdraw from life—indeed, your cowardice would rather hurry you back into the herd, the animal herd, away from the place where earnestness lives: being the single individual. O, you sanctimonious people with your patriotism which forbids you to be callous to the woes and welfare of the country. (JP 6:6580)

---

7. "Thorough Kneading of Reflection," *Søren Kierkegaard Newsletter*, Number 52 (December 2007), 11. In addition to being a wonderful translator, Edna was also known for her great home baked bread, which makes this bread-baking image of Kierkegaard's—kneading—all the more apt for a tribute to her.

We need to be jostled free from our entrenchments in the various crowds of our lives where we need to struggle with our personal responsibilities and individual Christian obligations. Every Christian minister knows about this problem when trying to cajole the congregation into ever greater commitment and involvement. These Christian ideas, upon which we, in this book, have been called to carefully consider, are just what is needed to disrupt our routines and "explode" our relativities (JP 6:6686).[8] In "the face of modernity's disdain for the infinite qualitative difference between the human and the divine," these Christian ideas hold out for us the possibility of a new way of life that is filled with "immense passivity, vulnerability and wounded openness."[9] That struggle is in large part the good fight of faith (1 Tm 6:12) that has all but been lost in the church today, but which historical Christianity has championed down through the generations.

Kierkegaard is famous for calling Christians to follow Jesus as well as believe in him—reminding us, in memorable ways, that belief without discipleship is empty or dead.[10] And that is because Jesus gives out no "discounts"—exempting Christians here and there, willy-nilly, from struggling to follow in his steps (JP 2:1848).[11] No, Christi-

---

8. See also JP 3:2959. These explosions can be superficial or profound. A wonderful musical example of this problem is the way the Brahms Handel Variations for Piano (1861) far out distance the Piano Concert No. 2 by Saint-Saens (1868), regarding the vexing problem of intellectual content in instrumental music. To compare these two piece, listen to Emanuel Ax, *Brahms: Variations & Fugue on a Theme by Handel, Etc.* (1992) SONY, SK-48046; and André Watts, *Tchaikovsky: Piano Concerto No. 1 & Saint-Saens: Piano Concerto No. 2* (1995) TELARC, CD-80386. Also note the caveat in Peter Kivy, *Music Alone: Philosophical Reflections on the Purely Musical Experience* (Ithaca: Cornell University Press, 1990), 218: "I find myself at present . . . unable to refrain from thinking that some musical works are profound yet unable, as well, to provide any rational grounds for my thinking it." Recall as well that music mattered deeply to Kierkegaard: "Everything ends with hearing—the rules of grammar end with hearing—the command of the law with hearing—the figured bass ends with hearing—the philosophical system ends with hearing—therefore the next life is also represented as pure music, as a great harmony—would that the dissonance of my life would soon be resolved in it" (JP 5:5161).

9. Simon D. Podmore, *Kierkegaard and the Self Before God: Anatomy of the Abyss* (Bloomington: Indiana University Press, 2011), 181, 182. An example of this wounded openness is reported on in Jack Schwandt, *The Hong Kierkegaard Library: A Crown Jewel of St. Olaf College*, Revised Edition (Northfield, Minnesota: Friends of the Kierkegaard Library, 2011), 161–62: "'My days are like shadows that declineth' [Ps 102:11]. So Jonathan Stenseth [1971–98] discovered early in his life; yet he was not defeated. Instead, he became a student of 'death, that teacher of earnestness.' The phrase is Kierkegaard's in 'At a Graveside,' one of *Three Discourses on Imagined Occasions*, a book Jonathan was reading in the spring of 1996 only a few weeks before the leukemia was discovered and he was married. . . . It helped prepare him for 'this final examination,' set by that new teacher. This examination, unlike the academic examinations at which Jonathan also excelled, was and always 'is equally difficult for all'" [TDIO 75, 102].

10. See Jas 2:26. See also the account of how the reading of Kierkegaard helped a Lutheran laywoman embolden her faith in Christ. Ann Dixon, "Nice Lutherans," *The Lutheran* (November 2003), 24.

11. On following in the footsteps of Jesus (1 Pt 2:23), see the classic novel by Charles Sheldon, *In His Steps* (1896; Grand Rapids: Spire, 1984). Note especially how Pastor Maxwell thinks Jesus would have him preach and also how best to spend his summers: "Preach fearlessly to the hypocrites in the church no matter what their social importance or wealth," and "[give] up the summer trip to Europe

anity is instead like a long train pulled by a locomotive engine. Kierkegaard explains why this is so and how the train has gone awry:

> Think of a very long railway train—but long ago the locomotive ran away from it. Christendom is like this. The ideal, the prototype was the locomotive, [representing the] perpetual motion which is the restlessness of the eternal. ... In the meantime generation after generation has imperturbably continued to link the enormous train of the new generation to the previous one, solemnly saying: We will hold fast to the faith of the fathers. Thus Christendom has become the very opposite of what Christianity is, ... the restlessness of the eternal. ... Christendom is tranquility—how charming, the tranquility of literally not moving from the spot. [But this is] the most peculiar characteristic. (JP 2:1933)

So the train has to be re-attached to the locomotive if we are to have any Christianity to practice and be blessed by. Central to this re-attachment is taking up again the practice of imitating Christ. "This is really the direction," Kierkegaard writes, "in which my whole productivity has tended" (JP 1:691). For indeed, Christianity "is the doctrine of and the instruction for being like Christ" (JP 2:1842). This is so, even though one may be an abject failure at it:

> Strictly speaking, to be a Christian is: to die (to die to the world)—and then to be sacrificed; a sword pierces his heart first of all (dying to the world), and then he is hated, cursed by men, abandoned by God (that is, sacrificed). In this way the essentially Christian is superhuman. [Now] I am incapable of this. I am able only to come so far out that I use "the prototype" as a source of humiliation, not for imitation. (JP 2:1899)

This is very helpful—because if we fail at imitating Christ we can still be involved by being humiliated by way of his example. For Kierkegaard this alternative course is strictly dialectical:

> Christ is the prototype, but as the prototype he jacks up the requirement even higher than the law. ... Then man despairs. But instantly the prototype changes and is also "the Savior," who holds out a rescuing hand to help him be like the prototype. He casts himself into the arms of the prototype. But the prototype changes again and is the Redeemer. This is the love of Jesus Christ. Inasmuch as there is to be striving, he is the prototype whom one ought to resemble, but the prototype is also the Savior and Redeemer who helps the Christian to be like the prototype. (JP 2:1863)

This is a startling—but truthful—characterization of the inner dynamic of Christian life. It shows how being humiliated by Christ's example can lead to redemption through Christ and the eventual following of him by his grace. Only in this way can

---

this year, using the money for something more worthwhile" (72–73).

faith and imitation, or becoming contemporaneous with Christ, go together. "Imitation there must be," Kierkegaard writes, "but not in such a way that one becomes self-important by it or seeks thereby to earn salvation" (JP 2:1877). And this imitation must not be forced upon us either, if it is to be genuine:

> Imitation is not the law's demand that a poor wretch of a man must torture himself. No, even Christ is against this kind of extorted discipleship. He would no doubt say to such a person, . . . let it come as a glad fruit of gratitude; otherwise it is not "imitation." Yes, one would have to say that such fearfully extorted discipleship is rather a perverted mimicking. (JP 2:1892)

Kierkegaard even adds that for all of the trauma inherent in following Christ and believing in him, there must also be a little room made for laughter (JP 2:1855).

Now because of Kierkegaard's concentration on following Christ, one could well suppose that my book is wrongheaded for trying to foster a Kierkegaardian parish ministry, since Kierkegaard did not want any such adjectival monstrosity made up about him, or any collection of sermons bearing his name:

> For all of his greatness, Kierkegaard's work was primarily negative. Kant said that the Scottish philosopher David Hume woke him from his dogmatic slumbers; this is a much-needed service that Kierkegaard has provided for many readers. But we should not try to be his disciples, or accept his views as our own, without critical examination. He certainly said often enough that he never wanted anyone to do that. Put very simply, he wanted us to think for ourselves and make our own decisions. He wanted no disciples. In the end, the desire of his heart was that we should become Christians, not Kierkegaardians.[12]

And so I have tried to use the thorough kneading of reflection throughout this book to examine ways in which Kierkegaard's presentations of the challenging ideas of Christianity may reform the church today—against all the naysayers. While I nevertheless still use the adjectival form of his name to describe this project—at its heart, I am promoting only Christ. And the ways that Kierkegaard does the same are of a great help in our time where quantity trumps quality,[13] the church is kept from making contributions to academic life,[14] helplessness—even before the sovereign Lord—is

---

12. Elmer H. Duncan, *Sören Kierkegaard*, Makers of the Modern Theological Mind, ed. Bob E. Patterson (Waco, Texas: Word, 1976), 136. Even so, see Thomas J. J. Altizer, *Mircea Eliade and the Dialectic of the Sacred* (Philadelphia: Westminster, 1963), 80: "Kierkegaard has had few true followers." So I would suppose that a good book on Kierkegaard for the renewing of the church would not sell well either! It would be like bringing out "a volume of verse," which in turn, is like "dropping a rose-petal down the Grand Canyon and waiting for the echo [when it hits the ground]." Scott Donaldson, *Poet in America: Winfield Townley Scott* (Austin: University of Texas Press, 1972), 294.

13. See Kenda Creasy Dean, *Almost Christian: What the Faith of Our Teenagers is Telling the American Church* (Oxford: Oxford University Press, 2010), 3: "I am personally not very much worried about the reduction in numbers where Christianity is concerned. I am far more concerned about the qualitative factor: what kind of Christianity are we talking about?"

14. See Catherine Pickstock, *After Writing: On the Liturgical Consummation of Philosophy* (Oxford:

deemed pathological,[15] passion and affection are banned from our cognitive projects,[16] political liberalism favors neutrality over religious insights,[17] Eastern religions are in ascendency,[18] and where Jesus is widely watered-down and domesticated.[19]

Blackwell, 1998), 253: "The Eucharistic sign, by contrast [to the necrophiliac sign of postmodernity], is able to outwit the distinction between both absence and presence, and death and life."

15. See Martin E. P. Seligman, *Helplessness: On Development, Depression, and Death* (1975; New York: W. H. Freeman, 1992), 168: "Can a psychological state be lethal? I believe it can. When animals and men learn that their actions are futile [Rm 9:16] and that there is no hope [Rm 7:24], they become more susceptible to death. Conversely, the belief in control over the environment can prolong life."

16. See William J. Wainwright, *Reason and the Heart: A Prolegomenon to a Critique of Passional Reason* (Ithaca, New York: Cornell University Press, 1995), 3: "The tradition I will discuss . . . places a high value on proofs, arguments, and inferences yet also believes that a properly disposed heart is needed to see their *force*."

17. See Nicholas Wolterstorff, "Why We Should Reject What Liberalism Tells Us about Speaking and Acting in Public for Religious Reasons," *Religion and Contemporary Liberalism*, ed. Paul J. Weithman (Notre Dame: University of Notre Dame Press, 1997), 180: "Liberalism, with its neutrality postulate, insists that . . . appeals [to the Scriptures in matters of public debate] must be silenced—or that those who present the appeal always have an additional, consensus populi, reason at ready."

18. See Philip Goldberg, *American Veda: From Emerson and the Beatles to Yoga and Meditation— How Indian Spirituality Changed the West* (New York: Harmony, 2010), 385 n. 24: "Indophiles like to point out that the religions that evolved from the Veda—primarily Hinduism but also Buddhism, Sikhism, Jainism, and their myriad variations—never started a holy war against another religion, never conducted an Inquisition or a Crusade, never burned heretics or exiled apostles, and never launched a conversion campaign."

19. See Dan Wakefield, *The Hijacking of Jesus: How the Religious Right Distorts Christianity and Promotes Violence and Hate* (New York: Nation Books, 2006), and Robert S. McElvaine, *Grand Theft Jesus: The Hijacking of Religion in America* (New York: Three Rivers, 2009).

Postscript

My Father in the Faith

"Life must be understood backwards, . . . but it must be lived forwards" (JP 1:1030), writes Kierkegaard in his nearly four thousand page, personal journal—which in its English translation by Howard and Edna Hong, amounts to six large volumes. This Christian author—this "spiritual adviser to the solitary" (JP 6:6459)—has become my father in the faith,[1] as I look back over the last few decades of studying his life and writings. Just as Martin Luther once said of Saint Augustine that his "keen judgment" was a blessing to him,[2] so Kierkegaard's judgments have been the same for me. In his journal, Kierkegaard notes that if it ever were to be published, its title should be "The Book of the Judge" (JP 6:6380). And his fundamental judgment is that Christianity has had all of its turbulence and difficulty ripped away from it—for, properly understood, Christianity is nothing but "mildness in severity." Just as in the Danish original, *Mildhed*, or mildness, rhymes with *Strenghed*, or severity—so in our faith and practice they belong tightly linked together. So what God has joined together, we should not put asunder![3] But in order to redress the situation, severity has to be the element emphasized[4] since it is the "dialectical factor" that thickens the soup, so to speak (JP 3:2873)—creating "the most intense agony

1. On the propriety of having a father in the faith, see Rom 4:12, 16; 1 Cor 4:15; Phm 1:10; and Jas 2:21—with the contrasting statement in Mt 23:9. As my father in the faith, Kierkegaard is in some ways like his own father: "[The] words with which my father interrupted all objections to his way of life [were]: This is the custom in my house" (JP 4:3841). And a reason for this short-circuiting of criticism is: "Actually, the best proof for the immortality of the soul, that there is a God, and the like, is the impression one has of this from his childhood, and therefore this proof, unlike those numerous scholarly and high-sounding proofs, could be stated thus: It is absolutely certain, for my father told me" (JP 2:1170).

2. Martin Luther, "Table Talks" (May 7, 1539), LW 54:352.

3. For a play on this passage from Mt 19:6, see Heiko A. Oberman, *Luther: Man Between God and the Devil*, trans. Eileen Walliser-Schwarzbart (New Have: Yale University Press, 1989), 160.

4. Luther says the same. See his "Lectures on Psalm 98" (1515), LW 11:274–75: "[It] is easy to teach what is good and preach what is true, but to sting the vices and reprove the wicked takes courage not to be afraid of the anger of those whom one reproves. . . . Therefore one must lift up the voice in the horn more than in the trumpet, for what is true is more easily heard than what is evil in us. And hence the trumpets are called silver, because they are pure and solid and true examples of heavenly things and they sound plain and clear. But the horn sounds more dull [but] not by its own fault, but by that of the hearer. For the latter is heard more reluctantly, the former more gladly. So the latter sounds harsh, the former clear, namely, to those for whom it sounds. . . . Therefore we all gladly hear and desire the future good, and it sounds clear to us. We want to rejoice with the saints, but we do not want to hear our sins reproved. The future joys please us, but we do not want to disturb our sins. Therefore we hear the trumpets even without a voice, but we do not want to hear the horn even with a voice. But surely this needs to be sounded most of all."

possible" (JP 4:5007).[5] And Kierkegaard for sure has distinguished himself in agonizing his readers!

Therefore he says in his journals that his task is "to apply a corrective to the established order, not to introduce something new" (JP 6:6693); that all he wants is "to starve the life out of all the illusions in which Christendom has run aground" (JP 6:6228); that it is a delusion to suppose that "if God does not intervene with punishment, then one is in excellent standing with him" (JP 3:2569); that "before God [we are] less than nothing" (JP 5:6135); and that "the human race is not progressing, except in knavish trickery" (JP 4:4981). "Good night, Ole!" as Kierkegaard would say (JP 4:4175)! Surely no one could think these are warm and fuzzy affirmations![6]

And Kierkegaard admits the same when he says, "I must always stand outside as a superfluity and impractical exaggeration," noting that "conditions are still far from being confused enough for proper use to be made of me. But it will all end with conditions getting so desperate that they must make use of desperate people like me and my kind" (JP 6:6709a). And he ramps this up by saying that "Christ is not love, and least of all according to the human notion of love. He was the *truth*" (JP 1:316). And so he adds that "to be a Christian is: to die to the world and then to be sacrificed. . . . I am incapable of this. I am only able to come so far out that I use the 'prototype' as a source of humiliation, not for imitation" (JP 2:1899). And again he writes that "Jesus was born of a virgin and thus . . . Christianity is not related to marriage, father, mother, child, but to every single individual human being as spirit. . . . It might be very good for Christianity to be represented by an unmarried person" (JP 1:570, 572); and that "the infant [and] the social mixer . . . are [only] the animal definition of what it is to be human" (JP 2:2067). Furthermore he says that "faith is always related to what is not seen—in the context of nature to the invisible, [but] in the spiritual context to the

---

5. On this understanding of how conceptual relations work, see my "Seek Simplicity and Distrust It: Paul R. Sponheim on Christian Theology," *dialog* 31 (Winter 1992), 36–41, with Sponheim's critique following (42–43).

6. And so all of Kierkegaard's writings, in one way or other, point to Matthew 7:14: "The gate is narrow and the way is hard that leads to life and those who find it are few" (RSV). This is true even though he rarely addresses this verse head on (UDVS 289–305, FSE 53–70). At one point, however, toward the end of his authorship, he does comment directly on this verse, as if in a summarizing way: "In the midst of this enormous population [or] swarm of 'Christians,' there now and then live some individuals, an individual. For him the way is hard—see the New Testament [Mt 7:14]; he comes to be hated by all—see the New Testament [Mt 10:22]; to put him to death is regarded as service to God—see the New Testament [Jn 16:2]. This is indeed a curious book, the New Testament; it proves to be right after all, because the individual, these individuals—yes, those were the Christians" (TM 120). Kierkegaard may have learned this severe focus from Luther. See, for instance, Martin Luther, "Commentary on Psalm 45" (1534), LW 12:217: "[Christianity is] dangerous and difficult." Luther's life shows this difficulty in his struggles against oppressive ecclesiastical hierarchy, corrupt monastic practices, and the degenerate university ethos. On these battles, see Heiko A. Oberman, *Luther: Man Between God and the Devil*, trans. Eileen Walliser-Schwarzbart (New Haven: Yale University Press, 1989).

improbable" (JP 2:1119); and that "God is no friend of the cozy human crowd" (JP 2:2078).

Not surprisingly, he also advises that "what our age needs is pathos (just as scurvy needs green vegetables), . . . a man who is able to short-suit reflectively all reflection" (JP 3:3129). He also notes that "to love God is possible only by clashing with all human existence (hating father and mother, hating oneself, suffering because one is a Christian etc.)" (JP 3:2453), but instead of that, we have "lowered the standard for being a Christian and thus have caught all the more. Instead of whales, we caught sardines—but countless millions of them" (JP 3:2979)! He goes on to say that "Christianity should not be lectured about. This is why Christ says, my teaching is food—this is to show that it ought to be existed in" (JP 1:482). Furthermore he says that "balloting is the downfall above all of Christianity, since it is a deification of the secular mentality and an infatuation with this world. . . . But Christianity is militant truth, assuming that here in this wretched world truth is always in the minority" (JP 4:4852). And Kierkegaard adds that "he who proclaims the law forces men into something; at least they try to hide themselves when faced with the law. But 'grace' makes them completely unconstrained. Face to face with 'grace' a person really learns to know what lies deepest in a man" (JP 2:1488). He also notes that "the main point in Christianity is that man is a spirit and spirit is diversity *per se*; Christianity's infinitely sublime thought is that each Christian becomes a Christian by different ways and means—always diversity, which is precisely what God wants, he (a detester of all mimicry, which indicates the absence of spirit) who is inexhaustible in creating diversity" (JP 4:4502). In addition he writes that "if the New Testament shall decide what is to be understood by being a true Christian, then being a true Christian very quietly—cozily, enjoyably—would be just as impossible as firing a cannon quietly" (JP 3:3619).

And so I end this severe litany with a few final statements. Kierkegaard writes that Christianity is "like water which in the reservoir is pure but is infected in passing through contaminated pipes. . . . Whenever something can be shared only through a medium, the quality of the medium is almost as important as the quality of that which is communicated through the medium. This shows what a dubious thing [it is to] talk about an objectively true proclamation of Christianity" (JP 3:3539). He also says that "thanking God for good days should first and foremost mean undertaking to examine oneself, how one clings to such things; it should mean that one learns to think lightly of all such things" (JP 2:1510). And so he says that Christ's "religion is of the spirit [and the] Spirit is: to live as if dead" (JP 4:4360); and that when one "gets down to brass tacks he finds that practicing Christianity is not very useful and that it is highly impractical" (JP 3:3352)! And finally he says that "joy proclaimed without mentioning the pain is only a sounding brass and a tinkling cymbal; unheeded, it whistles past the ear of the suffering one; it sounds on the ear but does not resound in the heart" (JP 2:2183). So while Kierkegaard knows that there is also joy in Christianity,[7] he knows

7. Kierkegaard even says more than this—that joy is central to Christianity—but note the

as well that it has to be strained through the sieve of suffering and sorrow if it is to be genuine.[8]

So while it was my parents, by the grace of God, who made me a Christian through the waters of Holy Baptism when I was but two months old—it has been the version of Lutheranism written down on Kierkegaard's many pages that has kept me, all these many years later, in "the household of God" (1 Peter 4:17). *Deo gratias!*

---

introductory qualification: "If this is properly interpreted, every man who truly wants to relate himself to God and be intimate with him really has only one task—to rejoice always" (JP 2:2186). And so he adds: "[Not] until a man is unhappily tormented in the world to the degree that his suffering is like misanthropy, not until then does Christianity come into being for him. All this beer-hall enthusiasm about living *gemütligt* [cozily] and having such a good life in animal-human categories and then putting the name of Christ on top of the cake every Sunday—that this cowardice is Christianity is, of course, a pure lie" (JP 4:4964).

8. On this point, Mt 13:21 is important. It is about showing how pain and suffering scares Christians away who initially liked the thought of believing in Christ. Kierkegaard's pseudonym, Anti-Climacus, develops this further: "Now the issue is: will you be offended or will you believe. If you will believe, then you push through the possibility of offense and accept Christianity on any terms. So it goes; then forget the understanding; then you say: Whether it is a help or a torment, I want only one thing, I want to belong to Christ, I want to be a Christian" (PC 115).

Epilogue

RONALD F. MARSHALL'S GATHERING of his scattered published essays creates a high water mark in Kierkegaard research. His essays published in *International Kierkegaard Commentary* on the Luther-Kierkegaard connection were among the very best comparative essays in that series.

The present collection also includes other essays, published and unpublished, on Kierkegaard's response to Luther, reflecting both his debt to and critique of the founder of the Protestant Reformation. Marshall also has a commanding knowledge of the secondary literature on both Luther and Kierkegaard in the English language, all of which he brings to bear on issues in contemporary Christian theology. The moral and social concerns addressed in Marshall's sermons reflect contemporary issues, but his response reflects the preacher-pastor-servant, not a social reformer such as Martin Luther King Jr. (1929–68). Marshall's emphasis is based upon historical and theological critique, a task he undertakes without becoming religiously, socially, and/ or culturally "preachy." His style is distinctively "declarative," even when cultivating the conceptual nuances in his writing. He does not attempt to convert the reader to his own or any other religious or philosophical viewpoint, although he constantly, competently, and clearly presents the Kierkegaard-Luther relation for our inspection, acceptance, rejection, further reflection, and edification. This book is not about "the secondary literature," although comments on previous research are far from absent.

One of the most beneficial effects of Marshall's efforts will be "to religionize" the study of Kierkegaard, to beckon us back to the primacy of the religious, the specifically Christian intent of his authorship. In philosophical circles, research has frequently centered on comparative historical studies of Kierkegaard with Socrates, Plato, Hegel, or Kant, etc. from the past. More recently, an assortment of thinkers who are primarily related to existentialism, postmodernism, and analytic philosophy have made distinctive contributions to our understanding of Kierkegaard. Then there are also studies of Kierkegaard's aesthetics, ethics, etc. All this effort testifies to the health of Kierkegaard studies in the philosophic spheres at this time. Marshall, by contrast, asks us to reconsider Kierkegaard as a religious thinker, specifically as a Lutheran, as one whose theological education was permutated by conflicting claims about religious and theological issues and whose life was lived in the area dominated by Lutheran theology and the forms of religious life that crystallized there. Luther, through his theology, the hymns he wrote, the church he founded, and the Protestant culture he incidentally initiated by the decisive theological changes he introduced, proved to be a major religious "power behind the throne[s]," of northern Germany and Scandinavia.

Marshall has put us deeply in his debt by recalling the importance of Luther to our attention in such focused detail. Although more by osmosis than direct inspiration, the reformer was the major religious influence underlying Kierkegaard's thought, especially Religiousness B, where his major purpose was to "reintroduce Christianity into Christendom" (PV 42). This effort compares well with Luther's posting of the ninety-five theses. Marshall's critical study honors Kierkegaard's effort while not evangelizing on its behalf. Marshall does something different: he bids us to consider Kierkegaard's theology simply as such; he suppresses the aesthetically decorative packaging such as "the stages on life's way" (SLW 476), thereby keeping the reader focused on Kierkegaard as a theologian, as a Christian writer, and as a genius who consecrates his literary gifts to the reintroduction of Christianity into Christendom.

As must be obvious: although Kierkegaard has a clear sense of the development of the conceptual distinctions he labors to establish, he is no systematic philosopher. Neither are his writings dominated by historical interests. Rather, he is a dialectical author. Not only are there "stages on life's way"[1] in his literary production, there are also stages on Kierkegaard's own personal way to be considered, for his writings cannot be separated from his person. The development of the concepts reflected in his writings is almost a mirror image of his own internal life and development. First and foremost, he thought through the concepts simply as such, and then he presented them in the most artistic philosophical literature *and* conceptually complex "treatises" since Plato, by showing and saying the conceptual content in its literary and philosophical expression in the same gesture.[2] Kierkegaard not only rethought Socrates and Athens, he simultaneously meditated upon the cultural, philosophical, and religious climate of his own Copenhagen, and in the same effort he expressed his critique of the degeneration of Christianity into Christendom.[3] Marshall's discussions of Kierkegaard's relations to the history of philosophy, to his critical appraisal of his own writings, and to the conceptual and public issues he vigorously confronted, are helpfully clarifying for today's Christian, Lutheran and otherwise.

With no intent of diminishing the "catch" of others who have previously fished in this pond, it must be said that Marshall's detailed mastery of the import of Luther's theology in Kierkegaard's existential thought has seldom, if ever, been matched in the history of Kierkegaard research. Lovers of either or of both of these theological radicals are deeply indebted to Marshall's efforts. However, there is more.

---

1. To reinforce both the dialectical structure of Kierkegaard's authorship, recall, for instance, that the authorship includes not only a "Diary of the Seducer," but also the moralistic injunctions of Judge William, a profound treatise on Christian ethics, an extended critique of the most important philosopher of the preceding generation, G.W.F. Hegel, a searing but loving critique of the ethical, religious, and theological pretensions of his time and place, and a large number of devotional discourses. Inwardly, his life was that of a penitent.

2. Interestingly, Dante's *Divine Comedy* rivals Kierkegaard's effort in the theological use of literature, but he lacks the variety of aesthetic forms used by Kierkegaard. Interestingly, Jean-Paul Sartre uses multiple literary forms in the service of his atheism.

3. The essays of the pseudonym, Judge William, is the primary vehicle for understanding Kierkegaard's complex and ironic relations to the conservative bourgeois culture as seen from the inside.

Marshall, the scholar, the preacher, and the priest, is not finished with us yet. The scholarly, analytic, and comparative effort noticed above seems complete in itself, and that is so. However, the volume includes several brief sermons. This is a surprise, to say the least! This last section adds to the theological depth and authority of the earlier sections. These sermons underscore the centrality of preaching in Lutheran churches for instruction, edification and as an invitation to the Eucharist. Each of the sermons is a theological and rhetorical masterpiece. The collection of Marshall's sermons is not a rival to Thomas à Kempis' *The Imitation of Christ* (1418–27) nor William Law's *A Serious Call to a Devout and Holy Life* (1728) and assumes no such pretensions. However, if it is true that clear theological thinking precedes and arms both inward piety and public obedience to the divine, Marshall's book benefits all, the pastor and the parishioner, and will instruct scholars for decades to come. These sermons are vivid testimonies of a preacher-scholar, who happened upon and who appropriated Kierkegaard's achievement for the strengthening of the Church in the fulfillment of its evangelical and edificatory ministries.

Robert L. Perkins
Senior professor of philosophy
Stetson University
DeLand, Florida

Selected Bibliography

Altizer, Thomas J. J. *The Call to Radical Theology*. Ed. Lissa McCullough. Albany: State University of New York, 2012.

Arbaugh, George E., and George B. Arbaugh. *Kierkegaard's Authorship: A Guide to the Writings of Kierkegaard*. Rock Island, Illinois: Augustana College Library, 1967.

Barnett, Christopher B. *Kierkegaard, Pietism and Holiness*. Burlington, Vermont: Ashgate, 2011.

Barrett, Lee C, III. *Kierkegaard*. Abington Pillars of Theology. Nashville: Abingdon, 2010.

Bukdahl, Jørgen. *Søren Kierkegaard and the Common Man*. Edited and translated by Bruce H. Kirmmse. Grand Rapids: Eerdmans, 2001.

Cappelørn, Niels Jørgen, Joakim Garff, Johnny Kondrup. *Written Images: Søren Kierkegaard's Journals, Notebooks, Booklets, Sheets, Scraps, and Slips of Paper* (1996). Trans. Bruce H. Kirmmse. Princeton: Princeton University Press, 2003.

Caputo, John D. *How to Read Kierkegaard*. London: Granta, 2007.

Come, Arnold B. *Kierkegaard as Theologian: Recovering My Self*. Montreal: McGill-Queen's University Press, 1997.

Cotkin, George. *Existential America*. Baltimore: The Johns Hopkins University Press, 2003.

Diem, Herman. *Kierkegaard: An Introduction*. Translated by David Green. Richmond, Virginia: John Knox, 1966.

Eller, Vernard. *Kierkegaard and Radical Discipleship*. Princeton: Princeton University Press, 1968.

Evans, C. Stephen. *Kierkegaard: An Introduction*. Cambridge: Cambridge University Press, 2009.

———. *Kierkegaard on Faith and the Self*. Waco, Texas: Baylor University Press, 2006.

Ferreira, M. Jamie. *Kierkegaard*. London: Wiley-Blackwell, 2009.

———. *Love's Grateful Striving: A Commentary on Kierkegaard's* Works of Love. New York: Oxford, 2001.

Garff, Joakim. *Søren Kierkegaard: A Biography*. Translated by Bruce H. Kirmmse. Princeton: Princeton University Press, 2005.

Goetz, Ronald. "A Secular Kierkegard." *The Christian Century* 111 (1994): 259–60.

Hall, Amy Laura. *Kierkegaard and the Treachery of Love*. Cambridge: Cambridge University Press, 2002.

Hannay, Alastair. *Kierkegaard: A Biography*. Cambridge: Cambridge University Press, 2001.

Heinecken, Martin J. *The Moment before God: An Interpretation of Kierkegaard*. Philadelphia: Muhlenberg, 1956.

Hong, Howard V., and Edna H. Hong, eds. *The Essential Kierkegaard*. Princeton: Princeton University Press, 2000.

Kirmmse, Bruce H. *Kierkegaard in the Golden Age of Denmark*. Bloomington: Indiana University Press, 1990.

———. *Encounters with Kierkegaard: A Life as Seen by His Contemporaries*. Translated by Bruce H. Kirmmse and Virginia R. Laursen. Princeton: Princeton University Press, 1996.

Krishek, Sharon. *Kierkegaard on Faith and Love*. Cambridge: Cambridge University Press, 2009.

Lebowitz, Naomi. *Kierkegaard: A Life of Allegory*. Baton Rouge: Louisiana State University Press, 1985.

LeFevre, Perry D. *The Prayers of Kierkegaard*. Chicago: University of Chicago Press, 1976.

Léon, Céline. *The Neither/Nor of the Second Sex: Kierkegaard on Women, Sexual Difference, and Sexual Relations*. Macon, Georgia: Mercer University Press, 2008.

Lippitt, John. *Kierkegaard and the Problem of Self-Love*. Cambridge: Cambridge University Press, 2013.

Lorentzen, Jamie. *Kierkegaard's Metaphors*. Macon, Georgia: Mercer University Press, 2001.

Lowrie, Walter. *Kierkegaard*. Oxford: Oxford University Press, 1938.

Malantschuk, Gregor. *The Controversial Kierkegaard*. Translated by Howard V. Hong and Edna H. Hong. Waterloo, Ontario: Wilfred Laurier University Press, 1978.

———. *Kierkegaard's Concept of Existence*. Edited and translated by Howard V. Hong and Edna H. Hong. Milwaukee: Marquette University Press, 2003.

Malik, Habib. *Receiving Søren Kierkegaard: Early Impact and Transmission of His Thought*. Washington, DC: Catholic University of America Press, 1997.

Marino, Gordon. *Kierkegaard in the Present Age*. Milwaukee: Marquette University Press, 2001.

Marshall, Ronald F. "Kierkegaard's Heavenly Whores." *Dialog* 31 (1992): 227–30.

———. "Taking Up Snakes in Worship." *The Bride of Christ* 20 (1996): 20–23, 41.

———. "Poisoning Baptism." *The Bride of Christ* 15 (1991): 9–13.

———. "Luther the Lumberjack." *Lutheran Quarterly* 10 (1996): 107–10.

———. "A Scandalous Christ." *The Christian Ministry* 28 (1997): 10–12.

———. "Our Serpent of Salvation: The Offense of Jesus in John's Gospel." *Word & World* 21 (2001): 385–93.

———. "Preaching against the Cross." *Lutheran Partners* 19 (2003): 24–29.

———. "Salvation within Our Reach." *Lutheran Forum* 31 (1997): 18–21.

———. "Christ as a Sign of Contradiction." *Pro Ecclesia* 6 (1997): 479–87.

———. "Psalmic Bishops." *Currents in Theology and Mission* 29 (2002): 40–44.

———. "Somber Lutherans." *Lutheran Forum* 38 (2004): 41–45.

———. "Luther's Alleged Anti-Semitism." *Logia* 21 (2012): 5–8.

Mercer, David E. *Kierkegaard's Living-Room*. Montreal: McGill-Queen's University Press, 2001.

Mulder, Jack Jr. *Kierkegaard and the Catholic Tradition*. Bloomington: Indiana University Press, 2010.

Nordentoft, Kresten. *Kierkegaard's Psychology*. Translated by Bruce H. Kirmmse. Pittsburgh: Duquesne University Press, 1978.

Oden, Thomas C. ed. *Parables of Kierkegaard*. Princeton: Princeton University Press, 1978.

Pattison, George. *Anxious Angels: A Restrospective View of Religious Existentialism*. New York: Saint Martin's Press, 1999.

———. *Kierkegaard's Upbuilding Discourses: Philosophy, Theology, Literature*. London: Routledge, 2002.

———. *The Philosophy of Kierkegaard*. Montreal: McGill-Queen's University Press, 2005.

Pelikan, Jaroslav. *From Luther to Kierkegaard: A Study in the History of Theology*. Saint Louis: Concordia, 1950.

Perkins, Robert L. *Søren Kierkegaard*. Richmond, Virginia: John Knox, 1969.

Podmore, Simon D. *Kierkegaard and the Self Before God: Anatomy of the Abyss*. Bloomington: Indiana University Press, 2011.

Polk, Timothy Houston. *The Biblical Kierkegaard: Reading by the Rule of Faith*. Macon, Georgia: Mercer University Press, 1997.

Pons, Jolita. *Stealing a Gift: Kierkegaard's Pseudonyms and the Bible*. New York: Fordham University Press, 2004.

Rae, Murray. *Kierkegaard and Theology*. London: T&T Clark, 2010.

Riviere, Wiliam T. *A Pastor Looks at Kierkegaard: The Man and His Philosophy*. Grand Rapids: Zondervan, 1941.

Roberts, David. *Kierkegaard's Analysis of Radical Evil*. New York: Continuum, 2006.

Roberts, Kyle A. *Emerging Prophet: Kierkegaard and the Post-Modern People of God*. Eugene, Oregon: Wipf & Stock, 2013.

Roos, Heinrich. *Søren Kierkegaard and Catholicism*. Trans. Richard M. Brackett. Westminster, Maryland: Newman Press, 1954.

Rosas, L. Joseph III. *Scripture in the Thought of Søren Kierkegaard*. Nashville: Broadman & Holman, 1994.

Stendahl, Brita K. *Søren Kierkegaard*. Boston: Twayne, 1976.

Sløk, Johannes. *Kierkegaard's Universe: A New Guide to the Genius*. Translated by Kenneth Tyndale. Copenhagen: Danish Cultural Institute,1994.

Smith, Joseph H., ed. *Kierkegaard's Truth: The Disclosure of the Self*. New Haven: Yale University Press, 1981.

Sponheim, Paul R. *Kierkegaard on Christ and Christian Coherence*. New York: Harper & Row, 1968.

———. *Love's Availing Power: Imaging God, Imagining the Word*. Minneapolis: Fortress, 2011.

Stewart, Jon. *Kierkegaard's Relation to Hegel Reconsidered*. Cambridge: Cambridge University Press, 2003.

Stokes, Patrick, and Adam J. Buben. *Kierkegaard and Death*. Bloomington: Indiana University Press, 2011.

Strawser, Michael. *Both/And: Reading Kierkegaard From Irony to Edification*. New York: Fordham University Press, 1997.

Swenson, David F. *Something About Kierkegaard*. Edited by Lillian Marvin Swenson. Minneapolis: Augsburg, 1945.

Thompson, Josiah. *Kierkegaard*. New York: Knopf, 1973.

Thomte, Reidar. *Kierkegaard's Philosophy of Religion*. Princeton: Princeton University Press, 1948.

Updike, John. "The Fork." In *Kierkegaard*, edited by Josiah Thompson. New York: Doubleday, 1972.

Walsh, Sylvia. *Living Christianly: Kierkegaard's Dialectic of Christian Existence*. University Park, Pennsylvania: University of Pennsylvania Press, 2005.

———. *Kierkegaard: Thinking Christianly in an Existential Mode*. Oxford: Oxford University Press, 2009.

Watkin, Julia. *The A to Z of Kierkegaard's Philosophy*. Lanham and Toronto: Scarecrow, 2010.

Westfall, Joseph. *The Kierkegaardian Author*. Berlin and New York: Walter de Gruyter, 2007.

About the Author

THE REV. RONALD F. MARSHALL has been the pastor at First Lutheran Church of West Seattle since he was ordained there in 1979. Prior to that, he served congregations in Pullman, Naselle and Chinook, Washington; and in Compton, Santa Monica and Pasadena, California. He has been married to Dr. Jane L. Harty since 1972 and they have three grown children: Susannah, Ruth and Anders.

He received a Bachelor of Arts in Philosophy from Washington State University in 1971, *magnum cum laude*, and was elected to Phi Beta Kappa. He also received a Master of Divinity from Luther Seminary, in St. Paul, Minnesota, in 1975; and a Master in Religion from Claremont Graduate School in 1978.

Pastor Marshall has published over fifty articles, specializing in the thought of Martin Luther and Søren Kierkegaard. Two of his better known essays are "Deathly Evangelism," which has been republished twice—the last time in the online journal, *Semper Reformandum*; and "Eaten Alive," a critique of the way The Book of Jonah has been retold in children's books. He has also published eight sermons. He is a student of Bob Dylan's songs, writings, paintings and movies. In 1989, Pastor Marshall published *Deo Gloria*—a history of First Lutheran Church of West Seattle from 1918–88; and in 2003, *Wittgenstein Reading the Comics*—a book on philosophical humor. In 2013 he published *Hunger Immortal: The First Thirty Years of the West Seattle Food Bank*, 1983–2013. He is also known for publishing, from 1990 to 2002, CERTUS SERMO: *An Independent Monthly Review of the Northwest Washington Synod of the Evangelical Lutheran Church in America*.

Since 2003 he has been teaching a four week class, open to the public, on *Reading the Koran in Four Weeks*—which he offers four times a year. Hundreds up and down the West Coast have taken this class. For more details on Pastor Marshall, go to flcws. org.

Name and Subject Index

Scripture Index